MW01515164

COMMUNITY CORRECTIONS

COMMUNITY CORRECTIONS

AN APPLIED
APPROACH

Dennis J. Stevens

University of Massachusetts-Boston

PEARSON

Prentice
Hall

Upper Saddle River, New Jersey 07458

Library of Congress Cataloging-in-Publication Data

Stevens, Dennis J.
    Community corrections : an applied approach / Dennis J. Stevens.
        p. cm.
    Includes bibliographical references.
      ISBN 0-13-113030-7
  1. Community-based corrections—United States. 2. Probation—United States. 3. Parole—United
States. I. Title.
    HV9304.S73 2006
    364.6'8—dc22

                                            2005008331

Executive Editor: Frank Mortimer, Jr.
Assistant Editor: Mayda Bosco
Executive Marketing Manager: Tim Peyton
Editorial Assistant: Kelly Krug
Production Editor: Jan Pushard, Pine Tree Composition, Inc.
Production Liaison: Barbara Marttine Cappuccio
Director of Manufacturing and Production: Bruce Johnson
Managing Editor: Mary Carnis

Manufacturing Manager: Ilene Sanford
Manufacturing Buyer: Cathleen Petersen
Senior Design Coordinator: Mary Siener
Cover Design: Anthony Gemmellaro
Cover Photo: Ken Kochey/Getty Images
Formatting and Interior Design: Pine Tree Composition, Inc.
Printing and Binding: R.R. Donnelley & Sons

Copyright © 2006 by Pearson Education, Inc., Upper Saddle River, New Jersey, 07458.
Pearson Prentice Hall. All rights reserved. Printed in the United States of America. This publication is protected by Copyright and permission should be obtained from the publisher prior to any prohibited reproduction, storage in a retrieval system, or transmission in any form or by any means, electronic, mechanical, photocopying, recording, or likewise. For information regarding permission(s), write to: Rights and Permissions Department.

Pearson Prentice Hall™ is a trademark of Pearson Education, Inc.
Pearson® is a registered trademark of Pearson plc
Prentice Hall® is a registered trademark of Pearson Education, Inc.

Pearson Education LTD.
Pearson Education Singapore, Pte. Ltd
Pearson Education, Canada, Ltd
Pearson Education—Japan
Pearson Education Australia PTY, Limited
Pearson Education North Asia Ltd
Pearson Educación de Mexico, S.A. de C.V.
Pearson Education Malaysia, Pte. Ltd

10 9 8 7 6 5 4 3 2 1
ISBN 0-13-113030-7

Dedicated to my children who always have my love:
David D. Stevens, Mark A. Stevens, and Alyssa P. Stevens

Contents

Part I

1   Community Corrections: An Overview   1

2   Approaches in Community Corrections   36

3   Entry Process, Sentence Strategies, and Intermediate Sanctions   72

4   Classification   112

Part II

10   Parole: Processes, Rights, and Services   322

Part III

Preface

As the American justice system winds and turns from changes in technology, medicine, the judiciary, and public sentiment, new avenues have been developed, new practices have been implemented, and new legal precedents have been set to carry community corrections (CC) into this new millennium. In the face of unparalleled growth accompanied by an incredibly huge budgetary crises, (CC) maintains a collision course with an equivalent dismay of burgeoning prison populations and heinous acts committed by defendants in programs designed to keep individuals from imprisonment. Policymakers have diversified the criminal justice objectives and shifted strategies to emphasize punishment and control practices that are more resonant with the get-tough attitudes of interest groups and the American public, but experience has documented that success can be equally available through less expensive avenues such as treatment and prevention. Few textbooks distinguish the push and pull strategies associated with punishment and treatment whereas many others present theoretical and often conceptual vignettes about programs, legal context of operations, abstract performance evaluations, and profiles of the type of client served by varies agencies. General belief systems and historical accounts that support various correctional strategies and practices are woven throughout this book so that when you read each chapter, you will have a better sense as to why certain strategies are used rather than others, and you will receive some historical information that helps you place those strategies into a specific time and place. That is, what will be revealed on these pages is that the predominant belief system of a specific era can and will establish the rationale and justification associated with correctional policy and practice. Regardless of how hard correctional personnel, volunteers, and vendors work, moving correctional participants closer to the goals of the correctional community has more to do with what policymakers, interest groups, and the public think because they control the purse-strings and the rationale that supports the correctional enterprise. In addition, outcomes are shaped by the intention of correctional participants who often engage in correctional strategies and programs under court authority. Once released from correctional supervision, many participants return to former lifestyles, sometimes because that is the only lifestyle that accepts them.

Although *Community Corrections: An Applied Approach* is a valuable resource of historical and current CC strategies, it also offers extensive case studies for students to better understand the contributions made by CC professionals. That is, *Community Corrections: An Applied Approach* is grounded in the experiences of CC professionals promoting this work as a handbook for the practitioner at justice academies, and it is rooted in a scholarly tradition to be used as a textbook for the student in college classrooms. This book provides relevant general information, key issues, and the experiences of practitioners, researchers, and CC to help guide a reader through the complex world of CC. In no way does this work imply that every attempt, issue, and strategy of CC is represented. However, as I reviewed the CC literature, it became apparent that several essential areas were largely neglected and were therefore incorporated into this work.

What Makes This Work Different?

Because this work is presented by an experienced practitioner and focuses on belief systems and their influences upon correctional policy and practice, classification systems, and special needs of correctional participants such as juveniles, female offenders, the elderly, the mentally ill and disabled, and sex offenders, this book exceeds the typical expectations of other works on the subject. It touches on female probation officers and parole officers, their experiences, and their historical accounts as a profession; it also describes traps (and resolutions) acted out by offenders to manipulate them.

I have worked in numerous correctional settings for over a decade, but to bring a fresh and realistic look to this work, I visited many facilities such as New York Shock Incarceration Camps, the Illinois Parole Adjustment Center, and the Massachusetts Trial Court (juvenile) Centers in Boston where I conducted interviews with colleagues, correctional personnel, and correctional participants. Rather than relying on outdated tables, I developed my own tables using up-to-date methods of discovery including discussions with those practitioners involved with the task at hand. As a classroom teacher, I generally dislike presenting students with antiquated icons that reinforce traditional perspectives wrapped in formal jargon that pushes students away from their studies, rather than engaging them. This book will engage readers at a student level and provide insightful reflections about the accomplishments and failures of correctional practices provided by the dedicated men and women in the corrections profession. A reader will gain a realistic insight into the world of community corrections and understand how and why it works.

DESIGN OF THIS BOOK

Community Corrections: An Applied Approach has 15 chapters, divided into three parts: Part I provides an overview, descriptions of approaches of correctional supervision, entry process, sentence and supervision strategies, and classification practices. Part II offers descriptions of pretrial release, diversion, probation, parole, and residential intermediate sanctions. Part III explores specific correctional populations such as juveniles, women, the elderly and the disabled, and finally, the mentally ill and sex offenders. Each chapter contains learning objectives, key terms and phrases, an introduction, insightful questions, a summary, and discussion questions.

I acknowledge that this work presents general information, key issues, and experiences of correctional practitioners, researchers, and participants to help guide your thoughts through the complex world of CC. I do not imply that every attempt, issue, and strategy of CC is represented. Also, because an issue or strategy is neglected does not imply that it is not an important part of corrections; it only means that given the size of this work, many strategies and issues were left out. Finally, because an estimated 8 out of every 10 defendants placed in institutional or CC care have alcohol or drug abuse issues, those issues are independently explored as they apply to the emphasis of the group discussed in each chapter.

Dr. Dennis J. Stevens

Acknowledgments

There are many people who provided excellent guideposts (and I probably should have listened to them more often). Without their help, it's doubtful this work would be in print. Acknowledgments are many, and hopefully I haven't missed anyone. If I have, sorry about that, I'll get you next time. However, for the most part, there are always the students to thank. After all, they had to listen to the lectures developed from the chapters of this work, ask the questions, and prepare the class projects to guide me through this process. My perspective has always been to write for my students as opposed to writing for my colleagues, but I collaborate with those colleagues, practitioners, and students who know the real answers.

Of those who inspired this work, kept me on track, and listened to my complaints, three names surface and deserve my warmest regards. First, my mentor and friend, Dr. Frank Schmalleger the great criminologist; second, Dr. Richard Bounds, the great forensic scientist, Mount Olive College, North Carolina; and my son, Mark A. Stevens, Manchester, NH, who contributed to sections of this work through his own experiences and continues to battle for his righteous place in the sun.

Acknowledgments include those who contributed to this work: Suzanne C. Koller, Court Appointed Special Advocate (CASA) volunteer for the Los Angeles County Superior Juvenile Court, Woodland Hills, CA; Dr. Nina Silverstein, University of Massachusetts-Boston; Dr. Eric Metchik, Salem State College (who was an early reader of the original chapters); Professor Tim Bakken, U.S. Military Academy at West Point: Dr. Darrel Irwin, University of North Carolina at Wilmington; Melanie Estes, Richmond, VA; Juvenile Intake Officer, Lori A. Gazerro, Commonwealth of Massachusetts; Sharon Brady, Division of Trial Court, Commonwealth of Massachusetts; BJS Statistician, Lauren E. Glaze, OJP, U.S. Department of Justice; Glenn S. Goord, Commissioner of NYDOCS; Dr. Cheryl Lirette Clark, Director of Shock Incarceration, NYDOCS; Superintendent Ronald Moscicki, Lakeview Shock Incarceration Correctional Facility, NYDOCS; James Flateau, Director of Public Information, NYDOCS; Linda Foglia, Assistant. Director of Public Information, NYDOCS; Lt. Sandra Amoia, Lakeview Shock NYDOCS; Tom Watson,

Inmate Atascadero State Hospital, CA; Governor Jane Swift, Commonwealth of Massachusetts; Commissioner Department of Corrections, Michael T. Maloney, Commonwealth of Massachusetts; Superintendent Elaine Lord, Bedford Hills Correctional Facility, NYDOCS; Superintendent Volunteer Services, Lisa Brennan, Bedford Hills Correctional Facility, NYDOCS; Kathy Boudin, Inmate, Bedford Hills Correctional Facility, NYDOCS; Judith Clark, Inmate, Bedford Hills Correctional Facility, NYDOCS; Warden John Sanfilippo, Lakes Region Facility, Laconia, NH; Warden Gwendolyn Mitchell, Central California Women's Facility, Chowchilla, CA; Warden Michel Rothwell, Sheridan Corrections Facility (fully dedicated drug rehab facility), Chicago, IL; Captain Stephen J. Wenderlich, Elmira Corrections, NYDOCS; Sheriff Michael G. Bellotti, Norfolk County, MA; Community Corrections Center Manager, Officer Chris Bell, Quincy, MA; Statewide Program Supervisor, Phyllis Buccio-Notaro, Community Corrections Massachusetts; Dr. Mary Ann Farkas, Marquette University; Dr. Kate King, Boise State University; Sheriff Frank Cousins, Essex County, MA; Sandra Brown, Manager, Women's Resource Center, Jamaica Plain, MA; Melissa Driscoll, a dedicated student at University of Massachusetts-Boston helped gather some of the contributors. Finally, thanks to Dr. Cindy Picou Stevens, Wentworth Institute of Technology, for continual encouragement.

The author would also like to thank the following reviewers: Shannon M. Barton, Indiana State University Terre Haute, IN., Karon M. Donahue, Waycross College Waycross, GA., James Jengeleski, Shippensburg University Shippensburg, PA., Arthur Lurigio, Loyola University Chicago, Chicago, IL., and Barbara Peat, Indiana University South Bend, South Bend, IN.

About the Author

Dr. Dennis J. Stevens received a Ph.D. from Loyola University of Chicago in 1991. Currently, he is an associate professor of criminal justice at the University of Massachusetts Boston. In addition to teaching traditional students, he has taught and counseled law enforcement and correctional officers at law academies such as the North Carolina Justice Academy and felons at maximum custody penitentiaries such as Attica in New York, Eastern and NC Women's Institute in North Carolina, Stateville and Joliet near Chicago, CCI in Columbia South Carolina, and MCI Framingham (women) and Norfolk in Massachusetts. Stevens has published several books and almost 100 scholarly and popular literature articles on policing, corrections, and criminology. He has been retained by state legislators, federal agencies, and foreign countries such as the Provincial Government of Canada, to aid in specific criminal justice investigations including drug trafficking, sexual assault, and correctional systems including sex offender programs, classification systems, and education. He has guided many sexually abused children in church-affiliated programs in New York, North Carolina, and South Carolina and has lead group crisis sessions among various police and correctional agencies. He is a former group facilitator for a national organization that specializes in court ordered cases of sexual offenders. Currently, he lives with his 14-year-old daughter Alyssa, near the sea, close to Boston and officiates at U.S. Swimming competitions because Alyssa is a competitive swimmer. He takes pride in his sons: David, who lives in Chicago, and Mark, who lives in Manchester, NH.

COMMUNITY CORRECTIONS

1

COMMUNITY CORRECTIONS: AN OVERVIEW

LEARNING OBJECTIVES

When you finish reading this chapter, you will be better prepared to:

- Describe the importance of studying community corrections.
- Identify two specific questions centered in a philosophical belief system that shape both community corrections policy and practice.
- Identify the criminal justice partners and reveal their individual functions.
- Identify the various types of offenses.
- Explain the primary role of community corrections.
- Identify the services provided by community corrections to participants.
- Characterize the differences between reported crime and clearance rates.
- Identify the various strategies of community supervision.
- Describe the goal of community corrections.
- Identify the rationale supporting community corrections.
- Identify and describe the characteristics associated with the Five Rs.
- Explain net-widening and describe its consequences.

KEY TERMS

Back-End Programs	Diversion Programs	Reconciliation
Civil Law	Front-End Programs	Rehabilitation
Clearance Rates	Net-Widening	Reintegration
Community Corrections	Parole	Restitution
Criminal Justice	Probation	Restorative Justice
Community	Public Safety	
Criminal Law	Recidivism Levels	

"Lots of people want to ride with you in the limo, but what you want is someone who will take the bus with you when the limo breaks down."

—Oprah Winfrey

INTRODUCTION

As the criminal justice community takes the spotlight in the media in its response to changes in technology, medicine, and the judiciary, and new threats including terrorism besiege the American people, huge correctional populations challenge an old guard's policies while legal precedent moves community corrections (CC) practice into a new decade—a new role. Old policy associated with punishment, incarceration, and control is as comfortable as riding in a limo, but at what expense? "Tough on crime" means getting tougher on criminals, which means the "lock 'em up and throw away the key" concept[1] or what we call, "cuff 'em and stac 'em." However, this perspective is incredibly expensive, has produced overcrowded prisons, and large segments of a free population are under correctional supervision.[2] Entire communities have changed their cultural icons to match correctional policy through a cumulative impact effect (explained later) as many community adults and juveniles are in the system, or are being processed out of the system, producing destabilized neighborhoods and dysfunctional families. Some offenders belong in prison and our most expensive remedy might well be considered for some of them,[3] but all offenders are not equal—most can change, and their change could enhance public safety as the criminal justice partners, including CC, meet new challenges. Beyond the scope of this work are criminal justice strategies to widen the net to apprehend, bring to trial, and sentence offenders wherever they live. This book examines the role of CC as an alternative to dated punishment and control perspectives and recommends that many offenders need another chance at making the right choices.

WHY STUDY CC?

When you think about prisons, images of threatening gun towers and indifferent barred cells might emerge. However, few images represent CC because it includes a variety of programs and services in a variety of settings. Few CC facilities or programs include gun towers or barred cells with the exception of shock incarceration camps. One good reason to study CC is because over 50 percent of the defendants before trial and over 80 percent of all convicted defendants are supervised through CC agencies and most of those individuals live among us.[4] Therefore, the best reason to study CC is because CC initiatives are the first option of most judges and it supervises more offenders than any other correctional enterprise.[5] A small portion of offenders is confined in prisons, jails, and other secure facilities. Studying CC means that each of us can aid our own communities to deal more effectively with the offenders who live among us (like it or not) and those new arrivals who may outnumber all of their predecessors. CC is about changing behavior without the use of institutional confinement. That is, changing behavior can be accomplished without gun towers.

FOCUS OF THIS BOOK

This book provides a glimpse into the intervention strategies employed by the criminal justice system to punish and treat adults and juveniles who made bad choices in their daily lives or were in vulnerable circumstances (i.e., poor, mentally or physically challenged). Although the focus of this book is about correctional services delivered in the community (i.e., probation, parole, residential intermediate sanctions), it is also about services provided to prisoners who eventually are returned to the community. When providing those services, the criminal justice community, and in this case corrections in particular, cannot ignore what the American public expects, which includes five simple things:[6]

- Safety from violent predators
- Accountability for the offense
- Repair of the damage done
- Education and treatment of the offender
- Involvement in making decisions

By implication, these are the very issues most Americans feel the criminal justice system is not accomplishing.[7]

In keeping with those thoughts, CC is moving toward those objectives with the expectation that its services are more efficient and less expensive than prison when supervising guilty defendants to avoid future bad choices, and at the same time, hold them accountable for an unlawful act. In addition, CC is designed to aid those in vulnerable circumstances through appropriate referral strategies that can enhance opportunities in a free society. However, a theme woven throughout this book focuses on philosophical beliefs or attitudes held by policy makers, interest groups, and the public that ultimately shape CC policy and practice. These belief systems are associated with two specific questions:

1. What factors lead an offender to crime? (causal factors of crime)
2. What is the best way to deal with offenders once they are in the corrections system? (correctional approaches)

The predominant belief system of a specific era can and will establish the ratio-nale and justification associated with correctional policy and ultimately practice. Said another way, moving correctional participants closer to the goals of the correctional community has more to do with what policy makers, interest groups, and the public think, than all the hard work performed by correctional personnel, volunteers, and ven-dors (contracted private providers). Somewhere between what policy makers, interest groups, and the public expect and mandate through policy, and what correctional per-sonnel, volunteers, and contracted vendors actually do, there are differences that this book will guide you through.

MAJOR IDEA OF THIS BOOK

This book argues that correctional programs delivered in the community can reduce crim-inal activities more often than programs delivered in prison to specific offenders. That is, crime-free lifestyles are more likely achieved through programs administered in a com-munity setting rather than in a facility (such as a high-security penitentiary) with those humbling gun towers. For instance, it would be easier to guide a participant to compliance with the rules of society if that individual actually lived in the community where the rules apply rather than in barred cells.[8] Exposing troubled men, women, and juveniles to the pains of imprisonment has produced unsatisfactory results, as evidenced by the number of convicts who return to a life of crime (and poverty) once released from prison and jail. One reason for this belief is that most offenders are individuals who made bad choices about their lifestyle, had unreasonable expectations about the relationships they entered into, and were extremely selfish. Alternatives to incarceration are necessary to bring order to a democratic society.

ASSUMPTIONS ABOUT YOU

More than likely, you are a college student or a justice academy trainee. You are probably a criminal justice major or in a closely related academic discipline, or your present or fu-ture occupation is closely related to the justice profession. More likely, you have com-pleted an introductory course in criminal justice and a corrections course or you possess some practical experience in one of the justice professions. However, even if you do not have those experiences, the stories offered in this work will be offered in an uncompli-cated fashion, without frills or 50-cent words. It is assumed that many of you currently hold or will hold an influential position in the justice system and will work to further the goals of CC. This final thought pushes the completion of this book because dedicated and knowledgeable professionals will continue to enhance CC and ultimately ensure public safety in our communities, but in an informed way.

CRIMINAL JUSTICE COMMUNITY

You already know that the criminal justice community is largely comprised of three partners, police, courts, and corrections, and that their ultimate goal is public safety.

> The ultimate goal of the criminal justice community Is public safety.

In part, this statement means that criminal justice personnel, volunteers, and contract vendors must: (a) defuse danger where it exists and (b) provide services without compromising individual Constitutional guarantees, especially due process.[9] Due process will be
discussed later but for right now what you need to know is that in a free society, the expectation is that its justice system will conduct its business without violating the individual rights of any constituent, including those rights of offenders, although their rights are
diminished rights (explained later).[10]

   In the final analysis, the job of everyone in criminal justice is public safety, and
ways to accomplish this aim are to reduce the risk of danger and to stop crime. Reducing
risk means just that: in volatile encounters, it is important to work toward reducing danger
and stopping crime. However, that may be impossible, because crime has accompanied
society since humanity banded together in ancient societies. Some experts say that crime,
believe it or not, is considered a strong indicator of a healthy society. They argue that
crime and society's response to crime provide camaraderie and unity among its members,
enabling a society to prosper.[11] A discussion about crime and its link to a healthy society
is interesting, but it is beyond the scope of this book.[12] Nonetheless, justice personnel
know they cannot stop crime, but they can control it within a legal framework.

   Constitutional rights concerning the justice community include, within limitations,
rights when confronted by police, rights when tried and convicted by the courts, and rights
when remanded to the supervision of a correctional agency. The justice process utilized
by any and all parts of the system must be the same, within guidelines, for each intrusion
or official action. Within the legal parameters as set forth by the Bill of Rights, the function of police is to arrest a suspect; the function of the court is the trial and sentencing of
an offender; and the function of corrections is to carry out the sentence of the court.[13]

> The function of criminal justice partners:
>
> • Police make arrests.
> • Courts conduct trials and impose sentences.
> • Corrections carries out the sentence of the court.

Most of the time, the court will sentence a defendant to serve his or her time while living
in the community—thus, CC is the largest part of most government (local or state) correctional systems.

> A **system** is a complex whole consisting of interdependent parts, whose operations are directed toward common goals and influenced by the environment in which they function.

Continuing with this thought in mind, each criminal justice partner has many divisions and literally hundreds of agencies and vendors within its system. One reason there are so many different agencies has to do with authority or jurisdictional issues. For instance, state probation agencies supervise defendants who are generally not confined whereas parole agencies supervise once-confined defendants who were conditionally released prior to serving their full prison sentence. The system of government in the United States is a federal system comprised of checks and balances, resulting in a fragmented government that produces a lot of replication in government services. One way to look at a federal system is to see that it encourages agency uniqueness and supports the notion that no single agency possesses an ultimate say over other agencies. That way, new ideas and practices have the greatest chance of surfacing. However, it would be useful to review the types of offenses defendants are charged with before beginning our CC adventure.

TYPES OF OFFENSES

There are primarily two sets of American public law that concern us most: *civil and criminal.*[14] Both sets of law prohibit or require specific action by the population. Both permit the government to assess penalties against those individuals who violate those laws.

Civil law is designed to protect a variety of interests, which can include family matters such as divorce, business relationships, and personal property. Civil law exists for the purpose of enforcing private rights. Civil law can also include remedies for slander and libel, as well as personal injury or wrongful death resulting from noncriminal negligence, intentional behavior, or improperly designed or manufactured products. Individuals found guilty of civil laws are generally given fines or community activities.

Criminal law is a body of law that regulates actions that can harm the interests of another individual, the state, or the federal government. Crimes such as murder and forcible rape violate an individual, but these crimes are also crimes against the state. These crimes involve stricter rules of procedure and burdens of proof and the emphasis of criminal law is on punishing an offender. Criminal law includes *treason, misdemeanor,* and *felon*y crimes.

Treason is usually a crime that is an attempt to overthrow the government. For instance, treason might be a conviction of a U.S. citizen for selling military secrets to a foreign government.

A *misdemeanor* is a criminal offense that is less serious than a felony or treason. It can be punishable through a jail sentence and generally carries a jail sentence of one year or less.[15] Normally, jail time is served in a local jail such as one operated by the county sheriff's office.

A *felony* is a serious criminal offense punishable by a death sentence in some areas of the country (and by the federal government). It usually carries a sentence of a year or more in a state or federal prison; however, a large number of first-time felons are given probation or other forms of a punitive sentence.[16]

INTRODUCTION TO CC

Crime and justice are complex systems. However, crime is nothing more than breaking the rules considered important by a specific society. Its justice system is one official response to rule-breakers.[17] The focus of this book is about one official strategy used by government to respond to offenders—CC. In sum:

> **CC** is a set of interrelated programs meant to prevent future criminal activity by providing opportunities that bolster accountability of offenders without compromising public safety.

Some CC programs focus on various methods of counseling, opportunities for educational and vocational improvement, methods of conflict resolution and anger management, substance abuse treatment, and victim services.

THE ROLE OF CC

The centerpiece of CC has boosted humane treatment with a focus on reform and an attempt to make an offender accountable. It provides professional services without incarceration to adult and juvenile defendants who are:[18]

- Arrested, released, and awaiting trial (pretrial release)
- Diverted from the justice process before, during, or after trial (diversion)
- Fined or have other forms of nonincarcerated sanctions imposed (intermediate sanctions)
- Found guilty but released from custody, provided Conditions of Freedom are met (probation)
- Released after serving time, provided conditions of release are met (parole)
- Provided alternative environments between probation and prison and aftercare (residential intermediate sanctions)

These descriptions are generalized to provide a brief frame of reference. More details are required, and that is the focus of this book.

SERVICES OF CC

The services of CC can be characterized as:

- Programs
- Treatment
- Supervision

The services of prison and jail include one additional characteristic—custody or confine-ment. However, CC services can include confinement through shock incarceration, and limited confinement, such as halfway houses and house arrest. In essence, programs relate to education, vocational training, and "how to" courses such as anger management. Treat-ment can be seen as improving or maintaining physiological and mental health and can in-clude substance abuse clinics, dental care, and medication. Supervision relates to surveillance and monitoring at various levels. Because many participants in CC originate from jails and prisons, we also discuss inmates as they apply to CC in this book.

ELIGIBILITY ISSUES AND CC

There are many scary stories about offenders in CC programs. For instance, Willie Horton was on work furlough in Massachusetts when he broke into a home and assaulted and raped a couple. You might recall the Horton case from old newspapers you've read and things you've heard since he changed the U.S. presidential candidacy of a Massachusetts governor in 1988.[19] Robert E. Stewart, too, was released to community corrections when he abducted his girlfriend and stole 10 thousand dollars. When identified during a traffic stop, Stewart shot an officer and fled. During the high-speed chase, Stewart crashed his vehicle into a telephone pole and died as a result of the accident.

You might be less comfortable with the use of CC as an alternative to imprisonment when you think about those stories and others such as those of Earl Shriner and Wesley Dodd. For instance, Earl Shriner's sexual attacks upon children bridged a span of 24 years. When he was 16, he was implicated in the strangling murder of a schoolmate, al-though he was too young to be prosecuted as an adult. Eleven years later, he kidnapped two teenage girls and spent 10 years in prison for those crimes. Before his 1987 release from parole, he stabbed, raped, and strangled a seven-year-old boy, then cut off the child's private parts and left him for dead. Authorities knew Shriner was extremely dangerous and knew he had hatched elaborate plans in prison to maim and kill children.[20] One of Shriner's fantasies was to possess a customized van with cages so he could kidnap chil-dren. Should Shriner have been paroled?[21] Today, states like Kansas keep potentially dan-gerous prisoners confined even after prison sentences have been served until his or her "mental abnormality no longer exists." You'll have a chance to read more about this un-usual community corrections strategy in Chapter 15.

How about Wesley Dodd? He was hung in Washington state for rape, torture, and murder of a four-year-old boy. His sexual predatory career lasted 15 years, punctuated by a few months of prison. Repeated misjudgments by psychiatrists and judges took note of his upbeat, apparently frank attitude. They argued that Dodd was treatable and placed him in CC. Dodd, however, made his position clear about crime when he commented that he enjoyed molesting children and would do whatever was necessary to stay out of jail to continue sexually assaulting children. During his trial, Dodd promised that if he was released or escaped, he would kill and rape again.[22]

In another case, Mary Lee Smith was a probationer who wanted continued community support.[23] At 17, she quit high school and moved many times with her husband, who was in the military. By 20, she had two children and was divorced. With few skills and less money, she turned to shoplifting, bad-check writing, and prostitution. She had a police record, but a prosecutor chose not to prosecute her. Her criminal conduct persisted, despite food stamps and other forms or welfare. Again Mary Lee Smith was apprehended, but this time she was prosecuted. If she went to jail, her children would become wards of the state. If you were the judge, what would you do?

Finally, Boston Massachusetts Superior Court Judge Maria Lopez became the target of severe criticism in 2002. A man dressed as a woman lured a boy into his car. When the boy refused to perform a sex act, the offender put a screwdriver to his neck. The offender plead guilty. Prosecutors asked for an 8- to 10-year prison sentence. Judge Lopez sentenced the offender to probation and house confinement, prompting public outcry. One critic said, "The sentencing speaks for itself." Proceedings to disbar the judge complicated her life so much that she sought a new career.

Clearly, personnel supervise heinous offenders but despite the sensational efforts of the media to entertain us, those heinous offenders are not as numerous within CC as expected.

Most criminal acts are "trivial and mundane affairs that result in little loss and less gain."[24] These garden-variety criminals, the researchers say, outnumber all other violators, although it's hard to say if every criminal act is trivial and mundane. Government statistics report that 85 percent of all federal prisoners and 53 percent of all state prisoners were in prison for nonviolent offenses (property crimes, drunkenness, and writing bad checks) in 1997.[25] As a guide, approximately two in every three prisoners are nonviolent offenders. Generally, nonviolent first-time offenders are preferred in CC programs when there is a choice, and although each strategy has its eligibility requirements and can influence decisions, more often it is not up to the agency to make those determinations. However, the reality is that most offenders are never known by the criminal justice community.

Reported Crime and Clearance Rates

Many offenders are never apprehended, let alone known by police, and would not be in the correctional system. Nearly all drug crimes, most property offenses, and almost all acts of violence within families are never reported to the police, let alone prosecuted.[26] Many surveys of high school seniors and others show that even extensive illegal drug taking among offenders, regardless of their age, does not result in an arrest.[27] Also, criminals are caught and convicted for less than one 10th of the serious crimes against others and for a fraction of one percent of illegal drug transactions.[28] These thoughts are consistent with government reports of crime and law enforcement clearance rates.[29] As you know, once a crime is reported to police (although many are not, as evidenced by the Uniform Crime Reports vs. National Incident-Based Reporting System),[30] an arrest might occur depending on many factors or what is referred to as the clearance rate.[31] The clearance rate is the difference between crime known by police and a subsequent arrest. For instance, nationwide, law enforcement agencies in 2002 recorded a 20 percent Crime Index clearance rate (2 crimes were cleared by an arrest out of 10 reported crimes). Some reported crimes will result in a higher arrest rate than other crimes and clearance rates can vary depending on the region of the country and the jurisdiction.

Crimes Cleared by Arrest

Percent of crimes cleared by arrest, 2002

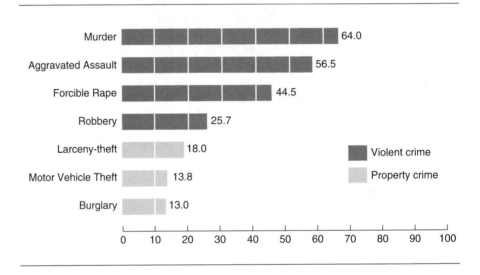

Printed with the permission of the FBI.[32]

It could be argued that law enforcement deals with visible "street" offenders most often as opposed to white collar, corporate criminals and upper class community members. It should also be acknowledged that law enforcement at all levels (federal, state, and local) intercedes in only the crime known or reported to the police—and most crime is never reported. Clearly, however, law enforcement, and especially local police, are both vital and necessary should Americans wish to live in a free society.[33] Nonetheless, experts argue that justice agencies support the interests of the dominant social class, resulting in fewer arrests and convictions of individuals in that social class than offenders in other social classes.[34] Other evidence reveals that when chronic predators, regardless of their social status, are arrested, it is usually on a lesser charge and therefore when sentenced, it is unlikely that they were identified as a heinous predator, especially in light of plea bargaining (typically 9 in 10 cases end in plea bargaining) and the manipulative skills of predators.[35] When offenders are in the correctional system, the type of correctional supervision provided for them varies depending upon their needs as determined through an evaluation or classification process (in Chapter 4) just as those agencies that administer CC programs vary.

Who Administers CC Programs?

CC is largely administered by state agencies, such as a department of corrections, but many programs are operated by local agencies such as a sheriff's office, a police agency, or a court system. Some are operated by federal agencies through the Bureau of Prisons. Additionally, many programs are delivered by private agencies contracted by federal, state, and local government. Contracting private agencies can be based on the knowledge that a particular agency has a strong expertise in a specific program area such as psychological assessments or is technologically better suited to deliver a specific service such as monitoring offender movements through an electronic bracelet probation program. In certain circumstances, a private agency, can be more cost-efficient than a public agency, especially in rural areas where a public agency might have few available resources. Also, private agencies can be managerially better suited to deliver specific programs because they can easily cross jurisdictional governmental borders, giving them greater flexibility. Despite the number of agencies administering CC programs, their immediate goals are similar.

Immediate Goal of CC

You learned that the ultimate goal of the criminal justice community is public safety and that the function of corrections is to carry out the sentence of the court. The immediate goal, however, of CC is to guide an offender to a crime-free lifestyle, regardless of the operating authority or model utilized to accomplish this goal.

> The immediate goal of CC is to guide an offender to a crime-free lifestyle by learning new behaviors and strategies for implementing those new behaviors.

Guide is an appropriate term because most offenders can overcome criminal options when they individually make a decision to change their behavior. That is, CC takes a positive view concerning the future of most offenders.

Why Programs Can Work in the Community

Although the public and the justice community see CC as "soft" on crime, it is the most common form of correctional supervision. There is a belief that only bricks and gun towers change criminal behavior.[36] Throughout its history, CC has been viewed as less punitive than imprisonment, and although there has been general support for the concept of community sanctions, current programs are viewed as inadequate. Maybe they are inadequate, but for reasons other than deficiency. When public support and resources are lacking, program quality suffers.

Certain environments can help an individual learn new behaviors among family and friends.[37] Think of an offender who may be a family's bread-winner. Incarceration would end contributions to the family, placing the family at-risk. A CC facility could allow an absence during the day for work. Family and friends may lend support to the offender who tries. Also, being at home or in a community correctional facility offers more comforts than prison and subsequently, more offenders can resolve conflicts faster. It is also less expensive to aid an offender at home or in the community than in prison. For some offenders, CC can change behavior, assuming an offender wants to change, without marching him or her through the cycle of violence reported in many prisons.[38] CC services are on the rise for many state and local governments.

However, another assumption of this book, based on experience, and the literature, is that not all violators want to change. However, what most corrections professionals have experienced and what must be clarified is that:

> The success of a CC program meeting its goals depends more on the intent of the offender as opposed to the "elegance" of the program.

Offenders sometimes manipulate even the most sophisticated of programs to gain a favorable response from a practitioner. Additionally, the success of correctional programs depends on the dedication of the practitioners (behaviorists) and/or clinicians (medically trained personnel), who provide services and evaluations, available resources, and both formal and informal correctional policy and regulations. Finally, in this regard there are many different ideas about the immediate goal of community corrections, but most agency mandates and their personnel want to aid offenders toward a crime-free lifestyle. Some say this thought represents a behavioral modification approach, and they might be right, but CC personnel agree that moving their client into a crime-free existence is their first objective. This thought is consistent with the American Probation and Parole Association's[39] perspective that views the purpose of CC as the productive *reintegration* (more on this perspective later in Chapters 2, 5, and 11) of offenders back into society.[40]

Therefore, *Community Corrections: An Applied Approach*'s goal is to demonstrate how CC can help an offender become an equal, crime-free participant in society without incarceration and, equally important, without compromising public safety. That way, everybody benefits. How CC meets these goals begins with knowing the primary strategies employed.

Community Correctional Strategies

Five primary strategies that relate to CC are used by the criminal justice community: *pretrial release, diversion, probation, early release and parole, and intermediate sanctions (including residential intermediate sanctions).*[41] The following descriptions will highlight those strategies, but each is discussed in a future chapter.

Pretrial Release is a practice designed as an alternative to pretrial detention of an arrestee and/or the release of an offender on commercial bond. These "suspects" are awaiting adjudication. In some cases, a pretrial release can be referred to as a procedural alternative to bail. Whether a suspect posts bail or is officially bailed out, these programs are short-term, narrowly focused programs.

Diversion is consistent with the CC goal of guiding offenders to crime-free lifestyles, because sometimes it is in the best interest of a suspect not to process him or her through the justice system. That is, if an individual is accused of a crime, but officials elect to forego either prosecution or punishment, it is in the best interest of the offender. The most common diversions are linked to specific conditions. For instance, drug or alcohol abusers can be diverted to treatment programs, family assault perpetrators can be diverted to counseling, and first-time petty offenders can be diverted to group sessions. It is believed that for some individuals, the formal process might be too harsh and a decision needs to be made by a judge and/or a prosecutor to avoid formal processing of certain suspects.

Probation is the most common strategy of corrections. Probation is a privilege extended to a guilty defendant. The defendant remains in the community under conditions and is supervised by probation personnel.

Early release and *parole* are similar in that they are strategies available to prisoners under certain conditions. In both cases, they can be conditionally released to a community under correctional supervision. Where parole is in place, there are several levels. These include intense parole, in which an offender is under constant surveillance by specialized parole officers, and regular parole, whereby the parolee reports to the parole center on a prearranged schedule and follows other limitations as set forth by the parole center.

Intermediate sanctions are between the two extremes of probation and prison. These sanctions consist of fines, restitution, community service, and work release. For some offenders, electronic monitoring and day reporting can apply to an intermediate sanction in some jurisdictions.

Residential intermediate sanctions resemble intermediate sanctions but involve the monitoring of living quarters or confinement under certain conditions of a defendant as opposed to prison or jail. An example can include shock incarceration, boot camps, and halfway houses.

RATIONALE SUPPORTING COMMUNITY CORRECTIONS

Although probation and parole have been around for a long time (and both are discussed in Chapter 7 through 10), California was one of the first states to enhance its CC programs in the 1960s. The California Probation Subsidy Program provided local communities with resources to manage their large CC caseloads. Part of the subsidy provided for counseling, employment training and job opportunity assistance, and specialized forms of guidance. Colorado and Oregon followed California's lead, but it took another decade for large-scale philosophical shifts to occur among different U.S. jurisdictions so that CC could be utilized more often.[42] Most community correction programs depend on state legislative appropriation of funds to increase the use of those programs. But a number of influential factors, particularly in the past few decades, justified their use. These include:

- Sentence reform
- Widespread drop in reported crime from 1994 to 2000
- Increase in general conviction rates
- Increase in correctional populations
- Prisons promote violence
- Overcrowded prisons
- Recidivism levels
- Economic downturns

Sentence reform: Several states attempted to reduce the rate of growth of their prison population through sentencing reform. For instance, Kansas' Sentencing Commission reforms enabled the courts to sentence 60 percent of nonviolent offenders to CC as an alternative to incarceration for minor parole violations in 2001, resulting in keeping 774 prison beds open for more serious offenders. In other states, officials are finding ways to close prisons or consolidate the number of corrections facilities. Also, some states released large numbers of prisoners into CC programs. In Washington, for example, the legislature and Governor Gary Locke approved an early-release law for nonviolent offenders. Washington state's Department of Corrections granted 350 releases in July 2003, the first month the law took effect. Georgia and several other states are considering "compassionate releases." Nonviolent elderly inmates are particularly expensive to incarcerate and, presenting no clear threat to public safety, are an appealing way to generate savings resulting in community corrections becoming the first choice of most judges. But it's not for every offender.

Widespread drop in crime from 1994 to 2000: This was reported by the FBI's Uniform Crime Report (UCR).[43] Individual police agencies report the aggregate number of reported incidents by offense type: murder, forcible rape, and so on, to the FBI. This widespread drop in crime could contribute to the use of community corrections as policy makers, interest groups, and making the public feel more confident about controlling criminals.[44]

The public is not as concerned with crime as it had been in the years when crime was trending upward. A 1994 survey by the Pew Research Center for the People and Press showed that 29 percent of the respondents thought that crime was the most important issue facing Americans.[45] Similarly, a Harris poll found that 37 percent of their respondents considered crime and violence to be among the most important issues for the government to address in 1994. By March 2002, only 10 percent of the individuals polled reported that crime and violence were major issues.[46] Terrorism, the economy, and international tensions topped the list that year, with unemployment following the top three.

Increase in general conviction rates: In 1996, state and federal courts convicted over 1 million adults of felonies. State courts convicted almost 998,000 adults of felonies in 1996, an average growth of approximately 5 percent every year since 1988 (667,366). From 1988 to 1996, the number of felony convictions increased faster than the number of arrests.[47] Because more defendants are being convicted, it is natural to assume that there would be a rise in the correctional populations.

Increase in correctional populations: An estimated 6.9 million persons were supervised by the correctional system in the United States as of December 2003. Of that number, almost 4.1 million defendants were on probation, 775,000 were on parole, 691,000 were in jail, and 1.4 million were in prison (see Table 1.1). State prisoners were estimated at 1.2 million, whereas federal prisoners were estimated at around 180,000.[48] The nation's prisons and jails held almost 2.1 million inmates, which was an increase of almost 40,000 more inmates than state, local, and federal officials held on the same date a year earlier.[49]

Overall, one out of every 140 American residents was incarcerated in prison or jail.[51] As confinement populations continue to rise and economic turndowns delay new prison construction, one result is more overcrowded prisons and jails.

Overcrowded prisons: Prison populations have continually increased year after year for the past 30 years. There are not enough prisons and jails to house all the offenders sentenced to confinement. Although local jails nationally were operating 6 percent below their rated capacity (safe number housed), state prisons were operating between 1 percent and 17 percent above capacity and federal prisons were 33 percent above their rated capacity.[52]

Yet, lack of space is only part of the problem. Unsafe or inhumane conditions exist in many prisons and jails.[53] One indicator is that as many as 40 states are under court order for failing to provide adequate conditions. Federal facilities are overcrowded too. Overcrowding in prisons, among other things, results in the early release of serious offenders, and therefore, those at-risk offenders might be more likely to re-offend than other offenders.[54] It might well be that prison was originally developed as a more humane way to control offenders over the gallows, public degradation, and punishment. But the current

Table 1.1   Persons Under Adult Correctional Supervision, 1995–2003[50]

Year	Correctional Population	Community Supervision		Incarceration	
		Probation	Parole	Jail	Prison
1995	5,342,900	3,077,861	679,421	507,044	1,078,542
1996	5,490,700	3,164,996	679,733	518,492	1,127,528
1997	5,734,900	3,296,513	694,787	567,079	1,176,564
1998	6,134,200	3,670,441	696,385	592,462	1,224,469
1999	6,340,800	3,779,922	714,457	605,943	1,287,172
2000	6,445,100	3,826,209	723,898	621,149	1,316,333
2001	6,581,700	3,931,731	732,333	631,240	1,330,007
2002	6,732,400	3,995,165	753,141	665,475	1,367,856
2003 Nov.*				691,301	1,226,175
2003 Dec.*	6,889,800	4,074,000	774,600		

Total estimated: Revised November, 2004. The above totals do not include 161,673 prisoners in federal prison and 110,621 federal offenders on probation in November and December of 2003.

primary mission of prisons is to control their populations as opposed to "custody with care." However, when prisons are overcrowded, it might be difficult for correctional staff to provide the appropriate care required to accommodate prisoners and ensure safety at the same time. One observer suggests that overcrowded facilities promote violence between custody staff and prisoners and between the prisoners themselves.[55]

Prisons promote violence: Because prisoners resort to violence once released, regardless of their previous experiences prior to incarceration, it is fair to say that prisons promote violence. Research shows that long prison sentences (more than two years) give rise to institutionalized prisoners who are more likely to commit more or new violent crimes once released.[56] That is, during confinement, many prisoners assimilate into the violent culture of prison life regardless of the crime that brought them to prison in the first place.[57] Of equal importance, there appears to be a parallel between the length of time a prisoner serves and his or her acceptance of violent crime as an option, once released, regardless of their previous criminal activity. Many prisoners became hardened violent offenders because of their prison experiences. It could be argued that for many prisoners, the physical separation from family members and friends, gap in employment, and general prison life experiences do not support even basic rehabilitation. For that reason, CC alternatives might prove to be a better choice for some offenders to bring them closer to the goals of corrections.

Recidivism rates: Approximately 7 of every 10 prisoners reoffend within three years of their release.[58] For purposes of this work:

> **Recidivism** is defined as a return to prison for a criminal offense other than a technical violation of parole.

Steering offenders or potential offenders away from choosing criminal lifestyles should be a priority of policy makers because about three in eight defendants had an active criminal justice status at the time of their current charged offense, including 16 percent on probation, 13 percent on pretrial release, and 6 percent on parole.[59] Some question how a loss of liberty and personal autonomy, a lack of material possessions, a loss of heterosexual relationships, and reduced personal security serve to punish offenders. Therefore, as an aid to social control, CC might be part of an evolutionary stage in the societal response to offenders, not to mention the expense of incarceration during a time when economic downturns affect most government programs.

Economic downturns: Severe fiscal problems in most states prompted policy makers to impose spending cuts on state correctional systems and their most expensive service is imprisonment.[60] As a result, CC is seen as the least expensive alternative. Prison officials realize spending cuts can be accomplished if the enormous growth in the prisoner population declines or is actually reduced, but as you already know, prison populations are on the rise. Prison administrators attempt to save money on everything from food to personnel overtime, while attempting to reevaluate tough-on-crime policies, including sentencing laws. But the largest outcome to the economic downturn is the greater use of CC, especially probation and parole.

In the early 1990s many states—particularly those in the northeast—were entering a stage of seeming "financial meltdown."[61] The National Conference of State Legislatures reported that 32 states had deficits for the fiscal year in 1991, including California which faced a $14.3 billion deficit.[62] When the states' fiscal year ended, a few states did not close their books, they closed their governments instead.

In 2000 alone, states spent $40 billion imprisoning approximately two million state and local inmates—more than one half of those funds or $24 billion was spent on incarcerating nonviolent offenders. All indicators are that prison populations will continue to rise through the remainder of the decade. These trends seemed to repeat themselves in 2003. For instance, the state of Washington reports the differences in the cost of confinement versus CC.[63]

Cost of Offender by Security Level in the State of Washington Fiscal Year 2003

- The average cost per bed (prison, prerelease, and work training release) was around $23,500 per year.
- Combined there were 12,432 work training release, pre-release, and prison beds available ($23,500 × 12,432 = $292,152,000).
- There were approximately 53,000 offenders on active supervision in the community.
- The average cost per offender on CC was around $780 per year ($780 × 53,000 = $41,340,000; difference between prison versus CC = $250,812,000 and 40,568 offenders)

Source: Washington Department of Corrections.[64]

Decreasing funds were only a part of the problematic equation facing corrections going into 2005. When states cut funds, CC programs, including probation and parole, are especially vulnerable because its "clients" are not those revered by policy makers or the public. Also, constitutional restrictions that compel specific performance and spending levels in prisons are not linked to CC. Litigation for noncompliance can be brought against a prison, yet CC can be starved of funds and performance is not necessarily protected by constitutional guarantees.[65] Cutting funds and performance for an agency whose primary goal guides offenders toward a crime-free lifestyle puts much of the burden on the community. Chief Probation Officer Barry Nidorf estimates that his deputies have on average only one hour and 47 minutes per year to devote to each probationer.[66] If the Chief accurately described a typical caseload among CC personnel, it would appear that participants might lack some services and CC personnel would work more than expected (or paid for).

- Welfare services are not needed if a bread-winner offender is allowed to remain in the community and keep his or her job (assuming he or she has one or through community correctional services can find one).[67]

- Victims' rights are served by making sure the offender is held accountable with the chance "to repair the damages they have caused."[68]
- Passive punishment increases recidivism (repetition of criminal behavior) levels by not correcting the problem.[69]

The National Council of State Legislatures reports that in 2005 it is expected that the top fiscal issue in seven states (Delaware, Georgia, Hawaii, Idaho, Kansas, Montana, and North Dakota) will continue to be corrections, despite all the cut-saving programs enacted over the past 10 years.[70] The top fiscal issues facing states in 2005 can include: health (30 states), K-12 education (26 states), budget (23 states), taxes (10 states), and transportation (5 states).[71] One way to understand these findings is to say that despite increases in the correctional population, it could be expected that correctional services and facilities are a major priority in keeping with its increases and importance.

LITTLE AGREEMENT ABOUT A COMMUNITY CORRECTIONS DEFINITION

There is little agreement about a definition of CC. Often it is defined depending on someone's practical experience and objectives.[72] For instance, some refer to community corrections as:

- Noninstitutional supervision designed to punish an offender
- Supervised options developed as alternatives to imprisonment or after conditional release
- Intervention that continues punishment in the community
- Programs conducted prior to being processed in the criminal justice system
- Intermediate sanctions conducted in the community
- The social control of persons whose behavior has brought them to the attention of the justice system
- Community rather than institutional confinement
- Citizen involvement
- Probation
- Parole

Each of these thoughts has a certain amount of merit and should any of them help you better understand the broad concept of CC, then it is probably useful to think in those terms. How should CC be defined in this new century?

CC DEFINED FOR A NEW CENTURY

For the purpose of better understanding the concepts in this book, any definition of CC should include a degree of the following characteristics:

- Reconciliation
- Rehabilitation

- Reintegration
- Restitution
- Restorative Justice

Development of the Five Rs are guided by the work of many researchers.[73] Intrinsic in the concept of the Five Rs is that each or more of these concepts should be a rallying point of CC services, regardless of the conviction status of the participant. That is, to guide an individual to a crime-free lifestyle through one or a number of programs, some part of the Five Rs should be visible in each program. Each of the Rs are outlined next but they are discussed in more detail throughout the book and linked to the community corrections highlighted services.

Reconciliation

Offenders should be personally accountable to the CC agency that provides services to them. Appeasement of the community services might be another way of describing the aim. That is, law-abiding community members should not be held financially responsible for the criminal acts of an offender. Offenders must be held financially responsible for services provided, and payment can be given in services rendered to the community or cash from the offender's employment, or through jobs provided by CC. Offenders should be charged for services provided by the CC program and those offenders can work off the fees or pay them in cash dollars. The two primary advantages that can be derived from reconciliation are that offenders are accountable and CC receives urgently needed funds to maintain and improve their rehabilitation programs.

Virginia offenders provided services to the community worth more than $428,000. In Kansas, more than 21 thousand hours of community service for governments and non-profit agencies was reported. And in Minnesota, the types of correctional services for which a fee is charged are:

- Probation
- Parole
- Supervised Release
- Intensive Community Supervision (ICS)
- Challenge Incarceration Program Phases II and III (CIP)
- Intensive Supervised Release (ISR)

What the state experienced was that when legislation was passed allowing CC to collect supervision fees, it was projected that $720,000 would be collected each fiscal year after the first year of implementation among 12,000 CC participants.[74] Although compliance expectations were not met the first year of the program (2002), the more experience CC personnel have with reconciliation methods, the higher the compliance ratio among their participants. Finally, 142 offenders in Virginia saved the state more than $325,000 through fees.[75]

Rehabilitation

Personal recovery and altering the attitudes and health of an offender so that re-offending is less likely is the objective of *rehabilitation.* CC rehabilitation primarily goes beyond recovery. Specifically, CC rehabilitation refers to altering the attitudes of an offender so he or she makes the decision not to re-offend. In the "free" world, helping clients "feel good" is the primary objective of a practitioner. But, in the world of corrections, the goal is not to make an offender feel good but rather to change behavior. Rehabilitation can relate to physical and mental recovery for the purpose of curbing recidivism levels, which will ultimately protect the public. The three most common physiological and psychological issues characteristic of most offenders supervised by correctional systems include:

- Alcohol and drug abuse
- Low self-esteem
- Lack of positive problem-solving skills

Troubled offenders continually make bad decisions and live in environments where other individuals may reinforce those decisions leading them to crime or self-destruction. This definition also suggests that a CC participant in "rehab" does not have to have been found guilty of a crime. CC rehab can include defendants who are diverted from the justice system, and upon successful completion of the program, criminal charges against the defendant will be dropped. In one sense, CC rehab, regardless of the client's justice disposition, can be looked upon as a preventive activity rather than a form of punishment.

For the purpose of clarification, guiding an offender to a crime-free existence is far different from the goals of a mental health practitioner who treats a client in the free world. This is to say that, typically, functioning offenders require guidance in learning new behaviors and strategies for implementing those new behaviors. For instance, elements of effective treatment are a complex process that can include the following:[76]

- Breaking through the denial perspectives and rationale of the offender.
- Confronting the offender with the crimes he or she committed.
- Helping the offender accept both responsibility and ownership of his or her crimes.
- Correcting cognitive errors or mental distortions that reinforce the offender's crimes.
- Developing empathy for victims by understanding victim fear and trauma resulting from actions initiated by the offender.
- Facilitating an offender's understanding of the sequence of events that led to his or her criminal activity.
- Establishing supervision conditions that minimize high-risk behaviors and situations.
- Developing relapse strategies and prevention skills.

- Identifying support networks including employers, family members, friends, teachers, and caseworkers.
- Referring offenders to appropriate clinicians, practitioners, instructors, law enforcement officers, and trainers.

The reason this idea is important is because unlike other forms of mental health treatment in which the primary goals are to reduce distress and enhance well-being, the goal of CC is to reduce the likelihood of an offender committing future crimes. Think of it this way: CC is a way of throwing a life raft to a temporarily troubled individual. Our concern is that this offender should not reoffend. It is hoped that a life raft can help offenders help themselves.

For some offenders, substance abuse can also be a pathway (but not a cause) of criminal activity. For many offenders, especially young troubled offenders, it is common to commit a crime to support a drug habit. Controlling substance abuse is a key to controlling crime, and CC rehab offers substance abuse programs more than any other program.

Reintegration

Reintegration prepares an offender to live crime-free without supervision in the community. Often, violators need a job, a place to live, emotional support, and an understanding of how things work. If those offenders were imprisoned, they probably struggled and lost their family relationships and friends as well as their self-esteem. Ideally, reintegration can also be produced through services aimed at "enabling the unable" by developing social and survival skills, remedying deficiencies in education, and increasing employability. For instance, often prisoners who have not been in the community for many years have lost touch with (or forgotten) the way life on the outside can be, especially in regard to technological advances such as bank teller machines and internet services.[77]

It is estimated that 600,000 adult and juvenile offenders arrive yearly on the doorsteps of communities nationwide.[78] Also, there are approximately 800,000 offenders on parole and 4,000,000 offenders on probation, and although prisoners returning to the streets are not the only focus of community corrections, there are few systematic comprehensive policies focusing on their personal success in the community. If we want offenders or potential offenders to comply with community standards (including the law), we should have kept them in the community in the first place. This is hardly a new thought. It is consistent with Daniel Glaser,[79] who suggests that prisoners should never be set apart from and out of communication with law-abiding persons any more than safety necessitates, especially if we ultimately wish to release them into the community with minimum risk. Preparation to return an individual to the community with a set of skills, an enhanced attitude, and even a job and a place to live should be the basic goals.

For instance, Kansas community corrections participants achieved a 95 percent employment rate in 1987. Virginia offenders paid child support for their families while saving more than $21,000 in welfare payments. Indiana offenders were offered education and employment services such as graduate equivalency degree (GED) classes.

> ## Protecting Communities by Helping Returning Inmates Find Work[80]
>
> In his 2004 State of the Union Address, President Bush proposed a 4-year, $300-million initiative to reduce recidivism and the societal costs of reincarceration by helping inmates find work when they return to their communities. The President's initiative, contained in his FY 2005 budget, will harness the resources and experience of faith-based and community organizations to help returning inmates contribute to society.
>
> Working together, the U.S. Departments of Labor (DOL), Housing and Urban Development, and Justice will assist exoffenders in finding and keeping employment, obtaining transitional housing, and receiving mentoring—three key requirements for successful re-entry.
>
> The proposal will expand on elements of a pilot project now underway at DOL (the Ready4Work Project). The groups participating in this pilot project have seen promising results: Exodus Transitional Community in East Harlem, NY was established five years ago by a group of exoffenders. In 2002, Exodus served 213 exoffenders with just 6 returning to prison. In 2003, Exodus served 290 with only 3 participants returning to prison.
>
> The City of Memphis, TN Second Chance Program was established three years ago by Mayor Willie E. Herenton. Second Chance has served more than 1,500 exoffenders over the past three years with only 4 returning to prison.
>
> The President's initiative will complement existing administration efforts to mentor the children of prisoners. Last year, $9 million was awarded to faith-based and community groups and the omnibus spending bill recently passed by Congress includes $50 million in additional funds.

Restitution

Restitution is centered in criminal accountability. It goes beyond a crime, the conviction, and punishment. If a defendant is merely punished, then it what way has the debt been satisfied relative to the victim? For instance, a defendant found guilty of drunk driving and involved in a car accident enters a plea agreement. The defendant can be ordered by the court to pay the victim for certain financial losses because of the crash.[81] This is known as restitution and may be part of the convicted person's sentence. Some states require automatic restitution. Restitution requests usually are attached to the presentence investigation (discussed in Chapter 8) prepared by the probation department.

What Does Restitution Cover?   Restitution can cover medical and funeral expenses, property loss or damage, counseling expenses, and other reasonable out-of-pocket expenses related to the crash. Restitution does not cover pain and suffering damages or punitive damage, which can be collected only in civil court under certain circumstances. State laws vary regarding whether the court must order full restitution. The financial assets of the defendant and whether the defendant is going to jail or prison can affect how quickly—or slowly—restitution will be collected. Restitution can be made in a single payment or in periodic payments over time. Payments are typically paid to the court and then forwarded to the victim. Depending on state law, the court may order a lien against the offender's property to pay restitution. In some states, wages may be garnished or other assets attached. Sometimes, restitution can be a huge amount. For instance, the Avanti Corporation was ordered (July 19, 2001) to pay over $182 million in criminal restitution to Cadence Design Systems Inc. for stealing its place and route code in 1991. The award does not include interest that Avanti will have to pay Cadence. Julius Finkelstein, deputy district attorney of Santa Clara County, said the interest will likely make the total award well over $200 million.[82] In some states, restitution can include payback for false and bogus checks to merchants, child support, and witness expenses. But often it is money paid to the state for victim relief. For instance, in Virginia more than $88,000 was repaid to victim programs between 1981–1984 and in Kansas $361,000 was paid to victim programs in 1987. CC programs must be seen as an extensive and structured set of activities geared toward these four outcomes, although it is unlikely that all four can fully be achieved at the same time. The purpose of these activities is to enable an individual to become more productive and law-abiding than before her or his admission to a CC program.

Restorative Justice

Restorative Justice is a form of restitution and it builds on the objective of reintegration by focusing on the victim in a process of reparation (social compensation for wrong). Financial interests are not the primary concern of restorative justice, thus setting it apart from restitution. The concept of restorative justice has been around for a long time, tracing back to tribal efforts of early societies. Most recently, it can be found in victims' rights movements of the 1970s–1980s.[83] Restorative justice is a:[84]

- Philosophy that views harm and crime as a violation of people and relationships.
- Holistic process that addresses the repercussions and obligations created by harm, with a view to putting things as right as possible.

In brief, Restorative Justice[85] holds that:

- Crime is about harm done to individuals and the community, and addressing crime meaningfully requires the response to be focused on that harm.
- Those who have been harmed by a crime need to have a primary, active role in determining what needs to be addressed, and they need to have a voice in how the resolution should happen.

- However the community chooses to respond to a crime, it should result in the needs of victims being significantly and meaningfully addressed.

- A focus on punishment is an inadequate response to addressing the harms done by crime. It doesn't touch on many important issues that need to be addressed. Holding an offender accountable for the harms caused and having the offender actively participate in how to make amends for the wrong done is of far greater value than punishment. The offender has incurred an obligation to victims and the community that needs to be met.

- Active community participation is essential to creating safe and healthy communities. The community as a whole, not the justice system in isolation, has the ability and resources to effectively respond to the harms of crime and to ultimately restore victims and integrate offenders into the community as healthy, whole contributing members of society.

A second approach to understanding Restorative Justice is to understand that restorative justice has a future focus, a focus on outcomes. When a harm has been committed in the community, there are three key groups that must be meaningfully responded to: the direct victims, the wider impacted community, and the offender.
Outcomes for victims should focus on:

- being given the opportunity to be acknowledged and heard
- having input regarding resolution to the offense
- having the harms done to them meaningfully addressed
- meaningful support services for healing and closure

Outcomes for the community should focus on:

- creating safe and healthy communities
- active and extensive partnerships with the justice system that lead to the integration of victims and offenders into the community as positive, contributing members

Outcomes for offenders should focus on:

- being accountable for the harm done
- taking an active role in determining how to make amends to victims and the community
- integration into the community as positive and productive citizens

Front-End, Back-End

There are front-ended and back-ended correctional programs. Front-ended programs are punishment options for initial sentences that are more restrictive than traditional probation but less restrictive than jail or prison. Back-ended programs are sanctions that move offenders from higher levels of control to lower ones for the final phase of their sentences, such as prison to parole. Front-end programs and back-end programs relate to intermediate sanctions by offering judges and correctional authorities increased punishment options. In earlier times, these individuals were placed on probation. Intermediate sanctions (especially front-end programs) may contribute to what is called net-widening because judges have more alternatives to confinement for offenders.

Net-Widening

Net-widening means increasing the number of offenders sentenced to a greater level of restriction (i.e., using an intermediate sanction as a stiffer punishment for offenders who would ordinarily have been sentenced to probation or a lesser sanction). Should a participant violate a program rule, the consequences would be inappropriate for this particular participant. Net-widening results in the sentencing of offenders to more restrictive sanctions than their offenses and characteristics originally warranted.

Following the recommendations of the 1967 President's Commission on Law Enforcement and the Administration of Justice, a nationwide explosion of diversionary programs was made available to defendants to keep them from the justice process.[86] However, an alarming trend developed. In part, the trend related to a documented failure of diversion to implement a reliable participant selection process that subsequently extended participant reach by increasing eligibility of programs to defendants who might not be eligible otherwise (i.e., increasing the candidate base to include defendants that would not necessarily attract justice sanctions or net-widening).

How could this happen? An individual engages in a minor infraction and is placed in a diversion (the topic of Chapter 6) program. But, if the program were nonexistent, that individual could have been released without sanction. The problem is that diversion programs are designed to keep individuals out of the system, as opposed to increasing the number of potential candidates into the system. Once in diversion, should a defendant violate a rule such as curfew, the defendant is now eligible for an official consequence or penalty. Studies show that some defendants are in the justice system that would not have been candidates prior to being placed into an alternative program that helped them avoid the process.[87]

The implications of net-widening are serious because the process results in the transfer of resources from those most in need of intervention to those who may require no intervention.[88] Net-widening results in depleting a CC program's resources and lessens its ability to properly intervene with those who really are in need of appropriate intervention. Instead of enhancing public safety, net-widening shifts resources from individuals with the greatest need.

SUMMARY

A good reason to study CC is because over 50 percent of the defendants prior to trial and over 80 percent of all convicted defendants are supervised through CC agencies and those individuals live among us. One focus of this book relates to troubled first-time offenders who made bad choices, and this work focuses on the nature and process of CC and the philosophical belief systems that shape correctional policy and practice concerned with the factors that lead to crime and how to deal with offenders once they are in the system. The focus of this book is that correctional programs delivered in the community can reduce criminal activities more often than programs delivered in prison for specific types of offenders. The ultimate goal of criminal justice partners comprised of the police, court, and corrections is public safety and the immediate goal of CC is to guide an offender to a crime-free lifestyle, regardless of the model utilized to accomplish this goal. The function of police is to make arrests, the courts conduct trials and impose sentences, and corrections carries out the sentences of the court.

Civil law protects a variety of interests, including family matters such as a divorce, business relationships, and protecting personal property. Criminal law is described as a body of law that regulates actions that can harm the interests of another individual, the state, or the federal government. Criminal law includes crimes such as murder and forcible rape. These crimes involve stricter rules of procedure and burdens of proof and the emphasis of criminal law is on punishing an offender. The role of CC is to provide a practical and humane alternative to imprisonment.

CC is described as a set of interrelated programs meant to prevent future criminal activity by providing opportunities that bolster accountability of offenders without compromising its mission. The focus of CC is to provide professional services to adult and juvenile defendants who are arrested, released, and awaiting trial (Pretrial Release); diverted from the justice process before, during, or after trial (Diversion); fined or subjected to other forms of nonincarcerated sanctions (Intermediate Sanctions); found guilty but released from custody provided conditions of freedom are met (Probation); released after serving time provided conditions of release are met (Parole); and provided alternative environments between probation and prison and aftercare (Residential Intermediate Sanctions). The services of CC can be characterized as programs, treatment, and supervision.

Justification that supports the use of CC has occurred as the realities of a new century demand attention: sentence reforms, widespread drop in reported crime from 1994–2000, increase in general conviction rates, increase in correctional populations, prisons promoting violence, overcrowded prisons, recidivism levels, and economic downturns. However, as new participants are added to community correctional programs designed to limit the impact of the justice system upon some defendants, the potential consequences of net-widening actually increase the candidate base to include defendants who would not necessarily attract justice sanctions.

Finally, although there are many jurisdictions providing correctional functions, one way to bring these agencies closer to their ultimate and immediate mission is to say that they should apply a range of guided supervision strategies, services, and programs couched in practices consisting of reconciliation, restitution, rehabilitation, reintegration, and restorative justice. Chapter 2 is about the four primary approaches of correctional supervision and helps describe the influences that shape correctional policy and practice.

DISCUSSION QUESTIONS

1. In what way might you agree with the explanation about the importance of studying CC?

2. Identify two specific questions centered in a philosophical belief system that shapes both community correctional policy and correctional practice.

3. Identify the criminal justice partners and reveal the function of each.

4. Identify and explain the various types of offenses.

5. In what way might you agree with the primary role of community corrections?

6. Describe the services provided by community corrections. Which service do you feel is the most important service and why?

7. Characterize the differences between reported crime and clearance rates. Why would a person who has been raped, robbed, or beaten not report to the crime to the police?

8. Describe the various strategies of community supervision.

9. Describe the goal of CC and explain in what way you agree and disagree with the goal.

10. Identify the justifications that support the use of CC. Of these, which justification would support the use of community corrections most and least?

11. Identify and describe the characteristics associated with the Five Rs. Explain which of these five characteristics is the most important one associated with the goal of community corrections.

12. Explain net-widening and describe its consequences. It what way might you guard against net-widening effects if you were in charge of the eligibility process?

NOTES

1. James Q. Wilson and George L. Kelling (1982). Broken windows: The police and neighborhood safety. *The Atlantic Monthly, 249*(3), 29–38.

2. Jeremy Travis (1998, June). *Plenary address.* Paper presented at the conference on international perspectives on crime, justice, and public order, Budapest, Hungary.

3. This thought should not be interpreted as taking a procapital punishment position. Frankly, I would never trust any government with such a final solution.

4. Bureau of Justice Statistics (2004). *Probation and parole in the United States, 2003.* Washington, DC: U.S. Department of Justice, Office of Justice Programs, NCJ

205336. Retrieved online January 11, 2005: http://www.ojp.usdoj.gov/bjs/pudf/ppus03.htm

5. Kathryn E. McCollister, Michael T. French, Michael Prendergast, Harry Wexler, Stan Sacks, and Elizabeth Hall (2003). Is in-prison treatment enough? A cost-effectiveness analysis of prison-based treatment and aftercare services for substance-abusing offenders. *Law & Policy, 25*(1), 63–82.

6. Reinventing Probation Counsel (2001). *Forming probation through leadership: "Broken Windows" model.* The Manhattan Institute, p. 17. Retrieved online January 11, 2005: http://www.cjtoday.com/pdf/7cjt1103.pdf

6. Edward J. Latessa and Harry E. Allen (1999), Corrections in the Community. (2nd ed.) Cincinnati OH: Anderson, 255.

7. Reinventing Probation Counsel (2001), 17.

8. Daniel Glaser (1997). *Profitable penalties: How to cut both crime rates and costs.* Thousand Oaks, CA: Pine Forge Press. Daniel Glaser (1995). *Preparing convicts for law-abiding lives. The pioneering penology of Richard A. McGree.* Albany: State University of New York Press.

9. Charles H. Logan (2001). *Criminal justice performance measures for prisons.* Bureau of Justice Assistance, Center for Program Evaluation. Retrieved online March 14, 2003: http://www.bja.evaluationwebsite.org/

10. Michael E. Smith (2001, June). *What future for "public safety" and "restorative justice" in community corrections?* National Institute of Justice, NCJ 187773. Retrieved online May 9, 2004: http://www.ncjrs.org/txtfiles1/nij/187773.txt. Also Leena Kurki (1999, September). *Incorporating restorative and community justice into American sentencing and corrections. Research in brief—Sentencing and corrections: Issues for the 21st century.* Washington, DC: U.S. Department of Justice. National Institute of Justice/Corrections Program Office, NCJ 175723. Retrieved online January 11, 2005: http://www.ncjrs.org/pdffiles1/nij/175723.pdf

11. Emile Durkheim (1984, 1933). *Durkheim: The division of labor in society.* Translated by W.D. Halls. New York: Free Press. Also see Kai T. Erikson (1966). *Wayward Puritans: A study in the sociology of deviance.* New York: Wiley. See pages 3–15 for a discussion about crime and society: "Durkheim made the surprising observation that crime was really a natural kind of social activity, an integral part of all healthy societies." 3.

12. Pursuing a study of the connection between society's response to wrong-doers and societal welfare might aid in a better understanding of the relevance of criminal sanctions in the American society, global societies, and even ancient societies. A recommended source in addition to Durkheim (see endnote 11): Heinrich Oppenheimer (1975). *The rationale of punishment.* Montclair, NJ: Patterson Smith (pp. 7–68 in particular). This work was originally published in 1913. Israel Drapkin (1989). *Crime and punishment in the ancient world.* Lexington, MA: Lexington Books (pp. 15–85 in particular).

13. Making an issue of the Bill of Rights is far more relevant that expected especially because the U.S. Patriot Act I and II can compromise the Constitutional rights of

many individuals. Perhaps in the time of terrorism and war, the U.S. government feels it necessary to violate the rights of others, despite the argument by many experts that the greatest test of the Bill of Rights is during acts of terrorism and war. Whichever position you take concerning this matter, it appears that most state and local justice agencies do not possess the same authority as federal agencies, at least at the time of this writing.

14. There is administrative law, too, that regulates daily business activities; violations of such regulations can result in warnings or fines, depending on their adjudged severity.

15. This rule of thumb depends on the jurisdiction, which includes authority—federal, state, local, tribal—and so on. In the Commonwealth of Massachusetts, defendants convicted of felonies in which a two-year sentence is imposed generally serve their sentence in a House of Corrections or county jail as opposed to a state prison. In Washington and several other states, a one-year sentence or less is generally served in jail.

16. Due to overcrowded conditions in state prisons, some state prisoners are transferred to county jails to serve their sentences. County or local facilities do not have to abide by the same standards state facilities do and for that reason, jails can be overcrowded and violate numerous standards without concern.

17. Wilson R. Palacios, Paul F. Cromwell, and Roger G. Dunham (Eds.). (2002). *Crime and Justice in America: Present realities and future prospects* (2nd ed.). Upper Saddle River, NJ: Prentice Hall, 1.

18. This thought is consistent with the American Probation and Parole Association. Retrieved online January 11, 2005: http://appa-net.org/

19. Michael S. Dukakis, then governor of Massachusetts, was a presidential candidate in 1988. For more information about Horton see J. J. Larivee (1993, October). Community programs: A risky business. *Corrections Today, 55,* 20–24.

20. J. Leo (1996, December 23). Changing the rules of a deadly game. *US News Online.* Retrieved online July 12, 2004: http://www.usnews.com/usnews/issue/23john.htm

21. R. Jerome, M. Eftimades, N. Gallo, and S. Sawicki (1995. March). Megan's legacy. *People Weekly, 43*(11), 46–60.

22. For details, see Edward Leberg (1997). *Understanding child molesters: Taking charge.* Thousand Oaks, CA: Sage.

23. Michael Braswell, Tyler Fletcher, and Larry Miller (1998). *Human relations and corrections* (4th ed.). Mount Prospect, IL: Waveland (pp. 19–21).

24. Michael R. Gottfredson and Travis Hirschi (1990). *A general theory of crime.* Stanford, CA: Stanford University Press, 16.

25. Bureau of Justice Statistics (2000). *Correctional populations in the United States for 1997.* Washington, DC: U.S. Department of Justice, Office of Justice Programs. Retrieved online May 14, 2004: http://www.ojp.usdoj.gov/bjs/pub/pdf/cpus9704.pdf

26. Daniel Glaser (1997). *Profitable penalties.* Thousand Oaks, CA: Pine Forge, 11.

27. Daniel Glaser (1997), 11.

28. Marcus Felson (2002). *Crime and everyday life,* (3rd ed.). Thousand Oaks, CA: Pine Forge, 9–12.

29. John Leo (1996, December 23). Changing the rules of a deadly game. *US News Online.* Retrieved online July 20, 2004: http://www.usnews.com. Also, see FBI, Uniform Crime Reports and Clearance Rates. Retrieved online January 11, 2005: http://www.fbi.gov/ucr/2004/6mosprelim04.pdf

30. The Uniform Crime Reporting (UCR) Program and National Crime Victimization Survey (NCVS) were designed to complement each other. The UCR Program's primary objective is to provide a reliable set of criminal justice statistics for law enforcement administration, operation, and management, as well as to indicate fluctuations in the level of crime in America. The NCVS was established to obtain and provide previously unavailable information about victims, offenders, and crime (including crime not reported to the police). Although the two programs employ different methodologies, they measure a similar subset of serious crimes. FBI. Retrieved online January 11, 2005: http://www.fbi.gov/ucr/ucrquest.htm

31. An offense is "cleared by arrest" or solved for crime reporting purposes when at least one person is (a) arrested or (b) charged with the commission of the offense and turned over to the court for prosecution (whether following arrest, court summons, or police notice). Although no physical arrest is made, a clearance by arrest can be claimed when the offender is a person under 18 years of age and is cited to appear in juvenile court or before other juvenile authorities. FBI. Retrieved online July 21, 2004: http://www.fbi.gov/ucr/ucrquest.htm

32. FBI. Uniform Crime Reports, Section III. Retrieved online January 11, 2005: http://www.fbi.gov/ucr/cius_02/pdf/3sectionthree.pdf

33. This thought is consistent with Chief Charles Ramsey, Metropolitan Police, Washington, DC, who argues that if history tells us anything, it tells us that if calls for these types of actions (arbitrary and unconstitutional use of police power) should occur in the future, we the police must be the first and the loudest to speak out. The chief was specifically responding to the illegal use of police power to aid nazi Germany's racial profiling of the Jews. He suggested that if the police of that day stood their ground, would outcomes have been different in Germany? See Dennis J. Stevens (2003). *Applied community policing in the 21st century.* Boston: Allyn Bacon (see p. 36 for Chief Ramsey's full perspective on this matter). And, Chief Charles H. Ramsey (2002). *Preparing the community for community policing: The next step in advancing community policing* (pp. 29–44). In Dennis J. Stevens (Ed), *Policing and community partnerships.* Upper Saddle River, NJ: Prentice Hall.

34. For a discussion about social class and criminal justice intervention, see Randall G. Shelden (2001). *Controlling the dangerous classes. A critical introduction to the history of criminal justice.* Boston: Allyn Bacon (especially pp. 2–14). Shelden suggests that the criminalization of the poor and minorities is, in effect, the duty of the justice community. Also, Jeffrey Reiman (1998). *The rich get richer and the poor get prison.* Boston: Allyn Bacon. Reiman postulates that the criminal justice community must fail in their conquest of lower class control to succeed. The state in a

capitalist society, as argued by Karl Marx some 150 years ago, is a committee of the capitalist social class.

35. For a closer look at this perspective, see Robert J. Meadows and Julie Kuehnel (2005). *Evil minds.* Upper Saddle River, NJ: Prentice Hall, 222.

36. For an in-depth discussion on this perspective, see Joan Petersilia (2001). *Measuring the performance of community corrections.* Retrieved online July 21, 2004: http://www.bja.evaluationwebsite.org/

37. Mary K. Shilton (1992). *Community corrections acts for state and local partnerships.* Washington, DC: American Correctional Association.

38. Joan Petersilia (2000, November). When prisoners return to the community: Political, economic and social consequences. *Sentencing and corrections: Issues for the 21st century.* Department of Justice. Retrieved online January 11, 2005: http://www. ncjrs.org/pdffiles1/nij/184253.pdf

39. American Probation and Parole Association. Retrieved online January 11, 2005: http://www.appa-net.org/

40. American Probation and Parole Association. Retrieved online January 11, 2005: http://www.appa-net.org/

41. Some writers like to include pretrial release (suspects who were arrested and are released to their own recognizance or they made bond) and are pending trial. However, few if any correctional systems offer programs to individuals pending trial or awaiting a final disposition unless trial is waved and a diversion program is suggested.

42. Dean J. Champion (1999). *Probation, parole, and community corrections.* Upper Saddle River, NJ: Prentice Hall.

43. See www.fbi.gov/ucr/ucr.httm

44. The UCR is a nationwide, cooperative statistical effort of nearly 17,000 city, county, and state law enforcement agencies who voluntarily report crime data brought to their attention. Not all police agencies participate. However, since 1930, the FBI has administered the program and issued periodic assessments of the nature and type of crime in the nation. Those reports show that crime has been slowing down. Although 2002 showed an increase, it is not as great as in previous years.

45. Nicholas R. Turner and Daniel F. Wilhelm (2002, December). Are the politics of criminal justice changing? *Corrections Today,* 74–76.

46. Bureau of Justice Statistics (2003). *Sourcebook of criminal justice statistics: 2002.* U.S. Department of Justice (Table 2.1). Retrieved online January 11, 2005: http://www.albany.edu/sourcebook. Those polled ranked terrorism, the economy, education, health care, and unemployment higher than crime and violence.

47. Bureau of Justice Statistics (2003). *Courts and sentencing statistics.* Washington, DC: U.S. Department of Justice, Office of Justice Programs. Retrieved online January 11, 2005: http://www.ojp.usdoj.gov/bjs/stssent.htm

48. Bureau of Prisons. Retrieved online January 11, 2005: http://www.bop.gov/

49. Bureau of Justice Statistics (2004, November). *Prisoners in 2003.* Washington, DC: U.S. Department of Justice, Office of Justice Programs, NCJ 205335. Retrieved online January 11, 2005: http://www.ojp.usdoj.gov/bjs/pub/pdf/p03.pdf

50. Dennis J. Stevens (2006). *Community corrections: An applied approach.* Upper Saddle River, NJ: Prentice Hall. Table developed after a review of the Bureau of Justice Statistics (2004, November). *Prisoners in 2003.* Also, Bureau of Justice Statistics (2004, July). *Probation and parole at yearend 2003.* Washington, DC: U.S. Department of Justice, Office of Justice Programs. Retrieved online January 11, 2005: http://www.ojp.usdoj.gov/bjs/pub/pdf/ppus03.pdf

51. Bureau of Justice Statistics (2004, November). *Prisoners in 2003.*

52. Bureau of Justice Statistics (2004, November). *Prisoners in 2003.*

53. For more detail, see Mary K. Shilton (1992), 2.

54. Judith Greene (2000). Controlling prison crowding. In Dennis J. Stevens (Ed.), *Perspective corrections* (pp. 178–180). Madison, WI: Coursewise.

55. Judith Greene (2000), 178.

56. For a closer look at the relationship between imprisonment and future violence, see Dennis J. Stevens (2000). The depth of imprisonment and prisonisation: Levels of security and prisoners' anticipation of future violence. In Dennis J. Stevens (Ed.), *Perspective: Corrections.* Madison, WI: Coursewise (pp. 81–88). This work offers a discussion about the pains of imprisonment and prisonization effects. Stevens does not take credit for those notions, because they were centered in the work of Donald Clemmer (1940–1958). *The prison community.* New York: Holt, Rinehart, & Winston. Originally, Stevens' work first appeared in the 1994 *Howard Journal of Criminal Justice, 33*(2), 137–157. Concerning the idea of violence in prison, see Dennis J. Stevens (1997). Violence begets violence. Corrections Compendium: The National Journal for Corrections. *American Correctional Association, 22*(12), 1–2. Also, for female prison violence, see Dennis J. Stevens (1998). The impact of time-served and regime on prisoners' anticipation of crime: Female prisonization effects. *Howard Journal of Criminal Justice, 37*(2), 188–205.

57. For a closer look at prisoner assimilation of violent norms and institutionalization, see Donald Clemmer (1958). For a closer look at the emotional pains of confinement, see Gresham M. Sykes (1958). *The society of captives.* New York: Princeton University Press. Sykes says "the deprivations or frustrations of prison life today might be viewed as punishments which the free community deliberately inflicts on the offender for violating the law. . . . It is not difficult to see this isolation as painfully depriving or frustrating in terms of lost emotional relationships, of loneliness and boredom. . . . What makes this pain of imprisonment bite most deeply is the fact that the confinement of the criminal represents a deliberate, moral rejection of the criminal by the free community" (pp. 64–65). As noted from the dates of these publications, assimilation into violence and the emotional pains of confinement have been perspectives that have been discussed for awhile and yet little has been done to address those issues, some might argue, such as Robert Johnson (1996). *Hard time: Understanding and reforming the prison.* Belmont, CA: Wadsworth.

58. There are many definitions for recidivism including repetition of criminal behavior and fingerprinted re-arrests for alleged crimes. See S. Clarke and A. L. Harrison (1992). *Recidivism of criminal offenders assigned to community correctional programs or released from prisons in North Carolina in 1989.* Report prepared for the North Carolina Sentencing and Policy Advisory Commission, Institute of Government. Chapel Hill: University of North Carolina at Chapel Hill.

59. For a closer look, see: Bureau of Justice Statistics (2003). *Criminal case processing statistics.* Washington, DC: U.S. Department of Justice, Office of Justice Programs. Retrieved online January 11, 2005: http://www.ojp.usdoj.gov/bjs/cases.htm

60. Karen Imas (2003, October). *The changing face of corrections in the current fiscal crisis.* The Council of State Governments/Eastern Regional Conference (pp. 5–9). Retrieved online January 6, 2005: http://www.csgeast.org/pdfs/ercoctbrief.pdf

61. Robert P. Corbett (1992). How did we get in this mess? In Donald Cochran, Ronald P. Corbett, Jr., Barry Nidorf, and Don Sites (Eds.) *Managing probation with scarce resources. Obstacles and opportunities* (pp. 1–8). U.S. Department of Justice, National Institute of Corrections.

62. Robert P. Corbett (1992). Also see National Conference of State Legislatures. Retrieved online January 6, 2005: http://www.ncsl.org/

63. Washington Department of Corrections. Retrieved online January 6, 2005: http://www.wa.gov/doc/doc.htm

64. Washington Department of Corrections. Retrieved online January 6, 2005: http://www.doc.wa.gov/

65. Robert P. Corbett (1992).

66. Karen Imas (2003), 6.

67. Judith Greene (2000), 178.

68. R. Moore and C. Brown-Young (2000, February). Washington's offender accountability act: A new approach to corrections. *Corrections Today, 2,* 60–63.

69. E. Viano (2000, July). Restorative justice for victims and offenders. *Corrections Today, 7,* 132–135.

70. National Conference of State Legislatures (2004). *State budget updates.* Retrieved online January 6, 2005: http://www.ncsl.org/print/fiscal/sbu2005-0411.pdf (p. 21).

71. National Conference of State Legislatures (2004), 21.

72. In fact, when thinking about a definition for community corrections, many textbooks and other sources were consulted. But, there was little consistency in definitions or in overall approaches to the subject. Works reviewed that led to this conclusion include: Dean J. Champion (1999). *Probation, parole, and community corrections* (3rd ed.). Upper Saddle River, NJ: Prentice Hall (pp. 269–270). Todd R. Clear and Harry R. Dammer (2000). *The offender in the community.* Belmont, CA: Wadsworth (pp. 26–29). Paul F. Cromwell, Rolando V. Del Carmen, and Leanne F. Alarid (2002). *Community-based corrections.* (5th ed.). Belmont, CA: Wadsworth. (p. 389). Edward J. Latessa and Harry E. Allen (1999). *Corrections in the community.* (2nd ed.).

Cincinnati OH: Anderson (p. 3). Marilyn D. McShane and Wesley Krause (1993). *Community corrections.* New York: MacMillan. (p. 4). Belinda Rodgers McCarthy, Bernard J. McCarthy, Jr., and Matthew C. Leone (2001). *Community-based corrections.* (4th ed.). Belmont, CA: Wadsworth. (p. 1). Other sources included the Bureau of Justice Statistics, National Institute of Corrections, and the American Probation and Parole Association, to name a few but there were many more.

73. Joseph Lehman, Trudy Gregorie Beatty, Dennis Maloney, Susan Russell, and Anne Seymour (2002). The three "R's" of reentry. *Justice Solutions.* Retrieved online January 6, 2005: http://www.appa-net.org/3R.pdf. Also see, Mark Umbreit (1999). *What is restorative justice?* St. Paul, MN: Center for Restorative Justice and Peacemaking. William J. Dickey and M. E. Smith (1998). What if corrections were serious about public safety? *Corrections Management Quarterly, 2*(3), 12–30. Thomas Cavanagh (2000). Restorative justice and the common good: Creating a culture of forgiveness and reconciliation. *Blueprint for Social Justice, LIII*(8), 48–54.

74. Minnesota Department of Corrections. Retrieved online January 6, 2005: http://www.doc.state.mn.us/

75. Mary K. Shilton (1992), 31.

76. Scott Matson (2002, October). Sex offender treatment: A critical management tool. *Corrections Today,* 114–117.

77. David M. Altschuler, Troy L. Armstrong, and Doris Layton MacKenzie (1999, July). Reintegration, supervised release, and intensive aftercare. *Juvenile Justice Bulletin.* Washington, DC: U.S. Department of Justice, Office of Justice Programs, NCJ 175715. Retrieved online January 6, 2005: http://ojjdp.ncjrs.org/jjbulletin/9907_3/intro.html

78. For more detail see Joan Petersilia (2000, November).

79. David Glaser (1997).

80. News Releases. The White House: George W. Bush. Retrieved online January 6, 2005: http://www.whitehouse.gov/news/releases/2004/01/20040123-4.html

81. *Financial recovery issues in court: Criminal process.* Retrieved online January 6, 2005: http://www.madd.org/home

82. Mike Santarini (2001, July 19). Avanti to pay $182 M restitution to cadence. *EE Times.*

83. There is an interesting narrative in Belinda Rodgers McCarthy, Bernard J. McCarthy, Jr., and Matthew C. Leone's (2001). *Community-Based corrections.* New York Wadsworth, 5–9.

84. The Center for Restorative Justice. Retrieved online January 6, 2005: http://www.sfu.ca/cfrj/intro.html

85. Eric Gilman (n/a). *What is restorative justice?* Retrieved online January 6, 2005: http://www.sfu.ca/cfrj/fulltext/gilman.pdf

86. Thomas G. Blomberg (1980). Widening the net: An anomaly in the evaluation of diversion programs. In Malcom W. Klien & K. D. Teilman (Eds.), *Handbook of criminal justice evaluation.* (pp. 571–592). Beverly Hills, CA: Sage.

87. Thomas G. Blomberg (1980).

88. Ross Jamison (2002). *Widening the net in juvenile justice and the dangers of prevention and early intervention.* Center on Juvenile and Criminal Justice. Retrieved online January 6, 2005: http://www.cjcj.org/pubs/net/netwid.html

2

APPROACHES IN COMMUNITY CORRECTIONS

LEARNING OBJECTIVES

When you finish reading this chapter, you will be better prepared to:

- Describe two conceptual political camps that shape correctional practice.
- Explain the historical evolution of official justice response towards wrong-doers.
- Describe two dominant perspectives about the causal factors of crime.
- Identify the four primary approaches.
- Link both causal perspectives to each of the four approaches.
- Explain the importance of studying these four approaches.
- Describe punishment as a corrections approach and explain its components.
- Explain in what way the mission of corrections could be furthered using a punishment approach.
- Discuss control as a corrections approach, describe its justification, and provide an example of how it could be utilized in community corrections, by law enforcement, and by the courts.
- Explain treatment as a corrections approach, discuss its justification, and identify some of its advantages linked to the Five Rs.
- Describe prevention as a corrections approach, explain its justification, and identify some of its advantages linked to the Five Rs.
- Identify different outcomes as the rationale pendulum swings.

KEY TERMS

Control Approach	General Deterrence	Selective Incapacitation
Collective Incapacitation	Prevention Approach	Specific Deterrence
Conservatives and Liberals	Procedural Criminal Law	Substantive Criminal Law
Just deserts	Punishment Approach	Treatment Approach
lex talionis	Retribution	

"We seldom attribute common sense except to those who agree with us."
—François Duc de La Rochefoucauld (1613–1680), French writer, moralist

INTRODUCTION

Chapter 1 implied that philosophical belief systems or attitudes held by policy makers, interest groups, and the public could shape correctional policy and practice. It was said that some of those attitudes address two specific questions:

1. What factors led an offender to crime? (causal factors of crime) "Did the offender commit the crime because he wanted to commit crime or did something push him over the edge?"
2. What is the best way to deal with an offender once in a correctional system? (approaches in corrections) "How should the correctional community respond to offenders?"

The way a person answers these questions has wide implication, especially if the person is a policy maker or influences policy makers. That is, policy, regulations, and enforcement of policies and regulations governing correctional programs, personnel, and their participants or clients can depend more on the broad political, philosophical, and social theme of the era than on the dedicated efforts of the courageous men and women who work and volunteer in correctional initiatives, including CC. This chapter explores "perceived" factors that some say cause crime, political themes associated with criminal law, historical perspectives of punishment, and the four chief approaches that characterize CC—punishment, control, treatment, or prevention. How are they connected? A young woman getting "stoned" because she enjoys "feeling free" would probably be treated differently in a correctional program (and during the arrest and trial) than a young woman who became addicted to illicit drugs a few months after being prescribed OxyContin for a painful surgery. But before discussing those perceived factors leading to crime and what to do about offenders in the correctional system, getting a clear view about the importance of this chapter is worth your time.

IMPORTANCE OF THIS CHAPTER

The centerpiece of this chapter and indeed this book is that both policy (directives, regulations, and enforcement initiatives) and approaches (punishment, control, treatment, and prevention) or strategies associated with models managing correctional populations are influenced by the attitudes of policy makers, interest groups, and the public regarding factors responsible for crime.[1] Keep in mind that correctional personnel, contract staff, and volunteers are obliged to follow policy and mandates. But there is often a difference between policy and practice.[2] That is, both official policy and everyday routine or practice of correctional workers can depend on "perceived" or alleged causal factors that influenced a guilty defendant toward crime. This chapter reveals those perceived factors and links them to broad political themes, which in turn helps policy makers shape official strategies or correctional approaches that should be employed when dealing with guilty defendants.

Policy makers and practitioners connect their own ideas about why a guilty defendant committed a crime and associate their own idea with a belief system or a body of knowledge to support their mending, tinkering, and performance of their version of the "best" model or approach in CC. That is, if a junkie gets high because she likes it, then she should be arrested, prosecuted, and sent to prison for a long time. One the other hand, if a drug addict was a war veteran and is "hooked" because of a combat wound treated with morphine, then maybe prosecution is inappropriate.

DIVERSION

There should be little doubt that custody is necessary for some defendants even in CC, but whether the court imposes a sentence upon a defendant to be served in jail through a community-related agency, there are largely four approaches (punishment, control, treatment or prevention) that await defendants. In the final analysis of how CC works, it is essential to understand the philosophy or attitudes of policy makers, interest groups, and the public, which ultimately shape the policy and practice of dedicated men, women, and volunteers who attempt to turn the life around of troubled people. Before going on, we should discuss the broad political themes that help many of us decide right from wrong.

BROAD POLITICAL THEMES

Many issues in criminal justice are complex, yet in an attempt to simply explain some of those issues, criticism comes easy to those who hold different ideas about life, liberty, and the pursuit of happiness. In this case, an attempt to learn about the attitudes of policy makers, interest groups, and the public can be characterized as belonging to one of two broad political camps:

1. Those reluctant to accept change, to preserve status quo and traditional values and customs, are generally against abrupt change—this is how we've always done it, they would say, "and it seems to me that is how community corrections should do its job." This group of individuals is referred to as *conservatives*.

2. Those tolerant of different views and standards of behavior in others. These individuals favor gradual reform and ideals that protect the personal freedom of the individual. This group is referred to as *liberals*. Liberals tend to be optimistic about

offenders in CC programs and feel that more programs should be offered through-out the system.

In a sense, it could be stated that conservatives are advocates of "tough" policies and liberals are advocates of "soft" justice policies.[3] How CC provides services to the offender might depend largely on the side of the broad political camp we accept most often. For instance, remember the young addicted man mentioned earlier in the chapter? Conservatives might not be concerned with the reason the young man used illicit drugs, whereas liberals might take another look at those reasons before deciding on how to deal with him once in the system. For instance, conservative thinking would suggest close monitoring of an offender on probation and any infraction of a rule would meet with the full conse-quences of the infraction. Conversely, liberal thinking might see close monitoring as an intrusion of an offender and only serious violations would be reported. Some might de-cide on a conservative approach for every question, but many could go back and forth, from liberal to conservative approaches, depending on the issue. Continuing along this line of reasoning, the way conservatives and liberals look at criminal law is different, too. Which approach in CC is considered a better strategy is influenced by conservative and liberal views, and those views include application of the criminal law.

Criminal Law

There are two types of rules in criminal justice. *Substantive criminal law* deals with crimes and their prosecution and *procedural criminal law* deals with process.

> ### Criminal Law
>
> Substantive criminal law defines crimes and procedural criminal law sets down criminal procedure. Substantive criminal law was originally common law, was later codified, and is now found in federal and state statutory law.
> Source: Findlaw.[4]

Substantive criminal law is a set of rules governing behavior of the public. Proce-dural criminal law is a set of rules governing behavior of the officials who administer jus-tice. Substantive criminal law defines lawful behavior and determines what constitutes a violation and the penalty for breaking the law. It creates or defines rights, duties, obliga-tions, and causes of action that can be enforced by law.

Procedural criminal law defines what officials can do (police can stop and search, judges can poll a jury, CC personnel can impose restrictions upon a participant) and how to do it (e.g., warrant, probable cause, conditional release). It prescribes the procedures and methods for enforcing rights and duties and for obtaining redress (as in a suit) and is distinguished from substantive law that creates, defines, or regulates individual rights.

Conservatives emphasize substantive criminal rules, whereas liberals emphasize procedural criminal rules. Both sides are adamant about which set of rules has priority.

The power of parole and probation officers must be enhanced to control parolees and pro-bationers—too many loopholes for offenders—versus the liberal perspective that the authority of parole and probation must be checked to protect democracy—too much power in the hands of government leads to tyranny (see Table 2.1).

One and only one category for every situation is not necessarily the way it works. Conservatives rely on getting tough on crime, whereas liberals see treatment as an answer, but conservatives can see treatment for certain violators, whereas liberals might consider "hard time." Which approach is better suited toward meeting CC objectives? Perhaps the best answer depends on your understanding about crime and punishment.

Historical Perspectives on Punishment

Early western history reveals that in kingdoms, tribes, and clans, when individuals broke cultural tradition or refused (or for reasons outside of their control such as mental incompetence) to comply with societal expectation, they were punished.[6] Often, those responses grew into an official response supported by monarchs, military leaders, or patriarchs of the day. Punishing individuals who broke societal rules and expectations is an unfortunate but necessary part of a surviving and healthy society. Of the various methods to control behavior, criminal punishment has been the most formal response because criminal behavior is the most serious type of behavior over which a society must gain control.[7] How closely does this thought compare with today's standards?

Early methods of punishment included banishing, crucifying, drowning, burning, throwing offenders off cliffs, quartering or dismembering, torturing, humiliating, and/or enslaving. Sometimes, violators were isolated in places such as convents, monasteries, insane asylums, or leper colonies, depending on the era. Strategies for less serious offenses included confiscating their property, fining them, destructing their home or property, and not allowing them to buy or sell property, to vote, or to marry.[8] That is, strategies to control offender behavior depended on the set of beliefs about the causality of crime, but punishment was administered in an arbitrary manner depending on the mood of the administrator.[9] Hopefully, you can see that there was a distinction in early practices to punish a violator as opposed to aiding his or her victim or an attempt to guide a violator

Table 2.1   Comparison between Substantive and Procedural Criminal Law[5]

Substantive Criminal Law	Procedural Criminal Law
Defines everybody's behavior	Defines official behavior
Defines rights, duties, and obligations	Describes how rights and duties are enforced
Determines what constitutes a violation	How to obtain redress (restore equality)
Identifies legal action	Identifies how legal action should be conducted
Supported by Conservatives	Supported by Liberals

Note: Both conservative and liberal agendas are not necessarily mutually excusive or polar opposites.

away from disruptive elements such as alcoholism. For instance, it was believed that if an offender were:

1. Demonic (evil), he or she had to be destroyed.
2. Out of touch with God, he or she needed to repent.
3. Poorly educated, he or she had to be trained.
4. Diagnosed as "sick," he or she required physical cure.
5. A witch, he or she must be burned.

Although monarchs and warriors, along with their hooded punishers, have been replaced with elected officials and confinement in 21st century America, the way modern society responds to violators is not very different from even ancient civilizations. When crime was seen as a deliberate act against the victim in ancient Athens, victims had the right to act out of anger and inflict physical punishment toward an aggressor to feel "cured."[10] In a modern nation, crime is a violation against all members of society, and therefore only government carries out the punishment of an aggressor. However, modern legitimate responses or the punishment of aggressors continues to flow from the beliefs held by policy makers, interest groups, and the public about the factors leading to crime. For instance, when a crime is committed, emphasis is on the intention or motive of the violator more than the crime itself. If the crime occurred because the violator wanted it to happen (getting stoned because the defendant wanted to get stoned) versus a factor that pushed the violator toward the crime (e.g., a traumatic early childhood experience or a violent abusive relationship), opinions about guilt will change, resulting in different official options. When we think about offenders, many of us accept one of two predominant beliefs about factors leading to crime: free will versus environmental factors.

TWO COMPETING VIEWS ABOUT CAUSAL FACTORS LINKED TO CRIME

Criminal justice agencies, including CC agencies, design strategies and programs consistent with popular ideas about causal factors of crime held by policy makers, interest groups, and the public. Although a study of crime causation or criminology is a vast study in itself, to simplify this thought, when we read about a terrible crime happening such as a woman killing her children, we wonder why she did it. For instance, we might ask: "Did she kill them because she wanted to kill them or did something drive her to it?" The instrumental factor that motivates an offender to commit a crime can be grounded in one of two competing views:

1. The *classical view* assumes human beings possess a free will and are capable of making rational decisions. They should be responsible for the crimes they commit because criminals are rational calculating machines.[11] The "best" method of control is punishment by enhancing pain to a point greater than pleasure.

2. An *environmental view* holds that decisions made by human beings are influenced by other factors such as the social environment, biological heritage, and psychological processes. Those factors, the thinking goes, should also be blamed for the decisions made by the offender.[12]

The Classical View: Free Will

The classical view of crime, as advanced by Cesare Beccaria and Jeremy Bentham during the Age of Enlightenment, argues that crime is a result of a rational or sensible decision and therefore, an offender exercises free will to commit crime.[13] Punishment should fit the crime. In contemporary America, when justice policy makers and practitioners accept the classical perspective, they look to the law for support and guidance.

Crime resides within the person and is "caused" by the way a criminal thinks, "not his environment."[14] A criminal psychologist reveals that when he began clinical work among prisoners, he believed that criminal behavior was a symptom of buried conflicts and was a product of early traumas and deprivation of one sort or another. He thought that people who turned to crime "were victims of a psychological disorder, an oppressive social environment, or both."[15] He holds a different perspective today, indicating that crime resides within the person and is caused by the way the offender thinks, not by the offender's environmental contributions.[16]

Focusing on crime through a free will perspective encourages due process standards and judicial restrictions.[17] That could be a good thing. But another product of this thinking validates methods of punishment and intense control as the best way to respond to violators. Part of this argument includes the idea that human beings avoid pain and seek pleasure. Make the pain of punishment greater than pleasure (of crime), these advocates say, and individuals will make the sensible decision to avoid crime.

Environmental Factors

In contrast to free will advocates, some behaviorists focus on environmental influences as causal factors leading to crime. Practitioners who accept an environmental perspective rely on methods of research in the field of criminology to aid them as they develop, maintain, and justify CC policy and practice. A simplified explanation is that environmentalists look at sociological, psychological, and biological aspects associated with an individual to determine the intent of a criminal act. Criminals are different even when they commit similar crimes. Social risk factors are different.[18] These factors include, *sociological* issues, such as family (rich or poor) practices or the early childhood experiences of an individual; social expectations and the social role of a child within his or her social universe; and his or her social structure, including the community where she or he grew up.[19] Social learning and labeling perspectives also play a role. That is, former and present living experiences enter into the causation equation. *Psychological* issues are included in environmental terms in the sense that some of us respond differently to varying situations such as in relationships and stressful events.[20] You might say that expectations about our relationships, how we respond to individuals when we are in a relationship, and events that occur in our lives might produce the criminal. For instance, an extremely selfish person in a loving relationship might demand sexual gratification regardless of the perspective or consent of a loved one (one difference between free will and the demand for sex in this example is that the offender cannot control the act to offend). Finally, environmentalists might add *biological* attributes to the list. For instance, some argue that among other biological issues, there are biological predispositions (weaknesses) toward drug addiction and violence that shape behavior.[21]

Some environmentalists add that we might want to see criminals as "human beings doing the best they can with what they have to work with."[22] For instance armed robbers (usually drug addicts), are not "seduced" into the sensationalism of crime. HIV-inflected, drug-addicted parents do not choose to leave their children at home without food or care while they hustle money for drugs.[23] In sum, from an environmental perspective, the cause of criminality (this does not include predatory offenders) or culpability can include politics (because crime is politically defined), economics, ideology, biology, and a historical context.[24] (See Table 2.2.)

Today, if a perception implies that a drug abuser "gets high" because the abuser wants to, then that abuser should be punished and imprisoned. This criminal sanction can be called a *punitive* (punishment) *approach* and is consistent with imprisonment and control as supported by the classical perspective of crime. Conversely, an environmental perspective supports the idea that a drug addict is a product of his or her social environment. Therefore, both the addict and the community require treatment of sorts. An environmentalist might think that drug addiction is a disease of society or a symptom of societal problems, and the individual is not necessarily immune to social diseases or the pressure of social demands. The debate continues. However, some take a position that utilizes both perspectives, especially in court. For instance, the degree of intent or how much free will was demonstrated during the commission of a crime can determine the level of guilt (more in this Chapter.)

Table 2.2 Two Competing Views About Causes of Crime[33]

Factors Causing Crime	*Classical View* Free Will and Rational Thinking	*Environment View* Environmental Influences
Strongest Factors That Influence Crime	Individual Desires[26]	Sociological, Psychological, and Biological[27]
Intervention Required	Individual[28]	Individual and Society[29]
"Best" Strategy	Punishment and Control[30]	Treatment and Prevention[31]
Desired Outcome	Punish and Deter[32]	Curb[33]

Look at it this way: The focus of a free will perspective is on the crime and the focus of an environmental perspective is on the criminal. Coming up with the "right" answer might be more difficult than expected. There is a lot of evidence to support both perspectives. Then, too, free will or environmental belief systems can justify the primary approach employed in CC.

BELIEF SYSTEMS AND CORRECTION APPROACHES

Although CC can deliver correctional services in numerous ways, most of those methods can be characterized through four models: punishment, control, treatment, and prevention. Each of these approaches is supported by a set of ideas or a philosophy that justifies services, programs, and supervision methods used when engaged with offenders, regardless of whether or not confinement is part of their sentence. CC cannot and does not operate in a vacuum. It is part of a correctional system that is part of the criminal justice community. Therefore, any philosophical discussion can easily relate to its partners as well.

A body of knowledge or a belief system linked to a correctional approach does more than shape policy and practice toward an approach of CC. It also shapes policy and practice associated with the conduct of correctional personnel, the management of the organizational structure, and the building designs of correctional centers and facilities. This includes:

- Hiring, training, and regulation of correctional personnel and volunteers
- Promotion and grievance process of personnel and offenders
- Regulations and classifications of correctional participants
- Monitoring, supervision, and surveillance techniques
- Management limitations and expectations
- Sanctions of those in diversion programs
- Policy of those in pretrial release programs
- Regulation and enforcement policy of those on probation and parole
- Institutional and community correctional services and programs
- Methods of change and accreditations
- Facility design and function

An approach can be politicized or part of a political platform such as the "get tough on crime" perspective. When a discussion arises because of a justice agency's regulation or law, it is often their philosophy or belief system that is debated, not necessarily the regulation or law. For instance, in a CC program where a "get tough on crime" principle is dominant, a minor offense might produce jail time for a violator in a diversionary program. The body of knowledge or philosophical belief system that supports a specific correctional approach or strategy offers a justification for the nature of sanctions and practices used and how they are administered.

PUNISHMENT APPROACH

One definition of punishment can be the infliction of a consequence in response to criminal conduct by those in authority. This thought is consistent with Andrew von Hirsch,[34] who adds that punishment should not be confused with its purpose. In part, the purpose of punishment is to be unpleasant and it is inflicted because of the conviction of a criminal act. But this notion advances the rationale that a harsh response by the justice community receives the benefit of an offense being "paid" or retaliation, and the effects of that action are expanded from a specific offender to the general public. From the cradle of early civilization to modern-day correctional practices, there are a lot of experiences linking punishment or punitive models to classical perspectives of crime and free will.

An "eye for an eye" or *lex talionis* as found in Exodus is also found in "hydraulic civilizations" organized around large-scale irrigation agricultures. Long before Christianity, organized civilizations existed.[35] Nonetheless:

> Then you shall give life for life, eye for eye, tooth for tooth, hand for hand, foot for foot, wound for wound, stripe for stripe.
>
> —Exodus 21–24

Those were empire states possessing tributary dominions and a hierarchical system of power and authority usually comprised of a rigid social class structure with a small elite and many slaves. Slaves and everyone between them and the elites were expected to behave in a certain way. It was as though behavior were programmed into the lifestyles of everyone. Behavior was grounded on compulsion (automatic) as opposed to consent (decision). For slaves, behavior inconsistent with those expectations had specific sanctions regardless of the *intent* of the person committing the act.

Punishment Model

The mission of the justice community is to administer punishment upon a guilty defendant and it should be commensurate with the seriousness of the crime. A punishment model can be characterized by a just desert, deterrence, and incapacitation perspective.

Overall, there are three categories that can characterize punishment as an approach to supervising offenders:

- Just deserts or retribution
- Deterrence
- Incapacitation

Just Deserts

> **Retribution** is a philosophical term suggesting actions that "get even" with a perpetrator. Social revenge suggests that individuals cannot exact punishment, but that the state will do so in their name. Retribution assumes that an offender willfully chose to commit an evil act, are responsible for their own behavior, are likely to commit similar acts again, and should receive the punishment they so richly deserve. Taking revenge upon a wrong-doer. Payback.

Just deserts can mean that aggressors "get what's coming to them" and is better known as retribution. Offenders deserve to be punished. Law is officially sanctioned as a means of regulating criminal behavior, regardless if the law is a "just" or an "unjust" law. A just deserts or retribution belief system advances the idea that a criminal is an enemy of society-at-large and deserves severe punishment. Punishment is considered to be a means of achieving beneficial and social consequences through application of a specific form and degree of punishment. There often is a conceptualized "fit" made between the crime and the punishment. In a modern just desert sanctioning system, the bases for determining a punitive sanction against an offender would be exclusively based on the seriousness of the offense.[36] Therefore, advocates of punishment see just deserts as a justice model, a fairness in the system that should administer punishment but fairly, based upon the seriousness of the crime committed. Defendants convicted of the same crime should receive the same sanction.

> **Just deserts** is a justice model that recommends the administration of punishment among guilty defendants based upon the seriousness of the crime committed—defendants convicted of the same crime should receive the same sanction.

There would be a scale prescribing offenses with penalties. Under a pure just desert system, all offenses would be linked to fixed penalties without regard for the character of the offender (i.e. age, circumstances, mental state, crimes of passion, etc.). For instance, after checking with several jurisdictions, following is a list of the 10 worst crimes, ranked from worst to least worst. How closely do you agree with this list?

The number of individuals (especially juveniles) who acted in concert with each other to accomplish a crime might intensify the level of crime severity.[37] Mandatory sentences (a specific length of time served in prison for a specific conviction, i.e., an armed robbery conviction automatically produces a seven-year prison sentence) would be supported by this belief system. Some add that a punitive (punishment) response is rooted in the personal need to retaliate or to avenge a "wrong" imposed upon property or person. Some argue that the "lust of vengeance" or the "thirst for revenge" are "so powerful that they rival all other human needs."[38] Retaliation through vengeance focuses on the offense and the past.

Severity of Crime Chart

1. Sexual battery; victim 12 years or older, offender uses or threatens to use deadly force.
2. Aggravated manslaughter of a child.
3. Kidnapping; child under age 13, perpetrator also commits aggravated child abuse; sexual battery; or lewd or lascivious battery, molestation, conduct, or exhibition.
4. Kidnapping; inflict bodily harm upon or terrorize victim.
5. Unlawful killing of human; unpremeditated and spontaneous.
6. Aggravated [forceful with a weapon] rape of an adult followed by homicide.
7. Sale or purchase of contraband drugs resulting in the drugs being dealt to victims under 12.
8. Aggravated rape of an adult; unpremeditated and spontaneous.
9. Money laundering, financial instruments totaling or exceeding $100,000.
10. Trafficking in illegal drugs.

Just deserts advocates are opposed to rehabilitation as the primary service provided by the justice system. They are opposed to determinate sentences (explained later) and early release programs (including parole) and see probation as too lenient a response.

It should come as no surprise that retaliation and vengeance continue to be used as the best way to deal with offenders.

Criticism of Just Deserts

The focus of just deserts and retaliation is on the crime and the past. Just deserts is a system of punishment that justifies itself simply because it's deserved. A counter-consideration is the principle of not deliberately causing human suffering where it might be avoided.[39] There are some moral issues connected to this perspective revealing an inadequacy in this new century. It might make more sense to focus on the victims of crime or on the future of an offender. In one sense, if the future were important, some offenders could be guided to a crime-free lifestyle and situations could be developed to prevent an incident from happening again (e.g., target-hardening techniques, such as in retail stores where management locks expensive product in special containers to prevent theft).

Also, correctional policy influenced by just desert advocates would less often favor early release for prisoners. One result would be that many prisoners would not be eligible for community corrections programs. A practice such as "good-time" or "good behavior" policies would be less available, a trend that seems to be popular among many correctional systems. And finally, parole requirements would be eliminated or difficult to reach for most prisoners.

Because a just desert perspective supports the premise that criminals "deserve to be punished," might this lay some groundwork for the use of unnecessary force and brutality toward a violator?

Turning retaliation inside out, there would tend to be an outpouring of public support for a mother who is so outraged by the sexual molestation of her child that she attacks and kills the suspect. The results of a trial might agree with public sentiment and she might go free. Does emotion dictate practice for the police, courts, and corrections when a just desert perspective dominates their thinking? There are many indicators that just deserts, retaliation, and vengeance have to do with official outcomes. We would like to say that when those outcomes seem "fair" or just, maybe it's okay. Yet arbitrary decisions that lack due process are alien to a democratic society. Finally, it is unlikely that just desert advocates would advance reconciliation, rehabilitation, reintegration, restitution, or restorative justice because none of these strategies would be considered punitive in nature.

Deterrence

Deterrence is another set of principles that support punishment. Unlike just deserts, which involves a backward focus, deterrence is centered on future crime. Because of the forward focus, its advocates argue that it serves a useful purpose because punishment has a deterrent (restraining) effect either specifically upon an offender (specific deterrence) or generally upon others who might consider a similar act (general deterrence). Deterrence assumes that if sufficient pressure is brought to bear, individuals "can and will change their behavior."[40] The knowledge of unpleasant consequences for proscribed acts will either prevent the commission of such acts altogether or minimize their frequency (general deterrence). It's a "pain versus pleasure" perspective—make the pain or punishment greater than the pleasure or crime and an offender will stop committing crime.[41]

Specific deterrence refers to the effects of sanctions on a specific person who receives those sanctions.

General deterrence refers to the population as a whole that might witness individual sanctions.

Criticism of Deterrence

An observation about deterrence is that it assumes most of us, if left to our own devices, would commit crime. Therefore, some of the implications arising from this thought are that correctional programs used to rehabilitate are less likely to accomplish their mission and reintegration plans will not work as expected.

Deterrence also assumes that in our quest to avoid pain, most of us make appropriate and rational decisions about our own behavior. However, there is evidence that many of us do not make rational or intelligent decisions even when we know the consequences. You might be hard-pressed to explain why people smoke cigarettes, abuse alcohol and drugs, or engage in family violence. Each of these decisions and many others might be as deadly as participating in a bomber's suicide mission.

There are reservations about the conclusion that deterrence works as well as the punishment seekers imply. After all, it has yet to be supported that the justice community can control human behavior in general, let alone the criminal activity of those under formal supervision. Specifically, most of us follow the law and live our life without committing crimes of violence. Evidently, there are other factors that deter most of us from harming others or ourselves. Those deterrents can be grounded in our social value system, influenced by religion, culture, living environment, expectations of others, and the pure desire to aid other individuals. Our belief is to develop, grow, and prosper in accordance with our social and spiritual expectations and legal obligations. Most of us rarely break the law, although it is easier to do than keep it.

Incapacitation

Incapacitation or imprisonment is the third category linked to a punishment model. Oddly enough, incapacitation is paradoxically opposite of a deterrence effect in that incapacitation sees a reduction in the capacity of offenders to offend if imprisoned for a long period of time. A growing conservatism tends to promote *Collective Incapacitation,* which can be defined as a policy of locking up any offender who is considered to be a crime risk as opposed to a *Selective Incapacitation,* which can be defined as targeting the most serious offenders for incarceration. By today's standards, that might imply imprisonment should be reserved for only the most violent of offenders.[42] Earlier sanctions left a permanent mark on an offender such as a branding their forehead, thereby warning others to beware of them. Other responses were equally cruel: a thief's hand might be severed or a liar's tongue removed. "Death and exile were also forms of incapacitation."[43] Nonetheless, thieves can use the other hand and liars can use other methods to communicate their deceit, just as predatory rapists would use items during the commission of their cruel crime.[44]

Criticism of Incapacitation

It is often believed that the length of a prison sentence has to do with the severity of the crime committed, and the length of time imposed and served is consistent with the length of time imposed and served for offenders convicted of a similar crime. Also, the length of confinement, supposedly, has a positive effect on the future outcome of an offender, once released. Additionally, there is an assumption that if a criminal is locked up, she or he can't commit crime. Each of these thoughts is not supported by the literature or experience.[45] Perhaps selective incapacitation might be more meaningful in the sense that prisons should only house violent offenders.

Criticism of Punishment Approach

Western ideals of punishment imply a passion for vengeance. Actually, vengeance is rooted in the need for security, especially in Western culture, where there appears to be a need to see retribution or vengeance carried out.[46] Then, too, many prisoners seem to accept violence and anger during their incarceration. Regardless of their lifestyle prior to prison, once released, they are more likely to engage in crimes of violence because of their prison experience.[47] Violence seems to perpetuate more violence.

Overpunishment. Increased punishment or overpunishment can have less of an effect on crime than expected. When the compliance point has been passed and the punishment continues, an offender ceases to care about the crime. For example, after an offender is released from prison, the stigma of imprisonment is carried for the remainder of the ex-convict's life. Many former convicts find it almost impossible to find gainful employment because of the stigma of imprisonment. Imagine if the ex-convict were mentally challenged, disabled, or elderly. What do you think their chances would be of survival in a free community after years of imprisonment? The temptation to return to a life of crime as a means of survival might become one of the few plausible responses available.

CONTROL APPROACH

Although a *control model* is the least complex of the correctional models, the idea of control is extensively practiced. Often times, control is used for the sake of control itself—thoughts of control are linked to confinement and to "close" or intense parole and probation. Simply put, convicted offenders, individuals considered a danger to society, or those accused of a crime must be restrained and closely monitored. Different from an incapacitation model where "lock 'em up and throw away the key" strategies are best, control as a correctional approach sees more than just prison time. To enhance public safety, control advocates believe strict enforcement of rules and regulations must apply to each and every offender.

Lost in the maze of a control perspective are quality services that personally enhance offenders. Supermax facilities such as Pelican Bay in California and Red Onion in Ohio and shock incarceration camps such as Lakeview in New York are the official responses of those who see control as vital and necessary. These ultimate control systems find funding among legislatures who accept a control model perspective of justice.

Along with this idea of control, correctional practices leading to reconciliation, rehabilitation, reintegration, restitution, and restorative justice are unlikely strategies for a correctional system to participate in because control or the means of control takes precedence over even the personal rights or recovery of a participant. But in what way is public safety served as this caged person is released? (And eventually most caged prisoners are released.)

Criticism of Control Approach

Control promotes violence, which ultimately cannot further public safety because most prisoners are eventually released and because many more are already in the community and under correctional supervision. At an extreme, consider the Federal Penitentiary at Marion (Illinois), a super-maximum-security unit, known as a modern day Alcatraz. It holds 400 of the federal system's most incorrigible inmates. Marion operates under a lock-down, meaning all prisoners are confined to their cells for 23 hours per day. Prisoners are allowed one hour of exercise outside their cell. As repressive as it is, advocates argue that locking-down the institution is the ultimate prevention of riots and various forms of violence.[48]

Human rights advocates criticize the repressive practices at Marion. Allegedly, numerous prisoners have been routinely chained to their concrete slab beds for several days. Although restraining prisoners is sometimes necessary, Amnesty International argues that officials at Marion violated numerous UN rules of conduct. Also, Human Rights Watch, another prison watchdog organization, investigated violations in supermax facilities across the nation and concluded that units in 36 states were in violation of human rights practices. Violations exist in the super-maximum-security unit for women at Broward Correctional Institution in Miami, where inmates were routinely handcuffed while outside their cell as a means of punishment, regardless of the infraction. At the supermax in Oregon, the administration was ordered to stop the practice of stripping inmates and having them earn back their clothing through good behavior. Often, these repressive measures are directed primarily at prisoners deemed violent or incorrigible (as reported by staff from a supermax facility). Yet, this approach is extremely limited because it reflects a belief system that emphasizes control without necessarily addressing the causes of violence, and whether those causes are institutional, individual, or a combination of the two.

There appears to be an illusion that America can "build" itself out of its crime problem or enhance its CC programs to include many more offenders. That is, more prisons can be built to accommodate the already overcrowded conditions that plague its system. Yet, as new prisons reach completion, they are populated to capacity in a short period of time. For instance, 528,000 new prison beds were built across the United States in the last decade, and yet correctional populations filled those facilities. Also, many CC caseworkers have doubled their workload in a short period of time and all indicators are that it will get worse before getting better (more on this in Chapters 8 and 10).

Control focuses on present issues as opposed to past issues or future concerns. Yet there is evidence that treatment, coupled with positive correctional programs and incentives, is more effective and efficient in maintaining order and safety than repressive and rigid custodial philosophy. Finally, widening the gap of hostility would produce more violence, fear, and hatred among those under correctional supervision.[49] Control does not attempt to aid those offenders who can be reformed.

Final Thoughts About Punishment and Control Approaches

The volume and nature of crime in America does not explain the dramatic growth of the correctional enterprise. The policies and practices that have shaped that expansion are numerous and diverse, yet those increases can be linked to the dominant view of punishment and control belief systems that advance such thoughts as "getting tough" and "waging war" on crime as a way to solve the crime problem.[50] By all accounts, crime is not necessarily any higher than it has ever been nor is the crime rate greater than similar industrialized countries. There is one exception to this generalization: the United States is characterized by an exceptionally high rate of homicide. In this regard, it could be argued that a high homicide rate is caused by the catastrophic interaction of a number of factors: availability of guns, high rates of economic urban inequality, criminalization and trade of illegal drugs, emergence of a "code of the streets" that encourages the use of violence, and finally the proliferation of violence in the media.[51] Nonetheless, high homicide rates do not explain the huge imprisonment rate because murder is rare in comparison to other crimes and most prisoners were convicted of crimes that are far less serious than murder.

There is also the belief that crime is far more serious today than in early America. Yet historical research shows that modern, industrial societies including the United States are significantly safer than the rural societies of previous centuries. In the United States, urbanization and industrialization are associated with a declining rate of violence. Western society, it could be said, is less violent then in previous periods.

As we turn to the high number of individuals under correctional supervision, it becomes clear that crime alone is not necessarily responsible for those huge correctional populations. One way to look at this argument is to see that the severity and pervasiveness of "street crime," drugs, and a redefinition of the poor (of all colors) as dangerous and "undeserving" populations seem to better explain the growth in the justice profession.[52] There is a feeling that the re-orientation of state policy around social control issues rather than social welfare issues enjoys widespread, bipartisan support.[53] Without an attempt to minimize crime and its effect (because CC operates primarily in the community), re-orientation can further public safety by enhancing treatment and prevention approaches among those it supervises.

TREATMENT APPROACH

Rehabilitation is the primary objective of treatment advocates. Ideally, treatment should and could be administered at all levels of criminal sanctions, including incarceration, without compromising public safety. Because many participants of community corrections have experienced the criminal justice system in total (including apprehension, trial, and incarceration), this section, like the previous sections, conceptually deals with the treatment model of response at the CC and prison level.

Specifically, the task of treatment in corrections is to provide a medical or clinical model approach for those under their care and supervision. Some of those models include programs that treat alcoholism, drug addiction, conflict resolution skills, and anger management skills among others. Other programs can aid the mentally and physically challenged, the neglected, and the underprivileged. What is known about treatment programs delivered in the community is that they can produce two to three times greater reductions in recidivism than treatment delivered in prison to similar populations.[54]

Drugs and Alcohol

As substance abusers are placed under correctional supervision, CC becomes a potential point of intervention to reduce or to help offenders eliminate their abuse. Drug and alcohol treatment among those imprisoned and those under CC supervision can result in reduced substance abuse, criminal activity, and associated problems, especially once those offenders are released from correctional supervision.[55] It is clear that the addicted correctional populations, whether institutionalized or in the community, are given a low priority for correctional managers.[56] For instance, from 1993 to 1996, the number of prisoners who needed substance abuse treatment climbed from 688,000 to 840,000.[57] The number of prisoners receiving treatment remained the same—about 150,000. In 1997, for instance, 1 in 10 state prisoners reported being treated for drug abuse since admission—a decrease from the 1 in 4 prisoners reporting such treatment in 1991.[58] Also, only 43 percent of the jail jurisdictions in America provided substance abuse treatment in 1998[59] and only 41 percent of those on probation participated in substance abuse treatment while under correctional supervision in 1995.[60]

On the other side of the coin, 8 of 10 of those individuals under correctional supervision have alcohol or drug issues as evidenced by Muriel Martin, supervisor of the Richmond Parole Unit in California, who estimates that 75 percent of her office's parolees' cases relate to underlying substance abuse problems.[61] Other agents in her department set the rates even higher—as much as 80 or 90 percent of their clients. Their concern is shared by many practitioners and clinicians alike who sometimes see that entire lives point to prison and a long nightmare of disadvantage and squalor.[62] Other people throw away their opportunities with bad choices or impulsive behavior. Either way, even official government statistics indicate that drugs and alcohol speed the route to incarceration and later homelessness.[63]

One estimate shows that states spend approximately 5 percent or less of their prison budget on drug and alcohol treatment and the federal government spends less than 1 percent.[64] This low priority continues, despite information that shows substance abuse treatment as beneficial. For instance, for every dollar spent on drug and alcohol treatment, California saves seven dollars in reductions on crime and health care costs.[65] Another way to understand this finding is to say that each day of treatment paid for itself on the day treatment was provided because of the avoidance of crime.[66] In essence, because crime declined by two thirds after treatment, that is to say that more treatment would reduce more crime.

Which product influences crime rates more—drugs or alcohol? The National Center on Addiction and Substance Abuse (CASA) says there is little question about the answer, although both drugs and alcohol are linked to crime.[67] More widely available than illegal drugs, alcohol is strongly correlated with sexual assault, aggravated assault, and child and spouse abuse. CASA says that a high percentage of homicides arise from disputes or arguments when alcohol is present, especially among family members. These findings are consistent with the aforementioned thoughts, which reveal that an estimated 80 percent of the men and women under correctional supervision are seriously involved with drug and alcohol abuse and the crimes it spawns prior to their conviction.[68]

CASA also reports a link between alcohol abuse and addiction and property crime. Among state prisoners, 17 percent of property offenders were under the influence of alcohol at the time of their crime; among federal prisoners, it was 9 percent. Releasing substance abusers from prison without treatment maintains the market for illegal drugs and keeps drug dealers in business; untreated substance abusers are likely to return to substance abuse and crime upon release. Recidivism is also related to drug and alcohol abuse.[69]

It is clear that substance abuse treatment is not as available as it should be, and when it is it appears that fewer complete it successfully than expected. For instance, one of three correctional participants in substance abuse treatment never finish it. Nearly two thirds of California drug offenders who began rehabilitation programs between July 2001 and June 2002 did not finish those programs, according to UCLA researchers who evaluated a California law that sends defendants to treatment rather than prison.[70]

However, it might surprise you that there are other methods of substance abuse intervention, such as vocational training, that can work among abusers under correctional supervision. For instance, classroom discussions about building a house are informative but if youths actually built one, they might learn more than the rhetoric.[71] One program is called Youthbuild, which is utilized in many jurisdictions. Some results show that 72 percent of the participants before Youthbuild used marijuana, 30 percent used hard drugs, and 76 percent used alcohol. After the program, 25 percent used marijuana, 6 percent used hard drugs, and 43 percent used alcohol. There were other results too, but what is known about drugs and alcohol is that they are pathways to crime, especially for young adults.[72] Apparently, programs like Youthbuild help juveniles in more ways than learning a trade.

Clinical

This more humane supervision system sees a high percentage of criminal behavior as potentially controllable through clinical intervention. This can be accomplished through two components, and both components must be genuinely present to accomplish that end: professional guidance and the willingness of the participant.

Clinical advocates report there are similarities between psychological and physiological conditions concerning the need for offenders to recognize the danger and undesirability of their criminal behavior. Then the offender needs to make significant effort to rid himself of that behavior. In fact, it will be argued that the treatment model cannot resolve or "remove" criminal behavior as one might remove an infected limb without the genuine support of the participant. In this model, participants are encouraged to see the rewards of positive behavior and are encouraged and equipped to adopt it as a model.

The medical model developed in the late 1920s and early 1930s under the leadership of Sanford Bates and the U.S. Bureau of Prisons (BOP) saw answers within a client. It then became necessary to:[73]

- Diagnose the individual problem.
- Develop a treatment program that might remedy the problem.
- Apply treatment.

When the client was rehabilitated, he or she would be released to aftercare in the community under the supervision of a therapeutic parole officer, who would continue casework therapy until the client was not a risk to the community. A medical model offered hope of individual well-being. It was the responsibility of corrections to "make the ill well." The "ill" would thus be passive recipients of beneficent therapy like patients in a hospital.

Finally, one goal of treatment is the indeterminate sentence and the assumption that an offender can be treated and given early release when he or she has been "cured." Are we to look on every offender as though he or she would commit crime, once released? First-time offenders can come to the right decision about their lifestyle if shown what the limits of those decisions are. It is better if a nonviolent offender is in the community receiving treatment toward conformity.

Treatment: Benedict Center

Benedict Center Women's Harm Reduction Program provides vital services in Milwaukee, WI as a sound alternative to incarceration for women offenders. It is a day program that provides child care and other programs for women. The goal is to support women in their efforts to construct responsible, healthy lives free of drugs and criminal involvement for themselves and their children. Approximately 200 women will be sent to the Benedict Center by the criminal courts, children's court, CC, treatment intake units, transitional living programs, shelters, and social workers in 2006.

Treatment relates to a holistic approach. Women become part of a caring community in which they encourage and mentor each other. After orientation, the participants are evaluated by a staff advisor who plans their individual programs and goals. For some women, immediate goals may be basic needs—shelter, food, clothing, mental health, or other medical care. Once goals are met, they are ready to set longer range objectives based on what the women want to achieve.

Program Components at Benedict Center

Alcohol and Other Drug Abuse (AODA) Treatment: a state-certified outpatient AODA treatment program using the harm reduction method.

Cognitive Skills Training: highly rated Moving On curriculum, which is designed exclusively for women offenders and based on social learning and relational theory.

Adult Basic Education Classes: women build skills needed for employment or further education and training.

High School Equivalency Degree (HSED) Program: women prepare to successfully complete their GED or HSED.

Women's Sexuality Group: specifically designed for women who have traded sex for drugs, shelter, or other commodities.

Anger Management: women analyze their own behaviors and learn how to change their responses to live more safely and communicate more effectively.

Stress Management: women develop a wide variety of coping strategies to deal with daily frustrations.

Cultural Diversity: women learn to appreciate other points of view and possibly change their way of thinking about people who are different from themselves.

Parenting and Family Nurturing Classes: assist women and their children to build more effective ways of communicating. The parenting group also works with women who are trying to regain custody of their children.

Women's Health: a broad range of health issues that invites health professionals to come to the groups. They share information about living with chronic health problems and ways in which women can prevent illness in themselves and their children.

HIV Awareness: women learn how to avoid sexually transmitted diseases through safe-sex practices and to protect themselves by learning how to establish personal boundaries.

Job Readiness: focuses as much on the characteristics needed to keep and be successful on the job as on the basics of how to apply and get hired. For women who are ready, actual job placement is brokered to other organizations that focus primarily on job placement.

Benedict Results

The Benedict center reports the following results for year end 2002:[74]

- 89 percent referred through Milwaukee County Misdemeanor Court met all of their court obligations.
- 43 percent had cases dismissed as the result of their participation.
- 40 percent had their sentences modified.
- 75 percent in the AODA component met at least one of their goals.
- 77 women participated in adult basic literacy classes.
- 78 percent raised reading scores between first- and third-grade levels.
- 67 percent raised math scores between first- and fourth-grade levels.

Criticism of Treatment Approach

Treatment does not imply that offenders should be cuddled or overprotected or allowed to do as they please, as many proponents of treatment seem to think. It is a fairly common belief among many elements of the criminal justice system that any program that is not punitive or restrictive is "soft" on criminals and consequently, weak. There is room for punishment and security in the treatment approach, but little room for treatment in the punitive approach. That is, the more humane treatment methods are intended to be used in conjunction with the employment of authority in a constructive and positive manner, but clients must be allowed to try, even if they fail. Authoritarian procedures, used alone, only give the offender more ammunition to support a self-image as an oppressed and impotent pawn of the power structure.

Helping offenders help themselves is not without critics. One of the most influential critics was probably Robert Martinson.[75] Martinson examined probation, parole, and incarceration and concluded that rehabilitation might be a difficult proposition. His perspective alluded that nothing worked, although his study was seriously flawed and Martinson himself recanted his claims. Another researcher says that Martinson's shortcomings were produced by providing insufficient qualification for the conclusions reached.[76] For instance, many of the programs Martinson reviewed were regarded as failures, but those programs were simply those that were starved of funds. Nonetheless, Martinson believed that supervisor and incarcerative strategies were workable, if they were properly administered, but most programs were poorly managed.[77] For instance, Martinson argued that the rehabilitative efforts of the correctional community had little effect upon recidivism.[78] Martinson's primary premise was that given the perspective policy makers, interest groups, and the American public held toward correctional programs of the 1950s, they were less likely to be appropriately funded, staffed, and managed. Finally, Martinson felt that most offenders could be rehabilitated but professional tools to accomplish the task were inadequate.[79]

Martinson's skepticism of the treatment ideal derived from his role from 1968–1970 in a survey of American studies on offender treatment programs, yet he was only one of three researchers. In fact, unknown to his colleagues,[80] Martinson published the now famous article, referred to as "nothing works" without their consent.[81] Nonetheless, at that time in correctional evolution, rehabilitation and diversion were considered crucial in the reform efforts of offenders. Martinson's critique appeared to have destroyed that perspective. Paradoxically, the idea that "nothing worked" appealed to the liberals and the conservatives alike.[82]

Liberals held a concern about the disparities of sentencing linked to rehabilitation that required indeterminate lengths of imprisonment and forced treatment. And conservatives favored anything that didn't discourage a just desert perspective linked to sentencing. If nothing works, longer prison terms and capital punishment could become a politically favorable position for conservatives. What became apparent, despite Martinson's recanted position that "some treatment programs do have an appreciable effect on recidivism," was that belief systems or philosophical models shape correctional practices because many correctional systems at the time abandoned treatment priorities.[83] Of interest, even today we know how to operate correctional programs, yet it appears that we are plagued with similar problems—belief systems that support antiquated notions of intervention among violators.[84] That is, policy and practice in the criminal justice community overall to curb the cycle of violence might be inadequately supported.

Then, too, treatment programs can fail and do fail. Often, it is not because a program lacks therapeutic integrity or competent therapists. Rather, they fail because offender "responsivity"-related barriers such as cognitive/intellectual deficits have not been addressed.[85] Also, an assumption taken by many opponents of correctional programs is that most offenders under correctional supervision do not possess the skills or the incentive to help themselves. The point is that many treatment programs do not work because of the way they are administered. The risk principle states that the intensity of the treatment intervention should be matched to the risk level of the offender. Ideally, there are three components of responsivity:[86]

- Match the treatment with the learning level of the offender
- Match the characteristics of the offender with those of the counselor
- Match the skills of the counselor with the type of program conducted

With that said, it is also true that offenders go into programs or engage in treatment with the primary goal of earning early release. After all, prisoners are largely offenders and at-risk individuals who might posses a common thread—that of lying to get what they want. To imply that they are "cured" might bring them closer to their goals. Yet, for that reason many experienced and dedicated clinicians and behaviorists work harder to motivate participants and sometimes, "convert" even at-risk individuals who characterize behavior that implies resentment toward the program. The conundrum is that correctional personnel and volunteers never really know which individuals will actually alter their behavior or know when that behavior will be affected as a result of a program, especially because it often takes more than a single program to aid behavioral change. That is, in my own experience at-risk individuals under correctional care (similar to college students) are selective listeners and it is hard to say when they will act upon disseminated information—behavior might change during the duration of the program (or class) or months and sometimes even years later.

Once free, they would be able to continue their life of crime. Extreme cases are usually offered with those criticisms. For instance, individuals who argue that treatment is highly overrated might offer high-risk offenders such as pedophiles to demonstrate the faults of correctional treatment.

PREVENTION APPROACH

A *prevention approach* refers to correctional initiatives designed to alter contributing factors that lead to criminal activities in institutional and community correctional populations. The goal is to avoid future crime, reduce victimization of others including offenders, and enhance community experiences.[87] For instance, altering alcoholic and drug abuse behavioral patterns among correctional populations (and the general public) will reduce crime, and equally important can break the cycle of violence. It will help offenders stay sober, which can result in getting and keeping a job, meeting and maintaining relationships with law-abiding individuals, and securing safe places to live.[88] It will help individuals lead a respectful life, and they will feel better about themselves (despite urges to run to the closest liquor store or drug pusher to relieve their loneliness, fears of failure, and frustrations). In this regard, the core elements of a prevention model are early intervention, judicial oversight, graduated sanctions and incentives, and collaboration among justice and treatment agencies. The results can include significant reductions in drug use, criminal offending, and family problems. And the ratio of the costs averted for each dollar invested can range from 3.2 to 7.7 depending on administration.[89] Intoxicated or stoned offenders, especially females, the mentally challenged, physically disabled, and the elderly are often victimized by other offenders (explained in Chapters 14 and 15).

The centerpiece of prevention initiatives is reintegration as associated with the Five Rs. The focus is on offenders and their release from correctional supervision. There are other processes in a preventive approach, but reintegration represents the largest effort associated with it.

Reintegration

A broad community correctional belief that emphasizes the achievement of useful and practical opportunities and skills by offenders, and the creation of supervised opportunities for testing, utilizing, and polishing those skills in community settings.

Reintegration is designed to guide a violator away from the roots of crime and the decisions that led to crime. Reintegration initiatives work better among violators in the community more so than those imprisoned.[90] Some examples include vocational training leading to employment opportunities, educational endeavors to achieve career advancement and critical skills, and/or counseling or group-facilitated programs that include conflict resolution or dispute management techniques intended to improve coping skills or progress in living skills. That is, the need to be unsupervised in the community as a contributing and trouble-free participant takes precedence.

Simply defined, a process of reintegration can include all activity and programming conducted to prepare an offender to return safely to the community and to live as a law-abiding citizen without supervision. To understand reintegration, we need to see the variables considered in decisions linked to releasing an offender to the community. Canada is advanced in reintegration programs, and their Canadian Correctional Service performs the following process for each prisoner:[91]

- Collect all relevant information about the offender that is available, including a judge's reason for sentencing and victim impact statements.
- Assess offender's risk level (likelihood to reoffend) and criminogenic needs (life functions that led to criminal behavior).
- Reduce offender's risk level by increasing knowledge and skills and changing the attitudes and behaviors that led to criminal behavior.
- Develop and implement programs and individual interventions that effect change in areas that contribute to criminal behavior.
- In cooperation with the offender, develop a plan to increase the likelihood that he or she will function in the community as a law-abiding citizen.

- Motivate and help the offender follow the correctional plan and benefit from correctional programs and interventions.
- Monitor and assess the offender's progress in learning and changing.
- Make recommendations to the National Parole Board as to the offender's readiness for release and the conditions, if any, under which he or she should be released.
- After release, help the offender respect the conditions of the release and resolve day-to-day living problems.
- Make required programs and interventions available in the community.
- Monitor the offender's behavior to ensure that he or she is respecting the release conditions and not indulging in criminal behavior.
- If required, suspend the offender's release, carry out specific intervention, and reinstate or recommend revocation of the release as appropriate.

The Service, in collaboration with Canadian courts, police, other federal departments and agencies, provincial government, municipalities, and voluntary organizations, considers reintegration a priority.[92] It is a smaller system than the correctional system in America and many parts of the aforementioned might be too expensive or too detailed to conduct on American correctional populations.

Reintegration Process at the Federal Level

The Re-entry Initiative envisions the development of model re-entry programs that begin in correctional institutions and continue throughout an offender's transition to and stabilization in the community. These programs will provide for individual re-entry plans that address issues confronting offenders as they return to the community. The Initiative will encompass three phases and be implemented through appropriate programs:

Phase 1—Protect and Prepare: Institution-Based Programs. These programs are designed to prepare offenders to reenter society. Services provided in this phase will include education, mental health and substance abuse treatment, job training, mentoring, and full diagnostic and risk assessment.

Phase 2—Control and Restore: Community Transition Programs. These programs will work with offenders prior to and immediately following their release from correctional institutions. Services provided in this phase will include, as appropriate, education, monitoring, mentoring, life skills training, assessment, job skills development, and mental health and substance abuse treatment.

Phase 3—Sustain and Support: Community Long-Term Support Programs. These programs will connect individuals who have left the supervision of the justice system with a network of social services agencies and community organizations to provide ongoing services and mentoring relationships.

Examples of potential program elements include institution-based readiness programs, institutional and community assessment centers, re-entry courts, supervised or electronically monitored boarding houses, mentoring programs, and community corrections centers.

Other Prevention Methods

Probation and parole services, which will be discussed in more detail in Chapters 7 through 10, were designed to represent the eyes and ears of the courts and parole commissions toward helping offenders to live a law-abiding life. To accomplish this task, officers guide offenders to solve social problems either through direct counseling and support or through a referral for treatment and support. Most of this aid provided to offenders falls primarily into one of the following categories: abiding by the general and special conditions of probation or parole, substance abuse treatment, vocational and employment assistance, resolving conflicts with interpersonal relationships, and the development of pro-social attitudes and associates.[93]

In part, prevention approaches adapted by probation and parole officers can help prevent future criminal acts by persons not on supervision by joining in partnership with community organizations and leaders. One such program is called Operation Spotlight.[94] Its process is a cross-agency interactive structure that is built on the "what works" research literature, organization change theory, high-performance team building, the tenets of structured family therapy, and upon proverbs drawn from human experiences that resemble common sense. The fundamental premise is that the probation profession, working in partnership with other community agencies, can deliver on the promise of public safety by directly reducing the number and severity of new crimes by at-risk offenders already in the community.

Health Prevention

Substance abuse treatment is key to helping injection drug users reduce HIV transmission risks. Linking HIV prevention programs and substance abuse treatment offers considerable potential but also challenges:[95]

- About one million people are active users of injection drugs (primarily heroin, cocaine, and amphetamines).
- Sharing syringes, drug solutions, and drug preparation equipment are primary routes for drug users to acquire and transmit HIV and hepatitis B and C.
- High-risk sexual behaviors often accompany high-risk drug use, further increasing the chances of transmission.
- About one third of AIDS cases every year are related to injection drug use.
- About 80 percent of corrections populations have serious substance abuse issues.

Many also have or are at high risk of having HIV or hepatitis. Substance abuse treatment and HIV services can help participants under community correction care, as well as their families, corrections staff, and the community at large. There are many health risks facing individuals under correctional supervision and protecting their health is a priority toward public safety and reducing crime. This prevention strategy, much like the reintegration strategy, can reduce victimization for individuals who are not under correctional authority. For that reason and because of the perceived minimal success of present correctional programs (recidivism rates range from 40 to 70 percent), many communities and governmental agencies are turning to a prevention approach as a solution.

DISADVANTAGES OF A BELIEF SYSTEM

Disadvantages of justice strategies that should be noted include vast sums of public treasure and resources that can be lost to uncertain causes. For example, the Office of National Drug Control Policy (ONDCP) shows that the U.S. government spent almost 20 billion dollars or a rate of about $614 per second on the "war on drugs" in the year 2004.[96] Click online to *http://www.drugsense.org/wodclock.htm* to see an up-to-the-minute dollar amount spent to control drugs. Drug users were generally sentenced to prison (except in a few states such as Arizona and California). In fact, the highest percentage of new admissions in both state and federal prisons were individuals convicted of drug use. State and local governments spent another 20 billion dollars during the same time period. Some critics argue the "war on drugs" principle is an expensive venture and the rationale or set of beliefs that justify it are redundant because illegal drugs continue to plague American residents.[97]

AS THE BELIEF PENDULUM SWINGS

As thoughts change about offenders and how to manage them, so does correctional policy and practice. For instance, earlier you saw that when individuals accept a free will perspective, they often depend on punishment and control approaches of correctional supervision. As that point of view changes, so does the approach to manage those offenders. Different approaches often change the hiring and training process, building design and equipment specifications, and the directives and methods of managing personnel. It has been shown that philosophical or belief systems shape CC approaches and strategies. With that said, consider that the United States is a vast country with almost 300 million people and numerous cultural perspectives. Imagine the incredible number of dominant belief systems in various regions of the country that influence and justify CC strategies. It is unlikely that, at any one time, all the people in America think the same way at the same time. Therefore, there are many competing and congruent beliefs about why individuals commit crime and the best way to respond to offenders. Thus, each correctional system is influenced by a different set of policy makers moving towards a common goal. As you can expect, each correctional system and each agency or operation within each system might well approve or disapprove of a different set of correctional practices for those individuals whom they supervise and those who supervise them.

SUMMARY

One assumption is that the criminal justice community will change the behavior of violators. The question is how—punish them or provide care. This chapter describes the conservative and liberal political perspectives shared by policy makers, interest groups, and the public. Conservatives think in terms of a rigid traditional status quo such as zero tolerance and no frill prisons, or specifically in terms of punishment and control. Liberals think in terms of care and treatment and are optimistic about the future of most offenders. Punishment advocates see general and specific deterrence, incapacitation, and just deserts or retribution as the best fit in dealing with violators. Control is paramount in the sense of supermax prisons, shock incarceration, and rigid CC strategies as acceptable responses to violators. Both punishment and control advocates tend to be conservatives. On the other hand, liberals rely on change and care or treatment and prevention. At the core of this chapter are those political agendas linked to a belief system dominated by factors of a causal nature characterized as free will versus environment.

Attitudes addressing why an offender committed a crime justifies a set of distinguishable correctional approaches couched in practices that justify punishment, control, treatment, and prevention. The way to respond to a violator depends on why the violator committed the crime. To a conservative, "stoned" violators who chose drugs because they like to get high deserve prison because they made a rational choice. The violators chose crime and deserve their just deserts—punishment. If the violators didn't learn from their mistakes after release and get stoned again, conservatives say that the punishment wasn't "hard" enough because the deterrence effect didn't take hold the first time around. The second time around, they believe more punishment should be applied, in the form of a more controlled environment, and then the violator will get the message.

On the other hand, liberals might see drug addiction as a symptom of societal inequalities and see treatment as the best official response to violators. Poverty, unemployment, inappropriate early childhood experiences, and few educational opportunities are the roots of crime.

The overall theme of this chapter (and this book) is that the performance of CC depends on broad philosophical, political, and social themes of the era.

Changes in a correctional policy and strategy occur as the "belief" pendulum swings. That is, as policy makers, interest groups, and the public change their ideas about the causes of crime, correctional practice through policy also changes.

DISCUSSION QUESTIONS

1. Describe two conceptual political camps that shape correctional practice. In what way do you identify with one or the other political camp?
2. Explain the historical evolution of official justice response toward wrong-doers.

3. Describe two dominant perspectives about the causal factors of crime. In what way do you accept one or the other perspective about causal factors?

4. Identify the four primary approaches.

5. Link both causal perspectives to each of the four approaches.

6. Explain the importance of studying these four approaches. Provide at least one example of these approaches employed by law enforcement, the courts, and corrections as illustrated in newspapers, on television, or your own experiences.

7. Describe punishment as a corrections approach and explain its components. Provide an example of each component.

8. Explain in what way any of the Five Rs could be furthered using a punishment approach.

9. Discuss control as a corrections approach, describe its justification, and provide an example of how it could be utilized in community corrections, by law enforcement, and by the courts.

10. Explain treatment as a corrections approach, discuss its rationale, and identify some of its advantages linked to the Five Rs.

11. Describe prevention as a corrections approach, explain its justification, and identify some of its advantages linked to the Five Rs.

12. Identify different outcomes as the rationale pendulum swings.

NOTES

1. To better understand how policy is developed, see Stella Z. Theodoulou (1995). *The nature of public policy.* In Stella Z. Theodoulou and Matthew A. Cahn (Eds.). *Public policy: The essential readings.* Upper Saddle River, NJ: Prentice Hall, 1–9.

2. This perspective is not limited to CC but most organizations of all varieties. Also, correctional personnel in this sense would include personnel from private agencies under contract to perform community corrections functions.

3. Samuel Walker (2001). *Sense and nonsense about crime and drugs.* Belmont, CA: Wadsworth, 14.

4. Findlaw. Retrieved online January 12, 2006: http://www.findlaw.com

5. Dennis J. Stevens (2006). *Community corrections. An applied approach.* Upper Saddle River, NJ: Prentice Hall.

6. For a closer look at the development of punishment and prisons in early European history, see Dennis J. Stevens (2006). A history of prisons: Continental Europe and England. *The Encyclopedia of Criminology.* New York: Routledge/Taylor and Francis.

7. Heinrich Oppenheimer (1975). *The rationale of punishment.* Montclair, NJ: Patterson Smith (p. 7). Originally published in 1913.

8. Heinrich Oppenheimer (1975), 12–18.

9. Israel Drapkin (1989). *Crime and punishment in the ancient world.* Lexington, MA: Lexington Books, 17–18.

10. Danielle S. Allen (2003). *Punishment in ancient Athens. Demous. Classical Athenian Democracy.* Retrieved online January 6, 2006: http://www.stoa.org/projects/demos/article_punishment?page=6&greekEncoding=UnicodeC

11. Derek B. Cornish and Ronald V. Clark (1999). Crime as rational choice. In Francis T. Cullen and Robert Agnew (Eds.), *Criminological theory: Past and Present.* Los Angeles: Roxbury, 254–257.

12. Randall G. Shelden (2001). *Controlling the dangerous classes: A critical introduction to the history of criminal justice.* Boston: Allyn Bacon, 32–33, 70, 78.

13. See Cesare Beccaria (1764). *Of crimes and punishment.* Also Jeremy Bentham (1789). *Introduction to the principles of morals and legislation.*

14. Stanton Samenow (1984). *Inside the criminal mind.* New York: Times Books (p. xiv).

15. Stanton Samenow (1984). p. xiii. This example is presented to help a student better understand the debate about the causes of crime.

16. Stanton Samenow (1984). p. xiv.

17. *Solesbee v. Balkcom,* 339 U.S. 9, 16 (1950). Due process is violated if a practice or rule offends some principle of justice so rooted in the traditions and conscience of our people as to be ranked as fundamental.

18. Curt R. Bartol and Anne M. Bartol (2006). *Criminal behavior: A psychological approach.* Upper Saddle River, NJ: Prentice Hall, 53.

19. Murray A. Straus and Richard Gelles (1990). *Physical violence in American families.* New Brunswick, NJ: Guildford. Also, Murray Straus (1991). Discipline and deviance: Physical punishment of children and violence and other crime in adulthood. *Social Problems, 38,* 133–145.

20. Hans Selye (1974). *Stress without distress.* Philadelphia: Lippincott. Hans Toch (2001). *Stress in policing.* Washington, DC: American Psychological Association (p. 189).

21. It is unlikely that everyone reading this simplified account will find every part of it acceptable. Yet the purpose is to show that there are two primary issues concerning the culpability of crime: free will and "other reasons." Other reasons are typically couched in eight categories: biological, psychobiological, psychological, sociological, social-psychological, conflict, phenomenological, and emergent. See Frank Schmalleger (2003). *Criminal justice today* (7th ed.). Upper Saddle River, NJ: Prentice Hall, 95.

22. Jeffrey Ian Ross and Stephen C. Richards (2003). *Convict criminology.* Belmont, CA: Wadsworth (p. 112).

23. Jeffrey Ian Ross and Stephen C. Richards (2003), 112.

24. Jeffrey Ian Ross and Stephen C. Richards (2003), 112.

25. Dennis J. Stevens (2006). *Community Corrections: An applied approach.* Upper Saddle River, NJ: Prentice Hall.

26. Stanton Samenow (1984), xiv.

27. Michael R. Gottfredson and Travis Hirschi (1990). *A general theory of crime.* Stanford, CA: Stanford University Press, 15–27.

28. Stephen G. Michaud and Roy Hazelwood (1998). *The evil that men do.* New York: St. Martin's Press, 137–154.

29. Daniel Glaser (1995). *Preparing convicts for law-abiding lives.* Albany: State University of New York Press (pp. 60, 122–135). Also, Murray Straus, Richard J. Gelles, and Suzanne Steinmetz (1980). *Behind closed doors: Violence in the American family.* New York: Doubleday, 7–33.

30. Derek B. Cornish and Ronald V. Clark (1999).

31. Elliott Currie (1985). *Confronting crime: An American challenge.* New York: Pantheon, 224–245.

32. John Douglas (1995). *Mind hunter: Inside the FBI's elite serial crime unit.* New York: Doubleday (pp. 320–329). Should the perspective of punish and deter be unclear, consider that every state and the federal government incarcerates a very high percentage of nonviolent offenders, including drug abusers, mentally challenged, and the elderly, most of whom might be punished and rehabilitated in a more encouraging environment as opposed to isolation and the high expense of prison. Many of us might think one way when it comes to intervention, but in practice, when it comes to responding to violators, the mood of the nation and the official policy is "cuff 'em and stack 'em."

33. Douglas B. Marlowe, Nicholas S. Patapis, and David S. DeMatteo (2003, September). Amenability to treatment of drug offenders. *Federal probation, 67*(2), 40–46. Retrieved online January 11, 2006: http://www.uscourts.gov/fedprob/2003Augfp.pdf. Faye S. Taxman (2002, September). Supervision: Exploring the dimensions of effectiveness. *Federal Probation, 66*(2), 14–27.

34. Andrew von Hirsch (1976) *Doing justice: The choice of punishments.* New York: Hill and Wang, 35.

35. For more detail see E. Adamson Hoeble (1954). *The law of primitive man.* Cambridge, MA: Harvard University Press. And Richard L. Henshel (1990). *Thinking about social problems.* New York: Harcourt Brace Jovanovich, 92–94.

36. More information see Thomas Ellsworth (1996). *Contemporary community corrections* (2nd ed.). Prospect Heights, IL: Waveland.

37. Linda J. Skitka, Andrea L. Piatt, Timothy U. Ketterson, and H. Russell Searight (1993). Offense classification and social facilitation in juvenile delinquency. *Social Behavior and Personality, 21,* 339–346.

38. Peter Marongiu and Graeme Newman (1987). *Vengeance.* Totowa, NJ: Rowman & Littlefield (p. 1).

39. Andrew von Hirsch (1976). p. xxxvii.

40. Richard L. Henshel (1990), 94.

41. For a consequence to serve as a deterrent, it should be swift, visible, and closely linked to the forbidden action to discourage future recurrences of that action; it should also be categorical, suggesting that anyone committing that specific act will receive the same punishment. Part of this perspective includes the idea that to frighten potential offenders, policy makers need to make the consequences of a specific crime vividly clear by establishing mandatory, definite consequences for the act. For instance, capital punishment is imposed upon guilty defendants in capital cases but executions themselves frequently don't happen. Therefore, offenders who could be capital punishment candidates do not fear its use. This does not necessarily advocate its use, but demonstrates the way deterrence should operate. See Dennis J. Stevens (1992). Research note: The death sentence and inmate attitudes. *Crime & Delinquency, 38*(2), 272–279.

42. Peter B. Greenwood (1983). *Selective incapacitation.* Santa Monica, CA: Rand Corporation. Also see Anthony Petrosino and Carolyn Petrosino (1999). The public safety potential of Megan's Law in Massachusetts. *Crime & Delinquency, 45*(1), 140–158.

43. Richard L. Henshel (1990), 94.

44. The goal of some predatory rapists is not necessarily penetration of their victims, especially sadist rapists, as described by N.A. Groth. (1979). *Men who rape: The psychology of the offender.* New York: Plenum.

45. Length of prison sentences for similar crimes seems to vary depending on a number of variables, including plea bargain practices. Also, differences of sentences might be reflected by the quality of lawyers—or the difference between a public defender and a private defense attorney. Sanctions could also depend on the prediction about an individual's likelihood of committing crimes in the future and what it would take to effectively control that person.

46. Eric Fromm (1983). The anatomy of human destructiveness. In K. Lorenz, *On aggression* (pp. 272–278). New York: Harcourt Brace Jovanovich. Fromm identifies two types of aggression: (a) benign-defensive aggression common in all animal species, phylogenetically programmed, aimed at preserving the species by either attack or flight when vital interests are threatened, and (b) malignant, destructive aggression that appears essentially uncontrolled (and is not phylogenetically programmed), more typical of human beings than animal species because humans are less driven by instincts. The relevance is that animals rarely fight to the death. Humans, in contrast, have no such built-in limits (because humans lack instinctual drives). Therefore, it is implied that aggression and/or vengeance is uncontrolled destruction of others because since it, indeed, occurred after the original behavior that produced a response. Also, see Curt R. Bartol (1995). *Criminal behavior: A psychosocial approach.* Upper Saddle River, NJ: Prentice Hall, (pp. 164–166). And Patricia Weiser Easteal (1990). *Killing the beloved: Homicide between adult sexual intimates.* Canberra, Australia: Australian Institute of Criminology, Studies in Law, Crime and Justice.

47. Dennis J. Stevens (1997). Violence begets violence. *Corrections compendium: The National Journal for Corrections, 22*(12), 1–2.

48. Practitioners (myself included) who have experienced tight controlled prison environments have also experienced greater prisoner violations, resentment, and above all, disrespect for their caretakers—or more than disrespect—anger.

49. John Irwin and James Austin (1994). *It's about time: America's imprisonment binge.* Belmont, CA: Wadsworth.

50. Katherine Beckett and Theodore Sasson (2000). *The politics of injustice: Crime and punishment in America.* Thousand Oaks, CA: Pine Force Press, 10–11.

51. Katherine Beckett and Theodore Sasson (2000). (pp. 8–9). Also see Henry H. Brownstein, (2000). *Social reality of violence and violent crime.* Boston: Allyn Bacon.

52. Randall G. Shelden (2001), 78.

53. Katherine Beckett and Theodore Sasson (2000).

54. Edward J. Latessa, Francis T. Cullen, and Paul Gendreau (2002). Beyond correctional quackery: Professionalism and the possibility of effective treatment. *Federal Probation, 66*(2), (43–49). Also see Joan Petersilia. (2003). *When prisoners come home: Parole and prisoner reentry.* New York: Oxford. And Lee Underwood, Debbie Kirkwood, and Ralph Fretz (2004). *Clinical utility and policy implications of a statewide community corrections treatment process.* Retrieved online July 30, 2004: http://www.cecintl.com/research.php

55. New York Department of Correctional Services. Retrieved online January 7, 2005: http://www.docs.state.ny.us/

56. Joan Petersilia (1997). A decade of experimenting with intermediate sanctions: What have we learned? In *Perspectives on Crime and Justice: 1997–1998,* Lecture Series, the National Institute of Justice, Washington, DC: National Institute of Justice, 3–5.

57. Bureau of Justice Statistics (1999, January). *Substance abuse and treatment, state and federal prisoners, 1997.* Washington, DC: U.S. Department of Justice, Office of Justice Programs, NCJ 172871. Retrieved online January 7, 2005: http://www.ojp.usdoj.gov/bjs/dcf/dt.htm#prison

58. Bureau of Justice Statistics (1999, January). *Substance abuse and treatment, state and federal prisoners, 1997.*

59. Bureau of Justice Statistics (1999, June). *DWI offenders under correctional supervision.* Washington, DC: U.S. Department of Justice, Office of Justice Programs, NCJ 172212. Retrieved online January 7, 2005: http://www.ojp.usdoj.gov/bjs/abstract/dwiocs.htm

60. Bureau of Justice Statistics (1997, December). *Characteristics of adults on probation, 1995.* Washington, DC: U.S. Department of Justice, Office of Justice Programs, NCJ 164267. Retrieved online January 7, 2005: http://www.ojp.usdoj.gov/bjs/abstract/cap95.htm

61. Sara Steffens (October 24, 2004). Drugs, alcohol pave highway to incarceration. *Contra Costa Times* (CA). Retrieved online January 7, 2005: http://www.mapinc .org/drugnews/v04/n1505/a02.html?144

62. *Analyses of substance abuse and treatment need issues analytic series A–7* (1998). Washington, DC: Office of Applied Studies, Substance Abuse and Mental Health Services Administration, U.S. Department of Health and Human Services.

63. *Analyses of substance abuse and treatment need issues analytic series A–7* (1998).

64. Bureau of Justice Statistics (1999, January). *Substance abuse and treatment, state and federal prisoners, 1997.*

65. Joan Petersilia (1995). A crime control rationale for reinvesting in community corrections. *Spectrum, 68,* 16–26.

66. Joan Petersilia (1995).

67. The National Center on Addiction and Substance Abuse. Columbia University, NY. Retrieved online July 30, 2004: http://www.activistcash.com/organization_overview .cfm/oid/318

68. Belenko, S. (1999). Research on drug courts: A critical review, 1999 update. *National Drug Court Institute Review, II*(2), 1–58. Judge Jeffrey Tauber (2000, June). Drug court practitioner. Fact sheet. *Drug Court Institute,* II(3). Retrieved online July 26, 2004: http://www.ndci.org/publications/EffectiveSanctionsFactSheet .pdf

69. Bureau of Justice Statistics (1994, September). Fact sheet: Drug and related crime. Washington, DC: U.S. Department of Justice, Office of Justice Programs, NCJ 149286. Retrieved online January 7, 2005: http://www.ojp.usdoj.gov/bjs/pub/pdf/ drrc.pdf

70. Anna Gorman (2004, September 23). *Report says 1 of 3 finish drug reh.* Los Angeles Times. Retrieved online January 7, 2005: http://www.latimes.com/news/local/ la-me-drug23sep23,1,4434531.story?coll=la-headlines-cali

71. Tim Cross (2004, April). What works with at-risk youths. *Corrections Today,* 64–67.

72. Office of Applied Studies (2002). *Department of Heath and Human Services. (SAMHSA).* Retrieved online July 24, 2004: http://www.oas.samhsa.gov/2k4/ detainedYouth/detainedYouth.cfm

73. Federal Bureau of Prisons. *Programs.* Retrieved online January 7, 2005: http:// bop.us

74. Benedict Center. Milwaukee, WI. Retrieved online January 7, 2005: http://www .benedictcenter.org/sam/profile2.cfm?ID=75

75. Robert Martinson (2001). What works? Questions and answers about prison reform. In Edward J. Latessa, Alexander Holsinger, James W. Marquart, and Jonathan R. Sorensen (Eds.), *Correctional contexts: Contemporary and classical readings* (Chap. 21). Los Angeles: Roxbury.

76. Rick Sarre (1999). *Beyond what works. 25 year jubilee retrospective on Robert Martinson.* Retrieved online January 12, 2005: http://www.aic.gov.au/conferences/ hcpp/sarre.pdf

77. Robert Martinson (1974). What works? Questions and answers about prison reform. *The Public Interest, 35,* (22–54). Also see Robert Martinson (1972). Paradox of prison reform. *The New Republic, 166,* 1, 6, 15, 29.

78. Robert Martinson (1974), 24.

79. Robert Martinson (1974), 24.

80. Douglas Lipton, Robert Martinson, and Judith Wilks (1975). *The effectiveness of correctional treatment.* New York: Praeger.

81. Rick Sarre (1999).

82. Francis T. Cullen and Paul Gendreau (1989). The effectiveness of correctional rehabilitation. In L. Goodstein and D. L. Mackenzie (Eds.), *The American prison: Issues in research policy* (p. 23–44). New York: Plenum.

83. Robert Martinson (1979). New findings, new views: A note of caution regarding sentencing reform. *Hofstra Law Review, 7,* 243–258.

84. Francis T. Cullen and Paul Gendreau (2000). Assessing correctional rehabilitation: Policy, practice, and prospects. *Criminal Justice, 3,* (109–114). Retrieved online January 5, 2005: http://www.ncjrs.org/criminal_justice2000/vol_3/03d.pdf

85. Sharon Kennedy (1999, February 1). Responsivity: The other classification principle. *Corrections Today,* 18–24.

86. Sharon Kennedy (1999).

87. Margot C. Lindsay (1999, June). Corrections and community partnership. In *Partnership for corrections: Six perspectives.* Washington, DC: Center for Community Corrections (pp. 1–20). Retrieved online January 7, 2005: http://www. communitycorrectionsworks.org/ART4WEB-CCC/ PDFspercent20ofpercent20booklets/ partnerships.pdf

88. Adele V. Harrell, Ojmarrh Mitchell, Jeffrey Merrill, and Douglas Marlowe (2003, February). *Evaluation of breaking the cycle.* The Urban Institute: A nonpartisan economic and social policy research organization. Retrieved online January 7, 2005: http://www.urban.org/Template.cfm?Section=ByAuthor&NavMenuID=63& template=/TaggedContent/ViewPublication.cfm&PublicationID=8338

89. Adele V. Harrell, Ojmarrh Mitchell, Jeffrey Merrill, and Douglas Marlowe (2003, February), 1.

90. Joan Petersilia (2003).

91. Donald A. Andrews (2000). Principles of effective correctional programs. In Laurence L. Motiuk and Ralph C. Serin (Eds.), *Compendium 2000 on effective correctional programming.* Correctional Service Canada. Ministry of Supply and Services 2001 (pp. 9–17). Also see Sharon M. Kennedy (2000). Treatment responsibility: Reducing recidivism by enhancing treatment effectiveness. In Laurence L. Motiuk

and Ralph C. Serin (Eds.), *Compendium 2000 on effective correctional programming.* Correctional Service Canada. Ministry of Supply and Services 2001 (pp. 18–21). Alan W. Leschied (2000). Implementation of effective correctional programs. In Laurence L. Motiuk and Ralph C. Serin (Eds.), *Compendium 2000 on effective correctional programming.* Correctional Service Canada. Ministry of Supply and Services 2001, 41–46.

92. Dennis J. Stevens (2000). Education programming for offenders. In Laurence L. Motiuk and Ralph C. Serin (Eds.), *Compendium 2000 on effective correctional programming.* Correctional Service Canada, Ministry of Supply and Services 2001, 57–63.

93. Harold B. Wooten (1999, June). Probation and parole supervision. In *Partnerships in corrections.* (pp. 111–143). The Center of Community Corrections. Retrieved online January 7, 2005: http://www.communitycorrectionsworks.org/ART4WEB-CCC/ PDFs percent20of percent20booklets/partnerships.pdf

94. Harold B. Wooten (1999).

95. Prevention among injection drug users (2002, October). *Drug use, HIV, and the criminal justice system.* National Center for HIV, STD Prevention, Centers for Disease Control and Prevention. U.S. Government. Retrieved online January 7, 2005: http://www.cdc.gov/idu/criminaljustice.htm

96. The White House Office of National Drug Control Policy (ONDCP), a component of the Executive Office of the President, was established by the Anti-Drug Abuse Act of 1988. The principal purpose of ONDCP is to establish policies, priorities, and objectives for the nation's drug control program. The goals of the program are to reduce illicit drug use, manufacturing, trafficking, drug-related crime and violence, and drug-related health consequences. Retrieved April 19, 2004: http://www.whitehousedrugpolicy.gov/policy/index.html

97. Ernest Drucker (1998, January/February). Drug and public health. *Public Health Reports.* U.S. Public Health Service (p. 114). Also, see *Drug sense: Drug war clock.* Retrieved online January 7, 2005: http://www.drugsense.org/wodclock.htm

3

ENTRY PROCESS, SENTENCE STRATEGIES, AND INTERMEDIATE SANCTIONS

LEARNING OBJECTIVES

When you have read this chapter, you will be better prepared to:

- Explain the criminal justice process leading an offender to CC.
- Describe the concept, process, and purpose of sentencing.
- Describe the contents and purpose of Presentence Investigation Reports.
- Identify the primary sentencing strategies used in the United States.
- Identify the causal perspective linked to crime that best justifies each sentence strategy.
- Identify the correctional approach that can be justified by each sentence strategy.
- Explain the rationale supporting the current trends in sentencing.
- Identify the methods of serving more than one sentence at a time.
- Identify and describe a range of intermediate sanctions imposed upon violators.
- Explain how the Community Corrections Act came about. Identify its goals and merits.

KEY TERMS

Civil Compromise
Concurrent Sentences
Consecutive Sentences
Determinate Sentencing
Diversion
Fines
Flat Sentences

Indeterminate Sentences
Intermediate Sanctions
Judicial Discretion
No Contest
Mandatory Sentences
Nolo Contendere
Nolle prosequi

Parole
Presumptive Sentencing
   Guidelines
Presentence Investigation
   Report
Restitution
Probable Cause

Probation	Structured Sentencing	Voluntary/Advisory
Sentence	Suspended Sentences	Guidelines
Sentencing		

> Liberty means responsibility. That is why most men dread it.
>
> —George Bernard Shaw (1856–1950)

INTRODUCTION

The focus of this chapter is on the responsibility of the justice community to ensure public safety while providing an efficient yet lawful system that makes violators accountable for their indiscretions and is capable of aiding in their reform. Some policy makers, interest groups, and segments of the public dread imposing criminal sanctions such as prison sentences upon violators whereas others promote capital punishment. However, freedom has a price that includes both individual accountability and government responsibility. George Bernard Shaw argues, "Liberty means responsibility." Part of the justice system's responsibility is to arrest, prosecute, and impose a sentence upon guilty defendants. One reality about public safety and reform is that some violators should be imprisoned for a very long time, but most can be held accountable and move toward crime-free lifestyles through conditional supervision in the community.

Although it is often argued that longer sentences deter violators, evidence from the United States, Canada, and Europe over the last 30 years shows a different story. That is, longer sentences increase recidivism levels for various reasons including the encouragement of violence, especially among nonviolent offenders.[1] Furthermore, swift and consistent punishment as opposed to harsh punishment or longer sentences has a direct impact on potential criminal behavior and limits the number and severity of offences committed.[2] Said another way, increasing the likelihood of apprehension and conviction will bring about a greater reduction in crime more often than longer sentences and harsher punishment.

Another finding is that high recidivism levels can be reduced through correctional treatment. Treatment has many benefits. For example, effective treatment programs cost about $3,500 per year (in 2002) per defendant. Savings during the first year after a defendant successfully completes a correctional treatment program are estimated at:

- $5,000 in reduced crime costs
- $7,300 in reduced arrest and prosecution costs
- From $23,000 to $43,000 a year per prisoner depending on the state in reduced incarceration costs.[3]

Each participant who completes a correctional treatment program and remains crime free can save taxpayers at least $37,000 or $37 million for every 1,000 success stories. What have states done to help themselves out of the correctional predicament centered in costly imprisonment and responsibility toward public safety? Prison sentences are incredibly expensive. In 2003, many states took measures to save money:[4]

- Illinois cut inmate education programs to save $5 million a year.
- Florida cut drug treatment for prisoners to save $7 million.
- Minnesota is charging prisoners room and board.
- Iowa prisons now serve desert only once a day.
- California prisons have stopped imprisoning drug addicts.
- Kentucky's governor gave 567 nonviolent inmates an early release from prison.[5]
- Many states repealed mandatory minimum sentencing laws for drug crimes.
- Washington lowered their inmate count by 1,800 through revised sentences perspectives.
- North Carolina's new sentencing guidelines call for harsh prison terms for violent crimes, but community level sentences for nonviolent, first-time offenders.[6]
- Connecticut, Louisiana, Mississippi, and North Dakota have reduced sentences for non-violent and first-time offenders by easing their mandatory minimum sentencing laws.
- Ohio released 4,000 prisoners earlier than expected and saved about $88 million.
- Texas, Oregon, California, Idaho, and Arkansas expanded the use of drug treatment to greatly lower prison costs (because about 80 percent of prison inmates have serious drug and alcohol issues problems).[7]

This chapter provides a description of the criminal justice process leading to correctional supervision. It identifies and explains sentence strategies and their links to causal factors of crime and to the various approaches of correctional supervision. It identifies and describes intermediate sanctions. Finally, it describes the contributing factors that led to the development of the Community Corrections Act that enhances community corrections in numerous ways.

CRIMINAL JUSTICE PROCESS LEADING TO CC

An individual can participate in a CC program in three ways:

1. Volunteer (some programs accept volunteer participants)
2. Diversionary recommendation
3. Sentenced by the court

   Volunteers: Individuals might wish to participate in a CC program to benefit from it. A person might feel potentially at-risk or might want to participate to further their knowledge about a specific subject. Finally, they might wish to learn or participate to better cope with a loved one.
   Diversionary recommendations: Will be covered in Chapter 6. What you need to know right now is that prior to a judicial sentence and at the discretion of police, courts, or other social agencies including schools, welfare, and private human services, an at-risk

What is the sequence of events in the criminal justice system?

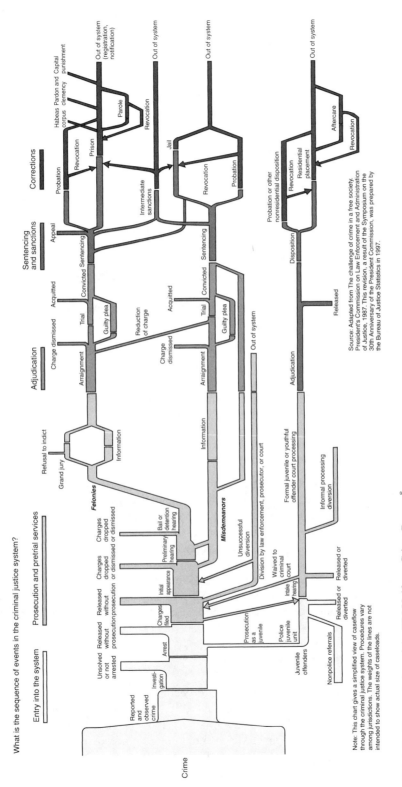

Note: This chart gives a simplified view of caseflow through the criminal justice system. Procedures vary among jurisdictions. The weights of the lines are not intended to show actual size of caseloads.

Source: Adapted from The challenge of crime in a free society, President's Commission on Law Enforcement and Administration of Justice, 1967. This revision, a result of the Symposium on the 30th Anniversary of the President Commission, was prepared by the Bureau of Justice Statistics in 1997.

Printed with permission of the FBI Uniform Crime Report.[8]

75

individual can receive a recommendation to participate in a program. The rationale of diversion is to keep an at-risk person out of judicial sentencing by providing an opportunity to change his or her behavior without judicial sanctions.

Sentenced by the court: Most participants are sentenced to correctional supervision.

Prosecution and Pretrial Procedure

After an arrest, the police offer information about the case and about the accused to the prosecutor.[9] The prosecutor's office will decide if formal charges will be filed with the court. If no charges are filed, the accused must be released. A prosecutor can also drop charges after making efforts to prosecute (*nolle prosequi*). A suspect charged with a crime must be taken before a judge or magistrate without unnecessary delay. At the preliminary appearance, the judge or magistrate informs the accused of the charges and decides whether there is *probable cause* to detain the suspect.[10] The accused is:

1. Informed of the charges against him or her at that appearance.
2. Advised of his or her rights.
3. Given the opportunity to retain a lawyer or have one appointed by the court if they are indigent.
4. Expenditures and funding sources: In 1999, an estimated $1.2 billion was spent to provide indigent criminal defense in the nation's 100 most populous counties. About 73 percent of the total was spent by public defender programs, 21 percent by assigned counsel programs, and 6 percent on awarded contracts. This $1.2 billion represents an estimated 3 percent of all local criminal justice expenditures used for police, judicial services, and corrections in these counties.[12]
5. Bail, bond, or an alternative arrangement is made (released on recognizance, conditional release, third–party custody depending on the case and the individual (a flight risk).[13] (Note: there will be more on pretrial release in Chapter 6). Should bail or an alternative be arranged and the obligations met by a defendant, the accused is released from custody or pretrial release to await trial appearance.

If the offense is not serious, the determination of guilt and assessment of a penalty may also occur at this stage. The court must also decide whether *probable cause* exists, granting the court detainment power over the accused.[14] A lack of *probable cause* will result in the case being dismissed. Subsequently, the accused is released.

Sufficient Probable Cause

A case can be sent to a grand jury, depending on state guidelines, when sufficient *probable cause* is present or the accused waives the right to a preliminary hearing. Depending on the seriousness of the crime, a determination of guilt and criminal justice sanction can occur at this time. More serious crimes proceed to a grand jury where it will be decided if the prosecutor offered sufficient evidence for a trial.[15] Not all jurisdictions

- Probable Cause—A reasonable belief that a person has committed a crime. The test the court of appeals employs to determine whether probable cause existed for purposes of arrest is whether facts and circumstances within the officer's knowledge are sufficient to warrant a prudent person to believe a suspect has committed, is committing, or is about to commit a crime. U.S. v. Puerta, 982 F.2d 1297, 1300 (9th Cir. 1992). In terms of seizure of items, probable cause merely requires that the facts available to the officer warrants a "man of reasonable caution" to conclude that certain items may be contraband or stolen property or useful as evidence of a crime. U.S. v. Dunn, 946 F.2d 615, 619 (9th Cir. 1991), cert. Denied, 112 S. Ct. 401 (1992).
- It is undisputed that the Fourth Amendment, applicable to the states through the Fourteenth Amendment, prohibits an officer from making an arrest without probable cause. McKenzie v. Lamb, 738 F.2d 1005, 1007 (9th Cir. 1984). Probable cause exists when "the facts and circumstances within the arresting officer's knowledge are sufficient to warrant a prudent person to believe that a suspect has committed, is committing, or is about to commit a crime." United States v. Hoyos, 892 F.2d 1387, 1392 (9th Cir. 1989), cert. denied, 489 U.S. 825 (1990) (citing United States v. Greene, 783 F.2d 1364, 1367 (9th Cir. 1986), cert. denied, 476 U.S. 1185 (1986).
- When there are grounds for suspicion that a person has committed a crime or misdemeanor, and public justice and the good of the community require that the matter should be examined, there is said to be a probable cause for, making a charge against the accused, however malicious the intention of the accuser may have been. And probable cause will be presumed till the contrary appears.
- In an action, then, for a malicious prosecution, the plaintiff is bound to show total absence of probable cause, whether the original proceedings were civil or criminal.

Source: The 'Lectric Law Library™[11] — http://www.lectlaw.com

require a grand jury. Some rely on the prosecutor to formally submit information to the court. If the grand jury or the court finds sufficient evidence, it submits an indictment (written statement of charges) to a trial court.

Once an indictment is filed, the accused is scheduled for arraignment.

Once Guilty

If the accused pleads guilty or pleads no contest—*nolo contendere* (accepts a penalty without admitting guilt)—the judge can accept or reject it.

Nadine Sanders, 42, was arrested January 20, 2003 by the Boston police. She was released on $500 cash bail and arraigned January 28, 2003. The charges were perjury, intimidation of a witness, and attempting to procure others to commit perjury. Nadine is the mother of a 23-year-old Boston man who faces a murder charge. The murder happened in front of a dozen witnesses including Nadine Sanders. The day after the murder, Nadine's home was searched and investigators discovered ammunition matching the casings found at the murder scene. Nadine was called before a county grand jury once her son was charged with murder in district court. Nadine allegedly tried to coerce witnesses not to testify against her son and gave information to the grand jury that contradicted what other witnesses said.[16]

No Contest Plea: *Nolo Contendere.* In Latin, "I do not wish to contend."

Nolo contendere is a plea by a defendant in a criminal prosecution that without admitting guilt subjects the defendant to conviction as in the case of a guilty plea but that does not bar denial of the truth of the charges in another proceeding (as in a civil action based on the same acts).[17] A no contest plea is similar to a guilty plea in that the accused can receive the maximum sentence for the crime provided by law.

Vince Neil of Motley Crue Pleads No Contest to Charge

Beverly Hills, CA: The lawyer for Motley Crue singer Vince Neil entered a no contest plea to a misdemeanor battery in an assault involving a record producer outside the Rainbow Bar and Grill in West Hollywood on April 28, 2002. In the club's parking lot, Neil struck his victim several times until he fell to the ground, breaking his elbow. A Superior Court judge ordered the 42-year-old singer to complete 100 hours of community service and pay restitution.[18]

An accused is guaranteed a trial by jury. Should a guilty verdict or guilty plea sentence be offered by a defendant, sentencing is determined.

Felony Convictions in State Courts: Method of Conviction, United States, 2000[19]

Offense	Jury	Bench	Guilty Plea
All offenses	3%	2%	95%
Violent offenses	9%	2%	89%
Drug offenses	2%	2%	96%

A sentence may involve one or a combination of a number of different elements, including incarceration (prison, jail), probation, and intermediate sanctions. Finally, in the matter of guilt and sentencing, there appears to be a continual debate about differences between public defenders and hired attorneys representing a defendants. Publicly financed counsel represented about 66 percent of federal felony defendants in 1998 as well as 82 percent of felony defendants in the 75 most populous counties in 1996.[20] Following are data provided by the Bureau of Justice Statistics that may help you develop a better picture of the debate between public and private counsel.[21]

- **Conviction rates** Conviction rates for indigent defendants and those with their own lawyers were about the same in Federal and States courts. About 90 percent of the federal defendants and 75 percent of the defendants in the most populous counties were found guilty, regardless of their attorneys.

- Of those found guilty, however, those represented by publicly financed attorneys were incarcerated at a higher rate than those defendants who paid for their own legal representation: 88 percent compared to 77 percent in federal courts and 71 percent compared to 54 percent in the most populous counties.

- **Sentence length** On average, sentence lengths for defendants sent to jail or prison were shorter for those with publicly financed attorneys than for those who hired counsel. In federal district court, those with publicly financed attorneys were given just under 5 years on average and those with private attorneys just over 5 years. In large state courts those with publicly financed attorneys were sentenced to an average of 2½ years and those with private attorneys to 3 years.

- **Racial disparity and the use of publicly financed counsel** Although 69 percent of white state prison inmates reported they had lawyers appointed by the court, 77 percent of blacks and 73 percent of Hispanics had publicly financed attorneys. In federal prison, black inmates were more likely than whites and Hispanics to have public counsel: 65 percent for blacks, 57 percent for whites, and 56 percent for Hispanics.

At this point, many offenders are remanded to the supervision of the department of corrections. Some are imprisoned, but most are placed into the community under a variety of correctional supervision conditions and surveillance options.[22]

> **Indictment:** Formal written statement framed by a prosecuting authority and found by a grand jury that charges a person or persons with an offense.

Purpose of a Penalty

Once an accused has been processed through the court and found guilty, the role of the judge is to impose a penalty or sanction. What is the purpose of a penalty? Some observers argue that the purpose of a penalty is couched in the belief that violators should be held accountable for their actions and the harm they have caused.

> If you believe that an underlying goal of the justice community is to identify individuals who have acted in an intentional way to hurt others and therefore should hold them accountable for their actions by imposing a penalty upon them, which approach of correctional supervision are you using to justify your thoughts?

Recall the various approaches of correctional supervision models in Chapter 2 (punishment, control, treatment, and prevention). If you see accountability and "payback" as "medicine" for a violator, then the model that best describes your thoughts is linked to the punishment model, specifically just deserts or retribution.

Sanction leads to Sentence
Guilt leads to Imposed Sanction
Trial leads to Verdict
Plea Bargain Negotiations
Arraignment Leads to Trial
Indictment Leads to Arraignment
Grand Jury Hears Evidence Leads to Indictment
Judge/Magistrate Reviews for Grand Jury
Prosecutor Files Charges
Arrest
Police Investigate
Crime Reported

Figure 3.1   Staircase Demonstrating Justice Process[23]

SENTENCE STRATEGIES

Importance of Reviewing Sentence Strategies

Because every offender under correctional supervision from those in solitary confinement to those in correctional substance abuse programs at a local YMCA have experienced the process of sentencing at some level, it is important for a justice professional or justice student to review sentence strategies. However, the focus is on CC and, accordingly, some sentences are not discussed such as life without parole and capital punishment. Nonetheless, most offenders know something about sentencing, especially as it relates to their case. But as an offender is processed through the justice system, they learn about sentence strategies associated with other cases from other offenders and from justice personnel and volunteers. In addition, knowledge of sentence strategies can aid CC practitioners and students to better understand some of the experiences of CC participants. Equally important, knowledge can influence change through an informed decision-making process that benefits everyone, especially if criminal justice is your profession.

An Example of Factors that Influence Sentence Strategies

The sentence imposed upon a defendant depends on many factors. Some of those factors include the prerogatives of the court, which are often guided by legislation and official directives. Other factors include belief systems held by policy makers, interest groups, and the public. As you already know, the core of those belief systems includes causal factors leading to crime (free will and environmental perspectives) and approaches of correctional supervision (punishment, control, rehabilitation, and prevention). With that said, after the guilt of a defendant is determined, the court imposes a sentence upon the defendant. That is, a sentence is the penalty imposed.

> **Sentencing:** The imposition of a criminal justice sanction by a sentencing authority such as a judge.

> **Sentence:** The penalty the court imposes upon a convicted offender.

General Sentencing Strategies

Think of it this way: The sentence or sanction imposed upon a convicted defendant will, in many cases, leave fewer choices for the defendant to make. Should confinement be part of a sentence, offenders will have little influence over its duration, its locale or region of the state where it will be served (if state jurisdiction applies), and the circumstances of their imprisonment. If it is a federal conviction, prison time can be served at a number of facilities across the country. Sentencing has to do with the conditions a convicted defendant will encounter with or without his or her consent, and offenders have few choices in the end result of any sentence. Realizing these thoughts at some level, most sentencing authorities attempt to find official solutions that maximize their correctional goals. As you know, most of those goals are couched in their beliefs about why defendants commit crime in the first place and how to respond to them at an official level. Furthermore, because many defendants are conditionally released from confinement (some even before serving any time in jail or prison), they become participants in a CC system. Therefore, it is helpful to review the most commonly used sentence strategies before examining intermediate sanctions or CC.

Sentence Process

Once a defendant has been processed through the justice system and stands in front of a judge, regardless of how the defendant got there, the defendant is sentenced. The defendant has either pled guilty or been found guilty through the judicial process, which could include a jury or a bench trial. To dispose of the case, a judge or a magistrate often has discretion in sentencing an offender. However, there are jurisdictions where state sentencing guidelines (for state cases) and federal sentencing guidelines (for federal cases) apply. Also, a judge's sentencing discretion is exercised within legislative boundaries often set by maximum and minimum penalties linked to sentencing guidelines.

> **Sentencing guidelines** are a set of standards established by legislatures, judges, or a sentencing commission to be followed by a judge when imposing a sentence. Divergence can be allowed but is usually accompanied by a statement of reasons prepared by the sentencing judge.

Sometimes, a sentencing commission oversees sentencing guidelines.

> A **sentencing commission** is an authorized group that develops a schedule of sentences that often reflects the gravity of offenses, prior record of offenders, and offenders' future prognosis of crime. The commission can include private citizens and justice personnel from the police, courts, and correctional community.

The task of a sentencing commission can be complicated because, public sentiment might hold a different perspective than judicial dictates, and at other times judges might disagree with the opinion of a jury.

Prior to imposing a sentence, a judge has other guides that can help guide a decision. For instance, a judge might hold a sentence hearing to consider evidence of aggravating or mitigating circumstances. There are also a number of investigative reports that can help a judge toward disposition. One such report is the Presentence Investigation Report (PSI) produced by a probation agency or another designated authority; this is discussed in more detail in Chapters 7 and 8.

Presentence Investigation Report (PSI)

A **Presentence Investigation Report (PSI)** is largely the task of a probation department and contains a personal history, along with an assessment and recommendations linked to the defendant.

A PSI is a confidential document about a defendant. The PSI carries a lot of weight concerning both a sentence as imposed by a judge and an early release recommendation from prison. Among federal and state probation officers, preparing a PSI acts as an "arm of the court."[24] The PSI actually recounts the government's version of the offense, inquires into the offender's criminal and social background, and evaluates the information gathered in terms of its reliance for determination of sentence. As the indeterminate, rehabilitative perspectives take hold, requiring an analysis of an offender's experiences, the PSI is not perceived to be an adversarial instrument that might favor the prosecutor or the defendant but rather a tool to aid the judge in better understanding the offender for the purpose of sentencing.

Sometimes, judges and parole authorities follow PSI recommendations and other times, they don't. For instance, in a high-profile 1998 case in Erie County, NY, after a lengthy, very publicized trial, the offender was found guilty on two counts of sodomy of a 13-year-old girl. Judge Michael F. Pietruszka sentenced the 33-year-old offender to a term of 13 months to 4 years as prescribed by state statue.[25] In the PSI, The Erie County Probation Department claimed the defendant was a "danger to society" and that if he were placed on probation or paroled, revocation (violating the conditions of probation and/or parole) was most likely. The prosecutor's office also contributed an opinion in the Buffalo newspapers indicating that the defendant was a heinous sex predator who preyed upon children through use of email. The probation officers who developed the PSI for this defendant, recommended a long-term sentence for the defendant, who was subsequently denied parole after two years of incarceration because of the contents of his PSI. The parole board took the contents of the PSI seriously despite all the "good-time" reports provided by New York Department of Correctional Services (NYDOCS). Also, although the prisoner successfully completed all of the required programs of the department of corrections, the conclusion was that he remained a danger to society. This notion seems to imply that either the programs provided by the NYDOCS were inadequate or the PSI contributes more influence than expected.

After serving his full prison sentence and, upon his release, the offender was labeled a level three (highest priority) sex offender and must comply with sexual offenders notification for 10 years after release. The offender's chances of getting a job, an education, or a safe place to live in New York are unlikely and should he wish to date a responsible individual, that may also be unlikely. One question is what will become of sex offenders, which currently number close to 300 thousand, in the United States?[26] (See Chapter 15 for more about sex offenders.)

Keep in mind that the afore mentioned facts only represent a window to the materials reviewed by the parole board. Continuing along this line of reasoning, it appears that the parole authority of New York put more emphasis on the PSI than the ability and evaluation of the rehabilitation programs and efforts of the NYDOCS. Could it be said that the probation personnel who completed the PSI held a "free will" perspective and thought that incapacitation was the best method of dealing with this prisoner?

DESCRIPTIONS OF SENTENCE STRATEGIES

Sentencing is a strategy or penalty model. Most jurisdictions use different sentencing strategies in their justice system, and of the strategies they do utilize, it is unlikely that their model includes every characteristic described. That is, because each jurisdiction is different due to its beliefs, resources, and experiences, it is likely that their official response to offenders, including sentencing strategies, are also different. Most sentence strategies can be characterized as flat, mandatory, presumptive, indeterminate, determinate, voluntary/advisory, life without parole, capital punishment, structured, suspended, or intermediate (see Table 3.1).

Flat Sentences

Sentences in 19th century America were comprised primarily of flat prison sentences. Flat prison sentences are a fixed amount of confinement to be served by a defendant. Generally, flat sentences were arbitrary decisions made by judges. There was little consistency between flat sentences and conviction records. For example, a defendant could get 15 years for shoplifting or 10 years for a murder conviction depending on how the judge felt on a particular day. Also, flat sentences allow little variation from the duration of the sentenced time imposed. For instance, a seven-year sentence implies that an offender will serve every day of the seven-year sentence prior to release. It could be said that advocates who believe all offenders make a choice about crime support this sentencing strategy and believe that the best way to respond to those violators is through retribution and incapacitation.

Mandatory Sentences

Mandatory sentences are fixed by statute for specific crimes and categories of offenders. Early release is unlikely. Unlike flat sentences, mandatory sentences are not imposed at the whim of the judge but are predetermined, often based on specific crimes and sometimes linked to the criminal history of an offender. It is expected that a prisoner will be confined for the duration of the prison sentence. For example, a 10-year prison sentence is automatically imposed upon every convicted participant in a drug transaction. This sentencing policy reflects a choice or free will causal perspective about crime and posits that the best approach in dealing with these offenders is through retribution—an eye for an eye. Most mandatory sentencing advocates see incapacitation as the best way to respond to offenders.

Table 3.1   Characteristics of Sentence Strategies[27]

Form of Sanction	Description	Approach of Correctional Supervision	Causal Factors of Crime
Flat sentences	Arbitrary sentence imposed by judge. Little consistency between crimes and sentences. Specific duration for a specific conviction. Little room for early release.	Retribution Incapacitation	Free will
Mandatory sentences	Fixed by statute for specific crimes. Consistency between crimes and sentences. Early release is unlikely. Prisoner serves the full sentence.	Just Deserts Retribution Deterrence Incapacitation	Free will
Presumptive guidelines sentencing	Ranges of time linked to categories of activities of the crime. Gives judge an "ordinary" sentence that can be imposed but allows for stiffer or lenient sentences depending on aggravating or mitigating factors.	Just Deserts Incapacitation	Free will
Indeterminate sentences	Minimum period to be served before release and a maximum period after which a prisoner can be re-leased. Eligibility depends on time necessary for treat-ment. Judge has discretion over minimum and maxi-mum durations. Sentence disparity is likely. Parole process has authority over an early release.	Incapacitation Deterrence Rehabilitation	Free will
Determinate sentences	Fixed term of incarceration. Dissatisfaction with treatment goals of indeterminate sentences. Can be reduced through "good time." No review by parole authority. Assumes consistency in sentences and an incentive for prisoners to behave while imprisoned.	Retribution Deterrence Incapacitation Rehabilitation	Largely free will and some en-vironmental
Voluntary/ advisory guidelines sentences	Based on previous sentencing policy that serves as a guide to a sentencing judge.	Retribution	Free will
Life without parole	Prisoner leaves prison when dead.	Retribution Incapacitation	Free will
Capital punishment	Death sentence.	Retribution Deterrence	Free will
Structured sentencing	Guidelines (offense and personal characteristics) for determining an offender's sentence. A compromise between mandatory and intermediate sanctions.	Incapacitation Rehabilitation	Free will some environ-mental
Suspended sentences	Defendant receives a prison or jail sentence but serving time is withheld pending conditional release. Probation.	Rehabilitation	Environmental
Intermediate sanctions	More restrictive than probation less restrictive than prison.	Rehabilitation Prevention	Environmental

There is also a mandatory minimum sentencing strategy. That is, in some jurisdictions, judges impose a mandatory minimum sentence unless there are aggravating or mitigating circumstances, in which case they might lengthen or shorten those terms, within narrow boundaries. For instance, a sentence may call for a six-month jail sentence for driving under the influence of alcohol conviction (DUI), and the judge can increase the six months to one year. But, the judge cannot reduce the minimum time to be served below the six-month minimum.

Mandatory sentences are linked with sentence reforms such as presumptive sentencing guidelines, truth-in-sentencing laws, and three-strikes laws. Each of these strategies requires incarceration for certain types of offenses for specified lengths of time, and each is discussed in more detail later in this chapter.

There are drawbacks to mandatory sentences even at the minimum level, especially because they allow a judge little discretion. Sometimes mandatory minimum sentences have some unexpected results. For instance, in Indiana, Mark Young was arrested as part of a marijuana conspiracy a few years ago.[28] Although everyone knew Mark had a previous juvenile record, everyone in the small farming community knew Mark straightened himself up. The arrest came as a surprise but the sentence shocked them more—life in prison based upon mandatory sentencing guidelines. While Young was being sentenced, the boxer Mike Tyson was on trial for rape in the same Indiana courthouse and received a few years in prison.

Then, there's 25-year-old Weldon Angelos, who was sentenced by Judge Paul Cassell (D. Utah) to 55 years, with no possibility of parole, for a first-time drug offense with possession of a gun on November 16, 2004. Calling the sentence "unjust and cruel and even irrational," Judge Cassell explains that he had no choice as mandated by federal mandatory sentencing guidelines.[29]

Additionally, it is likely that many policy makers and politicians use a mandatory sentence strategy for symbolic rather than practical reasons. Also, some prosecutors have refused to file charges against defendants bearing mandatory penalties. Prosecutors and judges use plea bargaining strategies to avoid mandatory type convictions (an offender can accept a guilty plea of nonmandatory crime). Then, too, juries have little influence over mandatory guidelines and often are unaware of elements that dictate sentences such as previous criminal histories and the use of weapons. Because of these reasons, the U.S. Supreme Court overturned the federal sentencing guidelines on January 12, 2005.[30] The high court ruled that the mandatory sentencing system violated Sixth Amendment rights. The high court's decision will ripple through state systems quickly for similar reasons.

Florida and Mandatory Sentencing

In 1999, the Florida Legislature enacted a minimum mandatory sentencing law called "10–20–Life" for criminals who possess or used guns to commit violent felonies or drug trafficking offenses.[31] This landmark reform requires a mandatory sentence of at least 10 years in state prison for any criminal convicted of possessing a gun while committing a violent felony. If the criminal actually shoots a gun while committing the crime, the initiative requires a minimum mandatory sentence of 20 years in state prison. If the criminal uses the gun to shoot another person and causes serious bodily injury or death, the initiative requires the courts to impose a mandatory sentence of at least 25 years and up to life in state prison.[32]

Michigan and Mandatory Sentences

A few days after Christmas in 2002, Governor John Engler ended Michigan's failed experiment with mandatory minimum drug sentences. The governor signed historic legislation repealing the Public Acts 665, 666, 670 that finally eliminated the state's Draconian mandatory minimum sentences for drug offenses. Now, sentencing guidelines are based on a range of factors and lifetime probation for the lowest level offenders has been replaced with a five-year probationary period. Previously, parole was denied on many drug possession offenders and that has now been repealed at the discretion of the parole board.[33]

Presumptive Sentencing Guidelines

Presumptive sentencing guidelines (PSG), sometimes called grid sentences, are contained in or based on legislation. They set out a range of penalties for an offense based on the seriousness of the offense and the offender's criminal history. Other factors, such as aggravating or mitigating circumstances, can be included in the guidelines. One purpose of PSG is to limit judicial discretion and to bring some consistency to prison sentences. Judges can depart from the guidelines in particular circumstances or upon giving reasons for a departure. It gives a judge an "ordinary" sentence that can be imposed; however, it allows for a stiffer or more lenient sentence depending on special aggravating or mitigating factors. Largely, PSG are sentences that meet the following conditions:

- Appropriate sentence for an offender in a specific case is presumed to be within a range authorized by guidelines established by a legislative body, such as a sentencing commission.
- Judges are expected to sentence within the range or provide written justification for departure.
- The guidelines provide for review of the departure, usually by appeal to a higher court. Presumptive guidelines might employ determinate or indeterminate sentencing components.

> **Presumptive Sentencing Guidelines** are guidelines developed by a sentencing commission centered on a quantitative scoring instrument evaluating the offender and the seriousness of the offense as opposed to the crime committed.

The first four states to adopt presumptive sentencing guidelines were Minnesota (1980), Pennsylvania (1982), Washington (1983), and Florida (1983). The Minnesota model focuses on controlling prison population growth and is often used as an example of the successful control of disparity and rising corrections costs. The Minnesota model uses a sentencing matrix of offense severity and offender's prior criminal history to indicate the appropriateness of the sentence. The matrix provides a range for specified offenses, penalties, and an additional range of penalties depending on the circumstances. Minnesota law classifies the crime of criminal sexual conduct into five categories: first-through fifth-degree criminal sexual conduct (see Table 3.2 for details).

It appears that often, advocates of PSG might accept a free will perspective as a crime causal link and consider the best approach to "cure" offenders is through an incapacitation process because, after all, they deserve the prison time imposed upon them (just deserts).[34]

Table 3.2 Presumptive Sentencing Guidelines: Penalties for Criminal Sexual Conduct in Minnesota

Name of Crime	Type of Activity	Maximum Penalty Provided by Statute	Presumptive Sentencing Guidelines Sentence (No Criminal History)
1st degree	Sexual penetration; certain sexual contact with victim under 13 years old	30 years; $40,000 fine	86 months in prison for penetration; 48 months in prison for contact with victim under age 13. Statutory law presumes an executed sentence of 144 months for all violations
2nd degree[34]	Sexual contact	25 years; $35,000 fine	48 months in prison; 21 months stayed sentence for "statutory rape."[a] Statutory law presumes an executed sentence of 90 months for crimes where the perpetrator uses or threatens to use force or violence, causes injury, uses a dangerous weapon, or creates significant fear on the part of the victim of imminent great bodily harm
3rd degree	Sexual penetration	15 years, $30,000 fine	40 months in prison; 18 months stayed sentence for "statutory rape"[a]
4th degree	Sexual contact	10 years; $20,000 fine	21 months stayed sentence; 12 months stayed sentence for "statutory rape"[a]
5th degree	Sexual contact; certain lewd conduct	One year; $3,000 fine (gross misdemeanor) Certain repeat violations punishable by five years; $10,000 fine	Sentencing guidelines do not apply to gross misdemeanor violations; felony violations are not ranked in sentencing guidelines and sentencing is left to court's discretion

[a]Statutory rape is defined as a criminal sexual conduct crime that has the following elements: (a) sexual conduct; (b) victim of a certain age; and for certain crimes, either; (c) familial relationship between the actor and the victim; or (d) use of a position of authority by the actor.

Source: Judie Zollar, Overview of Criminal Sexual Conduct Crimes.[35]

Indeterminate Sentences

Indeterminate sentences are minimum and maximum periods of prison time imposed by a judge (e.g., a three or five-year sentence).[36] In this instance, during the three-year period, the correctional system readies a prisoner for release through various methods that aid in altering a prisoner's attitudes and behavior (there is a concern toward reintegration). A parole authority would evaluate the "reformed" prisoner for possible conditional release after three years of incarceration and successful completion of all designated programs. In essence, the judge, correctional community, and a parole authority work in concert to release a "reformed" offender prior to the five-year sentence. In Texas, sentences range from death penalty for capital felony to state jail (see Table 3.3).

Indeterminate sentencing focuses on prison time to "fit" an offender rather than to "fit" the crime an offender committed. Before imposing sentencing, a judge can weigh each case on its own merits, which can include the intention of the offender during the commission of the crime as reflected in Table 3.3. Advocates of indeterminate sentencing argue that bringing a prisoner closer to conformity can be accomplished through incarceration. This thought obviously satisfies deterrence advocates because the prisoner now experiences the hardships of prison that will ultimately influence his or her future decisions about committing crime once released. They don't want to return to prison. However, treatment advocates, also support indeterminate sentencing based on the belief that an offender is optimistic about his or her future and wants to change especially while incarcerated because conformity leads to parole and freedom.

Determinate Sentences

Sentence strategies changed from an indeterminate sentence to a fixed or determinate sentence. "Determinate sentencing" was part of sentence reforms of the 1970s and includes early release of a prisoner based on "good-time credits" instead of a parole board review. This model implies that all offenders convicted of the same crime will receive the same sentence unlike the indeterminate model. For instance, in indeterminate sentencing a term for robbery could include imprisonment for not less than 2 years but not more than 15 years. Parole could be possible after two years after a review by the parole board. Determinate sentencing, on the other hand, mandates that guilty defendants convicted of the same crime receive the same sentence (e.g., three years for breaking and entering). Prisoners

Table 3.3   Punishment Ranges for Felony Offenses in Texas[37]

Felony				
Capital Felony	First Degree	Second Degree	Third Degree	State Jail Felony
Death penalty or life imprisonment	Life imprisonment or 5–99 years	2 to 20 years imprisonment	2 to 14 years imprisonment	180 days to 2 years

can be released at a specified time, minus good time credits or merits they earned while incarcerated without review by a board of any type. Once free, these former prisoners are not supervised by a parole officer. However, depending on jurisdiction, different forms of "reporting" could be expected.

> **Good-time** is an early release mechanism under determinate sentencing whereby a prisoner receives an automatic reduction in sentence for every day spent without violating a prison rule. Reduction time can also be earned by participating in educational programs, community service projects, and medical experiments.

"Good-time" credits vary from state to state and are not available in every jurisdiction. One thought behind good-time credits is that they are incentives for convicts and therefore an aid in managing a prison population. The downside of this thought is that some convicts are more concerned with reaching their own goals than the goals of the justice system. Additionally, some prisoners and correctional personnel can use good-time credit reporting for their own ends, inviting manipulation of the system.

An assumption of determinate sentencing is that all offenders are equal and should serve a similar sentence with options for early release and that an offender will be off the streets; so theoretically, crime will be better controlled.[38] Another assumption is that prisoners involved in programs have equal resources available to them as participants in similar programs in the free world. For instance, prisons might have libraries but those libraries have fewer resources than free libraries and are less often available to prison students because of short hours than free students. Therefore, an illusion about prisoner programs probably sets some prisoners up for failure, once released more often than expected.

> **Determinate Sentencing** is a fixed period of incarceration that can be reduced by "good-time" credits earned.

A typical example of punitive response in the sentencing process relates to California, where most offenders are sentenced for a set amount of time under California's Determinate Sentencing Law (DSL).[39] Once time is served, a prisoner is released and placed on parole.

Voluntary/Advisory Guidelines

Voluntary or advisory guideline sentences are based on previous sentencing policies of the court and are often built upon determinate or indeterminate models. Florida, Maryland, Massachusetts, Michigan, Rhode Island, Utah, and Wisconsin all experimented with voluntary/advisory guidelines in the 1980s. Most often, voluntary/advisory guidelines are not commonly imposed upon serious defendants and are followed at lower level courts more often when they are practiced. On the positive side, cases are disposed of quicker and there is probably more consistency between cases within a similar jurisdiction.

Structured Sentences

Structured Sentences are sentencing guidelines usually developed by a sentencing authority or commission that consist of a set of standards based on a combination of the offense and the personal characteristics of the defendant. Often, prior criminal history of the offender is the most important personal characteristic considered. The rationale for this sentencing strategy is what type of punishment a particular crime and criminal deserves.

Structured sentences were designed to save prison beds for violent offenders and use intermediate sanctions for lesser offenders. Structured sentencing tries to match correctional resources to sentencing policies.[40] Under structured sentencing strategies, sentences are more uniform and less subject to the individual discretion of judges or parole authorities. Structured sentencing is a compromise between mandatory sentences and intermediate sanctions. The justice community has yet to develop a clear consensus on the goals of structured sentencing.[41] The following lists the most frequently cited goals:

- Increase sentencing fairness.
- Reduce unwarranted disparity, either in the decision to imprison (dispositional disparity) and/or sentence length (durational disparity).
- Establish truth in sentencing.
- Establish a balance of sentencing policy with limited correctional resources.

Structured sentencing reforms can be used to deter potential offenders and incapacitate dangerous offenders. Sentencing reforms can also be used to reduce the likelihood and length of imprisonment for the so-called nondangerous offender.

Suspended Sentences

Sometimes a prison sentence is "suspended." A suspended prison or jail sentence is one that can be placed on hold if a defendant complies with specific conditions (i.e., probation or parole, both of which will be discussed in future chapters). However, what you need to know right now about probation is that it is generally viewed as the disposition of choice by the courts because probation populations' growth far exceeds that of institutional corrections. An offender on probation can remain free in a specific community but must abide by specific rules and conditions for a period of time. Rehabilitative advocates who tend to see confinement as problematic among most violators, especially nonviolent offenders, usually support probation sanctions.

> **Probation** is a sentencing option whereby an offender is not incarcerated but supervised in the community.

Federal Sentences

In most criminal federal courts, mandatory minimum statutes are widely used but often detested by federal judges. For the 90 federal districts within the boundaries of the United States, the median federal sentence in 1998 was 18 months.[42] The federal government incarcerated 163,493 prisoners in 2002 and 173,000 by year end 2003.[43] Of that number, 55 percent of all the incarnated inmates in federal prisons had been convicted of a drug offense; 11 percent had been convicted of weapons, explosives, or arson offense; and 10 percent had been convicted of an immigration charge. Table 3.4 shows the offenses for which federal inmates were incarcerated.

The real question is how many of those incarcerated will be released early and placed in a CC program? Of 99,000 federal offenders under community supervision, approximately 31,000 were on probation and 83,000 were under supervised release or on parole by year end 2003.

CURRENT TRENDS IN SENTENCING STRATEGIES

Trends in sentencing strategies are tied to belief systems or attitudes held by policy makers, interest groups, and the public. For instance, if the public thinks that the severity of the courts is not harsh enough upon defendants, there's a strong possibility that sentencing strategies will move toward sentencing strategies that are harsher. Consistent with this thought is a study from the General Social Surveys shown in Table 3.5.

Table 3.4   Federal Prisoners as of December 31, 2003

Conviction	Percent (Rounded)
Drug offenses	55
Weapons, explosives, arson	11
Immigration	10
Robbery	7
Property offenses	5
Extortion, fraud, bribery	4
Homicide, aggravated assault, and kidnapping offenses	3
Miscellaneous	2
Sex offenses	1
Banking and insurance, counterfeit, embezzlement	1
Courts or corrections (e.g., obstructing justice)	.5
Continuing criminal enterprise	0.4
National security	0.1

Percents rounded. N = Estimated at 163,493.
Source: TRAC.[44]

Table 3.5   Attitudes Toward Severity of Courts (%)

	1990			1993			2000		
	Too Harshly	Not Harshly Enough	About Right	Too Harshly	Not Harshly Enough	About Right	Too Harshly	Not Harshly Enough	About Right
National Response	3%	83%	9%	3%	81%	10%	8%	68%	16%

"I don't know" categories were omitted therefore percents might not sum to 100.
Question: In general, do you think the courts in this area deal too harshly or not harshly enough with criminals?
Source: U.S. Department of Justice.[45]

If these thoughts are typical across the nation, it should come as no surprise that tough sentencing strategies such as *three-strikes laws, truth in sentencing,* and *sentencing guidelines* were legislated by a number of states. That is, as the belief pendulum has swung, so has sentencing strategies.

Three-strikes laws are a unique form of mandatory sentencing under which offenders with three felony convictions are sentenced to life without parole. Washington was the first state to enact a Three Strikes Law sentencing program in 1993. California quickly followed. A double-digit drop in the homicide rates in California was attributed to the success of three-strikes laws. Certainly many factors play a role in lower homicide levels of any state, yet one reason for the rise in California's prison population beyond its expected levels is linked to three-strikes laws. By 1996, 22 states and the federal government had passed some form of three-strike legislation.

Truth in sentencing is a movement in both federal and state government spurred by anxious politicians, interest groups, and the public to provide more honesty in the sentencing of defendants. The amount of time violators serve in prison is almost always shorter than the time they are sentenced to serve by the court.[46] Prisoners released in 1996, for instance, served an average of 30 months in prison or 44 percent of their sentence.

The objective is to make offenders serve most of the sentence originally imposed. That is, a prisoner cannot be released from prison until he or she serves at least 80 percent (this percentage will vary depending on the jurisdiction) of the original sentence. For instance, if 10 years was the original sentence, the prisoner cannot be released through good time credits until the prisoner serves 8 years of the sentence. The federal government originally conceived this idea in 1984 when the Comprehensive Crime Control Act nearly eliminated good-time credits. Its goal was to dispose of parole.[47]

Criticism of Three Strikes

States that enacted broad "three-strikes" laws are finding that their judicial systems, prisons, and budgets are being strained past the breaking point by the huge volume of cases these laws create.[48] More defendants in those jurisdictions insist on a trial as opposed to accepting the three-strike provisions. Also, three-strikes laws can send offenders to prison for life on a nonviolent conviction. Then, too, many jurisdictions already have laws under which repeat or habitual offenders get substantially longer sentences. Punishment advocates say that increasing the "pain" (prison time) will reduce crime.[49] "Research by the Justice Policy Institute has shown that California counties that sent more people to prison under three-strikes laws over the last decade actually had less of a drop in violent crime than counties that used three-strikes laws more sparingly."[50] However, New York, a state without three-strikes, whose incarceration rate declined from 1994 to 2002, experienced a 20 percent greater drop in violent crime than "California, which Sam Clauder II, the man who pushed hard for California's three-strikes law in 1994, broke the bank expanding its prison system by more than 34,000 people during that same period."[51] But after its enactment, Clauder had to work even harder to restrict the law he helped enact. "After a couple of years, I could see it was a big mistake," said Clauder, the political director of Citizens Against Violent Crime (CAVC). "It was putting petty criminals in prison for life."[52]

HOW SENTENCES ARE TO BE SERVED

Deciding on how more than one prison sentence imposed on a single defendant should be served is a simple matter. That is, suppose a defendant receives two five-year terms. If these sentences are to be served at the same time by the same offender, it is called a *concurrent* sentence. Should a defendant serve one term after the other for a total of 10 years, it is called a *consecutive* sentence. Most often, judges have discretion over concurrent or consecutive sentences; however, in many jurisdictions, sentencing guidelines apply.

Concurrent Sentence is when the same prisoner serves more than one prison sentence at one time.

Consecutive Sentence is when one prison sentence is served after another prison sentence.

BRIEF HISTORY OF FLORIDA SENTENCING PRACTICES[53]

Prior to October 1983, Florida courts operated under an unstructured sentencing system allowing for a wide range of judicial discretion in the sentencing decision. Due to concerns regarding actual amount and percentage of time served, as well as a lack of uniformity in sentencing, the 1983 Florida Sentencing Guidelines were enacted October 1, 1983 and parole eligibility was abolished for almost all offenses committed after that date. The 1994 sentencing guidelines were enacted through the passage of the "Safe Streets Act." These guidelines were created with the recognition that prison resources are finite and that the use of state incarceration should be focused upon offenders who commit serious or violent offenses, or who offend repetitively. The 1994 guidelines repealed the grant of basic gain time, which had reduced prison sentences by one third. The structure of the 1994 sentencing guidelines had little similarity to the 1983 structure.

Under the 1994 structure, the total guidelines score determines the sanction and a range of length of sanction when state prison is applicable. The court has the discretion to increase or decrease the sanction by 25 percent. This provided for a relatively narrow range for the imposition of a sentence. The 1994 Sentencing Guidelines were significantly amended in 1995 through the passage of the "Crime Control Act of 1995."[54] The basic structure of the 1994 Sentencing Guidelines remained; however, point values were increased in a variety of areas and additional policy levers were created to provide for greater sanctions. At the same time, the "Truth in Sentencing" law was implemented, mandating that inmates serve a minimum of 85 percent of their court-imposed sentence, and the "Violent Career Criminal Act" was passed, which mandated that certain violent offenders must receive longer prison terms. The guidelines were slightly modified in both 1996 and 1997, again providing for increased sanctions and sanction length in certain instances. In February 2000, the Florida Supreme Court ruled in *Heggs V. State* that the 1995 Guidelines were unconstitutional due to a violation of the single subject rule of the Florida Constitution.[55] This allowed for adversely affected offenders with offense dates within a certain time period to be resentenced under the less strict 1994 Sentencing Guidelines.

Florida's Current Sentencing Structure

The Criminal Punishment Code ("Code"), a dramatic change from the previous sentencing policy, became effective for offenses committed on or after October 1, 1998. The Code contains features of both structured and unstructured sentencing policies. It maintains many of the goals of guideline sentencing but allows for greater upward discretion in sentencing, provides for increased penalties, and lowers mandatory prison thresholds.

The Code embodies the principles that:[56]

1. Sentencing is neutral with respect to race, gender, and social and economic status.

2. The primary purpose of sentencing is to punish the offender. Rehabilitation is a desired goal of the criminal justice system but is subordinate to the goal of punishment.

3. The penalty imposed is commensurate with the severity of the primary offense and the circumstances surrounding the primary offense.

4. The severity of the sentence increases with the length and nature of the offender's prior record.

5. The sentence imposed by the sentencing judge reflects the length of actual time to be served, shortened only by the application of incentive and meritorious gain-time.

6. Departures below the permissible sentencing range established in the code must be articulated in writing and made only when the circumstances or factors reasonably justify the aggravation or mitigation of the sentence.

7. The trial judge may impose a sentence up to and including the statutory maximum for any offense, including an offense that is before the court due to a violation of probation.

8. A sentence may be appealed only if the sentence is below the permissible sentencing range.

9. Use of incarcerative sanctions is prioritized toward offenders convicted of serious offenses and offenders who have long prior records, to maximize the finite capacities of state and local correctional facilities.

How defendants are sentenced:

As in the guidelines, the Code ranks all noncapital felonies in one of 10 offense severity levels—1 being the least severe (such as applying for a fake ID) and 10 being the most severe (such as non-capital murder or treason). Each of these rankings has a point value in each of three elements: primary offense, additional offense(s), and prior record. Point values escalate as the rank increases. Points are also provided for victim injury, legal status, and offenses returned for violation of community supervision, certain possession of firearms/destructive devices, and existence of a prior serious felony. Points from each of these categories are added and the result determines a recommended sentence. Under the Code,[57] any defendant can be sentenced to prison (regardless of the score) and the sentence may be up to the statutory maximum for that felony class as follows:

- Life felony may receive up to life in prison
- 1st degree felony may receive up to 30 years in prison
- 2nd degree felony may receive up to 15 years in prison
- 3rd degree felony may receive up to 5 years in prison

Under the Code, if total points are equal to or less than 44, the lowest permissible sentence is a nonstate prison sanction (such as community supervision, jail, or a fine). If total points exceed 44, state prison is mandated (absent a valid departure) and the minimum sentence is established by taking the total point value, subtracting 28, and decreasing the remaining value by 25 percent. This end result value is the lowest permissible prison sentence in months. More detailed information can be obtained by reviewing Florida Statute 921.[58]

Impact of Sentencing Guidelines and the Criminal Punishment Code

As the accompanying chart illustrates, defendants sentenced under the 1995 Sentencing Guidelines in conjunction with the "Truth in Sentencing Law" appear to serve the most time in prison. Although defendants are sentenced under both the Criminal Punishment Code and the "Truth in Sentencing Law," they appear to serve less time due to the lower point threshold that mandates a prison sentence.[59]

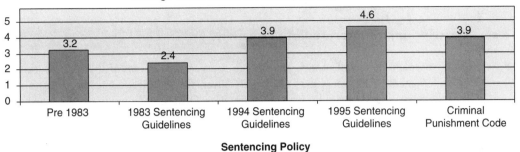

Average Years Served in Prison (Actual or Estimated)[60]

INTERMEDIATE SANCTIONS

Most sentences brought to bear on defendants exclude confinement. Most defendants are placed on probation and their prison sentence is suspended unless the defendant violates the conditions of probation. Although many of the following intermediate sanctions are detailed in future chapters, they are offered below in an abbreviated format for introduction purposes:

Intermediate Sanctions

Fines

Restitution

Diversion

Intensive supervision

Day reporting

Home confinement

Electric monitoring

Community service

Temporary release

Probation

Parole

Residential CC facilities

Halfway house

Intermediate sanctions can be interconnected. For instance, fines and community service are common sanctions for nonviolent young first-time violators. For example: 29-year-old Carrie Anne Drumm was convicted of raising $1,225 in donations from the retail gift store where she worked and also robbed the store of $17,800 in cash and merchandise. This Burlington, Vermont woman was sentenced to 45 days on a work crew, restitution to her employer, and probation for 5 years. Drumm pleaded guilty to the charges of lying to her coworkers that family members of hers were killed when they visited New York City on September 11, 2001.[61]

Descriptions of Intermediate Sanctions

Fines represent a sum of money paid to the court. A fine is one of the oldest forms of punitive sanctions known. Fines are largely given for a variety of less serious misdemeanor offenses committed by first-time offenders. Offenses that are typically punishable by a fine include minor drug possession (e.g., a small amount of marijuana), fish and game violations, shoplifting, traffic, civil rights, fraud, larceny, and even some first-time drunk driving cases. In more serious offenses or a case in which a defendant has a criminal record, judges combine a fine with other punishments, such as incarceration, community service, and probation. In many parts of the country, laws specify the maximum amount an offender may be fined for a particular offense. The judge is then free to impose a fine up to but not to exceed the prescribed amount. The court tries to structure fines in such a way that they are consistent, yet due to various income levels of defendants, what might be a reasonable fine for one offender might be an unreachable amount for another offender. Finally, a "day fine" is a penalty scaled to both the defendant's ability to pay and to the seriousness of the crime.

A **Fine** is a penalty imposed on an offender by the court requiring a specified sum to be paid. A fine can be a cash payment assessed by the judge in an individual case or determined by a published list of penalties. Fines can be paid in installments in many jurisdictions.

Day fine is a penalty scaled to both the defendant's ability to pay and to the seriousness of the crime.

Restitution: Whereas fines paid by a defendant go to the state (or federal or local government prosecuting the crime), restitution goes to the victim. Restitution is when a defendant is ordered to return or replace stolen or damaged property, to compensate a victim for physical injury, to cover medical and psychological treatment costs, or to pay funeral and other costs when a victim dies as a result of the action of the defendant. Sometimes, plea bargains are struck in which criminal charges are dropped altogether if a defendant admits guilt and completely compensates a victim, for example, for stolen property or a vandalized car. This type of arrangement may be called a *civil compromise.* In some cases, the "victim" is society, such as welfare and Medicare fraud schemes in which defendants may be sentenced to pay the state back the money that was defrauded or pay into a state victimization program.[62] The state or agency provides for each victim in different ways.

Restitution consists of payments made by a defendant to his or her victim for damages.

Restitution California Style

Many states have different ways of handling restitution. For example, in California, restitution fines are paid to the State Board of Control (BOC) Victims Restitution Fund.[63] The BOC Victims of Crime Program is the state agency responsible for administering the Victims Restitution Fund. The restitution fund is for victims of violent crimes who suffer out-of-pocket losses and who may be eligible to apply for financial reimbursement. The fund reimburses eligible victims for lost wages or support, medical or psychological counseling expenses, and other related costs. While an offender is incarcerated, inmates with court-ordered restitution fines have a specified percentage deducted from their wages and other trust account deposits for these fines. A defendant may also be ordered to pay restitution to the victim. This type of restitution is referred to as a direct order.

Diversion is when an individual is "diverted" out of the criminal justice system. Actually, it is a suspension of the prosecution of a charge for a period of time during which the defendant participates in a rehabilitation program or makes restitution, and after which the charges are dismissed if the rehabilitation or restitution is completed.[64]

One purpose of diversion is to allow a defendant to escape the stigma of a criminal conviction. Eligibility for diversion varies from one locality to another. Diversion programs are most often available to defendants charged with misdemeanors and nonviolent felonies. In some jurisdictions, diversion may be available to defendants charged with domestic violence, child abuse or neglect, traffic-related offenses, or even writing bad checks. The community, courts, and police conduct diversion programs. Advocates of diversion sanctions generally take a rehabilitation approach of supervision and often believe that those programs can act as prevention against future criminal activity. Also, these advocates generally see the crimes of a defendant as most often influenced by environmental perspectives as opposed to individual rational choices.

Diversion places defendants in the care of noncriminal justice agencies for services and programs instead of processing them through the courts or corrections. Their aim is to avoid the stigma of a conviction, therefore offsetting future crime.

Intense supervision can be probation or parole related. Often, intense supervision officers are armed and hold police powers over offenders, often amounting to more discretion than even sworn police officers. For example, an intense officer does not require *probable cause* or a warrant to enter the home of someone supervised nor must *probable cause* be evident for a personal search of the subject. There are many levels of supervision including high-risk (daily face to face), close risk (daily drug tests), intermediate risk (weekly), and reduced risk (monthly). This model of community corrections was developed once it was discovered there were a limited number of incarcerated individuals who, if given a highly structured environment, could be released to the community with minimal risk to the public.

Intense supervision is when a high-risk offender is monitored closely by officers who have small, limited caseloads allowing for frequent personal contracts, routine surveillance, and such other elements as frequent urine screening.

Day reporting centers are multipurpose facilities in the community where offenders are obliged to report daily and are required to spend their time on such activities as remedial education, job preparedness, drug counseling, and so on. Failure to appear or participate in specific activities such as drug testing could create grave consequences for the subject, such as revocation of conditional release from prison or jail or community supervision. Sometimes, subjects are required to call those centers by phone throughout the day to check in (e.g., after curfew hours). In some cases, subjects must contact their respective centers an average of 30 times during the week and take random drug tests.

Day reporting centers are facilities where offenders must report on a specific prearranged scale.

Home arrest and home confinement restricts an individual to his or her residence for a specific period of time.[65] There is usually one of three versions of home confinement, each with a different degree of restricted freedom, offering a range of sanctions at the local level:

- *Curfew* requires offenders to be in their residence during limited, specified hours, generally at night. The movements of an offender outside curfew hours are unregulated. This sanction may be coupled with other rehabilitative or service conditions.

- *Home incarceration* requires offenders to remain at home at all times, with very limited exceptions for religious or medical purposes. At a minimum, offenders are subject to random contacts across all hours covered by the condition to verify compliance.

- *Home detention* requires offenders to remain at home except for employment, education, treatment, or other pre-approved activities. Movement throughout the day is completely structured and movements must be pre-approved by correctional personnel. This sanction is often coupled with other rehabilitation programs or conditions. In many cases, electronic monitoring assists surveillance.

> **Home arrest and home confinement** restricts an individual to his or her residence for specific periods of time.

Electronic monitoring is when an offender is restricted to a residence except during preapproved leaves such as employment or rehabilitation sessions. An offender is sentenced to his or her home with restricted movements outside the home and an electronic device is strapped to the ankle of the offender. This device tracks an offender's movements.

> **Electronic monitoring** is continued location surveillance of an offender through electronic means such as an ankle bracelet.

Community service is when the court directs an offender to provide (free) services to the community such as clearing a park of debris. It can be part of or independent from restitution.

> **Community service** is performing tasks free of charge as directed by the courts.

Temporary release could include furloughs away from prison or jail, whereby an offender works or is on leave to tend to a personal problem or to prepare for release from prison.

> **Temporary release** is a furlough from confinement for a specific cause such as a funeral of a parent or work.

Probation is a court-ordered term of community supervision under specified conditions for a specific period of time that cannot exceed the maximum sentence for an offense. Supervision is most often provided through a correctional system whose authority is tied to state government. The frequency and method required of an offender to contact a probation officer is usually articulated in the *conditions of probation.*

> **Probation** is a criminal sanction whereby the court imposes conditions of freedom upon a guilty defendant.

Parole is a conditional release of a prisoner who has served part of a prison sentence and remains under the control of and in the legal custody of a parole authority. It is an early release from prison based on requirements set by the appropriate authority in jurisdictions where parole is permitted. Parole permits an offender the opportunity of living in a community. Violating parole restrictions or conditions can revoke an offender's parole resulting in a return to prison.

> **Parole** is a conditional release from prison, but the parolee remains under correctional supervision until the sentence is completed or parole is revoked.

Residential community correctional facilities provide high levels of both surveillance and treatment. Twenty-four-hour residency makes these facilities the community sanction that is closest to the total institutional setting of a prison or jail. The movements, behavior, and mood of the residents can be continuously monitored. Sometimes they are used as transitional stages for offenders who were previously confined. Residential community correctional facilities can be defined as residential settings for (a) housing adult offenders (b) with at least 70 percent of its residents placed by federal, state, or local criminal justice authorities; (c) operating independently from the detention operation of jail, prison, or other corrections institution; (d) permitting residents to leave the premises during the day for work, education, or community programs.

> **Residential CC facilities** are supervised environments where convicted offenders live and must be employed, but they can leave the facility for a limited purpose and duration, if preapproved. Examples include halfway houses, prerelease centers, restitution centers, drug treatment facilities, and work release centers.

Halfway house is a residence for offenders who might be in the release process from prison or in their first stages of return to the community. As the name suggests, halfway houses are halfway between prison and freedom. Offenders in halfway houses generally work and pay rent. They are allowed to leave only to report to jobs and they must return promptly at the end of their work schedule. Typically, halfway houses are oriented toward providing or brokering treatment services for their residents. Halfway house residents have greater freedom and responsibility than prisoners, but less freedom than ordinary citizens.

> **Halfway houses** are transitional residential community correctional facilities for offenders who are released from confinement yet are under supervision and treatment services as they prepare to enter the community.

COMMUNITY CORRECTIONS ACTS

Contributing Factors

Community Corrections Acts was developed through the active participation of many prominent individuals over a 30-year period. For instance, President John F. Kennedy enhanced federal financial support to a variety of local endeavors in the early 1960s. One result was that a number of community organizations and programs received funding marked for crime prevention programs. It was estimated at that time that 11 to 20 percent of the public participated in local crime prevention organizations.[65] Later, in 1965, President Johnson created the President's Commission on Law Enforcement and Administration of Justice. Its task was to make recommendations for enhancing the efficiency of the criminal justice system. One finding was that criminal victimization and the fear of crime were primary issues for the public. It was suggested that local communities should receive greater support to organize effective responses to those issues. The following decade, expanding the community's role in the war on crime and law enforcement's attention on crime prevention was encouraged through federal funding opportunities especially with the passage of the Community Anti-Crime Program of 1977 and the Urban Crime Prevention Program of 1980 (which provided funds directly to community organizations engaged in crime prevention activities). This led the way to Community Corrections Acts of 1991. However, this is not a federal movement but a state movement supported, in part, by the federal government.

Community Corrections Acts Defined

Community Corrections Acts (CCAs) are state laws that give economic grants to local communities to establish CC goals and policies and to develop and operate CC programs. Most CCAs transfer some state functions to local communities, decentralizing services and engaging communities in the process of reintegrating offenders. Along with the transfer of correctional responsibility from the state to the community, CCA provides financial incentives for counties, private citizens' groups, and private agencies to participate.

The Goal of CCAs

The goal of CCAs in various states is to make it possible to divert certain prison-bound offenders into local, city, or county level programs where they can receive treatment and assistance rather than imprisonment. However, goals vary from state to state. For instance, the most common goal in 14 states is expansion of sanction choices. Twelve states cite the promotion of state and community partnerships as the goal. Some CCAs focus on nonviolent offenders, whereas others merely include them. Some CCAs help communities move offenders out of local jails and into correctional programs that are less expensive and offer reasonable community protection. Financial incentives help communities manage more of their own correctional caseloads rather than ask the state to manage them. With these funds, local communities design, implement, and evaluate a complete range of local sentencing options.

Part of the rational is that because the family, friends, and jobs of a client are primarily in a specific community, local sanctions can be better designed to lend support to a client through the correctional treatment or prevention process. Although CCAs authorize and allow funding for a range of sanctions, including intermediate sanctions, they do more than that. CCAs implement community corrections philosophy by providing statewide structures that specify government and citizen roles and responsibilities in the planning, development, implementation, and funding of community sanctions.

CCAs and Minnesota

In 1973, Minnesota became the first state to adopt a CCA. Minnesota officials wanted to reduce fragmentation in criminal justice service delivery, control costs, and redefine the population of offenders for whom state incarceration was most appropriate. Communities throughout Minnesota accepted greater correctional responsibility for their less serious offenders, as long as the communities were also given state subsidies and control over those programs, which lead to their ultimate success that can be seen in Minnesota's low incarceration rate as compared to other states.

Kansas, Ohio, and CCAs

Kansas implemented a community corrections act in 1978 and included juveniles in their plans. They use home confinement, day reporting centers, halfway houses, electronic monitoring, and intensive supervised probation and parole. In Ohio, over 20 thousand offenders were in CC programs in 1993. Clients included nonviolent individuals who participated in both residential and nonresidential placement options. Some of these options included work release and halfway house programs. Some of the results produced through a study of those clients included the following:[66]

- A demonstrated willingness to comply with program rules and regulations.
- A motivation to work on individual treatment plans as described by program staff.
- A target population pool that consists primarily of nonviolent offenders, including misdemeanants, probation-eligible felony offenders, and parolees who are amendable to community sanctions.

Michigan and CCAs

The state of Michigan suggests that their Community Corrections Act program features several factors that distinguish Michigan as an innovator in shaping policy with the entire criminal justice system as follows:[67]

- Broad, statewide acceptance—Michigan has 44 Community Corrections Advisory Boards serving 72 counties.
- Data-informed, policy-driven systems—Michigan uses thorough analyses of sentencing data, jail use, sanctions, services, and assessments to appropriately match the program intensity and length of stays for offenders.

- Felony offender priority populations—Michigan targets certain felons for community corrections act programs and services.

It takes many individuals and groups to change the thinking, policy, and ultimately the practices of many institutions such as CC. This is not to say that the pendulum has swung in favor of CC, because the indicators are that imprisonment is enhancing its population at a faster rate than CC. Nonetheless, many regional and national associations have supported the CCA.

SUMMARY

This chapter provided a description of the criminal justice process leading to correctional supervision. It identified and explained sentence strategies. It revealed the links between sentence strategies and causal factors of crime and strategies and their link to various approaches of corrections. It identified and described intermediate sanctions. Finally, it described the contributing factors that aided in the development of the CCAs.

DISCUSSION QUESTIONS

1. Explain the criminal justice process leading an offender to CC.
2. Describe the concept, process, and purpose of sentencing.
3. Describe the contents and purpose of Presentence Investigation Reports. In what way do you see a PSI as beneficial to the courts, corrections, and the offender?
4. Identify the primary sentencing strategies used in the United States.
5. Describe each sentencing strategy and explain in what way you agree or disagree with it.
6. Identify the causal perspective linked to crime that best justifies each sentence strategy.
7. Identify the correctional approach that can be justified by each sentence strategy.
8. If you believe that an underlying goal of the justice community is to identify individuals who have acted in an intentional way to hurt others and therefore should hold them accountable for their actions by imposing a penalty upon them, which approach of corrections are you using to justify your thoughts?
9. Explain the current trends in sentencing, the rationale that drives them, and their outcomes. In what way might some of these trends aid corrections.
10. Identify the methods of serving more than one sentence at a time.
11. Identify and describe a range of intermediate sanctions imposed upon violators.
12. Describe the developments and merits of the Community Corrections Acts of 1991.

NOTES

1. Erika Fairchild and Harry R. Dammer (2001). *Comparative criminal justice systems* (2nd ed.). Belmont, CA: Wadsworth (pp. 222–270). Melissa E. Fenwick (2002). Imprisonment in an era of crime control. In Wilson R. Palacios, Paul Cromwell, and Roger G. Dunham (Eds.), *Crime & justice in America: Present realities and future prospect* (2nd ed., pp. 423–430). Upper Saddle River, NJ: Prentice Hall. Paul Gendreau, Clare Goggin, Francis T. Cullen, and Donald A. Andrews (2000). The effects of community sanctions and incarceration on recidivism. In Laurence L. Motiuk and Ralph C. Serin (Eds.), *Compendium 2000 on effective correctional programming* (pp. 18–21). Correctional Service Canada, Ministry of Supply and Services 2001. J. V. Roberts and L. J. Stalans (1997). *Public opinion, crime, and criminal justice.* Boulder, CO: Westview (p. 46). Dennis J. Stevens (1994). The depth of imprisonment and prisonisation: Levels of security and prisoners' anticipation of future violence. *The Howard Journal of Criminal Justice, 33*(2), 137–157. Among females, see: Dennis J. Stevens (1998). The impact of time-served and regime on prisoners' anticipation of crime: Female prisonisation effects. *The Howard Journal of Criminal Justice, 37*(2), 188–205. Dennis J. Stevens (1997). Violence begets violence: Study shows that strict enforcement of custody rules causes more disciplinary problems than it resolves. *Corrections Compendium: The National Journal for Corrections, 22*(12), 1–3.

2. Andrew Von Hirsch, Anthony Bottoms, Elizabeth Burney, and P.O. Wikström (1999). *Criminal deterrence and sentence severity: An analysis of recent research.* Portland, OR: Hart, 3–4.

3. *ACA 2003 Directory: Adult and juvenile.* Lanham, MD: American Correctional Association. Adult Correctional Budgets, Year 2002, 20.

4. Ronald Fraser (2003, February 18). Smart sentencing could cut prison costs, taxes. *The Toledo Blade* (Ohio). Retrieved online January 8, 2005: http://www.mapinc.org/drugnews/v03/n267/a07.html?1218

5. Kentucky Department of Corrections. Retrieved online January 8, 2005: http://www.corrections.ky.gov/

6. North Carolina Department of Corrections. Retrieved online January 8, 2005: http://webapps6.doc.state.nc.us/apps/offender/menu1

7. California expects its treatment programs will send 24,000 fewer persons to prison each year. A California DOC study said for every dollar invested in treating inmate substance abuse, taxpayers save about $7 in future costs. A similar analysis of saving money through treatment by Oregon's DOC showed a 5-to-1 savings ratio. But, Governor Schwarzenegger proposes cutting more than $90 million from inmate rehabilitation programs, such as education and substance abuse treatment, reports Mark Martin (2005, January 11). The California budget: Prisons. *San Francisco Chronicle* (p. 2). Spending taxes up-front to prevent problems can significantly cut unnecessary costs later in corrections, health, education, and welfare programs. Arkansas, Kentucky, and Oklahoma judges have the discretion to sentence offenders

convicted of nonviolent, nonsexual offenses to treatment as opposed to a prison term. Cutting correctly in Maryland: Executive summary (2003, February 20). *The campaign for treatment not incarceration.* Retrieved online January 13, 2005: http://www.treatnotjail.org/facts_cutting_summary.asp

8. Bureau of Justice Statistics (1997). *What is the sequence of events in the criminal justice system?* Washington, DC: U.S. Department of Justice, Office of Justice Program. Retrieved online January 7, 2005: http://www.ojp.usdoj.gov/bjs/pub/pdf/cjsflowco.pdf, Premission Granted by Clarksberg, FBI Communication Unit. WVA. Christy Nickles (304) 625-4995. 1.

9. Bureau of Justice Statistics (1997). *What is the sequence of events in the criminal justice system?*

10. A magistrate is a municipal, state, or federal judicial officer authorized to issue warrants, hear minor cases, and conduct preliminary or pretrial hearings.

11. The 'Lectric law library. Retrieved online January 8, 2005: http://www.lectlaw.com/def2/p089.htm

12. Bureau of Justice Statistics (2004, July). *Indigent defense statistics.* Washington, DC: U.S. Department of Justice, Office of Justice Programs. Retrieved online January 8, 2005: http://www.ojp.usdoj.gov/bjs/id.htm

13. Bureau of Justice Statistics (2004, July). *Indigent defense statistics.*

14. Bill of Rights, Amendment VI: In all criminal prosecutions, the accused shall enjoy the right to a speedy and public trial, by an impartial jury of the state and district wherein the crime shall have been committed, which district shall have been previously ascertained by law, and to be informed of the nature and cause of the accusation; to be confronted with the witnesses against him; to have compulsory process for obtaining witnesses in his favor, and to have the assistance of counsel for his defense.

15. Bill of Rights, Amendment V: No person shall be held to answer for a capital, or otherwise infamous crime, unless on a presentment or indictment of a grand jury, except in cases arising in the land or naval forces, or in the militia, when in actual service in time of war or public danger; nor shall any person be subject for the same offense to be twice put in jeopardy of life or limb; nor be compelled in any criminal case to be a witness against himself, nor be deprived of life, liberty, or property, without due process of law; nor shall private property be taken for public use, without just compensation.

16. Jared Stearns (2003, January 29). Murder defendant's mother faces charges. *Boston Globe,* 4.

17. The legal significance of a *nolo contendere* or "no contest" plea means "I will not contest it" (the charge) as found in Black's Law Dictionary 1048 (6th ed., 1990). A plea of *nolo contendere* is an admission of guilt that can subject a defendant to the same punishment received had the defendant plead guilty to the charges. See *United States v. Kahn, 822,* F. 2d 451, 455 (4th Cir. 1987). Furthermore, a defendant does not have the right to a no contest plea unless the court approves such a request. The concerns of the court to offer such a plea depend on, among other things, the inter-

est of the public in the effective administration of justice. The court must also see that the plea is knowingly and voluntarily made. See Fed. R. Civ. P. 11(b).

18. Josh Grossberg (2002, August 8). Crue's Neil wanted, Lee engaged. *Eonline.* Retrieved online November 26, 2004: http://www.eonline.com/

19. Bureau of Justice Statistics (2005, January 5). *Sourcebook of criminal justice statistics 2002. Felony convictions in state courts.* Albany, NY: U.S. Department of Justice, Office of Justice Programs (Table 5.46, p. 448). Retrieved online January 7, 2005: http://www.albany.edu/sourcebook/pdf/t546.pdf

20. Bureau of Justice Statistics (2004, July). *Indigent defense statistics.*

21. Bureau of Justice Statistics (2004, July). *Indigent defense statistics.*

22. If the case is a capital case, it is automatically reviewed by various courts of appeal.

23. Dennis J. Stevens (2006). *Community corrections: An applied approach.* Upper Saddle River, NJ: Prentice Hall.

24. Alfred R. D'Anca (2001). The role of the federal probation officer in the guidelines sentencing system. *Federal Probation, 65*(3), 20–24. Retrieved online January 12, 2005: http://www.uscourts.gov/fedprob/2001decfp.pdf

25. Due to the sensitivity of this particular case, the prisoner's name and DIN are withheld. However, they could be available, on a need-to-know basis, upon a written request to the author.

26. Bureau of Justice Statistics (2002, June). *Recidivism of sex offenders released from prison in 1994.* Washington, DC: U.S. Department of Justice, Office of Justice Programs. NCJ 193427. Retrieved online January 5, 2005: http://www.ojp.usdoj.gov/bjs/abstract/rsorp94.htm

27. Dennis J. Stevens (2006). *Community corrections: An applied approach.* Upper Saddle River, NJ: Prentice Hall.

28. *Mark Young's life sentence. Families against mandatory minimums (FAMM).* Retrieved online June 12, 2004: http://www.famm.org/famm1.htm

29. *Resources on Weldon Angelos. Families against mandatory minimums (FAMM).* Retrieved online November 26, 2004: http://www.famm.org

30. Charlie Savage (2005, January 13). High Court overturns sentencing guidelines. *Boston Globe,* p. A1, A20. Analysts say "the complex decision will enormously increase the discretionary power of federal judges in the short term, render less certain what sentence a defendant is likely to receive, and generate a flood of challenges to individual sentences" (p. A20).

31. State of Florida (2004, August). *10–20 life criminals sentenced to Florida's prisons: The justice impact upon Governor Bush's initiative upon armed felons.* Florida Department of Corrections. Retrieved online January 8, 2005: http://www.dc.state.fl.us/pub/10-20-life/

32. State of Florida (2004, August).

33. Laura Sager, executive director of Families Against Mandatory Minimums (FAMM), a nonprofit organization that spearheaded the drive for reform talks about

"failed sentencing" policies. "Harsh mandatory minimums, originally intended to target drug 'king pins' warehoused many nonviolent, low-level drug offenders at a very high cost to taxpayers." Judges should use discretion under sentencing guidelines to more closely fit the punishment to the crime and the offender.

Rep. Bill McConico (D-Detroit), sponsor of the bills, said, "This major step brings fairness back to the judicial system in Michigan." The reforms also had the strong support of former Michigan Republican Governor William G. Milliken, who called signing mandatory minimum drug sentences into law in 1978 "the worst mistake of my career" and campaigned for their repeal.

In 1998, FAMM led a successful drive to relax the "650 Lifer Law," the toughest drug law in the nation. That law mandated life without parole for anyone convicted of delivery or conspiracy to deliver 650 grams or more of heroin or cocaine.

34. On May 21, 2002, Governor Ventura signed into law a change in sentencing for some second-degree criminal sexual conduct offenses. Most notably, the law changed the presumptive sentence of a 90-month executed sentence of imprisonment that no longer applies to all second-degree offenders.

35. See *Minnesota Sentencing Code §§ 609.342 to 609.3451.* Also see, Judie Zollar (2002, October). *Overview of Criminal Sexual Conduct Crimes.* Minnesota House Research, State of Minnesota. Retrieved online October 2002: http://www.house.leg.state.mn.us/hrd/issinfo/ssovrcsc.pdf. There are a number of laws to which predatory offenders are subject in Minnesota. The purpose of these laws is to aid law enforcement in detection of crime and to further public safety (e.g., DNA analysis). The court must order persons convicted of or adjudicated delinquent for a sex offense to provide a biological sample for DNA analysis. This requirement also applies to persons convicted of other violent crimes listed in the law. If an individual was not ordered to provide this specimen at the time of sentencing, the offender must provide the specimen before release.

36. Judie Zollar (2002, October). *Overview of criminal sexual conduct crimes.* Minnesota House Research, State of Minnesota. Retrieved online January 8, 2005: http://www.house.leg.state.mn.us/hrd/issinfo/ssovrcsc.pdf

37. For a closer look at the criminal justice system in Texas. Retrieved online July 13, 2004: http://www.cjpc.state.tx.us/OffensesAndDefs/punishmentranges.pdf

38. However, in two studies on prison populations, it was learned that chronic offenders do not necessarily stop committing crime once imprisoned and that often, their crime sprees continue at similar levels as the streets. See the following for an in-depth look at those findings: David Eichental and James Jacob (1991). Enforcing the criminal law in state prison. *Justice Quarterly 8,* 283–303. Dennis J. Stevens (1997). Violence begets violence. *Corrections Compendium: The National Journal for Corrections, 22*(12), 1–2.

39. State of California's sentencing website: Retrieved online January 12, 2005: http://www.cdc.state.ca.us/ovsr/Helping percent20Crime percent20Victims.htm#RESTITUTION percent20FINES

40. Ronald F. Wright (1998, February). *Managing prison growth in North Carolina through structured sentencing.* National Institute of Justice, NCJ 168944. Retrieved online January 8, 2005: http://www.msccsp.org/resources/structured.pdf

41. *National Assessment of Structured Sentencing.* Washington, DC: U.S. Department of Justice, Bureau of Justice Assistance. February 1996. Retrieved online January 8, 2005: http://www.ncjrs.org/pdffiles/strsent.pdf

42. TRAC (2004). *Ranking federal judicial districts.* Syracuse University. Retrieved online January 8, 2005: http://trac.syr.edu/whatsnew/crl_trends/prisonsentence.html

43. TRAC (2004) and Bureau of Justice Statistics (2004). *Prisoners in the United States.* Washington, DC: U.S. Department of Justice, Office of Justice Programs (Table 3). Retrieved online January 8, 2005: http://www.ojp.usdoj.gov/bjs/pub/pdf/p03.pdf

44. TRAC (2004). *Ranking federal judicial districts.* Syracuse University. Retrieved online January 8, 2005: http://trac.syr.edu/whatsnew/. Also see Bureau of Justice Statistics (2004). *Prisoners in the United States.* Washington, D.C: U.S. Department of Justice, Office of Justice Programs (Table 1). Retrieved online January 8, 2005: http://www.ojp.usdoj.gov/bjs/pub/pdf/p03.pdf. Totals shown for federal prisoners is excluding prisoners held in U.S. territories.

45. Bureau of Justice Statistics (2002). *Sourcebook of criminal justice statistics, 2001.* Albany, NY: U.S. Department of Justice, Office of Justice Programs (Table 2.54, pp. 136–137). Retrieved online January 8, 2005: http://www.albany.edu/sourcebook/1995/toc_2.html

46. Bureau of Justice Statistics (2004, July). *Probation and parole in the United States, 2003.* Washington, DC: U.S. Department of Justice, Office of Justice Programs NCJ 205336. (Table 2 and Table 5). Retrieved online January 8, 2005: http://www.ojp.usdoj.gov/bjs/abstract/ppus03.htm

47. Bureau of Justice Statistics (1999, July). *Truth in sentencing in state prisons.* Washington, DC: U.S. Department of Justice, Office of Justice Programs, NCJ 170032 Retrieved April 23, 2004: http://www.ojp.usdoj.gov/bjs/pub/pdf/tssp.pdf

48. *Issue brief for congress: Crime control: The federal response* (2003, March 5). Washington, DC: Domestic Social Policy Division, The Library of Congress. Retrieved online January 8, 2005: http://usinfo.state.gov/usa/infousa/society/crime/crimegun1.pdf

49. NACDL. *Three strikes.* Retrieved online July 26, 2004: http://www.criminaljustice.org/MEDIA/pr000005.htm

50. *SF Gate.com Criminal Justice Reform.* Retrieved online January 8, 2005: http://sfgate.com/cgi-bin/article.cgi?file=/c/a/2004/07/06/EDG3K7ELAL1.DTL

51. *SF Gate.com Criminal Justice Reform.*

52. Kristina Horton-Flaherty (2002, March). Three strikes supporter has a change of heart, now want the law restricted. *California Bar Journal.* Retrieved online January 8, 2005: http://www.calbar.ca.gov/calbar/2cbj/02mar/page10–1.htm

53. The author developed this perspective for this chapter, but the work and credit belong to Stacey Heuston Anderson, Community Supervision Section Manager, Bu-

reau of Research and Data Analysis, Florida Department of Corrections. Also, Florida's websites aided in this venture: http://www.lectlaw.com/files/leg05.htm and http://www.5dca.org/Opinions/Opin2001/082701/5D00-3544.op.pdf

54. *An act to control crime by incarcerating violent criminals* (1995, February 22). U.S. Government. 104th Congress. 1st Session. Retrieved online January 8, 2005: http://www.lectlaw.com/files/leg05.htm

55. In The District Court of Appeal of the State of Florida. Fifth District. July Term 2001. *Barfield v. Florida.* Retrieved online January 8, 2005: http://www.5dca.org/Opinions/Opin2001/082701/5D00-3544.op.pdf

56. Executive Summary: Offenses committed on or after October 1, 1998. (2001). State of Florida, Department of Corrections (p. 2). Retrieved online January 8, 2005: http://www.dc.state.fl.us/pub/sg_annual/0001/executives.htm

57. Executive Summary: Offenses committed on or after October 1, 1998. (2001). p. 3.

58. Executive Summary: Offenses committed on or after October 1, 1998. (2001). p. 4.

59. Comparative Description. Statute 921 (2001). State of Florida, Department of Corrections (p. 6). Retrieved online January 8, 2005: http://www.dc.state.fl.us/pub/sg_annual/0001/dsec.html

60. This chart was developed by the author with data provided by Stacey Heuston Anderson, Community Supervision Section Manager, Bureau of Research and Data Analysis, Florida Department of Corrections. Dennis J. Stevens (2006). *Community corrections: An applied approach.* Upper Saddle River, NJ: Prentice Hall.

61. The committee on temporary shelter. Newsletter. Retrieved online November 26, 2004: http://cotsonline.org/index.php?id=30&backPID=20&begin_at=20&tt_news=27

62. Findlaw. Retrieved online November 26, 2004: www.findlaw.com

63. For more detail, see the state of California's restitution. Retrieved online July 15, 2004: http://www.cdc.state.ca.us/ovsr/Helpingpercent20Crimepercent20Victims.htm #RESTITUTION percent20FINES

64. Findlaw. Retrieved online January 8, 2005: http://dictionary.lp.findlaw.com/scripts/results.pl?co=lawcrawler.findlaw.com&topic=3d/3d6bd77b1366bc79504472aa641c f286

65. For more detail see: *Community correction punishments: An alternative to incarceration for nonviolent offenders,* by Marcus Nieto, May 1996. Retrieved online January 8, 2005: http://www.library.ca.gov/CRB/96/08/index.html#RTFToC14

66. Katherine Becket and Theodore Sasson (2001). *The politics of injustice: Crime and punishment in America.* Thousand Oaks, CA: Pine Forge (pp. 146–148).

67. Michigan Department of Corrections. Retrieved online January 8, 2005: http://www.michigan.gov/corrections/0,1607,7–119–1435—,00.html

4

CLASSIFICATION

After you read this chapter, you will be better prepared to:

- Identify the characteristics associated with most offenders entering the correctional system.
- Explain in what way some of those characteristics are associated with crime.
- Describe assessment and explain its function.
- Define classification and explain its importance to the correctional community.
- Describe the five general activities of the classification process.
- Identify the function of classification.
- Identify the confinement categories of classification.
- Describe the classification components found in corrections.
- Describe needs, risk, and criminogenic classification.
- Characterize the Level of Service Inventory (LSI–R) and its use.
- Identify and describe the four parts of an actual case management classification process.
- Describe the responsivity standards of classification and their function.

KEY TERMS

Assessment
Classification
Community Risk
    Classification
Criminogenic Assessment
Dynamic Risk Factors

First-time Offenders
External Classification
Internal Classification
LSI–R
Needs Classification
Recidivist

Responsivity
Severity-of-Offense Scale
Situational Offenders
Salient Factor Score
Static Risk Factors

Never mistake motion for action.

—Ernest Hemingway (1899–1961)

INTRODUCTION

Once guilty defendants are placed under institutional or CC authority by the courts, which services, including levels of supervision, should be provided to maintain public safety and protect the rights of defendants? Usually an "intake" assessment performed by a unit within the correctional system attempts to determine the risk and need levels of each defendant in an effort to allocate appropriate correctional services and levels of supervision for each participant. Largely, risk and need can be determined by the sentence imposed; physiological characteristics of the defendant, such as gender, age, and mental and physical health; policy; and resources of the correctional system. An intake assessment leads to the classification of each correctional participant and reclassification can occur many times while a defendant is under correctional authority.

During either an intake assessment or reclassification initiative, specific needs to aid a participant can be addressed such as occupation and vocational skills, education and social skills, mental health impairments, alcohol and drug abuse, and relationship expectations. Risk likelihoods can include the chances of an offender harming other offenders, correctional personnel, the facility, or himself or herself. Is the offender vulnerable to victimization during correctional supervision or will the offender prey upon other offenders? What's the risk of escape or absconding? What's the likelihood the offender will comply with the conditions of probation, parole, or residential confinement? These questions and many more are answered every day by correctional personnel through a process of assessment and classification to better serve the community and the offender.

Classification proceeds from two assumptions. The first assumption is that correctional participants vary in their "need" (i.e., dependencies, health, cognitive skills, and education) and their "risk" (supervision requirements).[1] To change the behavior of offenders while under correctional supervision by neutralizing or reducing needs and risks is designed so that once released from correctional supervision, offenders can live healthy and crime-free lifestyles. These objectives begin with an assessment of the individual leading to classification.

A second assumption associated with classification is that most offenders are treatable. However, treatment has a better chance of succeeding when defendants are sorted into groups based on their individual but similar needs and risk levels. This sorting out process or classification is the focus of this chapter.

It comes down to matching risks and needs of defendants with correctional services, whether those individuals are incarcerated, on probation or parole, or part of intermediate programs. Many offenders experience various levels of the correctional system: They come and go from probation to confinement and from confinement to parole. But I guess you're thinking that all defendants are equal. Let's see if you continue to think that way once you look over the next section.

CHARACTERISTICS ASSOCIATED WITH MOST OFFENDERS ENTERING CORRECTIONAL SYSTEMS

Defendants are not as similar as you might expect. Once placed in a correctional system, the system must provide numerous amenities as required by law, some of which include fulfilling needs and supervision. Determining "needs" and "risk" levels should be a simple task because defendants have a number of characteristics in common, as Table 4.1 demonstrates.

Table 4.1   Characteristics Associated with Most Offenders Entering Correctional System[2]

1. Antisocial/antiauthority attitudes, values, and beliefs (criminal thinking)
2. Procriminal associates and isolation from prosocial associates
3. Particular temperament and behavioral characteristics (e.g., egocentrism)
4. Weak problem-solving and social skills
5. Criminal histories
6. Family conflict, low levels of affection or cohesiveness, violence, psychological disadvantage evident among parents and siblings in the family of origin: criminal records, substance abuse, mental health problems, reliance on (as opposed to sometime use of) welfare, poor work habits, and unstable work history (as opposed to a low level of occupation)
7. A taste for risky activities, early adventurous exploration of adult pursuits (sex, drugs)
8. Early and diverse misbehavior (lying, stealing, aggression) in a variety of settings (home, playground, school)
9. Below-average verbal intelligence
10. Poor performance in school and, in particular, misconduct in school
11. Generalized difficulties or trouble in relationships with others (parents, siblings, teachers, peers, intimate others, employers)
12. A preference for leisure and recreational activities that are unsupervised and conducted in unregulated settings
13. Low levels of vocational or educational skills
14. Low levels of self-respect
15. Little self-control
16. Drug and/or alcohol issues
17. Act out of impulse

Keep in mind that at a young age, the behavior of many offenders is "dictated much more by instant impulse than by conscious reasoning," some practitioners believe.[3] Young people in particular act out on impulse, maybe for no more reason than how someone looks at them.[4] But it should be said that drug or alcohol abuse are major pathways[5] to crime for most offenders, and in part, those pathways are products or coproducts of other antecedent characteristics such as many of the characteristics listed in the Table 4.1.[6]

For example, a young male who practices little self-control, acts out of impulse, and is "high" is more likely to engage in criminal activity than someone who possesses high levels of self-control, thinks before acting, and refrains from getting high.[7] Some individuals can control their quick tempers (which some of us have), think before they act, and know when to stop when "partying" with friends, but others don't or don't care, according to my own experience with high-risk offenders.

Nonetheless, offenders have many personal problems, and when those problems are left unchanged, they "bode poorly for subsequent adjustment to community life after correctional authority ends: drug abuse, poor impulse control, lack of job skills, educational deficits, and so on."[8] Many offenders tend to live in unhealthy neighborhoods where inadequate health care is commonplace. There is also a tendency for offenders to engage in unhealthy lifestyles, and as they enter a correctional system, regardless if it's a facility or a community program, they have more health needs, than the average person.[9]

Finally, not all of the characteristics of offenders and their circumstances identified as risk factors are "bad" characteristics. For example, there is little inherently wrong with being male, being anti-authority in attitude, or possessing a taste for risk.[10] They are simply risk factors for criminal activity. Also, the validity of antisocial personality disorder (APD) as a meaningful concept has been hotly debated.[11] Some argue that there is no single type of abnormal personality prone to chronic rule violation; however, once socially labeled APD, expected characteristics are more likely to be observed by clinicians.[12]

In sum, a significant percentage of offenders demonstrate behavioral, physical, and mental problems that can often represent a clear and present danger to themselves and others, including correctional personnel and property as well as the community. To move closer to public safety, a correctional system must determine which services to provide an offender and what level of security or supervision is appropriate. Therefore, changing antisocial attitudes, reducing antisocial peer associates, promoting familial affection, increasing self-control and problem-solving skills, and reducing chemical dependencies would make a difference in the outcome of an offender.

How does corrections determine risk and needs? One answer is classification through assessment. That is, classification is one process that helps determine who gets what correctional services (custody levels, programs, treatment, and supervision).

Assessment Defined

Assessment is a comprehensive and integrated evaluation of an offender at the time of admission to a correctional system.[13] It involves the collection and analysis of information on each offender's criminal and mental health history, social situation, education, and other factors relevant to determining criminal risk and identifying offender needs.

Function of Assessment: Because assessment is the centerpiece for all future correctional decisions and recommendations throughout the management of the offender's sentence, it is the foundation for making informed and realistic classification decisions.[14] In addition, assessment data can act as a guide for correctional management to plan for anticipated resource requirements that might include clinicians, practitioners, and the search for private service venders to fulfill, for instance, specialized health needs.

Classification Defined

Classification is one result of the assessment process used when offender enters the correctional system, and depending on the system, this process is used throughout the offender's correctional experience. For the purposes of this book, classification is defined as a sorting process that helps match an offender with correctional services and supervision levels explained in Chapter 5.

Classification is a sorting process that helps match an offender with correctional services, including supervision levels.

Because each corrections system is linked to its own authority (e.g. federal, state, or local government and/or private authority), each has its own way of classifying defendants. Therefore, it goes without saying that each system has its own program standards and methods of evaluating corrections participants. Classification is important to community and institutional corrections for a variety of reasons. Primarily, classification:

- Sorts defendants into groups.
- Provides eligibility of services, including health care.[15]
- Provides eligibility of treatment for special needs participants.[16]
- Provides supervision levels.
- Guides decision making.
- Reduces bias.
- Improves placement potential of offenders.
- Helps manage resources and personnel assignment.
- Helps participants and their families find housing.
- Helps participants gain employment.[17]
- Helps participants and their families obtain welfare/food stamps/medication.
- Aids in legal challenges.[18]
- Simplifies and summarizes offender experiences.[19]
- Enhances predictions toward positive outcomes of the participant (through appropriate programs and supervision).[20]

Why Study Classification?

Because corrections services and supervision levels can influence the behavior of an offender in prosocial ways (including substance abuse, probation and parole violations, recidivism, and other aspects of criminal behavior), classification is one of the most important initiatives utilized by correctional systems. That is, the importance of studying classification is to better understand the eligibility of correctional services and supervision levels provided to an offender because the experiences of an offender before, during, and after correctional supervision are influenced by the competence of a classification process more than the dynamics or agenda of an offender.

As expected, one result arising from the different classification methods used in different jurisdictions is that an offender might receive a different classification "label" depending on the competence of the system. Therefore:

> It is vital for a "future" justice policy maker, interest group participant, or advocate of justice to accept the classification process as the single most important decision made about an offender after his or her conviction.

Classification Process

Classification can refer to six general activities that can be performed at different times while an offender is under correctional supervision regardless of whether the offender is institutionalized or in the community:

- A competent assessment based upon needs and risk indicators
- A systematic and uniform evaluation process of offenders
- A re-evaluation of participants to determine individual changes
- A grouping of offenders into a security category
- Providing appropriate correctional services to each group of offenders
- Predictive values that relate to a prevention model of corrections

As expected, the elements and the time frame of the classification process are different. For instance, the initial process can take up to a week in some jurisdictions and as little as a few hours in others. In most correctional systems, initial screening is conducted through a review of an offender's file, observations of correctional personnel, testing, and interviews. As part of the process, participants receive an oral and written orientation to the policies and program opportunities available at the agency.

A typical orientation would include information about which agency operates the program (center or facility), including names of administrators. In CC programs, new participants (regardless if participants were transferred from confinement, such as parolees) are interviewed and classified (again) by more than one caseworker, supervision expectations and rules are presented, and a participant's progress is, depending on the system, reviewed regularly. Sometimes these reviews are conducted at scheduled staff meetings.

If confined, a prisoner would learn about "head counts," personal cleanliness, social responsibility of participants (i.e., keeping areas clean and the ban on contraband such as drugs, magazines, and weapons), dress requirements, meals, transfers, medical, telephones, and visitation. They would learn about rules that apply to games they can play; mail they can receive and send; finances and money amounts on their person; and rules that cover the commissary, library, grievances, and rules of conduct. They would be told about eligibility for conditional release to a community center, depending on their classification.

Function of Classification

Some 50 years ago, the pendulum swung from a corrections model centered in a punishment model to a treatment model, producing a greater demand for CC. Although a treatment approach enhances the services of community corrections, oddly, "just desert" advocates also see an advantage in CC. They see CC as a way to punish violent offenders by making room in prison for them by separating out the nonviolent offenders and placing them in community corrections. Yet, to accomplish those aims, both camps (treatment advocates and just desert advocates), agree that the best way to separate offenders is through a systematic sorting process of offenders, which can be motivated by a treatment approach often leading to a prevention model of corrections. Today, the function of classification is to provide:

- Safety
- Control
- Method of providing programs

Safety is linked to the well-being of every individual supervised by correctional personnel. Safety also includes safety from:

- Each other
- Correctional personnel and their agents
- Processes governing offenders
- Facilities used to supervise participants

Control is linked to the correctional population at large, as well as correctional personnel and their agents (including privately owned agencies). Control is different from safety in that to control a correctional population means to keep them from destroying and/or abusing correctional property and each other. Control also implies that groups of offenders must perform tasks that include doing things many do not want to do (e.g., curfew), and obeying rules and regulations regarding contraband issues, (e.g., drugs, weapons, and other items that further unlawful or inappropriate behavior). Control can also translate to an operational strategy. That is, the classification information of a group of participants can help administrators operate a CC facility including personnel assignment and security measures.

Methods of providing programs include education, vocational training, and treatment linked to mental and physical health issues of participants. As you already know, participants enter community systems from a variety of life circumstances (including those from jail and prison), many live in poverty, and many have drug and alcohol issues. Classification helps guide the supervision staff to make informed decisions about correctional services in a safe environment. Classification instruments largely incorporate numerically weighted custody classification criteria and a scoring matrix.

How Assessment is Accomplished in Oregon

When offenders first enter the correctional system in Oregon, they are evaluated by an intake and assessment unit. Inmates participate in a number of written and verbal tests designed to assess various aspects of their academic and cognitive skills, English comprehension skills (for inmates with English as a second language), and mental health.[21] There are two group-administered, computer-scored assessment systems used in the intake and assessment process: Comprehensive Adult Student Assessment System (CASAS)[22] (an educational assessment) and the Personality Assessment Inventory[23] (a mental health assessment). Depending on their scores on either of these group tests, offenders may be interviewed by an education or mental health professional. They may also participate in individual testing designed to further identify areas of need/risk. Additional assessments include a series of questionnaires to evaluate levels of alcohol/drug use, existing work skills and certificates, family status, ethnicity, residency, native language, and religious background. The information obtained in the assessment process is used by the intake and Assessment counselors in the development of each inmate's plan while under Department of Corrections (DOC) care.

Nonetheless, there are distinctive differences between classification categories for imprisoned offenders and those living in the community.

CLASSIFICATION CATEGORIES

You now know that correctional services and correctional offenders are linked through classification regardless of the competence of the classification process or the intent of the offender. That is, for better or worse, eligibility of services, including supervision strategies and offender opportunities and experiences, are linked. Therefore, it seems that classification can be a predictive initiative because its process determines which services will be offered and under what conditions, based upon needs and risk determinants (explained later). But as you have probably already guessed, confinement classification and community classification initiatives are different.[24]

Confinement Classification

When an offender enters prison or jail, custody issues take precedence, yet the reality is that most prisoners are eventually returned to the community. Therefore, once custody risks are determined, re-integration issues such as future employment, housing, and welfare opportunities are relevant. Briefly, custody classification matches an inmate with services and supervision, which typically consist of:[25]

- External (matches custody level with security level) classification
- Internal (determines in-house custody or risk level) classification
- Community risk: prerelease (determines community risk; work furlough) assessment

External classification in prison. The process to help determine custody level of an inmate, which in turn influences the selection or section of a facility where a prisoner will be housed.[26] Assigning security level in prisons reveals that there are three security levels: maximum, medium, and minimum. From these three security levels, other levels are derived. For instance, from maximum security levels, supermax and close security levels were developed. Depending on anticipated levels of danger to other prisoners, correctional property, personnel, and themselves, a prisoner is assigned a level of supervision that will control that level of danger. Most prison and jail facilities have more than one security level.[27] For instance, a jail can hold maximum and minimum custody level offenders.

Internal classification in prison. The process of internal classification relies on factors found to be predictive of institutional conduct. Generally, internal classification systems use public and institutional risk factors. Prisons and jails use a variety of factors to predict risk or dangerous behavior of an offender. However, public risk and institutional risk factors seem to typify many of those factors. For instance, *public risk* characteristics of a defendant might include:

- Criminal violence history
- Age
- Escape and abscondance (bail jump) history
- Time of earliest possible release[28]

Institutional risk. The likelihood that a prisoner will be a danger to correctional staff and property, other inmates, or himself or herself. Some of the characteristics that influence institutional risk consist of:

- Marital status
- Prior criminal convictions *"static risk"*
- Current conviction/disciplinary record[29] *"dynamic risk factors"*

Martial status can include the number of years married or single. Static risk relates to the historical factors of the offender (e.g., age at first offence, prior criminal history) that can be used to assess long-term recidivism potential. The evaluation of change in offender risk level, however, requires the consideration of dynamic (changeable) risk factors. Although age is sometimes considered a dynamic risk factor, the most useful dynamic risk factors are those amenable to deliberate interventions (e.g., substance abuse, unemployment).[30] Recently, researchers revealed that policy implications for static risk and dynamic risk factors can include:[31]

1. Knowledge about static risk factors is sufficiently well developed that scales based on these factors can provide meaningful assessments of offenders' long-term risk potential.
2. For most contexts, evaluators would want to consider both static and dynamic factors. For example, an assessment of high risk by a static risk scale may suggest the need for incarceration. However, without a dynamic risk assessment, there is little information as to when the offender can be safely released.
3. Knowledge of dynamic risk factors is required to effectively treat and supervise offenders. Intervention efforts should focus on those characteristics (i.e., dynamic risk factors) most strongly related to criminal behavior.

Both public and institutional risk determinations relate to the custody level of a prisoner.[32]

Classification continues when new prisoners leave a correctional system's initial intake center and arrive at a specific security level prison or housing unit. This phase of classification is facility-based and often requires structured decisions on issues such as: housing units, programs, and work assignments. Internal classification addresses the questions of:

- Housing unit assignment within prison or jail
- Programs offered to prisoner
- Type of work offered to prisoner
- Privileges of a prisoner

Internal classification is an attempt to determine risk (danger and vulnerability) predictions to provide appropriate supervision of a prisoner with an eye toward safety, control, and supervision. This custody classification helps a system determine which security level prison or section of a facility in which to house an offender.

Community risk prerelease is an assessment phase leading to classification when prisoners are considered for release from a secure facility for work details, prerelease preparations, or parole. The type of risk to be assessed is focused on the likelihood of a prisoner committing a new crime. *Community risk* assessment is linked with needs associated with educational achievements, vocational skills, substance abuse, and relationships. For instance, we know that a prisoner has a greater chance of not committing another crime or what can be called recidivating if he or she has gainful employment.[33]

Additionally, the needs assessment could indicate if a prisoner has adequate vocational skills to seek and maintain suitable employment once released permanently or temporarily in the community.

For instance, the Idaho Department of Corrections' (IDOC) primary mission is associated with one of the Five Rs, a reintegration policy.[34] The IDOC feels that reintegration is a more prudent way to ensure public safety and move offenders toward a positive transition into the community. The IDOC correctional system supervises felony offenders in four community work centers located around the state. These facilities house both court-retained offenders and parolees. These facilities serve two purposes: First, they allow offenders to work while becoming reunited with families and the community. Second, they provide protection to the community by having the offenders subject to high accountability and security.

Correctional systems generally design classification components to prevent future crime, thereby enhancing public safety.

CLASSIFICATION COMPONENTS FOUND IN CORRECTIONS

Community corrections classification is typically unconcerned with external, internal, and community risk assessments, yet many of their participants originate from prison and jails, and those records tend to follow those offenders. Typical classification components in both institutional and community corrections are risk, needs, and criminogenic factors:

- Assessing risk (supervision) classification.
- Needs (programs) classification.
- Criminogenic (offender risk and criminogenic needs) assessment.

It is more likely that these three assessment categories (risk, needs, and criminogenic) are found in different forms throughout the American correctional system. Some systems rely more on one category than another system, and other systems merge these assessment categories. It might prove helpful to have a closer look at how risk, needs, and criminogenic categories are determined.

ASSESSING RISK IN COMMUNITY CORRECTIONS

Risk assessment is often a measure of the propensity of an offender towards violence as well as his or her easy manipulation by aggressive offenders. It is also an indicator of a potential suicide.

> Risk assessment provides a measure of the danger posed by an offender and the offender's vulnerability to victimization.[35]

One purpose of risk classification is to predict behavior of an offender while he or she is in the care and custody of corrections. One question answered by risk classification is the level of supervision to provide a specific offender during the correctional process which can include both residential confinement and community programs, such as probation and parole. In a word, risk assessment determines supervision: intense, high, medium, or low (these levels will be discussed later in this chapter). Criterion used to determine risk can consist of dynamic risk factors and static risk factors, as discussed in another section.

In correctional populations, risk classification is often centered on three traditional static risk categories that can be characterized as: severity of crime, first-time offenders and recidivists.

Severity of Offense Scale

Severity of an offense or the degree of harm that could result from a criminal act often plays a role in the supervision levels of prison and community initiatives. What crimes are viewed as the worst or most severe can be partially answered by a study conducted by the National Survey of Crime Severity Scale based on an ultimate score of 100 as illustrated in Table 4.2.

As made evident by the aforementioned severity list, after September 11, 2001, severity ideas have changed, but as you review this list, add your ideas to change the list to fit your environment. The idea of crime severity depends on many variables, which include who's asking, who's answering, and both of their life experiences and expectations. For instance, Brenda L. Vogel and James W. Meeker measured perceptions of crime seriousness in Washington, DC and Atlanta, GA among African Americans.[37] One conclusion arising from a sample of 621 participants shows that individual and community

Table 4.2   National Survey of Crime Severity: How People Rank Severity of Crime from 100.*

Severity Score	Offense
72	A person plants a bomb in a public building.
53	A man forcibly rapes a woman. As a result of physical injury, she dies.
48	A parent beats his young child with his fists. As a result, the child dies.
34	A person runs a narcotics ring.
30	A man forcibly rapes a woman. Her physical injuries require hospitalization.
21	A person kidnaps a victim.
18	A man beats his wife with his fists. She requires hospitalization.
17	A legislator takes a bribe of $10,000 from a company to vote for a law favoring the company.
15	A person, using force, robs a victim of $10. The victim is hurt and requires hospitalization.
9	A person, armed with a lead pipe, robs a victim of $1,000. No physical harm occurs.
6	An employee embezzles $1,000 from his or her employer.

*This table represents only a selection of 204 items, all scores are rounded, and, of course, based on current events.
Source: Marvin E. Wolfgang et al.[36]

characteristics, experiential variables, and the context in which a crime occurs influence judgments of crime severity as opposed to a specific event as offered in Table 4.2. Also, the justice community has a different line-up about severity than the public. For example, in different studies of police officers, severity of crime to those officers was linked with injury including sexual abuse or death of a child and injury or death of a colleague.[38] What is considered a severe criminally violent incident to a police officer might be understood differently by the American public, which includes the media, and especially television shows.[39] Then, too, severity of crime linked to a correctional system might be far different from the ideas held by the public and by those held by the police, as evidenced by the Corrections Severity of Crime List in Table 4.3. As you review Table 4.3, ask yourself what the events in the highest severity of crime list have in common.

It should be understood that severity of crime indicators are used by corrections to determine risk indicators of a defendant. How the court views severity can determine a criminal sanction and how a correctional system sees severity will determine the level of supervision for an offender regardless of where an offender is assigned within a correctional system.

First-Time Offenders

First-time offenders are those who commit one or more crimes but have no previous history of criminal behavior. Basically, there are few significant characteristics among first-time offenders. Neither gender, nor age, nor crime is consistent among these offenders. They may or may not have juvenile records, education, or employment prior to their criminal conviction.

First-time offenders who commit only the offense for which they were apprehended and prosecuted, and who are unlikely to commit future crimes, are called situational offenders.[40] The situation or condition of their existence led to a criminal act. For example, a battered child who attempts to take the life of her aggressor is unlikely to re-offend. Serious personal financial setbacks can prompt a company's auditor to commit the crime of embezzlement. Often, first-time offenders are placed in a diversionary component of the justice system. They are easy candidates for probation and often wind up in other community programs.

Recidivists

Recidivists might be considered the opposite of first-time offenders. That is, even after apprehension, prosecution, conviction, and supervision, these offenders continue to commit crime once released. These characteristics fit a specific offender who can be referred to as a career criminal. Recidivism has many definitions. For our purposes, recidivism is the reincarceration for a criminal offense (other than a technical violation of parole).[41] This definition is consistent with the idea that a recidivist is an offender returning to prison after

Table 4.3 Corrections Severity of Crime List

Highest	High
Escape attempt or aiding escape	Aggravated assault
Aggravated battery with deadly weapon upon correctional personnel; prisoners second	Aggravated battery
Armed robbery: Multiple, with injury	Aggravated child abuse
Burglary with assault	Arson
Inciting riot	Battery: Armed
Contraband sale and distribution in correctional facility	Extortion
Kidnapping	False imprisonment
Murder: First and second degree	False report of bombing
Sexual Battery: With violence, upon minor	Controlled substances: Importation, trafficking
	Introduction of contraband into detention facility
	Manufacture of explosives
	Robbery: Armed, strong armed
	Sexual battery: Other than capital or life felony

Moderate	Low
Armed trespass	Driving under the influence
Burglary	Leaving the scene of accident
Carrying concealed firearm	Battery
Forgery	Carrying concealed weapon
Grand theft	Disorderly conduct
Manslaughter	Gambling
Sale, delivery, possession of controlled substance	Offering to commit prostitution
Tampering with witness	Possession of marijuana: Misdemeanor
Worthless checks: Felony	Possession drug paraphernalia
Welfare fraud: Felony	Petit theft
Escape: Nonsecure facility	Trespass
	Worthless checks: Misdemeanor

once having been released. Be mindful that many released prisoners may commit crimes and elude detection or might receive other penalties for a conviction other than incarceration. Nonetheless, one implication of a recidivist is that his or her behavior has not been altered while in the care and custody of corrections. Therefore, it could be said that their behavior was not corrected, as expected. Sometimes these offenders are referred to as chronic, habitual, or repeat offenders.

Risk Assessment Scales: Federal Government Standards

Although each community program has its own standards of assessing risk, a close look at the U.S. Board of Parole's guidelines as updated in 2002 is often used as a guide. It is referred to as the Salient Factor Score (SFS). It measures six offender characteristics: prior convictions, prior commitments, age at current offense, recent commitments, probation/parole/confinement/escape status, and heroin/opiate dependence. The SFS appears to be as reliable a guide as other assessment instruments of its variety.[42]

Assessing Needs (Programs)

Needs assessments are linked to correctional services that enhance physical and mental health and services (e.g., programs that aid substance abusers) and treatment for diseases and depression.

> **Needs assessment** provides a measure of the offender's health and welfare requirements.[43]

Needs classification is practiced in both confined and community corrections settings. Its purpose is to identify which services are recommended for an offender. For example, programs can be offered in literacy, life skills (hygiene), substance abuse, health (mental and physical) treatment, and vocational training needs of a defendant. Medication capabilities can be an issue, because often the capability to prescribe, obtain, store, distribute, and document are relevant and legal issues faced by many correctional agencies. Also, contagious disease control is equally of concern in the sense that programs must be in place to detect, prevent, isolate, and control the spread of contagion. Emergency plans must also be in place to evacuate program and treatment participants. Emergency plans should also be in place to care for individual participants who suffer from various mental conditions. Keep in mind that offenders from the lower classes often have more health and mental issues than offenders from other social classes. Also, mental and health issues are a serious concern to correctional personnel and other offenders.

This assessment will aid in determining which community center or prison a defendant should be sent to within the system. Not every center has a complete range of available services. A needs assessment can include an initial assessment and re-assessment to determine the progress of treatment and programs. Needs assessment can be performed by a caseworker or a group of caseworkers. It can also be performed by intake personnel, who might or might not be as qualified as expected to conduct such assessments. However, recently there has been an interest in a third area of classification of assessment.

Assessing Criminogenic Categories

Criminogenic needs represent a different type of need other than physical, mental, and treatment type needs. The rationale is that needs in general are human necessities.

Third-generation assessment combines evaluations of offender risk and criminogenic needs to produce a more complete picture of both the likelihood of recidivism and mechanisms to reduce chances of failure.[44]

We all have needs. Some of us need help at school, some need personal time to solve problems, and some need friendship to make it through the day. Needs are the "deficits" or shortfalls that motivate behavior.[45] There is a difference, according to this perspective, between the needs of most people and the particular types of needs that can motivate a person toward criminal behavior. For instance, reducing chemical dependencies among offenders is at the top of the criminogenic list. Obviously, there would be more opportunities to help an offender toward a crime-free lifestyle if he or she were not dependent on drugs. Also, refer to the characteristics of typical offenders entering the correctional system at the beginning of the chapter. This list would provide more clues linked to criminogenic categories; however, antisocial attitudes, self-control, and impulsive behavior would certainly top the list under drug and alcohol abuse issues.

PROBATION AND PAROLE CLASSIFICATION

Probation and parole will be described in more detail in Chapters 7 through 10. However, participants in those community corrections strategies are processed in a similar fashion as a defendant convicted of crime and jailed (i.e., an orientation and an assessment).

Assessment forms are different depending on the belief systems held by those who developed them. That is, should a policy maker or interest group advocate, or even the public strongly accept, retribution as an appropriate correctional response toward offenders, different questions and scoring methods would tend to be utilized. For instance, the Level of Service Inventory is a new initiative designed to address concerns of policy makers, interest groups, and the pubic.

Level of Service Inventory

The Level of Service Inventory–Revised (LSI–R) is a quantitative survey of attributes of offenders and their situations, relevant to level of supervision and treatment decisions for persons aged 18 and older.[46] It is a predictive instrument that can predict outcomes in parole outcomes, success in correctional halfway houses, institutional misconducts, and recidivism. It can be used by probation officers, parole officers, and correctional workers at jails, detention facilities, and correctional halfway houses. It can also be used to: (a) provide a convenient record of factors to be reviewed as a quantitative decision aid in case classification and (b) assist in the appropriate allocation of resources.

Its advocates argue that this assessment can provide highly accurate predictions of how offenders with similar characteristics might behave in the future. There were a number of studies that evaluated the predictive value of the LSI–R prior to 2000. Most of those studies used samples of offenders in foreign prisons. Paving the way in the United States was a study representative of a 1,250-person sample served by community corrections facilities within the State of Ohio.[47] That study, although focusing on the predictive validity of the LSI–R, produced promising results.

One assumption of the LSI–R is that individual criminal behavior can be predicted with a certain degree of accuracy based on the outcomes of similar offender behavior.[48] The LSI–R consists of 54 items that are sorted into the following 10 substantive areas believed to be related to future criminal behavior:

1. Criminal history (10 items)
2. Education and employment (10 items)
3. Financial (2 items)
4. Family and marital (4 items)
5. Accommodations (3 items)
6. Leisure and recreation (2 items)
7. Companions (5 items)
8. Alcohol and drugs (9 items)
9. Emotional and personal (5 items)
10. Attitude and orientation (4 items)

Through an interview process, offenders are rated on items requiring either a "yes/no" response or the use of a structured scale ranging in value from 0 to 3. Based on these responses, the interviewer scores the offender on each item, totals the item scores, and determines the offender's overall risk level. Recently, the Pennsylvania Board of Probation and Parole (PBPP) selected the LSI–R as its risk classification tool because it introduces dynamic and more current factors into the risk assessment process, beyond the conventional use of static criminal history and demographic factors. Although the researchers recommended the LSI–R to the PBPP, they also revealed some reservations about some of the components of the instrument.

Other researchers also indicated that they were pleased with the predictive results of the LSI–R, which they studied in Scotland, but they argued that the research did not permit definitive statements about the predictive ability of the test. There were also concerns about differentiating between offenders who were at a medium and high risk of reoffending.[49] It also appears that the predictive utility of LSI–R may vary among different populations of offenders (e.g., women, drug misusers, and sex offenders) and further research might therefore explore the effectiveness of risk assessment tools with specific groups of offenders. Many states are considering the LSI–R and like the Sentencing Commission in Kansas in January of 2003, are conducting tests to determine the feasibility of LSI–R.[50]

CASE MANAGEMENT CLASSIFICATION PROCESS

In Chapter 5, case management strategies will be explained. This section shows how case management classification (CMC) can be employed.[51] Generally, CMC is a practical and easily administered interview and survey approach designed specifically for adult offenders in probation and parole agencies. Usually, the emphasis is on a strong relationship between the correctional supervisor and the participant during the classification and supervision process. Overall, CMC is a program that is supported by current reliable research that can guide the following four parts of the process:

- Attitude interview
- Objective background
- Behavioral observations
- Case manager's impressions

Attitude interviews address an offender's attitude about his or her crime, offense history, family, interpersonal relationships, current problems, and future plans. For each of these areas, one or two open-ended questions are followed by more specific questions designed to elicit the needed information. Interviews take approximately 45 minutes to conduct and 5 minutes to score. It is suggested that case managers incorporate their own skills and experience to develop individualized case plans. An example is provided in Table 4.4.

Objective background includes direct questions about family history. Did primarily your mother or father raise you? Do you have an intact biological family or other? What is the criminal history of your family members?

Behavioral observations include grooming and dress, self-confidence, attention span, comprehension, thought processes, affect, self-disclosure, and cooperation. These observations would come from the individuals during the interview process.

Case manager's impressions include a series of questions to be answered by the case manager. For instance, drawing on the aforementioned instrument, we can see how a case manager reports his or her impressions of a participant who has been assessed.

Using the instrument as described earlier, the hope is to learn a great deal about a participant to provide appropriate services and supervision. On one hand, these types of assessments are a great help, and on the other, they are only as good as the skill of the case manager, the time available, the quality of the services to which the participant might be eligible, and the truthfulness of the participant. Self-reports tend to be highly suspect, especially when dealing with individuals who have been involved with their own apprehension, prosecution and conviction.

JAIL AND CLASSIFICATION

Upon entry into most jails, inmates receive an inventory statement of their personal property. They also attend an orientation, are processed through classification, and move into general jail population as time (and space) permits. A classification form used in jails is typified by the one that follows.

Intake Classification Form[53]

Name		
Age: DOB SS#		
Address Telephone		
Sentence Information Offense Sentence/Bail Court		
Outstanding Legal Matters:		
Probation Officer/Court:		
Does individual claim to have any jail credits?		
Criminal Affiliations Codefendant(s)		
Enemies: STG Status:		
Incarcerated Family Members:		
Substance Abuse History		
Does inmate consider substance abuse a problem in his/her life?	Yes	No
Substance(s) Used: Quantity: Frequency:		
Last Use of Alcohol/Drug		
Medical History		
Does inmate take any medications? Type:	Yes	No
Communicable Disease Type:	Yes	No
Disabilities/Medical Condition Type:	Yes	No
Mental Health		
Does inmate claim that he has been diagnosed with mental illness? Type:	Yes	No
Has the inmate been hospitalized due to this illness?	Yes	No
Does the inmate take medication(s) due to his or her illness? Type:	Yes	No
Has the inmate been hospitalized due to this illness? Type:	Yes	No
Has the inmate ever attempted suicide? If yes, when was suicide last attempted?		
Is the inmate presently contemplating suicide?	Yes	No
Does the inmate exhibit signs of depression?	Yes	No
Are inmate's actions inappropriate/unusual?	Yes	No
Does inmate appear to be under the influence of alcohol/drugs?	Yes	No
Intake Caseworker's Signature Date		

Table 4.4 Sample Questions, Recommended Scoring Options, and Scoring Guide[52]

Questions	Scoring Options	Scoring Guide
Attitudes About Offense		
Tell me about the crime that got you into trouble. (If denied): What did the police say you did? a. How did you get involved in this offense? b. How did you decide to commit the offense? c. Which of your friends might have pushed you into this supposed crime?	Motivation for committing the offense: a. Emotional (anger, sex offense, jealousy) b. Material (monetary) c. Both emotional & material	a. Include assault (not robbery) b. Include prostitution, stealing, or selling drugs, car theft (not joy riding) c. Include stealing from parents for revenge Stealing primarily for peer acceptance Refusing to pay child support because of anger toward ex-spouse
Tell me more about the circumstances leading you to the offense.	Acceptance of responsibility for current offense a. Admits committing offense and doesn't provide excuses b. Admits committing offense but emphasizes excuses (drinking, friends, family, intimate other's behavior) c. Denies committing offense—that time	a. Takes responsibility while explaining circumstances b. Blames circumstances and does not take responsibility c. Denial of any significant aspect of offense (I helped watch for cops but my friend stole the money from the cash register)
Offense History		
Have you been in trouble before? Starting with the most recent, what prior offenses are on your record?	Felony or misdemeanor pattern: a. No prior offense b. Mainly misdemeanors c. No consistent pattern d. Mainly felonies	Include criminal traffic (DWI) and juvenile crime a. Don't score "a" if offender has more than two felonies b. Over 50 percent are felonies
Have you ever been armed when on the streets? Have you ever hurt someone when you were armed?	a. Yes b. No	Include sexual offense against a child.
School Adjustment		
What was your favorite subject in school?	a. Vocational b. Academic c. Gym d. No favorite subject	a. Include typing/short/hand b. Music or art

Table 4.4   Sample Questions, Recommended Scoring Options, and Scoring Guide (Continued)

Questions	Scoring Options	Scoring Guide
Did you have a favorite teacher?	Attitude toward teachers a. No favorite teacher b. Teacher chosen because of certain qualities that the offender admired; physical c. Other than physical d. Teacher chosen because of close personal relationship	Examples: a. She was hot b. She would help kids c. She would help me with my problems
Vocational and Residential Adjustment		
What was your most recent job? Distinguish part-time temporary; part-time regular; full-time temporary; full-time permanent.	Primary vocation a. Unskilled labor b. Semiskilled c. Skilled labor or white collar d. No employment history e. Student or recent graduate	a. Average person could do the job without trying b. Exclude jobs requiring no training or experience c. For homemaker, use prior vocation history
Family Attitudes		
How do you get along with your father?	Present feelings toward father a. Close b. Mixed or neutral c. Hostile	In multifamilies, use the person whom the offender identifies as father a. Include "we get along."
If you did something wrong as a teenager, how did your father handle it? What kind of discipline did he use?	Type of discipline father used a. Verbal or privilege withdrawal b. Permissive (let anything happen) c. Physical	If father did not live with offender during adolescence, do not rate item a. He always left it to mom
Interpersonal Relations		
Tell me about your friends? What do you like about them?	Offender's pattern of associates had been: a. Essentially noncriminal b. Mixed c. Mostly criminal	Focus is on associations, not only friends Marijuana use, alone, should not be counted as criminal a. Don't use "a" if offender committed offense with accomplices
Tell me about your relationships with girls (boys)?	Offender's opposite-sex relationship pattern generally is: a. Long-term (over 6 months) b. Short and long terms c. Short-term, less emotionally involved or little dating experience	b. Short-term relationships and/or no solid commitment to persons of the opposite sex

Table 4.4   Sample Questions, Recommended Scoring Options, and Scoring Guide (Continued)

Questions	Scoring Options	Scoring Guide
Feelings		
How would you describe your personality to me?	In describing self, offender: a. Emphasizes strength b. Emphasizes inadequacy c. Can't describe self	If offender gives positive and negative statements choose the one emphasized most. If both have equal emphasis, choose first one given. a. Choice "c" is designed to identify the offender who is incapable of showing insight complexity. I'm okay. I'm a nice person. I get into too much trouble.
Plans and Problems		
Aside from your legal problems, what is the biggest problem in your life right now?	Excluding legal problems, what does offender view as most important problem? a. Personal b. Relationships c. Vocational-educational d. Financial e. No big problems	a. Include Drinking or drugs Getting my head together b. Include Getting things straightened out with my fiancé Not getting along with my parents

Generally, if the offender has health insurance, that company would receive a statement of the physical examination (depending on jurisdiction) and medical history records would be requested from the insurance company. Should the offender not have insurance, state health agencies are contacted for records. Because many jail and prison facilities are smoke-free, offenders are advised of various services and treatment that might be available to help quit smoking. Finally, an inmate meets with representatives from community work services, a drug testing laboratory, and the probation department. Many nonviolent inmates are informed that they could be placed in a CC program if they follow the rules. Finally, in this regard, although the nation's jails held or supervised 762,672 offenders on June 30, 2003, jail authorities supervised 9 percent of these offenders (71,371) in alternative programs outside the jail facilities.[54]

RESPONSIVITY STANDARDS OF CLASSIFICATION

Just because an offender completes a substance abuse program does not mean the offender is "cured." There are many reasons an offender continues in a correctional program and not all of those reasons have to do with changing his or her behavior. Let Ernest Hemingway be your guide, "Don't mistake motion for action." That is, many offenders attend programs for the purpose of getting criminal charges dismissed, getting released from correctional supervision, or getting out of jail.

Responsivity is a way of delivering intervention in a style and mode consistent with the ability and learning abilities of an offender. It recognizes that individuals may be more responsive to certain correctional practitioners, clinicians, and teachers than others. Also, responsivity initiatives recognize the different abilities and motives of offenders to effect program and treatment outcomes. In addition, some of us learn at a different pace than others. Some responsivity considerations include:

- Level of maturity
- Level of psychological development
- Motivation and readiness to change
- Anxiety/psychopathy
- Social support for services
- Mental disorders
- Age
- Culture
- Intelligence

Classification and assessment, like everything in the criminal justice system, are a lot of difficult choices depending on the attitudes of policy makers, interest groups, and the public, which ultimately effects resources, policy, and enforcement of regulations.

SUMMARY

What correctional services should be provided to an offender is the focus of this chapter. There are three assumptions in this chapter: (a) offenders are treatable; (b) correctional systems must provide appropriate services (e.g., custody, programs, treatment, and supervision) to each offender; (c) sorting out offenders into categories or classification groups is the best way to provide appropriate services to them and maintain safety at the same time. It was shown that the offenders have different needs and risks. Characteristics associated with most offenders entering a correctional system included a list of 17 items from antisocial attitudes to impulsive behavior. It was suggested that most offenders have drug and alcohol abuse issues. Classification is a way to sort offenders toward correctional care. It is necessary because offenders are physically and psychologically different even though they may have committed similar crimes. They have different risks and need requirements. It is also necessary because each agency in each correctional system provides different services. Because classification determines the eligibility of supervision levels and programs for each offender under its care, it stands to reason that it has more to do with a defendant's experiences and his or her ultimate outcome than the individual offender's desires. Classification assessment generally refers to five activities: a systematic and uniform process, re-evaluation of participants to determine changes, a grouping of offenders into a security category, providing appropriate correctional services to each group of offenders, and predictive values that relate to a prevention model of care. Although confinement is concerned with external and internal issues, both confinement and community classification systems rely on an offender's risk (supervision), needs (programs), and criminogenic factors (a combination of risk and offender history) to help correctional personal make decisions about services and supervision levels.

The LSI–R was developed to aid in the decision to parole an inmate. Therefore, based on the assumption that an individual's criminal behavior can be predicted by assigning offenders to groups that have explicit reoffending probabilities, the LSI–R can be a tool to enhance public safety and curb recidivism levels.

Case management classification is a strategy that guides assessment in CC and includes attitude interviews, objective backgrounds, behavioral observations, and the case manager's impression of the offender. This method of assessment aids CC in many ways, but it is only as good as the skill of the case manager, the time available, and the truthfulness of the participant.

Once classified and participating in programs, offenders sometimes hold hidden agendas about completing a program other than wanting to change their behavior. For that reason, responsivity is a way of delivering intervention in a style and mode consistent with the ability and learning style of the offender. It recognizes that individuals may be more responsive to certain correctional personnel and programs than other personnel and programs. But it also recognizes that because of the differences among offenders as they engage in various programs (including treatment), it is understood that their ability to learn is also different. Responsivity evaluates levels of maturity and psychological development; motivation and readiness to change; anxiety/psychopathy; and other characteristics of the offender including age, culture, and intelligence.

Generally, good elements of effective classification and assessment include its purposeful application toward correctional goals, organizational fit, accuracy toward assessing outcome, ease or parsimony of use (distributed among different groups of participants), dynamic risk factors (which must be measured appropriately), effectiveness and usefulness, and practicality and ability to yield to consistent outcomes.

DISCUSSION QUESTIONS

1. Identify the characteristics associated with most offenders entering a correctional system.
2. Explain in what way some of those characteristics are associated with crime. What methods might you use to control several of those characteristics most salient among correctional populations?
3. Define assessment and explain its function.
4. Define classification and explain why it is important to study.

5. Describe the six general activities of the classification process. Which of these activities do you see as the most important activity linked to classification and why?

6. Identify the function of classification. In what way do you agree or disagree with it?

7. Identify the confinement categories of classification.

8. Identify the classification components found in corrections.

9. Describe needs, risk, and criminogenic classification. Which do you feel is the most important classification and why?

10. Characterize LSI–R and explain its function. In what way might it be suitable for other uses?

11. Identify and describe the four parts of an actual case management classification process. If you were a case worker, in what way might you change this process?

12. Describe the responsivity standards of classification and their function. In what way do these standards make sense?

NOTES

1. Curt R. Bartol and Anne M. Bartol (2005). *Criminal behavior: A psychological approach* (7th ed.). Upper Saddle River, NJ: Prentice Hall, 545.

2. Dennis J. Stevens (2006). *Community corrections: An applied approach.* Upper Saddle River, NJ: Prentice Hall. The following was reviewed for this table: Don Andrews and James Bonta (2004). *The psychology of criminal conduct.* Cincinnati, OH: Anderson. Curt R. Bartol and Anne M. Bartol (2005), p. 195–197. Michael R. Gottfredson and Travis Hirschi (1989). *A general theory of crime.* Stanford, CA: Stanford University (pp. 65–69). Jeffrey Ian Ross and Stephen C. Richards (2003) *Convict criminology.* Belmont, CA: Wadsworth (pp. 83–86). Jeffrey Ian Ross and Stephen C. Richards (2003). *Behind bars: Surviving prison.* Indianapolis, IN: Alpha Books (pp. 35–81). Stanton E. Samenow (1984). *Inside the criminal mind.* New York: Times Books (pp. 9–23). Nancy Shomaker and Mark Gornik (2002, October). Youthful offenders in adult corrections: A systemic approach using effective interventions. *Corrections Today, 64*(6), 112–113. Laura Tahir (2003, October). Supervision of special needs inmates by custody staff. *Corrections Today, 65*(6), 108–110.

3. Glen Castlebury (2002, October). Texas youthful offender program. *Corrections Today,* 102–104.

4. Don Andrews (1989). Recidivism is predictable and can be influenced: Using risk assessments to reduce recidivism. *Forum on Correctional Research, 1*(2), 11–18. Retrieved online January 8, 2005: http://www.csc-scc.gc.ca/text/pblct/forum/e012/e012j_e.shtml

5. S. Belenko (1999). Research on drug courts: A critical review, 1999 update. *National Drug Court Institute Review, II*(2), 1–58. Also, Judge Jeffrey Tauber (2000, June).

Drug court practitioner. Fact sheet. *Drug Court Institute,* II(3). Retrieved online January 8, 2005: http://www.ndci.org/publications/EffectiveSanctionsFactSheet.pdf

6. Curt R. Bartol and Anne M. Bartol (2006), 197.

7. Intent and opportunity must be present for an act (assuming there are laws in place) to be a criminal offense. In addition, the individual must possess the ability to commit the crime. Stanton E. Stanton (1984). *Inside the criminal mind.* New York: Times Books, 6–7.

8. Todd R. Clear and Eric Cadora (2003). *Community justice.* Belmont, CA: Wadsworth/Thompson, 75.

9. James M. Tesoriero and Malcolm La-Chance McCullough (1999). Correctional health care now and into the 21st century. In Roslyn Muraskin and Albert R. Roberts, *Visions for change* (pp. 329–350). Upper Saddle River, NJ: Prentice Hall. This writer adds that sometimes the hygiene of some offenders is so desperately in need of improvement that I have had to excuse myself rather than hag at the odor emitting from some offenders during sessions with them in various prisons.

10. Don Andrews (1989).

11. Curt R. Bartol and Anne M. Bartol (2005). p. 40, 196.

12. R. Blackburn (1988). On moral judgments and personality disorders: The myth of psychopathic personality revisited. *British Journal of Psychiatry, 153,* 505–512. Howard Becker (1963). *Outsiders: Studies in the sociology of deviance.* New York: Free Press, 8–9.

13. Larry Motiuk (1997, January). Classification for correctional programming: The offender intake assessment (OIA) process. *Forum on Correctional Services.* Retrieved online January 8, 2005: http://www.csc-scc.gc.ca/text/pblct/forum/e09/e091ind_e.shtml

14. John R. Weekes, Andrea E. Moser, and Chantal M. Langevin (1999). Assessing substance-abuse offenders for treatment. In Edward J. Latessa (Ed.), *Strategic solutions: The international community corrections association examines substance abuse* (pp. 1–39). Lanham, MD: American Correctional Association. Also, in prison systems, one aim is to provide rapid assessment, identify mentally disordered remanded prisoners, and speed their transfer from prison to health care, where a need is indicated. T. Weaver, F. Taylor, B. Cunningham, A. Maden, S. Rees, and A. Renton (1997). The Bentham Unit: A pilot remand and assessment service for male mentally disordered remand prisoners. II: Report of an independent evaluation. *The British Journal of Psychiatry, 170,* 462–466.

15. Kathleen Bachmeier (2003, October). Addressing quality health care in correctional setting. *Corrections Today, 65*(6), 76–78.

16. Laura Tahir (2003, October). Supervision of special needs inmates by custody staff. *Corrections Today, 65*(6), 108–110.

17. Shelly Morelock and Melissa Houston (2003, August). NIC provides practitioners skills to help offenders with re-entry, *Corrections Today, 65*(5), 42–45.

18. Dana A. Jones, Shelley Johnson, Edward Latessa, and Lawrence F. Travis (1999). *Case classification in community corrections: Preliminary findings from a national survey.* Annual Issue 1999, Classification and Risk Assessment, National Institute of Corrections, JICO–110. Longmont, CO.

19. Curt R. Bartol and Anne M. Bartol (2005), 535.

20. Curt R. Bartol and Anne M. Bartol (2006). p. 535.

21. Oregon Department of Corrections. Retrieved online January 8, 2006: http://www.doc.state.or.us

22. *Comprehensive adult student assessment system.* Retrieved online January 8, 2006: http://www.casas.org/01AboutCasas/01AboutCASAS.cfm?selected_id=197&wtarget= body

23. Psychological Assessment Resources. Retrieved online January 8, 2006: http://www.parinc.com/product.cfm?ProductID=163

24. Most of this discussion relied on Patricia L. Hardyman and Terri Adams-Fuller (2001). National Institute of Corrections. *Prison classification and peer training and strategy session: What's happening with prison classification systems?* September 6–7, 2000 Proceedings. Retrieved online January 8, 2005: http://www.nicic.org/pubs/2001/016707.pdf

25. James Austin (2001, February). *External and internal classification.* Paper presented at National Institute of Corrections Prison Classification Peer Training and Strategy Session: What's Happening with Prison Classification Systems? September 6–7, 2000. Washington, DC.

26. James Austin (2001, February).

27. American Correctional Association. *2003 Directory: Adult and Juvenile Correctional Departments.* Lanham, MD: ACA.

28. These items represent the official characteristics of the New York Department of Correctional Services. Retrieved online January 8, 2005: http://www.docs.state.ny.us/

29. Plea bargains never tell the whole story. That is, what is known about a guilty defendant relates to the crime or crimes admitted to through the plea bargaining process. It is difficult to tell what crimes were actually committed by an offender and sometimes it may even become a matter of law and regulation for criminal justice personnel to respond to items absent from those official records.

30. James L. Bonta (2002, August 1). *Approaches to offender risk assessment: Static vs. dynamic.* Public Safety and Emergency Preparedness Canada. Retrieved online January 8, 2005: http://www.psepc-sppcc.gc.ca/publications/corrections/199903_e.asp. Also Donald A. Andrews and James L. Bonta (1998). *The psychology of criminal conduct* (2nd ed.). Cincinnati, OH: Anderson. R. K. Hanson (1998). What do we know about sex offender risk assessment? *Psychology, Public Policy, and Law, 4,* 50–72.

31. James L. Bonta (2002, August 1). Donald A. Andrews and James L. Bonta (1998).

32. After confinement there are typically reclassifications (which might occur every 6 to 12 months thereafter) depending on the system. Reclassifications place a greater emphasis on actual institutional conduct centered in a *"just deserts"* model—if you pose less of a threat you get more privileges than if you pose more of a threat (you get the privileges you deserve). The overall goal is to use both *static* risk factors, such as the criminal history and current behavior (which could include criminal history), and *dynamic* risk factors, which might include a prisoner's institutional disciplinary records and performance in treatment and work assignments.

33. Roger H. Peters and Holly A. Hills (1999). Community treatment and supervision for offenders with co-occurring disorders: What works? In Edward J. Latessa (Ed.) *Strategic solutions: The international community corrections associate examines substance abuse* (pp. 81–93). Lanham, MD: American Correctional Association.

34. Idaho Department of Corrections. Retrieved January 8, 2005: http://www.corr.state.id.us/

35. Ray Sabbatine (2003, April). Risk management in jails: How to reduce the potential of negative outcomes. *Corrections Today,* 66–70. See also New York Department of Correctional Services. There are many definitions for risk assessment, but this definition is consistent with the correctional practitioners more than a conceptual description, largely offered by academics, which seems to ignore a participant's vulnerability to other offenders. Often, participant vulnerability plays a role in institutions as well CC program placement. In addition, suicide potentials are secured in a different way than others.

36. Marvin E. Wolfgang et al. (1985). *The National Survey of Crime Severity.* Washington, DC: U.S. Department of Justice, pp. vi–x.

37. Brenda L. Vogel and James W. Meeker (2001). Perceptions of crime seriousness in eight African-American communities: The influence of individual environmental, and crime-based factors. *Justice Quarterly, 18*(2), 301–320.

38. John M. Madonna and Richard E. Kelly (2003). *Treating police stress.* Springfield, IL: Charles C. Thomas (pp. 150–151). Hans Toch (2003). *Police stress.* Washington, DC: American Psychological Association (p. 180). Richard B. Parent (2004). Police use of deadly force in the Pacific northwest victim-precipitated homicide. In Vivian B. Lord (Ed.), *Suicide by cop* (pp. 31–43). Flushing, NY: Looseleaf Law Publications. Dennis J. Stevens (2003). Police stress. Before and after 9/11. In Heath Copes, *Police Stress,* 140–165. Upper Saddle River, NJ: Prentice Hall.

39. Katherine W. Ellison (2004). *Stress and the police officer* (2nd ed.). Springfield, IL: Charles C. Thomas, 52.

40. Martin R. Haskell and Lewis Yablonsky (1974). *Criminology: Crime and criminology.* Chicago: Rand McNally.

41. Dennis J. Stevens and Charles S. Ward (1997). College education and recidivism: Educating criminals is meritorious. *Journal of Correctional Education, 48*(3), 106–110.

42. You can measure your own SFS by going to a Web site that uses this measurement. One site is the Public Defenders Service for the District of Columbia. Retrieved online January 8, 2005: http://www.pdsdc.org/CriminalLawDatabase/salientfactorscore.asp

43. Determining their risk of escape, once confined, and their risk levels if on work furlong or released from prison.

44. Dana A. Jones, Shelley Johnson, Edward Latessa, and Lawrence F. Travis (1999).

45. Abraham H. Maslow (1962). *Towards a psychology of being.* Princeton, NJ: Van Nostrand.

46. Donald Andrews and James Bonta (ND). Level of service inventory–revised. Retrieved online January 8, 2005: http://www.cognitivecentre.com/assessment.asp?id=1

47. Christopher T. Lowenkamp and Edward J. Latessa (2000). *Race, gender, and the LSI–R: The predictive validity of the LSI–R on a sample of U.S. offenders.* Paper presented at the American Society of Criminologists in Los Angeles.

48. James Austin, Dana Coleman, Johnette Peyton, and Kelly Dedel Johnson (2003, January 9). The Pennsylvania Board of Probation and Parole. The Institute on Crime, Justice and Corrections at The George Washington University. Retrieved online January 8, 2005: http://www.pccd.state.pa.us/pccd/lib/pccd/stats/lsi_r_final_report.pdf

49. Gill McIvor, Kristina Moodie, Stella Perrott, and Fiona Spencer (2001). *The relative effectiveness of risk assessment instruments.* Unpublished report to The Scottish Executive, Social Work Research Centre—Annual Report. 2000.

50. Kansas Sentencing Commission Meeting (2003, January 9). Retrieved online January 8, 2005: http://www.accesskansas.org/ksc/KSC01092003.htm

51. *Case Management Classification: Assessment Instrument.* Revised August 1993. National Institute of Corrections. The CMC Assessment Instrument (formerly known as Client Management Classification) was developed under a LEAA grant in 1975 by Gary Arling and Gene Moen, Probation Officers, Wisconsin Bureau of Community Corrections. This instrument is used by the state of Washington, Department of Corrections.

52. Dennis J. Stevens (2006). *Community corrections: An applied approach.* Upper Saddle River, NJ: Prentice Hall. This work was guided by the correctional systems of Illinois, Massachusetts, New York, North Carolina, Washington, and Wisconsin.

53. Dennis J. Stevens (2006). *Community corrections: An applied approach.* Upper Saddle River, NJ: Prentice Hall. This work was guided by the correctional systems of Florida, Illinois, Massachusetts, New York, North Carolina, South Carolina, Texas, Washington, and Wisconsin.

54. Bureau of Justice Statistics (2004). *Prison and jail inmates at midyear 2003.* Washington, DC: U.S. Department of Justice, Office of Justice Programs. Retrieved online January 8, 2005: http://www.ojp.usdoj.gov/bjs/pub/pdf/pjim03.pdf

5

SUPERVISION STRATEGIES

After you read this chapter, you will be better prepared to:

- Identify organizational strategies that could help CC change.
- Describe some of the anticipated offender and community changes that would result from these organizational plans.
- Explain some of the obstacles that stand in way of implementing these changes.
- Describe the concept of "Amenability to Treatment" and explain its recent changes.
- Identify and describe generalized tasks performed by CC supervisors.
- Describe contact standards of supervision at an optimal and suboptimal level.
- Identify goals and the emphasized elements of case management.
- Describe similarities and differences between social work and case management.
- Identify a 10-step plan to aid a broker supervisor meet CC goals.
- Explain the 8-step model that incorporates the best of supervision strategies.
- Explain collaboration methods of case management and identify some of its obstacles.
- Describe "neutral zone" experiences and their relevance to CC supervisor strategies.
- Describe problems of casework assignments and strategies to remedy those problems.

KEY TERMS

Amenability to Treatment	Casework	Holistic Approach
Brokerage Supervision Model	Caseload	Neutral Zone
Case Management Model	Collaboration or Team Model	Social Work Perspective
		Workload Model

> There is no such thing as failure, only results, with some more successful than others.
>
> —Jeff Keller, Attitude is Everything, Inc.

INTRODUCTION

CC participants are comprised of a collection of largely guilty defendants from different backgrounds who originated from different justice agency processes. For instance, the courts could place a nonviolent defendant who has never served prison time on probation, whereas a violent offender could be released early from prison by an administrator and placed on conditional supervision or parole. First-time offenders could be conditionally released from jail or prison with correctional approval and placed in an alternative program that could include a range of sanctions from home confinement to shock incarceration. Also, offenders who showed mitigated circumstances (reducing the seriousness of a crime and its penalty) could be conditionally released from the justice process and put in an alternative sanction such as diversion or pretrial release programs. There are many other combinations, but the end result is similar—offenders with various experiences arrive at a community corrections agency from varies criminal justice agencies, yet all require correctional services, which can include supervision, treatment, programs, and residential custody at some level or another. You can see how difficult it would be to separate the various delivery CC practices as each agency is tasked with providing services but every agency is influenced by the practices of other agencies in a correctional system and the belief systems of their community, policy makers, and interest groups. For that reason and others, delivery styles associated with supervision strategies can be different but outcomes are similar, and when examining those strategies, it's best to look at conceptualized tasks such as caseloads and assessment strategies from a system-wide perspective to understand supervision strategies—the focus of this chapter. Think of it this way, each correctional enterprise, such as probation and parole, is amazingly different, and their participants have different backgrounds and experiences, but from the perspective of providing services and supervision to "clients," we can examine numerous similarities. In addition, some supervision strategies are more effective than others. That is to say that some supervision strategies are not necessarily failures, as Jeff Keller (quoted earlier) recommends. It is saying that some supervision strategies are more successful than others in some agencies, and less effective in other agencies. However, from the perspective of correctional personnel, it takes more than hard work to obtain the benefits that can be derived from quality CC supervision.

BENEFITS OF CC SUPERVISION

A caring rehabilitative effort on the part of CC can produce great benefits, which can include enhanced public safety and offender rehabilitation. For instance, young people who violate the law need to be held accountable for their offenses, and at the same time, consequences must include graduated methods toward preventing, controlling, and reducing further law violations.[1] There is evidence that the treatment provided to adults and juveniles in correctional residential facilities has lowered recidivism levels.[2] One assumption is that if the treatment that produced lower recidivism levels among those confined was adapted at the community level, it would follow that we could also expect lower recidivism levels from CC participants, such as probationers and parolees.[3] One implication from this thought is that quality treatment, regardless of the age or gender of the offender, may be an important factor in reducing recidivism among CC participants.[4] In fact, there are studies that show the supremacy of treatment efforts over punitive sanctions in bringing about reductions in recidivism.[5] Also, Joan Petersilia concludes that the "empirical evidence regarding intermediate sanctions is decisive: Without a rehabilitation component, reductions in recidivism are elusive."[6] The paradigm shift in the United States is to a treatment model, especially among CC agencies. Finally, taken as a whole, there is sufficient evidence from the aforementioned studies to conclude that some combination of treatment methods, with or without surveillance in the community, is effective in reducing the recidivism levels of many offenders.[7] That also translates to fewer victims and an enhancement of public safety.

CC ORGANIZATIONAL PLANS

To prepare troubled individuals to lead crime-free lifestyles through quality CC supervision, appropriate organizational and agency plans need to be designed, applied, or implemented, and appropriately funded and staffed.[8] In some cases, excellent plans might be designed and put into action, but because CC is only one piece of the criminal justice system, it is more likely that organizations and agencies outside of CC must assist in this venture. In this sense, CC personnel would have to facilitate those changes.[9] Following is a list and a description of organizational or agency strategies, in no particular order, that would help bring about furthering quality CC plans:

1. Acquire strategies to apply change
2. Clarify values, mission, and goals of agency
3. Decentralize
4. Broaden sentencing options
5. Improve classification systems that redefine offenders
6. Break down amenability to treatment perspectives
7. Develop methods of collaboration between justice agencies
8. Develop offender surveillance and supervision strategies

9. Put an emphasis on training and supervision
10. Promote cost effectiveness
11. Fulfill punishment requirements
12. Develop and implement professional methods to measure effectiveness
13. Prove success

Acquire strategies to apply change within programs and agency policy to aid in developing new practices and policy based on results of the evaluation process. Some of the most efficient organizational plans include collaboration from personnel and a review of the literature to see what works in CC.[10] In this regards, it also helps to study what strategies are being developed to help victims heal. Communities must be restored.[11] Does punishment dictate terms and conditions of supervision or are there other variables equally important?

Clarify values, mission, and goals of agency reveals that numerous personnel in many agencies are unclear about these variables. Clarification would aid in identifying and providing methods for measuring, evaluating, and communicating agency performance and accomplishments.[12]

Decentralize suggests that CC programs might be operated through local or state participation or private agencies and organizations, but at a local level. Break down authority and the decision making process of an agency—streamline command. Often, CC programs are sponsored through state departments of corrections and they can also be sponsored and/or managed by the local sheriff, police department, or court. Although state or federal authority might provide guidelines for many programs (and sometimes funding), a program might be administered at a grass roots level. It is at that level where authority, or at least a degree of authority, needs to rest. Some predetermined (and in writing) parts of authority should be with program operators.

Broaden sentencing options: It should come as no surprise that after two decades of an intense race to implement tough-on-crime sanctions (mandatory minimums, three-strikes and truth-in-sentencing legislation), sentencing, and correctional initiatives, by 2003 at least 18 states took legislative or administrative action to ameliorate the effects of stringent sentencing laws.[13]

Improve classification systems that redefine offenders implies changing a perspective about offender labels practiced in the criminal justice system including correctional labels. That is, changing the designation of a drug addict from a criminal label to a medical label to treat addicts in a clinical (medical) model as opposed to a punitive (punishment) model, as the state of California has recently passed into law. Classification methods must be developed and linked to various programs or strategies, which further the mission of community corrections and help in reliable predictions.[14]

Break down amenability to treatment perspectives because most often the construct of amenability to treatment reflects a tentative conclusion rather than a prediction linked to successful treatment or supervision (more later in this chapter). Using drug offenders as an example, little is known about what types of drug offenders are apt to succeed in rehabilitative programs.[15]

Develop methods of collaboration between justice agencies suggests justice agencies are unlikely to cooperate with each other, and in some instances due to differences in authority, that might be the case.[16] However, there are often a number of criminal justice agencies involved with a single offender. Police, the court and prosecutors, and other correctional personnel have probably dealt at different stages with the same offender, and therefore lines of communication and cooperation should be opened to effectively move an offender closer to the goal of community corrections.[17]

Develop offender surveillance and supervision strategies suggests closer monitoring of CC strategies in keeping with real life experiences. What is known about troubled offenders is that they can easily fall victim to failure as the correctional program unfolds with all its rules and directives. Many offenders had not lived by rules prior to their conviction. Surveillance strategies must be more amenable to real client behavior.

Put an emphasis on training and supervision is a given but in addition, training and clinical supervision of service delivery staff need to be emphasized in nontraditional programs. Problems attributable to inadequate training and supervision include unevenness in the delivery of services, inadequate attention to termination, and episodes of dysfunctional staff behavior (e.g., bickering, hostility, and inappropriate personal relationships between staff, other agency members, clients, and the family members of staff and clients).[18]

Promote cost effectiveness suggests that CC programs are less expensive than prison programs but cost effectiveness should be compared to similar programs in similar CC agencies.[19]

Fulfill punishment requirements represents a reality check in that CC personnel must be mindful that the individuals under correctional supervision are at risk of committing a crime and equally important, have engaged in criminal behavior. Official punishment can include a loss of privacy and other living options for these individuals. CC participants are offenders and this point is often lost among clinicians and practitioners.[20]

Develop and implement professional methods to measure effectiveness implies that ways of evaluating the success of every program and every individual in those programs must be in place prior to implementing a program and the entry of individuals in those programs.[21] To better serve the mission of CC and the community, professional guidelines must be linked to evaluation and staff and managers need the appropriate authority to change programs based on the evaluation reports.

Prove success means that agencies have to be able to show their effectiveness in costs and participant recovery.[22] Proving success can aid CC organizations and agencies to better manage those agencies (i.e., assigning personnel) and aid with funding (i.e., grants) and budget matters. That is, CC must be able to show their success stories to the public and those stories require documentation in some way that protects the confidentiality of CC participants, especially if those participants are minors.

There are a number of offender and CC changes that can be anticipated from organizational change. Being prepared for those changes can help CC move closer to its mission.

Anticipated Offender and Community Changes Due to Organizational Change

It is expected that there are a number of offender and community changes that should be expected from a CC endeavor depending on jurisdiction, program, resources, and policy of the agency performing the services. Following is a list, in no particular order, of offender and community expectations produced through CC planning:

1. Alter general criminal activity
2. Create and implement rehabilitative services
3. Prepare for relapse (substance abuse)
4. Expect deterrence
5. Enhance offender accountability
6. Heighten offender responsibility
7. Reduce prison and jail overcrowding
8. Enhance community experiences
9. Empower community participation

Alter general criminal activity suggests that potential offenders might rethink criminal intent, realizing they might be apprehended and sentenced to a community program that has consequences they want to avoid. For instance, some CC programs include public or community service. Some professionals, such as school teachers or dentists, and other concerned constituents, such as parents, might see community service as humiliating and/or bringing shame upon their family and/or friends and thus refrain from crimes such as drunkenness, property crimes, and/or road rage.

Create and implement rehabilitative services: The primary objective is to alter the behavior of offenders and clearly one way to accomplish that goal is to help an offender alter those influences that are pathways to crime such as substance abuse.

Prepare for relapse suggests what most practitioners know: Relapse is the most significant challenge that faces substance abuse dependence.[23] Programs must be developed to guide offenders through this process.

Expect deterrence relates to the idea that one CC job is to curb criminal activity linked to both an individual (specific deterrence) and to the general (general deterrence) population. Thus, its methods relating to surveillance and supervision must be professional and consistent, indicating to the client and others that CC cannot be manipulated.

Enhance offender accountability can include helping an offender feel more responsible and accountable for his or her criminal activity to others such as criminal justice personnel (i.e., enhancing accountability might help an offender to think before he or she acts).

Heighten offender responsibility suggests that in contrast to prison life, in which an offender makes few decisions about his or her lifestyle, CC clients make numerous decisions about their quality-of-life issues. When involved with CC, whether front-end noncriminal justice participation or probation, parole, or some other form of sanction, a client plays an active role in his or her progress.

Reduce prison and jail overcrowding suggests that more offenders in a community program rather than those imprisoned should impact prison populations today and tomorrow in the sense that as community programs work and help clients make law abiding decisions, they are less likely to reoffend.

Enhance community experiences include involving community residents who volunteer in local programs to help guide troubled individuals to crime-free lifestyles. Thus, those volunteers can enhance their personal positions in the community by helping the community control crime and at the same time, help community members improve their own lives through dedicated service in their community.

Empower community participation reveals that community support is vital to the success of most community programs. Empowerment, however, implies that the community participate in the decision-making process of the correctional enterprise. In part, the decisions of a correctional agency should not, and could not, continue to operate within isolation. The community must and should participate in correctional decisions.

This final idea can be guided by other justice agencies that have made tremendous gains in community relations. A CC model furthers the democratic concept, which is well underway in other governmental agencies such as community policing.[24] For instance, the community is empowered to influence the decision-making process of police in the sense of hiring, training, deployment, practices including use of force and hot pursuit, service priorities, and both promotional and disciplinary actions. There may be much to gain through an examination of community policing efforts; for instance, empowering community members and field correctional personnel in a decision-making process, which includes problem-solving initiatives of a community correction program. Limitations, expectations, and responsibility should be established and in writing prior to recruiting committee members.

Obstacles

CC planning and application has experienced numerous obstacles. Although it is impossible to list all of those obstacles, they are as varied as the number of offices and "rules" that guide them. However, the following list identifies the most prevalent obstacles:

- Fragmented national and local justice system
- Administrative or interagency problems
- Legal problems related to legislation
- Resource allocation or availability
- Belief systems of policy makers, interest groups, and the general public

Fragmented national and local justice system: The criminal justice system is made up of disconnected parts and elements and lacks what some might call coherence from agency to agency. It is also fragmented from top to bottom and from side to side. Therefore, gaining cooperation might appear to be difficult. For example, in one community, there may be more than one authority rendering decisions concerning policy.

Administrative or interagency problems: Due to the fragmentation of justice agencies, there are numerous jurisdictional overlaps of regulations, rules, and authority even within the administering agency. When problems arise, what supervisors have the authority to step in and handle the situation? Who to look to for guidance can be confusing among CC personnel. For instance, in Massachusetts, under the Trial Court or judges' authority, CC is operated under the direction of the sheriff through a deputy. In the CC center, managed by a deputy, are probation officers (state DOC employees), parole officers (state Law Enforcement employees), and substance abuse advisers and counselors who are county personnel. They work on the same cases.

Legal problems related to legislation: Simply providing CC alternatives does not necessarily mean sentencing prerogatives will automatically place offenders into those programs. That is, intermediate sentencing does necessarily conform to a correctional program. The correctional system itself is an intergovernmental crisis requiring an intergovernmental response.[25]

Resource allocation or availability: For a justice agency to refer candidates to an appropriate community corrections program can be complicated, especially if an agency is outside of the department of correctional services (or if CC is under different authority) in a given jurisdiction. Program staff and stability are important elements in reaching the goals of a CC agency and the goals of the referral agency. Getting to those referral agencies is a job in itself. Often those agencies have directives about their "clients" and where to refer them. Should a CC agency not be on the list because it is new or recently moved into a neighborhood, it takes planning, meetings, and assurances concerning the reliability of the agency to effectively deal with referred clients. Sometimes, as most practitioners know, referral agencies take the position that the soliciting CC agency holds what they consider "the wrong philosophy" or wrong mix of professionals to deal with "their" clients. Turf warfare is commonplace among public and private agencies of all types.

Belief systems of policy makers, interest groups, and the general public: The attitude of policy makers, interest groups, and the public on one hand, and justice professionals on the other, provides a forum that is in conflict about virtually everything from objectives to services to eligibility and even to characteristics of personnel and their professional styles. A new program placed in a community might face strong community resistance and in some cases, that resistance might become the undoing of an entire program. Strong and careful correctional leadership is required to guide policy makers, interest groups, and the community to appropriate participation. Why? Because it is their right in a democratic society and equally important, gaining their appropriate participation is the right step toward success. The corrections community cannot and should not be the only participant in balancing public safety and offender supervision and rehabilitation.

AMENABILITY TO TREATMENT TEST

Amenability to treatment has many meanings. For the purposes of this discussion, amenability to treatment will be defined as a documented willingness and capability toward treatment. Documentation refers to evidence obtained thorough interviews, records, and observations. The thinking goes that not every offender is amenable toward treatment and not every offender wants help. In some cases, that thought might have merit. However, amenability-to-treatment determinations are usually associated with past criminal history of offenders.[26] For the most part, psychometric risk-assessment instruments perform little better in predicting criminal recidivism than actuarial projections based predominantly on offenders' past antisocial behavior.[27] Therefore, as some argue, it is defensible to consider past criminal conduct in determining whether an individual based upon personnel history is a likely candidate to be treated.[28]

Many factors aid in ascertaining amenability levels of offenders. Sometimes this information is part of the PSI gathered for the court; it can be obtained during an intake process and it could be conducted prior to a participant's attendance in a CC agency or program. Of course, it can depend on the motivation of the offender. However, how effective any treatment might be has much to do with the ability of the treatment specialist or clinician. It is relevant to explain that the significance of any answer linked to amenability levels depends upon the ability, thoroughness, and expertise of the examiner, advises David X. Swenson.[29]

1. *Offender's response to previous treatment:* This can be documented through discharge summaries of former providers and collateral contacts of the examiner.[30]
2. *Offender's ability to formulate goals:* This is found in self-reported goals and demonstration of goal formulations by the client.
3. *Accepting personal responsibility:* A statement of personal accountability.[31]
4. *Attendance to previous treatment:* Records.
5. *Gains in previous treatment:* Statement of gains, explanations of personal change.
6. *Participation (verbal) in treatment:* Case summaries, collaboration with providers.
7. *Insight (connecting behavior and cause):* Evidence during interview.

8. *Reality contact:* Oriented and responsive to reality with no delusions, thought disorder, or hallucinations that significantly distort reality.

9. *Emotional reactance to situation:* Self-statement; MMPI;[32] collateral contact with victims, parents, and providers.

10. *Self disclosure:* Personal history and ease of disclosing history.

11. *Problem-solving skills:* Records and self-reported indicators. Goals reached.

12. *Motivation:* Personal statement, energy during interviews, and data in records.[33]

13. *Medication cooperation:* Regularly takes prescribed medications.

This list seems complete, although one other item requires attention. Supervision officers, (regardless where they work—in the field, at an office, or in a secured facility) receive a lot of resistance toward assistance of any kind from offenders, especially during early encounters. Supervision officers learn to neutralize offender resistance and use the anger or resentment, to the advantage of treatment, moving the offender toward compliance with an eye on public safety.[34] In this regard, a recommendation from William N. Elliott relates to what he calls the Three Rs concerning offender resistance:[35] Redirection (offenders tend to distract or divert a clinician), Reframing (offenders distort the truth about their criminality), and Reversal of responsibility (because of the excuses and justifications verbalized by offenders to explain their criminality).[36] This last point reveals that most offenders attribute their antisocial behavior to unfairness or societal injustices or they blame their victims for their crimes. That is, most offenders accept the environmental perspective about their criminal culpability.

Moving on with the discussion about amenability, especially among juveniles, the courts ask for evidence of amenability to treatment prior to transferring a juvenile to adult court. Amenability is used in substance abuse treatment and recently, among detained sex offenders after they served their sentences (more on this in Chapter 15).

In the past, before most offenders were placed in programs, the amenability of treatment question arose. But, this test has been challenged by the belief that every offender can benefit from correctional services. The driving force beyond this thought is that most prisoners are eventually released from prison into the community and those who aren't released tend to influence those who are released. Finally, keeping offenders busy with positive activities is probably wiser and less expensive in the long run. For example, a study on education among prisoners showed that it was far less expensive to educate prisoners than to re-incarcerate them after their release.[37] That is, there were huge differences in the prison return rates among those educated while incarcerated versus those who were not educated while incarcerated. Women prisoners in particular showed a very low return rate to prison over a three-year period after receiving an undergraduate degree while imprisoned. Also, once conditionally released to CC agencies, more often than other offenders, educated offenders complied with supervision conditions and busied themselves with employment and family matters. Apparently gainful employment opportunities can reduce recidivism rates.

It would appear that retribution advocates tend to support amenability of treatment (if they're criminals, they don't want change) whereas rehabilitation and prevention advo-

cates tend to support rehabilitation for all offenders, even knowing that not every participant in a CC program will change.

An Assumption of Rehabilitation

New treatment clinicians are usually under an assumption that they will change the behavior of all their clients in a CC program. Unfortunately, providing a quality program by a
dedicated and well-trained clinician or behaviorist does not mean that every participant
will change. There are many reasons a participant successfully completes a program and
some of those reasons have to do with being released from correctional supervision.
Maybe the participant wants to be released from supervision to "get high." One way to get
on the streets without being monitored by correction professionals is to successfully complete a correctional drug program. Many experienced correctional practitioners who provide services to both imprisoned and CC participants are mindful that some offenders
have different agendas for completing various intervention programs. Some corrections
participants merely want to show that they know more than the provider, others work hard
as students but lack the ability to change. One hope is that if a correctional provider works
hard enough, maybe many more offenders will change their minds about their interests.
Also, many practitioners, including myself, know that relapse can be part of success and
the participant must be prepared with appropriate "new" behavior to deal with that relapse. Behavioral practitioners realize that sometimes, a group participant or treatment
participant might do well in a group or during a treatment session, but gains can evaporate
once desperation sets in and the individual is alone.[38]

TASKS PERFORMED BY CC SUPERVISORS

Four general tasks are conducted by CC agencies. These tasks, to some degree or another,
are found system-wide from prisons, to jails, to CC services, including probation and
parole. However, in Chapter 7, the experiences of probation and parole officers will be examined in detail. Nonetheless, most tasks performed by community correctional personnel are characterized as:

- Law enforcement
- Counseling and education
- Informal assistance
- Supervision

Law Enforcement

Defendants in any correctional system must obey rules and regulations and, above all, the law.
These rules can include curfews, check-in procedures, participation in specific programs, payment of fines, restrictive liberties and movements, and restrictive social associations to name a

few. The laws refer to the law of the land. Some parole officers and some probation officers legally carry weapons, have police powers, and have the right to stop and search parolees. Then, too, each rule is designed to aid participant welfare in the sense of altering troubled decisions leading to illegal and inappropriate behavior, without compromising public safety.

Generally, balancing offender welfare and public safety is best accomplished by emphasizing tasks linked to reconciliation, rehabilitation, restitution, reintegration, and restorative justice. Specifically, each rule is designed to achieve the goals of CC, but recall that many individuals on probation and parole have a difficult time abiding by rules and laws in the first place.

Nonetheless, a participant is initially introduced to rules and expectations of a specific corrections agency through an orientation process. Each time a participant is transferred to another agency or even from program to program and prison to prison, orientation is repeated. That is, each agency has its own set of rules and regulations even within the same correctional system.

To ensure rule compliance, scheduled and unscheduled monitoring and surveillance are commonplace. For example, surprise urine tests ascertain drug use for both those in institutions and those in the community. Visits to homes or jail cells or places of employment help determine possession of unauthorized goods (contraband) or friends, and it aids in knowing the location on an offender. Other forms of surveillance are through electronic bracelets that can give the location of a specific participant at any time. Depending on the risk and needs levels of the offender as established through a classification process, supervision can be casual and informal to intense as explained in Chapter 4.

When a participant violates a rule, depending on the seriousness of the violation, privileges can be removed. For example, an agency might revoke (through an appropriate process) parole or conditional release and return a violator to prison or jail. If a violator is incarcerated, privileges such as visitation or television can be withdrawn. Decisions concerning those on probation can be made to send that violator to jail or prison to serve the balance of an imposed sentence. For less formal violations, additional conditions can be placed on the offender such as home or cell confinement when the offender is not at a scheduled event such as work or med-calls.[39]

Counseling and Education

Because one goal of corrections is to turn out a law-abiding population, one method of reaching this aim is through individual counseling, group encounters, and education. The behavior of most offenders, especially young offenders, who require attention is generally couched in substance abuse, anger, impulsiveness, and a lack of skills in conflict management and personal relationships. A three-year study by the National Center on Addiction and Substance Abuse at Columbia University shows that 1.4 million out of 1.7 million prisoners, while "high," stole property to buy drugs, had a history of substance abuse, or were jailed for violations of drug or alcohol laws.[40]

Other ways of reaching the correctional mission can include specialized treatment to deal with complicated problems for troubled individuals to make crime-free decisions in their community. By providing professional guidance and treatment, participants have a greater chance to learn new behavior and, equally important, to practice the new learned behavior. Often, counseling and education linked to community services are provided by numerous public and private agencies in a combined effort to aid a participant and to keep the community safe.

Equally important, education and training might include classes on how to read, hygiene, family skills, personal money management, and GED courses. Learning job skills can result in employment opportunities. Illiteracy and unemployment are common conditions among young offenders and those characteristics are linked to crime in many ways. In fact, approximately 30 percent of all incarcerated prisoners have not completed high school.[41]

Informal Assistance

Informal tasks of community correctional personnel are latent (present but unexpressed) tasks performed in the best interests of offender welfare and public safety issues. That is, most correctional personnel and volunteers are compassionate toward troubled individuals and want to help. However, many of the tasks performed by correctional personnel and correctional volunteers are often unreported and unrewarded. Additionally, many of those tasks are rarely mentioned in correctional job descriptions and can include but are not limited to:

- Assistance in helping participants obtain jobs
- Assistance in visiting family members (children removed from their custody or situations that include restraining orders)
- Applications for apartment rentals
- Reports to judges, parole boards, and governmental agencies about adjustments to the community by participants
- Admission to treatment and health services
- Welfare compliance such as food stamps and other benefits that might help participants move toward healthy and crime-free lifestyles

Correctional personnel and thousands of volunteers are hard-working advocates of correctional participants. Although there is some vagueness in the aforementioned categories, there are numerous examples of personnel and volunteers aiding participants throughout the country in different ways. Finally, one issue some have about these dedicated advocates is to understand the distinction between compassion and being "soft" on criminals. If the truth be told, many advocates believe professional supervision, treatment, and programs are at the core of curbing crime and, hence, reducing victimization. However, there are many different ways to supervise offenders.

Supervision

Many different techniques are used by CC officers when supervising an offender. Chapter 4 explained how to determine risk and needs among defendants, which is linked to supervision methods. However, many inconsistencies in supervision methods exist because of the numerous differences in agency policy, resources, public expectation, and correctional practice. There are also differences in risk, needs, and experiences of every offender. For example, offenders who require similar supervision to that of an imprisoned offender without that offender actually being imprisoned might be placed on intensive supervision. Regular supervision might be an appropriate strategy for an offender who requires a little less supervision, and medium, low, and administrative supervision strategies might be appropriate strategies for other risk offenders. Table 5.1 recommends surveillance techniques for some risk level offenders.

Table 5.1   Contact Supervision Levels[42]

Optimal Level	*Suboptimal Level*
Intensive supervision: 15 hours per month of supervision time	Not applicable
• 16 monthly face-to-face contacts; 4 in office and 12 in field	
• 8 monthly random curfew checks; 2 per week	
• 4 monthly face-to-face collateral contacts	
• 2 daily call-ins at wake-up and at curfew (no answering machines)	
• Daily checks with police department	
• Other collateral contacts as needed by phone	
• Urine analysis as needed	
High supervision: 8 hours per month of supervision time	High: 3 hours per month of supervision time
• 4 monthly face-to-face contacts; 2 in office and 2 in the field	• 2 monthly face-to-face contacts in office
• 1 home visit per month (counts as 1 face-to-face)	• 1 monthly collateral contact
• 4 collateral contacts per month	• Urine analysis as needed
• 1 record check per week	
• Other collateral contacts as needed by phone	
• Urine analysis as needed	
Medium: 4 hours per month	Medium: 1 hour per month
• 2 face-to-face contacts in office	• 2 quarterly face-to-face meetings in office
• 1 monthly face-to-face contact in field	• collateral contacts as needed
• 1 monthly collateral contact	
• Urine analysis if needed	
Low: 2 hours per month	Low: 1 hour per month
• 1 monthly face-face contact in office	• 1 face-to-face contact every 6 months
• 1 quarterly field contact	• Monthly written reports
• 1 monthly collateral contact for the first 6 months	
• Collateral contacts as needed thereafter	

SUPERVISION STRATEGIES

In general, three approaches are linked to supervision strategies in CC, although none of them are practiced as they will be conceptually outlined. What follows are idealized models of supervision strategies (case management, broker supervision, and team supervision). Hopefully, as you learn about supervision approaches, it will become clear that each of these strategies is couched in a rehabilitative model of corrections and that many CC supervisors believe that crime is a byproduct of inappropriate decisions influenced through social environmental factors including drug and alcohol dependencies, and the social and psychological triggers that promote addiction. With that said, in actual practice, most CC supervisors use a combination of these strategies to accomplish the aims of their agency. However, most of those strategies can probably be characterized as:

- Case management
- Brokerage
- Team or collaborative

Case Management

Case management is the preferred strategy of supervision in CC. It is a service delivery approach originally developed by social workers over 40 years ago to deal with a wide variety of offenders.[43] Case management is employed to:

- Reduce recidivism
- Address mental and physical disorders
- Reduce homelessness
- Track and monitor HIV/AIDS and other destructive diseases
- Track and monitor other serious offenses such as family violence and substance abuse

Case management employs caseworkers (CC supervisors, including probation or parole officers) who use a variety of techniques to serve correctional participants. However, a *holistic approach* is an attempted technique preferred by most caseworkers. That is, a caseworker addresses conditions within the entire life of a participant contributing to recidivism including:

- Unemployment
- Homelessness
- Substance Abuse

The holistic approach looks at contributing factors to re-offending potentials, rather than pinpointing a specific characteristic of a participant. Whether an offender is returning to the community after confinement or has remained in the community, a caseworker links a

> **Casework** emphasizes a holistic approach of supervision centered on a supportive one-to-one relationship with a participant.

participant with drug treatment programs, mental health services, and social service agencies during supervision and prior to correctional release.

> The case management approach emphasizes two elements:
>
> • Authority of a correctional caseworker
> • Relationship between caseworker and offender

Some say that the basic element in casework is the nature of the relationship between a caseworker and a correctional participant.[44] Most criticism about case management stems from that very relationship. Nonetheless, the focus of case management is on public safety and the assessed needs of a participan, and a participant's accountability to the victim and the community. The general tasks of a caseworker are:

• Assessing an offender's needs
• Designing a plan to achieve various objectives
• Working toward those objectives

The final phase is when a participant is released from community supervision because the participant completed the terms of a sentence or completed the terms of release conditions.

Close Relationship between Caseworker and Participant

In the true tradition of casework, a close relationship is established between a caseworker and an offender. However, this does not imply that an offender automatically becomes dependent on a caseworker. Many offenders find it hard to accept guidance in the first place. One implication of this thought is that the caseworker must "earn" the respect of a "client" prior to a participant's acceptance of the caseworker's leadership. Also, participants are not necessarily in community programs for extended periods of time; therefore, some caseworkers have the problem of resolving the issue of earning participant respect in a short period of time.

Social Work Perspective and CC Casework

An assumption of a social work perspective linked to CC casework is that participants can, and do, change their behavior when they are given the right tools at the right time. You might get the impression that a treatment approach influences the casework perspective whereas a punishment approach through retribution sees case management as a "soft on crime" approach. Also, most caseworkers accept the correctional models that support rehabilitation and prevention of future crime as the best approach toward offender welfare and public safety issues.

Caseworkers see behavior as complex and intertwined within an individual's social environment; therefore, social work strategy implies that problematic behavior can be isolated and treated. But, positive behavior can only be accomplished through a strong relationship between caseworker and participant, as discussed earlier. However, it is important to note that the motivational level of a participant plays an equal, if not a more important role, in correcting problematic behavioral patterns.

Furthermore, some "clients" in a typical social work relationship voluntarily enter into the relationship with a social worker. On the other hand, community programs are not based on a voluntarily relationship. A caseworker in a community program must resolve the issue between voluntary self-determination of the offender and the authority of a correctional supervisor. Although caseworkers require various degrees of authority over participants, it was revealed that the absence of coercion can enhance the relationship between a caseworker and a participant.[45] This idea is consistent with the rationale that to improve behavioral outcomes in a population considered "resistant to ameliorative interventions,"[46] coercion and authority must be minimized. However, as the caseworker establishes rapport with a participant, boundaries maintained in conventional casework are crossed, producing more self-disclosure, and more emotional support, often ending in a more tolerant caseworker who overlooks certain rule violations. Obviously, fewer revocations would occur under these conditions.

Evidence Casting Doubt on Case Management

In a study for the National Institute of Justice,[47] 1,400 arrestees between 1991 and 1993 who were linked to drug abuse and HIV were examined. Intense case management intervention was the primary method used to supervise those participants. The findings revealed that this intervention, delivered for 6 months to drug-involved arrestees, significantly reduced drug use and lowered recidivism.[48] Participation in the intervention was voluntary and as you know, participants in community programs are under the authority of their caseworker. In a sense, this thought might cast doubt on a case management perspective. Caseworkers need to understand this concern and compensate for it during supervision.

Brokerage Supervision

Brokerage supervision can be described as a strategy that focuses on obtaining (as opposed to providing) services for a participant. The correctional supervisor is not the primary agent of treatment as in the case management model. In a brokerage model, the supervisor's task is to assess the concrete needs of a participant (like the caseworker) and arrange for services, consistent with the assessment findings. That is, the supervisor "brokers" out services to other agencies. Think of it this way: Brokerage supervision means that a supervisor is a resource person, tasked with telling a participant where to go for services.

Recently, community personnel have been deluged with correctional participants. How does a correctional supervisor, almost regardless of where he or she is within the correctional system, have time and all the skills required to treat so many participants who have so many different needs?

Ideally, a community supervisor has a 10-step plan to follow to bring a defendant closer to the goal of a correctional agency.

- Inventory resources of community and other governmental agencies
- Develop resource banks complete with specialties and results
- Prepare community for arrival of specific offenders (i.e., sexual)
- Develop client contacts including contact person, phone numbers, address, and qualifications and waiting periods for entry into programs
- Develop a case plan for each caseload
- Refer participant to appropriate services
- Purchase services for participant (prepare necessary forms for managerial approval where necessary)
- Follow up on each defendant to determine level of participation
- Evaluate outcome of intervention
- Develop predictions based on intervention

As made evident by the steps in the brokerage model, this supervisor is a manager of resources; however, the case manager is engaged in both resources and evaluations. Evaluations take priority in determining the needs of an offender and, once that is accomplished, matching those needs to the resources. After needs and resources are matched, the supervisor continues to monitor the progress of the offender.

Paramount in a brokerage model is the relationship between the correctional supervisor with other agencies as opposed to the offender, as in the case management model. Also paramount in the brokerage model is the ability of the supervisor to make accurate evaluations (discussed in more detail in future chapters).

Casework and Brokerage Supervision

Ideally, a CC caseworker, through a one-to-one relationship, analyzes a participant, formulates a treatment strategy, implements the strategy, and evaluates the progress of a participant. The brokerage supervision's task assesses the needs of a participant and arranges for services to be provided consistent with his or her assessment findings. Both models move toward a similar mission. However, a merger of both strategies appears to be occurring among CC agencies. For example, Richard Enos and Steven Southern[49] propose a strategy model that incorporates both models in an eight-stage process:

- **Intake:** Orientation of rules, expectations, providers of services, and sanctions
- **Assessment:** History-taking, substance abuse evaluation, psychological assessment

- **Classification:** Risk assessments derived from offender's criminal history.
- **Referral:** Identify and refer services that enhance participant outcomes (i.e., half-way houses, substance abuse treatment, behavior modification programs, domestic violence centers, health care, housing).
- **Intervention:** Match available resources and services to offender's identified needs
- **Monitoring:** Keys to success include effective monitoring (electric surveillance devices, short confinement periods to aid cooperation with case manager, drug testing) and graduated sanctions for offenders who fail to comply with service plans.
- **Evaluation:** Determine if participant received services outlined in case management plan and whether participant benefited from those services (indicators of success include recidivism, response to intervention, urine drug screening, program attendance, and compliance reports).
- **Advocacy:** Testify or make recommendations in court on participant's behalf, negotiate pro bono services and obstructive bureaucratic practices, secure priority program placements, mediate difficult situations (e.g., arrange visitation with children). Identify and bring change to community conditions that contribute to a participant's revocation.

Casework Collaboration or Team Supervision

The third model of supervision is a more recent addition to CC agencies. It is a variation of the case management and brokerage approaches that involve the use of teams or collaboration of groups. That is, rather than a single supervisor or a single group of professionals overseeing a specific participant, a number of correctional supervisors or a number of groups might be responsible for a single participant. Whether it's between several supervisors (all of whom are from the same agency) or more than one group of supervisors from different agencies, collaboration means they are joined together to achieve a common goal in a relationship and its objectives.[50] More than one supervisor from the same or similar agencies is clear. Groups such as education, social work, mental health, and enforcement joined together might be harder to envision at first. For example, an intake evaluation is performed by several members of the team or a group, each emphasizing an area of expertise and authority. Substance abuse treatment professionals (e.g., county social workers) interview the participant during the intake process, as do supervision personnel (enforcement of CC rules such as drug testing schedules) and rule enforcers such as state probation officers. As you can see, a number of agencies can combine to provide services to a specific set of offenders as the Commonwealth of Massachusetts recently developed in their community corrections program through the Trial Courts of the Commonwealth. Deputies from the Norfolk Country Sheriff's Office (Boston), Office of Community Corrections, and the Massachusetts Department of Probation have personnel in a single facility to "team manage" CC participants. In other jurisdictions throughout the state, the team could be employed by a single agency but each member of the team is just that—a team player with specific skills. Part of the experienced thinking linked to offenders is that even among nonviolent offenders, when drug or alcohol dependence is present, participants are often dependent on more than one addiction at a time. For example, many addicts have multiple addictions. At the Norfolk community correctional center, for instance, the community personnel deal with caseloads in which their participants are dependent on cocaine, cannabis, and alcohol all at the same time. The team has to treat each addiction separately while trying to alter the everyday behavior of the participant.

Obstacles in Collaborative Models

Shared decision making and effective group processing is awkward for many personnel especially if they are accustomed to top-down decision making styles. Often, certain emotions and training perspectives require attention, in addition to the participant's requirements. Collaboration has many obstacles, which could include:

- Lack of knowledge regarding the role and expertise of other members of the team.
- Hierarchy of formal power differences.
- Lack of interpersonal skills and understanding of group dynamics.
- Turf issues.
- Different goals and authority.

Once differences are resolved, collaboration is probably the most useful and effective community strategy, but it is hardly cost-efficient and it is time-consuming. It has been noted that a number of authorities have attempted collaborative models, but because results were not immediate, available funds to operate those programs were reduced and those strategies ended long before appropriate assessments could be made.

How to Implement New Supervision Strategies

One problem of collaborative or team supervisor models is in their implementation because it is a fairly new approach to CC supervision. Also, because this book originates from an "applied" perspective, implementing new correctional strategies does fit the mission of this work. That is, whether the concern is to implement a team strategy or any other unproven strategy in a justice system including CC, lessons can be learned from other agency initiatives such as community policing. Often, when implementing a new strategy, particularly one that is considered to be a "cure-all," much like collaborative or team casework, policy makers, interest groups, and the public lose interest in waiting for results.[51] What to do? One answer comes from William Bridges who describes what he calls *"The Neutral Zone,"* a "very difficult time" where the boss is getting impatient and asking "How long is it going to take you to implement those changes?"[52] In retrospect, the Neutral Zone seems to be one of the experiences of CC programs. Correctional policy makers want quantifiable results and increasingly put pressure on a new strategy to demonstrate its success. Meanwhile, members of the new operation feel pressure to produce but find themselves unable to comply with their own job descriptions. Even principal planners become unable to successfully implement their design. Many began to question the virtue of the overall idea itself and the ability of those involved to carry it out. The experiences described are actually a normal part of a process of change. This unpleasant period of transition is known as the neutral zone, common to all organizations that apply and implement new strategies.

Bridges lists six steps to survive the neutral zone. These include:

1. Protect people from further change
2. Review policies and procedures
3. Examine reporting relationships and organizational structure
4. Set short-range goals
5. Do not promise overly high levels of performance
6. Help supervisors and managers learn what they need to function successfully

The time in the neutral zone can be a creative period if proper actions are taken prior to implementing a new strategy. Decisions can be made to minimize further changes within the agency and concentrate on making the current plan work. Policies and procedures can be examined and rewritten with the input of workers and supervisors. New procedures should take advantage of lessons learned to streamline operations and avoid problems previously experienced. Unproductive reporting relationships are changed and the organizational structure is modified to make communications easier and maximize the ability of the various components to accomplish their tasks and collaborate with other units. Each unit can be asked to develop short-term goals and focus on accomplishing those goals. Efforts can be made to establish more reasonable expectations as to what the new model can deliver and to communicate these new, less ambitious promises to stakeholders. Finally, opportunities for skill development can be provided for supervisors, equipping them to perform well in their assignments. It is suggested that when CC agencies change their supervisor strategy to meet 21st century knowledge, they review this neutral zone perspective and plan accordingly.

CASELOAD ASSIGNMENTS

Assigning a community correctional caseload often depends on jurisdiction and the criminal disposition of a defendant. If a defendant is conditionally released from prison, a parole authority or agency gets the assignment or case. When a defendant is conditionally released from jail, a community county agency might get the case. If the defendant is on probation, a probation agency is usually assigned the participant. Should the offender be in a diversion or pretrial program, specific agencies might supervise the participant. Assigning an agency might be a simple process depending on the penalty received by a defendant.

Assigning a CC supervisor in a specific agency might be more difficult. Many strategies can be used to assign defendants to community personnel supervisors. There are few if any set number of participants who enter any system because those numbers would depend on the courts and other agencies that feed community corrections. Although many different strategies are used throughout the country, many of those strategies can be characterized, such as the Conventional Model, Numbers game Model, Geographic Model, and Specialized Models of participant assignments.

Conventional Model: The conventional or traditional model of participant assignment is a random effort to distribute defendants to a community agency. That is, participants are assigned a specific correctional agency. But it is unlikely that an adequate system is in place to determine which correctional supervisor in an agency will become the supervisor of a specific participant. Random assignments imply that CC personnel must diversify their skill levels to deal with every need and risk category of participants. That is, from violent to drug-possession-type caseloads. In addition, many offenders are conditionally released to a CC agency and randomly assigned a supervisor. Inadequately prepared CC supervisors could underestimate the potential risk or needs of specific participants because of a lack of knowledge, especially if the confinement record of a defendant is used as the primary indicator of risk (to reoffend or use violence) and need (programs, such as substance control). That is, the crime that originally brought the defendant to be confined might not be an indicator of a participant's risk after confinement. For instance, defendants originally convicted of assault through a plea-bargain might in fact be violent predators who exhibit many of the traits of APD and are highly manipulative. Conversely, through offense escalation and prison experiences, nonviolent offenders might see violence as an appropriate response, once conditionally released from confinement.

Numbers Game Model: The numbers game model and the conventional model are similar. However, the numbers game model takes the total number of participants and divides that number by the number of community caseworkers. This model randomly assigns participants to personnel. That is, if there are 10 community caseworkers and 100 participants, each caseworker gets 10 new caseloads. If the maximum caseload is established at 35, once each caseworker has 35, the agency hires or transfers another caseworker to the unit.

Geographic Model: Assignment of participants based on a geographic model where caseworkers receive participants based on where a participant resides. Caseworkers living in rural areas receive smaller caseloads than caseworkers in urban areas because there is less travel time required on the part of caseworkers and participants.

Specialized Model: Assignment of participants is based on specialties of a specific caseworker. Should a caseworker possess skills and training such as those linked to drug or alcohol dependencies, it is likely that this caseworker is assigned drug or alcohol abusers more often than the other caseworkers.

Overall, you can see that the strategy used in a particular jurisdiction most often would depend on the correctional agency and system; the number of offenders assigned to a community agency; the mission of an agency; its resources, policy, and experiences; and finally, the belief systems in place. That is, when policy makers, interest groups, and the public of a specific jurisdiction rely upon a just desert rationale to support a local community agency, there is probably a difference in the quality of services and personnel available in that agency to handle specific caseloads. Justifying well-trained and talented community professionals might be less a priority to just deserters than those who see rehabilitation as an appropriate rationale.

Caseloads

The number of cases or a caseload that a supervisor manages at a given time is a matter of debate.[53] However, the literature is extensive concerning caseloads and dates to 1917.[54] At that time, it was suggested that a probation caseload standard of 50 offenders per officer was appropriate. Fifty was the standard until 1967, when the President's Commission on Law Enforcement and Administration of Justice lowered caseload averages to 35 participants per caseworker. Both of these numbers bore the stamp of "professional consensus": the National Probation Association, the American Correctional Association, the National Council on Crime and Delinquency, the U.S. Children's Bureau, and the National Council of Juvenile and Family Court Judges endorsed both the original 50-case standard and 35-case standard.

Probation Caseload Assignments

In the national probation bureaucracy of 50,000 employees, an estimated 11,500 directly supervise adult probationers, according to the National Institute for Justice Journal, producing an average caseload of 258 adult offenders versus an "ideal caseload" of 30.[55] One study calculates that only 4,420 of the nation's probation officers supervise felons, an average caseload of 337.[56]

In nearly 70 percent of cases, probation officers do not make "collateral contact" to verify such things as employment or attendance in drug treatment programs.[57] At any one time, one in nine adult probationers cannot be located because they have absconded.[58]

The American Probation and Parole Association (APPA) recommends a *caseload workload* model. The priority of the workload model is centered on supervision requirements that a correctional supervisor might have with a specific participant. Counting cases is different from accounting for differences in basic supervision strategies. One way to explain a workload model is to suggest that there is a differentiation of case supervision that is applied to different participants. Participants do not require an equal amount of supervision and services from an agency.

The APPA suggests that it is difficult to define an ideal caseload based on numbers because of the needs and risk levels of different participants. That is, some CC participants require more supervision time than other participants. For instance, high-risk and high-need offenders tend to require an estimated four supervision hours per month, compared to medium risk and medium need offenders who require two hours a month, and low risk and low need offenders who require one supervision hour a month.

Supervision Caseload

Case Priority	Hours per Month	Total Caseload
High	4	30
Medium	2	60
Low	1	120

Printed with permission of the American Probation and Parole Association, 2004.[59]

The APPA suggests that if the maximum number of hours available to any specific community caseload officer is 120 hours per month, then caseload can be comprised of 30 high priority cases, 60 medium priority cases, or 120 low priority cases. In all three instances, the officer would have a full workload (i.e., one where the number of hours needed to fulfill the minimum requirements on all the cases [demand] is equal to the amount of hours available to the officer [supply]). How well does caseload size work relative to recidivism?

Interesting enough, little evidence supports the view that smaller caseloads can lead to lower recidivism levels.[60] But many regular probation and parole officers (as opposed to intense probation officers, which will be discussed in Chapter 8) suggest that a "workable" caseload would range from 28 to 35 participants.[61] This finding is consistent with researchers who in 1997 said that the average caseload of probation officers should be 27 while the average caseload for intensive supervision caseload should be 24.[62] Based on the caseload numbers, it appears that many community systems hold similar expectations of their personnel. However, due in part to the typically large caseloads serviced by most CC officers, it is difficult to achieve quality service. Some counts show 70 caseloads for each caseworker as appropriate. Nonetheless, casework is extensively practiced throughout CC so much that any other method is considered ineffective.

APPA's Vision Statement: We see a fair, just, and safe society where community partnerships are restoring hope by embracing a balance of prevention, intervention, and advocacy.

APPA's Code of Ethics include: I will render professional service to the justice system and the community at large in effecting the social adjustment of the offender.
Source: APPA. http://www.appa-net.org/

Technology and Caseloads

Technology has entered the world of CC. However, at a time when fiscal austerity has touched each part of the correctional community, technological advancements are less available in many jurisdictions than expected. Some jurisdictions such as Los Angles

County, California use automation and computers to aid in their caseloads and rather than decreasing caseloads, it has an opposite effect. The county has approximately 50,000 adult probationers supervised by 340 probation officers including support staff.

The Los Angeles County Probation Department has developed the Automated Minimum Supervision Caseload (AMSC).[63] Approximately 65 percent of adult probationers are assigned to AMSC caseloads that utilize computers to monitor probationer compliance with court orders. Video orientation of probationers facilitates their instruction. The ratio of probationers to DPOs is 1,000 to 1. Also, the LA Probation Department developed a High Risk Offender program that targets offenders who pose a greater risk to the community and require a combination of supervision and monitoring. The staffing ratio in this program is approximately 200 adult probationers to 1 probation officer.

As you know, CC is operated by many enterprises including federal, state, county, municipal, and private agencies, each answering to their own authority and reaching for their own mission objectives. The APPA suggests that the diversity among service providers is substantial, and it is unlikely that a single uniform system is the answer.

SUMMARY

Supervision strategies provided by correctional systems and organizational efforts to shape those strategies are the focus of this chapter. CC organizational plans should include a broad range of goals such as: strategies to apply change, decentralization, broadening of sentencing options, improvement of classification systems that redefine offenders, developing methods of collaboration between justice agencies, developing offender surveillance and supervision strategies, promoting cost effectiveness, fulfilling punishment requirements, developing and implementing professional methods to measure effectiveness, and proving success. Also, anticipated offender and community changes caused by organizational change were explained, which included an array of components from altering general criminal activity, creating and implementing rehabilitative services, to empowering community participation. However, heightening offender accountability and reducing prison and jail overcrowding were also part of the list. Some of the obstacles that hinder organizational change included fragmented national and local justice systems, administrative or interagency problems, legal problems related to legislation, resource allocation or availability, belief systems of policy makers, interest groups, and the general public.

Amenability to treatment, or agreeable towards treatment suggests that some offenders are poor candidates for rehabilitation programs. However, with a paradigm shift toward treatment, the belief gaining ground is that all offenders can benefit from treatment, even the ones who are incarcerated. Better trained correctional personnel and volunteers can make a difference in the outcomes of correctional populations. This chapter identified and described generalized tasks of CC officers, which include law enforcer, counseling and education, informal assistance, and supervision. Various supervision strategies were explained including case management and its similarities and differences with social work perspectives. A 10-step plan that would aid "broker" supervisors was offered along with an 8-step model that incorporated the best techniques of the case management and broker approaches presented. Collaboration or team strategies of case management were discussed and some of their obstacles were revealed. How to implement new supervision strategies was offered by comparing the experiences from other justice agencies. Problems concerning casework assignments and strategies to remedy those problems were discussed.

DISCUSSION QUESTIONS

1. Identify organizational strategies that could help CC change.
2. Describe some of the anticipated offender and community changes that would result from these organizational plans. In what way might you disagree with at least two of these changes?
3. Explain some of the obstacles that stand in way of implementing changes. Are there any obstacles that you can describe that are missing from this list?
4. Describe the concept of "Amenability to Treatment" and explain its recent changes. What do you see as a strength of this perspective and what do you see as a weaknesses of it? Why would an offender not want help?
5. Identify and describe generalized tasks performed by CC supervisors. Which of these generalized tasks do you see as the most important task and why? The least important?
6. Describe contact standards of supervision at an optimal and suboptimal level.
7. Identify goals and the emphasized elements of case management.
8. Describe similarities and differences between social work and case management. Which other professions in criminal justice might also use social work perspectives in the performance of its duties?
9. Identify a 10-step plan to aid a broker supervisor meet CC goals.
10. Explain the 8-step model that incorporates the best of supervision strategies.
11. Explain collaboration methods of case management and identify some of its obstacles.
12. Describe "neutral zone" experiences and their relevance to CC supervisor strategies.

13. Describe problems of casework assignments and strategies to remedy those problems.

NOTES

1. Office of Juvenile Justice and Delinquency Prevention (2003, April). *Best practices in juvenile accountability: Overview.* Washington, DC: U.S. Department of Justice, Office of Justice Programs, NCJ184745 (p. 1).

2. Dale Parent (1990). *Residential community corrections: Developing an integrated corrections policy. Issues in residential community corrections policy and practice.* Washington, DC: U.S. Department of Justice. National Institute of Corrections (pp. 1–10). Nancy Shomaker and Mark Gornik (2002). Youthful offenders in adult corrections: A systemic approach using effective interventions. *Corrections Today, 64*(6), 112–114. Wayne N. Welsh and Gary Zajac (2004). A census of prison-based drug treatment programs: Implications for programming, policy, and evaluation. *Crime & Delinquency, 50*(1), 108–133.

3. Criminal Justice 2000, 3. Policies, Processes, and Decisions of the Criminal Justice System. Washington D.C., Office of Justice Programs, U.S. Department of Justice. Mark W. Lipsey (1999). Can rehabilitative programs reduce the recidivism of juvenile offenders? An inquiry into the effectiveness of practical programs. *Virginia Journal of Social Policy and Law, 6*(Spring), 611–641. Wayne N. Welsh and Gary Zajac (2004). A census of prison-based drug treatment programs: Implications for programming, policy, and evaluation. *Crime & Delinquency, 50*(1), 108–133.

4. Denise C. Gottfredson and William H. Barton (1993). Deinstitutionalization of juvenile offenders. *Criminology 31*(4), 591–611. Francis T. Cullen and Paul Gendreau (2000). p. 21. Mark W. Lipsey (1999). Can rehabilitative programs reduce the recidivism of juvenile offenders? An inquiry into the effectiveness of practical programs. *Virginia Journal of Social Policy and Law, 6*(Spring): 611–641.

5. Donald A. Andrews, Ivan Zinger, Robert D. Hoge, James Bonta, Paul Gendreau, and Francis T. Cullen (1990). Does correctional treatment work? A clinically relevant and psychologically informed meta-analysis. *Criminology, 28,* 369–404. Also, see Patricia M. Harris (1999). From research to results: Pathways to effective community corrections. In Patricia M. Harris (Ed.), *Research to research: effective community corrections. The International Community Corrections Association* (pp. 1–120). Washington, DC: The American Corrections Association.

6. Joan Petersilia (1997). A decade of experimenting with intermediate sanctions: What have we learned? In the National Institute of Justice (ed), Perspectives on Crime and Justice: 1997–1998 Lecture Series. Washington, DC: National Institute of Justice (p. 3).

7. David M. Altschuler, Tony L. Armstrong, and Doris L. MacKenzie (1999, July). Reintegration, supervised release, and intensive aftercare. *Juvenile Justice Bulletin.*

Washington, DC: JJB–175716. Retrieved online January 9, 2005: http://www.ncjrs .org/pdffiles1/175715.pdf

8. Vincent D. Basile (2002, December). A model for developing a reentry program. *Federal Probation, 66*(3), 55–58.

9. Idit Weiss and Yochanan Wozner (2002). Ten models for probation supervision compared across eight dimensions. *Journal of Offender Rehabilitation, 34*(3), 85–105.

10. Peter J. Delany, Bennett W. Fletcher, and Joseph J. Shields (2003, September). Reorganizing care for the substance using offender: The case for collaboration. *Federal Probation, 67*(2), 64–69.

11. Susan Sarnoff (2001, June). Restoring justice to the community: A realistic goal? *Federal Probation, 65*(1), 33–39. Retrieved online January 11, 2005: http://www .uscourts.gov/fedprob/2001junfp.pdf

12. Harry N. Boone, Jr. and Betsy A. Fulton (1996, June). *Implementing performance: Measures in community-based corrections.* National Institute of Justice, NCJ 158836 Retrieved online January 11, 2005: http://www.ncjrs.org/pdffiles/perform .pdf

13. For details prior to 2003, see Nicholas R. Turner and Daniel F. Wilhelm (2002, December). Are the politics of criminal justice changing? *Corrections Today, 64*(7), 74–75.

14. Curt R. Bartol and Anne M. Bartol (2005). *Criminal behavior: A psychological approach* (7th ed.). Upper Saddle River, NJ: Prentice Hall (p. 545).

15. Douglas B. Marlowe, Nicholas S. Patapis, and David S. DeMatteo (2003, September). Amenability to treatment of drug offenders. *Federal probation, 67*(2), 40–46. Retrieved online January 11, 2005: http://www.uscourts.gov/fedprob/2003Augfp .pdf

16. Mitzi A. Lowe, Joe Parks, and Charlotte Tilkes (2003, April). Using interprofessional collaboration to restructure detention program delivery. *Corrections Today, 65*(2), 70–73.

17. One good starting point is to review the literature on community policing strategies as many police agencies have undergone considerable change in the past few years. See how they went about changing their agency. See Dennis J. Stevens (2004). *Applied community policing in the 21st Century.* Boston: Allyn Bacon (pp. 21–31).

18. Kerry Murphy Healey (1999, February). *Case management in the criminal justice system.* National Institute of Justice, Research Action. Washington, DC: U.S. Department of Justice, NIJ 173409 (p. 19). Retrieved online January 10, 2005: http://www.ncjrs.org/pdffiles/155281.pdf

19. Lynne I. Goodstein and Doris Layton MacKenzie (1989). Issues in correctional research and policy: An introduction. In Lynne I. Goodstein and Doris Layton MacKenzie (Eds.), *The American prison: Issues in research and policy.* New York: Plenum (pp. 67–73).

20. Alan T. Harland and Wayne N. Welsh (1999) Toward the strategic management of correctional innovation: Putting what works information to work. In Patricia M. Harris (Ed.), *Research to results: Effective community corrections* (pp. 105–150). Lanham: MD: The International Community Corrections Association.

21. Felicia G. Cohn (2002, September). Valuing evaluation. *Federal Probation, 66*(2), 10–13. Retrieved online January 13, 2005: http://www.uscourts.gov/library/fpcontents.html

22. Faye S. Taxman (2002, September). Supervision: Exploring the dimensions of effectiveness. *Federal Probation, 66*(2), 14–27. Retrieved online January 13, 2005: http://www.uscourts.gov/library/fpcontents.html

23. Mark D. Litt and Sharon D. Mallon (2003, September). The design of social support networks for offenders in outpatient drug treatment. *Federal Probation, 67*(20), 15–21. Retrieved online January 13, 2005: http://www.uscourts.gov/library/fpcontents.html

24. For a working draft of community policing, see Dennis J. Stevens (2004), 4–13.

25. Mary K. Shilton (1992). *Community correction acts for state and local partnerships.* Maryland: American Correctional Association (p. 4).

26. C. C. Cottle, R. J. Lee, and K. Heilbrun (2001). The prediction of criminal recidivism in juveniles: A meta-analysis. *Criminal Justice and Behavior, 28,* 367–394. J. Monahan, H. J. Steadman, E. Silver, P. S. Appelbaum, P. C. Robbins, E. Mulvey, L. H. Roth, T. Grisso, and S. Banks (2001). Rethinking risk assessment: *The MacArthur study of mental disorder and violence.* New York: Oxford University Press.

27. James Bonta (2002). Offender risk assessment: Guidelines for selection and use. *Criminal Justice and Behavior, 29,* 355–379.

28. Douglas B. Marlowe, Nicholas S. Patapis, and David S. DeMatteo (2003, September), 44.

29. David X. Swenson (1999, November). *Adult certification evaluation: Adolescent certification to adult status for court.* Retrieved online January 9, 2005: http://www.css.edu/users/dswenson/web/psyeval/adolcertification.html. The process developed by Swenson is consistent with another observer who provides a plan for probation agencies. See Jennifer L. Ferguson (2002). Putting the "What Works" research into practice: An organizational perspective. *Criminal Justice and Behavior, 29,* 472–492.

30. This idea is congruent with Karl Hanson (2005, February). Twenty years of progress in violence risk assessment. *Journal of Interpersonal Violence, 20*(2), 212–217.

31. This thought is also consistent with Paul Gendreau, Claire Goggin, and Paula Smith (2003, December). Erratum. *Criminal Justice and Behavior, 30*(6), 722–724.

32. Minnesota Multiphasic Personality Inventory. For history and further descriptions of MMPI see Richard Niolon. *A history of MMPI.* Retrieved online January 9, 2005: http://www.psychpage.com/objective/mmpi2_overview .htm.

33. Other observers discuss a similar perspective concerning participant motivation specifically developed for employment in residential units. See Matthew L. Hiller, Kevin Knight, Carl Leukefeld, and D. Dwayne Simpson (2002). Motivatin as a predictor of therapeutic engagement in mandated residential substance abuse treatment. *Criminal Justice and Behavior, 29,* 56–75.

34. This thought is congruent with William N. Elliott (2002, December). Managing offender resistance to counseling. *Federal Probation, 66*(3), 43–45. Retrieved online January 13, 2005: http://www.uscourts.gov/fedprob/ 2002decfp.pdf

35. William N. Elliott (2002, December), 43–44.

36. William N. Elliott (2002, December), 45.

37. Dennis J. Stevens and Charles S. Ward (1997). College education and recidivism: Educating criminals is meritorious. *Journal of Correctional Education, 48*(3), 106–111.

38. For that reason, a relapse process must be part of every program and every group encounter. Think of it as a way to process failure. What to do when things happen must be regularly clarified to participants. Whether it is treatment toward sobriety, a program such as vocational skills, or group encounters dealing with anger issues, a process must be in place to deal with failure. If lifelines are arbitrary or don't exist, continued failure is more likely.

39. Some opponents of revocation standards (standards vary from jurisdiction to jurisdiction) should remember that CC populations have committed crimes probably because many of them were unsupervised at a time in their lives when it meant the difference between committing a crime or not committing a crime.

40. Gary Fields (1998, January 19). Study links drugs to 80 percent of incarcerations. *USA Today,* 84.

41. Bureau of Justice Statistics (2005). *Sourcebook of criminal justice statistics 2002, online.* Albany, NY: U.S. Department of Justice (p. 507, Table 6.39). Retrieved online January 9, 2005: http://www.albany.edu/sourcebook/1995/ pdf/t639.pdf

42. After a review of many caseload supervision strategies, Table 5.1 shows the recommendations that best distinguish between various levels. Do not assume that these suggestions are the best methods of supervising offenders; they are offered merely as an example. South Dakota Unified Judicial System: Court Services Adult Risk Assessment and Weighted Workload Management System. February 2, 1999. Information provided by National Institute of Corrections, NF 010982. This source was used as a guide, additions were added by author as needed after checking with other guides.

43. Kerry Murphy Healey (1999, February). *Case management in the criminal justice system.* National Institute of Justice, Research Action. Washington, DC: U.S. Department of Justice, NIJ 173409.

44. H. B. Trecker (1955). Social work principles in probation. *Federal Probation, 19*(1), 8–9.

45. *Case management with drug-involved arrestees.* National Institute of Justice, U.S. Department of Justice, NCJ 155281.

46. H. B. Trecker (1955). p. 4. Updates: T*imothy P. Cadigan, Bernadette Pelissier* (2003, September). Moving towards a federal criminal justice "system." *Federal Probation, 67*(2), 61–63. Peter J. Delany, Bennett W. Fletcher, and Joseph J. Shields (2003, September). Reorganizing care for the substance using offender: The case for collaboration. *Federal Probation, 67*(2), 64–69.

47. William Rhodes and Michael Gross (1997, March). *Case management with drug-involved arrestees: An experimental study of an HIV prevention intervention.* National Institute of Justice. Washington, DC: U.S. Department of Justice, NCJ 155281. Retrieved online January 9, 2005: http://www.uscourts.gov/fedprob/2003Augfp.pdf.

48. William Rhodes and Michael Gross (1997, March), 20–23.

49. Richard Enos and Steven Southern (1996). *Correctional case management.* Cincinnati, OH: Anderson (p. 2). Also Kerry Murphy Healey (1999, February). Case management in the criminal justice system. National Institute of Justice, U.S. Department of Justice, NCJ 173409.

50. Mitzi A. Lowe, Joe Parks, and Charlotte Tilkes (2003, April).

51. Dennis J. Stevens (2001). *Case studies in community policing.* Upper Saddle River, NJ: Prentice Hall (pp. 91–114).

52. William Bridges (1991). *Managing transitions: Making the most of changes.* Reading, MA: Addison-Wesley.

53. Michael R. Gottfredson and Don M. Gottfredson (1988). *Decision making in criminal justice: Towards the rationale exercise of discretion* (2nd ed.). New York: Plenum (pp. 181–184).

54. Hunter Hust III (1999). National Center for Juvenile Justice. Retrieved online January 9, 2005: http://www.ncjrs.org/html/ojjdp/jiabg_blltn_99_11/ curr.html

55. Joan Petersilia (1998). Probation in the United States. *Crime and Justice, 22,* 149–200. Also see Joan Petersilia (2001). *Reforming probation and parole: In the 21st century.* Maryland: American Correctional Association. Joan Petersilia (2003). *When prisoners come home: Parole and prisoner reentry: Studies in crime and public policy.* New York: Oxford University Press.

56. Michael Hotra (1998, May 22). *Missing persons: Most probation officers aren't watching criminals.* American Legislative Exchange Council, F.Y.I. pp. 8–9. More recently, Joan Petersilia (1998) claimed that "the average adult regular supervision caseload is reported to be 117 to 1" (p. 579).

57. Michael Hotra (1998). Joan Petersilia (1998), pp. 2–8. Only 12 percent of personal contacts between probationers and officers occur in the field; that is, at an offender's home or at his job. Also see Bureau of Justice Statistics (1997, December).

Characteristics of adults on probation 1995. Washington, DC: U.S. Department of Justice, Office of Justice Programs, NCJ–164267 (p. 8). Retrieved online January 9, 2005: http://www.ojp .usdoj.gov/bjs/abstract/cap95.htm.

58. Bureau of Justice Statistics (2004, July). *Probation and parole in the United States, 2003.* U.S. Department of Justice, NCJ 205336 (p. 4). Retrieved online January 9, 2005: http://www.ojp.usdoj.gov/bjs/pub/pdf/ppus03.pdf. A California sample of 4,047 parolees showed 27 percent absconded. See Frank P. Williams III, Marilyn D. McShane, and H. Michael Dolny (2000, March). Predicting parole absconders. *The Prison Journal, 80*(1), 36.

59. American Probation and Parole Association. Retrieved online January 10, 2005: http://www.appa-net.org/.

60. Bureau of Justice Statistics (1997, December). *Characteristics of adults on probation,* 1995. Washington, DC: Department of Justice, Office of Justice Programs, NCJ 164267. Thomas P. Bonczar. Retrieved online January 9, 2005: http://www .ojp.usdoj.gov/bjs/pub/ascii/cap95.txt. Also *The corrections yearbook, 1997* (1998). Camille Graham Camp and George M. Camp (Eds.). South Salem, NY: Criminal Justice Institute (p. 143).

61. An informal survey conducted by the author among 47 probation and parole officers in classes conducted at the North Carolina Justice Academy, Salemburg, North Carolina.

62. *The corrections yearbook, 1997* (1998), 143.

63. Los Angeles County Probation Department. Retrieved online January 9, 2005: http://probation.co.la.ca.us/adult/afield.html#AMSC

6

PRETRIAL RELEASE AND DIVERSION

After you read this chapter, you will be better prepared to:

- Define pretrial release and identify its standards of release.
- Identify the primary concerns of release and identify the established standards used to address those concerns.
- Describe the reasons many suspects fail to appear at court and how attendance can be improved.
- Identify the hardships of unnecessarily detained suspects.
- Explain cumulative impact and its effect upon a community.
- Define diversion and explain its rationale.
- Describe some of the history of diversion.
- Define pretrial diversion and explain its importance.
- Identify the standards that help guide diversion programs.
- Explain the link between substance abuse, juveniles, and crime.
- Describe drug courts and teen courts and explain their benefits.
- Identify successful diversion initiatives among the young.
- Explain the role restitution plays with diversion initiatives.

KEY TERMS

Accountability

Bail

Community Court

Community Service

Cumulative Impact

Danger Laws

Diversion

Drug Court

Labeling Perspective

Pretrial Detention

Pretrial Diversion

Release on Recognizance
   (ROR)

Restitution

Self-fulfilling Prophecy

Teen Court

Third-party Custody

> A government that robs Peter to pay Paul can always depend upon the support of Paul.
> —George Bernard Shaw (1856–1950)

INTRODUCTION

The justice community is not obliged to arrest, prosecute, and incarcerate every criminal suspect. Some offenders pose little risk and should be released from jail while awaiting trial or pretrial release, and others can be guided toward a crime-free lifestyle more often when diverted from judicial process. Pretrial release and diversion initiatives are the focus of this chapter. Through official discretions they can save scarce public resources reduce future criminality, and, more important, enhance public safety. The first part of the chapter examines pretrial release and the second part examines diversion along with juvenile drug initiatives tied into diversionary strategies. The final part of the chapter describes restitution as a diversionary initiate.

PRETRIAL RELEASE

Some of the issues leading to pretrial release are that Americans age 12 or older experienced about 24.2 million violent and property victimizations in 2001, advises the National Crime Victimization Survey (NCVS).[1] Around 14 million arrests occur each year. Of that number, about 2.2 million arrests are Index Crime Offenses: murder, rape, robbery, aggravated assault, burglary, larceny-theft, motor vehicle theft, and arson. One estimate shows that 56 percent of all suspects arrested for a crime of violence are released prior to a disposition of their case or what is called pretrial release.[2] Just 13 percent of murder defendants were released compared to 61 percent of assault defendants.

Pretrial release defined: It is the release of a defendant awaiting trial after an arrest. One role pretrial release plays is its link to Constitutional guarantees, an issue centered in the detainment of an unadjudicated suspect and the question of guilt. One assumption is that an arrest should not equal detention, except in limited cases.[3] Defendants who do not meet established standards for release remain in jail until trial. This practice is called pretrial detention.

Established standards: The goal of established standards is to determine whether the release of a defendant would compromise public safety and whether the suspect, once released, would make a scheduled court appearance. Discretion of justice practitioners is the most common method employed to determine if the established standards can be met by a defendant. Pretrial release's centerpiece rests on flight risk and public safety. To help determine "flight" and public safety concerns, established standards can include:

1. Seriousness of the offense
2. Defendant's criminal history
3. Defendant's ties to the community
4. Age and gender of the defendant
5. Eligibility criterion into pretrial release programs
6. Eligibility criterion into diversion programs
7. Risk assessment[4]
8. Substance abuse testing[5]

Despite the use of these established standards, 13 of every 100 released defendants arrested for a crime of violence fail to make a scheduled court appearance.[6] However, when practitioners address early or "primary" decisions in the processing of criminal cases such as pretrial release, it is acknowledged that a gap exists in obtaining extensive and credible information about defendants, which impacts both early decisions and all subsequent decisions in the justice process.[7]

Types of Pretrial Release

The majority of defendants are afforded an opportunity of release after an arrest. Most are released through a process referred to as bail. Bail is the most common mechanism used in the primary decision-making process associated with pretrial release/detention. It serves two objectives: (a) it helps ensure a reappearance of the accused in court and (b) it prevents unconvicted persons from suffering imprisonment unnecessarily.

> **Bail** is a surety or sureties deposited with the court, procuring the release of a person under pretrial custody for the purpose of ensuring the defendant's appearance at trial.[8]

Bail is categorized into two separate types:[9]

1. Financial release is accomplished through a bail bond. Despite a study demonstrating that defendants with strong ties to the community are likely to appear in court regardless of their economic status, the strategy to secure bail or a dollar amount is

used to encourage a defendant's appearance in court.[10] At the court's discretion, bail may be posted in cash or by a written guarantee called a bail bond, and usually represents a cash deposit at a reduced amount. Setting bail can take into account the financial condition, employment history, family situation and history, and prior criminal record of the defendant.[11] Thirty two percent of defendants released prior to case disposition were released under financial conditions that required the posting of bail, which can include:

a. Property bond: Involves an agreement made by a defendant as a condition of pretrial release requiring that property valued at the full bail amount be posted as an assurance of his or her appearance in court. If the defendant fails to appear in court, the property is forfeited. Also known as "collateral bond." Used less than 1 percent of the time by pretrial released defendants.

b. Deposit bond: The defendant deposits a percentage (usually 10 percent) of the full bail amount with the court. Bail is returned after the disposition of the case, but the court often retains a small portion for administrative costs. If the defendant fails to appear in court, he or she is liable to the court for the full bail amount. This type of financial release is used by 6 percent of all defendants and 10 percent of released defendants.

c. Full cash bond: The defendant posts the full bail amount in cash with the court. If the defendant makes all court appearances, the cash is returned. If the defendant fails to appear in court, the bond is forfeited. Full cash bonds are used less than 2 percent of the time by pretrial released defendants.

d. Surety bond: A bail bond company signs a promissory note to the court for the full bail amount and charges the defendant a fee for the service (usually 10 percent of the full bail amount). If the defendant fails to appear, the bond company is liable to the court for the full bail amount. Frequently the bond company re quires collateral from the defendant in addition to the fee. Surety bonds are the most common type of financial release (24 percent of all defendants and 37 percent of released defendants). See Figure 6.1 for a comparison.

2. Nonfinancial release. This is when a defendant is released from jail without the use of financial security or a financial bond as a court appearance guarantee. Just under one half of released defendants and 30 percent of defendants overall were not required to post a financial bond to be released after their arrest.

a. Release on recognizance (ROR): This is when the court releases a defendant on a signed agreement that he or she will appear in court as required. In this report, the ROR category includes citation releases in which arrestees are released pending their first court appearance on a written order issued by law enforcement or jail personnel. ROR (16 percent of all defendants and 26 percent of released defendants), was the type of nonfinancial release used most. Often, ROR is used when the defendant has (a) no previous convictions, (b) residential stability, (c) a good employment record, (d) reached adulthood.

b. Conditional release: This is when defendants are released under specified conditions. Monitoring or supervision, if required, is usually done by a pretrial services agency. In some cases, such as those involving a third-party custodian or

Type of pretrial release

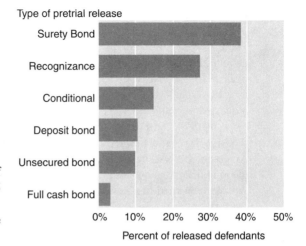

Figure 6.1 Pretrial Release of Felony Defendants in the 75 Largest Counties (2000)
Printed with permission of the Office of Justice Statistics.[12]

drug monitoring and treatment, another agency may be involved in the supervision of the defendant. Conditional release is used among 8 percent of all defendants and 14 percent of released defendants. Conditional release sometimes includes an unsecured bond and involves community correctional initiatives. The conditions will be covered in more detail later.

c. Unsecured bond: This is when a defendant pays no money to the court but is liable for the full amount of bail should he or she fail to appear in court. Unsecured bond is used among 6 percent of all defendants and 9 percent of released defendants.

Of defendants released on pretrial release in 75 of the largest counties in 2000, surety bond releases were employed 37 percent of the time, as Figure 6.1 shows. Released on recognizance accounted for 26 percent of the released defendants, conditional release accounted for 14 percent of the released defendants, 10 percent represented deposit bond releases, unsecured bonds were employed 9 percent of the time, and 2 percent of the defendants released previous to trial utilized full cash bonds.

Of the defendants who were detained in jail until court disposition, five out of every six had a bail amount set, but those defendants could not or would not post the money required to secure release.[13] The National Advisory Commission on Criminal Justice Standards and Goals revealed that almost 93 percent of felony defendants in some jurisdictions are unable to make bail.[14] Finally, in this regard, there is a growing movement toward pretrial detention as many dangerous offenders have engaged in crime while awaiting trial. In fact, 32 percent of those released through pretrial release initiatives to await trial committed another crime.[15] One fourth of those crimes were violent crimes including murder, rape, and robbery. For that reason several states have enacted *danger laws,* which limit the right to bail among specific types of offenders. It is easy to imagine that just desert advocates support danger laws and reject pretrial release programs associated with conditional release options.

Pretrial Release Reform

The passage of the *Federal Bail Reform Act of 1966* strengthened bail reform across the nation. This act contained provisions that represented departures from prior pretrial initiatives seeking consistency across jurisdictions; prioritized a list of options to consider before ROR, including a simple promise to appear when required by the defendant; and requested, in some cases, a surety bail through a commercial bail bonding agent.[16]

In 1970, the District of Columbia required that the threat to community safety, the risk of flight, and the seriousness of a crime be considered for pretrial release.[17] The American Bar Association called for the abolition of surety bail as an option, citing the long history of abuses associated with the practice.[18] In 1984, the Federal Bail Reform Act was amended to allow consideration of danger and preventive detention. Currently, at least 45 states, the federal government, and the District of Columbia specify a number of factors that must be considered in the release decision.[19] However, many defendants are only conditionally released from custody awaiting trial.

Pretrial Release Conditions

The conditions imposed on defendants vary, often depending on their dangerousness, their criminal history, the seriousness of the alleged crime, and the regulations of the jurisdiction. Yet, most conditions involve CC personnel at some level or another and can be characterized as:[20]

- Reporting regularly to a pretrial agency
- Maintaining a stable residence
- Finding and maintaining employment (if unemployed)
- Having a third party accept the custody or supervision of the defendant
- Participating in alcohol or drug treatment
- Obeying other probationary conditions such as curfew
- Remaining crime-free
- Refraining from interacting with complaining witnesses and criminal associates

Often, pretrial release includes participation in specific programs, restrictions, and rules.[21] Enforcement can be problematic in some jurisdiction for various reasons, including funding. Other jurisdictions such as Tucson, AZ, and Cincinnati, OH, order defendants to avoid alleged victims of the crime and any witnesses, such as in domestic violence cases. These "stay-away conditions" are enforced through employment of "mandatory" alternative housing for defendants until trial and the use of electronic bracelets.[22]

The idea is that jailing or even bringing to trial every offender is not the first choice of the justice community. For instance, many defendants are encouraged to attend substance abuse clinics in lieu of jail after an arrest for driving while intoxicated. Once the defendant successfully completes a prescribed program, the court can dismiss the charge of driving under the influence (DUI). Should the defendant be re-arrested for the same charge, it is unlikely that a program would be offered in place of a trial.

Failure to Appear

Researchers reveal that the reasons most defendants fail to appear (FTA) at a court appearance include everything from a lack of knowledge about the scheduled date to forgetfulness.[23] For instance, Rob Schwab, assistant administrator of the Pretrial Services Program in San Mateo, CA adds that some defendants willfully fail to appear, but for most FTAs the reasons are more complicated.[24] Some defendants lost their paperwork and forgot about an appearance date or did not know whom to contact to find out where and when to appear. Many defendants do not understand what they are supposed to do or fully comprehend the seriousness of the charges against them and the penalties for missing court.[25] Many defendants are afraid of the criminal justice system and are too fearful to ask simple questions. Many wrongfully equate a citation to appear on a misdemeanor as the functional equivalent of a parking citation. Other defendants think they have a valid excuse because they must work or have childcare or transportation difficulties. When the prerelease program in San Mateo realized that it had several categories of defendants with unacceptably high FTA rates, it initiated some simple notification and reminder procedures. Other factors unrelated to assets are better predictors of flight risk than financial criteria.[26]

Nonetheless, assuming the accused is crime-free while awaiting, missed trial appearances disrupt the court's schedule, delay the case, inconvenience victims and other witnesses, and waste valuable time and public funds. Many of the problems caused by defendants failing to appear can be minimized by improving communication between the court, defendants, and the pretrial services that play a key role in the process.

Pretrial Release and the Mentally Ill

Hardships of the pretrial process imposed upon many defendants after an arrest include the mentally ill, who, as a group, are often arrested, jailed, and convicted at higher rates than typical offenders.[27] For instance, a study of a special unit of a major metropolitan police department mandated to respond to incidents involving "emotionally disturbed persons" estimated that 5 percent of the dispatches per year involve a person with mental illness.[28] Other law enforcement agencies, such as the New York City Police Department, dispatch police officers to a person with mental illness every six minutes.[29] Other evidence that requires examination relates to Riker's Island, New York City's and the United States' largest jail populated with 8,000 prisoners. The average length of stay for all offenders is 42 days, however, for inmates with a serious mental illness, it is 215 days.[30] How many suspects arrested and jailed are homeless or impaired in any number of ways is anybody's guess, but individuals with mental and financial limitations are more likely to be jailed awaiting trial than others. In Chapter 15, the mentally ill along with other special groups such as the elderly, are discussed in more detail, but for right now, evidence reveals that the mentally ill are less likely to be candidates for pretrial release programs, diversion programs, or even probation.[31] However, general hardships of the pretrial release process are hardly limited to the mentally ill.

Hardships of Those Unnecessarily Detained

Studies have shown that suspects unnecessarily detained endure preventable hardships. These hardships are considered "preventable" because a change in the bail process would curb the hardships experienced through unnecessary detainment.[32] For instance, in comparison to early release defendants, detained defendants often:

- Plead guilty more often
- Are convicted more often
- Are sentenced to prison more often
- Serve full sentences more often

According to these researchers, their findings hold true even when other relevant factors are controlled, such as current charge, prior criminal history, family ties, and type of counsel.[33] The implication is that those not released while awaiting trial are less often candidates for CC programs, such as diversion and probation. Many individuals can face obstacles once released from jail; however, many have difficulty, even if jailed for a brief period following an arrest. It is easy to assume that most individuals detained awaiting trial tend to posses characteristics typical of the socioeconomic lower class more often than America's middle class because most middle class (and upper class) Americans have the available resources, networks, knowledge, and friends to help in their release efforts. Therefore, we can agree that many of the accused awaiting trial in American jails represent poor, unhealthy, and illiterate offenders more often than an affluent, healthy, and educated offender.[34] Continuing along this line of reasoning, it would seem logical that some of the challenges facing those detained would be their being hard-pressed to find a suitable, affordable place to live or to identify a family member or friend with whom to reside when released. Other challenges can include re-establishing eligibility for disability benefits under the state welfare programs and federal Supplemental Security Income (SSI), Social Security Disability Insurance (SSDI), and Medicaid programs; returning to a job that may or may not want them; or just getting back to daytime activity, which can include becoming involved once again in the life of loved ones and intimate others. Other challenges can include interruption of substance abuse treatment or altering a medication regimen, which may cause some postrelease difficulties and adjustments.

Then, too, detainment disrupts family routines and child-rearing practices, interrupts even meaningful employment, and imposes great financial and emotional costs upon family members and friends of the accused. Thus, it is in the interests of both defendants and the court to aid all defendants in meeting the conditions of release. Pretrial detention should be reserved for individuals likely to flee and dangerous offenders. Freedom at a price is not an American principle, some argue.

Cumulative Impact

Accepting the idea that the justice community primarily identifies, apprehends, and imposes sanctions on violators, it is likely that many more offenders from a high-impact crime jurisdiction versus a low-impact crime area await trial in jail and are incarcerated.[35] This in itself is not a great revelation, but consider the significance of what can be called *"cumulative impact."* Cumulative impact implies that in some high-impact communities, more than 10 percent of the adult males are arrested, convicted, and incarcerated in any given year.[36] It would follow that a high percentage of the community males were also jailed awaiting trial. It would seem reasonable that an almost equal number of individuals, if not more, would be returning to the community from jail and prison. The impact of this process would have a destabilizing effect upon a community as a whole, which, in turn, would exacerbate poverty, broken families, and unsupervised youth.[37] A good guess is that crime would tend to be recycled in those communities and CC strategies would be less likely available as policy makers, interest groups, and the public would see community programs as "soft on crime" and useless. Therefore, residence in poorly neighborhoods might be sentenced to confinement more often than CC programs.

However, criminal activity in any area cannot be ignored, including high-impact communities, despite the concerns of cumulative impact affects. Perhaps the justice process can be altered to provide stability through CC programs, including diversion initiatives, because stability and pubic order work well together.[38] That is, informal social controls such as families, neighbors, social organization, and friendships form the most important foundation for social order and public safety.[39]

Alternatives to Pretrial Release Standards and CC

The hardships of pretrial release can be minimized in a number of ways with an eye on public safety and assuring court appearances. In a recent study of the homeless awaiting trial for misdemeanors in San Francisco, a CC facility was used as a residence rather than jail until the defendant's court case was heard.[40] The program provided an alternative to jail, along with services specific to the client. An evaluation of a pilot program developed by the Center on Juvenile and Criminal Justice (CJCJ) demonstrates the benefits of diverting homeless misdemeanants into community-based services. The study compared a matched sample of "graduates" of CJCJ's Homeless Release Project (HRP) to other homeless misdemeanants who did not receive those services. The results show:

- HRP graduates were about half as likely to be arrested as the comparison group.
- Upon arrest, HRP participants were three times as likely to have their cases dismissed.
- Recidivism rates for the experimental group were 44 percent, whereas 71 percent of the comparison group recidivated.

The San Francisco Sheriff's Department supports the program. Sheriff Hennessey says that "This program ensures that homeless people will not sit in jail simply because they are homeless. It also ensures that people fulfill their court commitments. Keeping the homeless out of jail also saves the city money." The key is to balance public safety and control violators and available resources; it appears Sheriff Hennessey is mindful of that responsibility.

Pretrial Release Issues

It is known that at least one third of all defendants released through pretrial release strategies are re-arrested for a new offense, fail to appear, or commit another violation resulting in revocation of their pretrial release conditions.[41] These results give rise to issues of public safety. Therefore, it should come as no surprise that a number of jurisdictions are rethinking pretrial release. That is, some states have legislated *danger laws,* limiting bail to offenders who meet very narrow profiles.[42] It should be noted that the 1984 Federal Bail Reform Act allows federal judges to assess the danger of an accused to the community and to deny bail to defendants who are thought to be a danger. On one hand, it seems that there are hardships experienced by many suspects who are unnecessarily detained, and on the other hand, many offenders released from jail prior to their trial engage in additional crime. Perhaps this is what is meant when we consider that justice decisions are comprised of complex difficult choices.

If the National Association of Pretrial Service Agencies (NAPSA) has its way, performance, financial standards, and goals for pretrial release conditions of release while awaiting trial would be eliminated.[43] NAPSA insists that a presumption in favor of pretrial release should be a simple promise to appear by every defendant and services should be provided to those releasees that would in many cases be coordinated with other agencies. The Eighth Amendment to the Constitution does not permit excessive bail, nor excessive fines, nor cruel and unusual punishment. About half of those with bail amounts in 1996 had it set at $10,000 or higher. The average bail set was $31,000 and the average bail for murder defendants was set at $133,000.[44] However, in an unpublished report provided by Brian Reaves, a Bureau of Justice Statistics statistician, about 35,000 defendants (one in seven) jump commercial bail every year and bounty hunters return four out of five to justice.[45] Another report shows that an estimated 1 in 12 felony defendants released by state courts absconded before their trials and were still missing a year later. "Jumpers" are generally apprehended by bounty hunters comprised of an estimated network of 7,000 individuals who are paid approximately 10 percent of the bond value for recovery within a predetermined period.[46]

Pretrial Release Statistics

Of the accused arrested on felony charges in 40 of the nation's 75 largest counties, many were released as Table 6.1 reports.[47]

Of those defendants charged with the crime of murder, 13 percent were pretrial released; of those charged with the crime of robbery, 44 percent were pretrial released; but of those defendants charged with drug trafficking, 66 percent were pretrial released. A

Table 6.1   State Court Defendants Least Likely to Be Pretrial Released and Crimes Charged and Other Information, May 2000[48]

Type of Felony	Percentage Released	Type of Felony	Percentage Released	Released/ Denied	Percentage
Murder	13	Rape	56	Of those released; on own recognizance	26
Robbery	44	Burglary	49	Denied Bail	7
Drug trafficking	66	Theft	67	Rearrested while awaiting trial	16
Assault	68	Released Before Trial	62	Failed to appear in court	22
Weapons offenses	71	Probation violations	41	Of those failing to appear, after 1 year still fugitives	5
Felony driving offenses	73	Parole violations	23		

total of 68 percent of those charged with assault, 71 percent charged with weapons offenses, and 73 percent charged with felony driving offenses were released prior to their trial appearance date. Of those charged with rape, 56 percent were released; 49 percent of those charged with burglary and 67 percent of those charged with theft were released prior to trial. Overall, 62 percent of those defendants who lacked a criminal history were pretrial released. In addition, 41 percent of those who had revoked probation and 23 percent who had violated parole conditions were pretrial released. Of those pretrial released, 26 percent were released on their own recognizance (ROR) and 7 percent of the all the defendants were denied bail (or early release). Sixteen percent of those released prior to trial were rearrested, 22 percent failed to appear, and one year later, 5 of the 22 percent remained fugitives.

Federal Defendants and Pretrial Release: In recent study of federal defendants consisting of 34 percent of 56,982 defendants charged with a federal offense, almost one half of them were charged with crimes of violence, immigration, and drug trafficking offenses and were detained by the court for the entire pretrial period at a greater rate than other offenders. Defendants with a criminal history were ordered detained at a greater rate than first-time arrestees: 38 percent of defendants with at least one prior arrest were ordered detained compared to 27 percent of first-time arrestees.

DIVERSION

Most of us agree that an offender should be "accountable" for wrongdoings. Yet, some assume that accountability means punishment through confinement. On the other hand, if accountability and a behavior change can be accomplished through diversion, then it would make sense to utilize that initiative as often as circumstances permit. This idea is supported by the President's Task Force on Crime and is consistent with the Office of Juvenile Justice and Delinquency Prevention (OJJDP) concerning juveniles.[49]

Accountability and its rationale are different from administering punitive sanctions supported by a punishment philosophical perspective. Accountability can relate to rehabilitation and one component of rehabilitation that works well is accepting ownership of inappropriate behavior. Holding a violator "accountable" means that once a defendant is determined to have committed a law-violating behavior by admission or adjudication, he or she should be held responsible for the act through consequences or sanctions.

> "The concept of personal accountability for the consequences of one's conduct, and the allied notion that the person who causes the damage should bear the cost, are at the heart of civil law. It should be no less in criminal law."—The Final Report of the 1982 President's Task Force on Victims of Crime

The consequences or adjudication imposed upon a violator should be pursuant to law and should be proportionate to the offense. The response of the justice system should be applied swiftly, surely, consistently, and "graduated to provide appropriate and effective responses to varying levels of offense seriousness. Offender chronicity, which works best in preventing, controlling, and reducing further law violations."[50]

Accountability helps recovery. For instance, to change a chemically dependent violator, a defendant has to accept the reality of "dependency" and learn individually that he or she is solely responsible for his or her own recovery. It goes without saying that a chemically dependent violator also has to accept the fact that she or he made the decision to engage in substance abuse activity. The defendant must accept the "fault" of the crime.

Without individual responsibility and acknowledgement, it is unlikely that many would be reformed. *Accountability* means ownership of inappropriate behavior and eliminating the denial that often masks the problem. It is hoped that the diversionary program helps a defendant reach this point. That is, one goal of diversion is to change the behavior of the defendant, hopefully on a permanent basis, while enhancing public safety but sparing the incredible expense of confinement.

> **Diversion** is an alternative to an official process that could result in an alternative to arrest, prosecution, or incarceration.

Diversion programs allow an offender to live pretty much the way he or she did (minus criminal activity) prior to apprehension. The defendant can work, have fun with friends, and stay involved with family members without the stigma of official sanctions. A major conceptual rationale underlying diversion is that it reduces offender penetration into the justice system. That is, certain defendants "avoid the danger assumed to be associated with criminal stigmatization and criminal associations"[51] resulting in less future crime.

The thinking goes that some troubled people's misbehavior can be remedied more effectively in a CC program as opposed to a criminal justice sanction or jail.

With a youthful offender (18 to 29 years of age, depending on the state), for instance, diversion might consist of ordering that individual to a community service initiative rather than continuing to process the juvenile through the legal system. Community groups, the courts, police or private agencies, and federal or local government can operate diversion programs. Finally, in this regard, communities prosper through diversion in the sense that the unofficial justice system is addressing serious problems caused by a growing criminal and juvenile justice population by reducing reliance on traditional case processing and working to stem the "revolving door" syndrome.[52]

Eligibility

Generally, eligibility into diversion programs consists of first-time offenders. For instance, an arrested adult for DUI might be ordered to substance abuse counseling rather than face judicial consequences. Which violators are diverted most often from the official process to diversion programs?

- First-time offenders
- Nonviolent offenders
- Offenders who repeat minor offenses because of situations that cannot be resolved by the justice community
- Juveniles

The importance of diversion is that once an individual accepts participation, the justice process is suspended. In effect, an individual gets another chance before facing official penalties. Most first-time offenders appreciate the opportunity to change their behavior, but some reject a second chance. For instance, *community court* in Van Nuys, CA, was developed on a diversion principle to address quality-of-life issues of defendants such as drug addiction, alcoholism, homelessness, poverty, and mental health issues.[53] In October 2001, 399 arrests were processed as eligible for Van Nuys Community Court: an average of 2.2 arrests per day in four reporting districts that make up the Van Nuys (actually this is part of the Los Angeles Police Department) district. Over 280 of these arrests were for drinking in public and the remainder were for violations such as littering and illegal dumping. The court reported a 90 percent success rate for those defendants who took advantage of the community court, but they also reported that 50 percent of the arrestees never appeared in court. The program was implemented in 1999 and policy makers are working hard to enhance this initiative.

History of Diversion: Labeling

The use of diversion has a strong theoretical background based on stigmatization or "labeling" principles. Initially, labeling principles grew from Frank Tannenbaum's classic work on the "dramatization of evil"[54] and were furthered by Edwin Lemert's[55] statements about "secondary deviance." Howard Becker's[56] perspective confirmed the notion that social groups can create deviance through a labeling process beginning with certain (not necessarily criminal) acts called "deviant" and treating individuals who commit those acts as "outsiders."

Labeling Perspective[57]
    In its purest form:

- An individual is thought to be different from others (i.e., a juvenile delinquent, mentally challenged, an ex-convict).
- Authority (criminal justice community) provides a label or "tags" an individual.
- Others, or "an audience" respond to the label (as opposed to the person).
- The labeled person is more inclined to accept the label as that of an outsider because of how others treat him or her.
- The labeled person acts out the "labeled behavior" or behavior associated with the label.
- The new behavior of the "labeled" person matches the label or self-fulfilling prophecy.

A real concern is that a label can elicit negative responses toward the label as opposed to responses toward the person. Recall how some of your friends reacted toward another student who allegedly cheated on an exam at school or cheated on their significant other. Sometimes those responses are so strong and so overpowering for whatever reason that the labeled person has difficulty separating their real behavior from labeled behavior even when the label isn't true. The labeled individual may alter his or her behavior to fit the label and actually cheat. "You treat me like a cheater, so I might as well enjoy the benefits of being a cheater," might be a typical response from the labeled individual. Accepting the label and acting it out is called a *self-fulfilling prophecy*. Imagine how a youngster might behave if called a juvenile delinquent and, in fact, has not demonstrated delinquent behavior? Labeled individuals might conform to the behavior associated with the label and act out those expected patterns of behavior even when the individual never behaved that way in the past.

Criticism to Labeling

Some criticism about labeling perspectives is that it is largely untested; therefore, by definition, it is not a true theory. Becker acknowledges that point and recommends that this social reaction perspective should be empirically tested to determine its continuity.[58] Another criticism is its failure to explain primary deviance. Both Lemert and Becker believe that primary deviance is influenced by many different and changing variables. Is the labeling perspective a "causal" factor of crime?[59]

Becker qualifies his approach to social reaction theory by stating that some groups of rule-breakers may be able to choose alternative courses of action. However, it appears that labels are powerful devices that could motivate individuals to perform positively or negatively depending on many variables. The "power" of the label or social reaction depends on the authority of the group or person doing the labeling and the individual receiving it. The idea in diversion is not to label offenders as "jail birds."

Growth of Diversion

Pretrial release during the 1960s programs identified many defendants as simply being cycled through the system. Diversion began as a concept of interrupting that cycle by intervening in a balanced attempt to aid a defendant and the system at the same time. This balancing act or intervention was aimed at reducing the likelihood of a future arrest and to relieve an overcrowded justice system. The centerpiece of diversion was to suspend the official justice processing of a defendant's case. To this day, the suspension of forward prosecution of a case remains the hallmark of the diversion process.

Early diversion programs, such as New York's Manhattan Court Employment Project and Washington, DC's Crossroads Program, focused on socioeconomic concerns as the basis for arrest, thus they developed employment-based intervention strategies.[60]

Manhattan Court Employment Project and Crossroad

The Manhattan Court Employment Project in New York City and the Crossroad Program in Washington, DC were good examples of employment intervention strategies. Both programs utilized the employment program, Manpower Services, as their primary strategy. It was discovered that although this intervention was helpful, more than employment services were needed by defendants to accomplish the goal of reducing recidivism. The knowledge gained through those programs, along with a number of other programs, provided the basis for development of the field of pretrial diversion.

Pretrial Diversion

Pretrial diversion (PTD) is a form of probation authorized by most states, Washington, DC, and the federal government. Pretrial diversion is like deferred adjudication in that there is no finding of guilt. Eligibility can be at the pre-charge stage or at a point (prior to trial) at which a PTD agreement is effected. Participation in the program is voluntary and the participant must sign a contract agreeing to waive his or her rights to a speedy trial and presentment of his or her case within the statute of limitations.[61] The divertee must have advice of counsel, and if he or she cannot afford counsel, one will be appointed.

Optimally, the PTD program is tailored to the offender's needs and may include many employment and educational programs, including psychiatric care. For instance, the San Francisco Pretrial Diversion project provides first-time misdemeanor offenders with court-proceeding alternatives and services such as anger management; parenting, domestic violence, and substance abuse counseling; and job training; and education.[62] Many jurisdictions add restitution or forms of community service as part of the pretrial diversion program. Successful completion of program/termination from program results in a decline of prosecution.

Current Diversion Programs

Diversion programs have evolved throughout the United States in a variety of forms and use a broad set of approaches. Today, diversion programs incorporate basic practices with the overall goal of reducing recidivism through rehabilitation without linking a defendant to official justice sanctions. The correctional model that supports this strategy is couched in both rehabilitation and prevention philosophical models as opposed to just deserts and control models.

Standards of Diversion Programs

The National Association of Pretrial Services Agencies (NAPSA) developed a set of standards for diversion programs, that was updated in 1995. The standards describe diversion as "a strategy designed to offer nonpunitive case processing to selected individuals charged with a crime." NAPSA developed many sound standards to help guide diversion programs. For example, it:

- Offers persons charged with criminal offenses alternatives to traditional criminal justice or juvenile justice proceedings.
- Permits participation by the accused only on a voluntary basis.
- Allows the accused access to defense counsel prior to a decision to participate.
- Occurs no sooner than the filing of formal charges and no later than a final adjudication of guilt.
- Develops service plans in conjunction with the defendant that address the needs of that defendant and are structured to assist that person in avoiding behavior likely to lead to future arrests.
- Results in dismissal of charges or its equivalent if the divertee successfully completes the diversion process.

In some jurisdictions, the diversion process is established through legislation that provides for systematic application of appropriate standards and assessment principles. In other circumstances, participant agreements with prosecutors form the basis for the process. As expected, diversion, especially successful diversion, varies depending on many factors.

Diversion Services

Diversion programs offer a variety of services, including services through community referrals. Most diversion programs are comprised of three components:[63]

1. Treatment: To overcome problems leading to an offense
    -   Drug awareness and counseling programs
    -   Parental skills
    -   Decision-making or problem-solving skills
    -   Anger management
    -   Vocational skills
2. Sanction: Violators owe a debt to society
    -   Involves some form of community service such as volunteering at school program or crisis hotline
3. Supervision: It is expected that participants follow rules and requirements
    -   Drug tests
    -   Curfew
    -   Restrictions on peer association

The diversity of the types of interventions is often a response to the criminal justice population unique to each community. The strength of an effective diversion program is linked to its ability to match clients to the most appropriate intervention based on identified need, not just as a response to a specific crime. However, NAPSA says that what works best in diversion programs is:

-   Needs assessment
-   Individualized intervention plan
-   Contract with the defendant to delineate program requirements leading to a dismissal of the charges (success) or failure (continued prosecution)

Rehabilitation and prevention approaches support the diversion process. Also couched in these perspectives is the idea that a defendant is a member of a social environment that reinforces criminal culpability. Therefore, diversion programs are designed to aid the following without compromising public safety:

-   Enhance defendant reform
-   Reduce recidivism levels
-   Reduce cumulative impact affects

Thus, diversion aids the defendant, community, and the mission of the justice community. Furthermore, the most successful diversion programs are those that provide more intensive and comprehensive services.[64] Also, experienced caseworkers are essential to a program's success. For example, a program in St. Louis found that experienced caseworkers produced greater behavioral change than did less experienced caseworkers.[65]

Because diversion initiatives are utilized for first-time and often youthful offenders, especially juveniles, examining successful results among juveniles might be helpful in understanding why it is an important strategy.

JUVENILES AND DIVERSION

There is a great concern with inadvertently stigmatizing young, nonviolent offenders who committed petty acts that could be handled outside the formal system. Diversion is "an attempt to divert, or channel out, youthful offenders from the juvenile justice system."[66] Conceptually, diversion is based on the theory that processing certain youth through the juvenile justice system will do more harm than good.[67]

Many youths are arrested each year. For instance, in 2000, police agencies made an estimated 2.4 million arrests of persons under the age of 18. Juvenile arrests in 2000 consisted of 16 percent of all violent crime arrests and 32 percent of all property crime in the United States.[68] Interestingly, juvenile violent crime arrest rates in 2000 were at an all-time low since 1985, and 41 percent below the peak year of 1994. In Chapters 12 and 13, juveniles will be discussed in more detail, but for right now our focus is on juveniles and diversion. However, such a discussion must include substance abuse because substance abuse is a common characteristic of approximately 80 percent of all juveniles apprehended for criminal activities.[69] Therefore, breaking the cycle of juvenile crime implies that the cycle of substance abuse and juveniles must become part of any intervention strategy.

Substance Abuse and Juveniles

According to the National Household Survey on Drug Abuse, 11 percent of youths aged 12 to 17 reported current use of illicit drugs in 2001. This was an increase from 10 percent in 2000.[70] Among this age group in 2001, the percent using illicit drugs in the past 30 days prior to the interview was higher for boys (11 percent) than for girls (10 percent). Marijuana was the major illicit drug used for this age group. Eight percent of youths currently use marijuana.

Percentages (Rounded) of High School Students Reporting Drug Use (2002)[71]

Student Drug Use	Eighth Grade	Tenth Grade	Twelfth Grade
Past month use	10	21	25
Past year use	18	35	41
Lifetime use	25	45	53

Substance Abuse and Problematic Behavior

Youth substance abuse leads to many problems including the development of delinquent behavior, antisocial attitudes, and health-related issues.[72] Persistent substance abuse by young people leads to:[73]

- Academic difficulties
- Health-related problems (including mental health)
- Low self-respect
- Low self-confidence
- Poor peer relationships
- Physical or sexual abuse
- Involvement with the juvenile justice system

Additionally, there are consequences for family members, the community, and society.[74] Substance abuse among youth is strongly linked to delinquency. Arrest, adjudication, and intervention by the juvenile justice system are eventual consequences for many youth who engage in alcohol and other drug use argues the Office of Juvenile Justice and Delinquency Prevention in Washington, DC.[75] Check their website at: http://ojjdp.ncjrs.org/ But, substance abuse does not directly cause delinquent behavior, and delinquency does not directly cause alcohol and other drug use.[76]

Substance Abuse, Crime, and Diversion Initiatives Among Juveniles

Substance abuse includes both illicit drug and alcohol use. Drug use is related to crime in multiple ways. Most directly, it is a crime to use, possess, manufacture, or distribute drugs classified as having a potential for abuse (such as cocaine, heroin, marijuana, and amphetamines). Drugs are related to crime through the effects they have on the user's behavior and by generating violence and other illegal activity in connection with drug trafficking.[77]

Substance abuse is associated with both violent and income-generating crimes by youth. In turn, this increases fear among community residents and the demand for juvenile and criminal justice services, thereby increasing the burden on these resources. Gangs, drug trafficking, prostitution, and growing numbers of youth homicides are among the social and criminal justice problems often linked to adolescent substance abuse. And as the fear of crime intensifies, community members demand control and punishment as the primary response from the justice community as opposed to rehabilitation and prevention. On the other hand, community corrections advocates, through diversionary initiatives such as drug and teen court, see substance abuse guidance as the catalyst to change juvenile behavior toward drugs and alcohol, subsequently reducing crime and enhancing public safety.

There is a lot of evidence that links substance abuse and juveniles (and adults, too) to crime. In one study, it was learned that more than 39 percent of the youth confined were under the influence of drugs at the time of their current offense.[78] In another study of 113 delinquent youth in a state detention facility, 82 percent of them reported daily use of alcohol and other drugs just prior to admission to the detention facility, 14 percent were regular users (more than two times weekly), and 4 percent reported occasional use.[79] Finally, The 1996–1997 National Parents' Resource Institute for Drug Education (PRIDE) Study shows the percentage of 6th through 12th grade students who reported that they had used various substances and were involved in threatening or delinquent activities.[80] The percentage of youth who were involved in these activities and had not used alcohol or other drugs was substantially lower.

Substance abuse and youth, especially impulsive or quick-tempered youth, could easily overburden an already overworked justice system. Casper, a youth counselor at a detention facility in Charlotte, North Carolina made his position clear, "Take a hot-tempered kid, feed'em a beer or two and a hit of angel dust [cocaine], plac'em in a situation where he's 'dissed' [disrespected], and the next thing is, he's kic'en ass so bad, he whines up here. He's angry with the cops, the advocates who tried to help'em, the intake folks, and even the people who transported him here. If he's black or brown with a temper and a drug problem, he'll be a permanent guest of the state."[81]

Drug Court: As a Diversion Initiative

Title V of the Violent Crime Control Law Enforcement Act of 1994 provided initiatives to local government to develop *drug courts* that divert offenders from official process. One purpose of drug courts is to provide nonviolent, substance abusing youths and adults with sanctions and services necessary to change their deviant behavior.[82] Although there are drug courts for largely first-time offenders, many of their effects are directed at youths. The juvenile drug court is a unique community approach that attempts to build strong community partnerships and enhances the capacity of partners to assist in the habilitation of substance-abusing youth and, often, their families.

How Juvenile Drug Court Works

A juvenile drug court is a docket or a caseload within a juvenile court where selected delinquency cases, including status offenders, are referred. Youth referred to drug court are identified as having problems with alcohol and/or other drugs. The juvenile drug court judge maintains close oversight of each case. The judge leads and works as a member of a team that can be comprised of representatives from treatment, juvenile justice, social services, school and vocational training programs, law enforcement, probation, the prosecution, and the defense.[83] In this model, the juvenile's progress is generally monitored by a judge who relies on a variety of professionals to assess needs, recommend services, monitor behaviors, and apply sanctions when a lack of improvement is evident. The team decides on a plan to address substance abuse and related problems of a specific youth and his or her family.[84] The goals of the court are to:

- Provide immediate intervention, treatment, and structure in the lives of a juvenile who uses drugs through ongoing, active oversight and monitoring by the drug court judge.

- Improve the level of functioning in a youth's environment, address problems that may be contributing to drug use, and develop/strengthen their ability to lead crime- and drug-free lives.

- Provide juveniles with skills that will aid in leading productive substance-free and crime-free lives—including skills related to educational development, sense of self-worth, and capacity to develop positive relationships in the community.

- Strengthen families of drug-involved youth by improving their capability to provide structure and guidance to their children.

- Promote accountability of juvenile offenders and those who provide services to them.

Most communities that establish juvenile drug courts initiate programs that maximize intensive judicial intervention, including supervision of juveniles and the families of those juveniles. The rationale is that this level of intervention is not generally available through the traditional juvenile court process.[85]

The OJP Drug Court Clearinghouse and Technical Assistance Project advises that as of November 26, 2002, 47 states had implemented drug courts and three additional states were planning drug courts plus the District of Columbia, Puerto Rico, Guam, and two federal districts.[86]

One such program is the Youthful Diversion Program (YDP) in the Commonwealth of Massachusetts. The District Attorney's Office (DA) suggests that the YDP was created in response to widespread concern about the effects of underage substance abuse. However, a youthful offender, according to the DA, can include a first-time offender from age 17 to 21. Individuals who have been processed in the past through any other diversion program or criminal court system are ineligible. The referable offenses to the YDP are:

- Minor in possession of alcohol
- Possession of class D (possession of less than 3 grams of cocaine)
- Disorderly conduct
- Public drinking
- Disturbing the peace
- Minor purchasing or attempting to purchase alcoholic beverages
- Trespassing

Youths who enter the program are required to sign a contract in which they agree to participate in counseling and education and perform community services. The educational group provides young people with an opportunity to receive information about substance abuse and other high-risk behaviors. It is hoped that they will be able to apply their new knowledge to their own lifestyles. Successful completion of the program will result in the youth not having a court record for the offense that brought him or her to the attention of the court.[87] There is a sense that punitive sanctions are not necessarily the most attractive methods of aiding juveniles. Treatment and prevention are used as diversionary techniques to replace the typical process of the justice system. Additionally, although juveniles have a free will to choose their destiny, it is believed that the environmental issues can be persuasive tools in helping a juvenile make crime-free decisions.

Teen Courts

As in a traditional juvenile court, in teen courts young defendants go through an intake process, a preliminary review of charges, a hearing, and sentencing.[88] But teen courts are comprised of fellow teens. For instance, charges may be presented to the court by a 15-year-old "prosecutor." Defendants are represented by a 16-year-old "defense attorney." Other youth may serve as jurors, court clerks, and bailiffs. Some teen courts have a youth "judge" (or panel of youth judges) who choose the best disposition or sanction for each case.

> The rationale for teen court is that it takes advantage of the most powerful forces in the life of an adolescent—peer approval and reaction to peer pressure.

Another way to think about this is to say that youth typically respond better to pro-social peers than to adult authority figures.[89]

Teen courts are used for first-time juvenile offenders generally between the ages of 10 to 15 charged with a nonserious violation (e.g., shoplifting, vandalism, or disorderly conduct). Typically, young offenders are offered teen court as a voluntary alternative in lieu of more formal handling by the traditional juvenile justice system.

> Adults are involved in the teen court process as program administers and they are responsible for essential functions such as budgeting, planning, and personnel. In many programs, adults supervise courtroom activities and coordinate community service placements where youth work to fulfill the terms of their dispositions. In some programs, adults act as the judges while teens serve as attorneys and jurors. The key to a teen court program is the significant role youth play in the deliberation of charges and the imposition of sanctions on young offenders.

Teen courts are seen as a potentially effective alternative to traditional juvenile courts staffed with paid professionals such as lawyers, judges, and probation officers. In addition to the advantages of offenders being "judged" by their peers, the volunteer youth attorneys and judges probably learn more about the legal system than they could in a classroom. The presence of a teen court may also encourage the entire community to take a more active role in responding to juvenile crime. Teen courts offer at least four potential benefits:[90]

- **Accountability:** Teen courts help ensure young offenders are held accountable for their illegal behavior, even when their offenses are relatively minor and would not likely result in sanctions from traditional juvenile courts.

- **Timeliness:** An effective teen court can move young offenders from arrest to sanctions within a matter of days rather than the months that may pass with traditional juvenile courts. This rapid response may increase the positive impact of court sanctions, regardless of their severity.

- **Cost savings:** Teen courts usually depend heavily on youth and adult volunteers. If managed properly, they may handle a substantial number of offenders at relatively little cost to the community. The average annual cost for operating a teen court is $32,822.

- **Community cohesion:** A well-structured and expansive teen court program may affect the entire community by increasing public appreciation of the legal system, enhancing community-court relationships, encouraging greater respect for the law among youth, and promoting volunteerism among both adults and youth.

It's too soon to determine the effectiveness of teen courts because evaluation is in the early stages. However, regardless of the limited evidence, teen courts are increasingly in use across the United States.

Successful Diversion Initiatives Among Youth

It appears that recidivism is affected by diversion among juveniles. For instance, in the recent study, it was recommended that breaking the cycle between substance abuse and juvenile crime should become the primary goal of the justice community.[91] Why? Because the researchers discovered that substance abuse intervention programs could help reduce recidivism rates of even serious juvenile offenders. They argue that graduated sanctions work best. That is, graduated sanctions hold juveniles accountable for their actions and, at the same time, reward them for positive progress toward rehabilitation. Graduated sanctions utilize a carrot-and-stick approach to motivate the progress of juveniles in treatment: Good behavior (staying drug-free or avoiding delinquent actions) results in increased freedom or other rewards, whereas negative behavior results in severe restrictions or a more intensive therapeutic environment.[92] Based on an individual's progress, sanctions and therapeutic interventions can be made more or less intense. If an offender lapses into alcohol or drug (AOD) use and/or delinquent behavior at any point in the treatment process, graduated sanctions involving placing the juvenile in a high-security, more intense therapeutic environment are applied.

Another study focused primarily on probation and parole among juveniles and found similar results.[93] The impact of those interventions on recidivism was related most strongly to the juveniles' characteristics, particularly offense histories. Interestingly, interventions were more effective for juveniles who were confined for more serious crimes than those youths whose offenses were less serious, which offers good reason to believe that such noninstitutional interventions would be equally effective if used appropriately.

Those who support diversion cite studies such as the one in Colorado that compared an experimental group of diverted youth with a control group who received traditional juvenile justice strategies. The diversion program administered individual, parental, and family counseling, resulting in significantly lower recidivism rates than in the control group.[94]

The Adolescent Diversion Project in Michigan includes juveniles accused of serious criminal acts and juveniles with status offenses.[95] The study concluded that diversion could safely be extended beyond status and minor offenders. However, most of the defendants in the program admitted to criminal acts and the program reported lower recidivism rates than those reported for traditional court-processed cases.

The Rand Corporation also found that cases involving cocaine addiction and the use of rehabilitation and treatment outside jail were approximately seven times more effective than extended sentences, and two to three times more effective than those with shorter sentences who also tried rehabilitative strategies.[96]

The most successful diversion programs have been those that provide more intensive and comprehensive services.[97] The use of experienced youth caseworkers is especially important to a program's success. For example, a program in St. Louis, Missouri found that experienced youth caseworkers engendered greater behavioral changes in the youth than did less experienced caseworkers.[98]

CRITICISMS OF DIVERSION INITIATIVES

Diversion has it critics. Diversion's critics are numerous but help keep programs on track. Because criminal justice represents a host of difficult complex choices, critics play a key role in enhancing programs of every type including diversion programs. On one side of the dilemma are diverse participants with unlimited needs and risk categories. On the other side is a diverse justice community with its fragmented and limited authority, resources, goals, and missions in both public and private entities. With fragmentation comes conflicting expectations, findings, and conclusions from such a widespread, disjointed, and complicated social experiment.[99] Although many studies show that diversion programs are successful in reducing subsequent deviance, those studies are balanced by studies that find little impact. In certain cases, diversion programs were found to have detrimental properties, especially with recidivism.[100]

"Soft on Crime" Issues

Critics say diversion is "soft on crime." That is, violators deserve to be punished and that means one thing—prison or jail. For serious offenders, they might be right. However, convincing just desert and control advocates that rehabilitation and prevention are appropriate for some offenders is difficult because punishment and control rationales are entrenched ideals in the culture of many justice professions and are reinforced by the media as "the best response to offenders." Also, it is believed that success of the justice community depends on how punitively it responds to offenders. That is, the justice community responds after a wrongful act has occurred. Efficient and successful police organizations are measured by arrest rates, courts are measured by conviction rates and imposed long-term sentences, and corrections are measured by harsh supervision strategies. Nothing is wrong with those perspectives when utilized among certain violators.[101]

Budget Problems

When just desert and control advocates have authority over budget allocations linked to diversion programs, it is unlikely that appropriate resources are provided. Resources include funds, personnel, supplies, and, for that matter, even safe and appropriate buildings and places to conduct the business of the programs. Funds are also required to pay personnel, office expenses, facility rentals, and building maintenance.

Program Failures

Diversion programs are not always successful.[102] Some defendants fail to meet specified conditions and restrictions. For instance, some participants fail to meet program sessions, curfew, and restrictions. Others commit crime or engage in drug and alcohol activities.[103] In addition, diversion personnel fail because of enormous caseloads, lack of skill or training, failure to monitor defendants in an appropriate manner, failure to conduct program sessions professionally, or failure because of other priorities. Whatever the reasons for failure, they are costly to the community, the participants, and the mission of community corrections. Costs can include, among other things, increased victimization, funds, and community stability.[104] Other concerns raised about diversion programs include those related to prejudice, discrimination, civil rights violations, and the issue of net-widening.[105]

Juvenile Diversion Criticism

Researchers found that intervention, whether received in a traditional juvenile justice setting or in an alternative program, resulted in increased levels of perceived labeling and self-reported delinquency among youth. Two other studies supported this finding.[106] Other concerns raised about diversion programs include those related to prejudice, discrimination, civil rights violations, and the issue of net-widening. It should come as little surprise that conflicting expectations, findings, and conclusions emerged from such a widespread, disjointed, and complicated social experiment.[107] Although many studies show that diversion programs are successful in reducing subsequent deviance, these studies are balanced by studies that find no impact. In certain cases, diversion programs were found to have detrimental properties.[108]

RESTITUTION AND COMMUNITY SERVICES AS DIVERSION

Restitution can be part of a diversion program, can stand alone as a diversion strategy by itself, or can be part of community service. Restitution holds offenders partially or fully accountable for the financial losses suffered by the victims of their wrong-doings.[109] It can be imposed by both juvenile and adult criminal courts to compensate victims for out-of-pocket expenses and losses that are a direct result of a crime. It can be ordered by the courts. Restitution is practiced in many jurisdictions linked to many different processes, can be recommended to adults and juveniles, and can include community service. Monetary payment from an offender to a victim is the most common form of restitution. In some jurisdictions and depending upon the crime, monetary payment is made to an agency, which in turn provides for the loss incurred by the victim.

Community Services as a Diversion Initiative

Community service is a diversion initiative that orders defendants to perform "free labor" to benefit the community. Community services provided by an offender is referred to as "symbolic restitution" because restoration for the harm done is produced through work benefiting the entire community instead of a specific victim. The benefits arising from restitution and community service as diversion strategies include:

- Financial relief from losses incurred by a victim
- Enhancement of a defendant's comfort in the community
- Community is allowed to see defendant in a helping role
- Restitution and community service better fit the "crime"[110]
- Expense of processing a defendant through the entire system is saved
- Reduced confinement costs

Community service can help a defendant, especially a youth, in a feeling of accomplishment when the task is completed, and provides a way for the defendant to atone for the offense. In a sense, restitution and community service can restore some level of self-respect to the defendant.

In total, restitution and community service help create conditions for a defendant to atone for his or her mistakes and remain in the community as a valid member. It also allows an avenue for defendant, victim, community, and the justice system to build solidarity and enhance informal strategies of control. If Emile Durkheim, in his classic work about community solidarity, is correct, then it would be expected that the greater the bond between community members, the less likely an individual will engage in acts of deviance.[111]

Background of Restitution as Diversion

In the early years of America, imprisonment and fines were the chief punitive sanctions used by the justice system. In the decade that followed the 1982 passage of the Victim and Witness Protection Act, every state passed statutes addressing restitution, most following the lead of the federal model.[112] But states continue to amend their statutes, creating a patchwork of financial reparations for victims across the country. As of 1995, 29 states had followed federal law in mandating restitution in many cases, unless the presiding judge offers compelling reasons not to do so. Some states, however, mandate restitution only in cases involving violent crimes, whereas others mandate restitution only in cases involving property crimes. Concerning court cases, the court can order restitution after a guilty plea has been entered.

The amount to be given to a victim or a designated "victim" agency usually depends on the damage caused by the defendant. In some cases, the amount and the time frame in which the amount is to be paid should be in keeping with the ability of defendant. The order usually indicates how the funds are to be given to the victim—directly or through some probation office or court clerk.

SUMMARY

Pretrial release is release after an arrest but while awaiting trial, and chief concerns are flight risks and public safety. The established principles that help guide those concerns include seriousness of the crime; the defendant's criminal history, community ties, age, and gender; eligibility criterion into pretrial release and diversion programs; risk assessment; and substance abuse testing. Conditions of pretrial release include reporting to a pretrial agency, maintaining a stable residence, and among others, participating in alcohol or drug treatment programs and remaining crime-free. Sometimes defendants must refrain from interaction with complaining witnesses and criminal associates. Defendants who are unnecessarily detained tend to plead guilty, are convicted, are sentenced, and serve full sentences more often than others.

Cumulative impact implies that in some high-impact communities, more than 10 percent of the adult males are arrested, convicted, and incarcerated in any given year. The combined effect would destabilize a community as a whole, which in turn would exacerbate poverty, broken families, and unsupervised youth. Pretrial release and diversion programs can help stabilize communities.

Diversion is an alternative to an official process that could result in an avoidance of arrest, prosecution, or incarceration. One goal is to change the behavior of the defendant while enhancing public safety but sparing the incredible expense of confinement. A major conceptual rationale underlying diversion is that it reduces offender penetration into the justice system.

Diversion has a strong theoretical background based on stigmatization or "labeling" principles. The labeling process is described as starting with an individual who is thought to be different from others. Authority "tags" an individual and others (the audience) respond to the label, not the person. A labeled person is more inclined to accept the label as that of an outsider. Individuals processed through the justice system receive a label that can promote the acting out of the label even if the individual were law-abiding.

Pretrial diversion is like deferred adjudication in that there is no finding of guilt. Eligibility can be at the pre-charge stage and participation is voluntary. Standards that help guide diversion include the ideas, among others, that permit participation by the accused on a voluntary basis and that the accused have access to defense counsel. The services of diversion include treatment, sanctions, and supervision.

Because substance abuse is a common characteristic of approximately 80 percent of all juveniles apprehended for criminal activities, there is a link between diversion, juveniles, and substance abuse. Initiatives by local government include developing drug courts to help divert offenders from official process. One purpose of drug courts is to provide nonviolent, substance abusing adults and youths with sanctions and services necessary to change their behavior. Also, teen courts are much like traditional juvenile courts because young defendants go through an intake process and so on, but teen courts have other young people responsible for the process. Fellow teens are the lawyers, prosecutors, and judges.

The most successful diversion programs have been those that provide more intensive and comprehensive services toward substance abuse intervention programs, graduated sanctions, and rehabilitative strategies.

Restitution holds offenders partially or fully accountable for the financial losses suffered by their victims. It can be imposed by both juvenile and adult criminal courts to compensate victims for out-of-pocket expenses and losses that are a direct result of a crime. Community service is a diversion initiative that orders a defendant to engage in specific "free labor" to benefit the community.

DISCUSSION QUESTIONS

1. Define pretrial release and explain its standards of release. In what way might you agree with pretrial release?

2. Identify the conditions of pretrial release and its objectives Of those conditions, which do you feel are they most important issues? Least important? Why?

3. Describe the reasons many suspects fail to appear at court and how attendance can be improved. In what way might you agree with those reasons of not appearing?

4. Identify the hardships of unnecessarily detained suspects. How can many of the hardships experienced by some individuals be reduced?

5. Explain cumulative impact and its effect upon a community. In what way might you disagree with this perspective?

6. Define diversion and explain its rationale.

7. Describe some of the history of diversion.

8. Define pretrial diversion and explain its importance to the accused and to the justice system.

9. Identify the standards that help guide diversion programs. In what way do you agree with some of those standards and in what way might you disagree with them?

10. Explain the link between substance abuse, juveniles, and crime.

11. Describe drug and teen courts and explain their benefits.

12. Identify successful diversion initiatives among the young. In what way might a graduated program also work among adult offenders?

13. Explain the role restitution plays with diversion initiatives.

NOTES

1. Bureau of Justice Statistics (2003). *Sourcebook of criminal justice statistics 2002.* Albany, NY: U.S. Department of Justice, Office of Justice Programs, Estimated Number of Arrests (Table 4.1, p. 342). Retrieved online January 10, 2005: http://www.albany.edu/sourcebook/1995/pdf/t41.pdf

2. Bureau of Justice Statistics (2003). *Pretrial release and detention statistics.* Washington, DC: U.S. Department of Justice, Office of Justice Programs. Retrieved January 10, 2005: http://www.ojp.usdoj.gov/bjs/pretrial.htm

3. As the U.S. Supreme Court noted in a decision upholding the pretrial detention provisions in federal law for persons deemed to present a threat to the community, "(i)n our society liberty is the norm, and detention prior to trial or without trial is the carefully limited exception." *U.S. v. Salerno,* 481 U.S. 739 (1987).

4. John S. Goldkamp and Michael D.White (1998). *Restoring accountability in pretrial release: The Philadelphia Pretrial Release Supervision Experiments, Philadelphia.* Unpublished report. Crime and Justice Research Institute (pp. 154–157). Retrieved online January 13, 2005: http://www.ncjrs.org/rr/vol3_1/37.html

5. Christy A. Visher (1990). Using drug testing to identify high-risk defendants on release: A study in the District of Columbia. *Journal of Criminal Justice, 18*(4), 321–332. Adele V. Harrell, Ojmarrh Mitchell, Jeffrey Merrill, and Douglas Marlowe (2003, February 28). Evaluation of breaking the cycle. *The Urban Institute.* Retrieved online January 10, 2005: http://www.urban.org

6. Bureau of Justice Statistics (2000). *State court processing statistics. Felony defendants in large urban counties, 2000.* Washington, DC. U.S. Department of Justice, Office of Justice Programs (Table 20). Retrieved online January 10, 2005: http://www.ojp.usdoj.gov/bjs/pub/pdf/fdluc00.pdf

7. Pretrial Services Resource Center (2004). *Front-End decision making: A national perspective–1999.* Retrieved online January 10, 2005: http://www.pretrial.org/Front-Endpercent20Decision percent20Making.doc

8. David N. Falcone (2005). *Dictionary of American criminal justice, criminology, & criminal law.* Upper Saddle River, NJ: Prentice Hall, 19.

9. Bureau of Justice Statistics (2000). *State court processing statistics. Felony defendants in large urban counties, 2000* (p. 44).

10. C. E. Ares, A. Rankin, and H. Sturz (1963, January). The Manhattan Bail Project: An interim report on the use of pre-trial parole. *New York University Law Review, 38,* 68–95. John A. Carver. (1991). Pretrial drug testing: An essential step in bail

reform. *Journal of Public Law,* 5. John A. Carver, Director of the D.C. Pretrial Services Agency (1996, Spring). Pretrial urine testing: Implications for drug courts from a decade's positive experience. *On Balance,* 2–3.

11. John S. Goldkamp (1985). Danger and detention: A second generation of bail reform. *The Journal of Criminal Law & Criminology,* 76.

12. Bureau of Justice Statistics (2000). *State court processing statistics. Felony defendants in large urban counties.* Washington, DC: U.S. Department of Justice, Office of Justice Programs, 44.

13. Frank Schmalleger (2003). *Criminal justice today* (7th ed.). Upper Saddle River, NJ: Prentice Hall (p. 344).

14. Bureau of Justice Statistics. (2000). *State court processing statistics. Felony defendants in large urban counties, 2000,* 16.

15. National Advisory Commission on Criminal Justice Standards and Goals. *The Courts* (1973). Washington, DC. U.S. Government Printing Office (p. 37).

16. Bureau of Justice Statistics (2000). *State court processing statistics. Felony defendants in large urban counties, 2000,* 27.

17. U.S.C., Sec. 3146. Although the Bail Reform Act of 1966 only applied to federal courts and Washington, DC, many states emulated the federal law in creating a presumption in favor of release on recognizance in their own statutes.

18. *Findlaw Legal Dictionary.* Retrieved online January 10, 2005: http://www.findlaw .com

19. *American Bar Association Project on minimum standards for criminal justice, standards relating to pre-trial release* (1965). New York: Institute for Judicial Administration.

20. Pretrial Services Resource Center. 1010 Vermont Ave., NW Suite 300 Washington, DC 20005.

21. State of Texas Court System. Retrieved online December 1, 2004: http://www .state.tx.us/category.jsp?language=eng&categoryId=8.2. And, Todd R. Clear and Harry R. Dammer (2000). *The offender in the community.* Belmont, CA: Wadsworth, 126.

22. Barry Mahoney, Bruce D. Beaudin, John A. Carver, III, Daniel B. Ryan, and Richard B. Hoffman (2001, March). *Pretrial services programs: Responsibilities and potential.* NCJR 181939. Retrieved online January 10, 2005: www.ncjrs .org/pdffiles1/nij/181939.pdf

23. Barry Mahoney et al. (2001), 48.

24. Barry Mahoney et al. (2001), 49.

25. Barry Mahoney et al. (2001), 49.

26. Belinda Rodgers McCarthy, Bernard J. McCarthy, Jr., and Matthew C. Leone (2001). *Community-based corrections* (4th ed.). Belmont, CA: Wadsworth, 43.

27. Spencer P. M. Harrington (1999, May). *New Bedlam: Jails—not psychiatric hospitals. Now care for the indigent mentally ill. The Humanist, 59*(3), 1–3. Retrieved online May 14, 2004: http://www.findarticles.com/

28. Robert Panzarella and Alicea O. Justin (1997). Police tactics in incidents with mentally disturbed persons. *Policing: An International Journal of Police Strategies & Management, 20*(2), 326–338.

29. Unpublished statistic courtesy of James Fyfe, Director of Training, New York City Police Department. (2004).

30. Fox Butterfield (1998, March 5). Prisons replace hospitals for the nation's mentally ill. *New York Times,* A1.

31. Spencer P. M. Harrington (1999, May).

32. Stevens H. Clarke and Susan T. Kurtz (1983). The importance of interim decisions to felony trial court dispositions. *Journal of Criminal Law and Criminology, 74*; also see Michael R. Gottfredson and Don M. Gottfredson (1983). *Decision making in criminal justice: Toward a rational exercise of discretion.* New York: Plenum.

33. John Clark and D. Alan Henry (1996). *The pretrial release decision making process: Goals, current practices, and challenges.* Pretrial Services Resource Center from the National Institute of Justice, Abt Associates, Inc. (OJP–94–007). Retrieved online July 30, 2004: http://www.pretrial.org/ptrdecision1996.doc

34. Randall G. Shelden (2001). *Controlling the dangerous classes: A critical introduction to the history of criminal justice.* Boston: Allyn Bacon (pp. 16, 69–108).

35. Lawrence W. Sherman, Patrick R. Gartin, and Michael E. Buerger (1989). Hot spots of predatory crime: Routine activities and the criminology of place. *Criminology, 27,* 27–55.

36. Eric Cadora and Charles Swartz (2000). *Community justice atlas.* Center for Alternative Sentencing and Employment Services (CASES). Unpublished Report.

37. Todd R. Clear and Eric Cadora (2001). *Community justice.* Belmont, CA: Wadsworth, 2.

38. Wesley G. Skogan (1992). *Disorder and decline: Crime and the spiral of decay in American neighborhoods.* Berkeley, CA: University of California Press.

39. Emile Durkheim (1984, 1933). *The division of labor in society.* Translated by W.D. Halls. New York: Free Press. Also Todd R. Clear and Eric Cadora (2001). p. 2. And, Wesley G. Skogan and Susan M. Hartnett (1997). *Community policing, Chicago style.* New York: Oxford (pp. 237–241).

40. *Community-based treatment: The impact of the homeless pretrial release project* (2000, June). San Francisco, CA: Center on Juvenile and Criminal Justice.

41. Donald E. Pryor and Walter F. Smith (2002). Significant research findings concerning pretrial release. *Pretrial Issues, 4*(1), Washington, DC, Pretrial Services Resources Center. Retrieved online January 10, 2005: http://www.pretrial.org. Bureau

of Justice Statistics (1994, November). *Pretrial release of felony defendants, 1992.* National Pretrial Reporting Program. Washington, DC: U.S. Department of Justice, Office of Justice Programs, NCJ 148818. Retrieved online January 10, 2005: http://www.ojp.usdoj.gov/bjs/pub/pdf/nprp92.pdf

42. Joseph B. Vaughn and Victor E. Kappeler say that the first legislation linked to danger laws was the 1970 District of Columbia Court Reform and Criminal Procedure Act. See Joseph B. Vaughn and Victor E. Kappeler (1999). The denial of bail: Pretrial preventive detention. *Criminal Justice Research Bulletin, 3*(6), 1.

43. National Association of Pretrial Sentences Agencies. *The division of standards. Pretrial release standards introduction.* Retrieved online January 10, 2005: http://www.napsa.org/

44. Bureau of Justice Statistics (1994, November 21). *Pretrial release of felony Defendants, 1992.* Washington, DC: Department of Justice, Office of Justice Programs, NCJ–148818.

45. As stated in *The Economist,* June 19, 1999, p. 18; and reported by the National Center for Policy Analysis (NCPA) (2004). Retrieved online January 9, 2005: http://www.ncpa.org/studies/s233/s233.html#41

46. Michael K. Block and Steven J. Twist (1995, April). *Evidence of a failed system: A study of the performance of pretrial release agencies in California.* Washington, DC: American Legislative Exchange Council.

47. Bureau of Justice Statistics (2000, May). *Pretrial release and detention statistics.* Washington, DC: U.S. Department of Justice, Office of Justice Programs. Retrieved online January 10, 2005: http://www.ojp.usdoj.gov/bjs/pretrial.htm

48. Dennis J. Stevens (2006). *Community corrections: An applied approach.* Upper Saddle River, NJ: Prentice Hall. Data provided by Bureau of Justice Statistics (2000, May). Pretrial Release and Detention Statistics, Bureau of Justice Statistics (2003). *Felony defendants in large urban counties, 2000.* Washington, DC: U.S. Department of Justice, Office of Justice Programs, NCJ 202021 Retrieved online January 10, 2005: http://www.ojp.usdoj.gov/bjs/pub/pdf/fdluc00.pdf

49. Office of Juvenile Justice and Delinquency Prevention (2005). Washington, DC: U.S. Department of Justice, Office of Justice Programs. retrieved online January 10, 2005: http://ojjdp.ncjrs.org/

50. *Best practices in juvenile accountability: Overview.* April 2003. *JAIBG Bulletin.* Washington DC: U.S. Department of Justice, Office of Juvenile Justice Delinquency Prevention, NCJ 184745, 1.

51. Thomas Blomberg. *Lecture: Criminology 2002. Widening the net: An anomaly in the evaluation of diversion programs.* Florida State University. Retrieved online January 10, 2005: http://www.criminology.fsu.edu/crimtheory/blomberg/netwidening.html#1

52. The Board of Directors of the National Association of Pretrial Services Agencies, *Performance Standards and Goals for Pretrial Release and Diversion–Diversion* (1995 Revision), 21.

53. Craig Rhudy (2003, May). Van Nuys community court pilot project. *Law and Order, 51*(4), 58–61.

54. Frank Tannenbaum (1938). *Crime and the community.* New York: Columbia University Press.

55. Edwin Lemert (1951). *Social pathology.* New York: McGraw-Hill.

56. Howard S. Becker (1963). *Outsiders: Studies in the sociology of deviance.* New York: Free Press.

57. Dennis J. Stevens (2006). *Community corrections: An applied approach.* Upper Saddle River, NJ: Prentice Hall.

58. Howard S. Becker (1963).

59. Howard S. Becker (1963). Edwin Lemert (1951).

60. The Board of Directors of the National Association of Pretrial Services Agencies, *Performance Standards and Goals for Pretrial Release and Diversion–Diversion* (1995 Revision), 21.

61. U.S. Government Pretrial Diversion, 712 Pretrial and Diversion. Retrieved online January 10, 2005: http://www.usdoj.gov/usao/eousa/foia_reading_room/usam/title9/crm00712.htm

62. San Francisco Pretrial Diversion Project. Retrieved online January 10, 2005: http://www.sfpretrial.com/pretrialdiversion.html

63. Curtis J. Vander Waal, Duane C. McBride, Yvonne M. Terry-McElrath, and Holly VanBuren (2001, May). *Breaking the juvenile drug-crime cycle: Research report.* National Institute of Justice, NIJ186156. Retrieved online April 30, 2004: http://www.ncjrs.org/txtfiles1/nij/186156.txt

64. Joy D. Dryfoos (1990). *Adolescents at risk: Prevalence and prevention.* New York: Oxford University Press.

65. R. A. Feldman, T. E. Caplinger, and J. S. Wodarski (1983). *The St. Louis conundrum: The effective treatment of antisocial youth.* Englewood Cliffs, NJ: Prentice-Hall.

66. J. E. Bynum and W. E. Thompson (1996). *Juvenile delinquency: A sociological approach* (3rd ed.). Needham Heights, MA: Allyn and Bacon (p. 430).

67. R. J. Lundman (1993). *Prevention and control of delinquency* (2nd ed.). New York: Oxford University Press.

68. H. Snyder (2004). *Juvenile Arrests 2000.* Washington, DC: Office of Juvenile Justice and Delinquency Prevention.

69. H. Snyder (2004).

70. Substance Abuse and Mental Health Service Administration. *Results from the 2001 National Household Survey on Drug Abuse: Volume II, Technical Appendices and Selected Data Tables, August 2002.* Retrieved online April 30, 2004: http://www.samhsa.gov/index.aspx

71. *National Survey on Drug Abuse 2002.* Retrieved online January 10, 2005: http://www.samhsa.gov/oas/nhsda/2k1nhsda/vol1/toc.htm

72. Mental health problems, including depression, developmental lags, apathy, withdrawal, and other psychosocial dysfunctions, are frequently linked to substance abuse among adolescents. Substance-abusing youth are at higher risk than nonusers for mental health problems, including depression, conduct problems, personality disorders, suicidal thoughts, attempted suicide, and suicide. Marijuana use, which is prevalent among youth, has been shown to interfere with short-term memory, learning, and psychomotor skills. Motivation and psychosexual/emotional development also may be influenced. Office of Juvenile Justice and Delinquency Prevention (1998, May). *Drug identification and testing in the juvenile justice system.* Washington, DC: U.S. Department of Justice, Office of Justice Programs. Retrieved online January 10, 2005: http://ojjdp.ncjrs.org/PUBS/drugid/ration-03.html

73. Substance Abuse and Mental Health Services Administration (2002, December). *Emergency department trends from the drug abuse warning network. Preliminary estimates January to June 2002.* Also see Office of Juvenile Justice and Delinquency Prevention (1998, May). *Drug identification and testing in the juvenile justice system.*

74. Office of Juvenile Justice and Delinquency Prevention (1998, May). *Drug identification and testing in the juvenile justice system.*

75. J. D. Hawkins, D. M. Lishner, J. M. Jenson, and R. F. Catalano (1987). Delinquents and drugs: What the evidence suggests about prevention and treatment programming. In B. S. Brown and A. R. Mills (Eds.), *Youth at high risk for substance abuse.* Rockville, MD: National Institute on Drug Abuse (pp. 81–136). Donna Walker James (1997). *Comprehensive strategy for serious, violent, and chronic juvenile offenders.* Program Summary, American Youth Policy Forum. Retrieved online January 10, 2005: http://www.aypf.org/forumbriefs/1997/fb110797.htm

76. Ann H. Crowe (1998, May). *Drug identification and testing summary.* Washington, DC: American Probation and Parole Association.

77. Washington, DC: Office of National Drug Control Policy. Retrieved online January 10, 2005: http://www.whitehousedrugpolicy.gov/publications/factsht/crime/index.html

78. A. J. Beck, S. A. Kline, and L. A. Greenfeld (1988). *Survey of youth in custody, 1987.* Washington, DC: U.S. Department of Justice, Office of Justice Programs. Also see Ann H. Crowe (1998, May). *Drug identification and testing summary.* American Probation and Parole Association. Retrieved online January 10, 2005: http://ojjdp.ncjrs.org/PUBS/drugid/contents.html

79. J. J. De Francesco (1996). Delinquency and substance abuse: A brief analysis. *Journal for Juvenile Justice and Detention Services 11*(2), 77–78.

80. National Parents' Resource Institute for Drug Education. (1997). *PRIDE questionnaire report: 1996–97 National summary grades 6 through 12.* Atlanta, GA:

81. Personal communication. (2003, November 4). Former student.

82. Todd R. Clear and Harry R. Dammer (2001). *The offender in the community.* Belmont, CA: Wadsworth (p. 120).

83. National Council of Juvenile and Family Court Judges and National Drug Court Institute (2003). *Juvenile drug courts: Strategies in practice.* Washington, DC: U.S. Department of Justice, Office of Justice Programs, NCJ 197866. Retrieved online January 10, 2005: http://www.ncjrs.org/txtfiles1/bja/197866.txt

84. National Council of Juvenile and Family Court Judges and National Drug Court Institute (2003). And C. Cooper (Ed.). (1998, June). *Applying drug court concepts in the juvenile and family court environments: A primer for judges.* Washington, DC: US Department of Justice, NCJ 179318. And C. Cooper (2001, May). *Juvenile drug court programs. Juvenile accountability incentive block grants (JAIBG) Program Bulletin.* Washington, DC: US. Department of Justice, Office of Juvenile Justice and Delinquency Prevention, NCJ 184744.

85. Bureau of Justice Statistics (1998). Drug Court Clearinghouse and Technical Assistance Project. *Juvenile and family drug courts: An overview.* Washington, DC: US Department of Justice, Office of Justice Programs, Drug Courts Program Office, NCJ 171139.

86. Bureau of Justice Statistics (2003, February). Drug Court Clearinghouse and Technical Assistance Project. *Juvenile drug courts: Strategies in practice.* Washington, DC: U.S. Department of Justice, Office of Justice Programs. Retrieved online January 10, 2005: http://www.ncjrs.org/txtfiles1/bja/197866.txt

87. Jonathan W. Blodgett, District Attorney. The Commonwealth of Massachusetts. Office of the DA for the Eastern District. May, 2003.

88. Larry J. Siegel (2002). *Juvenile delinquency: The core.* Belmont, CA: Wadsworth (p. 287).

89. Jeffrey A. Butts and Janeen Buck (2000, October). *Teen courts: A focus on research.* Juvenile Justice Bulletin. Retrieved online January 10, 2005: http://www.ncjrs.org/html/ojjdp/jjbul2000_10_2/contents.html

90. National Youth Court Center. Retrieved online January 10, 2005: http://www.youthcourt.net/

91. Curtis J. Vander Waal, Duane C. McBride, Yvonne M. Terry-McElrath, and Holly VanBuren (2001). *Breaking the juvenile drug-crime cycle: Research report.* National Institute of Justice, NIJ186156. Retrieved online January 10, 2005: http://www.ncjrs.org/txtfiles1/nij/186156.txt

92. Curtis J. Vander Waal, Duane C. McBride, Yvonne M. Terry-McElrath, and Holly VanBuren (2001), 5.

93. M. W. Lipsey and D. B. Wilson (1998). Effective intervention for serious juvenile offenders: A synthesis of research. In R. Loeber and D. P. Farrington (Eds.), *Violent juvenile offenders: Risk factors and successful interventions.* Thousand Oaks, CA: Sage (p. 313–345).

94. M. R. Pogrebin, E. D. Poole, and R. M. Regoli (1984). Constructing and implementing a model juvenile diversion program. *Youth and Society, 15*(3), 305–324. Also C. E. Frazier and J. K. Cochran (1986). Official intervention, diversion from

the juvenile justice system, and dynamics of human services work: Effects of a reform goal based on labeling theory. *Crime and Delinquency, 32*(2), 157–176.

95. W. S. Davidson, II, R. Redner, R. Admur, and C. Mitchell (1990). *Alternative treatments for troubled youth: The case of diversion from the justice system.* New York: Plenum.

96. Jonathan P. Caulkins, C. Peter Rydell, William L. Schwabe, and James Chiesa (1997). *Mandatory minimum drug sentences: Throwing away the key or the taxpayers' money.* Santa Monica, CA: Rand Corporation. Rand report. Retrieved online January 10, 2005: http://www.rand.org/publications/MR/MR827/

97. J. Dryfoos (1990). *Adolescents at risk: Prevalence and prevention.* New York: Oxford University Press.

98. R. A. Feldman, T. E. Caplinger, and J. S. Wodarski (1983). *The St. Louis Conundrum: The effective treatment of antisocial youth.* Englewood Cliffs, NJ: Prentice Hall.

99. Office of Juvenile Justice of Delinquency Prevention (1999, September). *Detention diversion advocacy: An evaluation.* Washington, DC: U.S. Department of Justice. Retrieved online January 10, 2005: http://www.ncjrs.org/html/ojjdp/9909-3/contents.html

100. Ken Polk (1995). Juvenile diversion: A look at the record. In P. M. Sharp and B. W. Hancock (Eds.) *Juvenile delinquency. Historical, theoretical and societal reactions to youth* (2nd ed.). Upper Saddle River, NJ: Prentice Hall (pp. 124–174).

101. Thomas J. Bernard, Richard McClearly, and Richard A. Wright (1999). *Life without parole: Living in prison today.* Los Angeles: Roxbury. Daniel Glaser (1995). *Preparing convicts for law-abiding lives.* Albany NY: Sage.

102. D. G. Rojek and M. L. Erickson (1982). Reforming the juvenile justice system: The diversion of status offenders. *Law and Society Review, 16*(2), 241–264.

103. D. S. Elliott, F. W. Dunford, and B. Knowles (1978). *Diversion: A study of alternative processing practices: An overview of initial study findings.* Boulder, CO: Behavioral Research Institute.

104. S. B. Lincoln (1976). Juvenile referral and recidivism. In R. M. Carter and M. W. Klein (Eds.), *Back on the street: Diversion of juvenile offenders.* Englewood Cliffs, NJ: Prentice Hall.

105. For instance, one study found evidence of systematic differential treatment of African Americans; African American females, for instance, were more likely to be incarcerated for status offenses whereas their white counterparts were more likely to be diverted elsewhere. M. A. Bortner, M. L. Sunderland and R. Winn (1985). Race and the impact of juvenile deinstitutionalization. *Crime and Delinquency, 31*(1), 35–46.

106. D. S. Elliott, F. W. Dunford, and B. Knowles (1978). *Diversion: A study of alternative processing practices: An overview of initial study findings.* Boulder, CO: Behavioral Research Institute. Also, Office of Juvenile Justice of Delinquency

Prevention (1999, September). *Detention diversion advocacy: An evaluation.* Also S. B. Lincoln (1976). Also M. W. Lipsey, D. S. Cordray, and D. E. Berger (1981). Evaluation of a juvenile diversion program: Using multiple lines of evidence. *Evaluation Review, 5*(3), 283–306.

107. Office of Juvenile Justice of Delinquency Prevention (1999, September). *Detention diversion advocacy: An evaluation.*

108. Kim Polk (1995).

109. Office for Victims of Crime (1998, August). *New directions from the field: Victim's rights and services for the 21st century.* Washington, DC: U.S. Department of Justice. Office of Justice Programs, NCJ 172825. Retrieved online January 10, 2005: http://www.ojp.usdoj.gov/ovc/new/directions/pdftxt/bulletins/bltn16.pdf

110. Because prosecution is generally avoided when a diversion strategy is offered, it might be inappropriate to refer to the "act" as a crime because that has yet to be proven (the burden of proof is on the prosecutor to show that the defendant had, indeed, committed a crime).

111. Social solidarity and social deviance appear to be important elements of "community." Both enhance social awareness, social productivity, and ultimately, it can be implied—compliance. See Kai T. Erikson (1966). *Wayward Puritans: A study in the sociology of deviance.* New York: Wiley (pp. 3–6).

112. Office for Victims of Crime (1998, August). *New directions from the field: Victim's rights and services for the 21st century.*

PROBATION: NATURE, HISTORY, AND STATISTICS

LEARNING OBJECTIVES

After you finish reading this chapter, you will be better prepared to:

- Describe the justification that promotes probation.
- Define probation and identify its primary mission.
- Identify the advantages and disadvantages of probation.
- Identify the conditions of probation.
- Describe probationer rights and identify the chief legislation protecting probationers.
- Explain the relevance of diminished constitutional rights and preferred rights among probationers.
- Explain how probation works and identify some of its objectives.
- Articulate the historical development of "state" probation and identify some of the contributions of its early founders.
- Describe the historical development of federal probation.
- Describe the primary probation services and their programs.

KEY TERMS

Benefit of Clergy
Conditions of Probation
Courts of General
  Jurisdiction

Courts of Limited
  Jurisdiction
Courts of Record

Diminished
  Constitutional Rights
Electronic Supervision

Intense Supervision	Revocation	*Right* Mempa v. Rahy (1967)
Probation	Shock Probation	Gagnon v. Scarpelli (1972) *due*
Probationers	United States v. *privilege*	*process* John Augustus
Restitution Camp	Birnbaum (1970)	

> The greatest good you can do for another is not just share your riches, but reveal to them their own.
>
> —Benjamin Disraeli

INTRODUCTION

There were approximately 4.1 million offenders (about one in five were women and one in three were black) on state and federal probation in 2003.[1] As such, it is the most widely used criminal sanction in America. Probation is practiced in criminal justice systems all around the globe, in some form or another. Some of the primary factors that promote probation as the sentence of choice among the judiciary have to do with the incredible size of prison populations, which continue to expand each year despite reports that crime is on the decline. As you know, correctional populations have grown so rapidly in the past 10 years that no one expected prisons and jails to become one of the largest single expenditures for many jurisdictions.[2] New prisons require an enormous amount of planning and resources, which usually exceed public expectation and local support. These ideas are further aggravated by sentencing guidelines that regulate prison sentencing for a broader variety of misconduct than in previous periods of American criminal justice history and longer sentences than previously imposed. As expected, system overcrowding is commonplace (but then prisons have been overcrowded since the beginning of American correctional history).[3] In this regard, the life expectancy for prisoners is about the same as the life expectancy for a new prison, except that when new prisons are built, they are far more expensive than expected because of technological advances, human rights requirements that are dictated by legislation through policy makers and interest groups, and finally, the time and effort that must be devoted to public opinion.[4] The cost of maintaining prisons and jails can break state and county budgets and precipitate a return to emphasize treatment and sentencing reform rather than long prison sentences.

Then, too, as a nation, we tend to move back and forth between treatment and punishment approaches to justice, and sometimes not for all the right reasons. For instance, when treatment is a dominant perspective in a specific jurisdiction, laws are changed to shorten the time and methods of supervision among offenders who are released from prison far sooner than appropriate, but this action places the public at risk.[5] Also, other violent offenders are placed on probation or paroled out of prison and that can represent a serious threat to public safety.[6] Criminally violent offenders who lack any form of compassion for human beings, especially children (because they are easy prey), do exist, and if those offenders are confined, it is a prudent decision to keep them isolated.[7] During a

What Would You Do? Probation or Prison[11]

Let's assume you're a probation officer who discovered that one of your probation-ers, Mary Lee Smith, violated her conditions of probation.[10] You understand Mary Lee's circumstances. In fact, you have had similar experiences as Mary Lee, who is a year older than you. Instead, it's Mary Lee who is about to stand before Judge Randolph Quincy in a probation revocation hearing. When you graduated high school 10 years ago, you had a child you didn't want to give up, and your parents treated you as though you made some bad choices, so you didn't ask them for help, but they supported you anyways. For that, you're grateful. You found many poor paying jobs and with most of the money you earned, you paid child care and gave money to your mom. Of course, you knew it wasn't enough. You considered mar-riage so that your daughter could have a better life but you have a history of making bad choices, especially when it comes to men. Finally, you found a job you enjoyed at a nearby state juvenile corrections center. You received a lot of encouragement from your boss and the superintendent, and took advantage of a criminal justice scholarship program. You finished a degree in criminal justice and qualified for an entry-level position with the state's CC division. You advanced as the system grew and now, three years later, you are a probation supervisor in Judge Quincy's court.

You feel that Mary Lee is as much a victim as she is an offender. Married at 17, she quit high school and moved west with her husband who could not find a job. By the time she was 20, she had two children and was divorced, but working on a new husband who had served time in the local lockup. With child care to pay and skills that would command no more than minimum wage, Mary Lee turned to such income supplements as child care, shoplifting, and occasionally prostitution. Her shoplifting skills developed rapidly, and it was not long before she had a criminal record including several lesser offenses for petty larceny, which were disposed of by the prosecutor's declaration of *nolle prosequi*. Because stolen property was found at her home where she was also a caretaker, the Department of Social Ser-vices (DSS) was also on her case. In the past, Mary Lee received diversionary pro-grams and probation when she was apprehended and appeared in Judge Quincy's court. However, Mary Lee's criminal conduct has persisted, as has her inability to stretch her food stamps, welfare payments, and part-time minimum wage employ-ment into a satisfactory existence for herself and her children. To complicate mat-ters, the welfare safety net that helped keep Mary Lee and her children afloat will cease to exist by early next year. It would end earlier if she married the man (also unemployed) she is dating. He was good to Mary Lee and her children, a observa-tion you made several times and learned from information you gathered during the PSI that you prepared for the judge.

Judge Quincy called you into his chambers before sentencing. You pointed out Mary Lee's family obligations and the imminent possibility that the children would have to be placed in foster homes if Mary Lee were confined. Your PSI also reported that Mary Lee had taken in other children to earn an income, had been faithful in making restitution (for shoplifting), maintained a regular church relationship (for herself, her children, and the man she was dating), and promoted a satisfactory home environment for her children (aside from the stolen contraband). Also, evidence of substance abuse or even use was not evident. Although your report is professional, you sense that Judge Quincy has misgivings about Mary Lee and the professional level of your report. "Do you really believe this woman deserves to be in the community? You have found some redeeming features in her conduct, but I don't," he says. "Unfortunately, it appears to me that the only way she is going to learn to respect others people's property is to be deprived of her own freedom. I think the community is getting pretty tired of this kind of repetitive criminal conduct," Judge Quincy adds.

What do you say? You agree with the judge or not? Is there anything else you can do as a probation officer to help Mary Lee make a more successful adjustment regarding living within the limits of the law?

punishment phase, we imprison a lot of people, some of whom are misdemeanants, mentally challenged, young, innocent, elderly—the list goes on, but many could be supervised at home. (More later on specialized groups in Chapters 12 through 15.)

Nonetheless, there is little doubt that the public has more confidence in imprisonment than CC, including probation.[8] It is believed that if offenders are forced to be accountable and are physically prevented from committing crime on the street, justice is served.

On the other hand, probation is a humane alternative (and it's cheaper) than confinement. The promise of probation is in its opportunity to enhance the troubled lives of amenable people in exchange for quality lives. Probation and other CC strategies expand as America returns to treatment and recovery as a device to reduce prison sentences. Because offenders are often required to follow specific restraints and rules while on probation, which can include community service and victim restitution, you might say probation is controlled freedom. Yet some observers of probation reveal that there should exist a genuine concern for dangerous felons who are on probation.[9]

Critics of prison wonder about offender accountability—how can offenders learn to be accountable, self-reliant, and enhance their "greatest good" as expressed earlier by Benjamin Disraeli, especially with issues such as alcohol and drug dependency, when correctional personnel and secure facilities control every decision those offenders can make?

To better understand probation as a CC service, an explanation about the nature and the process of probation can help. The nature of probation is linked to its definition, conditions of probation, probationer rights, revocation, outcomes, descriptions about how probation works, objectives, history, statistics, and types of probation. Chapter 8 discusses the process of probation and its management and personnel along with various methods of delivery. When you have read both chapters, your knowledge about probation should be measurably improved, although you are cautioned to consider these chapters simply as guidelines because information about probation is generalized to clarify its contents and strategies change all the time.

THE NATURE OF PROBATION

What is Probation?

> Probation is a sentence imposed by the court upon a convicted offender, requiring the offender to meet certain conditions of supervision in the community.[12]

Generally, probation is given directly, but it may be combined with a period of confinement (often called shock probation or a split sentence) or be imposed in lieu of a suspended jail or prison sentence.[13] Probation is a court-ordered term of community supervision under specified conditions for a specific period of time that cannot exceed the maximum sentence for an offense. These conditions can vary depending on the jurisdiction, the belief systems of the public and policy makers, and the offender. Supervision is most often provided through a correctional system whose authority is tied to state government. Responsibility for enforcing the conditions of supervision in the community normally rests with a probation officer.[14] The frequency and method required of an offender to contact a probation officer is usually articulated in the *conditions of probation* (explained later in Chapter 8).

Sometimes probation is a sentence, other times it is a suspended sentence. There are two things probation is not: It is not confinement assuming conditions of probation are met by a probationer; and it is not an automatic right of a defendant. It was decided in *United States v. Birnbaum* (1970) that probation is a "privilege" or an entitlement provided by the courts.[15]

Probation is a privilege

When Probation Is Imposed Upon a Defendant

Probation can be imposed upon a defendant in a number of ways. For instance, the Bureau of Justice Statistics[16] advises:

- 54 percent of probationers had a direct sentence to probation.
- 25 percent received a sentence of incarceration that was suspended.
- 8 percent received a split sentence that included incarceration followed by probation.
- 13 percent had entered probation before completion of all court proceedings (including those who entered probation before final verdict).

Largely, defendants are granted probation through the court and they have not served jail time as part of their sentence, although there are variations in jail and probation combinations. For instance, a guilty defendant might receive a sentence of 30 days in jail and one year probation for a conviction of a simple assault unless the probationer violates conditions of probation. In addition, some states have combinations of prison and probation. Once probation is imposed upon a defendant, he or she becomes a probationer.

What is a Probationer?

> **Probationers** are criminal offenders who have been sentenced to a period of conditional supervision in the community.[17]

A probationer is required to abide by the restrictions and conditions of freedom ordered by the court and supervised through probation personnel. Violations can result in revocation (withdrawing probation) by the court and imposition of any sentence that might have been imposed before placing the offender on probation, such as 90 days in jail.[18] The probationer is often required to pay the cost of supervision to the jurisdiction that supervises the probationer, and may have additional conditions requiring payment of restitution, court costs and fines, public service, and various types of treatment.

Advantages of Probation

Advantages of probation for the corrections community include:

- Cost efficient in comparison to confinement
- Reduces overcrowded prisons and jails
- Reduces recidivism
- Provides supervision among those offenders who should not be confined (i.e., first-time nonserious offenders, young offenders, physically or mentally challenged offenders, mitigating circumstances)
- Provides supervision among violent offenders, sex offenders, and habitual offenders

Probation costs will be covered in more detail in Chapter 7 and 8, but for right now it would be helpful to know that the Department of Corrections in Georgia reported that in 2001, the average daily cost of probation was $1.49, as compared to the daily cost of housing an inmate in a minimum secured prison, which was $64.64. Across the country, the average daily cost of probation was $4.18 as compared to a high of $105.24 per offender for only food and health in prison.[19] In addition, 49 percent of all probationers had been convicted of a felony, 49 percent of a misdemeanor, and 2 percent of other infractions in 2003; 25 percent were on probation for a drug law violation and 17 percent for driving while intoxicated (DWI).[20]

Offender Advantages of Probation

There are many advantages of probation for the offender, including:

- Diverts offender from confinement system
- Eliminates stigma of prison sentence and avoids prisonization effect
- Allows offender to demonstrate a willingness to comply with a set of conditions that includes supervision
- Provides greater voluntary change toward reform than those incarcerated[21]
- Gives offender a chance to remain in the community among family and friends
- Allows offender the opportunity to pursue employment, school or trade, and religious activities
- Provides larger choice of service providers for treatment and programs

Disadvantages of Probation

Drawbacks that apply to probation can be characterized as:

- A relative lack of punishment for the just desert and control advocates who see punishment and confinement as the primary function of the criminal justice community.
- Possibility that some community members and victims of specific offenders might lose confidence in the criminal justice community when a defendant receives probation as opposed to harsher punishment.
- Increased risk to the community in the sense that almost one of every two probationers have been convicted of a felony prior to probation. Corrections supervision makes a difference for probationers, especially concerning reoffending, but reality indicates that supervision cannot consist of a 24-hour, 7-day-a-week observation of a convicted felon. Revocation rates indicate that many probationers violate the conditions of probation including violating the law.

Conditions of Probation

There are as many restrictions and conditions of probation as there are different jurisdictions that supervise it; however, there are many similarities (in no particular order), such as:

- Reporting to a probation officer or community center on a specific scale
- Maintaining residency at a specific address
- Curfew
- Employment
- No association with other offenders
- Compliance of laws and other regulations established in the conditions of probation

- Drug and alcohol free (greatest restriction)
- Victim restitution
- Community service
- Limited travel

This is not to say that someone on probation must meet all of these conditions. Each offender has different restrictions and conditions, depending on the order of the court and a number of other factors, including the perspective of the probation agency. Other conditions imposed upon a probationer include some of those mentioned in a national study by the U.S. Department of Justice.[22] This government report indicates that almost all of the probationers studied had conditions attached to their sentences that included many of those from the aforementioned list and the following:

- Monetary requirements ordered payment of supervision fees. As of 2001, the average monthly supervision fee charged offenders was around $29.80.[23] Fees can range from $5 to $60 per month depending on a probationer's income; for example, Massachusetts is $50. Only 41 states had authorized the imposition of some form of supervision fee as of 1996.
- Fines and court costs.
- Restriction from contacting any victim.
- Completion of specific training, human services (anger management), and educational programs.
- Limitations placed on movements, including directives to stay away from certain places, such as bars or businesses.
- Placed on electronic monitoring (bracelet program).
- Required to participate in other treatment programs, such as special psychiatric or psychological counseling, or domestic violence counseling.

A violation associated with a restriction or condition of probation could produce revocation (terminating probation). But, revocation is not automatic because probationers have rights.

Probationer Rights

Once a defendant is granted probation, it cannot be revoked or withdrawn unless "due process" concerns are met. Although probationers enjoy constitutional guarantees, those rights can best be described as *diminished Constitutional rights:* rights enjoyed by an offender that are not as highly protected by the courts as the rights of a nonoffender. A federal court of appeal helps clarify this position: "conditions which restrict freedom of speech and association are valid if they are reasonably necessary to accomplish the essential needs of the state and public order."[24] If a *preferred right,* such as the First Amendment, can be curtailed, then other rights can be curtailed under similar circumstances.

probationers right to council

right to due process

Nonetheless, in *Mempa v. Rahy* (1967) the United States Supreme Court provided a probationer's right to council if probation were revoked under a deferred sentencing statue. And, *Gagnon v. Scarpelli's* (1972) landmark case resolved many issues concerning due process protection for probationers prior to revocation:[25]

1. Revocation is considered at revocation hearing.
2. Probationer is informed in writing of the revocation charges.
3. Written notice is provided before the revocation hearing.
4. Probationer is allowed to attend the hearing and present evidence on his or her behalf.
5. Probationer has a right to challenge evidence and testimony.
6. Probationer has a right to confront witnesses and cross-examine them.
7. Probationer has a right to be represented by legal counsel.

United States Supreme Court Cases Influencing Probation

United States v. Birnbaum (1970): Probation is a privilege and not a right
Mempa v. Rahy, 389 U.S. 128 (1967): Right to Counsel
Gagnon v. Scarpelli, 411 U.S. 778, 93 S. Ct. (1972): Due process procedures extend to revocation

---

Due process as it applies to probation (and parole) furthers the "check and balance" principle of democracy and helps make the probational system subject to public scrutiny, as it should be.[26]

Revocation

Probationers are usually supervised by specific state personnel, but only a court process can reverse the court's benefit of probation. Data provided by the Bureau of Justice Statistics[27] for yearend 2003 advises:

- About three in five of the more than two million adults discharged from probation in 2003 successfully met the conditions of their supervision.
- The percentage of probationers discharged from probation supervision because of incarceration due to a rule violation or new offense varied from 21 percent in 1995 to 15 percent in 2000 to 16 percent in 2003.
- At yearend 2003, one in nine probationers had absconded (probationers who fail to report and could not be located).

How probation works depends on the jurisdiction. However, there are many similar characteristics that enable an examination of this CC initiative.

How Probation Works

> Legislative action places probation power with the courts to both grant and revoke it.

Primarily, only the courts have the power to grant and revoke probation, a fact previously mentioned but worth repeating. The authority of probation can usually be found in a state's criminal law. For instance, Massachusetts Criminal Law 276. 87 states that their superior court, district courts, and juvenile courts can put a defendant on probation before, during, and after trial with the consent of the defendant.

Most courts have a great deal of discretion over probation. Federal guidelines reinforce this power. The federal government permits all state and local courts having jurisdiction of the offenses for which probation may be used to place a defendant on probation. Thus, if the state provides only for felony probation, *courts of general jurisdiction* with the power to try felony cases have the authority to grant and revoke probation.[28] If misdemeanor probation is provided for, *courts of limited jurisdiction* may grant and revoke misdemeanor probation. In a few states, the power to probate is restricted to *courts of record.*

> **A Court of General Jurisdiction** is a court having unlimited (civil and criminal) trial jurisdiction, although its judgments are subject to appellate review.

> **A Court of Limited Jurisdiction** is a criminal court in which the trial jurisdiction is limited to hearing misdemeanor and petty cases.

> **A Court of Record** is a court whose acts and proceedings are kept on permanent record.

> ### For example, in the State of Florida, county courts, which are "courts of limited jurisdiction," handle:
>
> - County and city ordinance violations, including traffic infractions.
> - Minor offenses (misdemeanors) that provide for a maximum sentence of one year or less in the county jail.
> - Civil cases involving amounts of $15,000 or less, such as landlord-tenant and small claims disputes.

Circuit Courts, which are "courts of general jurisdiction," handle:

- Domestic relations cases such as dissolution of marriage (divorce), guardianship, and juvenile delinquency.
- Major criminal offenses (felonies), which can result in imprisonment in a state institution.
- Probate matters, such as the processing of wills and settling of estates of deceased persons.
- Civil cases involving amounts greater than $15,000.
- Appeals from county court judgments, except when a state statute or provision of the state constitution is held invalid.

Objectives of Probation

The primary objective of correctional systems, including probation, is protecting the community or public safety.

Avoiding confinement makes sense (assuming professional classification systems are employed) because the imprisonment experience shows that nonviolent first-time of-

---

The objectives of probation often change but generally include different goals of:

- Public safety
- Keeping defendant out of prison or jail
- Offender rehabilitation
- Keeping offender linked to family and employment
- Safety of victims
- Restitution monitoring
- Involvement of community resources and support

---

fenders may not require confinement to curb their criminal activities. Should the defendant be employed, community supervision would allow the probationer to provide for a family and continue with family activities including child care, regardless of the martial status of the probationer. In addition, some offenders might be more motivated toward reform in the community as opposed to confined offenders who experience the pain and the deprivation of prison life. Finally, involvement of community resources and support aids the CC system in surveillance strategies and offender opportunities for reform, in the sense of treatment and job skill training and job opportunities. The greatest threat to probation is its lack of clarity about its objectives: Is probation, for instance, a social service or is punishment?

Prevention practices play a role in furthering community safety in the sense that they reduce crime among offenders and get community members actively involved. Other community advantages include the preparation of the PSI. Because probation officers interview victims and make determinations about the risk of an offender to aid a judge with sentencing sanctions, prevention of future crimes can occur by referring victims to appropriate agencies for assistance. Reaching out to victims and the community can bring attention to victims and others, and to alternatives that could aid their quality-of-life experiences, such as domestic violence shelters and welfare resources.

Involving the community to the extent of personnel resources, such as volunteering, furthers public safety from the standpoint of knowledge and helps an offender feel a sense of belonging. But while all of this sounds good, it took several hundred years to reach this point.

HISTORICAL DEVELOPMENT OF PROBATION

Early America looked for alternatives to the punishment practiced in Western Europe and England.[29] In 18th- and 19th-century Britain, the severe punishments imposed on offenders, regardless of the seriousness of the crime committed, led judges and prosecutors to search for less harsh sanctions. During the time of King Henry VIII, for instance, no less than two hundred crimes were punishable by death, many of which were minor offenses. This harshness eventually led to discontent in certain progressive segments of English society concerned with the evolution of the justice system.[30]

Early procedures were used to circumvent the mechanical application of the criminal justice process and included the benefit of clergy, judicial reprieve and pardon, and release on recognizance (with or without surety).[31] Each of these procedures allowed the judiciary to impose sentences on a case-by-case basis.

Benefit of clergy originally provided an avoidance of secular forms of punishment for religious officials.

Benefit of clergy applied to the exemption of Christian clerics from criminal prosecution in the secular courts. The privilege was established by the 12th century and extended only to the commission of felonies. The ecclesiastical courts did not inflict capital punishment except in rare cases, in which event those adjudged guilty were turned over to local secular authorities for enforcement of the sentence. To receive benefit of clergy, a defendant was required to prove their literacy by reading a passage from the Christian Bible. Many criminals posed as clerics to obtain benefit of clergy and memorized Bible passages. In the 18th century, the reading test was abolished and everyone could claim this privilege for the first conviction of felony; later, the privilege was extended to women. Benefit of clergy thus mitigated the severities of English criminal law, which imposed the death penalty for many trivial offenses. Criminal law was ameliorated in the early 19th century, and in 1827 benefit of clergy was abolished as being no longer necessary. In the United States it was abolished in 1790 for all federal crimes, and in 1850, it disappeared from the state courts.[32]

Judicial reprieve was practiced by the 19th-century English courts to serve as a temporary suspension of sentence to allow a defendant to appeal to the Crown for a pardon. In the 1820s, the British government combined the Common Law surety and recognizance systems by releasing young offenders into the hands of employers.[33]

Release on recognizance with or without surety suggests that the English courts began the practice of "binding over for good behavior," a form of temporary release during which offenders could take measures to secure pardons or lesser sentences. Controversially, in due time, certain courts began suspending sentences.

Also, noncustodial sanctions such as probation and parole were used among juvenile offenders in France as early as 1830.[34] Portugal utilized a form of supervised parole among adult offenders in 1861. Saxony, Germany, and Denmark developed a classification system that allowed furloughs and conditional release for prisoners by 1871. European nations moved toward noncustodial sanctions in the 19th century in the form of a suspended sentence and community supervision.[35] However, in the late 21st century, recidivism was on the rise in Western Europe and many countries re-examined their position on suspended sentences and community supervision.

In America, particularly in the Commonwealth of Massachusetts, practices were developed known as "security for good behavior" or "good aberrance," in which, the accused paid a fee as collateral for good behavior, much like modern bail. Filing was also practiced in cases that did not demand an immediate sentence. Using this procedure, indictments were "laid on file" or held in abeyance.[36] To mitigate unreasonable mandatory penalties, judges often granted a motion to quash based upon minor technicalities or errors in the proceedings. Although these American practices were genuine precursors to probation, it is the early use of recognizance and suspended sentence that are directly related to modern probation.

Influential Individuals

Two names are most closely associated with the development of probation: Matthew Davenport Hill, an 18th-century English barrister and judge, and John Augustus, a 19th-century Boston boot maker.

When Matthew Hill became the Recorder of Birmingham England, a judicial post, he ordered the return of youthful offenders to one-day terms and returned them to their parents to supervise at home. Not all offenders were released to parents. If offenders demonstrated a promise for rehabilitation, but their parents seemed untrustworthy, those children were placed in the hands of generous guardians who willingly took charge of them. Hill had police officers pay periodic visits to these guardians in an effort to track the progress of the offenders and keep a running account.

In America, John Augustus, a Boston shoe cobbler, is credited as the "Father of Probation." Augustus was born in Woburn, MA in 1785. In 1841, although the Boston Police Court imposed a prison sentence upon an adult drunkard, Augustus persuaded the court to release him into his custody.[37]

In 1843, Augustus aided two girls, ages 8 and 10, and an 11-year-old boy, all of whom had been accused of stealing. By 1846, he had supervised about 30 children ranging in age from 9 to 16 years old.[38] Between 1841 and 1858, Augustus supervised approximately 2000 men, women, and children.[39] Augustus described his ongoing work with children before the court:

> In 1847, I bailed 19 boys, from 7 to 15 years of age, and in bailing them it was understood, and agreed by the court, that their cases should be continued from term to term for several months, as a season of probation; thus each month at the calling of the docket, I would appear in court, make my report, and thus the cases would pass on for five or six months. At the expiration of this term, 12 of the boys were brought into court at one time, and the scene formed a striking and highly pleasing contrast with their appearance when first arraigned. The judge expressed much pleasure, as well as surprise, at their appearance and remarked that the object of the law had been accomplished, and expressed his cordial approval of my plan to save and reform. Seven of the number were too poor to pay a fine, although the court fixed the amount at 10 cents each, and of course I paid it for them; the parents of the other boys were able to pay the cost, and thus the penalty of the law was answered. The sequel thus far shows that not one of this number has proved false to the promises of reform they made while on probation. This incident proved conclusively that this class of boys could be saved from crime and punishment, by the plan which I had marked out, and this was admitted by the judges in both courts. Printed with the permission of the American Probation and Parole Association.[40]

The Augustus "helper" model met with the scorn of law enforcement officials who wanted offenders punished, not helped,[41] and corrections professionals who were paid only when offenders were incarcerated.[42] Prudently, the court felt that not every offender should be imprisoned. John Augustus was unpaid for his services, which reveals a deeper commitment to aid others, and as such, probably the first volunteer of probation (see Table 7.2.)

First States to Legislate a Probation System

It probably comes as no surprise that because of John Augustus' influence, Massachusetts legislated the first state agent in 1869 to be present if court actions might result in the placement of a child in a reformatory. This action provided a model for modern caseworkers. Agents were to search for other placement, protect the child's interests, investigate the case before trial, and supervise the plan for the child after disposition. Massachusetts passed the first probation statute in 1878, mandating an official state probation system with salaried probation officers.[43] Interestingly, it was also the concern for mitigating the harshness of penalties for children that led to the international development of probation.

Public support for adult probation was much more difficult to come by. It was not until 1901 that New York passed the first statute authorizing probation for adult offenders, over 20 years after Massachusetts passed its law for juvenile probationers.[44] Other states quickly followed: by 1900, Vermont, Rhode Island, New Jersey, New York, Minnesota, and Illinois passed probation laws; by 1910, 32 more states passed legislation establishing juvenile probation. By 1923, many states adopted adult and juvenile probation laws (see Table 7.1).

Surprisingly, it was the federal government that resisted probation programs until 1925. By 1930, juvenile probation was legislated in every state except Wyoming. Today, probation is practiced in every state, Washington, DC, and the federal government.

History of Federal Probation

Most presentence investigations conducted early by the FBI (the probation component) were for violations of the White Slavery Act,[47] Dyer Act, and the Volstead Act.[48] There were approximately 34 bills sent to Congress between 1909 to 1925 to develop a federal probation system. One of those bills met rejection by Congress eight times until it finally won approval. It was sent to President Coolidge, the former governor of Massachusetts, who had first-hand experience with probation. Coolidge signed the American Federal Probation Act into law in 1925, establishing probation in federal courts. The director of the Federal Bureau of Prisons administered the program at that time. In 1930, there were eight federal probation officers nationwide. In 1940, responsibility for the administration of the system transferred to the Administrative Office of the U.S. courts. By 1950, there were 303 officers who supervised 30,087 caseloads, or over 1,000 cases for each officer.

Sentencing alternatives expanded with the passage of the Youth Corrections Act in 1950 (related to the sentencing and supervision of defendants aged 18 to 26), the Indeterminate Sentencing Act of 1958 (relating to adult defendants), the Criminal Justice Act of 1964 and the Prisoner Rehabilitation Act of 1965 (which established home furloughs, work release programs, and community treatment centers), and the Narcotic Addict Rehabilitation Act of 1966 (relating to drug treatment for addicted parolees). The staff grew to 1,148 and the supervision caseload grew to 59,534.

Since 1975, two major events helped promote the federal probation system: (a) the rehabilitation model in sentencing and supervision was supplanted by the crime control model and (b) pretrial services were established as a major component of the federal probation system. With respect to the former, enactment of the Comprehensive Crime Control Act of 1984 and the Sentencing Reform Act of 1984 replaced indeterminate sentencing with determinate sentencing. This legislation established the U.S. Sentencing Commission, which:

1. Regulated sentencing guidelines.
2. Elevated probation to a sentence in and of itself.
3. Eliminated parole.
4. Established supervised release as the new form of postconviction supervision.

Table 7.1   States with Juvenile and Adult Probation Laws: 1923

State	Juvenile	Adult
Alabama	1907	1915
Arizona	1907	1913
Arkansas	1911	1923
California	1903	1903
Colorado	1899	1909
Connecticut	1903	1903
Delaware	1911	1911
Georgia	1904	1907
Idaho	1905	1915
Illinois	1899	1911
Indiana	1903	1907
Kansas	1901	1909
Maine	1905	1905
Maryland	1902	1904
Massachusetts	1878	1878
Michigan	1903	1903
Minnesota	1899	1909
Missouri	1901	1897
Montana	1907	1913
Nebraska	1905	1909
New Jersey	1903	1900
New York	1903	1901
North Carolina	1915	1919
North Dakota	1911	1911
Ohio	1902	1908
Oklahoma	1909	1915
Oregon	1909	1915
Pennsylvania	1903	1909
Rhode Island	1899	1899
Tennessee	1905	1915
Utah	1903	1923
Vermont	1900	1900
Virginia	1910	1910
Washington	1905	1915
Wisconsin	1901	1909

Source: F. R. Johnson.[45]

Table 7.2 Events in the Development of Probation[46]

Year	Event
18th century	Matthew Hill, Recorder of Birmingham, orders youthful offenders to their homes.
1841	John Augustus asks Boston courts to release adult drunkards to his custody.
1878	The Commonwealth of Massachusetts formally adopts a probation system for juveniles.
1878–1928	35 states have passed juvenile and adult probation legislation.
1925	The federal government passes the American Federal Probation Act and most federal probation officers are volunteers.
1954	All states, the federal government, and Washington DC, have juvenile probation systems in place.
1956	All states but Mississippi have adult probation systems in place.
1958	Federal regulation supports split sentencing of reduced confinement periods followed by shock probation.
1973	National Advisory Commission on Criminal Standards and Goals endorses more extensive probation systems and programs.
1973	Minnesota is first state to adopt the CCA.
1974	Martinson's influential research reports that nothing works upon offenders, including programs.
1974	American Probation and Parole Association is conceived in Texas and endorses the case management system for probation.
1976	U.S. Comptroller General's study of probation concludes that the system inadequately provides services due to lack of funding and support.
1982	Georgia's ISP program claims to reduce recidivism.
1983	New Mexico develops electronic monitoring, which revolutionizes surveillance techniques of probation.
1987	New York develops its shock incarceration treatment program, which included "after shock" programs in the community.
1989	Government Accounting Office survey shows jurisdictions have adapted various probation strategies across the United States and that their results vary from jurisdiction to jurisdiction depending on many variables.
1991	U.S. Department of Justice funds intensive supervision programs and evaluations.
1996	City, state, and county New York probation agencies develop an integrated intergovernmental management team to conduct the services of probation across the state. Other jurisdictions monitor New York's lead in this effort.
1999	Massachusetts merges state probation officers with other local corrections personnel through the trial courts, which mandate a continuum of sanctions and services for offenders on probation, in custody of the sheriff, on parole, or in custody of the department of corrections. These intermediate sanctions programs are designed to provide sanctions and services at one location, a CC center.

5. Reformed "good time" provisions relating to service of prison sentences to a maximum of 54 days annually after completion of the first year of a sentence.

One result was that the percentage of a sentence served in prison increased before an offender would be released to the community (see Table 7.3).

Another important event was the adoption of the enhanced supervision philosophy, which focused on enforcement of court-imposed sanctions, risk control, and correctional treatment. Enhanced supervision refers correctional personnel participating in supervised programs or treatment along with their probationer. These developments, together with major technological changes, produced a variety of new officer specialties, including:

- Guideline specialists
- Drug and alcohol treatment specialists
- Mental health treatment specialists
- Community noncustody specialists (e.g., electronic monitoring treatment specialists)

Table 7.3   Important Federal Enactments Effecting Federal Probation[49]

Federal Action Enhancing Probation	*Effecting*
White Slavery Act of 1910	Made it a crime to transport women over state lines for immoral purposes
Dyer Act of 1914	Regulated the interstate transportation of stolen motor vehicles
Volstead Act of 1919	Prohibition of alcoholic beverages
American Federal Probation Act of 1925	Legislated probation in federal courts
Youth Corrections Act of 1950	Related to sentencing and supervision of defendants aged 18 to 26
Indeterminate Sentencing Act of 1958	Related to adult defendants
Criminal Justice Act of 1964	Established home furloughs, work release programs, and community treatment centers
Prisoner Rehabilitation Act of 1965	See Criminal Justice Act of 1964
Narcotic Addict Rehabilitation Act of 1966	Related to drug treatment for addicted parolees
Rehabilitation model in sentencing and supervision	Displaced the crime control model
Comprehensive Crime Control Act of 1984	Replaced indeterminate sentencing then in place with a determinate sentencing system.
Sentencing Reform Act of 1984	See Comprehensive Crime Control Act of 1984
Supervision philosophy of the 1990s	Promoted professional specialists
Mandatory minimum sentences of the 1990s	Provided longer sentences for drug traffickers
U.S. Sentencing Commission	Regulated federal sentencing policies

Shifting prosecutorial emphasis on drug traffickers, generated in part by congressional passage of mandatory minimum sentences for certain drug trafficking offenses in the late 1980s, dramatically affected the composition of supervision caseloads to the point where approximately 40 percent of all federal caseloads were drug offenders.

PROBATION SERVICES

The services provided by probation agencies across the United States depend largely upon their resources, experiences, policy, and public opinion in a given jurisdiction. A typical list of probation services provided include: presentence reports, counseling, job development, detox, substance abuse treatment, referral services, apprehension of absconders, and electronic monitoring devises. Some states provide different services to probationers than do other states, as indicated in Table 7.4.

PROBATION PROGRAMS

Probation systems provide numerous programs or plans of action for guilty defendants. The most common probation program is *Administrative Probation*. This program can be described as a form of noncontact supervision in which an offender who represents a low risk to the community may, upon satisfactory completion of half the term of regular pro-

Table 7.4   Services Provided by Probation Systems as of January 1, 2002

State	Presentence Reports	Family Counseling	Individual Counseling	Job Development	Detox	Substance Abuse Treatment	Referral Services	Apprehend Absconders	Electronic Monitors
Arizona	X	X	X	X	X	X	X	X	X
Colorado	X		X	X		X	X	X	X
Connecticut	X	X	X	X	X	X	X	X	X
DC	X	X	X	X	X	X	X		X
Georgia	X	X	X	X		X	X	X	
Illinois	X	X	X	X		X	X		X
Maryland	X		X	X			X		
Massachusetts	X								X
Nebraska	X						X		X
Tennessee									X
Texas	X	X	X	X	X	X	X	X	X
West Virginia	X		X	X			X	X	X
Total	11	6	9	9	4	7	10	6	10

Printed with permission of the *Corrections Year Book: Adults Corrections.*[50]

bation, be placed on nonreporting status until expiration of the term of supervision. In some jurisdictions that have administrative probation, the offender pays an initial or monthly processing fee, up to a specific amount, such as $50. Periodic record checks are completed to ensure the offender has not violated the law.

Regular probation consists of reporting to a probation officer at a specified time and place (usually the probation agency's offices) weekly or biweekly depending upon the conditions of probation as discussed earlier in this Chapter. Approximately three out of four probationers are required to regularly report to a probation authority in person, by mail, or by telephone.[51] It is expected that the probationer will remain within the boundaries of the conditions of probation and can have random drug and curfew checks.

Other programs, much like the probation systems that provide them, can vary depending on resources, experiences, and policy of various jurisdictions. Those programs vary depending on whether they are provided in systems or organizational structures that offer both probation and parole or just probation. In addition, probation agencies provided the following distinctive programs to constituents on January 1, 2002: restitution camp (limited compensation program), parenting classes, DWI programs, drug offender probation group homes, halfway houses, supervised home release, intensive supervision, community service, shock probation, and "other" programs (see Table 7.5).

Although many of these programs are detailed in other chapters, it is helpful to get an early look at them.

Restitution camp: Restitution is the practice of requiring offenders to compensate crime victims for damages offenders may have inflicted; there are several models of restitution including restitution camp, which can be described as symbolic restitution. Its rationale involves redress for crimes, payment of fines, and court costs, and is often applied when a guilty defendant is indigent. Often, it is used among juvenile offenders and can require housing for short periods of time.

Parenting classes: These classes instruct parents how to deal with their children and grandchildren. Often the subjects of these classes consist of hygiene, behavioral concerns, and conflict management. Often, these encounters consist of group instruction meeting perhaps once or twice a week. Sometimes, the entire family is present and sometimes only parents.

DWI Program: Can consist of, among other things, a weekly or daily meeting involving group discussions, films, and lectures. One efficient method is through the group process headed by a facilitator and it can consist of regular supervision or intense surveillance. DWI programs can include: *Drug offender probation (DOP):* DOP can be described as an intensive form of supervision that emphasizes treatment of drug offenders in accordance with individualized treatment plans. These programs can include elements of surveillance and random drug testing. Contacts and drug testing are often made by probation officers to ensure offenders remain drug-free.

Group homes: Group homes are dormitory type living arrangements are primarily for youthful offenders or special needs offenders such as sexual abuse victims,

Table 7.5   **Programs Available in Probation Agencies on January 1, 2002**

State	Restitution Camp	Parenting Classes	DWI Programs	Group Homes	Halfway Houses	Supervised Home Release	Intensive Supervision	Community Service	Shock Probation	Other Probation
Alaska			X		X	X	X	X		
Arizona	X	X	X	X	X	X	X	X		X
Colorado	X		X			X	X	X		X
Connecticut	X	X	X			X	X	X		X
Washington, DC	X	X			X	X	X			X
Georgia	X					X	X	X		X
Idaho	X	X		X		X	X	X		
Illinois	X		X			X	X	X		
Kentucky									X	X
Maryland	X		X				X	X		
Massachusetts	X					X	X	X		
Michigan	X					X	X	X		
Minnesota	X		X			X		X		
Mississippi	X					X	X	X	X	
Montana	X					X	X	X	X	
Nebraska	X						X	X		
Ohio				X	X	X	X	X	X	X
Pennsylvania	X					X	X			X
Tennessee							X	X		
Texas	X	X	X		X	X	X	X	X	X
Utah	X	X	X		X		X	X		
West Virginia	X		X			X	X	X		
Total	18	6	10	3	6	17	19	19	5	9

Printed with permission of the Corrections Yearbook (2003).[52]

abandoned victims, alcohol/drug abusers, the mentally ill or physically challenged, or nonviolent offenders.

Halfway houses: These houses are living quarters for offenders after a prison sentence has been serviced and before full release of an offender is granted. (For more information about halfway houses, see residential intermediate sanctions in Chapter 11).

Supervised home release: Offenders are restricted to living quarters at their permanent residence. They have a curfew, must submit to drug testing, and can only leave home to attend school, church, or employment. Sometimes electronic monitoring is used with this sanction. Supervised home release can also be a form of intense supervised house arrest in the community, including surveillance on weekends and holidays, administered by officers with limited caseloads. It is usually an individualized program in which the freedom of the offender is restricted within the community, home, or noninstitutional residential placement, and specified sanctions are imposed.

Intensive supervision: Critics say that increased use of regular probation poses a high risk for the community; therefore, many jurisdictions have adapted a more controlled form of intermediate sanction—intense supervision probation (ISP). ISP allows for closer monitoring of probationers through surveillance, drug testing, home and work visits, electric monitoring (bracelet), and house arrest.[53] Virtually every state and the federal government practice some form of ISP. Offenders receive closer surveillance, strict conditions, and more often require access to treatment than other probationers. The ISP offender is often a high-risk, high-need individual who is generally prison-bound. However, most jurisdictions prefer ISP to prison because it:

• Costs less than confinement alternatives.
• Helps an offender (through supervision) curb crime in the community.

Since the mid-1960s these programs have been aimed primarily at supervising adult offenders closely. In recent years, they have been designed for juveniles, too. Electronic monitoring is the most common strategy used with intense supervision as generally an offender is restricted to his or her permanent residence. Curfew, frequent drug testing, and specific restrictions are made concerning school, church and employment. The offender also attends classes and programs at community centers. Intensive supervision can be used for both felony and misdemeanor convictions such as sexual offenders. Electronic monitoring is also used in parole strategies, too. To give you an idea about the number of devices used across the United States, see Table 7.6. There is a front-end approach: an offender is sent directly to ISP before any confinement, a back-approach: an offender serves time such in the shock probation and enhanced supervision.

Sometimes jurisdictions contract with private vendors who monitor offenders on a twenty-four hour a day basis. Curfew violations are reported to probation staff for further investigation.

Other forms of ISP that should be mentioned, for instance, *Community control* is a form of intense supervised house arrest in the community, including surveillance on weekends and holidays, administered by officers with limited caseloads. It is usually an individualized program in which the freedom of the offender is restricted within the community, home or noninstitutional residential placement, and specified sanctions are imposed. As with probation, violation of any community

Table 7.6   Use of Electric Monitors in the United States during 2001

Type of Jurisdictions	Number of Jurisdictions	Number of Devises Used	Average Weeks Worn
Probation only	10	5,293	23
Probation and parole	19	9,208	12
Total	29	14,501	17

Printed with the permission of the the Corrections Yearbook (2003).[54]

control condition may result in revocation by the court and imposition of any sentence that it might have imposed before placing the offender on supervision. Often, the use of electronic monitoring as an enhancement to community control is used in conjunction with this form of probation. For example, in the Trial Court Program in the Commonwealth of Massachusetts (as discussed in Chapter 11) and the State of Texas, where it exists in all 20 judicial circuits throughout the state.

Another form of ISP that requires explanation is *enhanced supervision* because it resembles ISP conditions, but its (payroll and program) expenses are greater than a typical ISP program. It was established to provide a rigorous sanction and to better meet the needs of high-risk offenders.

Community service: In community service, an offender can be restricted to his or her permanent residence and work within the community under probation supervision and often within groups. Community service can be a condition of probation and as such a piece of another probation strategy.

Shock probation: This refers to split sentencing, which first appeared as a federal sentencing provision in 1958, although California imposed a combination of incarceration and probation for the same offender as early as the 1920s.[55] Shock probation follows a confinement period of somewhere between 30 to 180 days, and once released, the offender is resentenced to probation. The offender is "shocked" by confinement. For example, after six months of shock incarceration (which includes mandated treatment in New York), "graduates" begin a six-month shock probation program that also includes treatment and "close" supervision. The rationale of shock probation is that it helps as a crime is deterred in the sense that serving "time" is sufficiently traumatic to cause some offenders to want to avoid future jail sentences. Shock probation tends to satisfy critics of probation because confinement and the conditions of probation are punishment, and close supervision would add to public safety and offender accountability. Also, because offender reform is

---

In Ohio, shock probation allows a judge, at the judge's discretion, to release convicted criminals from prison before they are eligible for a parole hearing. Shock probation began as a scared-straight sort of program in the mid 1970s. It was designed to give a person a taste of prison life in the hopes that they wouldn't want to go back. It was very seldom used for criminals serving long sentences. The law was changed, revised, and added to when the lawmakers added something called Super Shock Probation. Super shock probation said that a person need only serve 90 days to be eligible for early release from prison. The prisoner could be let out at any time, no parole hearing was needed, no testimony, no nothing, only a judge to utter the words "let 'em go!"

Reprinted with the permission of Justice Junction www.justicejunction.com.[56]

largely a product of efficient treatment, punishment and control opponents see the mandated treatment while imprisoned and during shock probation as furthering rehabilitation.

"Other" programs: These can consist of day reporting centers, domestic abuse programs, programs for the mentally challenged, pretrial diversion, relapse prevention, sexual offender programs, work crews, and drug courts. Each jurisdiction has its own ideas about probation and the programs they offer. An explanation of one of the "other" programs that might help you better understand the diversity of probation program is domestic abuse programs. It is assumed that the intervention of the officer, the effective use of supervision tools designed to control an offender, and the use of treatment resources can enable the cycle of violence to be broken and provide an opportunity to have a positive impact upon the offender and ensure the welfare of the victim. Largely, the objectives[57] of domestic abuse programs can be described as four categories that:

- Provide close supervision and control of domestic violence offenders.
- Enhance the safety of domestic violence victims.
- Ensure that the batterer completes treatment.
- Coordinate the efforts of the courts, law enforcement, treatment agencies, and victim advocates with the probation agency's efforts to address the cycle of violence. Furthermore, most domestic abuse offender control programs consist of the following key elements:
- Completion of a lethality assessment of the offender.
- Supervision of the offender under the electronic house arrest intermediate punishment sanction.
- Completion of a batterer's treatment program and other counseling deemed appropriate for the offender.
- Geographic restrictions of offender's movement and whereabouts.
- Placement of a monitoring device within the victim's residence and use of a help/panic button to detect possible offender intrusion.
- Immediate response to violations from the victim's residence from both law enforcement and probation-parole personnel.
- Use of supervision tools such as drug screens and warrantless searches.

Things to Know about Probation Programs

As you read through the assortment of programs, familiar characteristics might appear within each such as surveillance, drug testing, and methods to alter the behavior of a participant toward a crime-free lifestyle regardless of the name of the program. Probation programs assume that most probationers want guidance in their life despite some of their comments and failures. One mission is to keep the defendant out of prison. Why? Because one of the greatest things you can do for another is not just share your riches, but reveal to them their own (as Benjamin Disraeli argues), through programs that help an individual see the right choices regardless of what the program is called.

Female Offenders—Walking Through Enhanced Supervision

Wendy Landry
Senior U.S. Probation Officer, Northern District of Texas

A NON-TRADITIONAL approach to supervising offenders can provide them with structure in a seemingly unstructured environment. Many of our offenders live on a chaotic roller coaster with very little chance of getting off the ride. A continuous frustration to many probation officers is getting offenders stable in the office only to send them back into their chaotic environment, where they return to their "normal" way of dealing with problems. When officers provide structure in an unstructured environment, offenders can learn coping skills that they will carry with them when they are not with their officer.

The Northern District of Texas, Garland Division, conducted a women's issues group that consisted of female offenders (mental health, drug, white collar, and general offenders) under federal supervision. The women's group revealed that many of our female offenders were suffering from depression and lack of motivation, which was exacerbated by their being overweight. We hypothesized that if we were able to get the offenders walking, then they would not only improve their physical appearance, but also their self-esteem and motivation.

A PROGRAM THEY COULD OWN

The women from the original women's issues group were approached with the idea of starting "their" own walking group, getting together one day a week to walk as a group. Several women became very excited about the concept and began not only to anticipate what would come from this group, but to help officers plan the program. This gave the women ownership of the program and therefore made them responsible for its success. Key to the success of this type of group is to allow the women to think they have the choice to attend; thus the officer doesn't have to waste time breaking through their guard. Although the group was not mandatory for any of the women referred, some were strongly encouraged to attend. Often this is important to get them to attend the group for the first time, after which their peers will keep them coming back.

Once plans were underway, the next step was to find a centrally located area in Dallas, Texas, that would provide walking trails with a relaxing atmosphere. We found this at White Rock Lake, located in the middle of the city, which made it easy for every participant to reach within 25 minutes. Other female offenders outside the women's issues group were referred to the walking group. For those women whose officers may not have considered referring them, we created a flyer for the lobby to entice interest. The wording of the flyer was developed by both officers and offenders. The flyer read: "Do you need some time for yourself? Would you like to be around other women who understand your circumstances? Would you like to feel better about yourself physically and do something about it?" Many offenders told us that the wording of the flyer really got them interested in the group.

To provide tangible means of measuring progress, a female deputy with the U.S. Marshals Office was asked to come in to calculate the group's body fat. Knowing that women would not show up for a group if they knew they were going to be weighed or measured, the officers sent out letters advising them that our first meeting would be in the office with a guest speaker. They were instructed to come dressed in shorts and t-shirts or bring this attire with them. Ironically, although they were instructed to bring shorts, not a single woman in the group did so. Although they did not know specifically what they were going to be subjected to with this guest speaker, we believe that they intentionally did not wear shorts in order to maintain control of what was going to happen in the group.

When the women arrived, the marshal was already in the room and the women naturally thought that she was a part of the group. When she was introduced as a U.S. marshal, every group member became paralyzed with fear that they had been tricked and were all going to jail. In general, these offenders had never had a positive contact with a U.S. marshal; their contact consisted of being arrested. One of the offenders had actually been arrested by this same deputy and was quick to announce this to the group. The women went through a series of emotions in just a few seconds; terror, which quickly turned to anger, and then a sense of relief when they realized they were not going to jail. The group immediately unified to revolt against getting their body fat measured. Officers attempted to defuse the revolt by stating that they would go first. In response, a participant stepped forward and said that she would go first. The offenders were given envelopes in which to place their results if they chose not to know their results immediately. They were then told that the deputy was sworn to secrecy and nobody had to know their percentage of fat. By the time the deputy completed everyone's test, including the officers, participants had loosened up and were joking with one another, sharing their body fat percentage with everyone in the group. By the time the class was over, the ladies had trust in the group, they had trust (for the first time) in the deputy, and they had found a way to laugh about a very uncomfortable situation.

We had not intended to walk during this first meeting; however, the group insisted we get started. Participants united and decided as a group that they would walk around the area for a short time. From this experience, they learned how to make a decision as a team, present it to the "boss," and execute their plan.

LEARNING LIFE SKILLS

The group experience begins before participants even leave the house: They experience their motivation to come to the group. Before attending this program, many offenders had little motivation to get out of bed, much less exercise. The walking group gives these women something to look forward to: talking with other women who understand what they are going through, knowing that someone cares if they show up or not, and doing something to make themselves feel better.

(*continued*)

(continued)

As the group has continued, it has become dear that the original hypothesis (walking will decrease depression while increasing self-esteem and motivation) underestimated the power of this group. There are many life skills that these women are learning without being aware of it and, because of this, there is no resistance so they are able to take the learned skills home with them. First, walking becomes a symbol of moving forward in life. Offenders are physically moving to achieve the goal of finishing that day's walk. Each woman shows up with a goal, whether it be to finish the walk, push to finish last week's territory in a shorter time, or even keep up with the fastest walker. They may have accomplished their goal just by showing up. They must learn to accept their accomplishments as well as their limitations.

Offenders are learning how to work as a team through leadership and encouragement. They are learning to make decisions together and plan for the future. For example, one day the officer got caught up at the office and was late getting to the lake. This left the woman with a dilemma: go ahead and walk or wait? As a group they determined that they would go ahead and walk, but walk the circular trail so they could watch for the officer's arrival. They further considered how to handle this situation in the future and determined which path they would take so that any late-comers would know where to find them.

Learning to set appropriate limits without feeling guilty is often a hard lesson for female offenders to learn. One day was very humid and hot. All the women were having a hard time finishing the normal walk, but Sharon in particular was having problems. Sharon, an extroverted single mother in her mid 30's, has a troubled teenager over whom she has little control. Sharon has been unable to set limits and stick to them without validation from her peers. On this particular day, Sharon's normal walking partner did not show up. Sharon was having great difficulty keeping up with the others and became more frustrated by the minute. This appeared to be a perfect opportunity to discuss accepting one's limits. We discussed the fact that many women have a hard time saying "no" and that it is important for them to listen to their minds and bodies to become aware of when they need to stop pushing. Sharon was given "permission" to tell the others in the group that they were pushing her too hard and she would not be keeping up. She was encouraged to do this without the guilt generally associated with saying "no." When she set her limit and accepted that she wasn't going to keep up with the rest of the group, she slowed down to a pace that was comfortable for her. She found support when another woman decided to keep her company. Her officer also stayed by her side until she finished the walk. This gave Sharon positive, experiential practice in being aware of her limitations, expressing these limitations appropriately, and following through with her wishes.

Learning alternative ways to deal with anger is another skill the women are building. One woman came to group one day annoyed about the lack of support she receives from her family of origin. As we walked, she talked about her frustration that she has always been there for her family, but when she needed them, they were nowhere to be found. As she became more agitated, she began to walk briskly until she was moving at a slow jog. After she released her anger, her pace naturally slowed back down. This process allowed her to express her anger in a physically healthy manner.

A Case in Point

The walking group, an apparently unstructured activity, in fact gave the offenders a loose, adaptable structure within which they were able to learn skills that have enhanced their lives and their supervision. However, it has helped Nicole in almost every aspect of her life. Nicole is serving a three-year term of supervised release for Using a Facility of Interstate Commerce to Promote and Facilitate Unlawful Activity Involving Prostitution. When she was first released from prison, she was very guarded and verbal about not letting probation know anything personal about her. As the weeks went on, she became very depressed and suicidal, and eventually wouldn't leave her home. She attended the original women's issues group only to keep her officer "off her back." However, during the group, she began to open up, finding a non-judging trust with her peers. Nicole was one of the first to jump at the opportunity to participate in the walking group. In fact, she pushed to get the group started early. The first day of the group was a turning point for Nicole. The deputy who measured our body fat was the deputy who had arrested Nicole on her instant offense. Although she was scared, she participated in the measurements, thanked the deputy for coming, and was able to joke that it was nice to see the deputy leave without her in handcuffs. Nicole has made remarkable progress in her personal life. Before the walking group, Nicole got up in the morning only to get her daughter off to school and promptly returned to bed. She suffers from major depressive disorder and was non-compliant with medications prescribed for this disorder. She used the excuse that she couldn't take her anti-depressant because she was afraid that it would make her gain even more weight. Until her supervision, Nicole had never worked a legal job in her life and was terrified of the rejection she might face if she began to seriously seek employment. Nicole came weekly to the walking group and made much progress. The first day we met at the lake, she could not locate the meeting place, but drove around the lake for an hour. Instead of becoming frustrated and angry, she realized how relaxed she felt just being close to the water. The following week, she was at the meeting place early and announced that she had been coming out to the lake daily to walk. Nicole quickly became a leader in the group, pushing others to try to pick up the pace and go a little further. Those who couldn't keep up developed the goal of being able to keep up with her in the future. Nicole became compliant with her medication and not only began to feel better, but was looking great. One day, Nicole complained to the group as they walked that she had filled out an application several months earlier at Wal Mart and was annoyed because she had never received a response. The group suggested that she take the initiative and follow up with Wal Mart. She took the group's advice and drove straight to Wal Mart, which hired her on the spot.

(continued)

LEVELS OF BENEFIT

The walking group has met regularly for the past seven months. During this time, we have had 15 offenders participate. The level of benefit varies from participant to participant. Three have found full-time professional jobs. Two of these women have informed their employers that they are participating in an exercise program and have asked for flexibility in their schedules on walking day to allow continued attendance. Their employers agree to this most of the time. Recently, one of the walkers admitted to her officer that she had used cocaine. Obviously, this is a serious violation of her supervision, in addition to being against the law. However, because of the working relationship she had built with her officer through her participation in the group, she admitted to feeling guilt for the first time ever in her life. She faced consequences for her actions and continues to walk weekly with the group. Another woman has attended every week without fail. Although she continues to be unemployed, she has become more active in the community, doing volunteer work and spending less time at home (which had been adding to her depression).

Not all participants have enjoyed the walking group. One woman came to the group a couple of times and decided that she did not like walking and hated the heat. Although she no longer participates in the group, it has been easier for her officer to break through her anger and supervise her because she knows her officer cares. Regardless of the level of personal benefit, offenders have become more open with their supervising officers, which allows officers to be proactive in their supervision of these offenders.

Conducting a walking group has given structure to the offenders in a non-traditional way. The group was started with the simple idea of forming a program with offenders so they could walk together. It has allowed offenders to physically move forward in their lives while learning valuable life skills. Skills learned in the group have helped not only the participants but also the officers. Offenders quickly realized that officers are human, that they care and are interested in offender's progress. In turn, offenders trust officers. Officers are given an opportunity to witness remarkably rapid progress emerging from a program that has enhanced their ability to supervise these women in the community.

Printed with permission of the U.S. Courts.[58]

Probation Statistics

A review of Table 7.7 and Table 7.8 will provide a better picture about the offenders involved in probation in the United States in 2003.

Table 7.7 Adults on Probation 2003

Region and Jurisdiction	Probation Population, 1/1/03	2003 Entries	Exits	Probation Population, 12/31/03	Percentage Change, 2003	Number on Probation per 100,000 Adult Residents, 12/31/03
U.S. total	4,024,067	2,229,668	2,179,847	4,073,987	1.2	1,876
Federal	31,330	13,989	14,449	30,599	−2.3	14
State	3,992,737	2,215,679	2,165,398	4,043,388	1.3	1,862
Northeast	629,503	233,044	247,722	614,825	−2.3	1,491
Connecticut	50,984	24,384	23,176	52,192	2.4	1,983
Maine	9,446	6,625	6,216	9,855	4.3	984
Massachusetts[a,b,c]	131,319	56,933	61,117	127,135	—	2,585
New Hampshire[d]	3,702	1,480	1,052	4,130	11.6	426
New Jersey	134,290	40,601	50,610	124,281	−7.5	1,907
New York[b]	132,966	39,590	48,261	124,295	−6.5	859
Pennsylvania[c]	130,786	52,072	45,652	137,206	4.9	1,454
Rhode Island	25,914	6,451	6,436	25,929	0.1	3,143
Vermont	10,096	4,908	5,202	9,802	−2.9	2,085
Midwest	937,378	606,152	607,511	936,387	−0.1	1,926
Illinois	141,544	63,000	60,090	144,454	2.1	1,542
Indiana	114,209	94,741	97,324	111,626	−2.3	2,424
Iowa	19,970	14,600	13,685	20,885	4.6	945
Kansas [c]	15,217	23,315	23,981	14,551	−4.4	725
Michigan[c,d]	174,577	130,857	129,029	176,392	1.0	2,364
Minnesota	122,692	59,517	71,484	110,725	−9.8	2,953
Missouri	54,584	26,512	25,486	55,610	1.9	1,305
Nebraska	16,468	15,845	13,901	18,412	11.8	1,432
North Dakota	3,229	2,332	2,059	3,502	8.5	737
Ohio[c,d]	215,186	146,723	142,616	219,658	2.1	2,573
South Dakota	5,088	3,261	3,129	5,236	2.9	933
Wisconsin	54,614	25,449	24,727	55,336	1.3	1,354
South	1,623,038	960,243	910,074	1,673,206	3.1	2,135
Alabama	39,713	15,152	15,213	39,652	−0.2	1,177
Arkansas	27,377	9,168	8,419	28,126	2.7	1,380
Delaware	20,201	13,962	15,242	18,921	−6.3	3,058
Washington, DC [c,d]	9,389	6,597	8,755	7,231	—	1,612
Florida[c,d]	291,315	257,539	261,212	287,641	−1.3	2,169
Georgia[e,a]	367,349	230,686	173,850	424,385	—	—
Kentucky[c]	24,480	16,165	11,949	28,696	17.2	921
Louisiana	36,257	13,875	13,455	36,677	1.2	1,120
Maryland	81,982	39,037	43,144	77,875	−5.0	1,890
Mississippi [c,f]	16,633	8,773	6,290	19,116	14.9	911

(continued)

Table 7.7   Adults on Probation 2003 (Continued)

Region and Jurisdiction	Probation Population, 1/1/03	2003 Entries	Exits	Probation Population, 12/31/03	Percentage Change, 2003	Number on Probation per 100,000 Adult Residents, 12/31/03
North Carolina	112,900	60,782	60,521	113,161	0.2	1,770
Oklahoma[d]	29,881	15,299	16,854	28,326	–5.2	1,082
South Carolina	41,574	14,760	16,287	40,047	–3.7	1,285
Tennessee[c]	42,712	24,256	24,132	42,836	0.3	968
Texas	434,486	200,450	202,947	431,989	–0.6	2,698
Virginia	40,359	30,669	29,365	41,663	3.2	743
West Virginia [c]	6,430	3,072	2,638	6,864	6.7	487
West	802,818	416,241	400,092	818,970	2.0	1,672
Alaska	5,229	973	796	5,406	3.4	1,185
Arizona[d]	66,485	39,115	39,795	65,805	–1.0	1,586
California[d]	358,121	180,636	164,059	374,701	4.6	1,441
Colorado[c,d]	57,328	28,954	30,985	55,297	–3.5	1,623
Hawaii	16,772	7,006	6,126	17,652	5.2	1,822
Idaho[d,g]	31,361	25,360	24,501	32,220	2.7	—
Montana	6,703	3,898	3,687	6,914	3.1	1,006
Nevada	12,290	5,869	6,000	12,159	–1.1	716
New Mexico	16,287	7,662	7,813	16,136	–0.9	1,186
Oregon	45,397	16,275	16,847	44,825	–1.3	1,662
Utah	10,646	5,429	5,696	10,379	–2.5	646
Washington[c,d]	171,603	93,132	91,921	172,814	0.7	3,767
Wyoming	4,596	1,932	1,866	4,662	1.4	1,255

Note: Because of incomplete data, the population for some jurisdictions on December 31, 2003 does not equal the population on January 1, 2003, plus entries, minus exits. Areas marked with—were not calculated.

[a]Data are for June 30, 2002 and 2003. Some data for June 30, 2002 were estimated.

[b]Due to change in reporting criteria, data are not comparable to previous reports.

[c]Data for entries and exits were estimated for nonreporting agencies.

[d]All data were estimated.

[e]Counts include private agency cases and may overstate the number under supervision.

[f]Data are for yearend December 1, 2003.

[g]Counts include estimates for misdemeanors based on admissions.

Printed with permission of the U.S. Department of Justice.[59]

Some highlights:

- Approximately 4.1 million offenders were on probation as of December 30, 2003.[61]
- The number of individuals on probation is the equivalent of almost one in every 53 adults living in America.

Table 7.8   Probation among the States, Yearend 2003

10 States with the Largest 2003 CC Population	Number Supervised	10 States with the Largest Percentage Increase	Percentage Increase, 2002–03	10 States with the Highest Rates of Supervision, 2003	Persons Supervised per 100,000 Adult U.S. Residents[a]	10 States with the Lowest Rates of Supervision, 2003	Persons Supervised per 100,000 Adult U.S. Residents[a]
Probation							
Texas	431,989	Kentucky	17.2	Washington	3,767	New Hampshire	426
California	374,701	Mississippi	14.9	Rhode Island	3,143	West Virginia	487
Florida	287,641	Nebraska	11.8	Delaware	3,058	Utah	646
Ohio	219,658	New Hampshire	11.6	Minnesota	2,953	Nevada	716
Michigan	176,392	North Dakota	8.5	Texas	2,698	Kansas	725
Washington	172,814	West Virginia	6.7	Massachusetts	2,585	North Dakota	737
Illinois	144,454	Hawaii	5.2	Ohio	2,573	Virginia	743
Pennsylvania	137,206	Pennsylvania	4.9	Indiana	2,424	New York	859
Massachusetts	127,135	California	4.6	Michigan	2,364	Mississippi	911
New York	124,295	Iowa	4.6	Florida	2,169	Kentucky	921

Note: This table excludes Washington, DC, a wholly urban jurisdiction; Georgia probation counts, which included probation case-based counts for private agencies; and Idaho, in which misdemeanor probation counts were not reported in 2003.

[a] Rates based on the estimated number of adult state residents on December 31, 2003.

Printed with the permission of the U.S. Department of Justice.[60]

- With 3,767 probationers per 100,000 adult state residents, Washington state had the highest rate of probation supervision; New Hampshire (with 426 per 100,000) had the lowest.

- At yearend 2003, more than half of all probationers were white (2,298,600); almost a third were black (1,209,000); and an eighth were of Hispanic origin (491,700).

- Forty seven percent of probationers had a direct sentence to probation; 29 percent had received a sentence of incarceration that had been suspended; and 9 percent had received a split sentence that included incarceration followed by probation. An additional 12 percent had entered probation before completion of all court proceedings (including those who entered probation before final verdict).

- At yearend 2003, one in nine probationers had absconded (had failed to report and could not be located).

- In 2003, 25 percent of probationers had a drug law violation; 17 percent were sentenced for DWI or under the influence of alcohol; 12 percent for larceny/theft; and 9 percent for other assault, excluding sexual assault and domestic violence. Fewer than 10 percent were sentenced to probation for domestic violence (7 percent), minor traffic offenses (6 percent), burglary (5 percent), fraud (4 percent), and sexual assault (3 percent).

Table 7.9   State Probation Budgets

Arizona	$56,000,594
Colorado	$52,861,835
Connecticut	$29,800,000
Washington, DC	$812,000,000
Georgia	$69,312,367
Illinois	$218,100,000
Nebraska	$14,512,771
Texas	$277,443,155
Wyoming	$10,922,466
Total	$1,490,953,168
Average	$165,661,463

Printed with permission of the Corrections Yearbook.[62]

- About three in five of the more than 2 million adults discharged from probation in 2003 had successfully met the conditions of their supervision. The percentage of probationers discharged from probation supervision because of incarceration due to a rule violation or new offense varied from 21 percent in 1995 to 16 percent in 2003.

Table 7.10   Cost per Day per Probationer in 2001

State	Overall	Regular	Intensive	Electronic[a]	Special[b]
Arizona	$3.60	$2.16	$17.22		
Colorado	$4.74	$1.71	$ 8.41	$ 2.49	$6.35
Connecticut	$1.70				
Washington, DC	$8.90	$8.90		$11.91	
Georgia	$1.58	$1.43	$ 3.62		$3.62
Illinois	$3.80	$3.50	$13.00	$ 5.00	$8.00
Nebraska		$4.33	$ 6.00		
Texas		$2.13			
Utah	$4.93				
Average	$4.18	$3.47	$ 9.77	$ 6.47	$5.99

[a] Supervision of a probationer that includes the use of an electronic monitoring devise such as an ankle bracelet, pager, voice verification telephone, or other electronic technology that assists probation officers in ascertaining an offenders' whereabouts.

[b] Includes special programming such as boot camp, substance abuse treatment program, or other programs and services. Imprisonment costs per day in 2003: $170.49 for juveniles, $64.80 for adults.[64]

Printed with permission of the *Corrections Yearbook*.[63]

Probation Budgets

Probation agencies across the United States spent an average of approximately $165,661,463 in 2001. See Table 7.9 for specifics:

To get a better picture, state budgets for probational services should be added to agencies that offer both probation and parole services. That totaled $1,464,871,971 in 2001. However, this total does not include states that offer parole separate from probation. Also, Table 7.10 offers a state per-day, per-probationer cost.

SUMMARY

Probation is a humane and less expensive alternative to incarceration. It was revealed that probation can provide advantageous programs that can alter the behavior of troubled offenders. Probation is a court-ordered term of community supervision under specified conditions for a specific period of time. It is described as conditions of freedom (i.e., curfew, drug and alcohol prohibitions, residence requirements) that can divert a guilty defendant from the consequences of imprisonment. Probationers have diminished constitutional rights compared with other citizens, yet revoking probation can only be accomplished through a court process. Public safety, keeping defendants out of prison, rehabilitation, and preserving family ties and employment are common goals of probation systems. Disadvantages of probation include a perceived lack of punishment, a loss of confidence in the justice community, and an increase in the risk of a community.

Origins of probation are traced to a shoemaker in Boston named John Augustus who asked a Boston court to release adult drunkards and wayward juveniles to his custody in 1843. Today every state, Washington, DC, and the federal government provide probation services and offer a wide array of programs. There were 4.1 million offenders on probation in 2003 and three in five of the more than two million adults discharged from probation had successfully met the conditions of their supervision. Costs per probationer is averaged at around four dollars per day, making this intermediate sanction helpful in a day when state budgets have been drastically reduced.

DISCUSSION QUESTIONS

1. Describe some of the rationale behind probation systems in the United States. In what way might you agree with the rationale supporting probation?

2. Define probation and identify its primary mission.

3. Identify the advantages of probation to the justice community and to a probationer. In what way might the community benefit from probation?

4. Identify some of the common conditions of freedom required of probationers. In what way do you agree with those conditions and in what way might those conditions preserve public safety?

5. Describe the rights of probationers and identify some of the chief legislation protecting them. In what way might you agree with probationer rights? Disagree?

6. Explain the relevance of diminished constitutional rights and preferred rights among probationers. In what way do you think that the rights of probationers should be increased or reduced?

7. Explain how probation works and identify some of its key components.

8. Articulate the historical development of "state" probation and identify some of the contributions of its early founders.

9. Describe the historical development of federal probation.

10. Describe the primary probation services and their programs.

NOTES

1. Bureau of Justice Statistics (2004, July). *Probation and parole in the United States, 2003.* Washington, DC: U.S. Department of Justice, Office of Justice Programs, NCJ 205336. Retrieved online January 9, 2005: http://www.ojp.usdoj.gov/bjs/pub/pdf/ppus03.pdf

2. Bureau of Justice Statistics (2004, November). *Prisoners in 2003.* Washington, DC: U.S. Department of Justice, Office of Justice Programs, NCJ 205335 Retrieved online January 9, 2005: http://www.ojp.usdoj.gov/bjs/pub/pdf/p03.pdf

3. Dennis J. Stevens (2006). The history of continental Europe and England prisons. *Encyclopedia of Criminology.*

4. Robert Sigler (2000, August). Prison costs rising even as crime declines. *USA Toady Magazine.* Retrieved online July 10, 2004: http://www.findarticles.com/p/articles/mi_m1272/is_2663_129/ai_63986732

5. Robert Sigler (2000).

6. Joan Petersilia, Susan Turner, James Kahan, and Joyce Peterson (1985). *Granting felons probation: Public risks and alternatives.* California: Rand Corporation (p. vii).

7. Stanton Samenow (1984). *Inside the criminal mind.* New York: Times Books (pp. 141–142). Curt R. Bartol and Anne M. Bartol (2005). *Criminal behavior: A psychological approach.* Upper Saddle River, NJ: Prentice Hall (p. 339). Bartol and Bartol say that mass murders are on the rise in the United States and estimate that mass murderers are responsible for as many as 3,500 to 5,000 victims each year. One concern is that the profile of the victims has changed from young females to children. Amber alerts have been developed by many police departments across the country in an attempt to curb this trend.

8. Alan T. Harland and Wayne N. Welsh (1999) Toward the strategic management of correctional innovation: Putting what works information to work. In Patricia M. Harris (Ed.), *Research to results: Effective community corrections* (pp. 105–150). Lanham, MD: International Community Corrections Association.

9. Joan Petersilia, Susan Turner, James Kahan, and Joyce Peterson (1985).

10. Michael Braswell, Tyler Fletcher, and Larry Miller (1998). *Human relations and corrections.* Prospect Heights, IL: Waveland (p. 19).

11. Dennis J. Stevens (2006). *Community corrections: An applied approach.* Upper Saddle River, NJ: Prentice Hall. This story was guided by Michael Braswell, Tyler Fletcher, and Larry Miller (1998). *Human relations and corrections.* Prospect Heights, IL: Waveland (pp. 19–20).

12. Bureau of Justice Statistics (1995, August). *Probation and parole violators in state prison, 1991: Survey of state prison inmates, 1991.* U.S. Department of Justice, Office of Justice Programs, Special Report NCJ 149076. Retrieved online January 10, 2005: http://www.ojp.usdoj.gov/bjs/pub/ascii/ppvsp91.txt

13. Bureau of Justice Statistics (1995, August). *Probation and parole violators in state prison, 1991: Survey of state prison inmates, 1991.*

14. Bureau of Justice Statistics (1995, August). *Probation and parole violators in state prison, 1991: Survey of state prison inmates, 1991.*

15. 421 F.2nd, cert. Denied, 397 U.S. 1044 (1970). Also see Roland del Carmen (1984). *Legal issues and liabilities in community corrections.* Paper presented at the annual meeting of ACJS, Chicago. And Roland del Carmen (1991). *Civil liabilities in American policing.* Englewood Cliffs, NJ: Prentice Hall.

16. Bureau of Justice Statistics (2004, July). *Probation and parole in the United States, 2003.*

17. Bureau of Justice Statistics (2004, July). *Probation and parole in the United States, 2003.*

18. This definition and supporting information is consistent with the State of Florida's, Department of Corrections. Retrieved online August 20, 2004: http://www.dc .state.fl.us/pub/annual/9697/stats/stat_cs.html#3

19. *The corrections yearbook: Adult corrections 2002* (2003). Camille Graham Camp & George Camp (Eds.). Middletown, CT: Criminal Justice Institute.

20. Bureau of Justice Statistics (2004, July). *Probation and parole in the United States, 2003.*

21. Daniel Glaser (1997). *Profitable penalties: How to cut both crime rates and costs.* Thousand Oaks, CA: Pine Forge.

22. Bureau of Justice Statistics (1997, December). *Nearly three-quarters of all probationers had some recent contact with their probation officers.* Washington, DC: U.S. Department of Justice, Office of Justice Programs, NCJ 164267. Retrieved online January 10, 2005: http://www.ojp.usdoj.gov/bjs/pub/press/cap95.pr

23. *The corrections yearbook: Adult corrections 2002* (2003).

24. *United States v Turner,* 44 F. 3d 900 (10th Cir. 1995).

25. *Gagnon v. Scarpelli,* 411 U.S. 778, 93 S. Ct. 1756 (1972).

26. This thought is linked to the federal system of government; that is, a check and balance political system.

27. Bureau of Justice Statistics (2004, July). *Probation and parole in the United States, 2003* (p. 4).

28. U.S.C.A. 3651. Also the following was used as a guide. Paul F. Cromwell, Rolando V. del Carmen, and Leanne F. Alarid (2002). *Community-based corrections* (4th ed.). Belmont, CA: Wadsworth.

29. The Minnesota Association of County Probation Officers was used as a source for this section. Their website is at: http://www.mncorrections.org/macpo/historyofprobation.htm

30. Department of Correctional Services. New York. Historical Archives. Retrieved online January 10, 2005: http://www.docs.state.ny.us/

31. United Nations Department of Social Affairs, Probation and related measures: 1951. (1972). In Robert Carter and Leslie Wilkins (Eds.) *Probation, parole, and community corrections* (pp. 81–89). New York: Wiley.

32. James R. Cameron (2001). *Frederick William Maitland and the history of English Law.* New York: Lawbook Exchange.

33. United Nations Asian and Far East Institute (1997). *Annual report for 1996.* Resource Material Series No. 51. Tokyo: United Nations Asian and Far East Institute for the Prevention of Crime and Treatment of Offenders (p. 119).

34. Dennis J. Stevens (2006). The history of continental Europe and England prisons. *Encyclopedia of Criminology.*

35. Sean McConville (1995). The Victorian prison: England, 1865–1965. In Norris Morris and David J. Rothman (Eds.), *The Oxford history of the prison: The practice of punishment in western society* (pp. 117–177). New York: Oxford University Press.

36. Department of Correctional Services. New York. Historical Archives. 2004.

37. Minnesota Association of County Probation Officers. Retrieved online August 21, 2004: http://www.mncorrections.org/macpo/historyofprobation.htm

38. Arnold Binder, Gilbert Geis, and D. Dickson Bruce, Jr. (1997). *Juvenile delinquency: Historical, cultural and legal perspectives* (2nd ed.). Cincinnati, OH: Anderson.

39. Harry Elmer Barnes and Negley K. Teeters (1959). *New horizons in criminology,* (3rd ed.). Englewood Cliffs, NJ: Prentice Hall, 554.

40. American Probation and Parole Association. *History of probation.* Retrieved online January 10, 2005: http://www.appa-net.org/media2004/probationhistory.htm

41. American Probation and Parole Association (2002). *The history of probation.*

42. A. R. Klein (1997). *Alternative sentencing, intermediate sanctions and probation.* Cincinnati, OH: Anderson.

43. National Center for Juvenile Justice (1991). *Desktop guide to good juvenile probation practice.* Pittsburgh, PA: Author. Retrieved online December 3, 2004: http://ncjj.servehttp.com/NCJJWebsite/pdf/insumaftercare.pdf

44. Edward J. Latessa and Harry E. Allen (1999). *Corrections in the community.* Cincinnati, OH: Anderson (pp. 112, 127–128).

45. F. R. Johnson (1928). Probation for juveniles and adults. NY: Century, 12–13.

46. Table developed by the author for this chapter after reviewing: Petersilia (2003); Edward J. Latessa and Harry E. Allen (1999); American Probation and Parole Association. *The history of probation* (2002), Department of Correctional Services. New York. Historical Archives (2004); Petersilia (1997); and Barnes and Teeters (1959).

47. It is reported that Jewish slaves were in ancient Egypt and have been found throughout history as a group who were often both enslaved and executed. The early ancestors of the Scots, Alba, and Picts were enslaved as early as the first century BC. In the sixth century, Pope Gregory first witnessed blonde haired, blue eyed boys awaiting sale in a Roman slave market. The Romans enslaved thousands of white inhabitants of Great Britain, who were also known as Angles. There are many documents that verify the bondage, kidnapping, and transporting of Brits to the Colonies as slaves. Some origins of white slavery can be found among the white captives held in African slave markets, people who were kidnapped by pirates during raids on the coasts of England, Ireland, and France. These slaves were very highly valued, especially by North African chieftains. The gold mining industry on the Gold Coast, modern-day Ghana, was also a magnet for the African slave trade, which continued long after the European nations agreed its abolition. White slaves were still held in North Africa as late as 1626. Around the 1470s, the Portuguese began to play a middleman role in the slave trade between the various African kingdoms. They imported slaves to the Gold Coast from Benin, Kongo, and Angola. But after 1540 the Portuguese involvement was curtailed when the Songhai Empire of Western Sudan increased the number of slaves it could trade with the Gold Coast merchants. The desperate need for labor in the gold mines led the Fanti and Asant of the Gold Coast to acquire their slaves in exchange for gold. The trade with North America and the Caribbean islands increased the demand for slaves from Africa. Initially though, labor on the sugar and tobacco plantations of the Caribbean and North American colonies was provided by white laborers. Many of these laborers were working-class people from Britain who had been kidnapped and transported to the West Indies to work as laborers there. But soon the English plantation owners found that their profits were lagging behind those of their fellow Europeans, Dutch, and Portuguese who used black slaves. When they discovered how much cheaper it was to use black slaves, as opposed to white laborers, the demand for African slaves increased dramatically. In the United States, white slavery included the transportation of youths to

slave markets, particularly for the sexual demands of others. See Brian M. Fagan (1998). *Clash of cultures.* Thousand Oaks, CA: Sage. And Eric Hopkins (1979). *A social history of the English working classes.* New York: Hodder Arnold H&S.

48. By the turn of the 20th century, temperance societies were prevalent in the United States. Concerned citizens had begun warning others about the effects of alcohol nearly 100 years earlier. However, enforcing Prohibition through the Volstead Act proved to be extremely difficult. The illegal production and distribution of liquor, or bootlegging, became rampant, and the national government did not have the means or desire to try to enforce every border, lake, river, and speakeasy in America. In fact, by 1925, in New York City alone there were anywhere from 30,000 to 100,000 speakeasy clubs. The demand for alcohol was outweighing (and outwinning) the demand for sobriety. People found clever ways to evade Prohibition agents. They carried hip flasks, hollowed canes, false books, and the like. While Prohibition assisted the poor factory workers who could not afford liquor, all in all, neither federal nor local authorities would commit the resources necessary to enforce the Volstead Act. For example, the state of Maryland refused to pass any enforcement issue. Prohibition made life in America more violent, with open rebellion against the law and organized crime. See David Pietrusaz (1998). *The roaring Twenties.* San Diego, CA: Lucent.

49. Dennis J. Stevens (2006). *Community corrections: An applied approach.* Upper Saddle River, NJ: Prentice Hall. The author developed Table 7.3 after reviewing the following: *Federal sentencing guidelines.* Retrieved online December 3, 2004: http://www.ussc.gov/2004guid/7b1_3.htm. Petersilia (2003): *U.S. courts and federal probation.* Retrieved online December 3, 2004: http://www.uscourts.gov/faq .html. William L. Selke and John Ortiz Smykla (1995). *Intermediate sanctions: Sentencing in the 1990s.* Cincinnati, OH: Anderson.

50. *The corrections yearbook: Adult corrections 2002* (2003), 214.

51. Bureau of Justice Statistics (2004, July). *Probation and parole in the United States, 2003,* 3).

52. *The corrections yearbook: Adult corrections 2002* (2003). p. 212.

53. William L. Selke and John Ortiz Smykla (1995).

54. *The corrections yearbook: Adult corrections 2002* (2003), 210.

55. Dean Champion (1999). *Probation, parole, and community corrections* (3rd ed.). Upper Saddle River, NJ: Prentice Hall (pp. 139–140).

56. *Justice Junction* (2001). Retrieved online January 14, 2005: http://www .justicejunction.com/

57. These guidelines are consistent with the North Carolina Department of Corrections. Probation-Parole Division. Revised January 2004. Retrieved online December 3, 2004: http://www.doc.state.nc.us/dcc/index.htm

58. Wendy Landry (2001). Female offenders: Walking through enhanced supervision. *Federal Probation, 65*(3), 46–49. Retrieved online January 10, 2005: http://www .uscourts.gov/fedprob/2001decfp.pdf

59. Bureau of Justice Statistics (2004, July). *Probation and parole in the United States 2003.*

60. Bureau of Justice Statistics (2004, July). *Probation and parole in the United States 2003.*

61. Bureau of Justice Statistics (2004, July). *Probation and parole in the United States 2003.*

62. *The corrections yearbook: Adult corrections 2002* (2003), 204.

63. *The corrections yearbook: Adult corrections 2002* (2003), 206.

64. *American Correctional Association 2003 Directory: Adult and juvenile* (2004). Lanham, MD: American Correctional Association (pp. 20, 25). Other sources include slightly different average totals such as *The correctional yearbook: Adult corrections* (2002). But two ideas should be clear (a) in criminal justice, sources often disagree and (b) criminal justice intervention is expensive.

PROCESS OF PROBATION AND THE ROLE OF PROBATION OFFICERS

LEARNING OBJECTIVES

When you finish reading this chapter, you will be better prepared to:

- Identify the influences that shape the process of probation.
- Describe advantages and disadvantages of executive and judicial branches of government linked to their operation of probation systems.
- Explain the negative and positive issues associated with probation.
- Clarify the primary roles performed by probation officers.
- Describe the range of responsibilities of probation officers.
- Describe the contradictions associated with probation officer performance.
- Identify the ultimate mission of probation officers.
- Describe various styles of delivery typified by many probation officers.
- Discuss the development of female probation officers.
- Explain the future of probation officers.
- Identify some of the competencies expected of probation officers and explain why those competencies might be helpful to a probation officer.

KEY TERMS

Absconders	Law Enforcer Role	Probation Officer Traps
Bureaucrat Role	Maternalist Orientations	Probation Officer Styles
Contradiction of Probation	Probation Management	Social Worker Role

I am a great believer in luck, and I find the harder I work the more I have of it.
—Thomas Jefferson (1743–1826)

INTRODUCTION

Chapter 7 described the nature of probation. This chapter focuses on the process of probation, which includes a description of the roles and responsibilities of probation officers
(POs). The probation process concerns the source of probation authority and addresses
both negative and positive issues linked to the most frequently used criminal justice
sanction—probation. Probation is an "agent of change," and as such, its process is guided
by policy that is always under scrutiny to keep pace with new challenges presented almost
daily in the 21st century. Things change, from technological advances to legalities mandating performance, from offender risk and need characteristics to correctional personnel
qualifications. Also, the huge correctional population growth in the past decades has produced an enormous, but fragmented, enterprise that delivers a service that is both antago-
nized and applauded, for different reasons, by conservatives and liberals alike. On the
playing field are the hard working men and women comprised of correctional personnel
who have the responsibility of supervising guilty defendants, some of whom are pleased
that they weren't institutionalized and others who should be. Correctional personnel, regardless of their work assignment (institutional or community), rarely select how and
whom they supervise.

Because probation policy and practice depend on many factors, authority, and initiatives, probation personnel performance (and programs) rarely fits a "single best model."
Nonetheless, there are some similarities and the correctional models in this chapter can
serve as a guide in characterizing and comparing various probation initiatives. Yet, one of
the most encompassing characterizations that will surface from this chapter is that what
policy makers, interest groups, and the American public think has more to do with how a
PO is legally bound to perform than the officer's ability, skill, and desire. There are, however, underlying principles of probation that influence policy and practice, which ultimately affect process and its outcomes.

UNDERLYING PRINCIPLES OF PROBATION

Probation is America's best and least expensive remedy for the criminal justice community. As expected, the underlying principles that shape probation policy and practice can
be couched in beliefs held by policy makers, interest groups, and the public about factors
associated with the causes of crime and their idea about the best correctional approach
when supervising offenders.[1] In keeping with this thought, proponents see probation as a
"soft" position toward offenders because violators have committed crime of their own free
will and therefore those offenders should get what's coming to them—punishment. For
conservatives, punishment translates to confinement. Probation is "babying" a criminal, a
just desert advocate might explain. Criminals are individuals who violate any form of the

law regardless of the significance of the law, argue just desert advocates. Punishment advocates believe probation is not the best way to punish a violator.

On the other hand, advocates of probation lean toward social environmental issues as factors that lead to crime and, as such, promote treatment and prevention as an advantageous approach when supervising guilty defendants. Conditions of probation, or what some call "conditions of freedom," are seen as punishment enough, and those conditions and personnel policy vary depending on who administers probation.

WHO ADMINISTERS PROBATION?

The U.S. Department of Labor reports that throughout America, federal, state, and local governments administer probation, but state governments operate most probation systems.[2] Although private industry provides contractual services to many state correction departments, it has yet to significantly contribute to probation systems. In some states, state government employs all (POs) and correctional treatment specialists, whereas in other states, local governments are the only probation employers. In still other states, both levels of government have probation authority. Currently, California and Texas have the highest probation and parole populations. Together, these two states account for about one fourth of the country's correctional supervision population.

Each jurisdiction has its own organizational structure; policies, function, and mission; and philosophy and procedures. Also, each jurisdiction has its own criteria for personnel, hiring and promotional strategies, as well as career expectations. What is evident upon a closer look at most probation agencies is that their procedures or policies are guided by the philosophical or societal belief systems that predominate the governmental agency with its responsibility. Therefore, each probation system has its own operational style of delivering probation services.

> **Probation management** is a department of government at the state, county, or city level that carries out probation functions, programs, and services pursuant to laws, policies, and rules.[3]

With so many different agencies operated by so many different jurisdictions, describing a typical organizational structure is challenging but necessary to get a sense of how probation services are delivered.

AUTHORITY

The branch of government given the legal responsibility over probation in each jurisdiction could make a difference in how probation services are delivered. Two branches of government are largely associated with probation authority:

- Executive branch of government
- Judicial branch of government

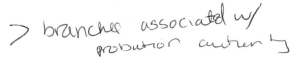 *branches associated w/ probation authority*

The executive branch has responsibility for state or local human service agencies, such as the departments of transportation, corrections, and welfare. When delivering services, executive branch personnel tend to be people-centered or human service guided. The judicial branch of government, on the other hand, largely has authority over the courts, and their personnel tend to be driven by laws more often than human service perspectives.

Probation services are operated by over 2000 separate agencies. Probation is exclusively under the executive branch of state government in 30 states (see Table 8.1). In

Table 8.1   Which Branch of Government Administers Probation

| State | Executive | | Judicial | |
	State	Local	State	Local
Alabama	X			
Alaska	X			
Arizona				X
Arkansas				X
California		X		
Colorado			X	
Connecticut			X	
Delaware	X			
Washington, DC			X	
Florida	X			
Georgia	X			
Hawaii				X
Idaho	X			
Illinois				X
Indiana		X		
Iowa				X
Kansas				X
Kentucky	X			
Louisiana	X			
Maine	X			
Maryland	X			
Massachusetts				X
Michigan	X			
Minnesota		X		
Mississippi	X			
Missouri	X			
Montana	X			

(continued)

Table 8.1   Which Branch of Government Administers Probation (Continued)

State	Executive		Judicial	
	State	Local	State	Local
Nebraska			X	
Nevada	X			
New Hampshire	X			
New Jersey				X
New Mexico	X			
New York		X		
North Carolina	X			
North Dakota	X			
Ohio				X
Oklahoma	X			
Oregon	X			
Pennsylvania				X
Rhode Island	X			
South Carolina	X			
South Dakota			X	
Tennessee	X			
Texas				X
Utah	X			
Vermont	X			
Virginia	X			
Washington	X			
West Virginia				X
Wisconsin	X			
Wyoming	X			
Total	30	4	5	12

Source: LIS, INC[5]

4 states, the local executive branch of government holds the responsibility of delivering probation and in 19 states, the judicial branch provides probation services of which most judicial branches are local as opposed to state governments. Also, in some jurisdictions, both executive branch and judicial branch probation authority operates side by side, such as in New York City and the state of New York. This mixed authority can usually be divided in the sense that the state of New York supervises one type of offender whereas the local government (New York City) primarily supervises another type of offender. Some supervision authority is more complex. For instance, in the Commonwealth of Massachusetts, probation is provided through the Trial Court of Massachusetts. The Chief Justice for Administration and Management of Massachusetts manages and administers the court

and probation. The Chief Justice employs approximately 7,000 state-paid employees in 130 locations.[4]

Which branch of government would be more efficient in delivering probation services? Some say that because the judicial branch is tasked with granting and revoking probation, it is likely to be managed more effectively by them than the executive branch. Others say that because the executive branch tends to manage the department of corrections and other social services, that branch could provide a wider array of professional services than the judicial branch, especially because most judges are trained in law as opposed to providing human services. Some believe that the judicial branch should focus on legality rather than rehabilitation. Also, as learned in Chapter 7, a probation system can be operated independently by a jurisdiction, and if the jurisdiction has a parole system, it can also be operated independently. Probation and parole can be operated by a single agency through either the judicial or executive branch of government, or both.

NEGATIVE ISSUES OF PROBATION

Probation is the most promising component of the criminal justice system, but is the most troubled.[6] Its troubles are rooted in the crisis of confidence directed at the criminal justice system by political leaders and the American public alike. Political leaders and the public influence the success of probation based on probationer crime reports and probationer noncompliance to the conditions of freedom.[7] Probation suffers from an image of "coddlers of criminals" and advocates of leniency during a popular trend towards severity.[8] Some actually see probation as wasteful and ineffective in the sense that community supervision does not necessarily reduce the likelihood of future crime.[9] Punishment advocates rest their case upon government statistics that report probation (and parole) violators comprised 30 percent of all the offenders in state prison for a violent crime in 1991. Specifically, probation and parole violators comprised 56 percent of all prisoners incarcerated for property offenses, 41 percent for drug offenses, and 85 percent for public-order offenses. Estimates show that criminals under correctional supervision (probation and parole):

- Commit 15 murders a day.[10]
- Nearly 4 of every 10 suspects arrested for a felony are already on probation, parole, or pretrial release from a prior conviction or arrest.[11]
- Nearly 45 percent of felony defendants arrested, and 15 percent of felony defendants charged with a violent crime, were on CC supervision—either probation or parole—at the very time they committed the new crime.[12]

Of an estimated 162,000 probationers returned to state prison in 1991 across the United States, collectively they were responsible for at least:[13]

- 6,400 murders (more than 50 percent of them were strangers)
- 7,400 rapes or sexual assaults (33 percent were under the age of 12)

- 10,400 assaults (50 percent were strangers, 10 percent were intimate others)
- 17,000 robberies (86 percent were strangers)
- 16,600 homes and business were burglarized
- 3,100 motor vehicles were stolen

From 1990 to 1993, the state of Virginia showed that 156 of the 1411 persons convicted of murder in that state were on probation at the time they committed the crime of murder.[14] Then, too, nationally 4 percent of those on probation absconded in 2003.[15]

> **Absconders** are still on probation, but they have failed to report and could not be located by the probation agency.[16]

Furthermore, an estimated 70 percent of those sampled in a national opinion poll felt the courts were not harsh enough on guilty defendants.[17] One implication arising from this finding is that the public lacks confidence in probation (and parole) and may see it as too lenient. For instance, one expert observed:

"Despite a proliferation of outstanding cutting-edge programs, for the most part and in most places, public regard for probation is dangerously low, and for the most part in most places, what passes for probation supervision is a joke. It's conceptually bankrupt and it's politically not viable."[18]

Finally, the American public sees probation as an alternative for certain types of offenders, "they still want strict and accountable alternatives that carry punishment based consequences for offender noncompliance."[19] This perspective implies that as of 2004, American society, may be closer to ancient notions of revenge-based justice as in "an eye for an eye" than a more productive perspective leading to the positive issues of rehabilitation.

POSITIVE ISSUES OF PROBATION

Some observers see the need for "effective community supervision of the millions of offenders in their midst who, unsupervised, pose public safety threats."[20] Does probation work because of sobriety produced through treatment programs, which in turn can reduce re-offending and ultimately enhance public safety?[21] Also, when probation is revoked because an offender violated curfew, for instance, is that a failure of supervision, or is it good supervision on the part of the probation officer who detected the violation?

For these reasons and many others, some suggest that for probation to become effective, the private sector should operate probation programs.[22] Offenders released on probation should post a financial bond guaranteeing behavior in accordance with terms of the release. If individual accountability is the answer to crime, then it must include the most powerful kind of accountability: financial responsibility.

In 1990, 69 percent of those who exited probation successfully completed their terms. This figure dropped to 59 percent in 1998.[23] In 2003, about three in five of the more than two million adults discharged from probation had successfully met the conditions of their supervision.[24]

Other prominent issues of probation include the notion that probation offers a greater voluntary change for an offender to reform than those incarcerated.[25] In this regard, Daniel Glaser cautions that the more male and female offenders are isolated from a law-abiding society and deprived of society's amenities, the more likely it is that offenders will reject the lifestyles and laws of that society.[26] Glaser argues that financial and social costs of confining an offender could be acceptable if it were known that confinement actually reduced crime. Also, David Eichental and James Jacobs reveal that when many offenders are sent to prison, their criminal activities are not necessarily reduced, but rather correctional administrations tend to ignore crimes—drug pushers continue to push drugs, sexual predators sexually assault others, and violent offenders continue their sprees of violence.[27]

Glaser adds that there are few indicators that higher penalties change crime rates despite the downward trend in crime rates during the early 21st century.[28] Andrew von Hirsch is more aggressive with his thoughts implying that prisons are downright wasteful, expensive, and ultimately destructive of self-respect.[29] Why do some feel so strongly against incarceration for all offenders? One answer might be consistent with clearance rates and funnel effect explanations as provided in earlier criminal justice courses. However, without an attempt at repetition, you will recall that most crimes including crimes of violence are never reported to the police, and of those crimes that are, few arrests follow those reports. Daniel Glaser[30] reports that nearly all drug crimes, most property offenses, and almost all acts of violence within families are never reported to police, let alone prosecuted. Marcus Felson adds that criminals are caught and convicted for less than 10 percent of their serious crimes against others and for a fraction of 1 percent of their illegal drug transactions.[31] Add those concerns with the enormous cost differences between incarceration and probation as discussed in Chapter 7, and it is hardly a contest (average: $64.64 per inmate per day at yearend 2002 versus $4.18 per probationer at yearend 2001).[32] The necessity of finding a reasonable alternative to confinement is a priority among criminal justice experts. Yet, no matter what alternatives are developed, professional personnel who perform numerous roles are required to carry out those alternatives.

ROLES, SELF-IMAGINATION, AND RESPONSIBILITIES OF POs

PO Roles

The roles and responsibilities of POs vary across jurisdictions. In fact, in a review of the literature, there are numerous categories, descriptions, and roles offered by numerous observers. With so many contributions, being certain which perspective has more merit than others can be a task.[33] Often, students have the impression that the job of POs relates specifically to monitoring the movements of probationers.[34] What you need to know about the job of a PO is that their roles and responsibilities vary depending on the jurisdiction and the needs and risk levels of probationers. It might be easier to understand the job of a PO by categorizing their roles, which can include the role of a law enforcer, which includes investigations, supervision, and analysis; the role of a social worker, which includes treatment, resource brokering or referrals, assessment, and evaluations; and the role of a bureaucrat, which includes the PO following the rules, regulations, and objectives of the jurisdiction that employs them.

Conceptual Roles of POs

- Law enforcer role: Investigation, supervision, and analysis.
- Social worker role: Treatment, resource brokering or referrals, assessment, and evaluations.
- Bureaucrat role: PO keeping rules, regulations, and objectives of the jurisdiction that employ them.

Each role is loaded with expectations and obligations, but it comes down to the protection of the public and the welfare of the probationer or control and counsel.[35] But let's not forget that probation personnel have to remain employed to perform their jobs. Nonetheless, these three roles—law enforcer, social worker, and bureaucrat—often conflict with each other, leading to the contradiction of probation as discussed later in this chapter. For now, the role of a social worker, as you read in this chapter, is comprised of two components referred to as (a) a resource broker or referrals and (b) a caseworker.[36] Ways to briefly explain the primary tasks associated with law enforcer and social worker, or more specifically, resource broker and caseworker, are listed in Table 8.2.

Table 8.2   General Skills Associated with Law Enforcer and Social Worker Roles[37]

Law Enforcer	Social Worker	
	Resource Broker	Caseworker
1. Assertion	1. Community development	1. Treatment planning
2. Supervision	2. Resource utilization	2. Counseling
3. Confrontation	3. Family resources	3. Family dynamics
4. Alcohol or Drug (AOD) crimes	4. Alcohol or Drug (AOD) resources	4. Alcohol or Drug (AOD) treatment
5. Differential risk	5. Sex offender resources	5. Sex offenders
6. Community partnerships		6. Psychological assessment
		7. Mental illness
		8. Mental retardation
		9. Psychopharmacology
		10. Group work

Robert Shearer reports that first, the technical level of the general skills increases as a department moves through a law enforcer to a resource broker to a social worker category.[38] Second, there is overlap in the three strategies. Third, there is a need for staff communication across all three strategies. This communication is important because during the course of supervision, probationers, staff, and intervention programs may change. This communication allows for professional override of an original strategy designation.[39] For example, a probation officer, for a variety of reasons, may need to be reassigned from caseworker to law enforcer. A probationer may also need to be reassigned to a PO who is primarily a caseworker.

During different periods through the history of probation, one of these three roles has dominated probation policy and practice.[40] Social worker orientation dominated the field until the mid-1970s, when the law enforcer role took precedent. The social work approach focused on brokering or referring of probationers to available services in the community to other agencies (e.g., alcohol and drug treatment, employment, mental health services, community services, etc.), instead of providing supervision agencies with the capacity to directly offer these services to offenders.[41] Two reasons for this change from social work to enforcer can be found in the "get tough on crime" perspective and the "nothing works" notions believed by policy makers, interest groups, and the American public. The enforcer role focuses on compliance of the probationer with the conditions of freedom and places more external control on the probationer (e.g., family violence therapy or group programs, drug tests, curfews, house arrest, more reporting and face-to-face contacts, etc.). The enforcer role places less emphasis on providing services to address underlying criminogenic (environmental) influences (as discussed in Chapter 10). For instance:

> Four principles guide environmental criminology (as it relates to community corrections). First, offenders, like all people, are constrained in their movements by their daily routines and streetscapes, and these constrained movements bring offenders into contact with possible crime opportunities. Second, locations vary in the opportunities for crime they present to people with an inclination to commit crimes. Third, offenders, like all people, read their environments for clues as to what types of behavior are feasible. And fourth, offenders, like all people, make choices based on their perceptions of rewards, risk, effort, and ability to be "excused." In short, environmental criminology investigates how offenders interact with their world and the consequences—including criminal acts—of these interactions. Printed with permission of Federal Probation.[42]

Does a dominate role of the enforcer work better than the social worker role? That is, in what way is public safety and probationer reform, including recidivism, impacted? Recidivism is due to an offenders' retaining criminogenic motivation or propensity and having access to opportunities for crime. That comes down to intent and opportunity. Therefore, for a PO to reduce re-offending, an important task is to provide or place offenders into treatment programs, based on the principles of effective rehabilitation, that diminish their "propensity for crime while reducing an offender's access to crime opportunities."[43] Joan Petersilia implies that the enforcer model does little to yield better probationer outcomes.[44] But overall, the research literature has not tested the different roles on offender outcomes. Nonetheless, what is clear is that belief systems held by those who develop probation policy have much to do with which role is dominant in a specific jurisdiction. As the "belief pendulum" swings, so do the roles and responsibilities of the men and women who supervise probationers.

Therefore, probation officers require many skills and must be flexible to change roles depending on their caseloads, which according to most POs, change often and may be influenced by their self-image of themselves.

Self-Image of POs

In light of the many roles POs play and in dealing with the issues of control and counsel inconsistencies, how do officers see their job? One study of POs finds that POs see themselves as possessing different roles depending on whom they are interacting with.[45] For instance, 81 percent of the sample identify themselves as a PO when they talk to a judge, 69 percent say they are a PO to personnel from social agencies, and 79 percent talk about being a PO with the their "client's" employers. POs want to be identified with correctional work, but don't want to have connection with the social worker profession, even if the PO delivers treatment of any kind. Less experienced officers, however, describe themselves as dealing with the therapeutic functions of probation as opposed to the experienced officers who tend to identify themselves with public safety while seeking to maximize a probationer's capabilities, largely through nontherapeutic methods.

In a similar study, researchers sent a survey to 417 adult POs in various jurisdictions.[46] The POs were asked to rate the appropriateness of 52 tasks performed at their jobs. As a result, seven categories were ranked by the PO according to their perceived degree of conformity to the role of the CC officers.[47] Those roles were:

- Referral function: Refering probationers to other community resources for treatment and care (e.g., substance abuse treatment).

- Advice and guidance: Providing information and helping to improve daily living experiences of a probationer (e.g., jobs and housing).

- Psychotherapy: Using techniques to learn about orientations and early childhood emotional problems. Only agreed upon for use with the "unduly suspicious," "reckless risk-taking," and "alcoholic probationer."

- Law enforcement: Detecting and apprehending violators. Only considered appropriate in two cases: when it is known for sure that a probationer attended Alcoholics Anonymous meetings or if probationer made court appearances without PO's knowledge.

- Environmental manipulation: Influencing personnel and volunteers that shape and monitor probationer's adjustment (e.g., speaking to a loan company on a probationer's behalf).

- Conduct establishment and enforcement: Using the PO's authority to attempt to coerce the probationer into behaving in accordance with the prevailing moral system of the community as perceived by the officer.

The roles a PO performs can vary often, as do their responsibilities.

Responsibilities of POs

POs are unique compared to other correction supervision officers. First, POs are "officers" of the court, and in this capacity, they perform PSIs with the responsibility of enforcing court orders that at times require these officers to perform a search, conduct an arrest if necessary, and seize evidence (in Chapter 10, there is a discussion about the differences and similarities between POs and parole officers). Their responsibilities associated with a PSI are to interview defendants, families, victims, witnesses, police officers, human service providers, and diagnostic clinicians to develop assessments of defendants. A part of their obligations may even include to: "examine all records and files in divorce, legal separation, annulment, custody and paternity cases in which orders or decrees have been entered to ascertain whether the persons to whom payments of money should have been made regularly."[48]

POs review sentencing recommendations with offenders and the families of those offenders before submitting them to the court. Often, POs appear in court to represent their department, present probation reports and respond to questions concerning probation recommendations.[49] A primary goal of POs is also to ensure community safety by monitoring an offender's activities to determine compliance with the conditions of probation and abstinence from further criminal acts.[50]

Table 8.3   Investigative Reports by Federal Probation Officers

Type of Investigation	1995	2000	2002
Total	169,113	203,845	NA
PSI	43,151	63,666	65,156
Collateral investigation for another district	33,293	46,341	52,047
Postsentence: Institution	2,217	NA	NA[a]
Pretransfer: Probation and parole	7,026	4,524	NA
Alleged violations: Probation and parole	26,629	29,976	35,577
Prerelease: For federal or military institution	15,425	23,639	27,117
Special: Prisoner in confinement	7,850	5,357	NA
Furlough and work release reports for Bureau of Prisons institutions	9,573	5,129	NA
Supervision reports	22,105	24,590	NA
Parole revocation hearing reports	1,844	623	NA

[a]Beginning in 2001, the source reported data only for four categories of investigative reports, thus those totals were not available.

Printed with permission of the Office of Justice Programs.[51]

The experiences of a PO can differ but only by degree. For instance, Table 8.3 reports the amount of investigative reports completed by federal POs. It is unlikely that a state PO completes as many different types of investigations such as prerelease investigations for the military as federal officers.

POs also supervise probationers; prepare an assessment of each probationer; and design specific plans to assist an individual probationer's return to society, which often requires referrals to treatment and program providers. A PO tends to act as a resource broker for services and some may be less personally involved with a probationer, because much time is spent as a resource broker: assessing offender needs, maintaining appropriate providers contacts, and linking the probationer with social service agencies that can appropriately address those needs.[52] Classification decisions of probationers are often based on standardized rating forms, especially Client Management Classification Guidelines, which itemize age, criminal record, and other pertinent attributes of each offender and then score each item.[53] Completing these forms takes about 90 minutes but can produce an optimum mode of supervision. Rationale and varieties of classification were presented in Chapter 4.

Yet, some POs accept the role of a therapeutic agent with the objective of helping each probationer solve social and psychological problems, depending on an officer's qualifications and job description.[54]

Finally, supervision, including surveillance of probationers, is expected at a high level of competence. Knowing the whereabouts of a probationer can include, depending on a PO's qualifications and training, supervision over electronic monitoring of participants and strategies, drug testing strategies at community centers, and administration and interpretation of psychological evaluations. Additionally, POs often operate CC programs such as work furloughs and arrange and participate in visitations with children and other family members of a probationer.

The Ultimate Mission of POs

Due to the range of a POs responsibilities, it is important to clarify their ultimate goal: To protect society from dangerous offenders while rehabilitating amenable offenders.

> The ultimate mission of a PO is to protect society from dangerous offenders while rehabilitating amenable offenders.

How do POs meet their ultimate mission? Strategies in probation are drawn from the social work field and are based on the caseworker model, as discussed in Chapter 5. A PO designs a treatment plan from information available about a probationer with an eye on the reintegration of the offender, but above all, public safety comes first. POs seek to prepare an offender to become an effective participant in the major social institutions of society, such as school, business, and church. This thought is consistent with Joan Petersilia, who argued that one of the critical lessons learned in the intermediate sanction era

Table 8.4   Range of Responsibilities of POs[55]

1. "Officers" of the court
2. (PSI) (investigation, interviews, and analysis)
3. Enforce court orders (arrests, searches, and seizing evidence)
4. Develop needs and risk assessment of defendants
5. Review sentencing recommendations (offenders, their families, and the court)
6. Appear in court on behalf of their department, present probation reports, and respond to questions concerning probation recommendations
7. Supervise probationers
8. Prepare specific diagnoses of each probationer
9. Design specific plans to assist individual probationers
10. Act as therapeutic agent
11. Provide referrals to treatment and program providers
12. Administer standardized rating forms
13. Surveillance: Testing, monitoring, and evaluating
14. Administration of community, center programs and facilities

(late 1980s–1990s) was the importance of supervision linked to clinical approaches.[56] Clinical approaches are more likely to lead to reductions in recidivism. In fact, in the 14-site study, researchers found that probationers with counseling services (e.g., employment, substance abuse, etc.) tended to have better probationer outcomes than those with merely surveillance functions.[57] Petersilia and Turner argued that probation supervision has the following objectives that focus on offender compliance:[58]

- Use the supervision period to engage the offender in a process of change.
- Assist the offender in understanding his or her behavior and becoming committed to behavioral change.
- Assist the offender in learning to manage his or her behavior and comply with societal norms.

Law enforcement activities including supervision are ongoing activities for a PO, while at the same time they also carry out social worker and bureaucrat obligations and expectations. As you can imagine, one result that can arise from the efforts of a PO is that the responsibilities of these three roles often conflict.

The Contradiction of Probation

A contradiction is something that is inconsistent, and in probation (and parole) a primary inconsistency exists between the primary directives associated with each role performed by PO. There are two distinctive parts to this contradiction. The first part relates to the primary function of probation, which includes both public safety and probationer welfare.

> **Contradiction of probation** is couched in its mission: Protection of the public and the welfare of the probationer.

In what way can these two opposing perspectives be accomplished? Some say the best way to protect the public is through incarceration. Others say that not every violator should be locked up. Nevertheless, the primary concern of a PO relates to the cornerstone of probation—control and counsel. In what way can a probation officer control public safety while at the same time guide a violator through rehabilitative initiatives, and keep the rules of the jurisdiction at the same time? Actually, it is the responsibility of the PO to act as an "agent of change" among probationers. Proponents of probation see this contradiction as impractical because the probationer is an involuntary participant in rehabilitation programs. They say that rehabilitation works best through the personal consent and commitment of a participant, but that is not the case among probationers. If they do not attend specific programs, they will pay the consequences. Therefore, probationers will give the appearance of reform during the probation period but resort to their criminal behavior once "off the hook." Is public safety best served through this process? The concern might have some merit as the role conflict of POs becomes clear. For instance, the Oklahoma Board of Corrections' probation and parole function statement is fairly typical of most responsibility statements for POs across the country:

Responsibility of Probation and Parole

It is the responsibility of Probation and Parole to protect the public, to protect the employees, and to protect the offenders entrusted in their supervision and custody through effective utilization of a continuum of supervision and intervention. The director shall ensure the utilization of a risk-based classification system that classifies offenders based on criminogenic needs, and establish supervision levels that address those needs. Each level of supervision will be clearly defined as to the expectation of supervision requirements.
Source: Oklahoma Board of Corrections.[59]

That is, the contradiction of probation can be seen between public safety and probationer reform. In addition, despite the directive of public safety and probationer rehabilitation, the first priority of the PO is the probation organization as opposed to the probationer, making other priorities suspect. Often, probationers understand the priorities of their PO and act out the role of recovery while actually withholding their real problems from the PO or agency referrals.

How do jurisdictions deal with the control-counsel contradiction of CC systems? One answer might be with the Virginia Department of Corrections, which recommends a balanced approach to CC supervision.[60]

The Virginia Department of Corrections answers part of the potential problem among POs. Many jurisdictions make similar presentations. Perhaps one reason that 1 of

---

Mission of the Virginia Department of Corrections

The mission of probation and parole programs is to enhance public safety by positively impacting offenders so they will lead pro-social and crime-free lives. The Community Corrections Division administers these programs and is committed to "A Balanced Approach" to offender supervision. In practice, this is accomplished through:

- Investigation and assessment of risk and needs
- Careful and focused plans of supervision
- Use of a wide variety of resources and treatment services
- Purposeful and proportionate application of sanctions for delinquency and noncompliance

---

every 10 POs leaves the profession every year has to do with the conflict that can develop between the responsibilities associated with the roles a PO must play.[61] There are few incentives or benefits offered to a PO, even for those POs who work extra hours and experience stressful encounters.

SERVICES PROVIDED BY POs

The basic services provided by probation agencies in the United States consist of detox, family counseling, apprehension of absconders, substance abuse treatment, job development, individual counseling, referral services, and presentence reports. It goes without saying that each jurisdiction delivers those services differently from other agencies. Of the agencies in the United States that provide only (as opposed to probation and parole) probation services, Table 8.5 shows the percentage of those agencies that provide the following services:

POs are facilitators of a defendant's readjustment to life in society and are providers of public safety to the courts and community through treatment, referrals, assessment, and evaluations.

Caseloads

POs work with people in all age groups representing many backgrounds, despite assignment to juvenile or adult probationers. They attempt to balance control and counsel directives while investigating, enforcing laws, referring probationers to various programs and treatments, and supervising criminals. It should be noted that POs working in rural settings, and in some cases in urban areas as well, could be assigned juveniles and adults,

Table 8.5 Percentage of Probation Agencies Providing Various Services

Service	Percentage Providing
Detox	36
Family counseling	55
Apprehend absconders	55
Substance abuse treatment	64
Job development	82
Individual counseling	82
Referral services	91
Presentencing reports	100

Printed with permission of *the Corrections Yearbook.*[62]

probationers and parolees. Their caseload can be in the 50 to 150 range, and they might travel more often than officers who work in other areas. It is likely that urban POs are assigned probationers consisting of similar needs and risks, but some probation officers in Chicago mentioned that they supervised "whoever walks in the door" of their agency.[63] Also, their caseloads can be as high as 2000, such as in California. Table 8.6 offers a better picture of the caseloads of POs in the jurisdictions that provide probation as an independent agency (without the connection to parole) as of January 1, 2002.

Table 8.6 Average Caseload per PO during 2001 by Type

State	Regular	Intensive	Electronic	Special
Arizona	60	25		
Arkansas	85			
Colorado	175	20		20
Georgia	251	40		40
Illinois	130	15		40
Michigan	75			
Nebraska	117	21	10	
Pennsylvania	15			
Rhode Island	314	72		59
Texas	116			
Wyoming	63	13		
Average	127	29	10	40

Note: Intensive includes electronic monitoring; caseloads vary depending on jurisdiction within state.
Printed with permission of *The Corrections Yearbook.*[64]

Of the states examined by the staff of the *Corrections Yearbook,* the average case-loads for POs ranged from 314 in Rhode Island to 15 cases in Pennsylvania.[65] Also, other states such as Maine have their own caseload configuration. For instance, in Region 1 (York and Cumberland counties), about 20 POs are employed.[66] Their roles are set up as follows:

- Two POs for sexual crimes (with a cap of 40 caseloads each)
- Two court officers (intake from court)
- One domestic violence PO (with a cap of 50 caseloads)
- One community confinement officer
- 16 field officers to handle a caseload of 2,400 with an average of 150 cases each. The recommended caseload is 85 maximum for each PO.

The hours a Maine PO works varies. They can work any time of the day or night. All cases are not equal. Some are high risk and need more than one visit per week. Over 1,200 of these cases are for felony crimes. There is a lot of "leg-work" for a PO in Maine as in most jurisdictions.

Also, specialized caseloads are common among POs. Probation systems routinely supervise sex offenders, drug users, DUI cases, and hyperviolent offenders by utilizing specialized caseloads. Most departments have found that specialization is an intelligent use of ever-diminishing resources. The problem is that they are losing resources as fast as they are gaining additional offenders.[67] This has resulted in the creation of case banks of less supervised offenders. Most of these case banks contain misdemeanor cases and class C felons. Finally, within any 48-hour period, there are at least 11 probationers arrested for serious probation violations.

STYLES OF DELIVERY

Studies on styles or strategies of POs reveal five probation officer styles: punitive, protective, welfare, passive, and bunker.[68]

1. A *punitive* style sees punishment and just desert as the most appropriate response to violators. This strategy sees the role of probational responsibility as that of a "guardian of middle-class morality." Threats and punishment practices keep probationers controlled, the thinking goes. Probationers are not to be trusted. After all, they are criminals.

2. A *protective* strategy focuses on protection of the community from the offender and protection of the probationer from the community. Direct assistance, lecturing, and alternately using praise and blame are part of this strategy.[69] For example, indecisive priorities might be seen in the practices of a PO involved with low-level sexual offenders required to register under mandates similar to Megan's Law. The officer could view notification as destructive and counterproductive for nonviolent, first-time offenders and attempt to find ways to exclude certain caseload offenders from registering.

3. The *welfare* strategy can be seen in a focus to improve the well-being of a proba-tioner. That is, the goal of the officer is to aid in the adjustment of the probationer to the community. The needs and capacities of the probationer determine services rendered. Emotional neutrality permeates the relationship.

4. The *passive* strategy implies that some probation officers prefer to perform as little as possible when supervising probationers.[70] These are the POs who "fake it" or who have an "ideal, trouble-free caseload."[71] Passivity in case management results in offender anonymity, which tends to produce a passivity in supervision that elevates an approach to case management, that some observers refer to as "harvesting the failures."[72] A description of that type of PO passivity is found given as:

> When probation and parole officers lacking resources and plausible technique are made re-sponsible for dispersed caseloads of individuals who proved themselves motivated offenders in the past, who are located where crime and vulnerable victims abound, and who are effec-tively anonymous because they are without formal or informal supervision for weeks on end, the agents are inclined to let nature take its course—to wait for police to arrest those offend-ers under their supervision who, unsupervised, commit new crimes.[73]

Obliviously, the passive strategy serves to undermine the rigorous enforcement of the conditions of probation and discourages any hope of rehabilitating an amenable offender. What about protecting society from a dangerous offender? Months may go by from the time a violation is detected to the point at which appropriate action, if any, is taken to meet the ultimate mission of probation. As an example, drug testing is scheduled in ad-vance in some jurisdictions, but test results are provided sometimes a week or more after the tests are administered. The passive officer is joined by the bunker officer.

5. A *bunker PO* is perhaps the most practiced style of delivering probation services and is conducted within the confines of an office. Referred to by the Reinventing Proba-tion Council as "fortress" or "bunker probation," this style of supervision relies on office-bound interactions with probationers, mostly during the working weekday hours of 8:00 a.m. to 5:00 p.m., to gather information and monitor offender compliance.[74] It is estimated that POs spend an average of 5 to 20 minutes once a month with offenders in an office set-ting where they depend on the offenders to give them truthful and accurate information re-garding their activities. Very little, if any, time is spent supervising offenders in the neighborhoods where they live, work, and play.[75]

In addition to these five styles, there are POs who conduct themselves as though they were law enforcers, timer-servers, therapeutic agents, and synthetic officers.[76] The law enforcer sees probation as a court order and their job is to insist on compliance to those orders because POs have the authority to keep the community safe. Timer-servers see their job based on requirements that must be met until they retire—"I don't make the rules, I just work here." The therapeutic agent is there to help the offender, and finally, the synthetic officer blends treatment and law enforcement components by "combining the paternal, authoritarian, and judgmental with the therapeutic." This officer feels offend-ers are wrong and responsible for their own behavior.

Before any style or strategy associated with delivering probation services can be judged, recall that often POs are limited by their caseloads, office and bench assignments, resources and policy, and many other influences. It is more likely that most POs want to perform their job in a professional way, but often must balance their services between "bureaucracy" dictates and the probational client. There are so many "probation styles" that it would be difficult to list all of them, but PO traps might make some PO problems clear.

Chief PO Bernie Fitzgerald in Boston says that "I think the way we operated was "fortress probation."[77] We sat inside our building and the police fed the child into the system. They brought the arrests in. We took the people after they had been arrested and processed them. Then the judges formed a disposition and placed them on probation. So the jobs were entirely separate. We didn't talk to one another; basically, it was two separate jobs. Probationers were coming in to report they were doing well and that they were going to school, or they were becoming gainfully employed, that they were complying with their curfews and their conditions of probation." Practice is changing in Boston and elsewhere. POs are being asked to document information provided by probationers. In one respect, that means the POs in Boston are going into the field and monitoring probationers.

PO Traps

POs and parole officers face several traps, regardless of the officer's gender or experience. Offenders usually try one or more of the following traps early in the supervision period as they interact with their probation or parole officer.[78] Their conversations might sound like this:

Different Religions Trap: In *my* religion, an offender might imply, we practice beliefs that subordinate women (or blacks, Latinos, children etc.). Therefore to treat *my* spouse or the victim (or a female PO) like a child is a religious matter. This conviction is a religious freedom issue.

Parent Trap: My parents got divorced and fought with each other all the time—that's why I'm so screwed up. My dad was a drunk and I want to be a good parent/spouse, but I can hear my parents fighting or see my father falling down drunk or (sigh) sexually abusing me . . .

Different Culture Trap: The PO or victim is not of *my* culture. If "you" were, you would know that in *my* culture things with women, for instance, are very different. This conviction shows a lack of sensitivity to diversity in this country.

Crazy-Maker Trap: I am highly educated and well-respected. This is a travesty. Why don't you spend time supervising bank robbers instead of me?

Violence Trap: *She/he* assaulted me! I only weigh 110 pounds or I am a very sick man. Listen to *me*. How could I terrify anyone? You can ask anyone, I never hurt anybody.

Recovery Trap: I've quit using drugs. I've been clean for two months now. Look how hard I'm trying. I'm doing this for you (or for the victim).

Cooperation Trap: You're right. I've been unaware of my anger. This experience is just what I needed. It took *you*, a brilliant PO, to show me the error of my ways.

Spouse or Children Trap: Look at her . . . just *look* at her (my victim). She uses drugs. Her grandparents have her kids. She can't keep a job. She keeps calling you up with untrue stories about me. I am trying very hard to be straight with you.

Pitiful Trap: I've lost my job. I don't have a car anymore. My dog ran away. I can't see my wife/husband or kids. She/he cleaned out the checking account. I have to pay these fines and *you're* on my case all the time. Why does all this happen to me. All I want is to live a normal life like other people.

Judicial Error trap: Even *she/he* (their victim/s) says it didn't happen. She/he told you this (crime I committed) is a mistake and that she/he loves/likes me. This is a huge miscarriage of justice by you people. I didn't (rob, beat, steal, rape, etc.) that person. (Or) You can tell that she really loves me, and I haven't accepted her advances.

FEMALE POS

American standards for female POs are couched in the historical development of the juvenile justice system as an expression of maternalist orientations about women in general. Elizabeth Clapp[79] argues for the importance of gender in shaping early welfare policy. Middle-class women reformers, accustomed to thinking of their role in society in terms of motherhood, initiated the campaign for the separate and different treatment of child offenders within the legal system during the 1890s. Those women saw wayward children as "innocents" in need of guidance as opposed to punishment and saw their duty as mothers to keep child offenders from mingling with adult offenders. Also, they felt that their duty was to give those innocents the protective guidance of a PO to keep from sliding further into criminality.[80]

For instance, Hannah Schoff (1853–1940) of the National Congress of Mothers stressed women's duty to be "mothers of all children." She saw the new juvenile court system as "the great work of guarding and guiding little children."[81] As a result of a Philadelphia police case in 1899, in which an eight-year-old girl, a boardinghouse slave, was arrested and imprisoned for arson, Schoff initiated a campaign for reform in the treatment of juvenile offenders. After securing the release and placement of that child in a foster home, Schoff studied the issue and drew up a series of bills for the Philadelphia legislature.[82]

Female reformers promoted maternalist roles by creating a system whereby POs (both men and women) would provide benevolent guidance and nurture children in trouble and work with the family to make sure that children were being brought up correctly. Elizabeth Rose argues that the work of the PO is often seen as an extension of the maternal role of women, which was seen as an especially appropriate role for women in the early days of American history.[83] Private women clubs attended by "the rich and famous" often paid the salaries of female POs and lobbied for the rights of women and children but strongly maintained that the role of women was that of "mothers."

Also, Anne Meis Knupfer[84] examined the ideologies, discourses, and practices of female POs in Chicago from 1900 to 1935. In her research, Knupfer reveals that maternalist organizations, especially the Chicago Woman's Club, influenced early probation work through both their financial support of female officers and their own participation as volunteer officers. Despite the rigorous training required of female POs, maternalist discourses continued to shape probation work, emphasizing the female officers' affective roles and dispositions. Although these POs had to deal with high caseloads and increased paperwork that compromised the extent to which they were able to carry out these roles, especially with delinquent girls, the maternalist rhetoric persisted. It might follow, therefore, that the paychecks of female POs during the development of probation to present times were tied to nurturing perspectives.

Today, the expectation of female POs continues to be centered in an application of maternalist behavior toward probationers despite basic training designed to move away from those perspectives. When female POs do not respond according to that expectation, it is not unlikely that some probationers are confused. For instance, a probationer named Brian says that "I thought I lucked out with this babe probation officer. Instead, she turned out to be worse than the men (officers). If I was ten minutes late for our appointment she climbed all over me. Damn ya'd think she could at least be nice to me. After all, she is a woman."[85]

However, it should be pointed out that some writers such as Roslyn Muraskin argue that women have been victimized by policies designed to protect them and that women have struggled to have changes occur for the "past several hundred years."[86] Although Muraskin has a valid point, perhaps what requires clarification is that the expectations of female POs were designed and reinforced by powerful women. The point is that the evidence suggests that prevailing societal belief systems during any specific era tend to often shape behavior than gender. How can the expectations about women be changed?

Number of Female POs

Of the states that employed probation systems independently from parole, Table 8.7 walks us through some of the percentages of male, female, and race of their PO. Of the states in this sample, they employed an average of 1,769 staff of which more than 50 percent were women and 75 percent were white officers as of January 1, 2002.

Also, of the 19,464 probation staff members, 46 percent were probation officers, 8 percent were supervisors, and 19 percent were support staff (of which most were female).

High percentiles of female versus male staff and POs are even employed by jurisdictions where a single agency supervises both probationers and parolees, as Table 8.8 demonstrates.

In sum, as of January 1, 2002 female staff members tend to outnumber male staff in these professions. Also, of the 20,695 probation/parole staff members, 54 percent (11,147) were probation/parole officers, 13 percent were supervisors, and 23 percent were support staff and were females. In addition, women might be strongly represented in PO jobs because a basic requirement is a college degree. Most men enter the criminal justice system as police officers where the qualifications routinely are: 21 years of age, a valid drivers license and a high school diploma. Another reason for low male participation might be that

Table 8.7   Probation Staff: Gender and Race (by %) on January 1, 2002

State	Total Employed	Male	Female	White	Black	Other
Arizona	2,008	44	56	77	5	18
Colorado	865					
Connecticut	365	54	46	73	18	9
Washington, DC	8,300	NA				
Georgia	1,396	45	55	71	28	01
Illinois	4,000	NA				
Massachusetts	1,739	55	45	78	13	09
Nebraska	362	40	60	95	03	02
Texas	97	39	61	51	16	33
West Virginia	228	36	64			
Total Average	19,464 (1,769)	45	55	76	13	11
Probation officer percentage	46					

All percents were rounded.
Printed with permission of *The Corrections Yearbook.*[87]

because, probation is considered "soft" on crime, men might feel that their skills might be inadequately used as a PO.

As a matter of continuity, the Home Office in the United Kingdom published a report in January 2004 that shows female POs formed 49 percent of the total POs in England and Wales in 1992. This proportion grew steadily and reached 61 percent by yearend 2002. For senior grades (all above main grade), a similar trend was apparent with women holding 33 percent of senior posts in 1992, but 50 percent by yearend 2002. The number of female chief POs has grown from 8 in 1992 to 18 in 2001 and 2002 (15 percent to 43 percent of all chief POs).

Gender Issues

Ever since the first female PO, Alzina Parsons Stevens, was assigned to the County Juvenile Court in Chicago in 1899, gender issues arose among female POs and parole officers.[89] At the workplace in general, gender inequity is deeply ingrained and often based on societal expectations and attitudes. Therefore, it should come as no surprise that female correctional personnel share similar gender inequity issues as female personnel in other professions. Female corrections personnel tend to be denied training, lack agency-sponsored opportunities for networking, and are limited by traditional organizational behavior.[90] One of the most pressing concerns of women's rights groups is the reform of sexist attitudes and practices within the criminal justice system.[91] One way to redress the problem is a major increase in the number of women in positions of power within the criminal justice system. But, the fact that women seem to hold many of the top positions does not necessarily change the problem because the policy makers, interest groups, and

Table 8.8   Probation and Parole Staff: Gender and Race (by %) on January 1, 2002

State	Total	Male	Female	White	Black	Other
Alaska	160	NA				
Arkansas	405	43	57	77	23	0
Delaware	584	57	44	80	19	01
Florida	3,770	42	58	61	31	08
Idaho	229	54	46	89	01	10
Kentucky	474	52	48	94	06	0
Louisiana	797	53	47	80	19	01
Maryland	1,204	32	68	47	52	01
Michigan	1,994	44	56	69	28	03
Minnesota	304	42	58	96	01	03
Mississippi	256	75	25	77	23	0
Missouri	2,151	37	64	82	17	01
Montana	176	58	43	99	01	0
North Dakota	76	42	58	100	00	00
Ohio	1,090	45	55	76	23	01
Oklahoma	452	62	38	78	10	12
Pennsylvania	1,090	59	41	76	13	11
Rhode Island	104	35	65	89	06	05
South Carolina	900	45	55	69	30	01
Tennessee	922	43	57	63	35	02
Utah	564	60	40	91	02	07
Virginia	1,491	47	53	72	27	01
Washington	1,406	40	60	83	06	11
Wyoming	148	41	59	95	01	04
Total	20,695					
Average	862	48	52	80	16	01
PO/Parole officer percentage	54					

All percents were rounded.
Printed with permission of *The Corrections Yearbook.*[88]

the general public continue to view women in "helper roles" that seem to support a maternalist expectation among women criminal justice personnel. Anthony Walsh casts some doubt on the effectiveness of more women in power positions as a strategy to meliorate the sexist attitudes and practices.[92] Walsh argues that not only are the attitudes of female POs regarding sexual assault more benign than those of their male colleagues, but also sex offenders processed by female officers received significantly more lenient conditions of probation. Apparently, based upon general expectations held by others, a self-fulfilling proficiency continues to enjoy support from the maternalist perspectives.

Preparing the Female PO Recruit

Training a PO can be challenging. For example, one of the most difficult skills a PO must acquire is the ability to properly supervise the aggressor of a domestic violence crime especially if the PO (or parole officer) is female and the aggressor is male.[93] There is the tendency on the part of the aggressor to try to bend the female PO to "his" will. That is a worldview that he, by virtue of being male, has (or so he portrays) "certain privilege." Probation and parole trainers argue that some women agree with that worldview.[94] This aggressor tends to probe the female PO during the initial interview. Generally, because the offender tends to be in denial about his crime despite a guilty conviction, he would "pour on the charm" to prove he is not like the person portrayed in the police reports. He often implies that the victim is not as smart, professional, or sophisticated as the female PO. He minimizes the amount of physical damage inflicted and ignores any pattern of behavior within the relationship. He focuses on how he is helping his victim, who he implies is obviously a lesser person than the PO. Most female POs expect these techniques from aggressors and his "charmed" dialogue fails. However, sometimes he succeeds. Nonetheless, probation trainers say that the female PO should remain firm, protect the victim, and enforce the court and restraining orders. In light of the offender's continued failure to manipulate most female POs, this offender would miss domestic violence classes or alcohol classes and violate curfew. He might exhibit rage, question sexuality, threaten loss of control, and make subtle remarks that could be taken as threats against the officer or her department. This becomes a regular routine that every specialist in domestic violence probation supervision has learned to expect. Preparing new officers for their role in probation and parole can be a difficult task depending on the orientations of the corrections student and their trainers.

QUALIFICATIONS FOR PO JOBS

Applicants are usually administered written, oral, psychological, and physical examinations. Background checks are extensive.[95] Good physical and emotional health are important. Most POs are required to complete a training program sponsored by their state or the federal government. Qualifications vary, but many qualifications are similar to the following list:

1. Applicants must have at least a bachelor's degree, preferably in a behavioral science field or with coursework emphasis in sociology, psychology, law enforcement, corrections, guidance and counseling, social work, or social welfare.
2. Applicants should be able to meet the following job requirements:
   a. Knowledge of interviewing and counseling techniques, and social casework principles or techniques.
   b. Knowledge of sociological principles, behavior principles, and child and/or adolescent psychology.

c. Knowledge of scope and function of social agencies, juvenile law, court process, and law enforcement.

A graduate degree, such as a master's degree in criminal justice, social work, or psychology, is helpful for advancement.

General Skills

Earlier it was suggested that there are four general tasks performed by community correctional officers: law enforcer, counselor and educator, informal assistant, and supervisor. POs must also possess a number of general skills or proficiencies that would aid them in their job performance. These general proficiencies can be sought among the hiring qualifications to some degree or another and should become the basis of preservice training and certification.[96] Those skills can include:

- Recording and documentation
- Time management
- Interpersonal communication
- Ethical decision making
- Cultural awareness
- Interview and assessment
- Legal procedures

A result of having officers with some knowledge or training in the aforementioned areas and training them further toward a greater proficiency would strengthen their effectiveness on the job, which ultimately adds to public safety and will aid probationers toward law abiding behavior. One purpose for presenting this information is to show the complexity of probation and parole jobs.

FUTURE OF POs

There has been a "rethinking" of the practices used by POs to deliver their services, argues Robert Shearer.[97] Some experts call for probation to be "reinvented."[98] Some experts suggest that probation needs to follow a new and enhanced model of community involvement so that probation is fundamentally reshaped.[99] For one, modern probation caseload assignments should be matched with PO expertise; that is, matching caseloads "needs" with a PO who can provide those needs.[100] Also, POs should be given the responsibility of working in the community using skills associated with community organizing, community problem-solving, and community interventions with a wide variety of offenders, both adult and juvenile. In a sense, community policing efforts couched in a "broken windows" perspective centered in problem-solving orientations seem to be the model recommended

The Culture of Correctional Personnel

Dr. Mary Ann Farkas
Marquette University

Exploring the organizational culture of correctional work has been a major interest of mine. I have used a variety of research designs to better understand the sentiment among corrections personnel. Most corrections recruits, regardless of whether they are tasked with institutional service or community service such as probation and parole, seem to develop an understanding of organizational values and norms based upon their interactions with other personnel, most notably colleagues and supervisors. Conclusions from my research imply that despite its paramilitary, hierarchical formal structure, correctional work may have a more influential informal culture at work. Although some officers adhere to the perceived formal values of order, security, and control, others emphasize a more flexible approach in managing inmates, providing basic human services, and utilizing people skills. The latter group learned that a more personalized, less rigid style gave them more control over their work environment, more security in their relations with inmates, and a more satisfying work experience. These correctional officers are usually older and more experienced than the others. There were instances in which officers experienced role conflict in their failed attempts to reconcile what they viewed as two competing goals—supervision or human service delivery. They resolved this dilemma by finding satisfaction in the extrinsic aspects of the job—pay and job security. Also, these officers held negative attitudes toward the job, offenders, coworkers, and supervisors. Consequently they usually left the organization early in their career.

Lack of leadership and participation in decision making were identified as major stressors for officers. The challenge for correctional leadership, then, is to clearly and collaboratively define the mission, goals, and values of their organization with their correctional staff—whether it is security and control or human service delivery. Correctional officers are less stressed and more satisfied with their job when they know what they are expected to accomplish and have a clear understanding of their role.

Dr. Mary Ann Farkas

by most present-day experts on probation change.[101] One implication of this thought is that POs should be given the training, authority, and prerogative to solve client problems, with influential input from their clients. Although the idea sounds novel and workable, an impression is that POs presently have little authority to make changes individually and case by case. The reality is that POs frequently make changes and solve client problems; however, rarely is the "extra mile" acknowledged by administrators. That is, POs tend to work very hard on behalf of their clients with an eye on public safety, but are rarely rewarded for efforts that are not part of their job descriptions.

Additionally, new challenges for the probation community arise in unexpected ways. For example, when California voters approved Proposition 36 in July 2001, it was with the intention of providing a rehabilitative alternative to the incarceration of those convicted of nonviolent drug offenses.[102] Although the jury is still out on whether the law and its attendant programs are working, the existing probation structure has been overwhelmed by the number of court referrals. Proposition 36 offers those convicted of a nonviolent drug offense an alternative: supervised probation and drug treatment. Initial predictions, at least by the initiative's proponents, were that the workload for POs would be significantly decreased because monitoring duties would be shared by probation departments and local treatment providers. Up to the summer of 2004, the reverse has been true.

For instance, Connie Havens, division director of the Orange County Probation Department, indicates that she anticipated an influx of 4,200 the first year.[103] But the numbers were almost 1,300 more probationers than expected. Havens' agency receives an average of 90 to 100 new cases every week, and as of 2003, the agency has only been funded to hire eight new probation officers.

Vicki Markey, deputy chief of the San Diego County Probation Department, reveals that her agency received probationers who should have been referred to summary probation, which is court supervision, or to a few days in jail, but who would not have been introduced to the formal probation system.[104] However, most of the new probationers have drug abuse issues and her agency can aid those probationers with those problems. Proposition 36 in California opens the door to treatment for many individuals who might not have tried to help themselves in the past. On the negative side of this situation, many of the POs in California are unsure if they are prepared to deal with so many drug abusive probationers.[105]

California's probation practitioners are up to the task of additional surveillance and drug testing. However, what these agencies have experienced in added growth would not necessarily represent a dilemma for probation executives because funds have been cut in California as they have across the country for CC systems and programs. Getting the job done professionally is seriously doubted.

Finally, some argue that probation requires "leadership committed to enforcing violation warrants, supervising offenders primarily in the community rather than in probation offices, and not directing POs to avoid dangerous areas."[106] Many POs, it is reported, actually fear for their personal safety and support carrying firearms, according to a national survey.[107] Two-thirds of parole and probation agencies permit officers to carry weapons all the time and most permit them to carry for specific duties like making arrests or transporting offenders. In some probation systems, POs are authorized to carry weapons as part of their daily assignments (AZ, DC, GA, IL TX, WV), in some only during transport, and in others during special circumstances. Probation and parole officers are authorized to carry weapons in a large number of states (AK, AR, CA, DE, FL, ID, KY, MD, MI, MS, MO, MT, ND, NY, OH, OK, OR, PA, SC, UT, VA, WA). It would appear that as the risk of POs (and parole officers) increases, the authority to carry weapons might become a standard within the next few years.

What is the best way to handle this problem? Certainly more advanced classification, more serious offenders imprisoned, and fewer probationer rights might be three thoughts worth considering. Probation is here to stay but necessitates many changes within its operation, authority, and among the experiences of the probation officer.

To provide an idea about job opportunities for probation officers, review the opportunity for a probation job in Illinois.

Illinois Probation Officers

Monitoring and evaluation of probation programs and operations to ensure compliance with state standards and guidelines. Among the programs and operations routinely monitored are:

- Adult investigation and supervision system
- ISP program
- Specialized DUI program
- Pretrial services programs
- Administrative sanctions programs
- Electronic monitoring and drug testing programs
- Operational standards for Illinois probation
- Juvenile assessment and supervision system
- Juvenile detention screening criteria
- Juvenile intake screening programs
- Probation supervision fees
- Public service and restitution programs
- Specialized sex offender supervision program
- Specialized drug offender supervision program
- Specialized domestic violence supervision program

SUMMARY

This chapter discussed the process of probation and the role and strategies of POs. The process is associated with the probational authority exercised by the executive and judicial branches of government and how a different focus is expected depending on which branch of government manages probation. The negative issues arising from probation include the crisis of public and official confidence because nearly 4 out of every 10 suspects arrested for a felony are already on probation and 10 percent of the other probationers become absconders. The positive issues of probation are that probation offers a greater voluntary change for an offender to reform than incarcerated offenders. More revocations of probationers can mean that probation officers are more efficient in detecting violators than in the past. Probationers set a number of traps for probation officers, which include different religion and parent traps, among others. The responsibilities of probation officers include a wide range of tasks but can be conceptually categorized as investigative and analysis, law enforcement, treatment and referrals, assessment and evaluation, and surveillance. Nonetheless, what is inconsistent about those responsibilities is the control versus counsel orientations. POs use the following conceptual styles in conducting their jobs: punitive, protective, welfare, passive, and bunker style supervision. Female POs jobs are couched in the historical development of the juvenile justice system as an expression of maternalist orientations about women in general. It is also revealed that female POs outnumber male POs. Preparations and qualifications were offered, as well as the suggestion that probation is one of America's best alternatives to incarceration provided it does not become a dumping ground for defendants where needs and risk have been inadequately decided.

DISCUSSION QUESTIONS

1. Identify the influences that shape the process of probation. In what way do you support this perspective?
2. Describe advantages and disadvantages of executive and judicial branches of government linked to their operation of probation systems.
3. Explain the negative and positive issues associated with probation.
4. In what way are greater probation revocations a positive outcome rather than a negative outcome?
5. Describe the range of responsibilities of POs.
6. Identify the types of investigative reports developed by federal POs.
7. Identify the ultimate mission of POs.
8. Identify the conceptual categories of PO responsibilities.
9. Describe the inconsistency within the conceptual categories of responsibility among POs. If you were a PO, in what way would you deal with this issue?
10. Describe the various styles of delivery typified by many POs. Looking to your future as PO, which style do you think you might demonstrate more often than the other styles and why?
11. Discuss the development of female POs and explain why maternalist orientations were dominant. In what way do you believe those perspectives are still in place in the American criminal justice system?

12. Explain the future of POs.

13. Identify some of the competencies expected of probation officers and explain why those competencies might be helpful to a probation officer.

NOTES

1. Idit Weiss and Yochanan Wozner (2002). Ten models for probation supervision compared across eight dimensions. *Journal of Offender Rehabilitation, 34*(3), 85–105.

2. Bureau of Labor Statistics (2004). *Occupational outlook handbook, 2004–05 Edition: Probation officers and correctional treatment specialists.* Washington, DC: U.S. Department of Labor. Retrieved online January 11, 2005: http://stats.bls.gov/oco/ocos265.htm

3. This definition is consistent with the New York Department of Correctional Services. Retrieved online January 11, 2005: http://dpca.state.ny.us/nysdpca/rulesregulations/347.htm

4. The Massachusetts Court System. Retrieved online January 11, 2005: http://www.state.ma.us/courts/admin/aotc.html

5. LIS INC., (1995) *State and Local Probation Systems in the United States: A survey of Current Practice,* CO: LIS INC.

6. R. A. Fox (2000). *Transforming probation through leadership: The "Broken Windows" model.* Manhattan Institute. Retrieved online January 11, 2005: http://www.manhattan-institute.org/html/broken_windows_4.htm#conclusion

7. W. J. Bennett, J. J. DiIulio, and J. P. Walters (1996). *Body count: Moral poverty and how to win America's war against crime and drugs.* New York: Simon and Schuster.

8. Daniel Glaser (1995). *Preparing convicts fore law-abiding lives.* Albany: State University of New York (p. 149).

9. M. O. Reynolds (2000). *Privatizing probation and parole.* National Center for Police Analysis. Retrieved online January 11, 2005: http://www.ncpa.org/studies/s233/s233.html#F

10. Bureau of Justice Statistics (2004, July). *Probation and parole in the United States, 2003.* Washington, DC: U.S. Department of Justice, Office of Justice Programs. NCJ 205336. Retrieved online January 11, 2005: http://www.ojp.usdoj.gov/bjs/pub/pdf/ppus03.pdf

11. Doris Layton MacKenzie et.al. (1999). The impact of probation on the criminal activities of offenders. *Journal of Research in Crime and Delinquency, 36*(4), 423–453.

12. Bureau of Justice Statistics (1995, August). *Probation and parole violators in state prison, 1991: Survey of state prison inmates, 1991.* Washington, DC: U.S. Department of Justice, Office of Justice Program, NCJ 149076. Retrieved online January 11, 2005: http://www.ojp.usdoj.gov/bjs/pub/ascii/ppvsp91.txt

13. Bureau of Justice Statistics (1995, August). *Probation and parole violators in state prison, 1991. Survey of state prison inmates, 1991.*

14. W. J. Bennett, J. J. DiIulio, and J. P. Walters (1996), 36.

15. Bureau of Justice Statistics (2004, July). *Probation and parole in the United States, 2003.* Also see Frank P. Williams III, Marilyn D. McShane, and H. Michael Dolny (2000, March). Predicting parole absconders. *The Prison Journal, 80*(1), p. 36.

16. Bureau of Justice Statistics (2004, July). *Probation and parole in the United States, 2003.*

17. Bureau of Justice Statistics (2002). *Sourcebook of criminal justice statistics 2001* (Table 2.54). Washington, DC: U.S. Department of Justice, Office of Justice Programs. Retrieved online January 11, 2005: http://www.albany.edu/sourcebook/

18. Walter J. Dickey and Michael E. Smith (1998, December). The report from the focus group on dangerous opportunity: Five futures for community corrections. *Rethinking probation: Community supervision, community safety.* Washington, DC: U.S. Department of Justice, Office of Justice Programs. Retrieved online January 11, 2005: http://www.ojp.usdoj.gov/probation/rethink.pdf

19. Mario Paparozzi (2003, August). Probation, parole and public safety: The need for principles practices versus faddism and circular policy development. *Corrections Today, 65*(5), 46–52.

20. Walter J. Dickey and Michael E. Smith (1998, December).

21. Walter J. Dickey and Michael E. Smith (1998, December).

22. M. O. Reynolds (2000). *Privatizing probation and parole.* National Center for Police Analysis. Retrieved online June 11, 2004: http://www.ncpa.org/studies/s233/s233.html#F

23. Bureau of Justice Statistics. (2004, July). *Probation and parole in the United States, 2003.*

24. Bureau of Justice Statistics. (2004, July). *Probation and parole in the United States, 2003.*

25. Daniel Glaser (1997). *Profitable penalties: How to cut both crime rates and costs.* Thousand Oaks, CA: Pine Forge.

26. Daniel Glaser (1975). *Strategic criminal justice planning.* Rockville, MA: National Institute of Mental Health. Also Daniel Glaser (1995). *Preparing convicts for law-abiding lives.* Albany: State University of New York Press.

27. David Eichental and James Jacobs (1991). Enforcing the criminal law in state prisons. *Justice Quarterly, 8,* 283–303.

28. Daniel Glaser (1995), 148.

29. Andrew von Hirsch (1976). *Doing justice: The choice of punishments.* New York: Hill and Wang, 89.

30. Daniel Glaser (1997), 11–12.

31. Marcus Felson (2002). *Crime and everyday life* (3rd ed.). Thousand Oaks, CA: Pine Forge.

32. American Correctional Association *2003 Directory: Adult and Juvenile.* Lanham, MD:, American Correctional Association (p. 20). Also see, *The corrections yearbook: Adult corrections 2002.* Camille Graham Camp & George Camp (Eds.). Middletown, CT: Criminal Justice Institute, 206.

33. For instance, Dan R. Beto, Ronald P. Corbett, and Gerald R. Hinzman (1999). Embracing key strategies for a national probation system, *Executive Exchange,* Huntsville: NAPE: George F. Cole and Christopher E. Smith (2005). *The American system of criminal justice,* (4th ed.). Belmont, CA: Wadsworth (pp. 301–307). Edward J. Latessa and Harry E. Allen (1999). *Corrections in the community* (2nd ed.). Cincinnati, OH: Anderson (pp. 260–265). D. E. Von Laningham, M. Taber, and R. Dimants (1966). How adult POs view their responsibility. *Crime & Delinquency, 12,* 97–104. Edward J. Latessa and Francis T. Cullen (2002, September). Beyond correctional quackery—professionalism and the possibility of effective treatment. *Federal Probation, 66*(2), 28–37. Robert A. Shearer (2001). Strategic alignment in community supervision of offenders. *Perspectives, 25*(3), 18–21. Faye S. Taxman (2002, September). Supervision: Exploring the dimensions of effectiveness. *Federal Probation, 66*(2), 14–27.

34. For instance, when I asked students at the University of Massachusetts Boston about the primary responsibilities of POs, most of them, including those students who were police officers, reported that POs generally monitor the whereabouts of probationers.

35. P. W. Hall and R. R. Smith (1981). Development of the probation counseling relationship scale, *Journal of Offender Counseling, 2*(1), 20–27. Also Dan R. Beto, Ronald P. Corbett, and Gerald R. Hinzman (1999).

36. George F. Cole and Christopher E. Smith (2005). Also see Robert A. Shearer (2001).

37. Dennis J. Stevens (2006). *Community corrections: An applied approach.* Upper Saddle River, NJ: Prentice Hall. Sources used to develop this table include: G. Cole (1989); Edward J. Latessa and Harry E. Allen (1999), pp. 260–265; Edward J. Latessa and Francis T. Cullen (2002, September); Robert A. Shearer (2001); Faye S. Taxman (2002, September).

38. Robert A. Shearer (2001), 18–21.

39. R. D. Hoge and D. A. Andrews (1996). *Assessing the youthful offender: Issues and strategies.* New York: Plenum.

40. Faye S. Taxman (2002, September).

41. Faye S. Taxman (2002, September).

42. Faye S. Taxman (2002, September). pp. 32–33. Also see, Edward J. Latessa and Francis T. Cullen (2002). Beyond correctional quackery—professionalism and the possibility of effective treatment. *Federal Probation, 66*(2), 28–38. Retrieved online December 27, 2004: http://www.uscourts.gov/fedprob/2002sepfp.pdf

43. Faye S. Taxman (2002, September), 33.

44. Joan Petersilia (1999). A decade with experimenting with intermediate sanctions: What have we learned? *Perspectives, 23*(1), 39–44.

45. A. P. Miles (1965). The reality of the POs dilemma. *Federal Probation, 29*(1), 18–22. And A. P. Miles (1965). Wisconsin studies the function of probation and parole. *American Journal of Corrections, 25,* 21–35.

46. D. E. Von Laningham, M. Taber, and R. Dimants (1966).

47. This study was also discussed in detail in Edward J. Latessa and Harry E. Allen. (1999), 260–261.

48. *Massachusetts criminal law and motor vehicle handbook: 2003 edition.* 276. 85A. New York: Gould (p. 683).

49. Bureau of Labor Statistics. U.S. Department of Labor: 2003. Retrieved online November 14, 2003: http://www.bls.gov/oco/ocos265.htm

50. George F. Cole and Christopher E. Smith (2005), 304–307.

51. Bureau of Justice Statistics. (2003). *Sourcebook of criminal justice statistics.* Albany, NY: U.S. Department of Justice. Table 1.77 retrieved online January 11, 2005: http://www.albany.edu/sourcebook/1995/pdf/t177.pdf

52. E. Carlson and E. Parks (1979). *Critical issues in adult probation: Issues in probation management* Washington, DC: U.S. Department of Justice, NCJRS 057667.

53. Daniel Glaser (1997), 21.

54. David Dressler (1969). *Practice and theory of probation and parole,* New York: Columbia University.

55. Dennis J. Stevens (2006). *Community corrections: An applied approach.* Upper Saddle River, NJ: Prentice Hall.

56. Joan Petersilia (1999).

57. Joan Petersilia and Steve Turner (1993). Evaluating intensive supervision probation/parole: Results of a nationwide experiment." *Research in brief.* Washington, DC: National Institute of Justice.

58. Joan Petersilia and Steve Turner (1993).

59. Oklahoma Board of Corrections. Retrieved online November 18, 2003: http://www.state.ok.gov

60. Virginia Department of Corrections. Retrieved online March 1, 2004: http://www.vadoc.state.va.us/offenders/community/overview.htm

61. Office of Justice Programs (1996). *Reducing demand through treatment.* Retrieved online December 26, 2004: thttp://www.ojp.usdoj.gov/reports/96wg/treat.htm. Also see Bureau of Labor Statistics. (2004). *Occupational outlook handbook, 2004–05 edition: Probation officers and correctional treatment specialists.*

62. *The corrections yearbook: Adult corrections 2002* (2003). Camille Graham Camp and George Camp (Eds.). Middletown, CT. Criminal Justice Institute (p. 214).

63. Personal communication with probation officers in Cook County Illinois and Los Angeles California. March 4, 2004. They wish to remain anonymous.

64. *The corrections yearbook: Adult corrections 2002* (2003), 195.

65. *The corrections yearbook: Adult corrections 2002* (2003), 196.

66. State of Maine. Minutes of Corrections Study Commission's meeting: September 24, 2003.

67. Personal communication with probation officers in Cook County Illinois and Los Angeles California March 4, 2004. They wish to remain anonymous.

68. For punitive, protective, and welfare PO see L. E. Ohlin, H. Piven, and M. D. Pappenfort (1956). Major dilemmas on the social worker in probation and parole. *National Probation and Parole Association Journal, 2,* 21–25. For passive officer see Daniel Glaser (1969). *The effectiveness of a prison and parole system.* IN: Bobbs-Merrill (pp. 292–295). Faye S. Taxman (2002, September). Supervision— exploring the dimensions of effectiveness. *Federal Probation, 66*(20), 14–27. For bunker see Robert A. Fox (2000). *Transforming probation through leadership: The "Broken Windows" model.* Manhattan Institute. Retrieved online November 14, 2003: http://www.manhattan-institute.org/html/broken_windows_4.htm#conclusion

69. Edward J. Latessa and Harry E. Allen (1999), 255.

70. Daniel Glaser (1995). *Preparing convicts for law-abiding lives.* Albany: State University of New York; (pp. 148–149).

71. C. L. Erickson (1977). Faking it: Principles of expediency as applied to probation. *Federal Probation, 4*(3), 36–39. Also Edward J. Latessa and Francis T. Cullen (2002).

72. Walter J. Dickey and Michael E. Smith (1998).

73. Walter J. Dickey and Michael E. Smith (1998), 20.

74. R. A. Fox (2000).

75. T. R. Bonczar (1997). Characteristics of adults on probation, 1995. *Special Report.* Washington, DC: Bureau of Justice Statistics.

76. Edward J. Latessa and Harry E. Allen (1999), 255–256.

77. Fitzgerald personal website. Retrieved online November 15, 2003: http://www.bostonstrategy.com/players/02_probation/01_fitzgerald.html

78. Carl Reddick and Don Chapin. *Domestic violence: A parole officer's perspective.* Paper presented at the fifth annual conference on Addiction & Criminal Behavior at St. Louis, MI, September 2004. This study was used as a guide for this section. Specifics were supplied by several POs who reviewed Reddick and Chaplin's study and made suggestions on how to generalize Reddick and Chapin's perspective. The POs were enrolled in inservice training programs at the North Carolina Justice Academy, Salemburg, NC. They wish to remain anonymous for obvious reasons.

79. Elizabeth Clapp (1998). *Mothers of all children: Women reformers and the rise of juvenile courts in progressive era America.* University Park, PA: Pennsylvania State University Press.

80. Elizabeth Clapp (1998), 87.

81. Elizabeth Clapp (1998), 90.

82. Women in American History Series. *Hannah Kent Schoff (1853–1940), welfare worker and reformer.* Encyclopedia Britannica.

83. Elizabeth Rose (2002). Book review for University of Illinois Press. American Society of Legal History.

84. Anne Meis Knupfer (1999). Professionalizing probation work in Chicago, 1900–1935. *Social Service Review, 73*(4), 478–496.

85. Personal communication with a probationer in Boston. June 2004.

86. Roslyn Muraskin (1999). Women and the law: Agenda for change in the twenty-first century. In Roslyn Muraskin and Albert R. Roberts (Eds.) *Visions for change* (pp. 369–379). Upper Saddle River, NJ: Prentice Hall. (p. 369).

87. *The corrections yearbook: Adult corrections 2002* (2003), 218.

88. *The corrections yearbook: Adult corrections 2002* (2003), 218.

89. Clarice Feinman (1994). *Women in the criminal justice system.* Westport, CT: Praeger.

90. Joseph R. Rowan (1996). Female correctional officers said to reduce prison violence. *Criminal Justice Newsletter,* April, *27*(7), 2–3.

91. Anthony Walsh (1984). Gender-based differences: A study of POs' attitudes about, and recommendations for, felony sexual assault cases. *Criminology, 22*(3), 371–387.

92. Anthony Walsh (1984).

93. In part, this perspective was learned by the author while teaching academic courses at the North Carolina Justice Academy. Many of the writer's students were probation and parole officers, police officers, and other professionals employed through the criminal justice system in the state and in the U.S. military.

94. Carl Reddick and Don Chapin (2004). *Domestic violence: A parole officer's perspective.* Paper presented at the fifth annual conference on Addiction & Criminal Behavior at St. Louis, MI, September 2004.

95. U.S. Department of Labor: Bureau of Labor Statistics. *Occupational outlook handbook.* Retrieved online September 4, 2004: http://www.bls.gov/oco/ocos265.htm

96. Robert A. Shearer (2001).

97. Robert A. Shearer (2001).

98. W. D. Burrell (2000) Reinventing probation: Organizational culture and change. *Community Corrections Report 7,* 53–54.

99. Dan R. Beto, Ronald P. Corbett, and James J. DiIulio (2000). Getting serious about probation and the crime problem, *Corrections Management Quarterly, 4,* 1–8. Also see Dan R. Beto, Ronald P. Corbett, and Gerald R. Hinzman (1999). And W. D. Burrell (2000). Also, *"Broken windows" probation: The next step in fighting crime.* (1999, August). New York: Center for Civil Innovation at the Manhattan Institute, Civic Report No. 7. Retrieved online December 14, 2004: http://www.manhattan-institute.org/html/cr_7.htm

100. Gerald R. Hinzman (1999). The matrix: A community corrections response to matching the offender with treatment resources. *Executive Exchange*. Huntsville: National Association of Probation Executives.

101. Reinventing Probation Counsel (2001). *Forming probation through leadership: "Broken Windows" model.* The Manhattan Institute. Retrieved online January 11, 2005: http://www.cjtoday.com/pdf/7cjt1103.pdf. Also James Q. Wilson and George L. Kelling. (2000). Broken window. The police and the neighborhood safety. In Willard M. Oliver (Ed.), *Community policing: Classical readings* (pp. 1–15), Upper Saddle River, NJ: Prentice Hall.

102. *TechBeat spring 2002*. National Law Enforcement and Corrections Technology Center. Retrieved online November 2003: http://www.nlectc.org/txtfiles/tbspring2002 .html

103. California department of corrections, division of community corrections. Retrieved online November 13, 2003: http://www.corr.ca.gov

104. California department of corrections, division of community corrections. Retrieved online November 13, 2003: http://www.corr.ca.gov

105. California department of corrections, division of community corrections. Retrieved online November 13, 2003: http://www.corr.ca.gov

106. Charles Lindner and Robert Bonn (1996). PO Victimization and fieldwork practices: Results of a national study. *Federal Probation, 60*(2), 16–23. And *"Broken Windows" probation: The next step in fighting crime. Manhattan Institute.*

107. Charles Lindner and Robert Bonn (1996).

PAROLE, NATURE, HISTORY, AND STATISTICS

LEARNING OBJECTIVES

After you finish reading this chapter, you will be better prepared to:

- Describe issues of collateral damage associated with the prison building boom.
- Define parole and identify its objectives.
- Explain functions of parole associated with parolees and corrections.
- Explain a three-phase strategy that helps inmates reintegrate into the community and includes whole or part of the recommended Five Rs.
- Describe the importance of preparole reports.
- Identify similarities and differences between parole and probation.
- Discuss the history of parole and contributions of influential practitioners.
- Describe 19th-century influences toward early release in Europe and England.
- Describe dynamics of the U.S. debate that developed between the first half of the 20th century versus the second half of the 20th century.
- Explain how parole eligibility can be determined.
- Describe good-time credits.
- Explain the current American mindset about early release.

KEY TERMS

Determinate Sentences	Mandatory Parole	Preparole Reports
Discretionary Parole	Zebulon Brockway	Dr. Samuel G. Howe
English Penal Servitude	Sir Walter Crofton	
Act of 1853	Captain Alexander	
Good-time Policies	Maconochie	
Indeterminate Sentences	Expiration of Sentence	

> History has demonstrated that the most notable winners usually encountered heart-breaking obstacles before they triumphed. They won because they refused to become discouraged by their defeats.
>
> —B. C. Forbes

INTRODUCTION

Parole is an early "conditional" release from jail or prison, saving confinement costs (e.g., $29,000 to house an inmate for a year as compared to $3,000 per parolee in California in 2003[1]) and providing prisoners an opportunity to demonstrate willingness to reform. However, parole has its critics because of cases such as one where a judge ordered Gerald Turner, the infamous "Halloween Killer" who inspired Wisconsin's sexual predator law, to serve 15 years in prison for violating his parole after authorities found hundreds of hard-core pornographic images on a computer drive in his room at a halfway house.[2] In 1973, Turner murdered and sexually assaulted a nine-year-old girl, Lisa French of Fond du Lac, on Halloween. The girl came to Turner's house while trick-or-treating. Turner was first paroled in 1992. He was taken back to prison a short time later, but a jury decided he was not sexually violent. Turner was granted parole again and placed at Foster Community Correctional Center in Madison in February 1998.

    Another case involves Christopher Shane Hyde, 30, who was a prisoner in Florida for murder and was eventually paroled. Four months after his release, Hyde walked into a funeral home and killed three people to steal their wallets.[3] The shootings at the Bell Funeral Home shocked residents of the close-knit coal town of 2,600, northwest of Birmingham, FL.

PUNISHMENT ADVOCATES AND PAROLE

Parole has many problems, especially when parolees commit loathsome crimes.[4] Punishment advocates believe prisoners should remain in prison for the full-term. Inherent in a punishment perspective is a focus on the past. As you already know, punishment advocates see prison as the place for punishment and it should be administered in a controlled, no-frill, environment (e.g., no televisions, educational programs, or workout equipment). Their perspective centers on a punitive criminal justice response toward all individuals who violate any law. The consensus? Build more prisons.

Additionally, punishment and control advocates argue that determinate sentences are counterproductive when "good-time" type credits toward early release are awarded to prisoners.

TREATMENT ADVOCATES AND PAROLE

On the other hand, treatment and prevention advocates might say, "Let's see who this guy is and make some informed decisions about how to change him." Treatment and prevention advocates tend to look to the future. With some crimes, the past should take precedence. But most prisoners hardly characterize Dr. Hannibal "The Cannibal" Lecter, played by Sir Anthony Hopkins in the 1991 movie, *The Silence of the Lambs.*

Collateral Damage

There is collateral damage from the prison-building boom fueled by the get-tough-on-crime attitudes of the last two decades. At least the boom has produced a lower crime rate in the 21st century, argue just desert advocates. However, there are more defendants currently imprisoned than at any other time in American history and the number of prisoners continues to climb—and not necessarily for convictions association with crimes of violence or because of an increase in the American population as some writers wish us to believe. For instance, of the 2.1 million offenders in state prisons, federal prisons, and jails, an estimated 50 percent of the occupants had been convicted of a nonviolent crime. There were an estimated 480 prisoners per 100,000 U.S. residents imprisoned as of June 2003, up from 411 at yearend 1995.[5] Huge increases in new arrivals to prison at a time when crime has declined might be hard to explain.

You already know that defendants are sentenced to prison more often and for longer periods of time, yet most are released. But because some jurisdictions have sharply curtailed education, job training, and other service programs, which includes treatment and appropriate rehabilitation programs, newly released prisoners are far less likely than their counterparts of two decades ago to find jobs, maintain stable family relationships, or contribute to the community or themselves in a positive way. For the most part, these offenders have no place to go and no money to help them find safe living environments or even to eat a well-balanced meal. For most of them, it does not take long before they once again engage in criminal behavior.

For the most part, prisoners are released to poor neighborhoods of large cities (regardless of where those prisoners lived prior to incarceration) and to its streets (one third lost their homes prior to their incarceration).[6] In addition, parole technology, parole officer training, and agency practices have increased dramatically in the last years. Consequently, former prisoners, including those on parole, are always one stop on the way back to prison.[7] For instance, recently the Little Hoover Commission, a nonpartisan, state-appointed watchdog group, blasted the current parole system in California—63 percent of parolees are returned to prison within 18 months of release. That equates to about 100,000 parolees each year (at yearend 2003) in California alone who return to a prison system holding about 162,000 prisoners.[8] California spends around $1.5 billion on its parole program and most of those funds are utilized to put parolees back in prison.

California prisons plan sweeping parole changes, spurred by budget pressures.[9] One of those changes includes reducing the number of parolees returned to prison. One estimate implies that approximately 15,000 fewer prisoners would be in the system by yearend 2005. New policies would allow violators to be monitored electronically, sent to home detention, or put on work release. Community prerelease programs would be expanded, as would oversight of parolees. Critics say the changes are aimed more at the bottom line than at prisoner welfare.

PAROLE DEFINED

The word parole comes from the French *parole d'honneur* or "word of honor."[10] Parole, in criminal law, is a pledge of good conduct by a person convicted of a crime as a condition of release from confinement prior to serving an entire prison sentence.[11]

Individuals on conditional release are subject to being returned to jail or prison for rule violations or other offenses.

Parole Defined

The term **parole** refers to both the process for releasing offenders from prison prior to the expiration of their sentences and to the period of conditional supervision in the community following imprisonment.[12]

Parole is early conditional release after jail or prison time before the entire incarceration period is served.

Of Those Paroled

Forty-five percent of state parole discharges in 2002 successfully completed their term of supervision, relatively unchanged since 1995. Forty-one percent were returned to jail or prison and 9 percent absconded.[13]

Prisoner Tom Watson[14] explains, "Both state and federal courts have consistently held that early release is exercised exclusively by the executive branch of government, and that parole occurs within the sentence of actual custody (i.e., early release).[15] The enforcement leverage that supports the parole conditions derives from the authority to return the parolee to prison to serve out the balance of a prison sentence."[16]

PAROLE GOALS

The ultimate goal of the justice community is public safety and in parole that means to protect the community from released prisoners.[17] The specific goal of parole is to supervise an offender after early release and promote a crime-free lifestyle by learning new behaviors and strategies for implementing those new behaviors. In CC, nowhere is this job more challenging for practitioners than among parole officers because most parolees were convicted of a felony resulting in a loss of family, jobs, relationships, and lifestyle experiences.

FUNCTIONS OF PAROLE ASSOCIATED WITH PAROLEE

Public safety is best served when conditionally released convicts contribute at a positive level to the community, especially through law-abiding behavior. How can that be accomplished? Probably at some level or another through the Five Rs.

- Reconciliation: Personal accountability. Providing financial contributions to community corrections services.
- Restitution: Criminal accountability. Financial reparation to victim/s and community.
- Rehabilitation: Personal recovery. Altering the attitudes and health of an offender so reoffending is less likely.
- Reintegration: Offender placement. Preparing an offender to live crime-free without supervision in the community.
- Restorative Justice: Victim personal recovery. Coming to terms with victims, families of victims and offenders, and community members.

Intrinsic to successful re-entry of a parolee is reconciliation, restitution, rehabilitation, reintegration, and restoration justice. For the purposes of this chapter, reintegration and restorative justice will be discussed, as these two goals are the most challenging aspects of parole while reconciliation, restitution, and rehabilitation have been discussed in Chapters 5 and 6.

Reintegration

Reintegration is the process of finding a convict meaningful employment and housing, restoring family relationships, and supervising an offender toward an independent, crime-free lifestyle.[18] Reintegration begins with understanding the needs of parolees and building a rapport—building trust. Many parolees have been accustomed to unstable relationships and have experienced the deprivation of freedom including custody practices of correctional personnel. Originally, if the offender had been a minimum risk, probation might have been the first choice of the court. But, because the defendant is conditionally released from jail or prison, the PSI, subsequent investigations and assessments, and all the other indicators may have recommended custody. And it is likely that most guilty defendants, especially those imprisoned, do not feel good about themselves.

This same person must now be guided through re-entry into a community that values (punishment and control philosophies) imprisonment more than release—even conditional release. Additionally, idleness, regimentation, and strict conformity to prison rules and acceptance of a prisoner subculture, including violence and anger, can become an obstacle for many parolees.

Then, too, the loss of time served can take its toll on family relationships, employment skills, housing, and all the other matters free persons take for granted. What about welfare and medical prescriptions (originally prescribed at the prison) and obtaining identification such as a driver's license or applying for a checking account? Completing application requirements for an apartment, electricity, and telephone service (to contact the parolee's parole officer) could be difficult if a parolee has limited resources (most do) and little family assistance. What about clothes, coats, and a toothbrush? Some might say that none of this concerns a parole officer, but without the focus of a parolee, a parole officer's job is exceedingly difficult. Finally, should the parolee be mentally challenged, lack English-speaking skills, or have serious health or medical issues, reintegration is complicated all the more. Reintegration is probably a larger job than expected and one that marks it as distinctively different than a probation process. That is, the focus of parole is on reintegration as opposed to conduct and behavior. Yet, one in five parolees leave prison without any postcustody supervision.[19] See Chapter 2 for details on reintegration at the Federal level.

Re-entry Strategies

There are many re-entry strategies (confinement to the community) across jurisdictions. To give you an idea about how re-entry models could work, one ideal process of re-entry initiative envisions the development of re-entry programs that can start in correctional institutions and continue throughout an offender's transition to and stabilization in the community.[20] Many of these programs try to provide for prisoner re-entry that addresses issues confronting prisoners as they return to the community. The initiative encompasses three phases, which often include whole or parts of the recommended Five Rs:

> Phase 1—Protect and Prepare: Institution-Based Programs. Services provided in this phase include education, mental health and substance abuse treatment, job training, mentoring, and full diagnostic and risk assessment.

> Phase 2—Control and Restore: Community-Based Transition Programs. These programs try to work with offenders prior to and immediately following their release from correctional institutions. Services provided in this phase try to include, as appropriate, education, monitoring, mentoring, life skills training, assessment, job skills development, and mental health and substance abuse treatment.

> Phase 3—Sustain and Support: Community Long-Term Support Programs. These programs try to connect individuals who have left the supervision of the justice system with a network of social services agencies and community organizations to provide ongoing services and mentoring relationships.

Examples of program elements include institution readiness programs, institutional and community assessment centers, re-entry courts, supervised or electronically monitored boarding houses, mentoring programs, and CC centers. Ideally, re-entry programs that begin upon entry into prison would be the goal of program initiatives. Because of the high number of prisoners, it is probably an unlikely initiative in correctional systems.

Restorative Justice

Explores the idea that fitting in and contributing to the community is not enough from the perspective of the victim/s, and all those who have been impacted by the action/s of the offender. It might not even be enough from the perspective of the offender, the arresting officers, and members of the court and community. A parolee (including those whose prison sentences have expired) must come to terms with victims, families of victims, families of offenders, community members, and officials. Think of family members who supported convicts while incarcerated with visits including food and clothes, letters, and humiliating experiences produced by justice personnel and the community. Resolution, or bridges, must be build to accommodate all those injured parities including the family and friends of the offender. It might follow that restorative justice is unlikely if an offender is unwilling.

Functions of Parole Associated with Corrections

The justice community would like to fulfill the following outcomes through parole practices.

- Deterrence of crime
- Punishment
- Decreases in jail and prison overcrowding
- Money savings
- Aid in incarceration control

Deterrence of crime is hopefully accomplished through surveillance strategies of the parole agency. Curfew, work requirements, and drug testing might aid in eliminating at least the opportunity to commit crime. However, the thought is that a parolee will realize that surveillance will detect criminal activity and therefore, it might not be in the best interest of the parolee to commit any crimes. Joan Petersilia makes a case that public safety is enhanced through parole surveillance and treatment.[21]

Punishment through parole is a continuation of the prison sentence in the sense that parolees are provided with stringent conditions of parole monitored by officers with discretion and police powers. For example, parole officers can enter the living quarters of a parolee without a warrant (more on parolee rights in Chapter 10.)

Decreases in jail and prison overcrowding is hopefully obtained through the early release of many inmates. The more offenders incarcerated, the more prisoners there are to be released. Another part of this function relates to the expense of confinement versus community supervision. For each day a defendant is on parole rather than confined, the state theoretically saves $21,114 per year and that would suggest one less defendant in prison.

Money savings suggests that the more defendants are on parole, the fewer prisoners, and that saves the state money because of the differences in the costs. Generally, the American Correctional Association reports that it costs an average of $64.84 per day per inmate compared to $6.94 per day per parolee.[22] Specifically, see Table 9.1 for estimates of costs in various states. See Table 9.2 for estimates of costs in states where probation and parole agencies operate under one management team.

You might wonder why there are differences in costs per day from state to state. It could be, among other things, that these costs reflect differences in payroll, rental space for offices, transportation, treatment and mental costs, and difference in monthly charges of parolee.

A closer look at a specific jurisdiction might help. For instance, the DOC in Georgia reports that it spends $23,554 per year (2003) for an inmate in a typical minimum security facility, $45,150 for an inmate in a typical medium facility, $58,920 for close security, $81,345 for maximum security, or an average of $48.66 per day per average of each inmate incarcerated.[25] But the state spends $1.50 every day for every probationer on average (not shown in the tables), up to an overall cost of $2.90 every day for every parolee and up to $6.00 every day for every parolee on electronic monitoring (see Table 9.1).

Aid in Incarceration Control implies that incentives such as parole "good-time" credits can often help maintain order inside prisons (discussed in this chapter). That is, early release can be linked to the "compliant" behavior of a prisoner.

Table 9.1   Costs per Parolee per Day in 2001: Parole Systems

States	Overall	Regular	Intensive	Electronic	Special
Arizona	$7.59	$6.92		$58.38	
California	$7.52				
Colorado	$9.85	$8.50	$17.85		
Connecticut	$17.00	$17.00	$17.00	$3.56	$17.00
Georgia	$2.90			$6.00	
Illinois	$1.45				
Kansas	$8.73				
Massachusetts	$5.67				
Nebraska	$8.50				
New York	$9.35				
South Dakota	$3.32				
Texas	$3.49	$2.84	$7.84	$2.66	$4.37
Utah	$8.22				
West Virginia	$3.57	$3.57			
Average	$6.94	$6.96	$14.23	$17.65	$10.69

Printed with permission of *The Corrections Yearbook* (2003).[23]

Table 9.2   Costs per Parolee per Day in 2001: Parole and Probation Systems

States	Overall	Regular	Intensive	Electronic	Special
Alaska	$4.15				
Arkansas	$1.75	$1.37	$1.75	$2.37	$3.75
Delaware	$5.12	$3.49		$10.00	$3.49
Florida	$4.07	$3.45	$8.33	$9.19	$8.76
Idaho	$3.90	$2.63	$8.51	$4.47	$3.64
Kentucky	$3.64	$3.64			
Louisiana	$2.12	$1.74		$3.02	
Maryland	$2.77	$2.77		$35.39	
Michigan	$7.73	$4.42	$12.68	$15.53	$59.27
Minnesota	$3.11	$2.87	$22.19	$5.25	
Mississippi	$1.72		$7.86		
Missouri	$3.34	$2.13	$5.94	$9.53	
Montana	$4.22	$3.43	$11.85	$11.85	
North Dakota	$3.54				
Ohio	$6.00				
Oklahoma	$1.87	$1.87			$1.87
Oregon	$5.10	$5.88	$10.85		
Pennsylvania	$8.62				
South Carolina		$2.80	$9.87	$16.77	
Tennessee	$3.65	$2.57			$4.72
Virginia	$4.13	$3.99	$6.05	$9.78	
Washington	$2.00				
Wyoming	$3.05	$3.05	$15.82		
Average	$3.89	$3.06	$10.14	$11.10	$11.45

Printed with permission of *The Corrections Yearbook*.[24]

Preparole Reports

In general, discretionary parole is rarely an automatic process. A typical model used by many states begins with the preparole report in determining whether a prisoner is suitable for discretionary parole. Parole boards consider a preparole report developed by parole officers including:

1. The recommendations made by the sentencing court, the prosecuting attorney, the defense attorney, and any statements made by the victim or the prisoner at sentencing.
2. The prisoner's institutional conduct history while incarcerated.
3. Recommendations made by the staff of the correctional facilities in which the prisoner was incarcerated.

4. Reports of prior crimes, juvenile histories, and previous experiences of the prisoner on parole or probation.

5. Physical, mental, and psychiatric examinations of the prisoner.

6. Information submitted by the prisoner, the sentencing court, the victim of the crime, the prosecutor, or other persons having knowledge of the prisoner or the crime.

7. Information concerning an unjustified disparity in the sentence imposed on a prisoner in relation to other sentences imposed under similar circumstances.

8. Other relevant information that may be reasonably available.[26]

Generally, preparole reports and other information by a parole authority are confidential and are not disclosed to anyone other than the board, the sentencing judge, the prosecuting and defense attorneys, the prisoner, the attorney for the board, and the staff of the board. Which states use preparole reports is explained in Chapter 10. However, prisoners believe their own disciplinary conduct record is crucial to obtain early release. Ironically, prisoners seem to behave better after a denial of a parole hearing because they believe denials are caused by misconduct.[27]

Parole Versus Probation

Chapter 8 focused on probation and this chapter's focus is on parole. Sometimes, characteristics between the two sanctions become clouded. Therefore, as a guide, Table 9.3 was developed to help clarify the major differences. However, from time to time in some jurisdictions, probation characteristics might well be described as those in parole categories and vice versa. Use this guide with caution.

HISTORY OF PAROLE

The development of parole is linked with the history of punishment and confinement in early European and English history. As you can imagine, attitudes held by policy makers, interest groups, and the public shaped those developments then, as they continue to do so today. A reasonable starting point for parole would be with the early English philosophy promoting punishment: "It's of little advantage to restrain the bad by punishment, unless you render them good by discipline."[40] The rise of imprisonment was associated with the belief that prisons were the place where punishment and discipline merged and discipline translated to forced labor.[41] Male prisoners labored on public projects and in military campaigns without pay or recognition.

Female prisoners worked at spinning, weaving, cloth making, milling of grains, and baking.[42] By the 17th century, convicts throughout Europe worked in shipyards and were chained to their beds at night. By the end of the 18th century, conditions of workhouses throughout England and Europe were appalling. Privacy was nonexistent. Prisoners without money starved. Sanitary conditions were deplorable. The exploitation of prisoners by

Table 9.3   Similarities and Differences between Parole and Probation (2003)[28]

Characteristic	Parole	Probation
Yearend 2003 estimates	760,000	4,000,000
Goal: Public safety	Yes	Yes
Established for purpose of rehabilitation	Yes	Yes
Used to control and deter crime	Yes	Yes
Used to relieve prison overcrowding and prison expense	Yes	Yes
Used as punishment	Continuation	Initially
Prepare (PSIs)	No	Yes
Prepare preparole reports	Yes	No
Officer of the court	No	Yes
How obtained by offender	Administrative act	Judicial Act
Definition[29]	Conditional release from prison under supervision after a portion of sentence has been served	Sentence served in community while under supervision
Offender convicted of crime	Yes	Yes
Percent of women	14%	23%
Felony convictions	97%	50%
Incarceration prior to parole[30]	96 percent served 1 year or more	Generally, no
Results of incarceration[31]	Loss of family ties, jobs and life experiences	None
Requirements during supervision[32]	Renewal of welfare, family ties, jobs, and personnel effects (i.e., drivers license, bank accounts, credit)	None
Officers can plan rehabilitation programs, act as therapeutic agents, and make referrals for treatment and programs	Yes	Yes
Officers had to help put life back together for offenders[33]	Harder due to lack of resources and support	Continuation
Focus of surveillance	Reintegration	Conduct and behavior
Conditions of freedom	Restrictive	Less restrictive
Societal stigma levels	High	Low in comparison
Supervision personnel	Executive branch of federal and state government	Executive and judicial branches of largely county government
Authority	Federal, state and local	Federal and state
Officers make assessments and predictions impacting sentencing[34]	No	Yes
Recommend remedial action or initiate court action when conditions of freedom are violated	Yes	Yes
Returned to prison or revoked (2003)[35]	41%	16%
Abscond[36]	9%	11%
Recidivism within three years[37]	62%	43%
Revoked without incarceration[38]		13%

Why Parolees Abscond (Escape or Flee Jurisdiction)[39]

One study of 863 California parolees shows characteristics of parolees who abscond most often:

1. Unstable living arrangements
2. Frequent unemployment
3. Previous parole violator
4. Large number of prior arrests
5. Single marital status
6. Previous felonies

The researchers found little difference between gender and absconders, but did find Hispanics were less likely than others to abscond.

other inmates and jailers resulted in the most vicious acts of violence imaginable.[43] England had to do something about the conditions and the prisoners, so they put prisoners on ships, some of which transported them to prisons in other countries and some of which never released them.

Transportation of English Prisoners

Transportation was a regular part of the penal system in early 18th-century England and Ireland, with convicts originally going to the American colonies.[44] America received an estimated 1000 convicts every year between 1596 and 1776. Upon arrival in America, the convict was sold to the highest bidder and thereafter was an indentured servant. Transportation to America ended in 1775 with the American Revolution and a new designation was selected. England transported approximately 160,000 prisoners to the Australia, Van Dieman's Land (Tasmania), and Norfolk Island prison colonies until 1853. One estimate reveals that up to one third of those transported died en route.[45]

Most prisoners receiving a transportation sentence were initially sent to the Hulks in London, and served the first part of their sentence in solitary confinement before being assigned to a convict ship leaving England. Transportation emerged as a humane alternative to public beatings and execution.[46] However, some say transportation was not prompted by humanitarian sentiments but demand for free laborers.[47]

At first, transportation was provided by a great number of the English Royal Navy's fighting ships. Eventually, some of those ships ended their days as prison galleys, defined as ("Hulks"), and were moored in coastal waters and stripped of sailing gear. Their upper decks were roofed over and the lower decks were converted to cells. For instance, one such hulk was the *Dromedary,* a ship of 20 guns that arrived in Bermuda in 1826 and docked for 37 years. They built a dock, a bridge, and barracks, which were eventually used in 1851.

Brutal punishment and degrading labor bred moral degeneration among the imprisoned and their keepers regardless of where they were confined. As a result, humanitarians came forward in Western Europe in the 18th century and rallied for human dignity, human rights, and separation of state power. Although many contributed, three influential practitioners were Alexander Maconochie, Sir Walter Crofton, and Zebulon R. Brockway.

Alexander Maconochie

Alexander Maconochie, a retired Royal Navy captain and former professor of geography at the University of London, replaced Sir George Arthur in charge of 2000 *twice-convicted* prisoners on Norfolk Island in 1840.[48] Prisoners on Norfolk Island had committed capital felonies in Australia and England more than once and received a capital sentence. Maconochie's first public report about conditions at Norfolk created an uproar among the free citizens of Van Diemen's Land who relied on the previous repressive regime for cheap labor from the colony. Maconochie did not spare the details in describing the vicious floggings, the heavy manacles, and the line of savage dogs kept tethered from shore to shore across Eaglehawk Neck to prevent escape from the hell of Port Arthur.[49] He described the prison compound as the "ultimate terror."

To better understand Captain Alexander Maconochie's motives, following is a line from a letter he wrote to Sir George Gipps at the English House of Commons in 1838: "punishment may avenge, and restraint may, to a certain limited extent prevent crime; but neither separately nor together, will they teach virtue."[50] Maconochie's plan was an incentive system called a "mark system" leading to a "ticket-of-leave." Once enough "marks" were earned through good behavior and hard work, the inmate was released from Norfolk Island and transported to Australia to live as a free man. The convicts could hardly believe what Maconochie outlined in the new regime, which involved two stages of treatment: punishment for the past, which they must meet with penitence, and training for the future, which they could embrace "with hope."

Under Maconochie's ticket-of-leave program, a prisoner would progress through stages of less restriction than the previous stage:

1. Strict custody and supervision when a prisoner arrives

2. Hard labor in work gangs

3. Freedom in certain areas of the island

4. Conditional release-ticket-of-leave

5. Complete freedom

Maconochie did not see the ticket-of-leave as parole (but Crofton and Brockway had) because Maconochie believed that a "reformed" prisoner should not be supervised.[51] Nonetheless, as the number of ticket-of-leave prisoners in Australia and England increase their punishment and control advocates successfully lobbied against Maconochie's system, bringing the "noble experiment" to a halt. Maconochie was removed from his office and returned to England. In 1867, transportation to Norfolk Island was discontinued.

Maconochie's last words about his ideas were delivered to a House of Lords select committee, and would ring down for centuries: "My experience leads me to say that there is no man utterly incorrigible. Treat him as a man, not as a dog. You cannot recover a man except by doing justice to the manly qualities which he may have—and giving him an interest in developing them."[52]

English Penal Servitude Act of 1853 to 1857

In the *1853 Penal Servitude Act,* only long-term prison sentences merited transportation, and in the *1857 Penal Servitude Act,* the sentence of transportation as punishment was abolished. Penal servitude was the term of imprisonment that included hard labor, served in England and Ireland, and transportation was used as an alternative sentence. That is, sentences of 7 years transportation or less were substituted by penal servitude for 4 years; 7 to 10 years transportation by 4 to 10 years; 10 to 15 years by 6 to 8 years' penal servitude; over 15 years' transportation by 6 to 10 years' penal servitude; transportation for life by penal servitude for life.

Therefore, records tend to put transportation and penal servitude together. This clumsy system of converting transportation to penal servitude equivalents ended with the Penal Servitude Act of 1857; subsequently, prisoners were sentenced directly to penal servitude if found guilty of offenses that formerly warranted transportation.[53] The law also provided a length of time that prisoners would be eligible for conditional release on the ticket-of-leave system.

The power of revoking or altering the license of a convict was exercised in the case of misconduct.

1. If, therefore, he wishes to retain the privilege, which by his good behavior under penal discipline he has obtained, he must prove by his subsequent conduct that he is worthy of Her Majesty's clemency.

2. To produce a forfeiture of the license, it is by no means necessary that the holder should be convicted of a new offense. If he associates with notoriously bad characters, leads an idle or dissolute life, or has no visible means of obtaining an honest livelihood, and so on, it will be assumed that he is about to relapse into crime and he will at once be apprehended and recommitted to prison under his original release.[54]

An assumption held by the enactors of the English Penal Servitude Acts was that prisoners were reformed after completing prison training programs, and once released, they would live crime- free lifestyles. The results of a royal commission's investigation revealed that prison programs were inadequate and that without supervision, ticket-of-leave holders had difficulty. One result from the commission's investigation was that police officers supervised ticket-of-leave persons.

Sir Walter Crofton

In 1854, Sir Walter Crofton was in charge of the Irish prisons. There were many pressing problems, but the most serious was overcrowding. Crofton implemented an incentive system guided by the "mark system" originally developed by Captain Maconochie.[55] Historically, Crofton's system impacted the way European prisons were operated by introducing the parole system. The Irish system punished prisoners for their crimes but prepared them for release by giving them options over release dates through good behavior.[56] Crofton felt that prison programs should be directed more toward reformation and "tickets-of-leave" should be awarded to prisoners who had shown achievement and positive attitude change. After a period of strict imprisonment, Crofton began transferring offenders to "intermediate prisons" where they could accumulate marks based on work performance, behavior, and educational improvement.[57]

Eventually they would be given tickets-of-leave and released on parole. Parolees were required to submit monthly reports to the police and a police inspector helped them find jobs and generally oversaw their activities. The concepts of intermediate prisons, assistance, and supervision after release were Crofton's contributions to the modern system of parole. American correctional systems were also impacted, because it was Crofton who introduced Zebulon Brockway and other American wardens to the Irish prison system at the first annual meeting of the National Prison Association in 1870 in Cincinnati, OH. Crofton's system of early release is considered the forerunner of the modern American parole system, and despite Massachusetts enacting parole legislation in 1837, it was Zebulon Brockway, the superintendent of the Elmira Reformatory in New York, who actually put a parole system into practice in 1876.

First Use of Word Parole

Use of the word **parole** for the early release from prison began with a letter from Dr. Samuel G. Howe of Boston to the Prison Association of New York in 1846. Howe wrote, " I believe there are many (prisoners) who might be so trained as to be left upon their parole (a promise made with or confirmed by a pledge of one's honor) during the last period of their imprisonment with safety."[58] Other accomplishments of Dr. Howe to protect the less fortunate can be seen by what he wrote for the governor of Massachusetts in another document, "But the immediate adoption of proper means for training, and reaching idiots, may be urged upon higher grounds than that of expediency, or even of charity; it may be urged on the ground of imperative duty."[59]

Zebulon Brockway

As superintendent of the House of Correction in Detroit, in 1869 Brockway introduced the indeterminate sentence for first-time offenders.[60] His ideas were incorporated in a Michigan statute but nullified by the courts. In New York, he organized the first state reformatory for adult males, built at Elmira, and was its first superintendent (1876 to 1900). He introduced a system of military training, physical training, education, and trade instruction, with incentives for good behavior. Many of Brockway's ideas can be traced to Sir Walter Crofton and Captain Maconochie. The success of Brockway's Elmira experiments led to the introduction of the indeterminate sentence in New York and in other states. In his book, Brockway wrote:[61]

> The very outward appearance of the reformatory—so little like the ordinary prison and so much like a college or a hospital—helps to change the common sentiment about offenders from the vindictiveness of punishment to the amenities of rational educational correction.

Brockway attempted to change public sentiment to allow for humane and effective forms of treatment for prisoners. Brockway's contribution to corrections goes beyond humanitarian accomplishments because indeterminate sentence provides for good-time conditional release from prison, or parole. In many areas, the New York Department of Correctional Service is a model used by many systems across America. Yet punishment and control philosophies have moved the justice system away from treatment and prevention to capital punishment.

Federal Parole History

In 1867, the first statute providing for the reduction of sentences of federal prisoners because of good conduct was enacted.[62] In 1902, a general revision of the good-time credit

Although the buildings that comprise Elmira Corrections have been updated, its one hundred fifty year history can easily be envisioned as you look around inside this walled city. Photo by Dennis J. Stevens.

Photo of a main lockdown area within Elmira Corrections. Photo by
Dennis J. Stevens.

statute was made. The schedule of good-time credits was made liberal and graduated so as
to increase with the length of sentence. In 1910, the federal parole system was actually developed. The Federal Juvenile Delinquency Act was approved June 16, 1938. Early release was the release from prison by expiration of sentence less good-time, it was termed
"mandatory release" rather than "conditional release" in 1956. Perhaps the most significant change for federal parole was when the U.S. Sentencing Commission recommended
that federal parole be abolished and parole be replaced by "supervised release for offenders convicted after November 1, 1987."[63] Offenders must serve a period of prison time
without being eligibile for parole. Once a prisoner serves the initial prison sentence, community supervision can follow. Nonetheless, the Parole Commission assumed jurisdiction
over parole grant hearings for code felony offenders confined in District of Columbia Institutions (effective August 5, 1998). The District of Columbia Board of Parole continued
to make postrelease supervision and revocation decisions for code cases.

Although federal parole is no longer available, it continues to supervise those remaining in the system. In fact, the Parole Commission was authorized a budget of
$9,876,000 at yearend 2002.[64]

The Parole Commission published a revised Desk Book on Training and Reference
Materials for hearing examiners and analysts as part of a program of staff training. Finally, the 21st Century Department of Justice Appropriations Authorization Act of 2002
extended the life of the Parole Commission until November 1, 2005.

U.S. Parole Commission Seal. Printed with permission of
the Office of Justice Programs.

19th-Century Influences toward Early Release in Europe and England

By 1900, the efficacy of isolating prisoners for long periods of time was called into question across Europe and England and the U.S. Labor law was the central and organizing factor of the daily life of prisoners in most countries.[65] On a typical day in a Belgian prison, prisoners arose at 5:00 a.m. to organ music as a call to prayer, breakfast, and work within the hour. After dinner, work continued until 9:00 p.m. Despite successful prison manufacturing producing goods, such as shoes, bedding, and baskets, prison labor was challenged.

Some reformers argued that profitable and productive prison labor were immoral. Their reasoning was couched in unfair competition because of differences in labor wage scales. When free labor works, paid labor does not. Many countries, including America, ignored those claims and continued prison labor as a self-sustaining enterprise. In Bavaria, Italy, and Spain, prisons allowed inmates to choose trades. However, some prisons forced prisoners to labor at places such as Devil's Island until they died. It was a desolate place in French Guyana and even in the 20th century, over 56,000 prisoners were transported to Devil's Island from France.[66]

Despite entrepreneur successes, prison culture promoted crime and, therefore, the growing presence of recidivism in European prison populations after 1865 spurred changes. The length of prison sentences and rehabilitation were less associated than expected. The longer a prisoner was incarcerated, the more likely the prisoner would resort to crime once released.[67] As a result, change came in the form of suspended sentences.

Courts determined the length of a prison sentence and then suspended it, allowing a first-timer to enjoy freedom as long as he remained crime-free.

Belgium led the way in 1888. After World War I, suspended sentences were adapted by many European nations including Eastern Europe, the Russian Socialist Federated Republic, Czechoslovakia, Romania, and Poland and spread to Asia, Latin America, Africa, and the Middle East.[68]

Supervised parole, another noncustodial sanction, was used among juveniles in France around 1830. Portugal utilized a form of supervised parole among adult offenders in 1861. Saxony, Germany, and Denmark developed an offender classification system allowing furlough and conditional release for prisoners by 1871. Even Russia abolished courts and prisons for children and raised the age for criminal liability from 10 to 17. European nations moved toward noncustodial sanctions and away from punishment models from 1900 to the 1960s. However, key issues facing approximately 350,000 prisoners in European prisons in the last few decades are the high cost of incarceration and uncontrolled violence and drugs.[69]

FIRST HALF OF 20TH-CENTURY INFLUENCES TOWARD PAROLE IN THE USA

Treatment Strategies and Indeterminate Sentences

Shifts in social thought about culpability of crime and treatment linked with excessive costs of incarceration, high recidivism rates, overcrowded facilities, and fears of growing homosexual promiscuity among prisoners produced changes in public sentiment.[70] Keep in mind that indeterminate sentences leading to parole focus on the offender and what can be done to rehabilitate him or her almost regardless of the crime committed by the offender. A treatment advocate might ask: "Who is the offender and what can we do to help this offender reform?" Forced labor in the United States was often challenged and eventually, all forms of forced labor became a question of legality. Prison workers can no longer compete with private industry. Concerning appropriate strategies of dealing with prisoners, although punishment and control approaches were an integral part of the justice system for guilty defendants, treatment or rehabilitation perspective took center stage from 1900 to the 1960s. Controlling criminal behavior was viewed through a treatment model that focused on rehabilitation.

Treatment Model

Given proper care and treatment, offenders can be changed into productive, law-abiding citizens. Casual factors of crime are associated with social influences more than free will perspectives. The emphasis is on future crime.

It was thought that prisoners could be treated for or cured of criminal behavior.[71] The emphasis of the rehabilitative philosophy was on the individual offender and the environmental and hereditary factors that might have contributed to his or her criminal actions. Clearly, free will advocates associated with punishment and control were less influential in deciding policy than treatment advocates.

> In the **indeterminate sentence,** legislation sets the minimum and maximum prison sentence for a particular offense; a judge specifies a prison term within the legislated parameters; a parole board (depending on jurisdictional guidelines) determines the actual time to be served by the prisoner. Therefore, conceptually, three different sources of authority work in concert: legislature, court, and paroling authority.

During that period, judges practiced wide discretion in how to sentence offenders; probation and parole were used extensively as alternatives to incarceration across the country. Because offenders were "treated" for criminal behavior, the public felt the professionals knew the most appropriate approach in dealing with criminals.

SECOND HALF OF 20TH-CENTURY INFLUENCES TOWARD PAROLE IN THE UNITED STATES

The treatment model reached its peak in popularity in the 1950s and 1960s. CC initiatives were popular. Halfway houses, diversion programs, and the increased use of probation kept offenders in the community in an attempt to avoid the stigma and other negative effects of imprisonment. The thinking was that if the prison staff could diagnose and treat the "badness," then the prisoner could be released when "cured." The justice system had relied on indeterminate sentence and parole. It should be cautioned that although indeterminate sentences and parole continue to be practiced in the United States even in the twenty-first century, their popularity has declined, as explained in the following sections.

Punishment Strategies and Determinate Sentences

Americans took on a conservative perspective about causes in crime and punishment and control perspectives became dominant approaches in corrections. An unpopular war in Southeast Asia, civil rights demonstrations, rising crime rates, and riots in urban America paved the way for a backlash against what some viewed as the lenient treatment of criminals in the late 1960s. Americans were angry, especially about crime and what to do about it. It is not important whether America was right or wrong, but that policy makers, interest groups, and the public can try to change legislation and what to do about crime. The push and pull of various perspectives that impact change is what provides the American system with predictions and visions of the future marked by challenges, expectations, advances preparedness, and technological developments.[72]

As a result, rehabilitation ideals lost favor as the primary underlying philosophy of the policy makers, interest groups, and the public. Research on correctional policy pub-

---

Punishment Model

The mission of the justice community is to administer punishment upon a guilty defendant and punishment should be commensurate with the seriousness of the crime. The characteristics of punishment are just deserts, deterrence, and incapacitation.

---

lished in the mid-1970s proclaiming that "nothing works" also hastened the end of the rehabilitative era. The stage was set for a pendulum swing in public opinion and thus "correctional policy moved toward an offense-based, punishment-oriented legal system."[73] Punishment perspectives characterized by just deserts, deterrence, and incapacitation took precedence over the treatment model prior to the 1960s.

Just deserts advocates are opposed to rehabilitation as the primary service provided by the justice system. They are opposed to determinate sentences that provide early release strategies including parole, and they see probation as too lenient a response toward offenders.

Liberals and conservatives alike attack the indeterminate sentencing model and treatment philosophies. Liberals see judicial discretion as creating a disparity among violators and imposing "unjust" sentences. That is, defendants guilty of the same crime should receive the same sentence and serve the same amount of time in prison. Conservatives feel the sentencing systems should make punishment more severe and certain, and place greater emphasis on deterrence and incapacitation. The system is too lenient in its response to violators; therefore, what is a violator's incentive to reform? Parole and treatment should be secondary if practiced at all.

Attacks on indeterminate sentences (which focused on treatment with an undetermined amount of time served in prison and the community) resulted in a shift in control of sentencing moving from the discretion of judges to legislatures and politicians. Policy makers recommended ranges of sentences for judges to follow in the name of fairness, certainty, and uniformity.

Legislative *determinate sentencing* systems of the 1970s were designed to reduce disparity, make sentencing more just, and punish offenders appropriately.[74] Some judges chose to ignore those guidelines, resulting in increased legislative involvement. Sentencing became politicized and the public and legislatures called for longer and tougher sentences.

Determinate Sentence Characteristics

Amount of time served depends on legislative statutes or guidelines, which mandate the period of time to be served before an offender is eligible (if at all) for early release. Emphasis is on the conduct of the offender while incarcerated.

CLOSER TO 21ST-CENTURY PAROLE IN AMERICA

Sentencing Commissions

In the 1980s, efforts arose to depoliticize structured sentencing initiatives. Several states created sentencing commissions that were supposedly free from political influence. These commissions represented an array of interests and were charged with creating sentencing guidelines that focused not only on the fairness of sentencing but also on prison crowding and the management of correctional resources. In some instances, these guidelines were not voluntary. Judges were required to follow the guidelines or provide written reasons for departing from them. Under the guidelines system, judges would impose a sentence upon an offender based upon a score that took into account the offender's prior criminal record and present offense. Determinate sentences focus on certainty of punishment and severity of crime and incorporate an exact amount of time or narrow sentencing range of time to be served in prison or in the community.

Parole Eligibility

A prisoner's eligibility for parole is determined by the court as set by law and regulation within the jurisdiction. An eligibility date for parole can be set in advance for a prisoner consistent with the jurisdictional statutes. That is, parole eligibility is never arbitrary. Generally, there are formulas that apply in each jurisdiction and, as expected, formulas vary depending on each state's regulations or statutes. There are many inmates who serve their full prison term imposed at trial. This process is called an expiration of sentence or "maxing" out of prison or time. However, there are two types of releases that influence the parole process.

Types of Parole Releases

The two types of releases from prison that influence the parole process are characterized as discretionary parole and mandatory parole:

> **Discretionary parole** is consistent with indeterminate sentences and exists when a parole board has authority to conditionally release prisoners based on a statutory or administrative determination of eligibility.

> **Mandatory parole** is consistent with determinate sentence strategies when prisoners are conditionally released from jail or prison after serving a specified portion of their original sentence minus any "good-time" earned for good behavior, which could include completion of formal programs such as vocational skills or education.

Mandatory release is guided by legislative stature or good-time laws (as opposed to a parole board). An inmate would enter the community automatically at the expiration of a maximum term minus credited time off. One reason mandatory release is used is because many states abolished discretionary parole and overcrowded prisons and fewer resources motivated many systems to develop a strategy of early release. Under the mandatory release option, prisoners serve time toward early release as opposed to parole where a date is automatically assigned for early release considerations.

Good-time can be defined as a reduction in sentence for good conduct of a prisoner. Prisoners receive days off from their minimum or maximum terms. Sometimes good-time credit can be produced by attending substance abuse clinics, educational and vocational programs, and anger management and conflict resolution classes. Not every state provides good-time the same way depending on policy and availability of resources. Good-time is provided as an incentive for cooperative behavior. It is usually administered and awarded by correctional personnel, such as those in social services. Often, it is automatically subtracted from a prisoner's sentence term. Good-time reductions are based on a prisoner's positive actions and are in effect in most states and the federal government.

Statistics of Prison Release Methods

Release from sentence can be accomplished through an expiration of the prison sentence or maxing out, discretionary parole (parole board), and mandatory parole (determinate sentences and good-time credits). Table 9.4 shows the method of release from state prison for selected years between 1980 and 2003. In 1980, of the 143,543 prisoners released, most were released to discretionary parole and fewer to mandatory parole.[75]

By 1990, the statistics are reversed—more prisoners were released to mandatory parole than discretionary parole. Also, approximately 9 percent (32,050) of those conditionally released were released to probation rather than parole. One explanation is that often short jail sentences (six months or less) and probation combinations, especially in southern

Table 9.4   Method of Release from State Prison for Selected Years 1980–1999

Year	All Releases*	Discretionary Parole	Mandatory Parole	Other Conditional	Expiration of Sentence
1980	143,543	78,602	26,735	9,363	20,460
1985	206,988	88,069	62,851	15,371	34,489
1990	405,374	159,731	116,857	62,851	51,288
1992	430,198	170,095	126,836	60,800	48,971
1995	455,140	147,139	177,402	46,195	66,017
1999	542,950	128,708	223,342	66,337	98,218

Note: Based on prisoners with a sentence of more than 1 year who were released from state prison. Counts are for December 31 for each year.

*Includes releases to probation, commutations, and other unspecified releases and excludes escapes, those absent without official leave, and transfers.

Printed with permission of the U.S. Department of Justice.[76]

states, were commonly imposed sanctions. Additionally, you might interested to knowing that of almost 54,000 women released in 1998, 41,000 were conditionally released: 14,000 parolees, 5,000 probationers, 20,000 supervised mandatory releasees, and 13,000 unconditional releasees. In a comparison, approximately 76 percent of both male and female releases consisted of conditional releases.

Table 9.5 shows the percentage trends of release from prison: discretionary parole, mandatory parole, and expiration of prison sentences for 1980 to 2000. In 1980, over 50 percent of released prisoners were discretionally paroled, 18.63 percent were released under mandatory guidelines, and 14.25 percent were released because those prisoners served their full prison sentence. In 1994, mandatory parole was greater than discretionary parole. In 1998, prisoners serving their full sentence prior to prison release were at the highest peak for the years shown until 2000 when almost 20 percent of released prisoners served their full sentence prior to release. Other overall data:

- Discretionary releases to parole dropped from 39 percent of releases in 1990 to 24 percent in 2000.

Table 9.5   Percent of Releases From State Prison by Method, 1980–2000

	Discretionary Parole	*Mandatory Parole*	*Expiration of Sentence*
1980	55*	19	14
1981	51	20	13
1982	51	24	14
1983	46	26	16
1984	45	28	16
1985	43	30	17
1986	43	31	15
1987	40	31	16
1988	40	30	17
1989	38	30	15
1990	39	29	13
1991	40	30	11
1992	40	29	11
1993	39	32	12
1994	35	36	12
1995	32	39	15
1996	30	38	17
1997	28	40	17
1998	26	40	19
1999	24	41	19
2000	24	39	20

*Percents rounded. Table developed for this chapter by the author using data from BJS and National Corrections Reporting Program.[77]

- Mandatory releases to parole have steadily increased from 116,857 in 1990 to 221,414 in 2000 (from 29 percent of all state prison releases to 39 percent).

- About 112,000 State prisoners were released unconditionally through an expiration of their sentence in 2000, up from 51,288 in 1990.

Discretionary releases of prisoners to parole supervision by a parole board decreased from 50 percent of adults entering parole in 1995 to 39 percent, or 178,800, in 2003; mandatory releases to parole supervision increased from 45 percent in 1995 to 51 percent (237,500) in 2003.[78]

How did this happen? One guess is that liberals saw discretionary boards as racists and conservatives or just desert advocates argued that discretion allowed prisoners to go free too early.[79] Other states such as New York also lean toward automatic release for parole among their 44 parolees after cutting their parole board's powers.

Although the federal government has directives to eliminate parole, temporary legislation has continued it through 2005. Finally, discretionary parole and mandatory release have similar conditions of release, but different recidivism levels, which is discussed in Chapter 10.[80]

PAROLE BOARD ELIMINATION

In a 1974 study, 50 federal judges were given 20 identical files of actual criminal cases and asked what sentences they would impose on the defendants.[81] The answers ranged from 20 years in prison and a $65,000 fine to three years in prison and no fine. The issue was debated in Congress for years. In 1984, U.S. Senator Edward Kennedy called federal criminal indeterminate sentencing "a national disgrace" and called for change. The result was Congress stripping federal judges of almost all sentencing discretion to eliminate disparities in prison terms. Instead, a complex series of sentencing "guidelines" were implemented in the federal system in 1987 that mandated sentencing according to a chart and a point system for adding up "factors" related to the crime and/or the defendant's criminal history.

In 1976, California's Governor Jerry Brown signed into law a set of criminal sentencing schemes that did away with parole in that state.[82] Significantly, where indeterminate or parole-eligible sentencing largely incorporated the idea that prisoners could be rehabilitated with incentives, the new California law abandoned rehabilitation across the board. "The purpose of imprisonment," the new law read, "is punishment." Other states followed California. That same year Maine abolished parole and six others–Pennsylvania, Arkansas, Ohio, Hawaii, Colorado and Delaware–lengthened prison sentences. Other states turned away from indeterminate or flexible sentencing and replaced it with guideline sentencing that guaranteed fixed prison terms. Within 10 years, 37 states had passed mandatory sentencing laws, and the prison population explosion was in full swing. Sixteen states and the federal government have abolished discretionary parole as of 2000 (see Table 9.6).

Part of the reason some policy makers favored an elimination of discretionary parole is perhaps associated with the threat of litigation by potential parolees who were declined.[83] Over the last few years, many cases have been filed in court seeking monetary compensation

Table 9.6 States that have Eliminated Discretionary Parole, as of 2000

All Offenders		Certain Violent Offenders
Arizona	Minnesota	Alaska
California[a]	Mississippi	Louisiana
Delaware	North Carolina	New York
Florida[b]	Ohio[d]	Tennessee
Illinois	Oregon	
Indiana	Virginia	
Kansas[c]	Washington	
Maine	Wisconsin	

[a]In 1976, the Uniform Determinate Sentencing Act abolished discretionary parole for all offenses except some violent crimes with a long sentence of a sentence to life.

[b]In 1995, parole eligibility was abolished for offenses with a life sentence and a 25-year mandatory term.

[c]Excludes a few offenses, primarily first-degree murder and intentional second-degree murder.

[d]Excludes murder and aggravated murder.

from parole board members for the release of prisoners who subsequently committed serious crimes. Overall, the paroling authority characteristics are found in Table 9.7 shows.

A more recent concern is possible liability for not releasing a prisoner who should have been released. As Rolando V. del Carmen implies, parole board members enjoy quasijudicial immunity and are therefore not liable for injuries caused by parolees.[85] Mississippi, for instance, spells it out this way: "The (parole) board, its members and staff, shall be immune from civil liability for any official acts taken in good faith and in exercise of the board's legitimate governmental authority."[86] Arizona and Alaska courts have indicated, however, that liability ensues under a narrow set of circumstances. How many jurisdictions will follow these leads remains to be seen. However, because parole is not a constitutional right, potential parolees may or may not be released at the discretion of the parole board.

Table 9.7 Overall Paroling Authority Characteristics on January 1, 2002

	States with Parole Boards	Full-Time Parole Boards	Total Board Members	Salaried Board Members	Total Support Employees	Number of Board Members to Grant Parole	Number of Board Members to Revoke Parole
Total	36	27	265	29	717	82	74
Average			7		21	2	2

Note: States that eliminated or deferred parole still require members to deal with previous parole decisions. Seven of the agencies noted allow staff members to conduct hearings in lieu of board members to grant parole and 10 allowed staff members to revoke parole.

Printed with permission of *The Corrections Yearbook*.[84]

On the other hand, conceptually determinate sentences suggest how much time will be served before an offender is eligible (if at all) for early release or before parole is determined by the correctional system (within guidelines). Although there is discussion about the process of early release, there is a strong movement to fix the problem of determinate sentences associated with early "good-time" practices. Why? Because in 1974, of 15,000 prisoners who were released on parole, 2,300 (16 percent) revoked parole in California, as compared with 85,000 (63 percent) out of 137,000 parolees in 2002.[87] Why the difference? Most prisoners served flexible sentences (e.g., 5 to 10 years) and a parole board had discretion in determining when prisoners were ready for release. When they could, prisoners usually showed the ways they were rehabilitated or had a job waiting for them or a family ready to aid them in re-entry. Prison officials approved of parole because it encouraged prisoners to improve and helped maintain order.[88] But California became the first state to take away the power of the parole board and eliminated flexible sentences, replacing them with fixed terms determined in advance by a judge. Prisoners were automatically released at the end of their term without review by a parole board, even though once released they were on parole.

Florida's Department of Corrections reports that parole was abolished in Florida in 1983 to allegedly eliminate judicial abuse and disparity in criminal sentencing. At the same time, Florida lawmakers, who felt many prisoners sentenced under the parole system had received disparate and disproportionate sentences, mandated that the Florida Parole Commission would be completely eliminated. However, 20 years later, more that 5,000 "parole-eligible" prisoners remain trapped in Florida's prisons while the Parole Commission fights to maintain its existence.[89]

TODAY'S MINDSET ABOUT PAROLE

What is today's American mindset about parole? One indicator reveals that when a random national sample was asked about whether prison systems rehabilitate prisoners so they are less likely to commit crimes in the future, three out of four say no.[92] Continuing along that line of thinking, parolees have not been rehabilitated in prison and therefore parolees continue to be "criminals and sick." Many say that there is a lot of support for ways to help prisoners. In addition, high revocation rates could mean parole officers work in keeping with the wishes of the public. That is, the more efficient a parole officer works, the more likely the officer will detect a parole violation. Finally, despite the seeming inconsistencies about public support, of the more than 470,500 parolees discharged from supervision in 2003, 47 percent had successfully met the conditions of their supervision.[93] Depending on your point of view, those statistics reveal that almost one of every two offenders who probably experienced the depravations and violence of prison life succeeded. In keeping with B. C. Forbes' thought that "history has demonstrated that the most notable winners usually encountered heartbreaking obstacles before they triumphed. They won because they refused to become discouraged by their defeats." Through offender hard work and the supervision of dedicated parole officers and probably many other individuals, one out of two is a good start.

Parole Decision Making: Sentences

The structure and function of parole is tied to the sentencing model used. As you already know, sentencing models (indeterminate, determinate, mandatory minimum, presumptive, and voluntary guidelines) have their own standards and mandates relating to an early release from prison prior to the full sentence served.

DEFINITIONS OF SENTENCE MODELS AT A GLANCE

Determinate: Sentences of incarceration in which an offender is given a fixed term that may be reduced by good-time or earned time.

Indeterminate: Sentences in which an administrative agency, generally a parole board, has the authority to release an offender and determine whether an offender's parole will be revoked for violations of the conditions of release. This model is consistent with parole objectives.

Mandatory minimum: A minimum sentence that is specified by statute and that may be applied for all convictions of a particular crime or a crime with special circumstances (e.g., robbery with a firearm or selling drugs to a minor within 1,000 feet of a school).

Presumptive sentencing guidelines: Sentencing that meets the following conditions: (a) the appropriate sentence for an offender in a specific case is presumed to fall within a range of sentences authorized by sentencing guidelines that are adopted by a legislatively created sentencing body, usually a sentencing commission; (b) sentencing judges are expected to sentence within the range or provide written justification for departure; (c) the guidelines provide for some review, usually appellate, of the departure. Presumptive guidelines may employ determinate or indeterminate sentencing structures and are based on two scales: the harm done by the crime and the offender's culpability.[90]

Voluntary/advisory sentencing guidelines: Recommended sentencing policies that are not required by law. Usually based on past sentencing practices, they serve as a guide to judges. The legislature has not mandated their use. Voluntary/advisory guidelines may employ determinate or indeterminate sentencing structures.

Printed with permission of the Office of Justice Programs.[91]

SUMMARY

Collateral damage associated with the prison-building boom fueled by punishment produces more new arrivals into prison during a time when crime is in on the decline. Parole was defined as early conditional release after jail or prison time before the entire incarceration period is served. The ultimate goal of parole is public safety in the form of protection of former prisoners and the specific goal of parole was reported as the supervision of an offender after early release to a crime-free lifestyle by learning new behaviors and strategies for implementing those new behaviors. Public safety is best served when conditionally released convicts positively contribute to the community through their law-abiding behavior and that behavior can, in part, be produced through reconciliation, restitution, rehabilitation, and reintegration strategies.

Deterrence of crime, punishment, decreasing jail and prison populations, and compensation for sentencing disparities are the functions of parole associated with corrections. Expiration of sentence, discretionary parole, and mandatory parole were described as the three types of releases and it was noted that there were more prisoners released through mandatory early release efforts than parole strategies. When parole and probation are compared, it is obvious that parolees represented more challenges because of their loss of family relationships and other living amenities. The history of parole suggests that "punishment advocates" saw parole as inappropriate concessions toward criminals and they did their best to demonstrate the weaknesses of parole and early release. Early European and English history of punishment and early release experiences were explored. The contributions of influential practitioners were revealed. The powerful debate that impacts parole (and most justice system issues) associated with the factors of crime and what to do about it once again surfaces in this chapter, and how those dynamics influence parole and its decline were revealed. The current American mindset about parole is that the public supports aid parolees and other offenders, but it is apparent that they want alternatives that carry punishment-based consequences for offender noncompliance.

DISCUSSION QUESTIONS

1. Describe issues of collateral damage associated with the prison-building boom. In your opinion, in what way can you both agree and disagree with this finding?

2. Define parole and identify its ultimate and specific goals.

3. Identify functions of parole associated with the parolee and describe the primary functions applicable to parolees in particular.

4. Identify functions of parole associated with corrections. In your opinion, in what way might you agree or disagree with those explanations?

5. Identify and explain types of release from prison or jail.

6. Describe the relevance of preparole reports.

7. Identify similarities and differences between parole versus probation.

8. Discuss the history of parole. Identify its major contributors and their contributions to parole. In what way do those early contributions influence today's parole objectives?

9. Describe 19th-century influences toward early release in Europe and England.

10. Describe dynamics of the U.S. debate that developed between the first half of the 20th century versus the second half of the 20th century.

11. Describe good-time credits used in mandatory parole. In what way do you agree with their use and in what way might their use be suspect?

12. Explain the current American mindset about early release. In what way might you agree or disagree with this perspective?

NOTES

1. California Department of Corrections. *Facts and Figures.* Retrieved online August 20, 2004: http://www.corr.ca.gov/CommunicationsOffice/facts_figures.asp

2. *"Halloween killer" violates parole, returns to prison.* (2003, April 7). Retrieved online August 20, 2004: http://database.corrections.com/news/results2.asp?ID=4575

3. *Alabama parolee held in funeral home killings* (2003, March 30). Retrieved online August 20, 2004: http://database.corrections.com/news/results2.asp?ID=4422

4. Morgan O. Reyonolds (2002). *Privatizing probation and parole.* National Center for Policy Analysis. Retrieved online August 18, 2004: http://www.ncpa.org/studies/s233/s233.html

5. Bureau of Justice Statistics (2003). *Prison populations.* Washington, DC: U.S. Department of Justice. Office of Justice Programs. Retrieved online August 10h 2004: http://www.ojp.usdoj.gov/bjs/prisons.htm

6. Jeffrey A. Beard and Kathleen Gnall (2003, August). The Pennsylvania approach to re-entry. *Corrections Today, 65*(5), 68–70.

7. Fox Butterfield. (2000, November 29). Often, parole is one stop on the way back to prison. *New York Times,* A1.

8. ABC News. Sacramento, California. *Parolees afforded more rights under reform agreement.* News 10. KXTV. Retrieved online November 23, 2003: http://www.kxtv10.com/storyfull.asp?id=5795

9. California prisons plan sweeping parole changes. (2003, November 13). *The Associated Press.*

10. Crowell, del Carmen (2002), 162.

11. Joan Petersilia (1993). *Criminal justice performance measures for prisons.* Bureau of Justice Statistics. Performance measures for the criminal justice system. Article prepared for the Bureau of Justice Assistance. Washington, DC: U.S. Department of Justice (pp. 19–60). Retrieved online November 12, 2003: http://www.bja.evaluationwebsite.org/html/documents/measuring_the_performance_of_com.htm

12. Bureau of Justice Statistics (1995, August). *Probation and parole violators in state prison, 1991: Survey of state prison inmates, 1991.* Washington, DC: U.S. Depart-

ment of Justice, Office of Justice Programs, NCJ 149076. Retrieved online December 15, 2004: http://www.ojp.usdoj.gov/bjs/pub/ascii/ppvsp91.txt

13. Five percent disposition was other or unknown at the time of the study. Bureau of Justice Statistics. *Probation and statistic findings.* Washington, DC: U.S. Department of Justice, Office of Justice Programs. Retrieved online November 14, 2003: http://www.ojp.usdoj.gov/bjs/pandp.htm#findings

14. Inmate Tom Watson, Shasta County Jail, 1655 West Street, Redding, CA 96001. For a complete view of Watson's statement, see his November 3, 2003 update site at: http://www.geocities.com/CapitolHill/Rotunda/4027/california_parole.htm

15. *Young v. Harper* (1997) 520 U.S. 143, 137 L.Ed., 2d 270, 117 S.Ct. 1148; *Morrissey V. Brewer* (1972) 408 U.S. 471, 33 L.Ed. 2d 484, 92 S.Ct. 2593, 2598.

16. *Id.* 92 S.Ct. at 2599.

17. This perspective is consistent with Frank Williams III, Marilyn D. Mc Shane, and H. Michael Dolny (2000). Developing a parole classification instrument for use as management tool. *Corrections Management Quarterly, 4*(4), 45–59.

18. Joan Petersilia (1993). Criminal justice performance measures for prisons (pp. 19–60). Also see Joan Petersilia (2003). *When prisoners come home: Public safety and reintegration challenges.* New York: Oxford University Press.

19. Joan Petersilia (2003), 16.

20. Bureau of Justice Statistics (2002). *Learn about prisoner reentry.* Washington, DC: U.S. Department of Justice, Office of Justice Programs. Retrieved online November 14, 2003: http://www.ojp.usdoj.gov/reentry/learn.html

21. See Joan Petersilia (1995). pp. 24–60. Also see Joan Petersilia (2003). pp. 14–18.

22. *The corrections yearbook: Adult corrections 2002* (2003). Camille Graham Camp and George Camp (Eds.). Middletown, CT. Criminal Justice Institute (p. 206).

23. *The corrections yearbook: Adult corrections 2002* (2003), 206.

24. *The corrections yearbook: Adult corrections 2002* (2003), 206.

25. Georgia Department of Corrections. Retrieved online August 7, 2004: http://www.dcor.state.ga.us/default.html

26. The Alaska Legal Resource Center, State of Alaska, Parole Division was used as a guide to develop this section.

27. See Jon L. Proctor and Michael Pease (2000, March). Parole as institutional control: A test of specific deterrence and offender misconduct. *The Prison Journal, 80*(1), 39–55. Retrieved online November 13, 2003: http://www.ncpa.org/studies/s233/s233n.html#10

28. Joan Petersilia (1995).

29. Bureau of Justice Statistics (2003). *Sourcebook of criminal justice statistics 2002.* Washington, DC: U.S. Department of Justice, Office of Justice Programs. Retrieved online March 14, 2004: http://www.albany.edu/sourcebook/

30. Doris Layton MacKenzie et al. (1999). The impact of probation on the criminal activities of offenders. *Journal of Research in Crime and Delinquency, 36*(4), 423–453.

31. Doris Layton MacKenzie et al. (1999).

32. Joan Petersilia and Steve Turner (1993). Evaluating intensive supervision probation/parole: Results of a nationwide experiment." *Research in Brief.* Washington, DC: National Institute of Justice.

33. Edward J. Latessa and Francis T. Cullen (2002, September). Beyond correctional quackery—professionalism and the possibility of effective treatment. *Federal Probation, 66*(2), 28–37.

34. Bureau of Justice Statistics (2004, July). *Probation and parole in the United States, 2003.* Washington, DC: U.S. Department of Justice, Office of Justice Programs, NCJ 205336. Retrieved online August 14, 2004: http://www.ojp.usdoj.gov/bjs/pub/pdf/ppus03.pdf

35. Bureau of Justice Statistics (2004, July). *Probation and parole in the United States, 2003.*

36. Morgan O. Reyonolds (2002). *Privatizing probation and parole.* National Center for Policy Analysis. Retrieved online November 14, 2003: http://www.ncpa.org/studies/s233/s233.htm

37. Bureau of Justice Statistics (2004, July). *Probation and parole in the United States, 2003.*

38. Dennis J. Stevens (2006). *Community corrections: An applied approach.* Upper Saddle River, NJ: Prentice Hall.

39. Frank P. Williams III, Marilyn D. McShane, and H. Michael Dolny (2000). Predicting parole absconders. *Prison Journal, 80*(1), 24–38.

40. Samuel Walker (1980). *Popular justice: A history of American criminal justice.* New York: Oxford Press (p. 42).

41. Patricia O'Brien (1995). The prison on the Continent: Europe, 1865–1965. In Norris Morris and David J. Rothman. *The Oxford History of the Prison: The Practice of Punishment in Western Society* (pp. 78–201). New York: Oxford University Press.

42. Dennis J. Stevens (2006). The history of prisons: Continental Europe and England. *The Encyclopedia of criminology and deviant behaviour.* New York: Routledge/Taylor & Francis.

43. Pieter Spierenburg (1991). *The broken spell: A cultural and anthropological history of preindustrial Europe.* New Brunswick, NJ: Rutgers University Press (p. 217).

44. David Shichor (1995). *Punishment for profit.* Thousand Oaks, CA: Sage (pp. 23–26).

45. *Early forms of punishment (2003).* Retrieved online November 14, 2003: http://notfrisco.com/prisonhistory/origins/

46. *British public record office (2003).* Retrieved online November 14, 2003: http://catalogue.pro.gov.uk/ExternalRequest.asp?RequestReference=ri2235

47. Early forms of punishment (2003).

48. Norval Morris (2002). *Maconochie's gentlemen: The story of Norfolk Island and the roots of modern prison reform.* New York: Oxford University Press (pp. 14–21).

49. Norval Morris (2002), 16.

50. Norval Morris (2002), i.

51. Norval Morris (2002).

52. John Clay (2001). *Maconochie's experiment: How one man's extraordinary vision saved transported convicts from degradation and despair.* London: John Murray Press.

53. *Bedforshire gaol records.* Retrieved online December 12, 2003: http://www.schools.bedfordshire.gov.uk/gaol/background/t&p.htm

54. William C. Parker (1975). *Parole: Origins, development, current practices and statutes.* College Park, MD: American Correctional Association.

55. Norval Morris (1995). The contemporary prison 1965–Present. In Norval Morris and David J. Rothman. *The Oxford history of the prison: The practice of punishment in western society.* New York: Oxford University Press (pp. 178–201).

56. Norval Morris (1995), 178–201.

57. Joan Petersilia (2000). *Parole and prison reentry in the United States.* American Probation and Parole Association. Retrieved online August 6, 2004: http://stars.csg.org/appa/perspectives/2000/summer/su00appa32.pdf

58. Philip Klein (1920). *Prison methods in New York state.* New York: Colombia University Press (p.417). Cited in U.S. Department of Justice, Attorney General's Survey of Release Procedures, 1939–1940, Washington, DC: U.S. Government Printing Office (p. 5).

59. Dr. Samuel G. Howe was a commissioner appointed by the governor to evaluate the less fortunate populations in Massachusetts in 1848. One account entitled, *On the causes of idiocy The evils which now infest Society are not inevitable,* outlined his plan to enhance the conditions of "idiots" in the Commonwealth of which Dr. Howe estimated numbered 571 residing in 77 towns throughout Massachusetts (p. 18). F. B. Sanborn (1891). *Dr. S. G. Howe—Philanthropist.* New York: Funk & Wagnalls. Also, Dr. Howe's wife was Julia Ward Howe (1819–1910), the author of "The Battle Hymn of the Republic." Julia was famous in her lifetime as poet, essayist, lecturer, reformer, and biographer. She worked to end slavery, helped to initiate the women's movement in many states, and organized for international peace—all at a time, she noted, "when to do so was a thankless office, involving public ridicule and private avoidance."

60. Zebulon Brockway (1969). *Fifty years of prison service.* New Jersey: Patterson.

61. Zebulon Brockway (1969), 163.

62. *History of federal parole programs (2002).* Retrieved online November 15, 2003: http://www.usdoj.gov/uspc/history.htm

63. *History of federal parole (2002).*

64. *History of federal parole (2002).*

65. Patricia O'Brien (1995). The prison on the continent: Europe, 1865–1965. In Norris Morris and David J. Rothman. *The Oxford history of the prison: The practice of punishment in western society.* New York: Oxford University Press (pp. 178–201).

66. Dennis J. Stevens (2005). The history of prisons: Continental Europe and England. *The Encyclopedia of Criminology and Deviant Behaviour.* New York: Routledge/ Taylor & Francis (pp. 485–487).

67. Norval Morris (1995).

68. Pieter Spierenburg (1995). The body and the state. In Norris Morris and David J. Rothman. *The Oxford history of the prison: The practice of punishment in western society.* New York: Oxford University Press (pp. 45–70).

69. Pieter Spierenburg (1995), 45–70.

70. Pieter Spierenburg (1995), 45–70.

71. The KCI Website. Formally the KOCH Institute. Retrieved online January 12, 2004: http://www.kci.org/publication/innovative_practices/intro.htm

72. Roslyn Muraskin and Albert R. Roberts (2005). *Visions for change: Crime and justice in the twenty-first century.* Upper Saddle River, NJ: Prentice Hall (p. 4).

73. The KCI Website.

74. L. I. Goodstein and D. L. MacKenzie (1989). Issues in correctional research and policy: An introduction. In L. I. Goodstein and D. L. MacKenzie (Ed.), *The American prison: Issues in research and policy.* New York: Plenum (pp. 67–73).

75. Bureau of Justice Statistics (2001, October). *Trends in parole, 1990–2000.* Washington, DC: U.S. Department of Justice, Office of Justice Programs, NCJ 184735. Retrieved online August 8, 2004: http://www.ojp.usdoj.gov/bjs/pub/pdf/tsp00.pdf

76. Bureau of Justice Statistics (2001, October). *Trends in parole, 1990–2000.* NCJ 184735.

77. Dennis J. Stevens (2006). *Community corrections. An applied approach.* Upper Saddle River, NJ: Prentice Hall. Bureau of Justice Statistics (2001, October). Also see National Center for Police Analysis. Retrieved online October 2003: http://www.ncpa.org/studies/s233/s233.html#F

78. Bureau of Justice Statistics (2004, July). *Probation and parole in the United States, 2003.*

79. Fox Butterfield (2000, November 29). Often, Parole is one stop on the way back to prison. *New York Times,* A1.

80. There is another type of parole referred to as a medical parole (e.g., prisoners with terminal illnesses such as full-blown AIDS [acquired immune deficiency syndrome]); 16 states use it sparingly when the convict poses no threat to the community.

81. Joseph T. Hallinan (2001). *Going up the river: Travels in a prison nation.* New York: Random House.

82. FPC and FDOC Annual Reports; Florida Statutes; FPC records; correspondence from Peter Peterson, FPC Director of Operations, 7/11/97; FPC Website: http://www.state.fl.us/fpc.

83. Rolando V. del Carmen (1988). *Civil liabilities of parole personnel for release, non-release, and revocation.* National Institute of Corrections. Retrieved online January 12, 2004: http://nicic.org/pubs/pre/004468.pdf

84. *The corrections yearbook: 2002 Adult corrections* (2003), 228.

85. Rolando V. del Carmen (1991). *Civil liabilities in American policing: A text for law enforcement personnel.* Englewood Cliffs, NJ: Prentice Hall (p. 7). Legal liabilities can include monetary awards for nominal, actual, or punitive damages and/or injunctions. Criminal liabilities can result in imprisonment, probation, fines, or other forms of criminal sanction. Administrative liabilities lead to dismissal, demotion, transfer, reprimand, or other forms of sanctions authorized by state law or agency rules or regulations. These points apply to police officers, but they also apply to all public officers. "Probation and parole officers, jailers, person officials, other personnel in the criminal justice system are liable," writes del Carmen (p. 7).

86. Mississippi Code of 1972, as Amended. 47–7–5. Retrieved online January 15, 2005: http://www.mscode.com/free/statutes/47/007/0005.htm. However, should prisoners feel that they were discriminated against, the parole board member could be scrutinized. Litigation outcomes might even be favorable toward a parole board member, but do members of a parole board wish to pursue public litigation?

87. California Department of Corrections website. http://www.corr.ca.gov/Offender InfoServices/Reports/Annual/PVRET2/PVRET2d2002.pdf

88. Fox Butterfield (2000, November 29).

89. *Florida parole.* Retrieved online January 2004: http://www.fplao.org/FloridaParole.html

90. Culpability for the purposes of presumptive sentence would be couched in the record of the offender. The rationale is that a succession of criminal acts would imply calculation or deliberate defiance of the law revealing the intent level of the criminal.

91. Bureau of Justice Assistance (1996, February). *National assessment of structured sentencing.* Washington, DC: U.S. Department of Justice, Office of Justice Programs. Retrieved online January 15, 2005: http://www.ncjrs.org/pdffiles/strsent.pdf

92. Bureau of Justice Statistics (2003). *Sourcebook of criminal justice statistics of 2001. Respondents ratings of several aspects of the prison system* (Table 2.20, p. 112). Retrieved online November 12, 2003: http://www.albany.edu/sourcebook/1995/pdf/t220.pdf

93. Bureau of Justice Statistics (2004). *Probation and parole in the United States in 2003.*

10

PAROLE: PROCESSES, RIGHTS, AND SERVICES

LEARNING OBJECTIVES

After you finish reading this chapter, you will be better prepared to:

- Identify conditions and special conditions of parole.
- Identify the inconsistency of parole: efficient parole practices and parolee crime.
- Describe the primary legislation protecting parolees and explain how it provides due process rights associated with revocation.
- Identify and explain the current issues of parole.
- Describe the key strategy in changing most prisoners and identify a state program that addresses this issue.
- Identify the primary services offered by parole agencies.
- Identify the primary programs offered through parole services.
- Describe the future expectations of parole.

KEY TERMS

Conditions of Parole
Exclusionary Rule

Inconsistency of Parole

Special Conditions of
Parole

Remember the four Rs: Respect for self, Respect for others, Responsibility for all your actions, and Reality.

—unknown

INTRODUCTION

Opportunities to accomplish the goals of a criminal justice agency are more likely during periods of change than at other times. Yet the enormous change confronting the justice community in the United States, including early release initiatives such as parole and good-time policies, reveals an incredible number of decisions being made every day. One truth is that many of those decisions are shaped by the attitudes of policy makers, interest groups, and the American public. Some want prisoners to grow old in prison whereas others want prisoners to be prepared to re-enter society. A common goal among both camps is to make violators accountable.

As each group and each member within each group gains input into the justice community, one thing is certain—the circle widens and as it widens, change within the justice community changes. In the midst of change, prisoners are re-entering the same community they left—the one where they engaged in the criminal activities that brought them to prison. Once again, they are emerging among old friends and family members. Once again, the old roadblocks consisting of drugs, alcohol, and violence are unchanged in those communities and among their friends and family members. Convicts entering those communities today, like those of yesterday, have felt the pains and deprivation of prison,[1] and that experience, it is argued by punishment advocates, is both payback for their crime and will lend itself to deterrence of future crimes for that offender and potential offenders. On the other hand, treatment and prevention advocates argue that many prisoners can reform if provided appropriate opportunities and professional guidance. CC, which includes parole, is part of our communities, not separate from them.[2] Consequently, parole systems require collaboration among various justice agencies to ensure public safety and offender rehabilitation. Whichever viewpoint makes sense is a point of debate, but what isn't debatable is that most often convicts return to the same communities comprised of the same daily routines from which they came, but as a different person.

The "get tough on crime" attitude of the last few decades resulted in more defendants serving prison time for crimes that once called for probation or diversion. In addition, prison sentences were longer than previously imposed. As a result, state and federal prisons and city and county jails were overcrowded. The enormous expense of imprisonment, higher recidivism rates, and limited government budgets prompted the justice community to find solutions to balance "get tough politics" with efficient justice sanctions including the use of alternatives to its most expensive sanction—confinement. Parole and early release initiatives are part of those answers.

Although decisions are made each day by parole professionals, the best that can be hoped for, aside from providing professional services within a legal framework, is that each decision is shaped by the Four Rs: respect for self, respect for others, responsibility for all your actions, and reality.

ESSENTIAL ELEMENTS OF A PAROLE SYSTEM

The American Correctional Association highlights a number of essential elements that should comprise an effective and efficient parole system.[3] Those factors are:

1. Flexibility in the sentencing and parole laws
2. Qualified parole board
3. Qualified parole staff
4. Freedom from political or improper influences
5. Parole assigned to a workplace position in the government administrative structure
6. Proper parole procedures
7. Re-release preparation within the institution
8. Parole personnel search
9. Proper attitude by the public toward the parolee

Some of the aforementioned might sound unreasonable, but obtaining a degree of each of these categories might aid in bringing a parole agency closer to its mission. But a missing truth is that without suitable resources to operate effective and efficient parole programs fitting the size and needs and risk of a parole population and dedicated personnel, it matters little how eloquent a process appears to be. Some states have huge financial resources to draw from, including many facilities and personnel. For instance, California has 32 re-entry facilities, one restitution center, and one drug treatment facility; most of these are operated by public or private agencies.[4] It also has 182 parole units and subunits across the state in 81 locations, 4 outpatient clinics, and over 3,000 parole officers and 102 clinicians on state payroll to serve among others and, 110,126 parolees, as of July 31, 2004.[5] California's parole recidivism tops 63 percent.

Inconsistency of Parole Elements

The aforementioned list of essential elements is a good starting point to understanding the issues surrounding parole. But there is an inconsistency requiring your attention between high parolee recidivism levels and revocation. With greater technology (e.g., computer tracking devices), more enhanced parole officer training, and more efficient surveillance strategies, it is more likely that parolee violations will be detected. When a parolee does not meet the conditions of parole (requirements that must be met) or breaks the law, a

---

Inconsistency of Parole

An inconsistency exists between efficient parole agencies and high recidivism levels of parolees. It does not necessarily follow that high recidivism levels among parolees means more violations committed by parolees. It could mean greater efficiency among parole personnel and fewer requirements to demonstrate guilt beyond a reasonable doubt in a streamlined process.

parolee can be returned to prison. In 2003, two of every five parolees were returned to prison.[6] Continuing along with this thought is the idea that the state does not have the burden of demonstrating guilt beyond a reasonable doubt about a parolee as it does among other defendants. Therefore, parole revocation is relatively easy to accomplish, especially because it requires a lower degree of certainty than trying a parolee on a new crime, and the legal process is more streamlined.

Conditions of Parole

In Chapter 9, we saw the various ways a prisoner could be released early from prison through parole or community supervision. Largely, conditions of parole are predicated upon enumerated conditions under the supervision of a parole officer. The conditions of parole vary from jurisdiction to jurisdiction. There are conditions of parole that benefit the community more than parolees. Because parole is fulfilling the obligations of an imposed jail or prison sentence in the community, it is both necessary and expected that conditions of parole will first serve public safety and second, help the prisoner adjust to community life. There are similarities in the conditions of parole as Table 10.1 shows.

Table 10.1   Conditions of Parole in Effect in 51 Jurisdictions

Conditions of Parole	Number of Jurisdictions	Percentages
1. Report to the parole officer as directed and answer all reasonable inquiries by the parole officer	49	96.1
2. Refrain from possessing a firearm or other dangerous weapon unless granted written permission	47	92.2
3. Remain within the jurisdiction of the court and notify the parole officer of any change in residence	46	90.2
4. Permit the parole officer to visit at home or elsewhere	42	82.4
5. Obey all rules and regulations of the parole supervision agency	40	78.4
6. Maintain gainful employment	40	78.4
7. Abstain from association with persons with criminal records	31	60.8
8. Pay all court-ordered fines, restitution, or other financial penalties	27	52.9
9. Meet family responsibilities and support dependents	24	47.1
10. Undergo medical and psychiatric treatment and/or enter and remain in a specified court-ordered institution	23	45.1
11. Pay supervision fees	19	37.3
12. Attend a prescribed secular course of study or vocational training	9	17.6
13. Perform community service	7	13.7
14. Obey all federal, state, and local laws	50	98.0

Source: Edward E. Rhine, William R. Smith, and Roland W. Jackson.[7]

Special Conditions

Parolees are compelled to comply with all special conditions imposed by their conditions of release and by parole supervision staff. Special conditions may include electronic monitoring, parole release to a CC center, prohibition from entering or working in establishments that sell or serve alcohol, in-patient or out-patient drug and alcohol treatment, sex-offender treatment, mental health treatment, or no contact with persons such as the victim of the crime or codefendants. For instance, special conditions of parole in South Carolina include: successful completion of a substance-abuse rehabilitation program; random drug tests; intensive supervision for an indeterminate period not to exceed 6 months; attending a mental-health care program for as long as may be necessary; being placed on electronic monitoring for an indeterminate period; and paying restitution, court costs, and supervision fees.[8]

Adults on Parole

The total number of individuals on parole in 2003 was 774,588 (see Table 10.2).[9] As you can see, there were a large number of entries (492,727) and exits (470,538). Typical of most CC programs and correctional systems, there are always a large number of defendants on the move.

   Outcomes.   Of more than 470,500 parolees discharged from supervision in 2003, 47 percent had successfully met the conditions of their supervision, 38 percent had been returned to incarceration, either because of a rule violation or a new offense, and 9 percent had absconded.[11]

U.S. Commission on Parole and Salient Factor Score

The U.S. Commission on Parole developed the Salient Factor Score (SFS02), which is an actuarial device used to evaluate the risk of parole violation by a prisoner if released to supervision.[12] It was recently revised to give better guidance in the scoring of the individual items. The score is a component of the commission's paroling policy guidelines for making parole release decisions. It is also employed in the guidelines for offenders in Washington, DC. The score comprises six criminal history items, including items such as number of prior convictions and commitments and age at the time of current offense. The total score ranges from 0 to 10, with the higher score indicating that the prisoner is a better parole risk.

RIGHTS OF PAROLEES

In Chapters 7 and 8, there was a discussion about diminished constitutional rights and preferred rights associated with probationers. Those principles and rights apply somewhat to parolees but in a different way. Although many important cases are associated with the rights of parolees, *Morrissey v. Brewer* is worth review.

Table 10.2   Adults on Parole 2003

Region and Jurisdiction	Parole Population, 1/1/03	2003 Entries	2003 Exits	Parole Population, 12/31/03	Percentage Change, 2003	Number on Parole per 100,000 Adult Residents, 12/31/03
U.S. total	750,934	492,727	470,538	774,588	3.1	357
Federal	83,063	33,590	31,088	86,459	4.1	40
State	667,871	459,137	439,450	688,129	3.0	317
Northeast	174,591	77,381	71,903	180,069	3.1	437
Connecticut	2,186	3,260	2,847	2,599	18.9	99
Maine	32	0	0	32	0.0	3
Massachusetts	3,951	6,305	6,552	3,704	−6.3	370
New Hampshire[a]	963	719	482	1,200	24.6	124
New Jersey	12,576	10,322	9,650	13,248	5.3	203
New York	55,990	25,049	25,186	55,853	−0.2	386
Pennsylvania[b]	97,712	30,870	26,338	102,244	4.6	1,084
Rhode Island	384	456	448	392	2.1	48
Vermont	797	400	400	797	0.0	170
Midwest	114,173	95,242	87,882	121,533	6.4	250
Illinois	35,458	32,476	32,926	35,008	−1.3	374
Indiana	5,877	7,304	6,162	7,019	19.4	152
Iowa[c]	2,787	2,787	2,475	3,099	11.2	140
Kansas[c]	3,990	4,146	3,991	4,145	3.9	207
Michigan	17,648	12,579	9,994	20,233	14.6	271
Minnesota	3,577	4,121	4,102	3,596	0.5	96
Missouri	13,533	10,407	8,720	15,220	12.5	357
Nebraska	574	839	763	650	13.2	51
North Dakota	148	585	507	226	52.7	48
Ohio	17,853	11,670	11,096	18,427	3.2	216
South Dakota	1,640	1,451	1,147	1,944	18.5	346
Wisconsin	11,088	6,877	5,999	11,966	7.9	293
South	219,849	104,142	96,351	227,668	3.6	291
Alabama	5,309	4,098	2,457	6,950	30.9	206
Arkansas	12,128	7,379	5,813	13,694	12.9	672
Delaware	551	217	239	529	−4.0	85
Washington, DC[a,b]	5,297	3,136	3,369	5,064	—	1,129
Florida	5,223	4,409	4,680	4,952	−5.2	37
Georgia	20,822	11,738	10,391	22,135	6.3	344
Kentucky[c]	5,968	4,719	3,115	7,572	26.9	243
Louisiana	23,049	13,468	11,452	25,065	8.7	766
Maryland	13,271	8,059	7,588	13,742	3.5	334
Mississippi[d]	1,816	1,103	963	1,816	0.0	87
North Carolina	2,805	3,214	3,342	2,677	−4.6	42

(continued)

Table 10.2   Adults on Parole 2003 (Continued)

Region and Jurisdiction	Parole Population, 1/1/03	2003 Entries	2003 Exits	Parole Population, 12/31/03	Percentage Change, 2003	Number on Parole per 100,000 Adult Residents, 12/31/03
Oklahoma[a]	3,573	1,995	1,521	4,047	—	155
South Carolina	3,491	1,025	1,306	3,210	−8.0	103
Tennessee	7,949	3,130	3,314	7,967	0.2	180
Texas[a]	103,068	32,847	33,644	102,271	−0.8	639
Virginia	4,530	2,779	2,475	4,834	6.7	86
West Virginia	999	826	682	1,143	14.4	81
West	159,258	182,371	183,313	158,859	−0.3	324
Alaska[c]	900	614	587	927	—	203
Arizona[b]	4,587	8,895	8,115	5,367	17.0	129
California[c]	113,185	148,915	152,305	110,338	−2.5	424
Colorado	6,215	5,298	4,954	6,559	5.5	193
Hawaii	2,525	906	1,191	2,240	−11.3	231
Idaho	1,961	1,486	1,118	2,329	18.8	236
Montana[c]	845	601	631	815	−3.6	119
Nevada	3,971	2,956	2,801	4,126	3.9	243
New Mexico	1,962	1,977	1,532	2,407	22.7	177
Oregon	19,090	8,059	7,380	19,769	3.6	733
Utah	3,352	2,300	2,353	3,299	−1.6	205
Washington[a]	95	45	35	105	10.5	2
Wyoming	570	319	311	578	1.4	156

Note: Because of incomplete data, the population on December 31, 2003 does not equal the population on January 1, 2003, plus entries, minus exits.

—Not calculated.

[a]All data were estimated.

[b]Data for entries and exits were estimated for nonreporting agencies.

[c]Excludes parolees in one of the following categories: absconder, out of state, or inactive.

[d]Data are for yearend December 1, 2003.

Printed with the permission of the U.S. Department of Justice.[10]

Morrissey v. Brewer (1972)

Morrissey v. Brewer[13] was the first U.S. Supreme Court decision to articulate a federal due process right for parolees to confront and cross-examine adverse witnesses at a revocation proceeding. *Morrissey* held that a parolee has "the right to confront and cross-examine adverse witnesses (unless the hearing officer specifically finds good cause for not allowing confrontation) . . . (though) the process should be flexible enough to consider evidence including letters, affidavits, and other material that would not be admissible in an adversary criminal trial."[14] A year later, *Gagnon v. Scarpelli (Gagnon)* extended *Morrissey* rights to probationers.[15]

In addition, the essence of parole is release from prison, before completion of sentence, on the condition that the prisoner abide by certain conditions and rules during the balance of the sentence.[16] Parolee's liberty while on the street is protected by due process, clarifies the American Law Institute.[17] Among other things, the U.S. Supreme Court said in *Morrissey v. Brewer*[18] that the minimum due process requirements for parole revocation are:

1. Two hearings are required:
   a. A preliminary hearing to determine whether probable cause exists that a parolee has violated any specific parole condition.
   b. A general revocation proceeding.
2. Written notice must be given to the parolee prior to the general revocation proceeding.
3. Disclosure must be made to the parolee concerning the nature of parole violation/s and evidence obtained.
4. Parolees must be given the right to confront their accusers and cross-examine them unless adequate cause can be given for prohibiting such cross-examination.
5. Finally, the *Morrissey* decision required that the hearing officer be neutral and detached.

Morrissey pleaded guilty and was convicted in 1967 of false drawing or uttering of checks. He was paroled by the Iowa Department of Corrections in 1968. Seven months later, parole was revoked because Morrissey violated the conditions of parole. He purchased a car under an assumed name and drove it without the permission of his parole officer. He had an accident and gave false information to the police. He also produced false documents. Morrissey never advised his parole officer of any of the proceedings. His parole was revoked once all the information surfaced.

A *hearing to revoke parole* differs from most criminal cases in many respects. Morrissey indicates that the final parole hearing should operate more informally than a criminal trial. "(T)here is no thought to equate this second stage of parole revocation to a criminal prosecution in any sense. It is a narrow inquiry; the process should be flexible enough to consider evidence including letters, affidavits, and other material that would not be admissible in an adversary criminal trial."[19] Differing levels of proof, rules of evidence, and procedure require the advocate to balance the unique needs of each proceeding.[20]

Exclusionary Rule

As previously mentioned, the level of guilt relevant to beyond a reasonable doubt is not addressed in *Morrissey*. Therefore, the likelihood of returning a parolee to prison is greater than during the original judicial process. Why?

For one reason, the *exclusionary rule,* which relates to search and seizure of evidence, does not apply to parole revocation hearings.

> ## Exclusionary Rule
>
> A rule of evidence that enforces the Fourth Amendment, in which the purpose is to deter police misconduct.

The exclusionary rule was applied to all illegally obtained evidence in state proceedings in the case of *Mapp v. Ohio.*[21] This case served to protect defendants against illegally seized evidence. In the case involving parolees, *Pennsylvania Board of Probation and Parole v. Scott,*[22] the court was asked if the exclusionary rule applied to parole hearings. The court ruled that the exclusionary rule does not apply because parole officers do not require warrants to conduct a legal search, and the burden of proof is lower in parole revocation hearings than in criminal court prosecutions. The rationale is that a parolee is actually a prisoner and prisoners have less expectation of privacy than others not under a correctional sentence. The rationale is that the exclusionary rule was created as a means of deterring illegal searches and seizures. The rule does not prohibit the introduction of illegally seized evidence in all proceedings or against all persons. It is applicable only where its deterrence benefits outweigh its social costs.

> ## Facts
>
> As a condition of Scott's parole, he was to refrain from owning or possessing weapons. Based on evidence that he violated this and other conditions of his parole, officers entered his home, searched, and found firearms. At his parole violation hearing, Scott objected to the introduction of this evidence on the grounds that the search was unreasonable under the 4th Amendment. Scott's challenge to the evidence was rejected. Thus, Scott's parole was violated and he was recommitted.

Much of the modern debate about the enforcement of the Fourth Amendment has focused on the wisdom of and constitutional necessity for the exclusionary rule, under which evidence obtained in violation of the Fourth Amendment is ordinarily inadmissible in a criminal trial. Liberals often support the rule because it is grounded in the Constitution, it is a deterrent to police misconduct, and it is helpful in the search for truth. On the other hand, abolishing the exclusionary rule has been a high priority for conservatives for more than thirty years because it limits police power.[23]

Legal Representation

A United States district court judge ruled in 2002 that the California parole system (which also implicates other state systems) failed to provide parolees in custody with timely hearings to determine if there were legal grounds to hold them, a violation of due process rights. Under a settlement from that case, a parolee must be appointed an attorney and receive a hearing within 10 days of arrest to determine if there is probable cause to file a charge of parole violation. The court also directed that parole revocation hearings must be heard by the board of prisons within 35 days of arrest. This suit further allows officers to direct parole violators who are not considered a danger to society to alternate programs, such as halfway houses or drug rehabilitation centers. It is estimated that three out of four parolees are substance abusers.

Rights Associated with Determinate Sentences

One (jailhouse lawyer) argues a twist to determinate sentences and good-time credits.[24] Once the state gives a prisoner "good-time" credits, the state might not be able to take them away, whatever the reason.[25] Good-time credits confer a liberty interest on prisoners as discussed in Chapter 9.[26]

A prisoner's good-time credits become vested when released from prison.[27] Therefore, once a determinant-term prisoner is released from prison, his good-time and associated credits become vested and the offender will have served his entire "actual custody" sentence. No matter what a state chooses to call it, "supervised released" or "early release," it falls squarely under the Morrissey definition of "parole,"[28] so when there is no more time left to be served to be released early from, the prisoner must be discharged.

Legal Cases Used in this Argument

Lynce v. Mathis (1997) 519 U.S. 433, 117 S.Ct., 137 L.Ed. 2d 63
Wolf v. McDonnell (1974) 418 U.S. 539, 44 S.Ct. 2963, 41 L.Ed. 2d 935
Gother v. Woods (9th Cir. 1995) 66 F. 3d 1097
Glouser v. Parrat (8th Cir. 1979) 605 F.2d 419
Younger v. Harper 117 S.Ct. 1148

Current Issues of Parole

Some of the current issues associated with early release strategies are:[29]

- Record number of prisoners are being released.
- Characteristics of parolees are rapidly changing.
- Sentencing and parole policy changes.
- Parole caseloads are rising.
- Parolees are being sent back to prison in record numbers.
- Parolees recidivism levels by type of release.
- Parolees are concentrated in a few urban areas.
- Handling drug offenders is key.

Record number of prisoners released. The number of prisoners being released to community supervision yearly is a little over 500,000 state prison inmates (or 1,600 a day—an increase of 46 percent from 1990) and 80 percent were released to parole supervision in 2001.[30]

Characteristics of parolees are rapidly changing. The characteristics of prisoners released and under community supervision have changed:

- More females (from 10 percent in 1995 to 12 percent in 2000 to 13 percent in 2003)
- Growing older (35 percent older than 35 years old)
- More have a history of failure on supervision (from 43 percent in 2000 to 47 percent in 2003)
- More drug law violators (35 percent)
- Will have spent more time in prison (e.g., in 1993 the average time imprisoned was 46 months, in 1996 50 months, and 1999 53 months).[32]
- More mentally ill (14 percent) and drug/alcohol involved (74 percent)
- More with infectious disease: 25 percent of all people living with HIV or AIDS in the United States in 1997 were released from a prison or jail that year

Sentencing and parole policy changes. Sentencing and parole policy changes include determinate and mandatory sentences initiatives. That is, 14 states abolished discretionary release for all inmates between 1977 to 1998 and truth-in-sentencing limits parole boards' power.

Parole caseloads are rising. Services, programs, and public tolerance have declined. Because building prisons takes money from services, fewer parole personnel are hired to take care of the expanding caseloads. For instance, the ideal caseload is 35:1, advises the American Parole and Probation Association. The average parole officer's caseload is about 70:1 If 80 percent of parolees on are on a regular caseload basis, that means two 15-minute face-to-face contacts a month. Due to policy makers, interest groups, and the public's lack of support, parole restrictions have widened and the fear of criminals, especially those on parole, has grown.

Printed with permission of the Office of Justice Programs.

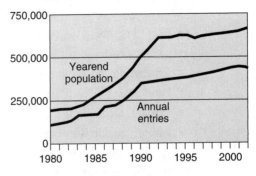

Annual State Parole Population and Entries to State Parole, 1980–2002[31]

Parolees are being sent back to prison in record numbers. As a result of a lack of support and public fear and demands, parole boards revoke parolees more quickly than in the past and technology helps uncover violations. Sixty two percent of those released from state prison will be rearrested with three years, indicating that success is declining: In 1983, 57 percent of parolees were discharged successfully. It could be said that parole violators are the main cause of the rise in prison admissions because they now account for 37 percent of all U.S. prison admissions. Something has changed. One change is the amount of crime committed by parolees. In Chapter 8 you were probably surprised by the crimes committed by those on probation. Parolees show similar results. During their average 13 months on parole in 1991, the 156,000 parole violators collectively committed an estimated:[33]

- 46,000 violent crimes
- 45,000 property crimes
- 24,000 drug offenses
- 9,000 other offenses

    In greater detail, based on convictions of the 156,000 parole violators collectively:[34]

- Murdered 6,800 people (50 percent were strangers)
- Raped or sexually assaulted 4,900 females and 600 males (21 percent were under the age of twelve; 47 percent under 18)
- Robbed 22,500 people (86 percent of them were strangers)
- Assaulted 8,800 people (14 percent of them were wives, ex-wives, girlfriends, and ex-girlfriends; more than half of them were strangers)
- Burglarized 23,000 homes and businesses
- Stole 4,800 motor vehicles

    Based on those offenders with a current conviction for a violent crime, probation violators were more likely to victimize a minor compared to parole violators (13 percent vs. 8 percent). Victim injury was also more prevalent among probation violators (60 percent) than parole violators (50 percent).

    Therefore, under these conditions, parole strategies are not meeting one of the primary directives: reducing overcrowded prisons.

A study of prison crowding conducted by the National Assessment of Structured Sentencing (NASS) concluded that to date, structured sentencing reforms have not demonstrated any appreciable effects on prison crowding. This is not to say that they could not have such an impact in the future. However, until the legislators and sentencing commissions become immune to "get tough on crime" pressures, there is little reason to believe that structured sentencing models will solve the prison crowding problem. Moreover, as state prisons remain crowded, they will continue to use discretionary early release programs.[35]

One recommendation made by NASS (2004) relates to mandatory minimum sentences. "It is clear from the experiences of many States that the increased use of mandatory minimum penalties is interfering with achievement of the dual goals of reducing disparity and controlling correctional population growth. A state should resist such provisions if they affect large proportions of its sentenced population."[36]

Parolees recidivism levels by type of release. The percentage of state parole discharges based on type of release influences successful completion of supervision as Table 10.4 shows. For instance, in 1990, 52 percent of those released from prison through discretionary parole successfully completed their parole supervision period

---

Rates of Successful Termination Higher when California Is Excluded

The size and make-up of California's parole population, combined with the low percentage of successful terminations (25% in 1999), affect the national rate of success for parole discharges. If data from California are removed from the analysis, the comparative rates of success for discretionary and mandatory parole change dramatically.

Overall, California accounted for nearly 30% of all state parole discharges during 1999. Discretionary parole, though available as a method of release, is rarely used in California. In 1999, more than 99% of California's parole discharges had received mandatory parole.

When California data are excluded, the success rate for all parole discharges rises to 53% (from 42%), and the rate for mandatory parolees increases to 64% (from 33%) in 1999 (see Table 10.3).

Table 10.3   Percentage Successful Among Parole Discharges in California and All Other States. 1995–1999

	California		Parole in All Other States	
Year	All Parole	All	Mandatory	Discretionary
1995	22.7	52.8	64.0	54.2
1996	23.8	56.6	71.6	55.8
1997	22.8	55.9	67.2	55.8
1998	24.3	54.5	65.7	55.2
1999	25.2	53.3	63.9	53.9

Note: Based on prisoners with a sentence of more than one year who were released from state prison.

Printed with permission of the U.S. Department of Justice.[38]

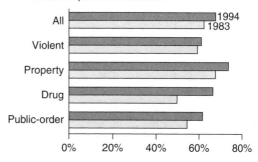

Percent of Released Prisoners Rearrested within 3 years, by Offense, 1983 and 1994

Offense of prisoners released

Printed with permission of the Office of Justice Programs.[37]

as compared to 24 percent who were released through mandatory parole initiative. In 1999, although more mandatory parolees successfully completed parole, a wide gap still existed between successful completion of discretionary and mandatory parole initiatives.

Parolees are concentrated largely in a few urban areas. For instance, 75 percent of all state prisoners in New York come from New York City. High percentages of urban parolees in Illinois come from Chicago, and that trend can be seen across the United States.

Handling drug offenders is key. For instance, practitioners report that 8 of each 10 apprehended offenders at every level have drug or alcohol issues as Table 10.5 demonstrates.

Table 10.4 Percentage (Rounded) of State Parole Discharges Successfully Completing Supervision by Method of Release from Prison, United States 1990–1999.

Year	All Discharges	Type of Release		Method of Release	
		First Release	Rerelease	Discretionary Parole	Mandatory Parole
1990	45	56	15	52	24
1991	47	61	17	53	25
1992	49	57	23	51	30
1993	47	65	23	55	34
1994	44	57	19	52	30
1995	44	63	18	54	28
1996	45	67	19	56	30
1997	43	63	17	56	31
1998	44	63	21	55	32
1999	42	64	21	54	33

Printed with permission of the U.S. Department of Justice.[39]

Table 10.5 Substance Abuse, Metal Illness, and Homelessness Among State Prisoners Expected to Release, Yearend 1999

Characteristic	Percentage (Rounded) of Expected Releases
Alcohol or drug involved at time of offense	84
Alcohol abuse	
Alcohol use at time of offense	42
Alcohol dependent	25
Drug use	
In month before offense	60
At time of offense	45
Intravenous use in the past	24
Committed offense for money for drugs	20
Mentally ill	14
Homeless at time of arrest	11

Printed with permission of the U.S. Department of Justice.[40]

> Handling drug offenders is key, argues Joan Petersilia. Parole violators returned to prison on drug offenses more than doubled since 1990. Serious underlying problems, few programs, and poor evaluations translate to recycled prisoners. Drug treatment among prisoners declined from 30 percent in 1991 to 24 percent in 1997.[41]

PAROLE SERVICES

Similar to probation services, parole services or systems provide services guided by state and federal resources, experiences, policy, and public opinion in their jurisdiction. The following services or systems are provided through 11 state parole agencies, Washington, DC, and the federal government (see Table 10.6). Also, 22 state agencies, Washington, DC, and the federal government (see Table 10.7) provide both parole and probation services that include: preparole reports (probation agencies conduct presentencing reports), family and individual counseling, job development, detox, substance abuse treatment, referral services, apprehension of absconders, and electronic monitoring devices as shown in Table 10.6 and Table 10.7.

Preparole reports can be described as written evaluations of a prisoner before release recommending his or her discretionary parole. Parole boards consider the preparole reports along with other information to determine parole options.

Family counseling relates to group guidance of a dysfunctional family through psychological techniques.

Individual counseling can be described as professional guidance of an individual by utilizing psychological methods, especially in collecting case history data, using various techniques of the personal interview, and testing interests and aptitudes.

Table 10.6   Services Provided by Parole Systems as of January 1, 2002[42]

Parole State	Preparole Reports	Family Counseling	Individual Counseling	Job Development	Detox	Substance Abuse Treatment	Referral Services	Apprehend Absconders	Electronic Monitors
Arizona	X		X	X			X		X
California	X	X	X	X	X	X	X	X	X
Colorado	X	X	X	X	X	X	X	X	X
Connecticut			X	X	X	X	X	X	X
Georgia	X			X		X	X	X	X
Illinois	X	X	X	X	X	X	X	X	X
Indiana						X	X		X
Kansas	X					X	X	X	X
Maryland	X		X	X		X	X	X	X
Massachusetts	X						X	X	X
Nebraska							X		X
New York	X	X	X	X	X	X	X	X	X
South Dakota	X		X	X			X	X	X
Texas	X	X	X	X	X	X	X	X	X
West Virginia			X				X	X	X
Washington DC	X	X	X	X	X	X	X	X	X
Federal government	X	X	X	X	X	X	X	X	X
Total	13	7	12	12	8	12	17	14	17

Although federal government is phasing out parole, there are still parolees in the process.

Note: Not every state offers parole or parole programs.

Job development can include job skill training and methods of obtaining employment such as how to complete a job application.

Detox can be described as detoxification from an intoxicating or addictive substance that is largely conducted in a ward or a clinic.

Substance abuse treatment generally relates to a 12-step program used by AA most often.

Referral services refers to services that are provided to a probationer but not performed by the organization doing the referral.

Apprehend absconders refers to locating parolees who have not reported to their parole office and could not be located through normal methods such as the use of telephone, U.S. mail, or through friends and family members.

Electronic monitors are methods used to monitor the whereabouts or movements of probationers such as a bracelet program.

Services provided by parole systems (Table 10.6) versus parole and probation systems in (Table 10.7) are similar. One difference rests with PSIs, as explained in Chapter 8, and preparole reports. Overall, writing reports, referral services, apprehension of absconders, and electronic monitoring seem to be provided most often by parole agencies.

Table 10.7   Services Provided by Parole and Probation Systems as of January 1, 2002[43]

Parole State	Pre-sentencing	Preparole Reports	Family Counseling	Individual Counseling	Job Development	Detox	Substance Abuse Treatment	Referral Services	Apprehend Absconders	Electronic Monitors
Alaska	X	X						X		X
Arkansas	X	X	X	X	X		X	X	X	X
Delaware	X			X	X	X	X	X	X	X
Florida	X	X						X	X	X
Idaho	X		X	X	X		X	X	X	X
Kentucky							X	X	X	X
Louisiana	X	X						X	X	X
Michigan	X	X						X	X	X
Minnesota	X	X	X	X	X			X	X	X
Mississippi	X	X		X	X			X	X	X
Missouri	X	X			X			X	X	X
Montana		X					X	X		X
North Dakota	X	X		X	X		X	X	X	X
Ohio	X	X		X	X		X	X	X	X
Oklahoma	X	X			X			X	X	X
Oregon	X	X		X	X	X	X	X	X	X
Pennsylvania	X	X		X				X	X	X
Rhode Island	X			X	X			X		X
South Carolina	X	X		X				X	X	X
Tennessee	X	X			X			X	X	X
Utah	X	X	X	X			X	X	X	X
Virginia	X	X					X	X		X
Washington	X	X					X	X	X	X
Washington, DC	X									X
Wyoming	X	X						X		X
Federal government	X									X
Total	24	20	4	12	12	2	11	24	19	26

Although federal government is phasing out parole, there are still parolees in the process.

Note: Not every state offers parole or parole programs.

PAROLE PROGRAMS

There are numerous programs or "plans of action" that parole systems provide for offenders. The most common parole program is *regular parole*. In jurisdictions where regular parole is the norm, the offender pays an initial or monthly processing fee, up to a specific amount such as 50 dollars. Periodic record checks are completed to ensure the offender has not violated the law and the parolee reports to a parole officer at a specified time and place (usually the parole agency's offices) weekly or biweekly depending upon the conditions of parole as discussed in Chapter 9. Government statistics report that approximately three out of four parolees are required to regularly report to a parole authority in person, by mail, or by telephone.[44] It is expected that the parolee will remain within the boundaries of the conditions of parole and might have random drug checks and curfew checks.

Other programs can vary depending on resources, experiences, and policy of various jurisdictions. Those programs vary depending on whether they are provided in systems or organizational structures that offer parole and probation and/or just parole. In addition, state parole agencies provided the following distinctive programs (either as stand alone agencies, as in Table 10.8 or in conjunction with probation agencies, as in Table 10.9)

Table 10.8   Programs Available in Parole Agencies on January 1, 2002[45]

State	Restitution Camp	Parenting Classes	DWI Programs	Group Homes	Halfway Houses	Supervised Home Release	Intensive Supervision	Community Service	Other Programs
Alaska					X		X	X	
Arizona						X		X	
California	X	X		X	X		X	X	X
Colorado	X	X	X		X	X	X	X	
Connecticut					X	X	X	X	
Georgia	X	X				X		X	X
Idaho	X	X		X		X	X		
Illinois		X			X	X	X		X
Indiana							X		X
Kansas	X				X		X	X	X
Maryland	X								
Massachusetts						X	X		
Michigan	X				X	X	X	X	X
Minnesota	X					X	X	X	
Mississippi						X	X		
Montana	X		X		X	X	X	X	
Nebraska							X		
New York		X						X	X
Ohio					X	X	X		X
Pennsylvania	X	X				X	X		X
South Dakota	X	X					X	X	
Texas	X	X			X	X	X	X	X
Utah	X	X			X		X		
West Virginia	X					X		X	
Washington, DC			X	X	X	X	X	X	X
Federal government*			X	X	X	X	X	X	X
Total	14	10	4	4	13	17	21	16	12

*Although federal government is phasing out parole, there are still parolees in the process.

Note: Not every state offers parole or parole programs.

to constituents on January 1, 2002: restitution camp (limited compensation program), parenting classes, DWI programs, group homes, halfway houses, supervised home release, intensive supervision, community service, and "other" programs. Other programs consist of drug courts, literacy programs, domestic violence and transitional case management, cognitive skills, shock parole, relapse prevention, and residential stabilization.

These parole programs are discussed in Chapters 3 and 9 and the information would be repetitive. However, electronic monitoring is also used in many parole strategies. To give you an idea about the number of devices used among parolees across the United States, see Table 10.10.

Sometimes, jurisdictions contract with private vendors who monitor offenders on a 24-hour-per-day basis. Curfew violations are reported to parole staff for further investigation. However, what follows are some specific parole programs.

Pennsylvania Prison-Based Drug Treatment for Parole Violators

Pennsylvania developed a program specifically for parole violators called Pennsylvania's Prison-Based Drug Treatment for Parole Violators. Pennsylvania learned what Joan Petersilia and most practitioners advise: handling drug offenders is key!

Table 10.9   Programs Available in Parole and Probation Agencies on January 1, 2002[46]

State	Restitution Camp	Parenting Classes	DWI Programs	Group Homes	Halfway Houses	Supervised Home Release	Intensive Supervision	Community Service	Other Programs
Arkansas	X	X				X	X	X	X
Delaware	X	X	X	X	X	X	X	X	X
Florida	X						X	X	X
Louisiana	X	X				X	X	X	
Missouri	X		X	X	X	X	X	X	X
Oklahoma	X						X	X	
Oregon	X	X	X	X		X	X	X	X
North Dakota	X		X	X	X	X	X	X	
Rhode Island	X						X	X	
South Carolina	X	X	X	X		X	X	X	
Virginia	X				X	X	X	X	X
Washington	X					X	X	X	X
Washington, DC								X	X
Wyoming						X	X	X	
Federal government*								X	X
Total	12	5	5	5	4	10	13	15	9

*Although federal government is phasing out parole, there are still parolees in the process.

Note: Not every state offers parole or parole programs.

Table 10.10   Use of Electric Monitors in 2001

	Number of Jurisdictions	*Number of Devices Used*	*Average Weeks Worn*
Parole-only Jurisdictions	17	35,180	18

Printed with permission of *The Corrections Yearbook.*[47]

This program is a residential program designed for parole violators who are returned to state prison not for a new arrest, but for a technical violation of the conditions of parole (e.g., failing routine drug tests or breaking curfew). This cycle costs states millions of dollars in custodial expenses and does little to address the drug problems that keep people cycling through the system. In Pennsylvania, technical parole violators account for approximately 30 percent of new prison admissions.

In 1998, Pennsylvania's Department of Corrections and Board of Probation and Parole collaborated to create a prison-based program to serve technical parole violators with substance abuse problems. Using federal funds, the state established two 60-bed Residential Substance Abuse Treatment (RSAT) programs in state prisons. In 2000, state officials added four more RSAT facilities to serve inmates statewide. Pennsylvania's RSAT programs are the only prison-based drug treatment programs in the nation that specifically target technical parole violators.

Instead of rejoining the general prison population after a violation, RSAT participants enter a three-phase program lasting 18 months:

- Six months of treatment in prison
- Six months of treatment while living in a halfway house
- Six months of less intensive treatment living on their own

The RSAT program delivers needed drug treatment while reducing the costs that would be incurred by simply putting parole violators back behind bars for one to three more years.

Like most correctional programs, Pennsylvania's Prison-Based Drug Treatment for Parole Violators faced challenges in resolving tensions between treatment and security goals and in delivering consistent treatment after participants left prison. It remains to be seen if resources will continue to be given to the program despite results suggesting parolees' experiences have been enhanced through it.

Texas' Super-Intense Supervision, Project RIO, and Special Needs Offender Programs

Texas developed a *Super-Intensive Supervision Program* (SISP), which is the highest level of supervision and offender accountability supervised by the Texas Department of Criminal Justice's Correctional Institutions Division or county jails for offenders on parole or mandatory supervision. The offenders remain in the program for the duration of their term of supervision or until removed by the Board of Pardons and Paroles. Some form of electronic monitoring monitors offenders 24 hours a day, 7 days a week. A single officer with a caseload ratio of 14:1 supervises the offenders who are released.

Project RIO (Reintegration of Offenders) is an effort by the Texas Parole Division and the Texas Workforce Commission to offer a wide range of employment assistance services to offenders statewide. The Texas Workforce Commission in collaboration with the Texas Department of Criminal Justice (TDCJ), the Windham School District, and the Texas Youth Commission (TYC) administers it. Project RIO started in 1985 and provides a link between education, training, and employment while an offender is incarcerated. It is designed to reduce recidivism through employment and employment skills. Project RIO officials feel that there is a strong connection between recidivism rates and employment. Even when one takes into account other factors such as age, risk score, race/ethnicity, and type of previous offense, post-release employment reduced rearrests and reincarcerations, Project RIO's records report.

An individualized treatment plan is developed to identify a career path for an offender and to guide placement decisions. Project RIO staff encourage participants to take advantage of educational and vocational services and assist offenders in obtaining documents necessary for employment. Unit or facility staff also provide placement services to give offenders practical work experience in their areas of training. After release, Project RIO staff provides exoffenders with individualized workforce development services, including job preparation and job search assistance. RIO participants attend structured job search workshops that focus on basic skills, such as completing a work application, preparing a resume, and performing in a mock interview. Project RIO staff certify prospective employees for the Work Opportunity Tax Credit program that provides a tax incentive to employers for hiring economically disadvantaged exoffenders.

Special Needs Offender Programs (SNOP) in Texas include Mentally Impaired (MI), Mentally Retarded (MR), Terminally Ill (TI), Physically Handicapped (PH), and Medically Recommended Intensive Supervision (MRIS) caseloads. SNOP maximizes the supervision of treatment of offenders diagnosed with mental impairments, mental retardation, terminal illness, and physical impairments by providing specialized supervision at a maximum ratio of 45:1 by 100 specialized officers with partial/full caseloads in 59 parole offices.

Washington, DC's SMART Initiative

Supervision and Management Automated Record (SMART) combines case management functions with an emphasis on agency performance.[48] At the Federal Court Services and Offender Supervision Agency (CSOSA), Director Paul Quander, Jr., says, "Our information system reflects our commitment to best practices and innovation. We recognize that accurate information is critical to our ability to protect the public."[49] CSOSA assumes probation and parole supervision of about 14,000 offenders from the District of Columbia Superior Court and the Washington, DC Board of Parole. The SMART initiative provides parole officers with up-to-date information about their caseloads and:

- Reduces paperwork toward a goal of a paperless office
- Provides automatic notification of events in support of CSOSA policies and procedures

- Tracks historical data
- Provides secure access from inside and outside the agency
- Presents a usable and navigable interface
- Produces management-level and operational reports
- Includes a fully searchable diary function
- Provides access via the Internet
- Assist senior managers in their supervisory role

Also, SMART consists of the following typical modules and functionality:

- Intake, including automatic assignments of cases to supervision teams based on offender demographics and round-robin cycles
- Reports, including detailed management-level caseload summaries
- Home page defaults to show caseload lists
- Security roles to restrict access to modules
- Replication of drug testing results
- Tracking of offenders in communities

New York City's Parole Restoration Project

Each year, technical parole violators—parolees who have not been re-arrested but have violated the terms of their parole (such as a failure to appear for an appointment)—spend months at Rikers Island in New York City. Special needs technical parole violators—including those with mental illness, women with sole custody of children, people with substance abuse treatment needs, and youth—remain in detention longer than other technical parole violators. The length of detention is longer because of the difficulty and time involved in placing special needs violators in appropriate community programs. *CASES' Parole Restoration Project* (PRP) works to restore otherwise prison-bound technical parole violators to parole and links participants to community services.

PRP serves detained technical parole violators with special needs, including individuals with mental illness, substance abuse problems, women with dependent children, and young people (aged 22 and under). After volunteering for the program's services, offenders are reinstated to parole supervision, which in turn mandates program participation. The mission of PRP is to restore its participants to parole supervision in a fair and affordable fashion that is consistent with public safety.

Special needs violators—PRP's target population—remain in detention longer than other technical parole violators (165 days on average, as opposed to 77 days) because of the difficulty and time involved in placing them in appropriate community programs. They are also more likely to be returned to prison instead of parole supervision, even though many could live in the community with appropriate monitoring and support. By linking special needs violators with community treatment options, appropriate violators are returned to parole supervision, freeing up costly jail space.

PRP seeks to increase the number of special needs violators returning to parole supervision by:

- Identifying eligible violators
- Assessing their treatment needs
- Linking them with community service providers
- Gaining support for the treatment plan from parole field staff and assigned legal representatives
- Recommending revoke/restore to the administrative law judge
- Monitoring participants for program compliance

CASES' is a public/private partnership drawing upon the collective resources and expertise of the New York State Division of Criminal Justice Services, the New York State Division of Parole, the New York City Department of Correction, Daytop Village, and the Women's Prison Association. [See their website: http://www.cases.org]

Virginia's Home Electronic and Telephone Monitoring

Virginia's home electronic and telephone monitoring (HEM) provides for strict curfew monitoring through a tamper-resistant transmitter worn on the ankle and a field monitoring device placed in the home of an offender. Offender's movements are closely monitored through random signals from monitor to transmitter. Offenders pay a $30 participation fee. This program was piloted during fiscal year 1990 to 1991 for parolees in Richmond and Winchester, VA. The program is available in all district offices and day reporting centers. HEM is used in conjunction with both intensive supervision and conventional supervision.

North Carolina's Mutual Agreement Parole Program

The Mutual Agreement Parole Program (MAPP) is designed to prepare selected inmates for release through structured activities, scheduled progression in custody levels, participation in community programs, and established parole dates.[50] It is a program that was established jointly by the Division of Prisons and the Parole Commission. MAPP participation is available to inmates who are within three years of parole and meet the following criteria:

- Must be in medium or minimum custody
- Must not be subject to a detainer or pending court action that could result in further confinement
- Be infraction-free for a period of 90 days prior to being recommended
- If sentenced under the Fair Sentencing Act, inmate is otherwise eligible for 270-day parole or community service parole

- If sentenced to life imprisonment, inmate must be recommended for participation by the Parole Commission

There should be a recognizable need on the part of the inmate for involvement in the MAPP program and the inmate should express a desire to participate in improving educational achievements, learning skills, participating in personal growth programs, and modifying specific behavior.

PAROLE STAFF

It probably came as a surprise in Chapter 8 that there are more female probation staff (55 percent female staff) and probation-parole staff (52 percent) than there are male probation-parole staff members. Also, there were approximately three white staff members out of every four and the fourth was comprised primarily of blacks or Hispanics. The percentage of parole staff is also skewed toward women and whites as Table 10.11 shows, based on the states evaluated by the staff at the Criminal Justice Institute in Middleton, CT.[51]

Keep in mind that the forementioned 10,481 parole workers and the 20,695 probation and parole staff, as discussed in Chapter 9 provide parole services to offenders. However, not all of the 20,695 officers who work in probation and parole agencies provide parole supervision. Furthermore, of the parole staff, 62 percent were parole officers, 13 percent were supervisors, and 23 percent were support staff.

Table 10.11   Parole Staff: Gender and Race January 01, 2002

State	Total	Male	Female	White	Black
Arizona	148	57%	43%	75%	01%
California	3,143	54%	46%	37%	28%
Colorado	120	53%	47%	74%	04%
Connecticut	89	57%	42%	75%	16%
Georgia	808	48%	52%	68%	30%
Illinois	461	65%	35%	46%	49%
Indiana	123	59%	41%	79%	18%
Kansas	151	53%	47%	85%	11%
Massachusetts	225	51%	49%	84%	11%
Nebraska	27	52%	48%	89%	11%
New York	2,389	46%	54%	53%	33%
South Dakota	39	64%	36%	97%	03%
Texas	2,715	39%	61%	43%	36%
West Virginia	43	54%	47%	98%	02%
Total	10,481	48%	52%	49%	31%
Average	749	53%	46%	72%	19%
Parole officer percentage	62%				

All percents rounded.
Printed with permission of *The Corrections Yearbook*.[52]

Future of Parole

Some call for the privatizing of both probation and parole.[53] Some think privatization would be more efficient in controlling parolees. Considering the inconsistency that exists between efficient parole agencies and high recidivism levels of parolees, privatization would be difficult to monitor.[54]

At least other government agencies, through the federal system, can make evaluations and recommendations of state systems. For instance, Colorado lawmakers are trying to understand how to make government more efficient after learning that an estimated 52 percent of all state prisoners end up behind bars after their release.[55] The policymakers, true to form, deliberated over additional legislation to control prisoners. However, Joe Ortiz, executive director of the Colorado Department of Corrections, painted a different picture of an overstretched system.[56] He reminded the lawmakers that they had cut an estimated $56 million from the Department of Corrections budget since 2001, which also ended most of the education and vocational training programs.

Additionally, it might be wise to consider a return of discretionary parole because recidivism levels are less than mandatory parole. There are benefits to the community when informed decisions are made by justice professionals. For example, the Iowa Board of Parole freed a record number of convicts in 2002 to 2003 using a philosophy of keeping violent offenders behind bars while granting early releases to lower risk inmates.[57] The approach appears to be easing Iowa's chronic prison crowding without endangering public safety. Paul Stageberg, a researcher for the Iowa Division of Criminal and Juvenile Justice Planning, says it appears that the parole board's new approach is succeeding because statistics indicate that criminal offenses by parolees have not increased, and violent crimes by those released are rare.

SUMMARY

Essential elements to efficiently operate a parole system are flexibility in sentencing and parole laws; a qualified board and staff free from political influences; appropriate procedures, especially re-release preparation prior to beginning the parole process; and above all, supportive policy and public attitudes toward the mission of parole. Resources and dedicated personnel are also required. However, an inconsistency exists in that an efficient parole agency produces more parole violators, implying that recidivism is not necessarily higher nor is that to say that the agency is less efficient. Reporting to a district office, following rules, answering questions truthfully, and remaining within a given jurisdiction are the most common conditions of early release conditions although those conditions vary across the nation.

Parolees have rights, as protected by the Constitution, and reaffirmed by the *Morrissey v. Brewer* case, which suggests that revocation is not an automatic issue. Other issues that should be at the forefront of parolee treatment are linked to: a record number of prisoners released, changed characteristics of parolees, sentencing and policing changes, rising parole caseloads, rising parolee recidivism, higher numbers of parolees concentrated in urban areas of the country, and handling of drug offenders. Services of parole agencies are guided by state resources, experiences, policy, and public opinion in specific jurisdictions and programs consisting of restitution camp, parenting classes, DWI programs, group homes, halfway and supervised houses, intensive supervision, and community services, which seem to be the mainstay of most parole programs. However, electronic monitoring is extensively used by most supervision agencies. The future of parole might do well to consider a return to sentencing models that enhance parole as a practical strategy as compared to an automatic release based on time served.

DISCUSSION QUESTIONS

1. Identify conditions and special conditions of parole. Which of these conditions are the most important conditions toward public safety and toward parolee rehabilitation?
2. Identify the inconsistency of parole, efficient parole practices, and parolee crime. In what way do you agree with the idea that an inconsistency does indeed exist?
3. Describe the primary legislation protecting parolees and explain in what way it provides due process rights associated with revocation.
4. Identify and explain the current issues of parole.
5. Describe the key strategy in changing most prisoners and identify a state program that addresses this issue.
6. Identify the primary services offered by parole agencies.
7. Identify the primary programs offered through parole services.
8. Describe the future expectations of parole.

NOTES

1. Deprivation as described in the classic work of Gresham M. Sykes (1966). *The society of captives*. New York: Atheneum (pp. 5–6). "Deprived of all activities of normal life," like caged animals.
2. Theodore M. Hammet, Cheryl Roberts, and Sofia Kennedy (2001). Health related issues in prisoner reentry. *Crime & Delinquency, 47*(3), 390–409.
3. American Correctional Association. (1969). *Manual of correctional standards.* Washington, DC: American Correctional Association (pp. 115–116).
4. Department of Corrections. State of California. Retrieved online August 8, 2004: http://www.corr.ca.gov/ParoleDiv/default.asp
5. California updates their correctional statistics on a monthly basis and sometimes a weekly basis depending on the information. Retrieved online August 8, 2004: http://www.corr.ca.gov

6. Bureau of Justice Statistics (2004, July). *Probation and parole in the United States, 2003.* U.S. Department of Justice, NCJ 205336. Retrieved online August 8, 2004: http://www.ojp.usdoj.gov/bjs/pub/pdf/ppus03.pdf

7. Edward E. Rhine, William R. Smith, and Ronald W. Jackson (1991). *Patrolling authorities: Recent history and current practice.* Laurel, MD: American Correctional Association, 161.

8. Department of Probation, Parole and Pardon Services. State of South Carolina. Retrieved online August 8, 2004: http://www.dppps.sc.gov/

9. Bureau of Justice Statistics (2004, July). *Probation and parole in the United States, 2003.*

10. Bureau of Justice Statistics (2004, July). *Probation and parole in the United States, 2003.*

11. Bureau of Justice Statistics (2004, July). *Probation and parole in the United States, 2003.* The remainder were still being processed.

12. *Final Rule: U.S. Parole Commission.* (2002, November 22). Doc. 02–29952. Federal Register, 67(228). pp. 70692–70694. (Rules and Regulations). Retrieved online March 2003: http://a257.g.akamaitech.net/7/257/2422/14mar20010800/edocket.access.gpo.gov/2002/02-29952.htm

13. *Morrissey v. Brewer,* 408 U.S. 471, 33 L. Ed2d 484, 494 (1972).

14. *Morrissey v. Brewer,* 408 U.S. 471, 33 L. Ed2d 484, 494 (1972), 489.

15. *Gagnon v. Scarpelli* (1973), 411 U.S. 778, 782, 791.

16. *Gagnon v. Scarpelli* (1973), 411 U.S. 778, 782, 791.

17. American Law Institute. American Bar Association. Committee on Continuing Professional Education. Retrieved online March 14, 2003: https://www.ali-aba.org/aliaba/f145promo.htm

18. *Morrissey v. Brewer,* 408 U.S. 471, 33 L. Ed2d 484, 494 (1972).

19. *Morrissey v. Brewer,* 408 U.S. 471, 33 L. Ed2d 484, 494 (1972), 486.

20. See, e.g., *N.Y. Exec. Law* §259-i(3)(f)(x) (preponderance of the evidence in final parole hearings); 9(G) N.Y.C.R.R. §8005.2 (rules of evidence for parole hearings).

21. *Mapp v. Ohio* 367 US 643 (1961).

22. *Pennsylvania Board of Probation and Parole v. Scott* 524 US 357, 118 S.Ct. 2014, 141 L.Ed.2d 344 (1998).

23. Timothy Lynch (1998). In defense of the exclusionary rule. Cato Institute's Center for Constitutional Studies. *Policy Analysis,* 319.

24. Thomas B. Watson, AT054128–4, Unit 16; Atascadero State Hospital, P.O. Box 7001, Atascadero, CA 93423–7001.

25. *Lynce v. Mathis* (1997), 519 U.S. 433, 117 S.Ct., 137 L.Ed. 2d 63.

26. *Wolf v. McDonnell* (1974), 418 U.S. 539, 44 S.Ct. 2963, 41 L.Ed. 2d 935; *Gother v. Woods* (9th Cir. 1995), 66 F. 3d 1097.

27. *Glouser v. Parrat* (8th Cir. 1979), 605 F.2d 419.

28. *Younger v. Harper* 117 S.Ct. 1148.

29. Guides in this section include: Joan Petersilia (2003). *When prisoners come home: Public safety and reintegration challenges.* New York: Oxford University Press (pp. 14–31). Retrieved online August 24, 2004: http://www.ojp.usdoj.gov/bjs/pub/pdf/ppus03.pdf. Joan Petersilia (1993). Criminal justice performance measures for prisons. *Performance Measures for the Criminal Justice System* (pp. 19–60). Washington, DC: Article prepared for the U.S. Department of Justice, Bureau of Justice Assistance. Retrieved online November 12, 2003: http://www.bja.evaluationwebsite.org/html/documents/measuring_the_performance_of_com.htm. Bureau of Justice Statistics (2004, July). *Probation and parole in the United States, 2003.* Bureau of Justice Statistics (1995, August). *Probation and parole violators in state prison, 1991: Survey of state prison inmates, 1991.* U.S. Department of Justice, NCJ 149076. Retrieved online December 15, 2004: http://www.ojp.usdoj.gov/bjs/pub/ascii/ppvsp91.txt. Bureau of Justice Statistics (2003). *Reentry trends in the United States.* Retrieved online August 20, 2004: http://www.seweb.uci.edu/users/joan/Images/prison_journal.pdf

30. Bureau of Justice Statistics (2003). *Reentry trends in the United States.*

31. Bureau of Justice Statistics (2003). *Reentry trends in the United States.*

32. Bureau of Justice Statistics (2003). *Reentry trends in the United States.*

33. Bureau of Justice Statistics (1995, August). *Probation and parole violators in state prison, 1991: Survey of state prison inmates, 1991.*

34. Bureau of Justice Statistics (1995, August). *Probation and parole violators in state prison, 1991: Survey of state prison inmates, 1991.*

35. *National Assessment of Structured Sentencing* (1996, February). Washington, DC: U.S. Department of Justice, Bureau of Justice Assistance. Retrieved online November 14, 2004: http://www.ncjrs.org/pdffiles/strsent.pdf. 144.

36. *National Assessment of Structured Sentencing.* (1996, February), 146.

37. Bureau of Justice Statistics (2001, October). *Trends in state parole, 1990–2000.* Special report NCJ 184735. Washington, DC. U.S. Department of Justice. Retrieved online November 14, 2004: http://www.ojp.usdoj.gov/bjs/pub/pdf/tsp00.pdf

38. Bureau of Justice Statistics (2001, October). *Trends in state parole, 1990–2000.*

39. Bureau of Justice Statistics (2001, October). *Trends in state parole, 1990–2000* (Table 16, p. 11).

40. Bureau of Justice Statistics (1995, August). *Probation and parole violators in state prison, 1991: Survey of state prison inmates, 1991.*

41. Joan Petersilia (2003), 1.

42. Dennis J. Stevens (2006). *Community corrections: An applied approach.* Upper Saddle River, NJ: Prentice Hall. Data developed after reviewing the literature, which includes: *The corrections yearbook: Adult corrections 2002* (2003).

Camille Graham Camp and George Camp (Eds.). Middletown, CT. Criminal Justice Institute (p. 210). Frank Lu and Laurence Wolfe (2004, July). Technology that works: An overview of the supervision and management automated record tracking (SMART) application. *Corrections Today, 66*(4), 78–80. Federal Court Services and Offender Supervision Agency (2004). *Community supervision services.* Washington, DC. Retrieved online December 28, 2004: http://www.csosa.gov/. Office of Justice Programs. *Learn about prisoner reentry* (2002). U.S. Department of Justice. Retrieved online November 14, 2003: http://www.ojp.usdoj.gov/reentry/learn.html. Melissa Sickmund (2002). *Juvenile offenders in residential placement: 1997–1999.* Washington, DC: Office of Juvenile Justice and Delinquency Prevention. Retrieved online December 28, 2004: http://www.ncjrs.org/pdffiles1/ojjdp/fs200207.pdf

43. Dennis J. Stevens (2006). Data developed after reviewing the literature, which includes: *The corrections yearbook: Adult corrections 2002* (2003). p. 214. Frank Lu and Laurence Wolfe (2004, July). pp. 78–80. Federal Court Services and Offender Supervision Agency (2004). Office of Justice Programs. *Learn about prisoner reentry* (2002). *The corrections yearbook: Adult corrections 2002* (2003), 214. Melissa Sickmund (2002), 4.

44. Bureau of Justice Statistics (2003). *Reentry trends in the United States.*

45. Dennis J. Stevens (2006). Data developed after reviewing the literature, which includes: *The corrections yearbook: Adult corrections 2002* (2003). p. 213. Frank Lu and Laurence Wolfe (2004, July). pp. 78–80. Federal Court Services and Offender Supervision Agency (2004). Office of Justice Programs. *Learn about prisoner reentry* (2002).

46. Dennis J. Stevens (2006). Data developed after reviewing the literature, which includes: *The corrections yearbook: Adult corrections 2002* (2003). p. 214. Frank Lu and Laurence Wolfe (2004, July). pp. 78–80. Federal Court Services and Offender Supervision Agency. Community supervision services (2004). Office of Justice Programs. *Learn about prisoner reentry* (2002).

47. *The corrections yearbook: Adult corrections 2002* (2003), 210.

48. Frank Lu and Laurence Wolfe (2004, July).

49. WAMU interview of Director Paul Quander, Jr. on Thursday, April 8, 2004 regarding women after prison. Washington, DC: Federal Court Services and Offender Supervision Agency. Retrieved online December 28, 2004: http://www.csosa.gov/.

50. It should be noted that there is no parole for federal prisoners who committed crimes after October 1, 1994 and were sentenced under Structured Sentencing. Only offenders who committed crimes before that date and were sentenced under Fair Sentencing or earlier criminal sentencing laws in NC may be considered for parole or MAPP.

51. *The corrections yearbook: Adult corrections 2002* (2003), 217–219.

52. *The corrections yearbook: Adult corrections 2002* (2003), 218.

53. Morgan O. Reyonolds (2002). *Privatizing probation and parole.* National Center for Policy Analysis. Retrieved online December 14, 2004: http://www.ncpa.org/studies/s233/s233.html

54. Frank P. Williams III, Marilyn D. McShane, and H. Michael Dolny (2000). Developing a parole classification instrument for use as a management tool. *Corrections Management Quarterly, 4*(4), 45–49.

55. Most paroled Colorado inmates end up returning to prison cell (2003, September 29). *Rocky Mountain News,* 12.

56. Most paroled Colorado inmates end up returning to prison cell (2003, September 29). *Rocky Mountain News,* 12.

57. Iowa grants paroles in record numbers. *DeMoines Register* (2003, September 19), 4.

11

RESIDENTIAL INTERMEDIATE SANCTIONS

LEARNING OBJECTIVES

After you finish reading this chapter, you will be better prepared to:

- Describe residential intermediate sanctions (RIS) and how they differ from other sanctions.
- Identify the reasons RIS were developed.
- Explain the link between belief systems and RIS rationale.
- Describe boot camps, explain their rationale, and identify their common characteristics.
- Explain conceptual differences between boot camps and shock incarceration.
- Describe the catalyst for change in shock incarceration.
- Describe the historical development of halfway houses.
- Explain the association of RIS and reintegration strategies.
- Describe a typical community residential program along with its treatment strategies.
- Characterize a restitution center and provide some of its rationale and criticisms.

KEY TERMS

Boot Camp

Drug and Alcohol
  Treatment Center

Halfway House

Relapse

Residential Intermediate
  Sanctions (RIS)

Shock Incarceration

Shock Probation

We must accept the reality that to confine offenders behind walls without trying to change them is an expensive folly with short-term benefits—winning battles while losing the war.

—Former U.S. Supreme Court Chief Justice Warren Burger

INTRODUCTION

This chapter describes residential intermediate sanctions (RIS) for offenders comprised largely of younger adults and juveniles who were prison-bound violators. These violators are placed in alternative but confined programs somewhere between probation and prison. Examples include boot camps, shock incarceration, and residential community correctional facilities that can include halfway houses, restitution centers, and drug and alcohol treatment centers. Some of these alternatives are more expensive than imprisonment, but many jurisdictions continue to try new methods to help troubled offenders in keeping with former U.S. Supreme Court Chief Justice Warren Burger's thoughts that "We must accept the reality that to confine offenders behind walls without trying to change them is an expensive folly with short-term benefits—winning battles while losing the war." CC is part of what works, although each jurisdiction has its own set of remedies. For example, here's how the state of Oklahoma explains it: "Community sanctions are legally binding orders of the court or paroling authority that deprive or restrict an offender's liberty or property. An intermediate sanction is any sanction that is more rigorous (unpleasant, intrusive, or controlling) than traditional probation but less restrictive than total incarceration."[1] There are significant differences between prison and residential intermediate sanctions.

DIFFERENCES BETWEEN TRADITIONAL PRISON AND RIS

Traditional systems such as state prisons and county jails confine general convicted populations (see Table 11.1). Residential intermediate facilities often confine prison-bound populations, but participants are selected from general convicted populations (e.g., age, crime, and criminal history). Residential intermediate facilities also house former inmates during a reintegration process into the free society. Punishment and control advocates lobby that prisons should emphasize custody and control. No frill prisons. However, treatment and prevention advocates lobby that residential intermediate facilities (and prisons) should emphasize reform and accountability. Both conservatives and liberals see residential

Table 11.1   Differences between Prison/Jail* and Residential Intermediate Housing[2]

Characteristic	Prison/Jail	RIS
Population	General	Targeted
Reintegration	Not a priority	Priority
Advocates	Punishment and control	Treatment and prevention
Primary function	Custody	Accountability and reform
Boot and shock camps	Military discipline	Close supervision is a guide toward reform
Supervision	Control	Social work model
Personnel	Public	Public and private
Management	Public	Public and private

*Some prisons and jails are operated by the private sector but conform to a public correctional authority.

intermediate sanctions as meaningful for different reasons: Control advocates see boot camps and shock incarceration as one way to make room in prisons for those who really deserve it, and they tend to applaud the military-type discipline of boot and shock camps; control is a necessary element leading toward reform. Liberals, on the other hand, see these alternatives as a second chance and feel the need for close supervision (not control) by some members of society to make the right decisions once released; close supervision is needed to help offenders toward reform.

Custody and policy in traditional corrections are most often organized and staffed by government (state, local, or federal) correctional personnel. Sometimes private venders are contracted to operate facilities, and often to administer services. Residential intermediate facilities are also managed and operated by correctional personnel, but they are also managed, staffed, and directed by private-sector employees. Sometimes, private organizations, including religious and other nonprofit organizations, operate and staff residential facilities. Also, private organizations tend to conduct business in ways that are compatible with business objectives, which include profit-making interests as opposed to government objectives that tend to ignore profit-making concerns.

ADVANTAGES OF MULTIPLE ORGANIZATIONS AND AUTHORITIES

What's the advantage to having many different operators of residential intermediate programs? The numerous levels of government and private organizations operating residential intermediate programs add variety and strength to the residential intermediate community. Each can learn from others and can act as "watchdogs" of various programs. At the same time, the many variations imply little uniformity in mission, policy, and practice. Variations exist throughout the country including differences in specific regions and even within municipalities. A residential intermediate facility situated on one city block could be operated completely differently, have different policies and mandates, and service a different level (risk and needs) offender than a facility a block away. In addition, one program or facility can be called by a name that reflects the characteristics of a set of practices and expectations that are far removed from the actual practices and expectations present. One implication of this thought is that this chapter should be looked upon as presenting conceptual models of residential intermediate programs. This does not mean the models presented are the "best" or the "only" models available. The purpose of this chapter is to acquaint you with general concepts of RIS.

WHY RIS DEVELOPED

RIS developed because evidence shows traditional probation and imprisonment are unproductive, especially for first-time nonviolent offenders. They are unproductive in the sense that the primary objective of probation is supervision and prison does not necessarily deter crime (inside or outside of prison) because once released, nonviolent prisoners are more likely to engage in crimes of violence because of their prison experiences.[3] Also, RIS tend to emphasize recovering from the troubles that brought an offender to the attention of the justice system in the first place.

Ultimately, it is hoped that RIS will aid offenders toward productive lifestyles. Other objectives of RIS include reducing prison overcrowding and allowing judges greater latitude in selecting punishment that more closely fits the circumstances of the crime and the offender.[4]

BELIEF SYSTEMS OR CORRECTIONAL APPROACH

Many observers of the American prison system argue that "prisons are economically and politically profitable for businesses and politicians, at the expense of communities from which prisoners are taken and in which prisons are built."[5] The notion that "harsher punishments and longer sentences reduce crime" is highly suspect. What we know about drug offenders, for example, can produce some insight into this thought. Defendants convicted of drug possession and other less serious nonviolent crimes have a greater opportunity to reform if placed in a less punitive environment than prison. After all, prisons are dangerous places. For that reason, when policy makers, interest groups, and the public see treatment and prevention as a more productive correctional approach, practices of the justice system favor RIS, including residential sanctions for some offenders.

Just deserts advocates look upon residential intermediate sanctions as a "weak" response to offenders unless military discipline is administered. Conversely, treatment and prevention advocates see RIS as punishment that comes closer to fitting the crime. Treatment and prevention advocates also see RIS as an opportunity to aid troubled offenders. The descriptions of boot camps, shock incarceration, and residential community corrections facilities (including halfway houses, restitution centers, and drug and alcohol treatment centers) should help your understanding of these strategies.

BOOT CAMPS

In 1983, Georgia and Oklahoma were the first states to operate *boot camps*. Ten years later, 25 states and the Federal Bureau of Prisons operated a number of boot camps across the country. The number of camps varies over time as new facilities open and others close.

As the name suggests, boot camps are modeled after military boot camp training and have an historical tie to earlier CC programs such as Scared Straight, "tough love," *shock probation,* and challenge programs such as Outward Bound.[6] The term boot camp conjures immediate, usually vivid images in the minds of most of us, among them one of a platoon marching in cadence under the stern leadership of a drill sergeant. This hard-nosed, sabre-voiced drill sergeant usually dons a wide campaign hat and yells in the ear of each "cadet." This strategy is generally referred to as an "in your face" approach.

Rationale of Boot Camps

Rationale that supports boot camp existence is that young offenders have not learned rudimentary discipline and respect for authority because of "failure of parenting, inadequate socialization, or adolescent rebellion."[7] A boot camp is designed as a crash course in discipline. Responding to the increase of juvenile arrests, several states and localities established juvenile boot camps modeled after boot camps for adult offenders.[8] Early camps emphasized military discipline and physical conditioning, but there were trends towards substance abuse treatment and education as objectives, in addition to military drills and discipline.[9] The following objectives aid in the development of boot camps to:

- Alleviate prison crowding
- Become an alternative to traditional incarceration
- Lessen recidivism
- Enhance self-discipline
- Educate
- Rehabilitate (substance abuse)
- Implement physical conditioning

These objectives can be obtained at a cost per individual lower than traditional incarceration probably because confinement time is reduced in boot camps.[10]

Common Boot Camp Characteristics

The media tends to focus on the confrontational element of boot camps, but practitioners appreciate those efforts because that is not their only concern.[11] In a 1991 survey of adult and juvenile boot camps, some of the common characteristics emerged:[12]

- A military-style environment
- Separation of boot camp participants from regular prison inmates when housed in co-located facilities
- An alternative to a longer term of traditional imprisonment
- Short confinement period (e.g., 14 to 120 days)
- Some hard labor
- Some supervision after confinement

For instance, when the State of Georgia implemented its Special Alternative Incarceration (SAI) in 1983 for nonviolent young offenders, their program was designed primarily as a 90-day experience in drill, hard work, and discipline in the military boot camp model. Afterward, another 90-day period of supervision was provided toward recovery and employment assistance. Observers across the country felt that "one size fits all." There was the thought that boot camps should be identical and planned around the following characteristics:

- First-time, nonviolent offenders
- Carefully selected participants
- Separation of boot camp participants from regular prison inmates
- Programs for male and female inmates
- Shorter confinement periods than prison sentences
- Some form of supervision, surveillance, or monitoring after confinement
- Revocations or violations of rules ends any relationship with boot camp alternatives

Successfully operating in a framework of military programs depends on specifically trained correctional personnel, the correctional population under their supervision, the resources of a program, and the mission or goals of boot camp.

Boot Camp Goals

Correctional practitioners try to fulfill six common goals through boot camp programs:[13]

1. Deterrence
2. Incapacitation
3. Punishment
4. Rehabilitation
5. Cost control
6. Reducing overcrowding

Some believe that military basic training can produce lasting behavior change and therefore, deterrence is a likely product of boot camp because participants would continue to behave in a more disciplined manner after release from prison.[14] Specific and general deterrence, focused on exposing the inmates to the realities of prison life, thereby deters them from committing future crimes and deters the general public from committing crime as they see the consequences for criminal activity.[15] The second goal can be reached because boot camp takes a violator off the streets for a period of time and therefore he or she is incapacitated or unable to commit crime on the streets. The third goal, punishment, can be achieved through rigorous activity. The forth goal, rehabilitation, is thought to be accomplished through the personal discipline learned during the program, and through therapeutic treatment programs where available.[16]

The fifth goal, cost control, can be achieved in boot camps because they confine a violator for a shorter period of time than traditional confinement. This goal played a key role in the Violent Crime Control and Law Enforcement Act of 1994, which offered state and local governments federal funds to plan, build, or expand boot camps. As a result, the sixth goal could be fulfilled by freeing prison space for violent offenders.[17]

Boot Camp Size

To offset overcrowding in prisons, large boot camp capacities are necessary, and to date that hasn't happened in every jurisdiction. A small boot camp (e.g., one with 50 beds) is not likely to produce a discernible reduction in the population of a large correctional system. In addition, large, congregate-care facilities have yet to prove to be effective in rehabilitating adult or juvenile offenders.[18] Small, community facilities, on the other hand, have proved to be more effective, both as an intervention with offenders and in terms of cost to the provider.

Boot Camp Design

Physical environment or boot camp design is an issue. It can be located in a general population facility, or it can stand alone. In some correctional systems, general population facilities co-locate prisoners of medium or maximum custody level prisoners with boot camp inmates. Housing is separate, and common areas of the facility, such as the gymnasium or cafeteria, are used by boot camp inmates and regular prisoners at different times. Prisoners are dressed in different color jumpers to distinguish classification. For example, Hays State Prison at Trion, GA, is a medium security prison with a boot camp unit within its prison compound.

Stand-alone adult boot camps avoid these operational concerns. Separation from more "hardened" prisoners reduces the potential of contraband and physical violence. Also, correctional personnel prefer stand-alone units.

Boot Camp Participants

Most boot camps have participant requirements that vary, depending upon jurisdiction, policy, and resources. Selection is often recommended by a judge, and sometimes it is recommended by correctional personnel during the diagnostic and classification process of a defendant into a prison system after a sentence is imposed. Often, boot camp caseworkers have the final decision regardless of classification recommendations. Those in boot camp are usually young, first-time offenders, engaged in nonserious crimes.

Other times, boot camps can be divided into two groups: probation boot camps and inmate boot camps. Offenders, male or female, in the probation boot camp are sentenced to the program directly by the court and are referred to as "detainees." Those in the inmate boot camps (referred to as "inmates") have received prison sentences. Assuming they meet the boot camp requirements and are asked to participate, in either case, they must volunteer for the program.

In a study on boot camp eligibility in eight states, researchers found the typical criterion described in Table 11.2.[19]

Boot Camp Costs

Most boot camp's time requirements are shortened versions of traditional incarceration sentences. For instance, if a prisoner has a two-year sentence imposed, it would be suspended for boot camp participation. Program length of boot camps in the United States averages almost five months with a range of three months to almost eight months in Louisiana.[21] Therefore, costs should be less despite the intense supervision once the offender is released. However, you probably realize that boot camps cost more per inmate per day than prison or jail facilities because they offer more programming and have more staff. Each moment of the day is monopolized with discipline-type exercises such as military marching drills and calisthenics. Therefore, costs are greater for a boot camp inmate than a traditional inmate, even if the time served were equivalent. But because of the significantly shorter residential stay in boot camps, savings are realized.[22] More specifically, of 52 camps polled by the staff at the Criminal Justice Institute,[23] the daily cost per inmate per day was $67.85, with a high in Nebraska of $195.61 per day compared to a low in Kansas of $39.23. An average estimate is $170.49 for confined juveniles per day and $64.80 for confined adults per day.[24]

Table 11.2   Program Legal Eligibility and Suitability Criteria Based on Individual Characteristics of Eight State Correctional Systems

State	Gender	Age	Mental Health Requirements	Physical Health Requirements	Free from Contagious Disease	Prohibition Against Homosexuality
Florida	M	18 to 25	Yes	Yes	No	No
Georgia	M	17 to 25	Yes	Yes	Yes	No
Illinois	M/F	17 to 29	Yes	Yes	No	No
Louisiana	M/F	Up to 39	Yes	Yes	No	Yes
Oklahoma	M	17 to 25	No	No	No	No
New York	M/F	16 to 29	Yes	Yes	No	No
South Carolina	M/F	17 to 24	Yes	Yes	Yes	No
Texas	M	17 to 25	Yes	Yes	No	No

Source: Doris MacKenzie and Claire Souryal.[20]

Federal Assistance to States

The federal government aids states in establishing boot camps for juveniles through federal funding or grants. States must follow guidelines to secure federal funding. Recently, the federal government[25] indicated that states can receive help for up to 10 military-style boot camps. The camps must be located on existing or closed military installations on sites to be chosen by the agencies.[26] Boot camps should provide:

1. Highly regimented schedules of discipline, physical training, work, drill, and ceremony characteristic of military basic training.
2. Regular, remedial, special, and vocational education.
3. Counseling and treatment for substance abuse and other health and mental health problems.

Boot Camps and Commercialism

The rise of boot camps for troubled youth has produced a trend toward private boot camps, wilderness programs, and academies of all types. In part, many of these privately owned facilities advertise both short-term (30 to 60 days) or long-term availability. They emphasize military discipline as a key to behavioral changes and their targeted market is school-aged youth, grades 4 through 12. They offer pictures of largely white teenagers in close drill with clean-shaven heads escorted by a brawny drill instructor. Some camps are coed and offer educational programs that would be accredited toward high school graduation. They also offer programs for substance abuse, psychological testing, and behavior modification programs.

Most are located in rural desolated regions. Some have the appearance of a vacation lodge and are in settings by the sea or in the mountains. Finally, their price range is from $6,000 to $12,000 a month, and if a youth is enrolled for a period of a year, tuition ranges from $3,000 to $6,000 a month. In each case, tuition payments are requested in advance of a participant's arrival at camp. Some brochures include financial resources that might be available, including mortgage refinancing information.

Most camps advertise that they help troubled teens and offer testimonials from children and parents. Finally, several judges interviewed say they would allow troubled youth enrollment in a private boot camp because it would save public funds.[27] Generally, if an offender could not successfully complete a private program, a second intermediate sanction would be unlikely depending on the circumstances, such as a death in the family.

Profiles of Boot Camps

Texas Boot Camps operate two facilities that are co-located as part of a prison facility and local government operates five facilities. Their total capacity is almost 1,000 prisoners including 70 females. Philosophically, Texas' boot camps were designed to expose offenders to the realities of incarceration and to facilitate a positive change in offender behavior. To achieve this objective, the program uses summary punishment, confrontation, and re- habilitation in a military-style environment. The prison-based boot camps and the locally operated facilities are managed by a Community Supervision and Corrections Department (CSCD), with the support of the administrative judicial district judge. The targeted popu- lations for boot camp participants is from 19 to 29 nonserious, nonviolent offenders who are prison- or jail-bound. Boot camp operating costs per inmate ranged from $18 to $50 in 1997, depending on the location. Differences in costs depend on the personnel assigned to a program. Most participants are in the program for 90 days, less than 6 percent receive treatment while in local program, and none receive treatment while in the prison program. Fifty percent of their time is spent in work-related activities and 31 percent is spent in in- terpersonal activities. Structured aftercare services are available for locally operated pro- grams, but no aftercare is available for the prison-based programs. Reports on recidivism levels are inconclusive.

Camp Reams: Ohio Department of Rehabilitation and Correction.[28]   Camp Reams is a minimum-security facility on the grounds of Southeastern Correctional Institution (SCI). The camp is Ohio's first boot camp and is comprised of two buildings, one for pro- gramming and staff offices and one for inmate housing. One hundred beds are available. The camp is administered and supervised by the Unit Commander who reports directly to SCI's warden. After confinement, intense supervision is conducted in the community.

To be eligible for boot camp placement, offenders must be 18 years of age or older, in good physical and mental condition, and not engaged in violent crime. Additional screening is done at the reception centers, including medical, psychological, educational, and substance abuse assessments.

Initially, the program consists of a 90-day component, with advanced military-style training designed to emphasize behavioral conformity through repeated drills, hard labor work assignments, and physical training. Also, Adult Basic Education classes, completion of the GED program, substance abuse counseling, values clarification, decision-making skills training, and employment skills development are featured. The second phase of the program consists of another 90 days in a halfway house under limited supervision. Fi- nally, the offender serves the remainder of a sentence under parole supervision/postrelease control for six months.

Georgia's Comprehensive Correctional Boot Camp Program.   This program was built on military-style discipline, compulsory drug education modules, and postrelease follow-up in the community.[29] The Comprehensive Correctional Boot Camp Program in- cludes four types of facilities:[30] Two are inmate boot camps and intensive treatment pro- grams that house sentenced prison inmates; the other two are probation SAI/boot camps and probation detention centers that house persons who are sentenced to the boot camps as a condition of probation.

Maryland's Herman L. Toulson Correctional Boot Camp.   This camp has four fe- male and almost 300 male youthful offenders who completed the program in 2000.[31]

Eighty inmates completed their GED, 136 completed the basic literacy course, 179 completed a substance-abuse intervention program, and 85 completed vocational training. Two hundred sixty eight inmates completed an employment readiness course and 58 inmates completed a fiber-optic cable installation training course through the Anne Arundel Community College.

Do Boot Camps Work?

One study investigated recidivism among 480 male graduates, aged 16 to 40 years, who attended a southern boot camp.[32] Over a three-year period, 58 percent of the sample was returned to prison. Among the strongest predictors of recidivism were inmates' perceptions of boot camp as merely an expedient avenue to early release, future expectations of success, resilience, and several personality traits. However, age at first arrest, prior criminal history, and peer association and influence also played a primary role in these recidivism levels. It could be argued that a better method of inmate selection for boot camps must be used if recidivism levels are to be reduced.

In another study of three juvenile boot camps, participants who completed the residential program and graduated to aftercare showed marked improvements in many areas but not necessarily in recidivism levels.[33] For example, three fourths of the participants at one camp improved their performance in reading, spelling, language, and math by one grade level or more. In another facility, the average juvenile boot camp participant improved reading, spelling, and math skills by one grade level. In addition, a significant number of participants found jobs while in aftercare. But when recidivism was measured, significant reductions were not noted between the recidivism rates of juvenile boot camp participants and those of the control groups (youth confined in state or county institutions, or released on probation).

Boot Camps Conclusions

Explicit "get tough" promises made by volatile politicians to expand the use of boot camps generally find support among just desert advocates who see a lack of discipline as the principle vehicle leading to crime. Continuing along that line of reasoning, military-style boot camps would provide the discipline to make the "right" decisions. That is, boot camp supporters seem to draw a straight line from free will to discipline to crime and somehow that line ends at boot camps. In many ways, their thoughts make sense.

However, in some jurisdictions reluctant correctional administrators face a political rush to create boot camps; they may also have "lost control of boot camp development when choices about key design features were shifted from administrative to political area."[34] Some correctional executives used boot camps to reap public relations benefits. Some results helped cool the fervor over boot camps, at least regarding their impact on recidivism levels because some studies have shown "no significant difference in postrelease recidivism of boot camp graduates compared to nonparticipants."[35] Also, OJJDP's evaluation of juvenile boot camps found no significant differences in postrelease outcomes.[36] Intermediate improvements were also found, such as boot camp inmates who were less alienated by their prison experience than traditional inmates. Boot camps house offenders that would otherwise be imprisoned. Many boot camps limit eligibility to nonviolent first-time offenders. They select offenders who otherwise would receive probation and intensively supervise graduates, thereby increasing return-to-prison rates for technical violations. Cost-wise, boot camps tend to be more expensive per participant than if the participant spent the same number of days in prison. These alternatives to incarceration programs differ, as do their success rates, for a variety of reasons. The effects of boot camps on recidivism and rehabilitation are inconclusive.

SHOCK INCARCERATION

Shock incarceration (SI) is difficult to describe in general terms because of jurisdiction, program variety, and resource differences that are present across the country. There are policy makers and their constituents who think of shock incarceration typified by Dale Parent, "In a sense, shock incarceration is a program that can be—at least in perception—all things to all people."[37]

What Is SI?

SI is an alternative to traditional prison for younger, nonviolent offenders. It provides shorter incarceration periods and intense supervised aftercare. SI provides strict military-style discipline, unquestioning obedience to orders, and highly structured days with drill and physical activities. But its focus is upon therapeutic programs such as substance-abuse treatment, education, and other programs that address reintegration.[38] Most shock programs are designed toward total learning control that fosters involvement, self-direction, and accountability.

Differences Between SI and Boot Camp

The terms SI and boot camp are often used interchangeably. During a review process of boot camps, various jurisdictions, including practitioners, referred to their programs as "boot camps" or "shock" regardless of the focus or structure of their practices. One observation is that many boot camps seem to have evolved into shock incarceration systems. There are observable distinctions between boot camps and shock incarceration as illustrated in Table 11.3. However, those characteristics seem to overlap, implying that a model of either program might, at times, be unreasonable or inadequate.

SI facilities are usually managed through a state's department of corrections, whereas boot camps can be operated by variety of organizations and governmental agencies. SI facilities (including shock parole and shock probation) are more often public systems operated by state employees. It's not uncommon to see privatized boot camps operated by commercial entities, state programs, and county programs operated by sheriff deputies. SI's intended population tends to be youthful offenders between the ages of 18 to 29, whereas boot camp populations are geared toward juveniles. SI's focus is therapeutic in a highly structured organizational environment linked to stable resources, whereas boot camps tend to rely on regimented discipline linked to organizational uncertainties about management, policy, and resources.

Although both generally provide military drills, SI has specific terms such as six months confinement; boot camps tend to provide supervision within a wide range of confinement, which can run from seven days or a little longer.

The rationale of SI is to impress upon offenders the seriousness of their crimes without imposing a long prison term, although they continue the spirit of physical training like that of boot camps.[39] However, SI philosophy tends to lean upon therapeutic and educational challenges to change the attitudes of the violator as opposed to military training. On the other hand, most often the rationale linked to boot camps is that military basic training in and of itself leads to a lasting behavioral change in an offender.[40]

Although both groups of participants must meet specific criteria, SI's populations are processed through courts and state classification caseworkers who recommend SI to a

Table 11.3   Differences between SI and Boot Camp[41]

Characteristic	SI	Boot Camp
Management	State through their department of corrections	Numerous organizations and various governmental agencies including the federal government
Privatization	No	Yes
Population	18 to 29	Juveniles to age 25
Primary theme	Therapeutic in a highly structured environment that relies on regimented discipline	Regimented discipline
Organizational structure and funding	Stable	Unstable
Period of confinement	180 days	7 days to 180 days
Military drills	Yes	Yes
Rationale	Impress offender with seriousness of crime without imposing a long prison term	Military basic training causes lasting behavior change
Components that change behavior	Therapeutic and educational programs	Military discipline
Participants	Prison-bound	Volunteers, enrolled, diverted from criminal justice system, jail or prison-bound
Managers	Managers have equal or similar status as prison superintendents	Managers usually report to prison superintendents
Aftercare	Intense parole supervision for 6 to 12 months	None to some

violator (violators can accept or reject recommendation). SI participants are largely individuals who were prison-bound and volunteer for the SI option, if offered. Boot camp participants must also meet specific criteria but they can be volunteers (or enrolled by parent/s); individuals diverted through the CJ system by the police, prosecutors, or courts; or can be jail or prison-bound. Keep in mind that not every jurisdiction has SI units or boot camps.

SI confinement is generally followed by intense supervision and boot camps may or may not have a supervision requirement (aftercare programs) after completion. SI programs are probably more efficient because of their consistency and treatment emphasis. For instance, at boot camps, substance abuse programming is confined to "off hours"— during the evening and on the weekend. Moreover, boot camp programs are conducted over a brief duration (e.g., one week to six months), which is inconsistent with what is known about the length of effective drug treatment. In essence, boot camp programs, although well intentioned, lack individual conformity, structure, and too little participation time is spent in them to produce appropriate results.

Together, these aspects of drug treatment programming in boot camps may undermine the purpose and efficacy of the programs.

Finally, there are many variations of boot camps and shock incarceration that incorporate many of the characteristics of both alternatives. Often, those variations are less likely to be considered CC systems. But, they are clearly alternatives to traditional prisons, boot camps, and SI. For example: The Family Resource Center at Lakes Region Facility in New Hampshire emphasizes family values. It is designed to be a child-friendly environment. It is a safe and nurturing environment where incarcerated parents and their children who visit can maintain and further develop family bonds.[42] In June 2002, it housed 326 males and 53 females. As of July 29, 2004, women inmates were removed from the facility and transferred to Shea Farm Halfway House. Military drills are not part of the daily routine, but the programs work simultaneously to address the needs of the offender population. For instance, most programs emphasize family values, character development, and are designed to develop ownership of their lives. After 90 days of successful program time, graduates exit to either the "academy" (confinement) program or strict probation and often go directly to drug and alcohol treatment. This program is specifically for nonviolent, nonsexual offenders who may either have failed at initial probation or for whom the state feels that one more attempt at a community option is appropriate. New Hampshire records show a recidivism rate of approximately 28 percent.[43]

Selection Process

Selection criteria impacts a shock program in several ways, such as age barriers that would reduce the pool of potential candidates in a program and a widened offense criterion that might possibly deter rehabilitative efforts.[44] Physical and mental restrictions may reduce the ability of SI to achieve major goals by reducing the pool of inmates to rehabilitation programs. That is, not everyone would or could participate in every activity—impacting unity. Therefore, the selection process is relevant to SI basic operations and achievements.

SI as a Catalyst for Change

The SI experience is designed to induce stress.[45] Studies have shown that stress levels peak early when an individual is confined. To "shock" inmates into compliance or "going straight" can be accomplished with less confinement than more (depending on the prisoners). Studies show that many inmates are interested in learning about ways to improve themselves through education and treatment during periods of high emotional stress.[46] Doris MacKenzie and Clair Souryal suggest that within a period of several months, as stress levels taper off, the desire to change also tapers off.[47] The desire for change is related to the emotional distress experienced at the onset of the prison term. As you can imagine, these thoughts reveal that chances for improvement for some inmates are more likely when they first start their prison sentence.

The SI advantage is the combination of stress produced through forced physical participation and participation in rehabilitative programs that includes educational and vocational pursuits. The point is that this combination should produce "shock" graduates who wish to make positive contributions in their community, once released. However, because the basic program functions as a catalyst for change, a question remains relating to the effectiveness of the rehabilitative programs linked to shock activities.

Shock Treatment

Examination of the most and least often used treatment interventions offered at SI facilities suggests that most programs are oriented toward pragmatic skill-building as a means of helping inmates cope with problems and stressors they would face on returning to society. These approaches were identified by researchers[48] as "psychoeducational" and they focused on the following:

- Development of motivation and commitment (to overcome dependence)
- Development of life skills (e.g., fiscal management, communication skills, constructive use of time)
- AIDS education and prevention
- Relapse prevention strategies
- Development of an aftercare plan to access community resources after release

Traditional psychotherapeutic approaches, designed to uncover and deal with the offenders' underlying psychological and emotional problems, are used infrequently, researchers argue. Detoxification, pharmacological interventions, individual therapy, and family counseling were rarely used at SI facilities. The absence of programs addressing the unique psychosocial characteristics of the offender, either through individual or small group therapies, raised questions about the effectiveness of SI treatment programming. In response to these findings, keep in mind that a conflict does exist between security and treatment. That is, the job of correctional personnel including counselors leans on public safety. Their job priorities vary from a counselor in a different setting for obvious reasons.

Shock Findings

A group of 387 females and 1,546 males who participated in the Oklahoma Shock Incarceration Program (SIP) were compared with almost 3000 traditional prisoners.[49] A survival analysis was conducted to determine the difference in recidivism rates for the two groups. Recidivism rates were lower for the male inmates in the SIP group than for the male inmates who participated in conventional incarceration, and equal for the two groups of female inmates.

Shock Programs

The Illinois *Impact Incarceration Program* (IIP) is a voluntary program for nonviolent first-time and second-time offenders from ages 17 to 35 who had been sentenced up to eight years in prison.[50] The impetus for the Illinois program was prison crowding, but the program, as developed, included rehabilitative programming to improve basic education, reduce drug and alcohol abuse, and build offenders' self-esteem and life skills. A substantial aftercare component was built into the program incorporating both electronic detention and parole. The IIP uses a structured environment to address the problems that have led to the inmates' criminal activity based on three components:

- Military physical training stressing highly structured and regimented routines
- Substance abuse education, treatment, and counseling, together with basic education, life skills training, and aftercare preparation
- Gradual reintroduction to the community

The program is 120 days, with the first two weeks consisting of orientation to military bearing and physical activities. Inmates wear white jump suits to identify them as new recruits, or "ghosts." The next 90 days focus on building self-esteem through programs and treatment. The final two weeks consist of aftercare preparation for release to the community.

Aftercare is 90 days and is designed to gradually reintegrate the graduate into the community. This consists of electronic detention, random drug tests, and physical spot checks. Also, each participant is required to complete 35 hours of programs consisting of education, employment, community service, substance abuse treatment, or group therapy.

Michigan's shock incarceration program is called *Special Alternative Incarceration* (SAI).[51] Phase I of Michigan's program involves a highly disciplined regimen of 90 days consisting of military-style exercise, meaningful work assignments, and other programming such as secondary education and substance-abuse treatment. Phase II involves intensive supervision in the community, usually in a residential "halfway house" setting. Phase III involves supervision of offenders similar to the way in which probationers are supervised. Phase I and III are mandatory, and Phase II is determined by assessing a particular offender's need for residential placement.

The military discipline portion of the program is designed to break down streetwise attitudes so staff can teach positive values and attitudes. Offenders take classes in job-seeking skills, substance-abuse awareness, and anger management. They are also enrolled in General Educational Development preparation and Adult Basic Education. They perform a variety of tasks, including conservation work, recycling, park maintenance, and snow removal near senior housing.

The SAI program includes an intensive postrelease program and may include Phase II, which is placement for up to 120 days in a residential setting or on electronic monitoring. For prisoners, Phase III includes parole for 18 months or for the balance of the minimum sentence, whichever is longer. The first four months of parole are under intensive supervision, which can include daily supervision, including nights and weekends, if needed.

While in postrelease, offenders are expected to work or go to school at least 30 hours per week. They submit to random drug tests and participate in any counseling and training.

Colorado's *Youthful Offender System* (YOS) was designed to break down gang affiliations.[52] YOS is a "middle tier" between the Division of Youth Corrections (juveniles) and the Department of Corrections (adults) for violent youth felons. YOS combines a firm, disciplined regime with a full schedule of academics, work, interpersonal relations, and prevocational skills within a positive peer culture that reinforces prosocial behavior. Youth between 14 to 18 years of age charged with a violent weapons-related Class Two through Class Six felony or chronic juvenile offenders who have been directly filed by the district attorney into district court and convicted as adults are eligible. The court can suspend the adult sentence and commit the youth to the program. All sentences to YOS are determinate sentences of three to seven years and include a mandatory intensely supervised community-release program of 6 to 12 months. Here's how it works:

Intake, Diagnostic, and Orientation (IDO) (30 to 45 days) transfers an offender to the custody of YOS, orients the offender to the program, and implements a comprehensive diagnostic process. IDO emphasizes group discipline and group incentives in the context of a highly structured routine and an intense physical regimen. IDO establishes the attitudes and behaviors required for the offenders' effective participation in the positive peer culture that characterizes Phase I, which provides intensive residential programming in a secure facility. An offender can remain in Phase I for eight months to six years. This is a functional approach within a positive peer culture. Each resident engages in education, cognitive restructuring, and other programs to meet their needs.

Phase II is a three-month pre-release program that supports redirection programs and establishes the basis for an effective and well-planned Phase III community reintegration. Phase III is the community supervision and reintegration component of the program that provides intensive supervision and surveillance of the youth offenders in the community. This phase is a highly structured, intensely monitored program designed to protect the public and facilitate the habilitation of the YOS resident. A graduated decrease in the supervision intensity accompanies positive program participation, measurable attainment of defined goals and objectives, and increasingly prosocial involvement. This phase implements the ideas learned in Phase II through an interactive partnership of state and community agencies.

Females in Military-Style Programs

Although female inmates participate in boot camps and SI programs in New York, Illinois, New Hampshire, and other jurisdictions, the findings are not conclusive. Boot camps and SI facilities began accepting females in the early 1990s. However, concerns arose for female inmates in these programs because their dropout rate was higher than male inmates in similar programs.[53] Perhaps things have changed since a 1992 study that noted military-style programs were designed for male inmates and hardly fulfilled the special needs of female inmates.[54] The study noted the following concerns:[55]

- Female inmates are more likely to have children and be the sole parent for those children. Military-style programs restricted, or even banned, visitation, creating difficult situations for mothers and their children. Also the programs did not teach parenting skills.

- Female inmates are more likely to have a history of physical or sexual abuse. Although female inmates were four to five times more likely than male inmates to have been victims of physical or sexual abuse, most camps had no programs to help them cope with or avoid victimization. Derogatory boot camp tactics tended to retraumatize domestic violence victims.

- Female inmates are more likely to have a different history and pattern of drug use than males. Most substance abuse treatment used therapies designed for males.[56]

- Female inmates are more likely to have been unemployed before imprisonment. Boot camps did little to prepare women for employment after release.

- Female inmates at boot camps reported high stress levels, which may be why they tended to drop out of boot camp at a higher rate than male inmates. Stress stemmed from a physical training regimen designed for males; drill instructors' "in your face" tactics; lack of other female participants, often leading to isolation within the camp; and cross-gender supervision.[57]

Some recommendations made to help reduce female dropouts in military-style programs can include:

- Using women staff members as role models
- Addressing participants' prior victimization by building self-esteem and emphasizing empowerment and self-sufficiency
- Using nonaggressive program management styles[58]

Living in "Shock:" New York Style

Physical training begins at five in the morning for all inmates and correctional personnel (including the superintendent, psychologists, caseworkers, and instructors) at New York's Lakeview Shock Incarceration facility.[59] Inmates arrive at the facility in a group and for the next six months (other than a few who "wash out"), they eat as a group, study as a group, and sleep as a group. Anger management, substance abuse, and family relationship sessions, to name three programs, are conducted throughout the day and night and all inmates participate in every program throughout the six-month period. Every minute is planned and accounted for. There are no leisure minutes other than the supervised period when inmates can write letters to loved ones and that too is conducted for the group at a specific time.

Objectives of SI are similar to boot camps but shock emphasizes a therapeutic or treatment approach with an aim toward developing law-abiding citizens. SI encompasses drill and ceremony, physical training, work, and education, to which are added a heavy emphasis on substance abuse education, treatment, and the development of personal responsibility. These combined objectives are visible with SI, which has enjoyed popular support even from "get tough" advocates.[60]

The New York SI objectives are to:[61]

- Treat and release selected state prisoners earlier than their court-mandated minimum period of incarceration without endangering public safety
- Reduce the need for prison bed space

Graduation from New York SI is the only systemic way New York inmates can be released from prison before their minimum parole eligibility date.[62] New York operates some of the largest shock programs in the nation with a capacity in 2003 for almost 1300 males and 169 females at four different facilities located in the state at Summit, Monterey, Moriah, and Lakeview.[63]

Daily Schedule for Offenders in New York SI Facilities

A.M.	
5:30	Wake up and standing count
5:45–6:30	Calisthenics and drill
6:30–7:00	Run
7:00–8:00	Mandatory breakfast/cleanup
8:15	Standing count and company formation
8:30–11:55	Work/school schedules
P.M.	
12:00–12:30	Mandatory lunch and standing count
12:30–3:30	Afternoon work/school schedule
3:30–4:00	Shower
4:00–4:45	Network community meeting
4:45–5:45	Mandatory dinner, prepare for evening
5:45–9:00	School, group counseling, drug counseling, pre-release counseling, decision-making classes
8:00	Count while in programs
9:15–9:30	Squad bay, prepare for bed
9:30	Standing count, lights out

New York State Department of Correctional Services, Lakeview Shock Incarceration Camp. Photo by Dennis J. Stevens with permission by the superintendent.

The discipline continues during breakfast, lunch, and dinner. Photo by Dennis J. Stevens with permission of the superintendent.

Forty percent of an inmate's time is in treatment and education, which are divided as follows:

- Physical training, drill, and ceremony (26 percent)
- Treatment and education sessions to treat addictions (28 percent)
- Academic education (13 percent)
- Hard labor on facility and community projects (33 percent)

Physical Training, Drill, and Ceremony.   Each morning from 5:45 to 7:00 A.M., participants perform calisthenics and run. Throughout the day, inmates march to and from activities in platoon or squad formation. Three times a day, formal company formations of platoons muster before physical training, work, or school and evening programs.

Once they graduate, they return to their respective community but remain under DOC intense supervision for another six months.

Work.   Participants perform six hours of hard work per day while in SI, arranged in two three-hour periods before and after lunch. Camp is located adjacent to state conservation land where SI inmates maintain public use areas. Inmates also work on the ground of the SI camp and on municipality projects around the facility. Inmates who graduate SI perform 650 hours of hard work.

Females and males during calisthenics and drill beginning at 5:45 A.M.
Photo by Dennis J. Stevens with permission of the superintendent.

Network.   This therapeutic approach has been used in DOC facilities since 1978, but because of recent budges cuts, the program now functions in SI facilities. Network emphasizes a decisional approach to problem solving and building self-esteem using a five-step model taught in 12 sessions. An emphasis on family issues and parenting skills is part of most SI curriculums because around 75 percent of the female inmates and half of the male inmates are parents.

Inmates are formed into platoons and they live together as a unit; they hold a Network community meeting daily to resolve problems and reflect on their progress. Network helps inmates adjust to community living and develop socialization, decision-making, and critical thinking skills.

All staff, officers, counselors, supervisors, teachers, and support staff in SI facility are trained in Network methods so that the skills are reinforced in every aspect of every program. Community agencies and volunteers are also encouraged to participate. For instance, The Network Program objectives are grouped into three basic areas:

- Responsibility for self
- Responsibility to others
- Responsibility for the quality of one's life

Network teaches that to make responsible decisions, participants must consider their own wants and needs, the effect they have others, and their own particular situations. It

Female inmates at Lakeview participate in a Network session. Photo by Dennis J. Stevens with permission of the superintendent.

teaches them that responsible behavior results from recognizing the differences between wants, needs, and learning appropriate ways of meeting those wants and needs. One emphasis is couched in the perspective that criminal behavior and substance abuse are negative, dysfunctional attempts to meet one's needs versus a sense of self-worth and personal pride, which are the foundations of a responsible lifestyle.

Substance Abuse Treatment.   New York emphasizes alcohol and substance abuse treatment. All SI inmates are required to participate in Alcohol and Substance Abuse Treatment (ASAT), a drug education and group counseling program for 6 hours per week.

ASAT is based on the 12-step recovery program of Alcoholics Anonymous and Narcotics Anonymous and is staffed by trained substance abuse counselors. Materials from the Network program are also included in the curriculum. All materials are in English and Spanish.

Education.   Improved educational achievement is a central objective of New York's SI program. All inmates spend 12 hours in academic work each week and some spend more. Over the course of their stay, participants complete at least 260 hours of academic education including remedial education, basic high school equivalency classes, and preparation for the GED. Offenders who have completed high school or obtained a GED spend these hours as tutors or literacy volunteers. In fulfillment of the Network concept, this education program also draws on community resources and volunteers.

Intense Community Supervision.   Intense Community Supervision is called "aftershock." Operated by the New York Division of Parole, the goals of aftershock are similar to SI's objectives with an emphasis on substance abuse counseling. Caseloads usually consist of one parole officer for every 19 SI graduates. Home visits, drug testing, and curfew checks are routine. Many graduates of aftershock are hired by contracted companies who supply services to the participants, such as Vern Institute of Justice and the Fellowship Center in New York City.

Saving Money in New York

The NYDOCS reports that SI saves money for state taxpayers in two ways: by reducing expenditures for care and custody and avoiding capital costs for new prison construction. If SI were not available, 40 percent of the SI participants would go to medium security facilities. Shock graduates are released from the New York SI program 354 days before their earliest possible release without the shock program. Some further facts about the New York's Shock program are:

- For each 100 SI graduates, NYDOCS saves approximately $2.73 million, which it otherwise would have spent for the care and custody of those inmates.[64]
- For 3,140 releases from SI as of July 2004, there was an estimated savings in program costs of one billion dollars since its inception in the late 1980s.[65]

- Only 32 percent of shock graduates return to prison within three years of release compared to a return rate of 40 percent among shock-eligible nonparticipants and 48 percent among shock dropouts, who together serve an average of 18 months in prison.[66]
- New Yorkers saw a budget savings of $878 million in operating costs because, without SI inmates would have spent at least another 12 months in prison. Those longer prison stays would also have necessitated $126 million in capital construction of the additional prison beds that would have been necessary to house them.[67]

NYDOC reveals that one of the least publicized components of SI is community service conducted by inmates. Each year, supervised crews of shock inmates perform thousands of hours of community service as part of their daily routine. It is estimated in 2000 that they performed 1.2 million hours of community service. If the municipalities that were helped had hired laborers at a federal minimum wage of $5.15 per hour to accomplish those tasks, it would have cost the community around $6.2 million. SI in New York appears to provide many benefits for its eligible inmates and for the community.

HALFWAY HOUSES

Policy makers who focused exclusively on punishment under community supervision now realize that extending treatment or other needed services can reduce the odds of recidivism and enhance public safety.[68] The employment of a *halfway house* is halfway between prison and the community, and it is there that an offender can better prepare to enter the community.

Historical Development of the Halfway House

The concept of a transitional residence for prisoners probably had its origins in England and Ireland during the early 1800s. In America, the Massachusetts Prison Commission in 1817 attempted to establish a temporary residence to house destitute former prisoners but failed. The Massachusetts Legislature felt that promoting common living arrangements for offenders would enhance crime. They would "contaminate" each other.

In 1845, the Isaac T. Hooper Home in New York City opened its doors to female offenders and continues to operate today. It was the world's first halfway house for released female prisoners and eventually became the Women's Prison Association and Home managed by Abigale Hooper Gibbons, a famous prison reformer.[69]

Another New York City facility, Hope House, opened in 1896, supported by private funds. Early in the 1900s, Hope Houses opened in many cities across the nation, including Chicago, New Orleans, and San Francisco. Those attempts eventually failed because of a lack of funds, a "contamination" belief, and the Great Depression, which weakened any government promise of financial support. The rebirth of the halfway house came as a result of an awareness of the high recidivism levels among released prisoners. In 1954, numerous halfway houses opened in the United States, such as the Crenshaw House in

Los Angeles and Dismas House in St. Louis. Private and religious groups pioneered the halfway house movement in the United States.

In 1961, Attorney General Robert Kennedy provided federal funds to advance publicly operated halfway houses for youthful offenders. The attention of halfway homes led the way to the Prisoner Rehabilitation Act of 1965. One result arising from this legislation was that it authorized the Federal Bureau of Prisons to establish community residences for adults and youthful offenders and justified state and private halfway houses, day reporting centers, restitution centers, work furlough centers, and correctional treatment facilities outside of prison walls. It promoted transfers of federal prisoners to privately sponsored halfway houses.

Referrals to a Halfway House

The primary way an individual enters a halfway house is as a former prisoner who has been conditionally released or paroled from prison. The purpose of a halfway house referral is to have a place to live while being "processed" out of the system. The halfway house provides the participant with a place to sleep and an address from which to apply for referrals to community health services including welfare, job training, and development, and to help secure personal identification such as a driver's license.[70] Halfway houses also provide authorities with an opportunity to continue surveillance of an offender and to aid an offender in treatment options while preparing to enter the community.

Other methods of referral are when prisoners have not been released through parole but are in the process of release. While at the halfway house, these individuals remain under DOC supervision because they remain prisoners until their release date, which is sometime in the future, assuming all things move along without disciplinary problems, such as violating curfew or getting drunk. A violation could result in returning an inmate to prison to serve the remainder of a prison sentence.

Most paroled inmates do not reside in halfway houses. A third way an inmate could be referred to a halfway house once paroled is after living in the community, when unanticipated problems arise such as unemployment or health issues. A halfway house could accept a referral from a supervising agency to aid a parolee until the problem is resolved.

At the federal level, the U.S. Bureau of Prisons established prerelease guidance centers in many cities across the country. Offenders are referred to a prerelease guidance center months before a prison release for the purpose of freeing prison space, aiding the offender toward reintegration, and saving on prison costs. From the perspective of the offender, he or she can attend school, seek employment, and find a place to live before an actual release. Many states have followed the model of the federal government.[71]

Halfway Houses and the Legal System

Much of the push toward halfway houses came after the decriminalization of public drunkenness that followed the adoption of the Uniform Alcoholism and Intoxication Treatment Act of 1971. The Uniform Act mandates the provision for a continuum of

Alcohol Abuse Recovery Homes (Halfway Houses)

Darrell Irwin[72]
University of North Carolina at Wilmington

Alcoholism researcher George Valliant says that when doctor, family, and patient agree that the patient has an illness that requires treatment, the provision of treatment can begin.[73] Within community corrections halfway house models, there are two types of housing for alcoholic offenders: one is a nonpunitive shelter to the actively drinking offender and another is an alcohol-free halfway house for the destitute participant trying to say sober.[74] Following sobriety and rehabilitation, many alcoholics are referred to alcohol abuse recovery homes or, as they are commonly known, halfway houses. Halfway houses are bridges between inpatient hospitalization and the outside world. The idea of "halfway in" and "halfway out" is common whether the purpose of the program is alcoholic or psychiatric treatment or offender rehabilitation among offenders. Proponents of the halfway house movement consider its experimental and innovative nature as one of its strengths.

A one-day census of the nearly one million people in drug treatment in 1994 in the United States found that 24,348 were in halfway or recovery houses.[75] The halfway/recovery house is rated by the American Society of Addictive Medicine (ASAM) as ASAM Level III.1, suitable for a population of clinically managed low intensity patients. This care level targets clients that have unsafe living environments, need time to develop their recovery skills, and have manageable medical or psychological problems.[76]

After referral to a halfway house, alcoholics are expected to perform the daily tasks of living and working. Alcoholics living in halfway houses are sometimes attempting these tasks for the first time in their lives. Royce and Scratchley recognize the emphasis on habilitation, stating a "supportive environment is more necessary when the patient has been a homeless drifter or otherwise leading an unstructured life."[77]

A structured living situation benefits the homeless or those who come from a home that contributed to their alcoholism such as female alcoholics living with abusive drinkers. Halfway houses offer less formal settings in which alcoholics develop personal relationships with other residents and staff. The halfway house is often designed to create a family atmosphere providing a surrogate family that was often missing in the alcoholic's home life. For others, the family home may provide the support and stability needed for recovery.[78] The alcoholic may become more autonomous by holding down a job, however the alcoholic must return to the house at night after work.

coordinated services intended for all alcoholics. When states began following the Uniform Act, the criminal justice system was removed as a sanction for public drunkenness and replaced by an alternative health care system that was designed to deal with public inebriates. Halfway houses were one alternative institution that emerged in this new health care approach to alcoholism.

In short, the move toward decriminalization involved a removal of criminal sanctions and a substitution of the use of health care facilities for alcoholics. Inebriates could no longer be denied treatment because of previous withdrawal from treatment or relapses after treatment, reflecting the chronic nature of alcoholism. In effect, the Uniform Act and decriminalization of public drunkenness made all treatment for alcoholism voluntary. For the alcoholic who may be lacking social support and not yet assured of recovery, the halfway house became an option in the continuum of care.

An Example of a Typical Halfway House

Oxford Houses represent a typical concept in self-run, self-supported recovery houses.[79] The first Oxford House was started in Washington, DC in 1975 and has spread to 39 states and 263 cities. Presently, there are 630 Oxford Houses that are chartered to a group of individuals who are recovering alcoholics and drug addicts. Oxford House charters are free, but each group of individuals that reside in the houses must follow three conditions to keep their charter. These conditions are:

- The house must operate using democratic principles
- The group must be financially self-supporting
- Any resident who uses drugs or alcohol is immediately expelled

Oxford Houses and other self-run halfway houses are nonprofit, tax exempt, publicly supported corporations that proliferated as a result of the Anti-Drug Abuse Act of 1988. This federal legislation, *PL–100–690,* requires each state to establish a revolving fund to make loans to cover the security deposit and first month's rent for groups of recovering individuals who wish to start a recovery home. These individuals receive the knowledge and support from Oxford House to establish and operate a successful house. Once a charter is granted, often with help from local members of Alcoholics Anonymous or Narcotics Anonymous, a recovering individual can reside in an Oxford House as long as he or she does not drink or use drugs. Expulsion is the penalty once a majority of residents (51 percent) believe that any member has relapsed into using alcohol or drugs. However, there is no pressure on anyone in good standing to leave. Pressure from authorities is not often conducive to recovery from alcoholism. Peer pressure is often a more effective substitute and therefore utilized by these self-run recovery houses.

Economics of Halfway Houses

Treatment of alcoholism is often viewed from a "continuum of care" perspective. Although this ranges from initial detoxification to primary residential treatment to outpatient care, the actual availability and affordability of care are issues that concern alcoholics and their loved ones. An important criteria for medical payment is cost effectiveness and level of care. Much of alcoholism treatment and aftercare is paid for by third-party payees such as medical insurance and managed care companies.

Special Populations and Halfway Houses

Female alcoholics confront special challenges in the treatment of alcoholism. These challenges begin with finding a suitable program for treatment. A study conducted by the Association of Halfway House Alcoholism Programs of North America reported that, among a representative sample of nationwide halfway houses, 56 percent served men only, 35 percent were coed, and only 9 percent served women only.[80] Further, the 161 coed houses only reserved 19 percent of all available beds for women. Another survey, conducted in New York State, found that in 45 inpatient alcoholism facilities, only 17 percent of all beds were allocated for women.[81] The problem of treatment of women alcoholics appears to be systemic.

Treatment Results

Alcoholics commonly stay three to six months in halfway houses following hospital treatment. During this time, the halfway house will try to equip its members with self-sufficiency skills before returning them to the community. A follow-up study of men who were admitted to halfway houses in Ontario, Canada showed that in a three-month period, 51 percent of them had an officially recorded drunkenness episode.[82] This proportion was similar to a control group of men who had not entered the halfway house. A second finding was that the subsequent incidence of drunkenness among the halfway house residents was unrelated to the length of stay at the halfway house.[83]

Another study on treatment and relapse in a halfway house found that only about 20 percent of alcoholic halfway house residents were sober six months after discharge.[84] The researcher found that the tensions existed in halfway houses over adherence to group norms. Residents must submit to the authority structure of the house. The main exertion of authority came from the staff, but the residents were interested in reducing that authority. From the tension created in such a residence came a typology of residents within the halfway house. The majority of these residents were labeled "regular guys" who are found in greater numbers in halfway houses and who relapse more frequently. One conclusion from this study was that recovery and relapse are a group phenomenon that happens within a given social context. Houses may produce relapse when recovery is intended. Intergroup relations within such a treatment setting produce several types of friendship groups. Although not actively discouraging residents from associating with one another outside the houses, it was clear to Rubington that when these friendship groups extend after treatment, a certain number of relapses were inevitable. The two types of relapses that frequently occurred were paired relapse, when either two residents left treatment together and got intoxicated, or sequential relapse, when one person relapses and another feels compelled to follow his or her example.[85] The researcher argues that "the test of a halfway house's success is the number and kinds of sober roles ex-residents perform after membership and the kinds of groups in which they perform them."[86]

To view the recovering alcoholic in a halfway house setting locates the marginality of coping styles of those clients utilizing this treatment modality. Treatment models must match alcoholics with approaches ranging from the promotion of a healthy self-concept, interactional group therapy, and coping skills treatment within the halfway houses. The paradox becomes how one might achieve the "creation of environments—not programs— capable of supporting sober individuals in low-income housing once formal treatment ends."[87] Levels of program intensity vary among halfway houses. At one end exists a group living situation and at the other end exists an inpatient rehabilitation center. The battle for recovery in alcoholism often requires the care provided by the structured environment found in a halfway house setting.

Uses of Halfway Houses

Although the function of halfway houses seems to be consistent with their original intent, a safe haven while offenders attempt to reintegrate back into society, the role of halfway houses has changed from that of a shelter to that of a facilitator. In light of the number of prisoners utilizing their facilities and the knowledge of various needs required of offenders to alter their behavior, this thought should come as no surprise. For instance, there is a link between alcohol and crime:[88]

- Among the 5.3 million convicted offenders under the jurisdiction of corrections agencies in 1996, nearly 2 million, or about 36 percent, were estimated to have been drinking at the time of the offense. The vast majority, about 1.5 million, of these alcohol-involved offenders were sentenced to supervision in the community—1.3 million on probation and more than 200,000 on parole.

- Alcohol use at the time of the offense was commonly found among those convicted of public-order crimes, a type of offense most highly represented among those on probation and in jail. Among violent offenders, 41 percent of probationers, 41 percent of those in local jails, 38 percent of those in state prisons, and 20 percent of those in federal prisons were estimated to have been drinking when they committed the crime.

Most offenders have drug or alcohol abuse problems prior to incarceration; therefore, it makes sense for halfway houses to aid offenders with their problem to alter the criminal behavior. In addition, halfway houses are facilities for more than adult former prisoners. Today, many halfway houses cater to other groups such as juveniles, probationers, the accused awaiting trial, and offenders directly sentenced for treatment, ordered by a judiciary eager to secure service, and supervision for offenders.

More than 600,000 prisoners leave prisons and jail in a given year to begin the difficult transition that many often fail.[89] Sixty two percent are expected to be arrested at least once within the next three years and 41 percent will be returned to jail or prison.[90] A halfway house is halfway out of prison and halfway back into the community.[91] Some halfway houses also function as prerelease guidance centers. The idea of gradual release into the community by former prisoners has benefits in the sense of helping an inmate move closer to a crime-free lifestyle.[92] The term "halfway house" seems obsolete. A more accurate description of halfway houses for the 21st century might be "community corrections residential facility."[93]

COMMUNITY RESIDENTIAL CENTERS

Community residential centers (CRCs) are nonconfining residential facilities for adults and juveniles who have been or are being processed through the justice system. CRCs are intended as alternatives for individuals not suited for probation or in need of a period of readjustment to the community after incarceration. Most CRCs provide transitional and extensive services for youthful offenders and juveniles and some specialize in specific client groups. As implied, many halfway houses have evolved into community residential centers and provide (or contract) specialized treatment.

Reasons for Change of Halfway Houses to CRCs

The change of halfway house services to CRCs was influenced by several factors:

1. Dramatic acknowledgment of assessed needs of individuals under DOC supervision
2. Beliefs changing from a punishment to a treatment approach
3. Reconciliation, restitution, rehabilitation, and reintegration taking center stage
4. Correctional acceptance of the reintegration mission

Dramatic acknowledgment of assessed needs of individuals under DOC supervision. As previously mentioned, alcohol and drug abusers are crowded into prisons, parole, and probation caseloads. To help alter the behavior of those offenders, their own alcohol and drug issues require attention. There are also other assessed needs that promote CRCs. For instance, an estimated 283,800 mentally ill offenders were held in the nation's state and federal prisons and local jails at midyear 1998.[94] An additional 547,800 mentally ill people were on probation in the community.[95] Offenders identified as mentally ill were more likely than other offenders incarcerated or on probation to have committed a violent offense. An estimated 13 percent of the mentally ill state prisoners had committed murder, 12 percent rape or sexual assault, 13 percent robbery, and 11 percent assault. Nearly one in five violent offenders in prison or jail or on probation were identified as mentally ill. Also, over 40 percent of the mentally ill were unemployed prior to the judicial process. If they are going to be released, they will need jobs or a form of support.

Beliefs have changed from punishment to treatment approaches. The pendulum continues to swing because of expectations that have not been reached regarding the high recidivism rates and higher incarceration costs. CC options are less expensive to operate.

As the net widens to include more middle class citizen prisoners, their family members, networks, and friends influence imprisonment options more often than former generations. Of course, this is not to say that the pendulum of beliefs cannot swing back.

Reconciliation, restitution, rehabilitation, reintegration, and restorative justice are taking center stage.   Experts have learned that CC services emphasizing all or part of the Five Rs are more likely to turn troubled behavior around. Less concern with custody issues provides a focus on the Five Rs.

Correctional acceptance of the reintegration mission.   Reintegration, in particular, seems to be woven into most community programs. Many professionals are aware of the success of the reintegration movement in the mental health field and hope to earn similar successes in CC. The role of mental health has changed in corrections because corrections is legally obliged to provide needed health services to all participants including those in CC. This thought is consistent with the President's Commission on Law Enforcement and Administration of Justice of 1965. That is, it called for mobilization and change of the community and its institutions, which includes CC.

Some argue that to achieve the objectives of reintegration, CC needs to meet the following criteria:[96]

- A location and interaction within a community that offers opportunities to fit an offender's needs
- A nonsecure environment (the offender's home, a surrogate home, or a community residence) in which the offender lives as a responsible person with minimal supervision
- Community-based education, training, counseling, and support services
- Opportunities to assume (or learn) the normal social roles of citizen, family member, student, or employee
- Opportunities for personal growth

CRC Treatment

The various needs and risks of offenders in CRCs (and elsewhere throughout the correctional system) would stagger your imagination. For instance, many offenders are referred to the courts as a result of their mental health problems,[97] a trend that is more likely to continue regardless of federal legislation to do otherwise.[98] Some centers operate 24-hour crisis intervention counseling to aid mentally ill participants who have addictions and others provide close supervision over suicide risks. Inside some CRCs, intervention is underway for survivors of suicide attempts and sexual abuse and incest, support groups for offenders with learning disabilities and basic literacy programs, basic and updated job skills training, hygiene training (how to keep clean), and drug and alcohol counseling and prevention intervention. The finest textbooks in corrections cannot adequately explain the enormous effort made by most correctional personnel to aid those under their supervision and care, nor can they describe the painful experiences of most correctional participants.

Addiction has powerful biological and behavioral dimensions. For many, treatment is a long-term process that involves multiple interventions and attempts at abstinence.[99] Often, offenders might have both an addiction and a mental illness. Many community residential centers focus on Alcoholics Anonymous and Narcotics Anonymous as part of the overall abstinence program. Even the most severely addicted offenders can participate in treatment and reduce their drug use. But the benefits do not stop there. Every dollar invested in correctional treatment, whether it's CRCs or day-reporting centers, reduces the cost of drug-related crime, criminal justice costs, and theft by four to seven dollars.[100] When health care savings are included, total estimated savings could be as high as a ratio of 12:1.[101] Treatment also improves the stability of family and community life and improves an individual's employment opportunities. Helping offenders to support themselves would reduce welfare support to many families and individuals, which would represent another large savings and, equally important, pave the way for many individuals to take pride in their own achievements.

CRC Programs

A previous chapter explained that a significant percentage of offenders demonstrate behavioral, physical, and mental problems that often represent a clear and present danger to themselves and others, including correctional personnel and property and the community. To enhance public safety, correctional systems that include CRCs determine offender needs and risks through assessment process.[102] Offenders are then placed in programs that fit their needs and at risk levels that do not compromise public safety.

However, CRC programs are frequently criticized. For example, the merits of Alcoholics Anonymous and Narcotics Anonymous tend to be debated whether promoted through a correctional system or independently, and from time to time they are attacked in court. CRC residents must memorize and act out the 12 Steps of AA. Participants must demonstrate an understanding of the program, design a postrelease plan, chair an AA or NA meeting, and participate in the affairs of the program. The latter might include house chores, such as cleaning the facility, attending house meetings, working outside the program, and of course, remaining sober and clean.

A national survey of CRCs of more than 1,000 agencies in 1991 found a combination of drug treatment and work-release programs. The three most frequent types of services provided to clients were job development, drug testing, and counseling. In descending order, their clients were in prison prerelease, were inmates, and were on probation. In 1991, more than 16 offenders were diverted from incarceration into CRC. The rate of program completion was more than 70 percent and the failure rate totaled 3 percent.[103]

Another study examined the effectiveness of various levels of coercion during substance abuse counseling and determined that legally referred clients (offenders under supervision) do as well or better than voluntary clients in and after treatment.[104]

Despite some variation in findings, empirical studies have largely supported the use of coercive measures to increase the likelihood of an offender's entering and remaining in treatment. Sometimes offenders mask their use of illegal substances, including alcohol and narcotics, in a variety of ways. Some ways are inventive and other ways are less than imaginative. One problem is when CRC offenders mask their use of illegal substances with prescription medications, either to get high or to cover illegal drug use. This technique presents a challenge to CRC caseworkers and counselors.[105]

A Typical CRC in Florida

The Bradenton Drug Treatment Center in Tampa, FL operates as a residential therapeutic community treatment program housing approximately 70 youthful (16 to 24 years of age) offenders in Manatee County.[106] The program is designed to address the needs of offenders who have been sanctioned to probation or community control and have been identified as having a chronic substance abuse problem. The program is broken into three treatment components with Phase I of the program operating through a cooperative effort between the Florida Department of Corrections staff and the contract treatment staff of Operation Par Inc.

Phase I lasts six months and includes programs such as anger management, problem-solving skills, stress management, parenting skills, financial planning, leisure skills, and relapse intervention groups.

Phase II is three to six months of residential treatment in a nonsecure facility operated by Operation Par Inc. This phase provides the offender with transitional housing, as well as continued substance abuse treatment programming. Offenders in Phase II prepare themselves for life in the community through a transition curriculum. Phase III lasts from six to nine months and consists of community supervision, job development, education and vocational training, and continued outpatient aftercare substance abuse treatment.

RESTITUTION CENTERS

Restitution centers (RCs) are facilities that receive court-ordered remand of offenders who must reside in the facility, work, compensate victims for their losses, face their victims in victim-offender reconciliation sessions, learn to appreciate the impacts of their criminal behavior on victims, and save money for use on their return to the community.[107] Restitution or compensation to victims for their losses at the hands of the offender also implies the restoration of something to its rightful owner or condition. Specifically, RCs are residential facilities in which offenders voluntarily participate in activities designed to assist the offender in paying back individual victims of crime and society as a whole. Residents pay room and board fees (e.g., $20 a day). Activities include community service work, full-time employment, counseling programs, and educational programs.

RCs: A National Perspective

Most residential RCs are designed as a diversion program and to teach participants to become accountable to victims.[108] A victim may be an individual or society as a whole. Residential RCs have also been designed to provide a positive environment for offenders to cultivate productive law-abiding behaviors. The programs in RCs may encompass a number of components like those found in CRC but the focus is on victim restitution and system reconciliation. If possible, restorative justice may well follow restitution and reconciliation principles. Research has found that restitution can create an atmosphere of reconciliation between the offender and victim(s). It has also been discovered that citizens are more willing to support programs that provide a tangible redress for criminal acts and assurances for public safety.[109] For instance, in Texas, the court can place an offender in a community corrections facility (CCF), such as an RC, for a period of no less than 1 month and no more than 24 months.[110] Residents work full time, perform community service restitution, and attend educational and rehabilitative programs. Residents' income covers part of the cost of room and board, restitution to victims, familial obligations, and court-ordered fines and fees.

Effectiveness of Community Residential Programs

Recent studies on the effectiveness of CC programs including halfway houses and CRCs reveal that most information on the subject is suspect because most assessments linked to effectiveness describe processes or correctional activity rather than outcomes.[111] There is an urgent need to produce easy-to-read data that shows evidence-based outcomes. But evaluation of effectiveness of community residential houses including halfway houses should also require consideration across three dimensions:[112]

- Humaneness
- Recidivism
- Cost studies

Humaneness is a vital component to community residential centers of all types. They are more humane than prisons. There are some thoughts that it is difficult to measure whether humaneness objects have been reached in favor of more quantifiable data such as recidivism.

Recidivism is more complex to measure than expected because participants represent parolees, probationers, pretrial detainees, work releasees, and furloughees. They also are under federal, state, and local jurisdiction, making it difficult to compare outcomes. Recidivism studies that do exist show success with about 71 percent of the participants tested, and in-program rearrest rates of 2 to 17 percent.[113] Other recidivism studies of alcohol abusing participants show success rates ranging from 70 to 80 percent; driving under the influence rates can be significantly reduced with CRC treatment as high as 92 percent.[114] On the whole, recidivism studies of CRC participants perform no worse than offenders who receive other correctional sanctions. But there is evidence that CRC residents have more needs than other offenders.

Finally, there are some general criticisms about CRC:[115]

- Many CRCs inadequately assess offenders' needs and risk levels
- There are few distinctions made between offenders based on risk

- Qualifications of staff are not as high as expected.
- Staff turnover is high, probably because of low pay and burnout.
- Generally, many CRC facilities can be classified as one step above "three hots and a cot" by some offenders.
- The public supports the CRC mission on the surface but rejects the idea that CRC facilities are situated in their neighborhood and especially not on their block.

SUMMARY

RIS is characterized by prison-bound violators placed in an alternative confinement program somewhere between probation and prison (e.g., boot camps, shock incarceration, and residential CC facilities that include halfway houses and community restitution centers). Key differences between RIS facilities and jail or prison are that RIS emphasizes reintegration, treatment and prevention, accountability and reform, close supervision as a guide toward reform, the social work model, and the fact that public and private organizations can operate them. RIS developed because traditional probation emphasizes supervision and imprisonment does not necessarily deter crime, especially for first-time offenders.

Boot camps tend to be less expensive than other forms of confinement largely because they are shortened versions of traditional incarceration. The rationale behind boot camp existence is that young offenders have not learned rudimentary discipline and respect for authority because of a failure of parenting, inadequate socialization, or adolescent rebellion. A boot camp is designed as a crash course in discipline. Therefore, military discipline and physical conditioning are emphasized but some are moving toward education and treatment. Boot camps tend to house younger, nonviolent offenders. SI is also an alternative to traditional custody and provides strict military discipline with highly structured days, but focuses on therapeutic programs, educational advancement, and reintegration of offenders. It has an aftercare component based on intense parole strategies. Unlike boot camps, SI tends to have a stable organizational structure, is operated by state government, and is more structured toward inmate reform. Many inmates in SI were originally sent to medium security facilities that would have cost the state more money than SI, and SI's recidivism levels are lower when aftercare is provided.

Halfway houses were once largely for prisoners on their way to freedom after a prison term. They have evolved into CRCs that provide treatment and employment opportunities in a drug- and alcohol-free environment. CRC programs emphasize reintegration and are now for defendants who are being processed through or being processed out of the justice system. The change of halfway houses and other similar facilities to CRCs was influenced by several factors: dramatic acknowledgment of assessed needs of individuals under DOC supervision; beliefs changing from a punishment to a treatment approach; reconciliation, restitution, rehabilitation, and reintegration taking center stage; correctional acceptance of the reintegration mission; and lower cost of halfway houses as compared to prisons.

RCs are facilities that receive court-ordered remand of offenders who must reside in the facility, work, compensate victims for their losses, face their victims in victim-offender reconciliation sessions, learn to appreciate the impact of their criminal behavior on victims, and save money for use on their return to the community. Most residential restitution centers are designed as a diversion program to reduce the number of commitments to prisons, to address declining appropriations from legislatures, and to pay back victims of crime. Although it is difficult to evaluate the outcomes of restitution centers, it was suggested that humaneness along with recidivism and costs become part of an equation to determine effectiveness. Studies have shown that recidivism levels of RC participants perform no worse than offenders who receive other correctional sanctions. But there is evidence that RC residents have more needs than other offenders. Finally, there are some general criticisms about RC, which among others include the idea that CRC inadequately assess offenders' needs and risk levels.

DISCUSSION QUESTIONS

1. Describe RIS and explain in what way they differ from other criminal justice sanctions.
2. Identify the reasons RIS were developed.
3. Explain the connection between the belief systems or correctional approaches that support RIS.
4. Describe the primary characteristics of most boot camps and provide some of the rationale that supports their existence.
5. In what way might boot camps be more effective than other criminal justice sanctions?
6. Describe SI and explain the merits of its selection process.
7. Explain conceptual differences between boot camps and SI.
8. Describe the catalyst for change in SI and its aftercare.
9. Describe the historical development of halfway houses and explain why halfway houses evolved into what they are today.
10. Explain the association of RIS and reintegration strategies.
11. Describe a typical community residential program along with one of its treatment strategies.
12. Characterize a restitution center and provide some of its rationale and criticisms.

NOTES

1. State of Oklahoma. Department of Corrections. Retrieved online August 20, 2004: http://www.doc.state.ok.us/CommSentence/comm_sanctions.htm
2. Dennis J. Stevens (2006). *Community corrections: An applied approach.* Upper Saddle River, NJ: Prentice Hall.

3. Norval Morris and Tonry Michael (1997). *Between prison and probation: Intermediate punishment in a rational sentencing system.* New York: Oxford University Press. William M. DiMascio (1997). *Seeking justice: Crime and punishment in America.* New York: Edna McConnell Clark Foundation. Jeffrey Reiman (2000). *The rich get richer and the poor get prison.* Boston: Allyn & Bacon. Randall G. Shelden (2001). *Controlling the dangerous classes: A critical introduction to the history of criminal justice.* Boston: Allyn & Bacon.

4. William M. DiMascio (1997).

5. William M. DiMascio (1997). Randall G. Shelden (2001.)

6. Dale G. Parent (1989). *Shock incarceration: An overview of existing program.* Washington, DC: US Department of Justice (xii).

7. Billie S. Erwin (1996). Discipline in Georgia's correctional boot camps. In Doris L. MacKenzie and Eugene E. Herbert (Eds.), *National Institute of Justice Report: Correctional boot camps: A tough intermediate sanction* (Chapter 12). KCI Website. Retrieved online December 29, 2004: http://www.kci.org/publication/bootcamp/docs/nij/Correctional_Boot_Camps/table_context.htm

8. Michael Peters, David Thomas, Christopher Zamberlan, Caliber Associates (1997, September). *Boot camps for juvenile offenders: Program summary.* Washington, DC: Office of Juvenile Justice and Delinquency Prevention, Department of Justice, Office of Justice Programs.

9. United States General Accounting Office (GAO) (1993). *Prison boot camps: Short-term prison costs reduced, but long-term impact uncertain.* Washington, DC. Retrieved online August 20, 2004: http://www.gao.gov/

10. Doris MacKenzie and Claire Souryal (1994). *Multisite study of corrections boot camps.* KCI Institute (Chapter 18). Retrieved online December 28, 2004: http://www.kci.org/publication/bootcamp/docs/nij/Correctional_Boot_Camps/chpt18.htm. B. Borque and S. Hill (1996). *A national survey of aftercare provisions for boot camp graduates.* Washington, DC: National Institute of Justice, U.S. Department of Justice. Dale College and Jurg Gerber (2002). Rethinking the assumptions about boot camps. In Wilson R. Palacios, Paul F. Cromwell, and Roger G. Dunham (Eds.) *Crime and justice in America: Present realities and future prospects* (2nd ed., pp. 382–393). Upper Saddle River, NJ: Prentice Hall.

11. Michael Peters, David Thomas, Christopher Zamberlan, and Caliber Associates (1997). Also see C. Puzzanchera (2002). *Juvenile court placement of adjudicated youth, 1989–1998.* Washington, DC: Office of Juvenile Justice and Delinquency Prevention. Retrieved online December 29, 2004: http://www.ncjrs.org/pdffiles/164258.pdf

12. Doris MacKenzie and Claire Souryal (1991). Rehabilitation, recidivism reduction outrank Punishment as main goals. *Corrections Today, 53*(6), 90–92, 94–96.

13. Dale G. Parent (1996). Boot camps and prison crowding. In Doris L. MacKenzie and Eugene E. Hebert, (Eds.), *Correctional boot camps: A tough intermediate sanction* (Chapter 16). Washington, DC: National Institute of Justice, Office of Justice

Programs, U.S. Department of Justice. Retrieved online January 15, 2005: http://www.kci.org/publication/bootcamp/docs/nij/Correctional_Boot_Camps/table _context.htm

14. Susan T. Marcus-Mendoza (2001). *A preliminary investigation of Oklahoma's shock incarceration program.* State of Oklahoma, Department of Corrections. Retrieved online December 28, 2004: http://www.doc.state.ok.us/DOCS/OCJRC/OCJRC95/ 950725d.htm

15. Mark W. Osler (1991). Shock incarceration: Hard realities and real possibilities. *Federal Probation, 55*(1), 34–42.

16. Dale G. Parent (1995). *Planning a boot camp: An overview of five critical elements.* Paper presented at the Office of Justice Programs Boot Camp Technical Assistance Workshop, Atlanta, GA, April 1, 1995.

17. Dale G. Parent (1994). Boot camps failing to achieve goals. *Overcrowded Times, 5*(4), 8–11. And Dale G. Parent, R. Bradley Snyder, and Bonnie Blaisdell (2001, August). *Boot camps' impact on confinement bed-space requirements: Final Report.* National Criminal Justice Reference Service. Retrieved online December 28, 2004: http://www.ncjrs.org/pdffiles1/nij/grants/189788.pdf

18. J. J. Wilson and J. C. Howell (1993, December). *Comprehensive strategy for serious, violent, and chronic juvenile offenders.* Program Summary. Washington, DC: Office of Juvenile Justice and Delinquency Prevention, Office of Justice Programs, U.S. Department of Justice.

19. Doris MacKenzie and Claire Souryal (1994).

20. Doris MacKenzie and Claire Souryal (1994).

21. *The corrections yearbook: Adult corrections 2002* (2003). Camille Graham Camp and George Camp (Eds.). Middletown, CT. Criminal Justice Institute, 132.

22. Eric Peterson (1996). *Juvenile boot camps: Lessons learned.* National Institute of Justice, Fact Sheet 36, 1996.

23. *The corrections yearbook: Adult corrections 2002* (2003), 132.

24. *American Correctional Association 2003 Directory: Adult and juvenile* (2004). Lanham, MD: American Correctional Association (pp. 20, 25). Other sources gave slightly different average totals such as *The correctional yearbook: Adult corrections* (2002). But two ideas should be clear: (a) in criminal justice, sources often disagree and (b) criminal justice intervention is expensive.

25. From the U.S. code online via GPO Access. Part H—Boot camps: Sec. 5667f. Establishment of program. Retrieved online December 28, 2004: http://frwebgate .access.gpo.gov/cgi-bin/getdoc.cgi?dbname=browse_usc&docid=Cite:+42USC5667f

26. *Juvenile residential facility census, 2000: Selected findings.* Washington, DC: U.S. Department of Justice, Office of Justice Programs. December 2002. NCJ 196595. And BJS. *Juveniles in public and private residential custody facilities* (Table 6.9).

27. Personal communication with several juvenile judges in the Commonwealth of Massachusetts.

28. Department of Corrections. State of Ohio. Retrieved online December 26, 2004: http://www.drc.state.oh.us/web/reams.htm

29. Gerald T. Flowers, Timothy S. Carr, and R. Barry Ruback (1991). Special alternative incarceration evaluation. Atlanta: Georgia Department of Corrections. And Andy E. Bowen (1991, October). Making boot camps bigger and better. *Corrections Today,* 84–87.

30. John Keenan (1996). In *National Institute of Justice Report: Correctional boot camps: A tough intermediate sanction.* Georgia Department of Corrections. Retrieved online December 28, 2004: http://www.kci.org

31. See Maryland Department of Corrections. Retrieved online December 29, 2004: http://www.dpscs.state.md.us/doc/

32. B. B. Benda, N. J. Toombs, and M. Peacock (2002). Ecological factors in recidivism: A survival analysis of boot camp graduates after three years. *Journal of Offender Rehabilitation,* 35(1), 63–85.

33. Eric Peterson (1996).

34. Dale G. Parent, R. Bradley Snyder, and Bonnie Blaisdell (2001, August). *Boot camps' impact on confinement bed space requirements: Final report.* National Criminal Justice Reference Service. Retrieved online December 28, 2004: http://www.ncjrs.org/pdffiles1/nij/grants/189788.pdf

35. Dale G. Parent, R. Bradley Snyder, and Bonnie Blaisdell (2001, August). Also Doris MacKenzie and Claire Souryal (1994).

36. Institute for Criminological Research and American Institutes for Research. (1992). *Boot camps for juvenile offenders: Constructive intervention and early support-implementation evaluation final report.* New Brunswick, NJ: Rutgers University.

37. Dale G. Parent (1989). *Shock incarceration: An overview of existing program.* Washington, DC: U.S. Department of Justice (xi.).

38. Cherie L. Clark, David W. Aziz, and Doris L. MacKenzie (1994, August). *Shock incarceration in New York.* National Institute of Justice, NCJ 148410.

39. J. Burns, J. F. Anderson, and L. Dyson (1997, May). What disciplinary rehabilitation unit participants are saying about shock incarceration. NCJ 168996. *Journal of Contemporary Criminal Justice, 13*(2), 172–183.

40. Susan T. Marcus-Mendoza (2001). *A preliminary investigation of Oklahoma's shock incarceration program.* State of Oklahoma. Department of Corrections. Retrieved online December 28, 2004: http://www.doc.state.ok.us/DOCS/OCJRC/OCJRC95/950725d.htm

41. Dennis J. Stevens (2006). *Community corrections: An applied approach.* Upper Saddle River, NJ: Prentice Hall.

42. New Hampshire Department of Corrections (2005). Retrieved online February 27, 2005: http://www.state.nh.us/nhdoc/fcc/index.html

43. New Hampshire Department of Corrections (2005).

44. Dale Colledge and Jurg Gerber (2002). Rethinking the assumptions about boot camps (pp. 382–397). In Wilson R. Palacios, Paul F. Cromwell, and Roger G. Dunham (Eds.), *Crime and justice in America: Present realities and future prospects* (2nd ed., p. 386). Upper Saddle River, NJ: Prentice Hall.

45. Doris Layton MacKenzie and Claire Souryal (1994), 13.

46. Doris MacKenzie, D. Wilson, and S. Kider (2001). Research findings from prevention and intervention studies: Effects of correctional boot camps on offending. *The Annals of the Academy of The American Academy of Political and Social Science, 126,* 1–15. Also see U.S. Department of Justice (2003, June). *Correctional boot camps: Lessons from a decade of research.* Washington, DC: Department of Justice, NCJ 197018. Retrieved online December 28, 2004: http://www.ncjrs.org/pdffiles1/nij/197018.pdf (8–11).

47. Doris Layton MacKenzie and Claire Souryal (1994). p. 13. Experienced correctional personnel can verify this finding in that during the first few months when a noncareer criminal prisoner arrives to serve his or her prison sentence, the prisoner is so filled with uncertainty and stress that the prisoner will conform to almost any directive given by correctional personnel. It is for that reason it is often argued that prison sentences should be reduced to a few years because it is at that point they are most amendable to change and can avoid prisonization affects. See Dennis J. Stevens (2000). The depth of imprisonment and prisonisation: Levels of security and prisoners' anticipation of future violence. In Dennis J. Stevens (Ed.), *Perspective: Corrections* (pp. 81–88). Madison, WI: Coursewise.

48. The Center for the Study of Crime, Delinquency, and Corrections (Southern Illinois University at Carbondale) collected data in 1992 and the first 6 months of 1993; the study results reflect the adult boot camp substance abuse programming that was offered during this time period. Also see Ernest L. Cowles, Thomas C. Castellano, and Laura A. Gransky (1995). *Boot camp: Drug treatment and aftercare interventions: An evaluation review.* NIJ Research in Brief, NCJ 155062. Retrieved online December 28, 2004: http://www.ncjrs.org/txtfiles/btcamp.txt. These researchers referred to boot camps only in their titles when they were evaluating what appears to be shock camps. One reason for this could have been the dates of the research. Since that time, the distinction between the two has become clearer.

49. Susan T. Marcus-Mendoza (2001).

50. Robert J. Jones and Steven P. Karr (1996). The development and implementation of Illinois' impact incarceration program. In *National Institute of Justice Report: Correctional boot camps: A tough intermediate sanction.* Retrieved online December 28, 2004: http://www.kci.org/publication/bootcamp/docs/nij/Correctional_Boot_Camps/table_context.htm

51. Department of Corrections. State of Michigan. Retrieved online December 28, 2004: http://www.michigan.gov/corrections/0,1607,7-119-1435-5043—,00.html

52. Department of Corrections. State of Colorado. Retrieved online December 28, 2004: http://www.doc.state.co.us/Facilities/YOS/yos.htm

53. Merry Morash, Tim Bynum, and Barbara Koons (1998). *Women offenders: Programming needs and promising approaches.* Research in brief. NCJ 171668. Washington, DC: U.S. Department of Justice, National Institute of Justice. Also, Doris L. MacKenzie, Lori A. Elis, Sally S. Simpson, and Stacy B. Skroban (1996). Boot camps as an alternative for women. In Doris L. MacKenzie and Eugene E. Hebert (Eds.), *Correctional boot camps: A tough intermediate sanction* (Chapter 14). Research Report, NCJ 157639. Washington, DC: U.S. Department of Justice, National Institute of Justice. Retrieved online January 15, 2005: http://www.kci.org/publication/bootcamp/docs/nij/Correctional_Boot_Camps/chpt14.htm

54. Dale G. Parent (2003, June).

55. Dale G. Parent (2003, June). Also Merry Morash, Tim Bynum, and Barbara Koons (1998). And for SI see Cherie L. Clark, David W. Aziz, and Doris L. MacKenzie. (1994, August). In addition, this author visited several shock camps in New York in 2002 and interviewed male and female inmates, correctional personnel, and caseworkers. One characteristic confirmed through several discussions was that most of the programs were designed for young males and rarely included or engaged females. For instance, although there were many scheduled programs for anger management, there were few scheduled programs for parenting classes.

56. The author found few if any AOD programs designed specifically for females or those that were gender-free at any of the New York SI facilities visited in the summer of 2002.

57. M. Morash, T. Bynum, and B. Koons (1998). Also see D. L. MacKenzie, L. A. Elis, S. S. Simpson, and S. B. Skroban (1996). Further evidence supporting this position was found by the author during a summer 2002 visit to New York SI facilities. For instance, during the 5:45 A.M. physical exercise in the yard, female inmates were performing jumping-jack exercises. Upon closer observation, it became clear that many of the female inmates were in pain because they were not equipped with appropriate protective undergarments. When the superintendent was asked about this observation, there was no response. For clarification, see the photo of female inmates in the Living in "Shock:" New York Style section of this chapter.

58. R. A. Lewis, M. Jones, and S. Plant (1998). *National multisite process evaluation of boot camp planning grants: An analysis of correctional program planning.* San Francisco: National Council on Crime and Delinquency and the U.S. Department of Justice, National Institute of Justice. Also see, Merry Morash, Tim Bynum, and Barbara Koons (1998).

59. The author was present at several 5:45 sessions and witnessed this requirement of all inmates and staff.

60. Doris Layton MacKenzie and Claire Souryal (1994, September).

61. Cherie L. Clark, David W. Aziz, and Doris L. MacKenzie (1994, August).

62. To guide this chapter, the author visited several SI camps throughout Massachusetts and New York. Without the cooperation of the New York Department of Corrections, this chapter would not be as detailed and updated.

63. All four facilities have been accredited by the American Correctional Association. Most of the information that follows for New York is contained in *Executive Summary: New York State DOCS Shock Incarceration 2001 Legislative Report.* Department of Correctional Services. Available through Department of Corrections, Director of Information.

64. Cherie L. Clark, David W. Aziz, and Doris L. MacKenzie (1994, August).

65. Cutting-crime Shock saves taxpayers $1B (2004, Autumn). *DOCS Today, 13*(10), 6. New York State Department of Correctional Services. Retrieved online December 29, 2004: http://www.docs.state.ny.us/PressRel/DOCSToday/Autumn2004edition.pdf

66. *Executive Summary: New York State DOCS Shock Incarceration 2001 Legislative Report.* Department of Correctional Services. Available through Department of Corrections, Director of Information (p. 4). And also *Cutting-crime Shock saves taxpayers $1B (2004, Autumn).* Cherie L. Clark, David W. Aziz, and Doris L. MacKenzie (1994, August).

67. *Cutting-crime Shock saves taxpayers $1B* (2004, Autumn).

68. Douglas Young, Faye S. Taxman, and James M. Byrne (2002, August 20). *Engaging the community in offender reentry.* NCJS. Retrieved online December 28, 2004: http://www.ncjrs.org/pdffiles1/nij/grants/196492.pdf

69. Sarah Hopper Emerson (Ed.). (1897). *Life of Abby Hopper Gibbons, told chiefly through her correspondence.* Edited by her daughter, Sarah Hopper Emerson. Two volumes. New York: Putnam.

70. *Executive summary.* Vera Institute of Justice. Retrieved online December 28, 2004: http://www.vera.org/publications/publications_2c.asp?publication_id=15&publication_content_id=264&section_id=16&project_id=&sub_section_id=5

71. James Beck (1979). An evaluation of federal community treatment centers. *Federal Probation 43,* 5. And Paul Gendreau, M. Shilton, and P. Clark (1995, May). *Intermediate sanctions. Making the right move. Corrections Today, 57*(1), 28–65.

72. Darrell Irwin (2005). *Inmates in halfway house society.* Written specifically for this chapter. Dennis J. Stevens (2006). *Community corrections: An applied approach.* Upper Saddle River, NJ: Prentice Hall.

73. George E. Valliant (1983). *The natural history of alcoholism.* Cambridge, MA: Harvard University Press, 300.

74. George E. Valliant (1983), 300.

75. Substance Abuse and Mental Health Services Administration (1996, June). *Overview of the FY95 national drug and alcoholism treatment unit survey 1980–1994.* Retrieved December 29, 2004: http://www.samhsa.gov/index.aspx

76. American Society of Addictive Medicine (1996). *Patient placement criteria for the treatment of psychoactive substance disorders,* (2nd ed.). Chevy Chase, MD. Also, see, ASMD's website. Retrieved online December 29, 2004: http://www.asam.org/

77. J. E. Royce and D. Scratchley (1996). *Alcoholism and other drugs.* New York: Free Press, 252.

78. J. E. Royce and D. Scratchley (1996), 252.

79. Oxford House: The concept (2004). Retrieved online December 29, 2004: http://www.oxfordhouse.org/main.html

80. Marian Sandmaier (1980). *The invisible alcoholics.* New York: McGraw-Hill, 216.

81. Marian Sandmaier (1980), 216.

82. H. M. Annis and C. B. Liban (1976). *A follow-up study of halfway house residents and matched non-resident controls.* Toronto, Canada: Addiction Research Foundation.

83. H. M. Annis and C. B. Liban (1976). Also Earl Rubington and Martin S. Weinberg (Eds.). (2002, August). *The study of social problems: Seven Perspectives* (6th ed.). Oxford, England: Oxford University Press.

84. Earl Rubington (1995). Elderly homeless alcoholic careers. In Thomas P. Beresford and Edith Gomberg (Eds.), *Alcohol and aging* (pp. 370–389). Oxford, England: Oxford University Press (p. 371). Also Earl Rubington and Martin S. Weinberg (2004). *Deviance: The interactionist perspective.* Boston: Allyn & Bacon.

85. Earl Rubington (1995), 377.

86. Earl Rubington (1995), 373.

87. P. Koegal and M. A. Burnam (1988). Alcoholism among homeless adults in the inner city of Los Angeles. *Archives of General Psychiatry, 45,* 1011–1018.

88. Bureau of Justice Statistics (2001). *Criminal offenders statistics.* Washington, DC: U.S. Department of Justice, Office of Justice Programs. Retrieved online December 28, 2004: http://www.ojp.usdoj.gov/bjs/crimoff.htm#lifetime

89. Further, it is estimated that over 3 million former prisoners are in general population as of 2002. See Harry Holzer, Steven Raphael, and Michael A. Stoll (2003). *Can employers play a more positive role in prisoner reentry? The Urban Institute.* Belmont, CA: Wadsworth. Retrieved online December 28, 2004: http://www.newtexts.com/newtexts/cluster.cfm?cluster_id=114#head_1

90. Marta Nelson and Jennifer Trone (1996). *Why planning for release matters.* New York: Vera Institute of Justice, State Sentencing and Corrections Program, NCJ 189666.

91. Aaron Beck (2000). *State and federal prisoners returning to the community: Findings from the Bureau of Justice Statistics.* Washington, DC: Bureau of Justice Statistics.

92. National Institute of Corrections (2003, March 3). *Transition from prison to the community.* Washington, DC: Department of Justice. Retrieved online December 28, 2004: http://www.nicic.org/

93. George Rush (1992). *The dictionary of criminal justice.* Guilford, CT: Duskin.

94. Bureau of Justice Statistics (1999). *Mental health and treatment of inmates and probationers.* Retrieved online December 28, 2004: http://www.ojp.usdoj.gov/bjs/pub/press/mhtip.pr

95. Bureau of Justice Statistics (1999). *Mental health and treatment of inmates and probationers.*

96. Belinda McCarthy, Bernard McCarthy, and Matthew C. Leone (2001). *Community-based corrections,* (4th ed.). Belmont, CA: Wadsworth (pp. 4–5). Also, Paul F. Cromwell, Rolando V. Del Carmen, and Leanne F. Alarid (2003). *Community-based corrections.* Belmont, CA: Wadsworth (p. 11). The idea sounds novel, but the literature has been exploring this perspective for some time. For instance, Daniel Glaser (1964). *The effectiveness of a prison and parole system.* Indianapolis: Bobbs-Merrill. Also see Daniel Glaser (1973). *Routinizing evaluation.* Washington, DC: National Institute of Mental Health. Glaser argues that among other things, it is highly unlikely for offenders to learn the rules of a free society while locked up in prison.

97. D. Michaels, D. Zoloth, and P. Alcabes (1992). Homeless and indicators of mental illness among inmates in New York City correctional system. *Hospital and Community Psychiatry, 32,* 150–155.

98. Washington Report, 108th Congress, Number 14, ACJS July 28, 2003. A group of legislators from both parties and both houses have introduced legislation designed to divert mentally ill offenders from the criminal justice system into more effective treatment programs, ending the revolving door for nonviolent mentally ill people for whom jail is their only treatment facility. The bills (S.1194 and HR 2387) were introduced by Sen. Mike DeWine (R–Ohio) and Rep. Ted Strickland (D–Ohio), who had won passage three years ago of a modest bill to establish grants for mental health courts. The new bill would expand that effort by $100 million a year for a variety of programs, both state and local, and for mental health and criminal justice agencies, through 2008. The grants could be used to help jails increase their treatment of mentally ill offenders, provide aftercare programming, divert some out of the system, train criminal justice personnel to recognize mental illness, and provide courts with more options.

99. Donald G. Evans (2002, October). ICCA's Legislative forum is a success. *Corrections Today, 64*(6), 18–19.

100. Donald G. Evans (2002, October). Also see Andrea Barthwell's presentation at the International Community Corrections Association annual legislative forum, May 20–21, 2003, Washington, DC. Barthwell argues that illegal drugs cost society $143.4 billion a year.

101. Treatment reduces transmission of blood-borne pathogens such as HIV and hepatitis C.

102. Refer to the classifications to better understand this requirement.

103. B. Huskey (1992, October). The expanding use of CRCs. *Corrections Today, 12,* 1–7.

104. David Farabee, Michael Prendergast, and M. Douglas Anglin (1998). The effectiveness of coerced treatment for drug-abusing offenders.*Federal Probation, 62*(1). Retrieved online August 20, 2004: http://www.uscourts.gov/fedprob/1998junefp.pdf

105. Sam Torres (1998). Monitoring prescription medication use among substance-abusing offenders. *Federal Probation, 62*(1), 11–16.

106. Florida Department of Corrections. Retrieved online December 28, 2004: http://www6.myflorida.com/pub/pqannual/1999/programs_available.html

107. Edward J. Latessa and Harry E. Allen (1999). *Corrections in the community.* Cincinnati, OH: Anderson (p. 390).

108. TDCJ–Community Justice Assistance Division. *Agency Brief March 1999.* Department of Corrections, State of Texas. Retrieved online December 28, 2004: http://www.tdcj.state.tx.us/publications/cjad/rc97.pdf

109. Texas Department of Criminal Justice. *Agency Brief March 1999.* Retrieved online August 20, 2004: http://www.tdcj.state.tx.us/publications/cjad/rc97.pdf

110. Department of Corrections, State of Texas. Retrieved online December 28, 2004: http://www.tdcj.state.tx.us/publications/cjad/rc97.pdf

111. Mario Paparozzi (2003, August). Probation, parole and public safety: The need for principled practices versus faddism and circular policy development. *Corrections Today, 65*(5), 46–48.

112. Edward J. Latessa and Harry E. Allen (1982). Halfway houses and parole: A national assessment. *Journal of Criminal Justice, 10,* 153–156.

113. B. Huskey (1992, August). The expanding use of CRCs. *Corrections Today, 54*(8), 70–74.

114. Paul Friday and Robert Wertkin (1995). Effects of programming and race on recidivism: Residential probation. In J. Smykla and W. Selke (Eds.), *Intermediate sanctions: Sentencing in the 1990s* (pp. 209–217). Cincinnati, OH: Anderson.

115. These criticisms were guided by Edward J. Latessa and Harry E. Allen (1999). *Corrections in the community.* Cincinnati, OH: Anderson (393) and the experience of the author and his correctional students.

12

JUVENILES:
THE DEPENDENCY ERA

LEARNING OBJECTIVES

After you finish reading this chapter, you will be better prepared to:

- Describe conceptually the role "dependency" plays in the link between the justice community and children.
- Identify some of the early responses toward young wrongdoers in early America.
- Describe how close ties within the family play a role in initiatives toward wayward children.
- Characterize how mass immigration shaped an urbanized American population and lead to their exploitation.
- Describe the role poverty had in shaping child-labor practices and poorhouses.
- Characterize the efforts of the child-savers.
- Describe what is meant by *patens patriae* and its effects upon juveniles in early America.
- Describe the rise of state institutions in America and their impact upon juveniles.
- Characterize the 19th-century shift to treatment and prevention among juvenile offenders.
- Explain the ideas that surfaced promoting the development of the Illinois Juvenile Court of 1899.
- Identify the achievements of the Illinois Juvenile Court Act of 1899.
- Describe the criminal state of mind perspective and *mens rea* and the role they play among juvenile offenders.
- Identify some of the results in saving one child from a career of crime.

KEY TERMS

Child Protectors
Child-Savers
Culpability
Dependency
Illinois Juvenile Court
   Act of 1899

Juvenile Justice System
Parens Patriae
Mens Rea
Stubborn Child Law
Status Offenders
Contributors Names

Charles Lorring Brace
Henry Bergh
Etta Wheeler

"Remember the Four Rs: Respect for self, Respect for others, Responsibility for all your actions, and Reality."

—Unknown

INTRODUCTION

American history is strongly linked with initiatives of adults in their attempts to *protect* youths or what can be called dependency initiatives. Dependency initiatives are the focus of this chapter and it will argued that those initiatives continue to influence policy and practice of community corrections among juveniles in the 21st century. In one sense, child protectors help maintain dependency strategies among our young. Chapter 13 will emphasize criminal justice initiatives, which include the prosecution of youths or what can be called delinquency initiatives. In this regards, it took a criminal justice system to create juvenile delinquency. In the words of one juvenile police investigator, "One way to solve our juvenile delinquency problem is to use that four letter word—wait."[1] The words of the officer have merit because many believe that as an offender ages, the less likely it is that he will commit crime.[2] And, of course, juveniles will eventually become adults. For that reason, punishment and control advocates are anxious to control youthful offenders for long periods of time until they cease to be a threat.

Liberal advocates, on the other hand, recommend that corrections provide strategies through CC initiatives that aid juvenile offenders because, they believe, troubled youth have been denied appropriate guidance and care during childhood and consequently cannot make "right" decisions toward productive lifestyles or what can be called a dependency perspective.[3]

Nonetheless, younger people are more likely to be arrested as compared to adults because they commit crimes in groups and are highly visible because their crimes tend to be in public places, such as in schools, retail shops (shoplifting), and on the streets, including public transportation.[4] The Office of Juvenile Justice and Delinquency Prevention (OJJDP) reports that although arrests among juveniles are declining, juvenile arrests for drug abuse violations increased 59 percent from 1993 to 2002 as compared to 33 percent increase among adults.[5] But new dangerous strategies are practiced by youths. The signs are everywhere: kids bringing guns and drugs to junior high, high school boys engaged in "posses" to "rack up body counts" of the number of girls "sacked," mall rats "streaming" through the aisles of a department store and grabbing stacks of clothing before making their getaway, tagger crews "mapping the heavens" spray painting their three-letter monikers on overhead freeway signs.[6]

At-risk children are no longer ghetto youths but may also be affluent suburban youths. Some argue that the attitude and lifestyles of the poor have moved into middle-class neighborhoods,[7] and to maintain social order, the criminal justice system must control this dangerous class of individuals.[8] In what practical way has the justice community responded to "renegade" children, as some observers call them?[9] More drug arrests among juveniles can imply greater abuse of drugs among juveniles, especially those living in poverty, but it can also mean stricter enforcement among substance-abuse violators, which represent almost 13 percent of all current juvenile arrests.[10] For instance, television viewers across the nation witnessed the commando raid of a Charleston, South Carolina, suburban high school in late 2003.[11] Gun-toting police burst into the school, ordered students to the floors, and searched for drugs with the aid of K9 dogs. The police did not find any drugs.

One fact is that many youngsters, which includes those living in poverty and middle class neighborhoods, respect themselves, others and their property, and are responsible for their actions. But as the "Unknown" speaker who is quoted at the beginning of the chapter suggests in the Three Rs, what about the Fourth R, or reality? What is the reality related to initiatives taken by adults when responding to youths?

As it turns out, official initiatives of adults to control youngsters runs deep in American history, particularly the history of poor immigrant and wayward children.[12] What might surprise you is that religious organizations and private enterprise, some of which capitalized on the vulnerability of children, conducted intervention initiatives allegedly designed to protect children. Actually, it was state government that legislated provisions through "child-saver" moments to safeguard the youth of America from misguided religious organization, private enterprise, and suspect practices of intervention. Another result, however, was the creation of the juvenile delinquency system discussed in Chapter 13. That is, the 21st-century juvenile justice system embraces two distinct and often opposing components—dependency and delinquency—and both concepts can be found supporting policy and practice in modern American CC systems.

DEPENDENCY

Dependency refers to "needing something," a person who is not self-reliant. Child dependency is that portion of the juvenile justice system that handles the victimization of children through child abuse and parental neglect. Some jurisdictions refer to the dependency component as abuse and neglect, dependency and neglect, child welfare, or child protection. Dependency of children might be dealt with through adult court, Department of Social Services (DSS), Department of Youth Services (DYS), and numerous other agencies including nonprofit private organizations depending on the jurisdiction. In addition, the juvenile justice system generally has jurisdiction over situations involving conduct directed at (rather than committed by) juveniles, such as parental neglect, deprivation, abandonment, and sexual and physical abuse.

Most states distinguish such behavior from delinquent conduct to lesson the effect of any stigma on children as a result of their involvement with the juvenile justice system.

Policy makers, interest groups, and the public who see treatment and prevention as an appropriate response toward youngsters favor CC programs and see offender accountability and responsibility techniques as appropriate strategies to change troubled youth. They rely on treatment and integration strategies for youths as the best response toward most juvenile offenders. Centered in the belief that youth need to remain in the community to best learn how to live in the community as a law-abiding resident, these advocates would try to persuade policy makers and interest groups to emphasize community supervision as opposed to confinement. That is, you might call these advocates child-protectors. Confinement should be reserved for chronic and largely adult criminal offenders.

Child-protectors argue that a categorization of American's youth as delinquents is in part arbitrary because youth without appropriate family resources are more often subject to criminal justice sanctions than children from affluent families.[13] They argue that the actions of children, which include criminal behavior, are often symptoms of other characteristics or problems encountered by children as opposed to criminal acts committed with malice and criminal intent.[14] For instance, some children are truant from school. A juvenile who is truant can become a **status offender.**[15] A status offender can be adjudicated a delinquent. However, one reason a status offender might "skip" school is because of physical abuse.[16] Bruises and low-levels of self-esteem are visible to others, or so some status offenders believe. Others might feel ashamed of their abuse and "want to hide." We also know that delinquent children suffer abuse and neglect at greater rates than the general population.[17] In fact, the number of dependency hearings is more numerous than delinquency hearings.[18]

CHILD-PROTECTORS OR CHILD-PROSECUTORS?

Dependency or child protectors and delinquency or child prosecutors emerged over time in American history. But those strategies were not that of an enlightened child prosecutor or child protector until well into the 20th century, when those strategies were designed to treat children not as small adult offenders, but as child victims less accountable for their condition and more entitled to rehabilitation than punishment.

Despite concern for the welfare of children in early America, there were few if any special facilities or programs that were specifically designed for appropriate custody or protection.[19] Also, separate laws, courts, or advocates to help guide their behavior were virtually nonexistent. Reform came through concerned individuals and nonprofit organizations leading to a juvenile justice system. Some of the events that led to child-reform and the American juvenile justice system included:

- Early responses to wrongdoers
- Close ties with family
- Urbanized population exploitation produced by mass immigration

- Poverty, child labor, and poorhouses
- Child-savers
- *Parens patriae*
- Rise of state institutions: Reform schools
- 19th-century shift to treatment and prevention
- Illinois Juvenile Court Act of 1899

Early Responses to Wrongdoers

Prior to the mid-1700s, serious juvenile crime in America was uncommon. Punishment and the discipline of children were parental responsibilities and the responsibility of other adults in the community.[20] The advantages of community participation are obvious in the sense that children were supervised in every activity of community life whether their own parents were present or not.[21] One result of this form of supervision would affect opportunities of a child to engage in deviance and at the same time, would lessen victimization by outsiders and insiders alike.[22]

Laws were eventually passed to punish parents who would not control the behavior of their own children. Serous disobedience toward parents resulted in a child's apprenticeship in a trade of some type.[23] As America grew and its perception of crime and punishment changed, laws and the official response to juveniles also changed. Prior to that time, children were viewed as small adults and treated as such. Sometimes those ideas about small adults were complex. For example, the Puritans who lived in early New England believed their children were little Adams and Eves—born sinners.[24]

When a Puritan child exercised his or her will and displayed aggression, the elders believed parents were actually engaged in a battle with the devil over the soul of the child.[25] Parents had to keep control of their children and it was appropriate, so much that it was a legal responsibility, for parents to use whatever means were available to control wayward children. For instance, letting a child cry until the child fell asleep from exhaustion, depriving a child of love and attention, and withholding food until the child submitted to the will of the parents were all common practices. It was the responsibility of a parent to break a child's will on the assumption that broken wills led to rule compliance.

From a legal perspective, the *stubborn child law* was passed in 1648 in Massachusetts.[26] It established a clear legal relationship between children and parents. It made it a capital offense for a child to disobey parents. This statue stated in part:

> If a man have a stubborn or rebellious son, of sufficient years and understanding . . . which will not obey the voice of his Father or the voice of his Mother, and that when they have chastened him will not harken unto them; then shall his father and mother being his natural parents, lay hold of him, and bring him to the Magistrates assembled in court and testify unto them, that their son is stubborn and rebellious and will not obey their voice and chastisement, but lives in sundry notorious crime, such a son shall be put to death.[27]

Close Ties with Family

Youngsters had relatively close ties with family and community until the age of puberty right up to the late 18th century. Runaway and unknown children in the community were treated differently. They received harsh treatment up to the late 19th century.[28] Also, urban youths in the 18th and 19th century involved in serious crimes received similar punishment as adults—imprisonment, whippings, and death. However, youths who committed petty crimes such as stealing or vandalism were viewed as wayward children or victims of neglect and were placed in community asylums, reform schools, and settlement houses.[29] Those facilities provided discipline and hard labor as avenues toward a "reformed" child. The harsher the discipline and the harder the labor, the more likely the child was, indeed, reformed.

Many practices toward youngsters were influenced by the reality that they often produced an income for their families. That is, at ages as young as six and seven from the colonial period through the 19th century, many children worked. They provided parents with a form of social security, unemployment insurance, and yearly support.[30] As soon as a child was capable, it was expected they would contribute to the support of their parents. Poor children worked hard labor as apprentices to wealthy landowners or ship captains. In sum, wayward children, including immigrant children and those without parents, were confronted by a harsh justice and community system. On the other hand, privileged children who violated the law were treated on an informal basis and were often diverted from the official process (much as they are today).[31]

Urbanized Population Exploitation Produced by Mass Immigration

In 1853, the United States began surveying railroad routes to the Pacific, mapping four different routes. Poster, flyers, and advertisements went to Europe and the rest of the world extolling the virtues of coming to America for "free land."[32] Agents of steamship lines and railroads attracted thousands of immigrants to the United States with words such as "the land of opportunity" and "land of a second chance." Many believed America was the "land of milk and honey." As a result, the United States welcomed over 4,311,465 newcomers, between the years of 1841 to 1860, many of them children. Ellis Island in New York processed 2,251 immigrants in its first day of business after being rebuilt from a fire in 1900. In 1907, a record number (1,285,349) of immigrants were admitted to the United States.[33]

As you can imagine, there were numerous problems generated by urban growth and one of those problems was the product of poor children. Immigrants were largely crowded into urban neighborhoods where children filled public schools and mastered diverse street trades.[34] Institutions and organizations geared up to deal with the requirements of immigrants and their children and public funds were spent in every area of urban life from orphanages to kindergartens.[35]

It might be difficult to believe, but estimates from 1854 counted the number of homeless children in New York City at approximately 34,000. Many of those children were thrown out of their homes, were runaways, or simply tried to survive after their parents died.[36] Their conditions were deplorable. Many were near starvation, few had warm clothing in winter, and almost none had any medical care. These children became known as "street Arabs" and added to the stereotypes of the dangerous class.[37] Because these children faced problems with street violence, many of them formed gangs and were a growing problem for police. Of course, some were arrested and even those as young as five years of age were often thrown in jail with adults. There was a "reign of terror" against many children of the poor during the 18th and early 19th centuries.[38] Children were placed into notorious workhouses (about which Charles Dickens wrote), textile mills, mines, ships, and prisons.[39]

Living conditions for immigrants in particular were difficult to describe, jobs were scarce, and labor in the north and New England was cheap because of child labor and in the south because of slavery. Without extended family (grandparents, aunts, uncles) members to rely upon in times of need, young families fell apart. This thought is consistent with 20th century findings in that children in single parent homes are more likely to become victimized than children where two parents are present due in part to the amount of supervision afforded by two partners as opposed to one.[40] Children had to work if they could find jobs. Food was scarce. Job safety was nonexistent, causing many young men and children to be killed in accidents at sea and at other places of work. This left women and children to make their own way living as best they could. Disease from living in unsanitary quarters led to early deaths of overworked mothers. Orphanages were built to care for as many children as could possibly be taken in. Adults could pay for the care on a weekly or monthly basis but if the payments stopped, the child became a *ward of the court* and was "disposed" of as social workers saw fit.[41]

Poverty, Child Labor, and Poorhouses

Social life in early urban America was characterized by two outwardly contradictory trends: an affluent elite comprised of merchants, professionals, and government officials who established what they considered to be a "refined lifestyle" and the indigent poor.[42] Urbanization and industrialization generated a concern by the elite that certain segments of the population were susceptible to the influences of a decaying environment. At the time (although there seem to be traces of this notion alive and well today), there was an assumption that the refined "world" of the elites would never advance if the dangerous class were left to its own devises.[43] The dangerous class was comprised of the poor, single, criminal, mentally ill, unemployed, and immigrants.

Children of destitute families left home or were cut loose to make out as best they could. Wealthy families tried to absorb vagrant youth as apprentices or servants as best they could. The affluent class held a general assumption that vagrant and delinquent children were considered a group that might be "saved" by a combination of state and community intervention. But that meant a child had to be confined, disciplined, and work at hard labor for the sake of child's welfare. In response to those ideas, local jurisdictions developed poorhouses (almshouses), workhouses, and settlement homes. One result was that the poor, insane, diseased, and vagrant were also crowded into those poorhouses along with destitute children. Unhealthy conditions existed in most poorhouses, which fostered violence, corruption, and disease.[44]

Not all child employment was conducted by the poor. Many youngsters were eager to escape from parental surveillance and went to live and work in places such as the mills in Lowell, MA. Company agents recruited other youngsters. For example, Sarah Hodgson left Rochester, NH, to work at the mill in Lowell, Massachusetts in 1830 when she was 16. Sarah's parents operated a prosperous 75 acre farm and did not need her wages to survive. Sarah traveled to Lowell with two friends, Elizabeth and Wealthy, with whom she roomed in one of the company's boardinghouses. Older than Sarah and experienced at mill work, Wealthy acted as a watchful eye and wrote seperate, reassuring letters to Sarah's parents.[45]

Child-Savers

In 1817, prominent New Yorkers formed the *Society for the Prevention of Pauperism.* Although the society concerned itself with attacking taverns, brothels, and gambling parlors, they were concerned with the moral training of poor children. Soon other groups concerned with the plight of poor children formed. Their focus was on extending governmental control over youthful activities (drinking, vagrancy, and robbery). In addition, rapid industrialization and a lack of regulation led many employers to look to the youth of the nation for cheap labor. No laws or generally accepted standards protected youngsters in the workplace.[46] The exploitation of children was rampant by both commerce and the justice system of the day.

Child-savers thought children presented a threat to the moral fabric of society. Due to the influence of the child-savers, state legislatures enacted laws giving courts the power to commit children who were runaways or criminal offenders to specialized institutions usually operated by charitable groups such as religious organizations.

The most prominent of the care facilities developed by child-savers was the House of Refuge in New York, established in 1825.[47] Its mission was to protect children by removing them from the streets and reforming them in a family-like environment. The majority of the children admitted were status offenders placed in the institution by court order, and their length of stay depended on need, age, and skill. Once confined, youths were required to do piecework provided by local manufacturers or to work part of the day in the community. The House of Refuge was often operated as though it were a prison, with strict discipline and absolute separation of the sexes. Harsh programs drove many children to run away. Reformers fought to reduce the backbreaking hours of hard labor performed by children and they won their first successes in urban industries. Farms were left out of the early halting attempts to end hard labor for children.[48] Eventually, the House of Refuge and similar facilities were legally bound to take a more lenient approach.

Charles Loring Brace and the Orphan Trains.   As an alternative to a House of Refuge, another child-saver, Charles Lorring Brace, a New York philanthropis helped develop the Children's Aid Society in 1853.[49] He launched the "orphan trains" program that helped an estimated 150,000 to 200,000 children find homes. A home environment, as opposed to institutional confinement, was the building block of a law-abiding population. Brace's care led to the "free-home-placing-out" or the orphan trains of children between 1854 and the early 1930s.

Orphan trains worked this way: In the west and mid-west, Brace believed that God-fearing homes could be found for children out of big cities.[50] The history of the railroads is deeply tied to the history of the "Orphan Trains Era." Railroads were the most inexpensive way to move children westward from poverty-filled homes, orphanages, poor houses, and the streets. Children were taken in small groups of 10 to 40 under the supervision of at least one "western" agent and traveled on trains to selected stops along the way. As an orphan train stopped in a town, the children were herded off and presented to townspeople, who would hand-select their choices of a child to adopt. Children not adopted returned to the train hoping for better luck in the next town. The Orphan Trains were an early form of foster care.

Parens Patriae

The literature suggests that some, but not all, child-savers rationalized control over children through the English concept of *parens patriae* (state is the parent of a child), often for their own purposes, including the continuance of middle- and upper-class values and the perpetuation of a child labor system consisting of marginal and lower class skilled workers. With no attempt to minimize the enormous effort of many child-savers, basic moral and legal rights of children were often violated: Children were simply not granted the same moral or constitutional protections as adults.

This idea of *parens patriae* continues to dominate the American juvenile justice system in the 21st century. Therefore, it could be said that American juvenile justice is rooted in English Common Law, founded on three assumptions about age and criminal responsibility:

- Children under the age of 7 were recognized as incapable of possessing criminal intent.
- From age 7 to 14, offenders were not responsible unless the state proved the offender could clearly distinguish between right and wrong.
- Youths 14 and older were assumed to be responsible for their actions and deserving of punishment (the burden was on the defendant to prove he or she was not responsible).

Historical Background of Parens Patriae

Parens patriae can be traced to medieval England's chancery courts where it was a means of the crown to administer landed orphans' estates.[51] The King of England was considered the "father" of the English people and equally important, he held legal authority as such. Therefore, the King also had the responsibility and obligation to protect and care for the English children.[52] By the 19th century, this responsibility and obligation developed into the practice of state wardship over children. If a child had no parents or if parents were deemed unfit, the state assumed legal guardianship over those children. The chancery court furthered English law mandating needful children as a ward of the state under the protection of *parens patriae.* The English chancery court seemed almost passionate toward children: welfare and protection of a child was their primary goal rather than punishment (as in an adult English court). The state would act as a guarantor of the trust and intervene when a child's rights were jeopardized.[53] This function today is performed by the courts when dealing with matters relating to children under the Child, Youth, and Family Services Act or the Children's Law Act. In America, the child-savers used *parens patriae,* which supported the legal basis for court intervention between children and their families. American police arrest adults for the purpose of punitive action, but when it comes to children, arrests are made for the purpose of protection and reform. Therefore, even the thought of taking a juvenile into custody is a different process guided by different regulations and different laws compared with taking an adult into custody. Many police officers are confused about this process, one officer says, because of the confusion and the extra paperwork required in juvenile custody, many officers avoid juveniles offenders.[54] That thought might be good for the aggressor but sets the juveniles up for failure in that a juvenile feels he or she can get away with anything. Also, this avoidance of taking juveniles into custody is not in the best interests of the victims or the individuals who witnessed the victimization.

Rise of State Institutions: Reform Schools

It's a stone's throw from a house of refuge to a "reform school" for vagrant children. *Parens patriae* can easily support the concept of reform school. That is, a child is in custody for the purpose of reform. In fact, even today, many juvenile practitioners believe that if the state can take control of troubled children at very young ages, the state could "turn those children around," says a Kansas City police officer.[55] Many officers, court personnel, and juvenile training school personnel are under the impression that children with the potential of becoming major criminals are visible at very young ages. This thought is consistent with some criminologists. For instance, Stanton Samenow argues that as young as five years of age, the characteristics of an aggressor are visible.[56] That is, behavioral characteristics consistent with APD are observable in the behavior of young children and it is recommended that their behavior and cognitive functioning (thinking, especially problem-solving skills) be enhanced "before it's too late."[57]

State institutions opened in Westboro, Massachussets in 1848, and Rochester, New York a year later. They opened in Maine, Rhode Island, and Michigan in 1906.[58] Children worked in the institution, learned a trade, and sometimes received basic education. For the most part, they were racially and sexually segregated, disciplined harshly, and quality hygiene care was unlikely. Girls admitted to the Western House of Refuge in Rochester, New York were often labeled as criminal, despite the reality that they were previously abused and neglected children. They were subject to harsh working conditions, strict discipline, and intense labor. The primary difference between a house of refuge and a reform school was that the reform school was financially funded and operated by the state or local government as opposed to a charity or a religious organization.

Reform schools attempted to be humanitarian. This is not to say that the state provided better conditions than previous operators of homes for children. The increasing criminal rates among children and a lack of appropriate alternatives to deal with them hastened the development of state intervention that included juvenile court. Institutions and organizations geared up to deal with the requirements of children and public funds were spent in every area of urban life from social clubs to sports teams, orphanages to juvenile courts, from kindergartens to legislation, including the Illinois Juvenile Court Act of 1899.

Summary Before 1899

- Little difference seen in a child's behavior between delinquency and dependency
- No separate process, policy, or organizational structure for youthful offenders
- No specific legal process of delinquency or dependence
- Poor children and immigrant children treated as if criminals
- Youth legally treated about the same as adults
- No distinction by age or ability to commit crime
- Youths had no constitutional "rights"
- State seen as father of children (continuing myth of affluent male dominance)
- Reform developed by child protectors through nonprofit organizations

---

Nineteenth Century Shift to Treatment and Prevention

It was felt that the juvenile justice system should avoid the trappings of the adult criminal process with its confusing rules. The idea of crime and punishment among children was to be abandoned. Children were to be treated and rehabilitated and the procedures from apprehension through institutionalization were to be clinical rather than punitive. Child-savers believed that the environment shaped the behavior of juveniles more than "free will" factors. Accordingly, treatment and prevention strategies were emphasized more often than punitive strategies linked to punishment and control philosophies.

The first major movement in the United States to protect children occurred in 1874 with the case of Mary Ellen, when the court appeared to recognize that children did have a right to not being treated inhumanely.[59] Mrs. Wheeler, a volunteer church worker, was visiting an elderly woman in the tenements of New York City when she learned about an eight-year old girl named Mary Ellen. This child had been indentured at the age of 18 months. Mary Ellen was frequently beaten, and her cries for help were often heard throughout the community. Authorities told Etta Wheeler they could not intervene because there were no laws protecting children. Etta Wheeler went to Henry Bergh, of the New York Society for the Prevention of Cruelty of Animals for help. The case was taken to court under laws that normally protected animals. One result was that the child's guardian was sentenced to a jail sentence of one year. Mary Ellen was placed in the home of Etta Wheeler. In 1875, Henry Bergh helped create the New York Society for the Prevention of Cruelty to Children (NYSPCC) because so many cases of maltreated children were being brought to the Society for the Prevention of Cruelty to Animals.[60] One of the more shocking abuses disclosed by the New York Society for the Prevention of Cruelty to Children (NYSPCC) were those in what were called "baby farms," private nurseries and homes akin to modern unlicensed daycare facilities. Infants were found sleeping on bare floors, filthy, unattended and starving, while older children were warehoused in unsuitable quarters where unscrupulous operators profited from the fees and public appropriations.[61]

Child labor was a problem addressed at the very first NYSPCC meeting. One notorious form of abuse was effectively terminated by the NYSPCC between 1879 and 1885, working with the United States Immigration Service and a foreign consulate. This was the infamous "padrone system" whereby desperate, well-intentioned European or Irish families were duped into sending their children to America to a sponsor of their own nationality who promised jobs, training, and care for a time, after which the children were to be sent home. Instead, like "Oliver Twist," children were brutalized, forced to beg, entertain, or steal to support the padrone.[62]

As the 19th century drew to a close, the radical concept of organized child protection had been accepted and replicated throughout the nation and the world. In New York City (Manhattan and the Bronx), the NYSPCC had investigated 130,000 complaints, aided 370,000 children, sheltered 84,000 children (at its own expense) and prosecuted 50,000 cases at a conviction rate of 94 percent.[63] Not only were new laws in place with a growing number of agencies to enforce them, there was also a growing recognition of society's responsibility for the protection of children. The realities that surfaced promoting the development of the Illinois Juvenile Court of 1899 included the following ideas listed in no particular order:

- Children should not be held as accountable adult transgressors.
- The objective of a juvenile justice system should be to treat and rehabilitate rather than punish.
- Disposition should be predicated on analysis of the youth's special circumstances and needs.
- Separate courts should be established for delinquent and neglected children.
- Children should be separated from adults in courts and institutional programs.
- Probation programs should be developed to assist the court in making decisions in the best interests of the state.
- Juveniles should not be treated the same as adults.
- There should be serious distinctions made by age.
- Juveniles have no constitutional "rights."

The child-saving movement culminated in the passage of the Illinois Juvenile Court Act of 1899.

Illinois Juvenile Court Act of 1899

The primary result of the Illinois Juvenile Court Act was to halt adult exploitation, abuse, and punishment strategies toward youthful offenders. The child was to be treated and rehabilitated, and the procedures from apprehension through institutionalization were to be clinical rather than punitive. Child-savers believed that the behavior of a child is a product of the child's social environment.[64] The Illinois Juvenile Court Act achieved the following:

- Established juvenile delinquency as a legal concept.
- Made a distinction between delinquency and dependency.
- Established the age of a delinquent to be 16.
- Established a court and a probation program specifically for children.
- Detention facilities and reform for children came under state control.
- Juvenile courts were developed in virtually every jurisdiction by 1925.

Interpretations of its intentions differ, but unquestionably the Illinois Juvenile Count Act established juvenile delinquency as a legal concept. For the first time, the distinction was made between children who were neglected and those who were delinquent. Delinquent children were those under the age of 16 who had violated the law. Most important, the act established a court and a probation program specifically for children. In addition, the legislation allowed children to be committed to institutions and reform programs under the control of the state.

Other states quickly developed their own juvenile court system. For example, in 1903, Judge Ben B. Lindsey of the Denver Court (served 1901–1927) passed "An Act Concerning Delinquent Children." Judge Lindsey was a leading reformer of juvenile justice methodologies.[65] Lindsey held that a child under 16 years of age who had committed a criminal act would be charged with improper conduct. He or she would be prosecuted as a juvenile disorderly person rather than as a criminal under the general statutes.[66]

By the 1920s, noncriminal behavior in the form of incorrigibility and truancy from school was added to the jurisdiction of many juvenile court systems. Of particular interest was the sexual behavior of young girls and the juvenile court enforced a strict moral code on working-class girls, not hesitating to incarcerate those who were sexually active. Programs of all kinds, including individualized counseling and institutional care, were used to cure juvenile criminality. By 1925, juvenile courts existed in virtually every jurisdiction across the United States.

As cities and the country grew, everything that happened in the second half of the 19th century and in the 20th century happened first to and for children. When the stages of childhood and youth were extended through compulsory education, the commercialization of entertainment and leisure, and the reform of abusive child-labor practices, urban children were the first beneficiaries.[67] In the early 1900s, community intervention began by way of probation. This, however, showed how ineffective untrained probation officers could be at handling delinquents. As a result, college-trained personnel, graduate social workers, professional psychologists, and psychiatric consultants who tried to reform youths moved into the ranks of juvenile justice agencies.

Melanie Estes

Fresh out of college with a four-year degree in Criminal Justice, I was surprised to find such a wide range of career opportunities in this field. I was also shocked to learn that the competition for these jobs was fierce. I knew I wanted to work with juveniles but wasn't sure where to start. Upon completing a job interview at a local children's home, I knew that this was the job for me. The jobs opened at that time were entitled Youth Counselors. Within three weeks I was offered the job. Proud to accept this position I was off to train for my future career at United Methodist Family Services (UMFS) in Richmond, VA. Trainings included: CPR and first aid, certification in a nurse's assistant program, crisis wave, and many group management classes. The first aid and nurse's assistant were both very important because this job would require medication administration. Crisis wave is the name of a self-defense/restraint technique that would enable me to both keep myself safe as well as the kids. As for ongoing group management classes, those would come in handy to communicate with the youth, build trust with them, and ultimately help them complete the program. The program at UMFS was created to help youth who were considered "at-risk." With an average stay of six to nine months, it was UMFS's goal to return the child to their home, help prepare them for independent living, and help them regain enough control of their behaviors to be placed in a less restricted environment. At-risk youth include: youth from broken homes due to abuse, neglect, or because their parents were incarcerated; youth released from juvenile detention facilities; and youth sent to the program by court officials as a diversionary strategy. Our staff worked hand in hand with caseworkers, probation officers, social workers, parents (both birth and foster), treatment specialist, and psychiatrists.

My job description includes: developing and implementing therapeutic goals; role modeling and teaching basic living and social skills; documenting progress notes; developing strategies for challenging behaviors; assessing high risk situations; serving as a liaison for those listed earlier, distributing medication on a daily basis; and interactively cooking, cleaning, and participating in all activities with the youth. Within a year I was promoted to Senior Youth Counselor. In addition, I was responsible for the youth housed in campus.

Recently, I was given the added responsibility of managing and training staff members to do the jobs I liked best. Although I don't make much money, I do get more reward from my job then I ever dreamed possible. It has proven to be a challenging career that promotes growth and is an ever-changing, fast-paced field of work. I have built relationships with the kids that continue to be rewarding. The benefits of these very relationships and the accomplishment of seeing just one youth succeed far outweighs the joy I could ever get from a huge paycheck!

Unclear Motives

The preventive initiatives of many adults upon early juvenile wrongdoers were to "save" children from becoming criminals. But the good intentions of some of those child-savers who helped develop a juvenile justice system were not always altruistic. Equally important, it is a misunderstanding of history that the dependency component was a movement to protect abused and neglected children. Whatever motivated child-savers of the past, the question asked today of modern child-savers relates to the denial of due process and the morality of their actions. For instance, in modern America, does the system protect those juveniles who need protection and does it prosecute those offenders who should be prosecuted? Might the answer depend on other answers? It seems that the juvenile justice system is vague in its execution of their responsibilities due in part to the ambiguous and complex nature of the task in itself. For instance, how the justice community views the juvenile criminal state of mind and *mens rea* can determine whether CC sanctions will be provided or whether the offender will be tried as an adult and if convicted, will be incarcerated with adult convicted felons.

Criminal State of Mind and *Mens Rea*

Young children mostly equate "wrong" with "punished." Adults understand that certain acts are wrong even though consequences do not follow and that other acts are right even when they do lead to punishment. Children younger than six years of age think that accidentally breaking something valuable is worse than intentionally breaking something of less value.

In part, it is the intension of the individual prior to an act that impacts the degree of guilt, if any, on the part of an actor. What an alleged violator thought prior to a violent altercation can make the difference during litigation between a self-defense verdict versus a first-degree or second-degree murder verdict. At what age is behavior linked to criminal intent?

Throughout the late 18th century, "infants" below the age of reason (traditionally age seven) were presumed to be incapable of criminal intent and were exempt from prosecution and punishment.[68] However, children as young as seven stood trial in criminal court. If those children were found guilty, they were sentenced to prison and even death. The mission to help troubled children was stated clearly in the laws that established juvenile courts and thus, juvenile court has the prerogative of informally diverting cases from its judicial action in keeping with Judge Lindsey's perspective, as mentioned earlier.[69]

Understanding *mens rea,* the Latin for "guilty mind," relates to the *intent* requirement of the law, probably with the exception of some acts involving fault or negligence, which must be linked to the defendant to demonstrate guilt.[70] That is, the implication of *mens rea* is its connection to *culpability* (responsibility, deserving of blame).[71] Accidents happen. Criminal acts, on the other hand, are often linked to the desire or the intention of the defendant to fulfill the act. Although *mens rea* is highly debated and subject to various interpretations, its applicable level of culpability that applies to each element of a specific crime is usually defined by a general provision within a jurisdiction's criminal code or by the statute that defines a particular crime.[72] For instance, the Texas Penal Code, Chapter 6.02 and 6.03, advises that "a person does not commit an offense unless he intentionally, knowingly, recklessly, or with criminal negligence engages in conduct as the definition of the offense requires. . . . a conscious objective or desire to engage in the conduct or cause the result." A guilty mind implies an actor knows what he or she is doing. The act is punishable because a violator had the intent to commit the crime, or injury, to another person. The American legal system requires a prosecutor to link a defendant with criminal intent to carry out a criminal act; otherwise, a reasonable doubt exists and the defendant can be found innocent. With that said, a position argued is that because youths do not understand the consequences of their behavior, in what way could they have the intention to commit a crime?

During the latter part of the 18th century, children younger than seven were considered incapable of *mens rea* and therefore exempt from criminal liability from their actions. Youths above seven years of age were prosecuted and a penalty including capital punishment was imposed similar to that of an adult. Although most jurisdictions do not routinely impose adult sentences upon youths any longer, many states judicially waive juveniles to adult criminal court (this will discussed in more detail in Chapter 13), and many states have legislated more punitive responses upon youth. Each state differs as to its age requirements. Equally important, after a juvenile is found guilty of a crime and subject to community corrections supervision, assessing needs and risk is influenced by the intent of the defendant at the time of the crime. One way to ascertain "intent" can be found in the "degrees" of a conviction. For instance:

Assault—First-Degree: A person knowingly engages in conduct that creates a grave risk of death, amputation, or serious bodily injury. Example: *A physical altercation whereby victim is stabbed with a screwdriver, causing serious bodily injury.*

Burglary—First-Degree: A person knowingly enters or remains unlawfully in a building or occupied structure with the intent to commit a crime against a person or property. Example: *A person enters a home and assaults a victim.*

Burglary—First-Degree: A person knowingly breaks an entrance into or remains unlawfully inside a building or structure with the intent to commit a crime against a person or property. Example: *A person enters an unlocked home and steals jewelry, a DVD, and cash.*

A juvenile probation officer in the San Fernando Valley in California says that she is always careful in the presence of juvenile offenders, but the ones she monitors closer than others are the ones convicted of a first-degree crime such as assault.[73] She adds that "degree" can depend on other factors such as legal representation.

Saving One Child

One of the best predictors of adult offenders is their juvenile criminal history.[74] If a juvenile offender is placed into a CC system, in part, one responsibility of the system aside from supervision and care is to aid the offender to change; (i.e., to stop reoffending). Therefore, saving one child has much to do with the priority of CC—public safety. Thus, saving a child from a criminal career also saves victims.

Saving one juvenile from a life of crime is depicted by an observer who estimates that an average career criminal commits between 68 to 80 serious crimes over a 10-year period including four years as a juvenile.[75] Also, there are tangible and intangible costs that such crimes impose on victims, the community, and the criminal justice community. For instance, expenses borne by the justice community for an arrest, investigation, processing, punishment, and productivity losses caused by incarceration are estimated at $1.3 to $1.5 million dollars for each offender (based on 1998 expenses). Of course, there is no way to estimate the costs linked to pain and suffering and diminished quality of life imposed on victims. Saving a child has benefits to everyone, especially future victims.[76] Note that the aforementioned estimates are tentative but they do provide an opportunity to see the kind of costs associated with a typical criminal.

SUMMARY

Dependency refers to an individual who needs something from others to survive and can be described as a person who is not or cannot be self-reliant. Child dependency is that portion of the juvenile justice system that handles the victimization of children through child abuse and parental neglect. Some jurisdictions refer to the dependency component as abuse and neglect, dependency and neglect, child welfare, or child protection. Many public and nonprofit agencies participate in protecting children.

Some of the events that led to child reform and the American juvenile justice system included early responses to wrongdoers; close ties with family; urbanized population

Career Profile: Juvenile Court-Appointed Special Advocate Volunteer

Suzanne C. Koller is a Court-Appointed Special Advocate (CASA) volunteer for the Los Angeles County Superior Juvenile Court. She has been a CASA volunteer with the Child Advocate office for eight years. Although Suzanne had little college before her appointment to CASA (although raising three daughters is an experience of its own), she received practical training from a division of social service, including client encounters that were monitored by experienced advocates for several months before given her first client. Officially, she advocates for abused and neglected children in the dependency court system. They range in age from birth to 18. Her responsibilities include: maintain complete records about the case; interview parties involved in the case, including the child; determine if a permanent plan has been created for the child; assure that the child's best interest is being represented at every stage of the case; attend court hearings and make written recommendations to the court on what decision is best for the child; monitor the case and participate in any planning or treatment team meetings; and remain actively involved in the case until formally discharged by the court. Suzanne says that there are roughly 1,200 frightened and confused children that enter the Los Angeles Dependency Court System each month. For two decades, a growing network of CASA volunteers have stepped in to work on behalf of these children. Suzanne believes that a CASA makes a tremendous difference in the life of these children. But she also suggests that anyone wanting to become an advocate must hold a deep conviction in their soul that these children really need a guiding light. The most successful advocates are persons who love children and hold a great deal of respect for them and their future. Disappointment is commonplace and most advocates are prepared to deal with children who make poor decisions about their life, even after an advocate guides them to a better environment. Suzanne says that relapse is expected, but strong advocates deal with those issues. The rewards are never immediate and sometimes it takes years to see even a small thank-you smile, but when it comes, it's an incredible experience.[77]

exploitation produced by mass immigration; poverty, child labor, and poorhouses; child-savers; *patens patriae;* the rise of state institutions: reform schools; 19th-century shift to treatment and prevention; and the Illinois Juvenile Court Act of 1899.

Protection or dependency strategies promoted in part through *parens patriae* have existed since the beginning of American history and continue today through agencies such as the DSS and DYS. As urbanization exploded in the United States through immigration, child protectors intervened through religious and private organizations to aid poor children and lead them to orphanages and other methods of protecting them from criminal victimization and labor exploitation. For instance, orphan trains were used as a way to find families for city children in rural communities. There was no separate legal process, policy, or organizational structure for youthful offenders. The state's response eventually included reform schools. It was not until the Illinois Juvenile Court of 1899 that a juvenile justice system was developed and with it came the institution of delinquency.

In addition, the intent of adults concerning initiatives toward youngsters was suspect. The point was made that children mostly equate "wrong" with "punishment." Children younger than six years of age think that accidentally breaking something valuable is worse than intentionally breaking something of less value. Older children and adults give more regard to people's intention. The importance of this thought relates to *mens rea,* asking at what age behavior is linked to criminal intent? For instance, during the latter part of the 18th century, children younger than seven were considered incapable of *mens rea* and, therefore, exempt from criminal liability from their actions. Youths above seven years of age were prosecuted and a penalty including capital punishment could be imposed, similar to that of an adult. Although most jurisdictions no longer impose adult sentences upon youths, many states judicially waive juveniles to adult criminal courts. A discussion of the prosecution of youths and other justice strategies will continue in Chapter 13.

Finally, a brief overview was presented revealing the results of saving one child from a criminal career. An estimated 68 to 80 serious crimes over a 10-year period (including 4 years as a juvenile) and approximately $1.3 to $1.8 million in criminal justice expenses for each child could be saved through appropriate initiatives including those offered through CC.

DISCUSSION QUESTIONS

1. Describe conceptually the role "dependency" plays in the link between the justice community and children.
2. Identify some of the early responses toward young wrongdoers in early America. In what way do you agree and disagree with those early remedies?
3. Describe how close ties within the family played a role in initiatives toward wayward children in early America. In what way might family ties change the outcomes of modern-day teenagers?
4. Characterize how mass immigration shaped an urbanized American population and led to their exploitation. In which third-world countries do you see similar trends?
5. Describe the role poverty shaped in regard to child-labor practices and poorhouses. How would you have responded to youngsters if you owed a mill in those times?
6. Characterize the efforts of the child-savers. In what way might those efforts have been beneficial toward youngsters and also exploitative of youngsters?
7. Describe what is meant by *patens patriae* and its effects upon juveniles in early America. In what way does *patens patriae* continue to shape juvenile policy among the police, the courts, and CC.
8. Describe the rise of state institutions in America and their impact upon juveniles.
9. Characterize the 19th-century shift to treatment and prevention among juvenile offenders.

10. Explain the ideas that surfaced promoting the development of the Illinois Juvenile Court of 1899. In what way do you agree with those ideas?

11. Identify the achievements of the Illinois Juvenile Court Act of 1899.

12. Describe the criminal state of mind perspective and *mens rea* and the role they play among young offenders. Describe in what way age impacts the guilty mind.

13. Identify some of the benefits of saving one child from a career of crime.

NOTES

1. Personal communication with author (2004, August 4). Boston Police Department.

2. Michael R. Gottfredson and Travis Hirschi (1990). *A general theory of crime.* Stanford, CA: Stanford University Press, 107–108.

3. Michael R. Gottfredson and Travis Hirschi (1990). p. 90. Also, Robert Sampson and John Laub (1993). *Crime in the making: Pathways and turning points through life.* Cambridge, MA: Harvard University press, 4–9.

4. Office of Juvenile Justice and Delinquency Prevention. *Juvenile arrests 2002* (2004, December). Washington, DC: U.S. Department of Justice, NCJ 201370. Retrieved online December 29, 2004: http://ojjdp.ncjrs.org/ojstatbb/crime/qa05101.asp?qaDate=20040801

5. Office of Juvenile Justice and Delinquency Prevention. *Juvenile arrests 2002* (2004, December).

6. Wayne S. Wooden and Randy Blazak (2003). *Renegade kids, suburban outlaws: From youth culture to delinquency.* Belmont, CA: Wadsworth, 1–4.

7. PBS Transcript Version (2004). *People like us: Social class in America.* Retrieved online December 30, 2004: http://www.pbs.org/peoplelikeus/resources/transcript.pdf, 32.

8. Randall G. Shelden (2001). *Controlling the dangerous classes: A critical introduction to the history of criminal justice.* Boston: Allyn & Bacon, 16–19.

9. Wayne S. Wooden and Randy Blazak (2003), 2.

10. OJJDP Statistical briefing book. *Easy access to FBI arrest statistics: 1994–2001.* Retrieved online March 27, 2004: http://ojjdp.ncjrs.org/ojstatbb/ezaucr/asp/ucr_display.asp

11. The aftermath of this police raid has produced litigation against the police, the school, and the officials involved in the raid by concerned parents and others including the American Civil Liberties Union's (ACLU) Drug Policy Litigation Project. Retrieved online March 27, 2004: (http://www.aclu.org/DrugPolicy/DrugPolicy.cfm?ID=10972&c=19) The ACLU has filed a lawsuit on behalf of 20 more students alleging Fourth Amendment violations. Additionally there are concerns that some motives behind the raid involved racial discrimination because about 75 per-

cent of the students were white, whereas 75 percent of those caught in the raid were black. However, most of the families involved in various lawsuits have specifically requested that the ACLU represent them.

12. *Children in urban America project.* Marquette University, Department of History, Milwaukee, WI. Retrieved online March 24, 2004: http://134.48.55.172:8000/cuap/index.shtml

13. Leonard P. Edwards (1992). The juvenile court and the role of the juvenile court judge. *Juvenile and Family Court Journal, 43*(2), 1–45.

14. Curt R. Bartol and Anne M. Bartol (2005). *Criminal behavior: A psychosocial approach* (7th ed.). Upper Saddle River, NJ: Prentice Hall, 40–41.

15. Wayne S. Wooden and Randy Blazak (2003), 5.

16. Leonard P. Edwards (1992), 4–6. For excellent descriptions on how the behavior of children is easily misunderstood, leading toward criminal justice intervention, see Edward Humes (1996). *No matter how loud I shout.* New York: Simon & Schuster. Especially children raised by the state, 106–120.

17. Susan Datesman and Michael Aickin (1985). Offense specialization and escalation among status offenders. *The Journal of Criminal Law and Criminology, 75,* 1246–1275. Also Brianne Gorod (2000). *The significance of risk. An examination of deprivation and delinquency in the lives of status offenders.* Retrieved online January 16, 2005: http://www.childwelfare.net/activities/interns/2000summer/BrianneGorod2.html

18. Howard A. Davidson (1997). The courts and child maltreatment. In Mary Edna Helfer, Ruth S. Kempe, and Richard D. Krugman (Eds.), *The battered child* (5th ed.). Chicago: University of Chicago Press. Also see Marvin Ventrell (1998). Evolution of the dependence component of the juvenile court, 3. Retrieved online March 13, 2004: http://naccchildlaw.org/documents/evolutionofthedependencycourt.pdf

19. J. Herbie DiFonzo (1995). Deprived of fatal liberty: The rhetoric of child saving and the reality of juvenile incarceration. *University of Toledo, College of Law, 26,* 855.

20. Randall G. Shelden (2001), 197.

21. Jeanne Boydston, Nick Cullather, Jan Ellen Lewis, Michael McGrerr, and James Oakes (2002). *Making a nation: The United States and its people.* Upper Saddle River, NJ: Prentice Hall, 83.

22. Murray Straus (2000). *Beating the devil out of them: Corporal punishment in American families and its effects on children* (2nd ed.). New Brunswick, NJ: Transaction Publishers, 18–24.

23. W. Lance Bennett (1994). *Inside the system: Culture, institutions and power in American politics.* New York: Harcourt Brace.

24. Jeanne Boydston, Nick Cullather, Jan Ellen Lewis, Michael McGrerr, and James Oakes (2002), 81–84.

25. Larry J. Siegel (2002). *Juvenile delinquency: The core.* Belmont, CA: Wadsworth, 267–283.

26. John R. Sutton (1993). *Stubborn children: Controlling delinquency in the United States. 1640–1981.* Berkeley, CA: University of California Press, 11–14.

27. John R. Sutton (1993), 11.

28. During the first half of the 19th century, the population exploded due to an increased birthrate and expanding immigration and the rural poor and immigrants were attracted to urban commercial centers. Employment was a major draw. For instance, in 1720, 12,000 people lived in Boston, 10,000 inhabitants were in Philadelphia, 7,000 lived in New York, and Newport and Charleston were home to almost 4,000 each. By the eve of the American Revolution, Philadelphia had grown to 30,000 residents, New York to 25,000, and Boston reported 16,000 residents. These cities were ports, centers for the fur trade, and centers of commerce.

    By 1850, urban population increased from 5 to 15 percent and jumped to 40 percent by 1900 and 51 percent in 1920. New York had more than quadrupled its population in the 30-year stretch between 1825 and 1855—from 166,000 in 1825 to 630,000 in 1855. See J. J. Macionis and V. N. Parrillo (1998). *Cities and urban life.* Upper Saddle River, NJ: Prentice Hall (pp. 21–52). Also, The United States Historical Census Data Browser. Retrieved online December 29, 2004: http://www.census.gov/prod/2002pubs/po102-ma.pdf

29. Randall G. Shelden (2001), 197–198. Also see Larry J. Siegel (2002), 268.

30. Joseph F. Kitt (1977). *Rites of passage: Adolescence in America, 1790 to the present.* New York: Basic Books, 23–24.

31. Joseph M. Hawes (1971). *Children in urban society: Juvenile delinquency in nineteenth-century America.* New York: Oxford University Press. And Joseph M. Hawes (1991). *The children's rights movement: A history of advocacy and protection.* New York: Twayne Pub.

32. T. L. Bernard (1992). *Inside the system: Culture, institutions and power in American politics.* New York: Harcourt Brace, 43–49. Also see David Rothman (1998). *Social inequality.* Upper Saddle River, NJ: Prentice Hall, 4–8.

33. T. L. Bernard (1992), 47. Also see David Rothman (1998).

34. David Nasaw (1986). *Children of the city.* New York: Oxford University Press, 14–16.

35. John Mack Faragher, Mari Jo Buhle, Daniel Czitrom, and Susan H. Armitage (2000). *Out of many: A history of the American people* (3rd ed.). Upper Saddle River, NJ: Prentice Hall, 58–60.

36. John Mack Faragher, Mari Jo Buhle, Daniel Czitrom, and Susan H. Armitage (2000), 988.

37. Meg Greene Malvasi (1999, August 3). *History for children and street Arabs.* Retrieved online March 14, 2004: http://www.suite101.com/article.cfm/history_for_children/18538

38. Randall G. Shelden (2001), 197.

39. Randall G. Shelden (2001), 197–198.

40. Murray Straus (2000), 27.

41. John Mack Faragher, Mari Jo Buhle, Daniel Czitrom, and Susan H. Armitage (2000), 333.

42. J. J. Macionis and V. N. Parrillo (1998).

43. Randall G. Shelden (2001), 16–19, 73–74. Also see, Larry J. Siegel (2002), 267–294.

44. John Mack Faragher, Mari Jo Buhle, Daniel Czitrom, and Susan H. Armitage (2000), 380–387.

45. Jeanne Boydston, Nick Cullather, Jan Ellen Lewis, Michael McGrerr, and James Oakes (2002), 288.

46. Jeanne Boydston, Nick Cullather, Jan Ellen Lewis, Michael McGrerr, and James Oakes (2002). Also see, Lewis W. Hine (2001). *The empire state building. Children at work 1908–1912.* New York: Prestel.

47. David Nasaw (1986). *Children of the city.* New York: Oxford University Press.

48. David Nasaw (1986).

49. Sanford J. Fox (1970). Juvenile justice reform: A historical perspective. *Stanford Law Review, 22,* 1187.

50. Jim McCarty (1997, July). *Rural Missouri.* Retrieved online March 14, 2004: http://www.rootsweb.com/~mogrundy/orphans.html

51. John R. Sutton (1993). *Stubborn children: Controlling delinquency in the United States. 1640–1981.* Berkeley: University of California Press.

52. Harry E. Allen and Clifford E. Simonsen (2001). *Corrections in America: An introduction* (9th ed.). Upper Saddle River, NJ: Prentice Hall, 467–468.

53. Harry E. Allen and Clifford E. Simonsen (2001), 469.

54. Personal communication with police officer in Dorchester. January 2004.

55. Personal communication with police officer. June 2003. The officer wished to remain anonymous.

56. Also, Stanton Samenow (1984). *Inside the criminal mind.* New York: Times Books, 53–59.

57. Stanton Samenow (1998). *Before it's too late.* New York: Times Books, 37.

58. Larry J. Siegel (2002), 267–294.

59. *Child maltreatment.* Department of Education, Government of Newfoundland and Labrador (2003). Retrieved online December 29, 2004: http://www.edu.gov.nf.ca/child/Main.htm

60. Judith S. Rycus, Ronald C. Hughes, and Jewell K. Garrison (1989). *Child protective services: A training curriculum.* Washington, DC: Child Welfare League of America. Mary Ellen's Court Statement: "My name is Mary Ellen _____. I don't know how old I am; my mother and father are both dead; I call Mrs. C_____ momma; I have never had but one pair of shoes, but can't recollect when that was; I have no

shoes or stockings this winter; I have never been allowed to go out . . . except in the night time, and only in the yard (to use the outdoor privy); my bed at night is only a piece of carpet stretched on the floor underneath a window and I sleep in my little undergarment with a quilt over me; I am never allowed to play with other children; momma has been in the habit of whipping me almost everyday; she used to whip me with a twisted whip—a rawhide; the whip always left black and blue marks on my body; I have now on my head two black and blue marks which were made by momma with the whip, and a cut on the left side of my forehead which was made by a pair of scissors in momma's hand; she struck me with the scissors and cut me; I have no recollection of ever having been kissed and I have never been kissed by momma: I have never been taken on momma's lap or caressed or petted; I never dared speak to anybody, because if I did I would get whipped; I have never had . . . any more clothing than I have on at present . . . .; I have seen stockings and other clothes in our room, but I am not allowed to put them on; whenever momma went out, I was locked up in the bedroom; . . . I don't know for what I was whipped; momma never said anything when she whipped me; I do not want to go back to live with momma because she beats me so." [60] Mary Ellen was placed in a loving home, married, raised a family of her own, and died at the age of 92 in 1956. Source: New York Society for the Prevention Of Cruelty to Children. Retrieved online August 20, 2004: http://www.nyspcc.org/beta_history/index_history.htm

61. New York Society for the Prevention Of Cruelty to Children. Retrieved online March 24, 2004: http://www.nyspcc.org/beta_history/index_history.htm

62. New York Society for the Prevention Of Cruelty to Children.

63. New York Society for the Prevention Of Cruelty to Children.

64. Judith S. Rycus, Ronald C. Hughes, and Jewell K. Garrison (1989).

65. Sanford J. Fox (1996). The early history of the court: The future of children. *The Juvenile Court, 6*(3), 29–39.

66. Laoise King (2003, April). Colorado juvenile court history: The first hundred years. *The Colorado Lawyer, 32*(4), 63–65.

67. Jeanne Boydston, Nick Cullather, Jan Ellen Lewis, Michael McGrerr, and James Oakes (2002), 622–628.

68. Howard N. Snyder and Melissa Sickmund (1999). *Juvenile offenders and victims: 1999 National Report.* Washington, DC: U.S. Department of Justice, Office of Juvenile Justice and Delinquency Prevention, NCJ 178257, 86.

69. Howard N. Snyder and Melissa Sickmund (1999), 86.

70. Negligence refers to acts that a reasonable person would not do or the failure to do something that a reasonable person would do under the same or similar circumstances. Its interpretation is generally guided by the criminal code or statutes of a given jurisdiction.

71. For instance, a typical "culpability" provision can be found in the Pennsylvania Consolidated Statutes. Crimes and Offenses (Title 18). Part I. Preliminary Provisions. Chapter 3. General Requirements of Culpability include:

(a) Minimum requirements of culpability: Except as provided in Section 305 of this title (relating to limitations on scope of culpability requirements), a person is not guilty of an offense unless he acted intentionally, knowingly, recklessly, or negligently, as the law may require, with respect to each material element of the offense.

(b) Kinds of culpability defined: A person acts intentionally with respect to a material element of an offense: if the element involves the nature of his conduct or a result thereof, it is his conscious object to engage in conduct of that nature or to cause such a result; and if the element involves the attendant circumstances, he is aware of the existence of such circumstances or he believes or hopes that they exist.

A person acts knowingly with respect to a material element of an offense: if the element involves the nature of his conduct or the attendant circumstances, he is aware that his conduct is of that nature or that such circumstances exist; and if the element involves a result of his conduct, he is aware that it is practically certain that his conduct will cause such a result.

A person acts recklessly with respect to a material element of an offense when he consciously disregards a substantial and unjustifiable risk that the material element exists or will result from his conduct. The risk must be of such a nature and degree that, considering the nature and intent of the actor's conduct and the circumstances known to him, its disregard involves a gross deviation from the standard of conduct that a reasonable person would observe in the actor's situation.

A person acts negligently with respect to a material element of an offense when he should be aware of a substantial and unjustifiable risk that the material element exists or will result from his conduct. The risk must be of such a nature and degree that the actor's failure to perceive it, considering the nature and intent of his conduct and the circumstances known to him, involves a gross deviation from the standard of care that a reasonable person would observe in the actor's situation.

72. Sue Titus Reid (2001). *Criminal law* (5th ed.). New York: McGraw Hill, 36.

73. Personnel communication with a juvenile PO employed by the state of California who wishes to remain anonymous.

74. Michael R. Gottfredson and Travis Hirschi (1999), 107.

75. Mark Cohen (1998). The monetary value of saving a high-risk youth. *Journal of Quantitative Criminology, 14*(1).

76. This explanation was also addressed by Howard N. Snyder and Melissa Sickmund (1999), 82.

77. Prepared by the author for this chapter based upon information provided by Suzanne Koller.

13

JUVENILES:
THE DELINQUENCY ERA

LEARNING OBJECTIVES

After you finish reading this chapter, you will be better prepared to:

- Describe delinquency and status offender behavior.
- Explain why official response went from dependency to harsh penalties.
- Describe the juvenile justice process starting with an arrest.
- Describe the relevance of juvenile waivers to adult court.
- Explain the rationale behind probation and intense probation.
- Identify a school curriculum that can help youths reduce antisocial characteristics.
- Identify several of the programs that aid juveniles towards compliance.
- Identify the primary U.S. Supreme Court decisions that shaped due process for juveniles.
- Define Habeas Corpus and explain its use.
- Identify similarities in the juvenile and adult justice systems.
- Identify differences between juvenile and adult justice systems.

KEY TERMS

CHINS	Juvenile Delinquency	Status Offenders
Delinquents	Prevention and Control	*Kent v. United States (1966)*
Habeas Corpus	Act of 1968	*In Re Gault (1970)*
Juvenile Waivers	PINS	*In Re Winship*

> We are born weak, we need strength, helpless, we need aid; foolish, we need reason. All that we lack at birth, all that we need when we come to man's estate, is the gift of education.
>
> —Jean Jacques Rousseau (1712–1778)

INTRODUCTION

Dependency strategies toward juveniles were explored in Chapter 12, which included a historical account from early American history to the beginning of the "delinquency era" with the development of the first juvenile court system in 1899. This chapter is about the institutionalization of juveniles through the criminal justice system. The chapter begins with an explanation of delinquency and status offenders and describes the juvenile justice process, including descriptions of juvenile waivers from juvenile court to adult court for some offenders. Special CC programs designed largely for juveniles are described, including probation. Although Jean Jacques Rousseau seems right in his assumption that children are dependent upon adults for education and reason, I wonder if Rousseau ever thought that the criminal justice system would be one of the important contributors of child protection through juvenile legislated rights. In this regard, the U.S. Supreme Court brought forth several important cases discussed in this chapter, which developed the boundaries criminal justice professionals must follow. Finally, similarities and differences between juvenile and adult justice systems are offered to help present a better understanding of the juvenile justice system.

DELINQUENTS AND STATUS OFFENDERS

Delinquency is a failure to comply with both rules and laws. Juvenile offenders are a component of the juvenile justice system that handles violations of rules and laws committed by minors such as truancy, theft, and assault. There are approximately 1.8 million juvenile delinquency cases heard by the courts each year.[1]

In the 21st century, the juvenile justice system exercises jurisdiction over two distinct categories of juvenile offenders: *delinquents* and *status offenders*. Delinquent children are those who fall under a jurisdictional age limit that varies from state to state and who commit an act in violation of the penal code of that state.[2] The delinquency component of the court may also include "status offenses:" truancy, running away, or alcohol possession. Status offenses are violations that are age-specific or discriminatory depending on how you want to view this perspective.[3]

Status offenders are commonly characterized in state statutes as persons or children in need of supervision (PINS—persons in need of supervision or **CHINS**—children in need of supervision). Most states distinguish such behavior from delinquent conduct to lessen the effect of any stigma on children as a result of their involvement with the juvenile court.[4] For instance, the district court in Alexandria, VA, reports that there are two types of CHINS cases:

- *CHINS Supervision Cases* involve children who are failing to attend school as required by Virginia law or who are running away from home.
- *CHINS Services Cases* involve children who may be out of control at home and are in need of services or assistance that the community can provide.[5]

The district court mandates that a child's failure to attend school must first be addressed by the Alexandria City Public Schools and the child's parents.[6] Each school, the report says, has a social worker that is available to assist parents with concerns they may have about how their child is performing in school. In most instances, the school system looks to the parents of children through the fifth grade to be responsible for their child's actions, such as attending school. From the 6th grade through the 12th grade, the child and the parents are both responsible for the child's attendance at school and in other matters.

In addition, juvenile courts in general across the country have jurisdiction over situations involving conduct directed at (rather than committed by) juveniles, such as parental neglect, deprivation, abandonment, and abuse.[7] Most states distinguish such behavior from delinquent conduct to lesson the effect of any stigma on children as a result of their involvement with the juvenile court system.[8] Juvenile courts also have jurisdiction over conduct directed at juveniles such as parental neglect, deprivation, abandonment, and both sexual and physical abuse.

Number of Persons under 18 in the United States

The U.S. Census reports that at yearend 2000, one in every four persons living in the United States was under the age of 18.[9] That is, of 281 million residents, 72 million were juveniles. Most of those juveniles were between the ages of 5 and 13. And as you can expect, 69 percent of those youths were white, 17 percent were Latino, and 15 percent were African American or black. Although the juvenile population has been increasing, it represents a smaller share of the total population because the older population is living longer due to medical technology. One estimate is that by 2020, youngsters will represent 16 percent of the U.S. population.[10]

What is a Juvenile in Legal Terms?

A juvenile is a youth at or below the upper age of original jurisdiction of a court in a State.

Oldest Age for Original Juvenile Court Jurisdiction in Delinquency Matters: 2002

Age 15	Connecticut, New York, North Carolina
Age 16	Georgia, Illinois, Louisiana, Massachusetts, Michigan, Missouri, New Hampshire, South Carolina, Texas, Wisconsin
Age 17	Alabama, Alaska, Arizona, Arkansas, California, Colorado, Delaware, District of Columbia, Florida, Hawaii, Idaho, Indiana, Iowa, Kansas, Kentucky, Maine, Maryland, Minnesota, Mississippi, Montana, Nebraska, Nevada, New Jersey, New Mexico, North Dakota, Ohio, Oklahoma, Oregon, Pennsylvania, Rhode Island, South Dakota, Tennessee, Utah, Vermont, Virginia, Washington, West Virginia, Wyoming

Note. Some states report individuals as young as 14 confined in their state residential facilities, such as Connecticut.
Source: National Center for Juvenile Justice.[11]

State statutes define which youth, based on age criteria, are under the original jurisdiction of the juvenile court. In most states, the juvenile court has original jurisdiction over all youth charged with a criminal law violation who are below the age of 18 at the time of the offense, arrest, or referral to court. Many states have higher upper ages of juvenile court jurisdiction in status offense, abuse, neglect, or dependency matters—often through age 20.[12]

From Dependency to Harsh Penalties

The mission to help troubled youth was instrumental in developing the laws that helped establish juvenile courts that flourished in the first half of the 20th century. This compassionate notion led to practical and policy differences between adult and juvenile court. In the next 50 years, most juvenile courts had exclusive jurisdiction rights over youth under 18 charged with violating a crime. A juvenile court, often at its own discretion, could:

- Waive jurisdiction over a juvenile whereby the juvenile would be tried in adult court.
- Divert a juvenile out of the system thereby bypassing judicial action.
- Conduct formal criminal proceedings against the juvenile.
- Impose a sanction to be carried out at a juvenile residential center or facility.

Regardless of the offense, juvenile court outcomes ranged from warnings to probation to training schools to treatment to waivers to adult courts. Dispositions were tailored to best meet interests of the child and treatment lasted until the child was "cured" or became an adult.

Public confidence in the treatment model waned as due process protections for juveniles were emphasized in the 1950s and 1960s. Treatment and confinement practices had not produced the expected results. The U.S. Supreme Court required juvenile courts to become more formal (like adult courts) yet retain some of their distinctive differences. Due process guarantees would be applied to juveniles in a number of ways through the Juvenile Delinquency Prevention and Control Act of 1968 (amended 1974), which recommended that children charged with noncriminal offenses be handled outside the juvenile court system. However, across the nation, there were a number of legislative state changes in response to the mood of the nation about juveniles and about which correctional approach would best "fit" a juvenile offender regardless of whether the juvenile was involved in a crime or a status offensive as Table 13.1 shows. Some states declare their goals and objectives in exhaustive detail, reports the OJJDP, even to the point of listing specific programs and sentencing options.[13] Other states mention only the broadest of aims, whereas others remain silent on the subject of juvenile justice, at least in their statutes.[14] Many juvenile court "purpose" clauses or objectives have been amended over the years, which reflect philosophical or rhetorical shifts in a states' overall approach to juvenile delinquency. At of the end of the most recent legislative session (2002 or 2003,

Table 13.1 Correctional Approaches Stated in Juvenile Justice Systems[18]

Balanced Treatment/ Prevention	Control/ Treatment	Control	Punishment	Diversion/ Treatment	Punishment/ Treatment[18]
Alaska	Georgia	New Hampshire	Connecticut	Washington, DC	Arizona[19]
Florida	Iowa	New Mexico	Hawaii	Kentucky	Colorado
Idaho	Louisiana	North Dakota	North Carolina	Massachusetts	Delaware
Illinois	Michigan	Ohio	Texas	South Dakota[20]	Nebraska
Kansas	Mississippi	Tennessee	Utah	West Virginia	South Carolina
Maryland	Missouri	Vermont	Wyoming		
New Jersey	Nevada				
Pennsylvania	Rhode Island				
Wisconsin	South Carolina				
Some Treatment/ Prevention	**Some Control/ Treatment**	**Some Control**			
Alabama	Arkansas	Arkansas			
California	California	Maine			
Indiana	Florida	Montana			
Iowa[21]	Illinois	New Jersey			
Minnesota	Maine	Texas			
Montana	Massachusetts	Wyoming			
Oregon	Minnesota				
Washington	New Jersey				

Note: categories are not mutually exclusive. Most states seek to protect the interests of the child, the family, the community, or some combination of the three.

In 17 states, the purpose clause incorporates the language of the balanced and restorative justice approaches, emphasizing offender accountability, public safety, and competency development. Purpose clauses also address court issues such as fairness, speedy trials, and even coordination of services. In nearly all states, the code also includes protections of the child's constitutional and statutory rights.

Caution: Policy and practice are two different matters.

depending on the state), Paul Griffin and Melanie Bozynki proposed that most state juvenile court objectives and policies can be placed into five categories and as a matter of discussion, the author made an attempt to match each category with a correctional approach:[15]

1. Balanced and Restorative Justice (BRRJ) clauses: This is when the state's policy makers advocate that the justice community, including juvenile courts, balance their practices to support three specific initiatives: public safety, offender accountability to victims and the community, and the development of offender skills necessary to live law-abiding and productive lives in the community. It would appear that this directive tends to favor a treatment and preventive approach, which can include CC initiatives more than the other corrections approaches of punishment and control. It would also appear that the policy makers in these states see social environmental influences as major contributors to crime as opposed to free will perspectives.

2. Standard juvenile court act clauses: This is where the juvenile justice shall provide each juvenile offender with care, guidance, and control that will enhance the welfare of the juvenile, but toward the best interest of the state. When a child is removed from his or her parents, the court will fill the parental gap. These objectives or policies can be interpreted as a perspective couched in *parens patriae* or what seems to describe the primary philosophical characteristics of control and treatment approaches.

3. Legislative guide clauses: This is when four objectives are emphasized by state statue: (a) to provide for the care, protection, and wholesome mental and physical development of children involved with the juvenile court; (b) to provide a program of supervision, care, and rehabilitation as opposed to criminal sanctions against children who commit delinquent acts; (c) to remove a child from the home only when necessary for his or her welfare and in the interests of public safety; (d) to assure all parties their constitutional and other legal rights. The characteristics of this clause seem to support a control approach to justice practices.

4. Directives emphasizing punishment, deterrence, accountability, and public safety: That is, in at least six states, the juvenile justice system is directed to "get tough on juvenile offenders," in that policy directs community protection, offender accountability, crime reduction through deterrence, or outright punishment, either predominantly or exclusively. Retribution and just desert policies seem to be officially supported in those states and it is expected that those policy makers tend to believe that free will is the greatest contributor of juvenile crime.

5. Clauses with traditional child welfare orientations: These clauses exist in at least four states (including Washington, DC), which emphasize the promotion of the welfare and best interests of the juvenile as the sole or primary purpose of the juvenile court system or what can be referred to as a liberalness that seems to emphasize diversion and treatment. These policy makers would tend to look at the social environment as the root causes of crime.

The National Center for Juvenile Justice and the OJJDP[16] imply that certain states tend to emphasize specific criminal justice approaches as explained in Chapter 2 that could ultimately reflect CC practices. (See Table 13.1)[17]

Most states have legislated punitive sanctions and practices against juveniles as the perspectives of policy makers,[19] interest groups, and the public move away from treatment and prevention.[20] Some of those punitive sanctions removed classes of juvenile offenders from juvenile court jurisdiction to adult court authority or waivers from juvenile jurisdiction to adult courts (more on waivers later) in this chapter.[21] Many policy and practices of the juvenile justice system also took on an adult justice perspective toward other classes of juvenile offenders.[22] Therefore, no matter the position taken by the legislative body of a state to mandate care and comfort to a child offender, should regulation also provide prosecutors an opportunity to waive a child to adult court, in the final analysis, some children continue to suffer the consequences of adult behavior.[23]

Imposed Dispositions upon Juvenile Offenders[24]

The justice system in most jurisdictions can impose the following upon juvenile offenders:

- Release
- Diversion
- Judicial waiver to criminal court
- Probation under supervision
- Boot camp
- Monitoring to verify compliance with court orders
- Electronic home monitoring
- Removal from the family home to residential placement
- Payment of pay restitution to the victim or to a victim fund
- Require offender to apologize to the victim
- Community work service
- Payment of a fine
- Completion of a chemical use assessment and follow
- Treatment
- Completion of a psychological evaluation
- Offender must attend school
- Completion of special classes or programs
- Offender must, learn new skills
- Other court-ordered sanctions

JUVENILE PROCESS THROUGH JUSTICE SYSTEM

The stages of processing juveniles through the justice system are described in Figure 13.2.[25] Although every jurisdiction is unique due to its own practices and tradition, descriptions of juvenile justice processing are generalized, highlighting a common series of decision points. Keep in mind that throughout the process, the police, prosecutors, juvenile probation, and the courts can use discretion to release, divert, and informally halt the process of disposition depending on local statues, practices, and on the merits of the case, the violation, and the circumstances of the accused. However, the first step of a juvenile entering the system is through an arrest.

Juvenile Arrests

The first decision of police is to arrest a juvenile. In 2002, there were approximately 2.4 million arrests of persons under the age of 18 (see Figure 13.1). The most serious nonviolent

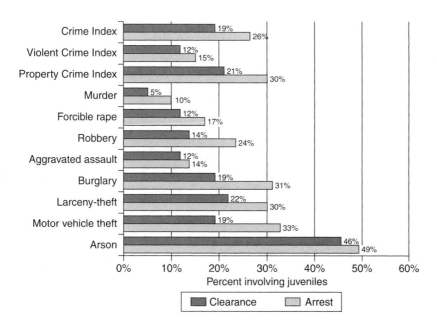

The Juvenile Proportion of Arrests Exceeded the Juvenile Proportion of Crimes Cleared by Arrest in each Offense Category, Reflecting the Fact that Juveniles are More Likely to Commit Crimes in Groups and are More Likely to be Arrested than Adults

Figure 13.1

Source: *Crime in the United States 2001* (Washington: DC: U.S. Government Printing Office, 2002 Tables 28 and 38.

WHAT DO ARREST STATISTICS COUNT

To interpret the material in this bulletin properly, the reader must have a clear understanding of what these statistics count. The arrest statistics report the number of arrests made by law enforcement agencies in a particular year—not the number of individuals arrested, nor the number of crimes committed. The number of arrests is not equivalent to the number of people arrested because an unknown number of individuals are arrested more than once in the year. Nor do arrest statistics represent counts of crimes committed by arrested individuals, because a series of crimes committed by one individual may culminate in a single arrest, or a single crime may result in the arrest of more than one person. This latter situation, where many arrests result from one crime, is relatively common in juvenile law-violating behavior because juveniles are more likely than adults to commit crimes in groups. This is the primary reason why arrest statistics should not be used to indicate the relative proportion of crime committed by juveniles and adults. Arrest statistics are most appropriately a measure of flow into the criminal and juvenile justice systems.

Arrest statistics also have limitations for measuring the volume of arrests for a particular offense. Under the UCR Program, the FBI requires law enforcement agencies to classify an arrest by the most serious offense charged in that arrest. For example, the arrest of a youth charged with aggravated assault and possession of a controlled substance would be reported to the FBI as an arrest for aggravated assault. Therefore, when arrest statistics show that law enforcement agencies made an estimated 202,500 arrests of young people for drug abuse violations in 2001, it means that a drug abuse violation was the most serious charge in these 202,500 arrests. An unknown number of additional arrests in 2001 included a drug charge as a lesser offense.

WHAT DO CLEARANCE STATISTICS COUNT?

Clearance statistics measure the proportion of reported crimes that were resolved by an arrest or other, exceptional means (e.g., death of the offender, unwillingness of the victim to cooperate). A single arrest may result in many clearances. For example, 1 arrest could clear 40 burglaries if the person was charged with committing all 40 of these crimes. Or multiple arrests may result in a single clearance if the crime was committed by a group of offenders. For those interested in juvenile justice issues, the FBI also reports information on the proportion of clearances that were cleared by the arrest of persons under age 18. This statistic is a better indicator of the proportion of crime committed by this age group than is the arrest proportion, although there are some concerns that even the clearance statistic overestimates the juvenile proportion of crimes.

For example, the FBI reports that persons under age 18 accounted for 24 percent of all robbery arrests but only 14 percent of all robberies that were cleared in 2001. If it can be assumed that offender characteristics of cleared robberies are similar to those of robberies that were not cleared, then it would be appropriate to conclude that persons under age 18 were responsible for 14 percent of all robberies in 2001. However, the offender characteristics of cleared and noncleared robberies may differ for a number of reasons. If, for example, juvenile robbers were more easily apprehended than adult robbers, the proportion of robberies cleared by the arrest of persons under age 18 would overestimate the juvenile responsibility for all robberies. To add to the difficulty in interpreting clearance statistics, the FBI's reporting guidelines require the clearance to be tied to the oldest offender in the group if more than one person is arrested for a crime.

In summary, although the interpretation of reported clearance proportions is not straightforward, these data are the closest measure generally available of the proportion of crime known to law enforcement that is attributed to persons under age 18.

Printed with permission of the U.S. Department of Justice.[26]

charges in over 40 percent of the juvenile arrests were comprised of larceny-theft, simple assault, drug abuse violations, and disorderly conduct. Twenty six percent were female and 71 percent were white. Approximately five percent of the juvenile arrests in 2002 were for the violent crimes of aggravated assault, robbery, forcible rape, and murder; 16 percent were female and 44 percent were black offenders. Also, 1 in 11 juveniles arrested was under the age of 13. Once an arrest is completed, police generally have four choices:

1. Release
2. Diversion
3. Refer to prosecutor's office
4. Detention while awaiting disposition

1. **Police Release Juvenile:** After a review of the case, police might determine that in the best interests of public safety and the youth, it would be best to release the individual to his or her guardians. In 2002, approximately 30 percent of all juveniles taken into custody were released from further justice process.[28]

2. **Police Refer Juvenile to Informal Diversion:** Juveniles who are not referred to juvenile court and not released are generally diverted to informal alternative programs that can be operated by the police but many times are operated by community public and private organizations. Referral stops the judicial process, assuming the juvenile successfully completes the diversion program (i.e., cleaning parkways, attending substance abuse meetings). The major premise behind diversion is that juveniles need not help stigmatization. Some of their problems can include poor relationships with family, poor school performance, or chemical abuse issues. With diversion, the youth has the responsibility to fulfill an obligation (problem-solving skill groups, counseling, school attendance, curfew) so as to avoid having his or her case handled formally in court.[29]

3. **Police Refer Juveniles to Prosecutor's Office:** After interviews with the victim/s, offender, and parents, and considering a youth's prior contacts with the juvenile justice system, the police might refer a youth to the prosecutor's office. In 2003, the police referred an estimated 85 percent of all delinquency cases to juvenile court through the prosecutor's office. The remaining referrals were made by parents, victims, schools, and POs. (Federal regulation requires that a juvenile be securely detained for no longer than six hours and in an area that is not within sight or sound of adult inmates).[30]

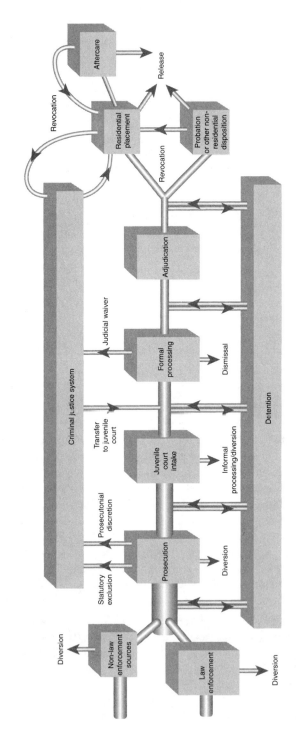

Figure 13.2 Process of Juvenile Criminal Justice System
Printed with the permission of the U.S. Department of Justice.[27]

4. **Police Place Juveniles in Holding Facility or Detention:** Sometimes a juvenile appears to be a danger to himself or others and depending on the seriousness of the crime and evidence, can be placed in a holding or detention facility while awaiting disposition. In all states, a detention hearing must be held within a time period defined by statute, generally within 24 hours. At the detention hearing, a judge reviews the case usually prepared by police, juvenile probation officers, or detention workers and determines if continued detention is warranted. As a result of the detention hearing, the youth may be released or detention continued. Detention can continue during the entire judicial process based on the crime, danger potential, risk, and statue warrants confinement.[31]

5. **Prosecutor's Office Refers Case to Juvenile Court Intake or Diversion:** Intake can consist of juvenile POs and members of the prosecutor's office. Court intake reviews the merits of the case, circumstances of those accused, evidence, youth's record, and seriousness of the crime, and can also look at the accounts of the victims and conduct interviews with them. Youthful diversion programs provided by the prosecutor's office are usually based on a belief that not all cases are best handled through a formal complaint and court hearing.[32] Generally, the only referable cases to a diversion program are first-time offenders who engaged in:

   a. Possession of alcohol

   b. Possession of drugs at the Class D level

   c. Disorderly conduct

   d. Public drinking

   e. Disturbing the peace

   f. A minor purchasing or attempting to purchase alcohol

   g. Trespassing

Youths who enter a program sign a contract in which they agree to participate in counseling or substance abuse guidance, education, and community service. Successful completion results in the youth not having a court record for the offense that brought them to the attention of the court.

1. **Juvenile Court Intake:** Court intake has the (almost sole) authority to dismiss the case; handle it informally, such as through a diversion program; or request formal intervention by juvenile court based on the merits of the case. (In adult court, this action might lead to an automatic court process but among juveniles the decision to prosecute belongs to juvenile court intake.)

2. **Informally Processing/Diversion:** About one half of all cases referred to juvenile court intake are handed informally. Most informally held cases are dismissed whereas others are diverted out of the system but conditions are placed upon the juveniles.

3. **Informal Diversion Conditions:** If a case is not dismissed and not referred to court, the juvenile voluntarily agrees to specific conditions for a period of time. These conditions are often outlined in a written agreement called a "consent

decree." Conditions can include victim restitution, school attendance, drug counseling, friendship avoidance, and curfew. In most jurisdictions, an informal disposition must be accompanied by an admission of guilt. Juveniles are often monitored by POs. This process is sometimes called *"informal probation."* If the juvenile successfully completes the process, the case is dismissed. If the juvenile fails to meet the conditions, the intake decision may be to formally prosecute the case, and the case will proceed just as it would have if the initial decision had been to refer the case for an adjudicatory hearing. If the juvenile violates rules and conditions set by the court, the juvenile may be required to appear in court and more severe consequences may be imposed.

4. **Formal Processing:** During the court process, dismissal is based on a number of factors produced from the case such as a lack of evidence or a not-guilty finding. A juvenile's case can be transferred or judicially waived to criminal court, or a case can continue toward final deposition.

5. **Judicial Waiver:** In nearly all adjudicatory hearings, the determination that the juvenile was responsible for the offense(s) is made by a judge; however, in some states the juvenile is given the right to a jury trial. Waiver into criminal court can depend on age, circumstances of the crime, and criminal history, as discussed earlier.

6. **Adjudication:** Between the adjudication decision and the disposition hearing, an investigation report is prepared by probation staff. Once the juvenile is adjudicated a delinquent, a disposition plan is prepared and needed support systems and programs are checked for availability. Psychological assessments, diagnostic tests, or a period of confinement in a diagnostic facility might follow. At this point, a disposition hearing generally takes place unless the juvenile is released, which can imply that a not-guilty finding was determined.

7. **Disposition Hearing:** At the disposition hearing, dispositional recommendations are presented to the judge. Most juvenile dispositions are multifaceted and can include additional requirements such as drug counseling, weekend confinement in the local detention center, and community or victim restitution. A term of probation may be for a specified period of time or open-ended. Review hearings are held to monitor the juvenile's progress and to hear reports from probation staff. After conditions of the probation have been successfully met, the case is terminated.[33]

8. **Probation:** The most severe disposition ordered in 63 percent of the cases in which the youth was adjudicated delinquent.[34] During a period of probation supervision, a juvenile offender remains in the community and can continue normal activities such as school and work. However, the juvenile must comply with certain conditions. This compliance may be voluntary: the youth agrees to conditions in lieu of formal adjudication. Or compliance may be mandatory following adjudication: the youth is formally ordered to a term of probation and must comply with the conditions established by the court.

9. **Residential Placement:** The judge may order a juvenile to be committed to a residential placement facility. Residential commitment may be for a specific or indeter-

minate ordered time period. In October 2000, there were 110,284 juveniles in 3,061 juvenile (public and private) centers across the United States (not including juveniles in adult prisons, jails, or mental health facilities).[35] Some of those residential placements could include boot-camp-type facilities. Concerning public facilities, it cost taxpayers an average estimated cost per day of $170.49 for each juvenile compared to confined adults at $64.80 per day per prisoner, as of September 20, 2002.[36] In many private facilities, family or community members of a confined youth will often pay the costs of confinement.

10. **Aftercare:** When a juvenile offender completes a residential program and supervision continues in the community for a designated period of time. During this period the juvenile is under supervision of the court, the juvenile corrections department; or some other agency designated by the court, prosecutor's office, or statute. Crowded juvenile residential facilities, unacceptably high recidivism rates, and escalating residential costs are among the factors that fostered "intensive juvenile aftercare." It is believed that juvenile offenders, while under aftercare, during their transition to the community, would benefit in such areas as family and peer relations, education, jobs, substance abuse control, mental health, and recidivism.[37]

11. **Delinquency Cases Handled by Juvenile Courts:** In 2002, U.S. juvenile courts processed an estimated 1.3 million delinquency cases.[38] These cases involved juveniles charged with criminal law violations.[39] The number of delinquency cases handled by juvenile courts increased 44 percent between 1989 and 1998. During this time, the number of drug law violations increased 148 percent, person offense cases increased 88 percent, public order offense cases increased 73 percent, and property offense cases increased 11 percent.[40]

JUVENILE WAIVERS TO ADULT CRIMINAL COURT

All states have established legal mechanisms whereby some juveniles may be prosecuted within the criminal justice system. Some juveniles face mandatory or automatic waiver to adult courts whereas in other jurisdictions prosecutors or judges utilize discretion in placing juveniles under criminal court authority. There is a current trend toward an increasing number of juvenile cases waived to adult criminal courts and a current trend toward more punitive criminalized sentences imposed among juveniles in the early 21st century. One report shows that juvenile courts waived 47 percent more delinquency cases to criminal court in 1996 (approximately 10,000 cases) than in 1987.[41] Isn't it true that the media describes various forms of unfairness applied to some adults in the justice system? One question is in what way are American children protected when adult justice is applied to them?

As official response moved from helping to punishing, waiving (processing) juveniles from juvenile court to adult court became an easier process. In 1999, 46 states and Washington, DC had statutes allowing judicial waiver.[42] In recent years, the number of juvenile offenders transferred into the adult criminal justice system has increased. There are three basic transfer mechanisms:

- Judicial discretionary waiver
- Statutory or mandatory exclusion
- Concurrent jurisdiction[43]

Most standards combine these concepts in some way or simply allow a waiver whenever the court finds "good cause" such as the state of Kansas or whenever the accused is not a "proper subject" for juvenile treatment (Missouri and Virginia).[44]

Waiver provisions vary in their provisions and in their degree of flexibility. As of 1999, there were no waiver provisions in four states (see Table 13.3). Some state waiver provisions are entirely *discretionary* on the juvenile court whereas in one state (Connecticut), it is mandatory to waive a juvenile under specific conditions.[45] In other mandatory states, proceedings against a juvenile are initiated in juvenile court. In other provisions, there is a rebuttal or *presumptive* in favor of waiver, and in other states waivers are *discretionary* and *mandatory* once the juvenile court judge determines that certain statutory criteria have been met. The juvenile court has no role other than to confirm that the statutory requirements for mandatory waiver are met. Once it has done so, the juvenile court must send the case to a court of criminal jurisdiction.[46]

However, all states and Washington, DC allow adult criminal prosecution of juveniles under some circumstances.[48]

- The most common waiver is the judicial discretionary waiver provision whereby the juvenile court judge has the authority to waive juvenile court jurisdiction and transfer the case to criminal court.[49] If standards call for courts to exercise discretion to waive jurisdiction when the interests of the juvenile or the public would be better served or when the public safety or the public interest requires it. Or when a juvenile does not appear to be amenable to treatment or rehabilitation within the juve-

Table 13.3   States with Judicial Waiver 1999

No judicial waiver	Massachusetts, Nebraska, New Mexico, New York
Discretionary waiver	Alabama, Arkansas, Florida, Hawaii, Idaho, Iowa, Maryland, Michigan, Mississippi, Missouri, Montana, Oklahoma, Oregon, South Dakota, Tennessee, Texas, Vermont, Washington, Wisconsin, Wyoming
Mandatory waiver	Connecticut
Discretionary and mandatory waiver	Delaware, Georgia, Indiana, Kentucky, Louisiana, North Carolina, Ohio, South Carolina, Virginia, West Virginia
Discretionary and presumptive waiver	Alaska, Arizona, California, Colorado, District of Columbia, Kansas, Maine, Minnesota, Nevada, New Hampshire, Pennsylvania, Utah
Discretionary, presumptive, and mandatory waiver	Illinois, New Jersey, North Dakota

Source: U.S. Department of Justice[47]

nile system. The specific factors that determine lack of amenability vary, but typically include the juvenile's offense history and previous dispositional outcomes.

- In most states, judicial waiver provisions are limited by age and/or offense criteria. Many statutes instruct the court to consider the availability of dispositional alternatives for treating the juvenile and the time available for sanctions, as well as public safety and the best interests of the child when making waiver decisions.

- In some states, a combination of the youth's age, offense, and prior record places the youth under the original jurisdiction of both the juvenile and criminal courts. In these situations where the courts have concurrent jurisdiction, the prosecutor is given the authority to decide which court will initially handle the case. This is known as *concurrent jurisdiction, prosecutor discretion,* or *direct filing.*

Waiver Debate

However, due to the increasing number of delinquency cases waived into adult criminal courts, and the increasingly punitive criminalized delinquency court, some believe the American justice system is losing in its mission to treat children differently than adults.[50] Child advocates and public defenders are alarmed about automatic transfers.[51] Juveniles prosecuted in adult criminal court include a high percentage of abuse victims, mentally ill and educationally limited children, and children of color. Children convicted in adult courts face more severe and, often mandatory penalties than children convicted in juvenile courts. In some states, these children stand to lose collateral rights such as the right to vote before they have had a chance to enjoy them. Also:

- One study, comparing New York and New Jersey juvenile offenders, shows that the rearrest rate for children sentenced in juvenile court was 29 percent lower than the rearrest rate for juveniles sentenced in the adult criminal court.[52]

- A Florida study compared the recidivism rate of juveniles who were transferred to criminal court versus those who were retained in the juvenile system and concluded that juveniles who were transferred recidivated at a higher rate than the nontransfer group. Furthermore, the rate of reoffending in the transfer group was significantly higher than the nontransfer group, as was the likelihood that the transfer group would commit subsequent felony offenses.[53]

Some experts also argue that defense attorneys and public defenders seem ill-prepared to handle cases of children who appear in adult criminal courts.[54] It stands to reason that public defenders, much like some judges, prosecutors, and POs assigned the adult system, are often inexperienced in recognizing the needs and characteristics of younger defendants.[55] Finally, imprisoning youth offenders in adult prisons also places those juveniles in real danger. For instance, correctional personnel, including correctional officers, caseworkers, and classification evaluators, although compassionate toward younger offenders, tend to lack appropriate training in uncovering needs and risks of younger prisoners.[56]

- Children in adult institutions are 500 percent more likely to be sexually assaulted, 200 percent more likely to be beaten by staff, and 50 percent more likely to be attacked with a weapon than juveniles confined in a juvenile facility.[57]

What Contributed to an Official Change from Protection to Prosecution?

The correctional approach pendulum shifted from treatment to punishment aided by the media, some argue.[58] In the 1980s and 1990s, the media sensationalized juvenile offenders. In Denver, Colorado for instance, the predominant newspaper of the city printed 44 front page stories and 48 editorials of the topic of juvenile in the summer of 1993. During the previous summer, the same newspaper printed 2 front page stories and 3 editorials about juvenile offenders.

Another study from the same period reveals that of 141 articles about serial rape in the mainstream press, most furthered the fear of crime and reported that females should submit to attackers or die.[59] Most of those articles reported rape in terms that intensified reader fears as most readers identify with the victims. Serial rapists were depicted in articles such as "Fraternities of Fear: Gang Rape" in *MS* as young, out-of-control males. It's little wonder that criminologists took advantage of the opportunity and dubbed juvenile offenders as "super-predators" and warned the public of an unprecedented wave of youth violence.[60] One check of government statistics during that period reveals that violent crime among juveniles was not seriously climbing.[61] Finally, the literature is replete with evidence linking the fear of crime with irrational behavior, including harsh punitive practices toward juveniles, and in this case, juvenile waivers to adult criminal courts.[62] The push and pull for an appropriate approach toward juveniles is a complicated discussion producing complicated outcomes that are often misinterpreted, depending on who is doing the looking. Although some suggest harsh sentences, others suggest a response somewhere between harsh and not harsh or an intermediate sanction.

When some researchers conducted face-to-face interviews with youthful offenders, many of whom had been transferred to the adult system in Florida, the findings were curious. One way to interpret those findings is to say that juvenile prisoners reported that the experience of adult confinement was "beneficial."[63] Two concerns emerge from these findings. First: policy makers might believe that the threat of adult punishment will result in lowered juvenile crime rates. The fact is that although there has not been extensive current research into the deterrent effects of stricter laws, the evidence that does exist shows that deterrent effects of harsher punishment are minimal or nonexistent, and that waiving juveniles in an adult court can result in higher rates of reoffending.[64] Second: criminals including juvenile criminals, lie all the time about everything.[65] That is not to say that some heinous juvenile offenders should remain in confinement.

Therefore, to save juveniles from an uncertain future and to save community resources, intermediate sanctions seem productive for juveniles and the community.[66] Intermediate sanctions as a regular form of criminal penalty for juvenile offenders might include a greater use of diversion, probation, home confinement, community programs, and boot camps.

JUVENILE COMMUNITY CORRECTIONS PROGRAMS

Juvenile strategies, like adult strategies, are often linked to diversion, restitution, and community service. The thought is that keeping, an offender out of the justice system can be more helpful to specific individuals regardless of their age. The conditions set for juveniles might be more in keeping with their ability to pay and their age than adults, yet there are probably more similarities than there are differences and that thought can be extended to include most CC programs for juveniles. However, due to the philosophy of "protecting" children, official community supervision is generally more consistent among juveniles than among adult offenders. Nonetheless, probation is a common form of CC.

Probation

Of those juveniles on probation in 2000 (see Table 13.4), 22 percent were female and 30 percent were black. Also, characteristics of the adjudicated cases ordered to probation in

Table 13.4   Probation As a Court Disposition

Q: How many delinquency cases receive probation as the most restrictive disposition?

A: Probation was ordered in 58 percent of the more than 1.1 million delinquency cases that received a juvenile court sanction in 2000.

	Delinquency Cases Disposed, 1985–2000			
	Waived to Criminal Court	Placed	Probation	Other Sanctions
1985	7,092	104,827	428,149	169,892
1986	7,304	114,950	438,649	182,575
1987	6,806	112,028	434,794	193,228
1988	6,746	110,677	435,112	189,182
1989	8,015	125,607	425,773	190,080
1990	8,298	131,248	469,615	206,030
1991	10,688	132,415	506,876	244,392
1992	10,235	138,387	531,528	266,668
1993	11,228	144,940	516,964	267,910
1994	12,067	159,929	563,005	296,911
1995	10,406	161,260	616,783	307,484
1996	10,713	165,202	650,187	347,720
1997	9,104	171,281	681,399	352,080
1998	8,151	168,466	674,789	331,085
1999	7,076	159,949	669,602	311,381
2000	5,581	156,491	658,771	309,822

Printed with permission of the U.S. Department of Justice.[68]

2000 consisted of 23 percent of juveniles who had committed crimes against a person (violence), 40 percent against property, 13 percent drugs, and 24 percent public order.[67] Probation may be used at either the "front end" or the "back end" of the juvenile justice system: low-risk offenders or as an alternative to prison for more serious but usually first-time offenders. During a period of probation, a juvenile offender remains in the community and can continue activities such as school, work, and sport activities. In exchange for community supervision, there are sometimes voluntary or informal conditions of probation and other times mandatory or formal conditions of community supervision. More than half (52 percent) of juvenile probation dispositions in 1996 were informal (i.e., enacted without a formal adjudication or court order).

Often, the probation design includes items meant to control and rehabilitate a juvenile. For instance, a juvenile may be required to meet regularly with a probation supervisor, adhere to a strict curfew, and complete a specified period of community service. In this manner, keeping tabs on a defendant through regular checks and having them stay off the streets at night might discourage night activities that could include alcohol abuse; being involved in community activities might help a juvenile feel as though he or she is "paying back" for their crime, thus enhancing their own self-respect and involvement with the community. The conditions of probation may also include provisions for the revocation of probation should a juvenile violate the conditions. If probation is revoked, the court may reconsider its disposition and impose a stricter sanction.

Juvenile Intense Probation

Juvenile intense probation supervision (JIPS) is a juvenile justice strategy whose effectiveness has yet to be substantiated. In some juvenile probation offices, the typical caseload is fewer than among adults. Juvenile POs, especially "intense" officers, might carry a caseload of 20 to 16 clients that see their caseloads on a daily bases. Police-probation partnerships have been used to further strengthen the intensity of juvenile intensive supervision because the police can add a component of surveillance to the probation services. JIPS programs usually include mandatory substance abuse treatment and alcohol and drug testing. Target populations for JIPS would include offenders who were "confinement bound." JIPS placement usually restricts violent offenders such as sex offenders, those committing crimes with a firearm, and those offenders committing grievous bodily harm.

One study reports that JIPS programs are effective alternatives to incarceration among juveniles even if recidivism levels were similar due to costs to conduct JIPS programs.[69]

What Works?

Other than regular probation, studies show that the following intervention strategies can enhance juvenile offenders:[70]

- Guided group processes that can reduce school crime and disorder and improve the overall school environment

- Structured social learning programs that teach new skills (how to interact with the opposite sex, problem-solving skills, etc.) and reinforce behavior and attitudes
- Cognitive behavioral programs that target attitudes, values, peers, substance abuse, and anger
- Family-based interventions that train family on appropriate behavioral techniques
- Graduated sanctions within structured intervention approaches
- Team collaboration intervention
- Electronic monitoring within JIPs programs
- School curriculums that promote social competence, further academic attainment, and reduce the risk of antisocial behavior
- JIPs
- Intense aftercare

Furthermore, a "compendium of programs" can be summed up in nine program principles that lead to positive outcomes for young people:[71]

1. Quality of implementation
2. Caring, knowledgeable adults
3. High standards and expectations
4. Parent/guardian participation
5. Community involvement
6. Holistic approaches
7. Youth as resources/community service and service-learning
8. Work-based learning
9. Long-term services, support, and follow-up

The following don't work as well as the aforementioned list.[72]

- Drug prevention classes focused on fear and other emotional appeals
- Drug education
- Talking cures
- Nondirective interventions
- Self-help programs
- Increasing cohesion or the unity of criminal groups
- Targeting noncrime producing factors?
- Fostering self-regard or self-esteem
- Radical nonintervention (doing nothing)
- Targeting low-risk offenders

The Massachusetts Experiment[73]

To maintain public safety and aid troubled youth, the legislature of Massachusetts enacted boot camps, residential programs, and school-based programs for high-risk juveniles. Those programs did not serve their clients as well as expected. One result was the Massachusetts General Law (MGL) Chapter 211F, which established the Office of Community Corrections (OCC) in 1996. OCC's jurisdiction is in the judicial branch of the Massachusetts Trial Court (as opposed to DOC). Its purpose is to reduce overcrowding in prisons and jails through what can be called a graduated sanction. The primary targeted offender is the step-out-of-jail, early release "drug-related" client under a county sheriff's supervision. Programs were designed to promote public safety by developing community-based corrections programs for appropriate offenders and mandates that the OCC collaborate with all criminal justice agencies in the Commonwealth.

The juvenile offender's resource center (JRC) was approved for operation in 1999. Other juvenile centers followed as their success became apparent. The juvenile centers collaborated with the DYS, the Office of the Commissioner of Probation (OCP), Boston public schools, and other human service agencies. Most juveniles entering the program are referred by the court once adjudicated a delinquent and through DYS. DYS referrals are generally youth in custody with the intent of "stepping them down" to the community.

Each referral is classified by one of four levels. Level I requires basic supervision. Level II requires drug testing only. Level III receives part-time programming including after school programs, community service, drug testing, and electric monitoring. And Level IV receives full programming, which includes intense supervision in terms of electronic monitoring (ELMO), substance abuse counseling, and courses such as life skills and anger management. Referrals can be required to participate in programs generally taken by a different level client depending on a caseworker's evaluation.

ELMO

Keeping the community safe and offenders under tight supervision can be accomplished through electronic monitoring or the "bracelet," which is required of all Level IV participants. Being in other than a preapproved place is automatic termination from the program and means a return to DYS or jail. Electronic monitoring has proved its worth because it aids in determining location and helps youth stay straight. For instance, peer pressure and drugs and alcohol are significantly correlated. When JRC participants show others their bracelet, it's an easy out not to engage in risky behavior. That way they blame conformity on the bracelet even if they're "dared" to perform inappropriate behavior.

DRUG TESTING

All participants referred to JRC must submit to random drug testing. This test is a color-coded system that meets the stands of the APPA. Juveniles have responded well to the use of consequences and rewards depending on the results of their drug screens. Our experiences show that some juveniles have multi-addictions and it becomes very hard on them to help themselves. Often, recommendations are made to the court for further treatment in a residential setting.

COMMUNITY SERVICE

Most juveniles referred to JRC have some type of restitution as part of their probation conditions. They fulfill their requirements through community service programs that use a variety of sites and tasks to help keep the juveniles interested and concerned with the community and their victims. Some sites include Greater Boston Food Bank, Pine Street Inn, AIDS Action Community, Franklin Park Zoo, and the New England Aquarium.

EDUCATION

At each facility, public school education is provided for each participant. At many centers, certified public school teachers instruct students onsite. Through small class sizes, curriculums centered at the student's level of interest, and a focus on issues that impact these students, the participants take a great interest in their advancement. One issue is preparing students to return to their home schools as achievers. Often the students feel as though they are helping themselves and not wasting their time on subjects that might not help them better themselves.

GROUP THERAPY

Most juveniles referred to JRC have extensive histories and struggles with abstinence, problem-solving strategies, family relationships, and a lack of self-control. Groups are designed to provide substance abuse, awareness services, anger management, and violence prevention. Also, life skills and health education are required of Levels III and IV. Awareness of victims' feelings is emphasized. Accountability and the impact of delinquent behavior on community and family is also stressed. One idea is to link youth with their community and their feelings because many feel neglected (and probably are by both community and family).

TEAM MEETINGS

As a form of checks and balances, the team approach was adapted as the method of juvenile processing. Intervention is a team effort comprised of teachers, clinicians, JRC and OCC staff, probation, DYS, and the monitoring staff who meet weekly to review each participant. Decisions are made about transition, increasing sanctions, and responses to behavioral problems. There is also a treatment team meeting conducted while the youth is present. At those meetings, the juvenile has an opportunity to ask questions, make statements, and learn more about his or her case. These meetings also help JRC personnel learn about the home environment of the youth under their supervision, especially because aftercare services are often sought by juveniles or recommended by various team members. By keeping close contact with juveniles, helping them to step back into their communities is vital to the success of the program.

RESULTS

Due to the short time period of operations, results are inconclusive. However, an official report by the Suffolk County JRC shows that aftercare services are important to the success of many of the participants and that when provided, youths have a better chance of reintegrating back into their home schools and communities without reoffending. The way most JRC personnel see it, reoffending is one goal for the youth and helping to develop a productive member of the community is their reward.

- Boot camps centered primarily on military basic training
- School-based leisure time enrichment programs?
- Scared straight programs
- Rehabilitation programs that use vague unstructured counseling
- Residential programs for juvenile offenders using challenging experiences in rural settings

Home Confinement and Electronic Monitoring

Home confinement restricts juvenile offenders to their home during specified periods of time and under specified conditions. For instance, the juvenile can leave home to attend school and maybe the library (at preapproved times). While at home, only family members can be present. As part of the home confinement strategy, an offender is fitted with an unremovable devise that emits a signal that can in some jurisdictions transmit the location of the offender to the probation department.

School, Drugs, and Community Prevention Approaches of Delinquency

As you expect, youths who start offending early in childhood are more likely to become serious, chronic offenders than those who start offending during adolescence.[74] Early intervention is crucial to preventing delinquent behavior and understanding the factors related to delinquency are essential to effective early childhood intervention. For instance, we know that there is a significant link between drug use and juvenile crime. Ways to curb drug use among youth could benefit from knowing the results of a poll that shows peer pressure, lack of parental supervision, and drug availability as the three most influential factors leading to drug use among teenagers.[75]

That is, adolescent drug abuse is highly correlated with the behavior of best friends, especially when parental supervision is weak regardless of the social class or race of the child.[76] Where feelings of alienation run high among inner-city youths, affiliation with other drug users helps them deal with their feelings of inadequacy, stress, and recognition.[77] Much like their counterparts in suburban neighborhoods, those youths often join with other unsupervised youths of all social groups who seek friendships in an attempt to enhance their feelings of belongingness and to learn the techniques of drug use. The relationship is reciprocal: Users seek friends who engage in these behaviors and associating with drug abusers leads to increased levels of drug abuse.[78]

It would make sense that because education is a compulsory effort by society to guide youths, it could do more to enhance intervention at the level of peer groups and perhaps also influence parental supervision standards through informal workshops and brochures. This thought is consistent with a study that shows kindergarten through high school programs or K–12, whose curriculums promote social competence and academic attainment and reduce the risk of antisocial behavior.[79] Education can further social skills and promote social competence through curriculums that promote:

- Prosocial norms
- Problem-solving skills
- Social interaction skills
- Conflict resolution
- Violence prevention
- Antibullying programs
- Causes/consequences of violence
- Proactive behavior
- Cooperative learning

Other interventions are necessary in some cases to aid in the development of the child, which could include a referral to other agencies by specified school personnel.

Other Prevention Approaches

Many programs and individuals help prevent delinquency. The justice community does not own the franchise on diverting youth away from crime, nor should they. Prevention is everybody's job. Although only a few descriptions follow, they represent some of the hundreds of successful programs found nationally that prevent delinquency.

Lansing, MI, School District and Truancy. Lansing's school district and the Citizens United to Track Truants (CUTT) help to reduce truancy among school aged children. They hold a belief that a strong correlation exists between school attendance and delinquency. CUTT volunteers, all senior citizens, work from an office provided by the Lansing Police Department.[80] Volunteers staff a hotline where volunteers take calls on reported truants. They also receive daily attendance data from the K–12 schools in the district. Volunteers make house calls for chronic truants. Some CUTT volunteers patrol Lansing neighborhoods. They are equipped with radios and when they spot truants, they contact the police. Literature, seminars, and presentations are made throughout the school district to inform students and parents about the program.

During the first year of truancy initiatives (1997–1998), Lansing experienced an 11 percent reduction in the number of juveniles accused of crimes during school hours, in the second year (1998–1999) that percentage was 27 percent, and in the third year (1999–2000) it was 33 percent. Also, during the 1996–1997 school year, 34 percent of the students in the Lansing School District missed more than 10 days of school, but that number fell to 23 percent the following school year, and an estimated 18 percent the year after that.[81] It is unlikely that CUTT is 100 percent responsible for these successes because everyone in the community played a role in helping students to stay in school and out of trouble. But, it is likely that the concern of CUTT played a key role in influencing the participation of others.

Vietnamese Youth Outreach in Roanoke, VA. In May 1997, several community and local government agencies (including Refugee Immigration Services, the local housing authority, Roanoke's school district, health and social services, and the police department) formed an alliance to aid Vietnamese youth in Roanoke's large Vietnamese community.[82] Most Vietnamese refugees do not understand or trust many of the Roanoke's city services including education, health and welfare, and the justice system. Conversely, many locals do not understand the Vietnamese language or their cultural mores. The FBI's Uniform Crime Reports indicated that the level of crime in Roanoke was not a significant problem, but there was growing concern that disaffected Vietnamese youth were being recruited into organized gangs by transient Vietnamese refugees from other communities. Programs were designed to create positive activities and involvement for Vietnam youth in the community.

Education is at the core of the intervention on all sides, including the cultural program and tutoring of Vietnamese youth, outreach citizenship training of Vietnamese adults, and cultural diversity training for all public personnel in Roanoke. An important resource for the outreach project is the Vietnamese Youth Group, organized through the Catholic Church. Adult community leaders conduct Vietnamese language and history classes and provide recreational and cultural activities. The resource specialist also convenes regular after school tutorial sessions with a small number of Vietnamese youth. To expand Vietnamese adults' understanding of the justice system, the resource specialist has translated criminal justice system terminology into Vietnamese. Other cities such as Boston are tailoring a similar program to meet the needs of youth in their city.

Missouri's DYS Acts. Nationwide, most confined juvenile offenders are held in facilities with more than 110 offenders and the custody staff are usually comprised of correctional officers whose primary objective is control.[83] These realization, combined with high juvenile recidivism rates, motivated Missouri's DYS to develop smaller units, staffed by college trained behavior specialists, who rely on the group process and personal offender development rather than punishment and isolation as the best medicine for delinquent youths.[84] DYS obtained abandoned schools and other nonthreatening environments, including a former convent, to house smaller groups of juvenile offenders. From the day an offender enters a DYS facility, youths spend virtually every moment of their time with a team of 9 to 11 other youngsters and a staff of behavioral specialists. The emphasis of every DYS program is re-entry, and once released, DYS provides aftercare programs supervised by service coordinators and "trackers" who are typically college students or residents of the youth's home community.[85] Specialized attention, one-on-one relationships formed between young people and the staff, and few locked doors add to Missouri's DYS plan, which has produced interesting results.[86] For instance, in February 2003, a DYS recidivism analysis found that of 1,386 juveniles released from custody in 1999, just 111 (8 percent) were sentenced to prison and 266 (19 percent) were sentenced to adult probation.[87] Another 228 youths (16 percent) were recommitted to DYS for breaking rules or committing a new crime (a total of 43 percent). Compared with states that measure youth recidivism in similar ways, Missouri's results concur. For instance, a 2000 recidivism study in Maryland found that 30 percent of youths released from juvenile custody were incarcerated within three years of their release.[88] In Louisiana, 45 percent of the youths released from juvenile custody in July 1999 through June 2001 were reconfined or placed on probation by June 2002.[89] In Florida, 29 percent of youths released from juvenile custody from July 2000 through June 2001 were returned to juvenile custody, sentenced to prison, or placed on probation within 12 months.[90] Also, in this regard, Missouri's DYS budget for 2002 breaks down to $103 for each youth per day compared to Louisiana's $270 per juvenile, Maryland's $192 per juvenile, and Florida's $271 per juvenile per day.[91] Finally, recall that the average cost per day in the United States was $171 per day for each confined juvenile.[92] It seems Missouri is on the right track.

Incarcerating Connecticut's Youthful Offenders.   Connecticut law indicates that adult criminal liability is applied at age 16.[93] The term youthful offender, however, refers to offenders between the ages of 14 to 21. In 2003, Connecticut reacted to the growing trend of youth violence by passing laws that allow teens as young as 14 to be tried as adults and confined under the supervision of the department of corrections. The spectrum of juvenile housing units address offender needs, but custody and control are primary directives. Youthful offenders in Connecticut are divided by an objective classification process. Restrictive housing needs, chronic disciplinary offenders, and security risk groups (gangs) are housed in isolated units. Training, counseling, and discipline are featured. "Training is provided through a predominantly adult (correctional officer) mindset."[94] Some of the results of Connecticut's youthful offender program are that offenders who have been declared unmanageable in other youth settings have been remanded to placement in specialized units where "staff intervention and the facility's physical plant" have been successful in returning these offenders to the unrestricted general population, and ultimately, back to society.[95] Also, staff members have learned interaction techniques that enable them to connect with young offenders and establish in those offenders, "a new appreciation for authority figures in their lives."[96] Finally, "the opportunities for Connecticut's youthful offenders are given the opportunity "to choose better paths for their lives."[97]

Youth Crime Watch of America.   One national program that applies the principles of risk-focused prevention is the Youth Crime Watch of America, Inc. (YCWA).[98] YCWA is a nonprofit organization that establishes youth crime watch programs throughout 500 sites in the United States and other countries. Youth and youth advisors trained in YCWA methods currently run programs in elementary, middle, and high schools, neighborhoods, public housing sites, recreational centers, and parks. YCWA originated in Miami, FL, in 1986 and has three primary goals:

- Provide crime-free, drug-free, and violence-free environments for healthy learning and living

- Instill positive values, foster good citizenship, and build self-confidence in youth while instilling a sense of personal responsibility and accountability

- Enable youth to become a resource for preventing drug use and other crimes in their schools and neighborhoods

When YCMA was first being developed some 20 years ago, several high school principals were receptive to the concepts of YCWA and the Law Enforcement Assistance

Administration provided funds to develop a handbook for student voluntary participants. Students ran the events of YCWA and adult voluntary advisors guide their activities.

YCWA was recognized by Presidents Reagan, Bush, Clinton, and George W. Bush and has received many national honors and awards, including being named a U.S. Department of Education Exemplary Program of Excellence. In 1999, Congress and President Clinton endorsed a request to provide $1 million of funding to YCWA and the Department of Education earmarked an additional $500,000.

In 2002, YCWA emphasized a "watch out, help out" commitment, which encouraged youth to look for problems within their school and community and to become actively involved in solving those problems. Motivated by the principle of good citizenship, YCWA has enabled participants to greatly reduce crime, violence, and drug use in their communities and neighborhoods. For example, after the formation of a youth crime watch program in 1994, Leto High School in Tampa reported a 72 percent drop in crime. In 1995, Carol City High School in Miami reported a 45 percent decrease in student crime after beginning its youth crime watch. To learn more, try the YCWA website at: http://www.ycwa.org/

Southeastern Michigan Spinal Cord Injury Center. The Southeastern Michigan Spinal Cord Injury Center has developed a highly effective program in which youthful victims of gun violence, now paraplegic or quadriplegic, go before groups of students to show them, by personal example, the consequences of using guns. Their testimonials touch students as no classroom text or lecture can and the schools can work with police, victim groups, and the victims themselves to make such presentations possible.

Gun Safety in Miami-Dade. In Miami-Dade County, FL, several groups came together to cosponsor a Gun Safety Program following a report of 137 handgun incidents in the public school system during the school year. The K–12 program features a comprehensive curriculum, teacher training, youth crime watch, parent education, and media involvement. The partners include the national Center to Prevent Handgun Violence, the Dade County School Board, Youth Crime Watch of Dade County, local agencies, and the Miami-Dade Sheriff's Department.

Examples of San Francisco and Alexandria Programs. In San Francisco, many elementary schools let youths settle their problems. That is, youngsters who have been trained as mediators use their skills to help classmates peacefully resolve playground disputes. The mediation training, conducted by Community Boards of San Francisco, involves youth as young as fourth grade who learn how to help keep playground disputes from escalating into physical confrontations. Teachers and administrators credit the program with substantially improving the climate of the whole school, not just the playground area.

Other types of programs include the Untouchables in Alexandria, VA. This club helps young men to develop pride and self esteem by employing a holistic approach to empower the participants with knowledge and skills to increase their physical, emotional, intellectual, and spiritual levels of functioning so that the members will live, work, play, and socialize in a productive and healthy manner. Adult role models serve as mentors.

Drug Prevention Basics.   In 2002, the ONDCP argued that parental influence has a powerful impact when it comes to deterring kids from substance abuse and recommends:[99]

- Parents should find ways to communicate and spend time with their children, even if it means participating in activities they won't enjoy.
- Parents should not "give up" trying to communicate with and discipline their children, even though teens may fight their parents for more independence.?
- Parents need to talk to their kids about the dangers of drugs. The teens said that although their parents had talked with them about sex, none had a conversation explicitly about drugs.

The importance of this perspective is to understand that not all children have parents who have the first clue about a meaningful experience let alone conversation with their children. For that reason, many children are thrown to the criminal justice system for a remedy. The sad truth is the justice system can never take the place of a parent—even a bad parent—especially while the child is dependent. It has also been proven that family-based treatment programs can reduce adolescent drug abuse.[100] Although there are many influences that further drug abuse (e.g., peer relationships, family, school, neighborhood environments) and social or cultural norms that can act as a predator or place some children at risk, family-based treatment programs significantly reduce drug abuse. Things the family does together have a great impact on preventing drug use and reducing its use. Thus, justice services need to move into the parental business and help parents help their children. As far-reaching as this sounds, police officers could become public school teachers, which means earning educational degrees and certifications to teach specific courses to youngsters in our classrooms (without their guns).[101] In that way, police would play a professional leadership role in communities and prevent crime of all varieties from occurring. Also, because officers would be on the front lines, they could effectively deal with troubled youths and guide others to productive law abiding lifestyles.

Juvenile Recidivism

Some facts about juvenile recidivism are that youths known to the justice community by age 13 are responsible for a disproportionate share of serious violent crime. That is, 40 percent of all males and 34 percent of all females with a criminally violent career had been seen by the justice system by age 13.[102] Similar results were found among chronic offenders—over 50 percent of both male and female chronic offenders had their first referral by age 13. In addition, over 50 percent of males and almost 75 percent of females who enter the juvenile justice system never return on a new referral. Thus, the juvenile system seems to be working more productively than less productively.

JUVENILE RIGHTS: MAJOR U.S. SUPREME COURT DECISIONS

Concerned about increases in juvenile delinquency and the need to safeguard children's rights, especially due process, in 1974 Congress passed the Juvenile Justice and Delinquency Prevention (JJDP) Act (Pub. L. 93-415, September 7, 1974). The act created the National Advisory Committee for Juvenile Justice and Delinquency Prevention, which developed juvenile justice standards that established due process guarantees to juveniles.[103]

Those standards were influenced by three landmark U.S. Supreme Court decisions: *Kent v. United States (1966), In Re Gault (1970),* and In *Re Winship.*

Kent v. United States, 383 U.S. 541 (1966)[104]

The major conclusions of Kent v. United States involved transfer of jurisdiction. The juvenile defendant is entitled to certain essential due process rights: (a) a hearing, (b) representation by an attorney, (c) access to records involved in the transfer, and (d) a written statement of reasons for the transfer.

In *re Gault,* 387 U.S. 1 (1967)[106]

One result was habeas corpus availability for juveniles. The *Gault* decision by the U.S. Supreme Court ruled that, in proceedings that might result in commitment to an institution, juveniles have due process rights, which include:

1. Reasonable notice of changes
2. Counsel
3. Questioning witnesses
4. Protection against self-incrimination

Habeas Corpus: A writ ordering a detained person into court for a decision on whether the original detention is lawful. A writ of habeas corpus is a judicial mandate to a prison official ordering that an inmate be brought to the court so it can be determined whether or not that person is imprisoned lawfully and whether or not he should be released from custody.[107]

In *re Winship,* 397 U.S. 358, 1970

Justice Brennan delivered the opinion of the Court and indicated that proof beyond a reasonable doubt, which is required by the Due Process Clause in criminal trials, is among the "essentials of due process and fair treatment." The U.S. Supreme Court ruled that the "reasonable doubt standard" should be required in all delinquency adjudications.

Kent v. United States, 383 U.S. 541 (1966)

Procedural Background

In 1961, while on probation from an earlier case, 16-year-old Morris A. Kent, Jr., was arrested and charged with housebreaking, rape, and robbery. Kent confessed to the offenses and offered information on several similar incidents. Anticipating that the District of Columbia Juvenile Court would consider waiving its jurisdiction over Kent and remitting him for trial to the criminal system, Kent's attorney filed motions requesting a hearing on the issue of jurisdiction and seeking access to the juvenile court's social services file on Kent. The juvenile court judge did not rule on this motion. Instead, he entered an order stating that the juvenile court was waiving jurisdiction over Kent after making a "full investigation." The judge did not describe the investigation or the grounds for the waiver.

When Kent was indicted in criminal court, Kent's lawyer moved to dismiss the criminal indictment, arguing that the juvenile court's waiver had been invalid. That motion was overruled and Kent was subsequently tried in criminal court and found guilty on six counts of housebreaking and robbery. He was sentenced to 30 to 90 years in prison.

On appeal, Kent's attorney again challenged the validity of the waiver. Appellate courts, however, rejected the appeal, refused to scrutinize the juvenile court judge's "investigation," and accepted the waiver as valid. In appealing to the U.S. Supreme Court, Kent's attorney argued that the judge had not made a complete investigation and that Kent had been denied his constitutional rights simply because he was a minor.

U.S. Supreme Court's Decision

The U.S. Supreme Court ruled the juvenile court order waiving jurisdiction invalid, holding that Kent's counsel should have had access to all records involved in the waiver decision and that the judge should have provided a written statement of the reasons for the waiver. The Supreme Court also held that waiver hearings do not need to conform to all the formal requirements of a criminal trial, but that they must measure up to "the essentials of due process and fair treatment." In particular, the court held that juveniles facing waiver are entitled to:

- Representation by counsel
- Access to social services records
- Written statement of the reasons for waiver

Printed with permission of the Office of Juvenile Justice and Dequincy Prevention.[105]

Kent Waiver Criteria

In an appendix to its opinion, the Court in *Kent v. United States* detailed the following "criteria and principles concerning waiver of jurisdiction":

> An offense falling within the statutory limitations . . . will be waived if it has prosecutive merit and if it is heinous or of an aggravated character, or—even though less serious—if it represents a pattern of repeated offenses that indicate the juvenile may be beyond rehabilitation under Juvenile Court procedures, or if the public needs the protection afforded by such action.

> The determinative factors that will be considered by the Judge in deciding whether the juvenile court's jurisdiction over such offenses will be waived are the following:

> 1. The seriousness of the alleged offense to the community and whether the protection of the community requires waiver.
> 2. Whether the alleged offense was committed in an aggressive, violent, premeditated, or willful manner.
> 3. Whether the alleged offense was against persons or against property, greater weight being given to offenses against persons especially if personal injury resulted.
> 4. The prosecutive merit of the complaint; that is, whether there is evidence upon which a Grand Jury may be expected to return an indictment (to be determined by consultation with the [prosecuting attorney]).
> 5. The desirability of trial and disposition of the entire offense in one court when the juvenile's associates in the alleged offense are adults who will be charged with a crime in [criminal court].
> 6. The sophistication and maturity of the juvenile as determined by consideration of his home, environmental situation, emotional attitude, and pattern of living.
> 7. The record and previous history of the juvenile, including previous contacts with [social service agencies], other law enforcement agencies, juvenile courts and other jurisdictions, prior periods of probation to [the court], or prior commitments to juvenile institutions.
> 8. The prospects for adequate protection of the public and the likelihood of reasonable rehabilitation of the juvenile (if he is found to have committed the alleged offense) by the use of procedures, services, and facilities currently available to the Juvenile Court.

Source: U.S. Department of Justice.[106]

The Core Requirements of the Juvenile Justice and Delinquency Prevention Act Primarily Address Custody Issues

The Juvenile Justice and Delinquency Prevention Act of 1974, as amended, (the Act) establishes four custody-related requirements:

- The "deinstitutionalization of status offenders and nonoffenders" requirement (1974) specifies that juveniles not charged with acts that would be crimes for adults "shall not be placed in secure detention facilities or secure correctional facilities."
- The "sight and sound separation" requirement (1974) specifies that "juveniles alleged to be or found to be delinquent and [status offenders and nonoffenders] shall not be detained or confined in any institution in which they have contact with adult persons incarcerated because they have been convicted of a crime or are awaiting trial on criminal charges." This requires that juvenile and adult inmates cannot see each other and no conversation between them is possible.
- The "jail and lockup removal" requirement (1980) states that juveniles shall not be detained or confined in adult jails or lockups. There are, however, several exceptions to the jail and lockup removal requirement. Regulations implementing the Act exempt juveniles held in secure adult facilities if the juvenile is being tried as a criminal for a felony or has been convicted as a criminal felon. In addition, there is a 6-hour grace period that allows adult jails and lockups to hold delinquents temporarily until other arrangements can be made. Jails and lockups in rural areas may hold delinquents up to 24 hours under certain conditions. Some jurisdictions have obtained approval for separate juvenile detention centers that are collocated with an adult jail or lockup facility.
- The "disproportionate confinement of minority youth" requirement (1992) specifies that states determine the existence and extent of the problem in their state and demonstrate efforts to reduce it where it exists.

Regulations effective December 10, 1996, modify the act's requirements in several ways:

- Clarify the sight and sound separation requirement—in nonresidential areas brief, accidental contact is not a reportable violation.
- Permit time-phased use of nonresidential areas for both juveniles and adults in collocated facilities.
- Expand the 6-hour grace period to include 6 hours both before and after court appearances.
- Allow adjudicated delinquents to be transferred to adult institutions once they have reached the State's age of full criminal responsibility, where such transfer is expressly authorized by State law.

The revised regulations offer flexibility to states in carrying out the act's requirements. States must agree to comply with each requirement to receive Formula Grant funds under the act's provisions. States must submit plans outlining their strategy for meeting the requirements and other statutory plan requirements. Noncompliance with core requirements results in the loss of 25% of the state's annual Formula Grants Program allocation.

As of 1998, 55 of 57 eligible states and territories were participating in the Formula Grants Program. Annual State monitoring reports show that the vast marjority are in compliance with the requirements, either reporting no violations or meeting *de minimis* or other compliance criteria.

Other Court Cases that Shaped Juvenile Practice[108]

Breed v. Jones (1975) ruled that juvenile adjudication for violation of a criminal statute is equivalent to a criminal court trial. The double jeopardy clause of the Fifth Amendment applied to juveniles' court proceedings as it did adult proceedings.

Oklahoma Publishing Co. v. District Court (1977) ruled that a state court could not prohibit the publication of information obtained in an open juvenile proceeding. When photographs were taken and published of an 11-year-old boy suspected of homicide and the local court prohibited further disclosure, the publishing company claimed that the court order was a restraint in violation of the First Amendment. The Supreme Court agreed.

Smith v. Daily Mail Publishing Co. (1979) involved the discovery and subsequent publication of the identity of a juvenile suspect in violation of a state statute prohibiting publication. The Supreme Court declared the statute unconstitutional because it believed the state's interest in protecting the child was not of such magnitude as to justify the use of a criminal statute. Criminal trials are open to the public, but juvenile proceedings are meant to be private and confidential, which ordinarily does not violate the First Amendment right to free press discussed in the *Oklahoma Publishing Co. v. District Court (1977)*.

Fare v. Michael C. (1979) despite *parens patriae,* helps define the relationship between a PO and a juvenile probationer. Michael C., a juvenile, was arrested for murder. After being advised of Miranda Rights, Michael C. requested the presence of his PO, whom he confided in about the murder. The PO later presented testimony in court that helped convict Michael C. of the crime. The defendant appealed the murder conviction based on an alleged confidential relationship. The high court reasoned that POs work for the state and not the client. Therefore, conversations with POs are not shielded by lawyer-client privilege. This means that information provided by probationers to POs can be disclosed despite any obligation on the part of the PO.

Eddings v. Oklahoma (1982) ruled that a defendant's age should be a mitigating factor in deciding whether to apply the death penalty.

Schaff v. Martin (1984) upheld a statute allowing for the placement of children in preventive detention before their adjudication. The Supreme court concluded that it was not unreasonable to detain juveniles for their own protection.

New Jersey v. T.L.O. (1984) determined that the Fourth Amendment applies to school searches. The Supreme court adopted a "reasonable suspicion" standard, as opposed to the stricter standard of "probable cause," to evaluate the legality of searches and seizures in a school setting.

Thompson v. Oklahoma (1988) ruled that imposing capital punishment on a juvenile murderer who was 15 years old at the time of the offense violated the Eighth Amendment's constitutional prohibition against cruel and unusual punishment.

A series of U.S. Supreme Court decisions made juvenile courts more like criminal courts but maintained some important differences

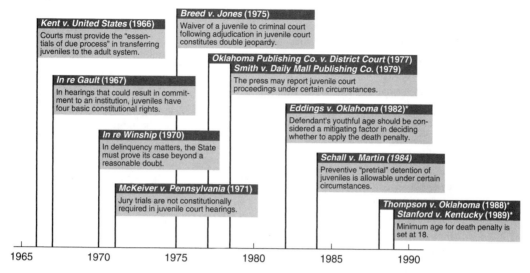

Source: Printed with the permission of the U.S. Department of Justice.[109]

Stanford v. Kentucky and Wilkins v. Missouri (1989) concluded that the imposition of the death penalty on a juvenile who committed a crime between the ages of 16 and 18 was not unconstitutional and that the Eighth Amendment's cruel and unusual punishment clause did not prohibit capital punishment.

Veronica School District v. Acton (1995) held that the Fourth Amendment's guarantee against unreasonable searches is not violated by the suspicionless drug testing of all students choosing to participate in interscholastic athletics. The Supreme Court expanded power of public educators to ensure safe learning environments in schools.

United States v. Lopez (1995) ruled that Congress exceeded its authority under the Commerce Clause when it passed the Gun-Free School Zone Act, which made it a federal crime to possess a firearm within 1,000 feet of a school.

However, recent studies of legal representation of juveniles have found that despite the constitutional requirements set forth in juvenile justice standards, juveniles in many regions of the country are still not represented by counsel. Three out of six states surveyed reported that on average less than 50 percent of juveniles charged with delinquency were represented by legal counsel.[110] This lack of counsel has been attributed to several factors:

- Parents' reluctance to retain an attorney
- Inadequate public defender legal services in nonurban areas

Table 13.5   Similarities of the Justice System for Juveniles and Adults[111]

Discretion exercised among police, court, and corrections

Right to Miranda warnings

Protection from prejudicial identification procedures

Procedural safeguards with an admission of guilt

Court protection during procedures

Right to an Attorney

Pretrial Motions

Plea bargaining

Hearing Rights

Appeal Rights

Proof beyond a reasonable doubt standard

Pretrial Release and Detention

Bail and Bail denial

Imposed Penalties

Diversion

Probation

Confinement

Table 13.6   Differences between Juvenile and Adult Justice Process[112]

	Juveniles	Adults
Primary purpose	Rehabilitation & Protection	Punishment
Jurisdiction of systems	Age	Nature of offense
Arrests	Detained & adjudicated	Arrested & convicted
Status offenses	Apprehended for acts that would not be criminal if committed by an adult	
Openness and formality of procedures	Informal and private	Formal and public
Release of information	Cannot be released	Must be released to the media
Involvement of parents	Highly involved	Not involved
Ppretrial release	Into parental custody	Might get bail
Right to jury trial	No constitutional right	Have jury rights
Role of judge	As a wise parent	Neutral
Search and seizure	In school without a warrant or without probable cause	Cannot be searched without a warrant or probable cause.
Permanence of record	Sealed when the age or majority is reached	Permanent
Prosecution	Juvenile court intake decides	District attorney decides
Death penalty	Not generally	Yes, depending on jurisdiction

SIMILARITIES AND DIFFERENCES BETWEEN JUVENILE AND ADULT LEGAL SYSTEMS

There are many similarities between juvenile and adult legal systems as demonstrated in Table 13.5. See Table 13.6 for differences between juvenile and adult justice systems.

The similar and different expectations for juveniles and adults are idealized but often result in a similar outcome. For instance, although juveniles are taken into custody and adults are arrested, both are deprived of freedom. It is important to recognize that American society rejects the use of adult criminal law labels in juvenile proceedings primarily because it is believed that juveniles can be rehabilitated. Yet at the same time, many juvenile codes stress punishment as opposed to prevention and treatment as noted earlier.

SUMMARY

Delinquent behavior is defined as juvenile behavior that breaks laws whereas status offenders are defined as juvenile behavior that fails to meet established expectations of conduct such as school truancy. Juveniles were defined generally as youths 18 and under but different states have different legislation concerning the age of minor in their jurisdiction. The juvenile justice system was described in some detail beginning with an arrest to prosecution to trial to diversion, probation, or confinement. One poll among youngsters shows that their use of illegal drug use was influenced through peer groups, lack of parental supervision, and the ease of obtaining drugs. As the pendulum swung from treatment to punishment, juvenile were waivered into adult courts more often. School curriculum and community programs that help youths curb drug use and violence were described and juvenile rights were examined through U.S. Supreme Court decisions that provided rights among juveniles. For instance, *Kent v. U.S. (1966)* provided due process rights to juveniles in the form of a hearing and representation, *In re Gault (1967)* provided for protection against self-incrimination, and *In re Winship (1970)* provided "reasonable doubt standard."

The similarities between juvenile and adult justice systems were identified. Some of those findings include Miranda warnings, protection from prejudicial identification procedures, and procedural safeguards with an admission of guilt. Differences between juvenile and adult justice systems were also identified and included punishment versus rehabilitation and protection, age versus offense, detainment versus arrest, and role of judge is seen as a "wise parent" versus a neutral role.

DISCUSSION QUESTIONS

1. Describe delinquency and status offender behavior and explain in what way that behavior might be different from the behavior of earlier generations of youths.

2. Explain why official response went from dependency to harsh penalties. In what way do you agree with the change?

3. Describe juvenile waivers into adult court and the benefits gained through this process.

4. Describe the important components in the juvenile justice process starting with an arrest.

5. Explain the rationale and behind probation and intense probation and describe the primary benefits of probation among juveniles and the justice system.

6. Identify a school curriculum designed to reduce antisocial characteristics and increase prosocial opportunities among today's youth. In what way do you agree and disagree with those curriculum items?

7. Identify several CC programs that aid juveniles toward compliance and describe in what way they impact juvenile behavior.

8. Identify the three primary U.S. Supreme Court Decisions that shape criminal justice intervention activities and explain their impact among both the justice system and the offender.

9. Define Habeas Corpus and explain its use. In what way do you agree with Habeas Corpus? Disagree?

10. Identify similarities in the juvenile and adult justice systems and explain in what way some of those similarities are advantageous and disadvantageous to juveniles.

11. Identify differences between juvenile and adult justice systems and explain in what way those differences might be advantageous and disadvantageous to juveniles.

NOTES

1. U.S. Department of Justice, Office of Juvenile Justice and Delinquency Prevention. *Juvenile arrests 2002* (2004, December). Washington, DC: U.S. Department of Justice, NCJ 201370. Retrieved online December 29, 2004: http://ojjdp.ncjrs.org/ojstatbb/crime/qa05101.asp?qaDate=20040801

2. Larry J. Segal (2002). *Juvenile delinquency: The core.* Belmont, CA: Wadsworth, 277.

3. D. P. Mears (1998). Evaluation issues confronting juvenile justice sentencing reforms: A case study of Texas. *Crime & Delinquency, 44*(3), 443–463.

4. R. Dembo, K. A. Cervenka, B. Hunter, and W. Wang (1999). Engaging high-risk families in community based intervention services. *Aggression and Violent Behavior, 4*(1), 41–58.

5. Alexandria, Virginia District Court (2003). Retrieved online December 31, 2004: http://ci.alexandria.va.us/courts/jdrdc/jdrdc_chins.phtml

6. Alexandria, Virginia District Court (2003).

7. Oklahoma Criminal Justice Resource Center (1999).*Preliminary analysis of the Beckham County juvenile drug court.* Oklahoma City, OK: Oklahoma Criminal Justice Resource Center, Oklahoma Statistical Analysis Center, 21–36.

8. J. Alexander, C. Pugh, and B. Parsons (1998). *Blueprints for violence prevention: Functional family therapy.* Boulder, CO: Center for the Study and Prevention of Violence. Retrieved online December 31, 2004: http://www.colorado.edu/cspv/.

9. U.S. Census Bureau (2001, October). *Census of U.S. population: Summary file.* Retrieved online December 31, 2004: http://www.census.gov/population/cen2000/phc-t9/tab01.txt

10. U.S. Census Bureau (2004). *National population estimates.* Retrieved online December 31, 2004: http://www.census.gov/popest/national/

11. Melanie Bozynski and Linda Szymanski (2004). National overviews. *State Juvenile Justice Profiles.* Pittsburgh, PA: National Center for Juvenile Justice. Updated February 4, 2003. Retrieved online December 31, 2004: http://www.ncjj.org/stateprofiles/

12. Office of Juvenile Justice and Delinquency Prevention (2002, April 25). *Statistical briefing book.* Washington DC: U.S. Department of Justice Retrieved online December 31, 2004: http://ojjdp.ncjrs.org/ojstatbb/html/qa085.html

13. Patrick Griffin and Melanie Bozynski (2004). National overviews. *State Juvenile Justice Profiles.* Pittsburgh, PA: National Center for Juvenile Justice. Washington DC: U.S. Department of Justice. Retrieved online December 31, 2004: http://www.ncjj.org/stateprofiles/

14. Howard N. Snyder and Melissa Sickmund (1999, September). *Juvenile offenders and victims: 1999 national report.* Washington, DC: U.S. Department of Justice Officer of Juvenile Justice and Delinquency Prevention (p. 87). Retrieved online March 14, 2004: http://ojjdp.ncjrs.org/ojstatbb/html/qa250.html

15. Patrick Griffin and Melanie Bozynski (2004).

16. P. Torbet and L. Szymanski (1998). *State legislative responses to violent juvenile crime: 1996–97 Update.* Bulletin. Washington, DC: U.S. Department of Justice, Office of Justice Programs, Office of Juvenile Justice and Delinquency Prevention. Cited in Howard N. Snyder and Melissa Sickmund. (1999). p. 87. All states have established legal mechanisms whereby some juveniles may be prosecuted within the criminal justice system.

17. As you review the criteria, you might take exception to some of the interpretations of author, but the intention of this exercise is to demonstrate the differences of the policy and practices of juvenile justice jurisdictions.

18. Dennis J. Stevens (2006). *Community corrections: An applied approach.* Upper Saddle River, NJ: Prentice Hall. This table was developed after a review of Howard N. Snyder and Melissa Sickmund (1999, September). *Juvenile offenders and victims: 1999 national report.* Washington, DC: Officer of Juvenile Justice and Delinquency Prevention (p. 98). Retrieved online March 14, 2004: http://ojjdp.ncjrs.org/ojstatbb/html/qa250.html Also, see Patrick Griffin and Melanie Bozynski (2004). Iowa Department of Corrections mandates available on their website: Retrieved online January 1, 2005: http://www.state.ia.us.

19. Added by author after a review of other Office of Justice and Delinquency Prevention materials and to show remainder of the states not mentioned: Howard N. Snyder and Melissa Sickmund. (1999). *Juvenile offenders and victims: 1999 National Report.* Washington, DC: U.S. Department of Justice, Office of Juvenile Justice and Delinquency Prevention, NCJ 178257, 87.

20. Based on waiver provisions and sentencing structure. Howard N. Snyder and Melissa Sickmund. (1999), 89.

21. Based on waiver provisions and sentencing structure. Howard N. Snyder and Melissa Sickmund. (1999), 89.

22. Based on waiver provisions and Iowa Department of Corrections mandates available on their website. Retrieved online January 1, 2005: http://www.state.ia.us

23. Howard N. Snyder and Melissa Sickmund (1999, September), 170.

24. Charles Puzzanchera (October, 2000). *Juvenile court placement of adjudicated youth, 1988–1997.* Washington, DC: U.S. Department of Justice. Retrieved online December 31, 2004: http://www.ncjrs.org/txtfiles1/ojjdp/fs200015.txt

25. OJJDP. 2003. Retrieved online March 14, 2004: http://ojjdp.ncjrs.org/facts/caseflow .html.

26. Howard N. Snyder. (2003, December.) *Juvenile Arrests 2001. A Message From OJJDP.* Available online at www.ojp.usdoj.gov/ojjdp

27. Howard N. Snyder and Melissa Sickmund (1999, September). *Juvenile offenders and victims: 1999 national report.* Washington, DC: Office of Juvenile Justice and Delinquency Prevention. p. 98. Retrieved online March 14, 2004: http://ojjdp.ncjrs .org/ojstatbb/html/qa250.html

28. Howard N. Snyder and Melissa Sickmund (1999, September), 97.

29. Howard N. Snyder and Melissa Sickmund (1999, September), 99.

30. Howard N. Snyder and Melissa Sickmund (1999, September), 100.

31. Howard N. Snyder and Melissa Sickmund (1999, September), 100.

32. In this case, the District Attorney for the Eastern District in the Commonwealth of Massachusetts program is for juveniles aged 17–21 and provides first time offenders with the opportunity to receive services in lieu of going through the traditional court process.

33. Howard N. Snyder and Melissa Sickmund (1999, September), 100.

34. A. Stahl, T. Finnegan, and W. Kang (2002). *Easy access to juvenile court statistics: 1985–2000* (data analysis and presentation package). Pittsburgh, PA: National Center for Juvenile Justice (producer). Washington, DC: U.S. Department of Justice Office of Juvenile Justice and Delinquency Prevention. Retrieved online August 20, 2004: http://ojjdp.ncjrs.org/ojstatbb/probation/qa07101.asp?qaDate=20030811

35. *Juvenile residential facility census, 2000: Selected findings.* (December 2002). Washington, DC: U.S. Department of Justice, Office of Justice Programs, NCJ

196595. And Bureau of Justice Statistics. *Juveniles in public and private residential custody facilities* (Table 6.9).

36. *American Correctional Association. 2003 Directory. Adult and juvenile* (2003)., 20, 25.

37. David M. Altschuler. (1998, December). *Reintegrating juvenile offenders into the community.* Retrieved online August 20, 2004: http://www.ncjrs.org/txtfiles/ fs000234.txt

38. OJJDP reports that "arrest statistics have been used as the main barometer of juvenile delinquent activity over the past decades. Unfortunately, many juvenile offenses go unreported and thus do not become a part of the national statistical picture. Indeed, many minor offenses committed by juveniles are considered part of growing up and are handled informally rather than by arrest and adjudication. It is critical to get a firm understanding of the range and prevalence of juvenile offending—from minor fights on playgrounds to aggravated assaults involving weapons." *Office of Juvenile Justice and Delinquency Prevention. An overview (2003).* Retrieved online August 20, 2004:http://ojjdp.ncjrs.org/ojstatbb/offenders/ overview.html

39. Anne L. Stahl. *Delinquency cases in juvenile courts, 1998.* Washington, DC: U.S. Department of Justice Office of Juvenile Justice and Delinquency Prevention. Retrieved online March 14, 2004: http://www.ncjrs.org/txtfiles1/ojjdp/fs200131.tx

40. Anne L. Stahl. *Delinquency cases in juvenile courts, 1998.*

41. Howard N. Snyder and Melissa Sickmund. (1999, September), 143, 171.

42. Howard N. Snyder and Melissa Sickmund. (1999, September), 171–173.

43. Adapted from material compiled by Patrick Griffin in 2000 for the National Center for Juvenile Justice's State Juvenile Justice Profiles website. OJJDP statistical briefing book. Retrieved online September 20, 2004: http://ojjdp.ncjrs.org/ojstatbb/ html/qa086.html.

44. Patrick Griffin, Patricia Torbet, and Linda Szymanski (1998). *Trying juveniles as adults in criminal court: An analysis of state transfer provisions.* Washington, DC: National Center for Juvenile Justice. Retrieved online March 20, 2004: http://www.ncjrs.org/pdffiles/172836.pdf, 13.

45. Contrary to the popular CBS television show, *Judging Amy,* staring Amy Brenneman.

46. Patrick Griffin, Patricia Torbet, and Linda Szymanski (1998), 13.

47. Howard N. Snyder and Melissa Sickmund (1999, September). *Juvenile offenders and victims: 1999 national report.* Washington, DC: Office of Juvenile Justice and Delinquency Prevention (p. 98). Retrieved online March 14, 2004: http://ojjdp .ncjrs.org/ojstatbb/html/qa250.html

48. Patrick Griffin, Patricia Torbet, and Linda Szymanski (1998), 13.

49. Patrick Griffin, Patricia Torbet, and Linda Szymanski (1998), 13.

50. Charles M. Puzzanchera. (2002). *Juvenile court placement of adjudicated youth, 1989–1998,* NCJRS. Retrieved online March 14, 2004: http://www.ncjrs.org/txtfiles1/ojjdp/fs200202.txt

51. Malcolm C. Young. (2000). *Providing effective representation for youth prosecuted as adults.* Series: Bureau of Justice Assistance Bulletin. Executive Director, *The Sentencing Project.*

52. Jeffrey Fagan (1996). *The comparative advantage of juvenile versus criminal court sanctions on recidivism among adolescent felony offenders, 1, 21, 27.* Unpublished manuscript on file with the ACLU. ACLU Fact Sheet on the Juvenile Justice System. Retrieved online March 15, 2004: http://www.aclu.org/.

53. Donna M. Bishop et al. (1996). The transfer of juveniles to criminal court: Does it make a difference? *Crime & Delinquency 42,* 171–183. Jodi Lane, Lonn Lanza-Kaduce, Charles E. Frazier, and Donna M. Bishop (2002). Adult versus juvenile sanctions: Voices of incarcerated youths. *Crime & Delinquency, 48*(3), 431–455.

54. Howard N. Snyder and Melissa Sickmund. (1999), 142–145.

55. Vincent Schiraldi and Mark Soler (1998, March). The will of the people: The public's opinion of the violent and repeat Juvenile Offender Act of 1997. *Justice Policy Institute.* Retrieved online January 16, 2005: http://www.justicepolicy.org/article.php?list=type&type=85

56. Dennis J. Stevens (1997). Violence begets violence: Study shows that strict enforcement of custody rules causes more disciplinary problems than it resolves. *Corrections Compendium: The National Journal for Corrections, 22*(12), 1–3.

57. Martin Forst, Jeffrey Fagan, and T. Scott Vivona (1989). Youth in prisons and training Schools: Perceptions and consequences of the treatment-custody dichotomy. *Journal of Juvenile & Family Court, 40,* 1–9. Zvi Eisikovitz and Michael Baizerman (1983). Doin' time: Violent youth in a juvenile facility and in an adult prison. *Journal of Offender Counseling, Services & Rehabilitation, 6*(5). Also see ACLU Fact Sheet on the Juvenile Justice System. Retrieved online January 16, 2005: http://www.aclu.org/.

58. Katherine Beckett and Theodore Sasson (2000). *The politics of injustice: Crime and punishment in America.* Thousand Oaks, CA: Pine Forge, 184–185.

59. Dennis J. Stevens (2000). *Inside the mind of the serial rapist.* New York: Author's Choice, 18. Those publications include: *Ebony, Essence, Glamour, Good Housekeeping, Ladies Home Journal, Maclean's, Mademoiselle, McCall's, MS, Nations Business, Newsweek, NY Times, People Weekly, Psychology Today, Redbook, Reader's Digest, Scholastic Update, Time,* and *Teen.*

60. William Bennett, John DiIulio, and John Walters (1996). *Body count.* New York: Simon and Schuster.

61. Official state-sanctioned punishment among juveniles has become serious business. For instance, between 1977 and 1999, 12 persons who committed their crimes while children were executed in the United States. During the same period, at least 30

mentally retarded prisoners were put to death. Amnesty International (1998, December 3). *The conveyor belt of death continues.* Retrieved online January 2, 2005: http://web.amnesty.org/library/Index/ENGAMR510981998?open&of=ENG-2AM

62. Wesley G. Skogan (1990). *Disorder and decline: Crime and the spiral of decay in American cities.* New York: Free Press. James Q. Wilson and George L. Kelling (2000). Broken windows: The police and neighborhood safety. In Willard M. Oliver (Ed.), *Community policing: Classical readings* (pp. 1–15). Upper Saddle River, NJ: Prentice Hall.

63. Jodi Lane, Lonn Lanza-Kaduce, Charles E. Frazier, and Donna M. Bishop (2002).

64. Frontline: *Juvenile justice. PBS.* (2004). Retrieved online January 2, 2005: http://www.pbs.org/wgbh/pages/frontline/shows/juvenile/stats/kidslikeadults.html

65. Stanton E. Samenow (1984). *Inside the criminal mind.* New York: Times Books (p. 21). Also see Curt R. Bartol and Anne M. Bartol (2005). *Criminal behavior: A psychosocial approach.* Upper Saddle River, NJ: Prentice Hall (p. 70).

66. Norval Morris and Michael Tonry (1991). *Between prison and probation: Intermediate punishments: Towards a rational sentencing system.* Oxford, England: Oxford University Press, 17–35.

67. U.S. Department of Justice, Office of Juvenile Justice and Delinquency Prevention. *Probation as a court disposition* (2000). Retrieved online August 20, 2004: http://ojjdp.ncjrs.org/ojstatbb/probation/qa07103.asp?qaDate=20030811

68. U.S. Department of Justice, Office of Juvenile Justice and Delinquency Prevention. *Probation as a court disposition* (2000). Retrieved online August 20, 2004: http://ojjdp.ncjrs.org/ojstatbb/probation/qa07103.asp?qaDate=20030811

69. Richard G. Weibush (1993). Juvenile intensive supervision: The impact of felony offenders diverted from institutional placement. *Crime & Delinquency, 39,* 68–89.

70. David M. Altschuler (1998). *Reintegrating juvenile offenders into the community: U.S. Department of Justice, Office of Juvenile Justice and Delinquency Prevention.* Intensive community-based aftercare demonstration program. Retrieved online March 21, 2004: http://www.ncjrs.org/txtfiles/fs000234.txt. Eileen M. Garry (1997). *Performance measures: What works?* OJJDP Fact Sheet. See also G. A. Wasserman, K. Keenan, R. E. Tremblay (2003, April). *Risk and protective factors of child delinquency.* Washington, DC: U.S. Department of Justice, Office of Justice Programs, Office of Juvenile Justice and Delinquency Prevention, Child Delinquency Bulletin, March 2003, NCJ 193411 (p. 8). Dennis Jay Kenney and Steuart Watson (1999). *Crime in the schools: Reducing conflict with student problem.* National Institute of Justice. Retrieved online January 16, 2005: http://www.ncjrs.org/txtfiles1/177618 .txt. National Institute of Corrections (2001). *Promoting public safety using effective interventions with offenders.* Retrieved online January 16, 2005: http://www .nicic.org. Lawrence Sherman, Denise Gottfredson, Doris MacKenzie, John Eck, Peter Reuter, and Shawn Bushway (1998). *Preventing crime: What works, what doesn't, what's promising.* National Institute of Justice. Retrieved online January 16, 2005: http://www.ojp.usdoj.gov/nij/

71. Eileen M. Garry (1999, November). *A compendium of programs that work for youth.* U.S. Department of Justice, Office of Juvenile Justice and Delinquency Prevention, OJJDP Fact Sheet #121, U.S. Department of Justice, Office of Justice Programs.

72. Eileen M. Garry (1999, November).

73. Dennis J. Stevens (2006). *Community corrections: An applied approach.* Upper Saddle River, NJ: Prentice Hall. Written for this publication with data provided by Lori A. Gazerro, Juvenile Intake Officer, Commonwealth of Massachusetts.

74. Barbara J. Burns, James C. Howell, Janet K. Wiig, Leena K. Augimeri, Brendan C. Welsh, Rolf Loeber, and David Petechuk (2003, March). Treatment, services, and intervention programs for child delinquents. *Child Delinquency: Bulletin Series.* Washington, DC: U.S. Department of Justice, Office of Justice Programs, NCJ 193410.

75. Bureau of Justice Statistics (2002). *Sourcebook of criminal justice statistics: 2000. Respondents' perceptions of factors determining whether a teenager tries illegal drugs* (Table 2.5). Albany, NY: U.S. Department of Justice, (p. 102). Also, some empirical evidence is available at G. A. Wasserman, K. Keenan, & R. E. Tremblay (2003, April). *Risk and protective factors of child delinquency. Child delinquency series bulletin.* Washington, DC: U.S. Department of Justice, Office of Juvenile Justice and Delinquency Prevention, Child Delinquency Bulletin, NCJ 193411 (p. 8).

76. Delbert Elliott, David Huizinga, and Scott Menard (1989). *Multiple problem youth. Delinquency, substance abuse and mental health problems.* New York: Springer-Verlag. And Thomas Dishion, Deborah Capaldi, Kathleen Spracklen, and Li Fuzhong (1995). Peer ecology of male adolescent drug use. *Development and Psychopathology, 7,* 803–824.

77. C. Bowden (1971). Determinants of initial use of opioids. *Comprehensive Psychiatry, 12,* 136–141.

78. John Bradshaw (2002). *Healing: The shame that binds you.* New York: Health Communications Inc. Also Terence Thornberry and Marvin Krohn (1997). *Peers,* drug use and delinquency. In David Stoff, James Breiling, and Jack Maser (Eds.), *Handbook of Antisocial Behavior,* (218–233). New York: Wiley. Retrieved online March 21, 2004: http://www.next-step-recovery.org/index.html#i1

79. G. A. Wasserman, K. Keenan, and R. E. Tremblay (2003, April).

80. Dennis J. Stevens (2002). *Case studies in community policing.* Upper Saddle River, NJ: Prentice Hall, 132–133.

81. Personal communication with members of CUTT and the Lansing School District.

82. Dennis J. Stevens (2002), 201–202.

83. *American Correctional Association. 2003 Directory. Adult and juvenile* (2003). p. 25.

84. Dick Mendel (2004, February). Show & tell: Missouri's division of youth services acts as a nation model. *Corrections Today, 66*(1), 56–59.

85. Dick Mendel (2004, February), 58.

86. Department of Social Services. Division of Youth Services. Missouri. Retrieved online January 3, 2005: http://www.dss.mo.gov/dys/

87. Dick Mendel (2004, February), 58.

88. Dick Mendel (2004, February), 59.

89. Dick Mendel (2004, February), 59.

90. Dick Mendel (2004, February), 59.

91. Dick Mendel (2004, February), 59.

92. *American Correctional Association. 2003 Directory. Adult and juvenile* (2003)., 20, 25.

93. Brian Evelich (2002, October). Incarcerating Connecticut's youthful offenders. *Corrections Today, 64*(6), 86–89.

94. Brian Evelich (2002, October), 89.

95. Brian Evelich (2002, October), 88.

96. Brian Evelich (2002, October), 89.

97. Brian Evelich (2002, October), 89.

98. See Gerald A. Rudoff and Ellen G. Cohn (2002). Youth crime watch of America: A youth-led movement. In Dennis J. Stevens (Ed.), *Community and community policing* (pp. 132–156). Upper Saddle River, NJ: Prentice Hall.

99. Parental Influence (2002). *Update: National youth anti-drug media campaign. Prevention basis for families.* U.S. Department of Health and Human Services, Substance Abuse and Mental Health Services Administration.

100. Patrick Zickler (2002). Family based treatment programs can reduce adolescent drug abuse. In *Parental Influence: Update: National Youth Anti-Drug Media Campaign.* U.S. Department of Health and Human Services, Substance Abuse and Mental Health Administration, 4–7.

101. Dennis J. Stevens (2004). *Applied community policing in the 21st century.* Boston: Allyn Bacon.

102. Howard N. Snyder and Melissa Sickmund. (1999), 80.

103. Howard N. Snyder and Melissa Sickmund. (1999), 88.

104. Law cases. Retrieved online March 24, 2004: http://www2.law.cornell.edu/cgi-bin/foliocgi.exe/historic/query=*/toc/ percent 7B38797,0,0,0 percent 7D/pageitems= percent 7Bbody percent 7D

105. U.S. Department of Justice: Office of Juvenile Justice and Delinquency Prevention (2000, June). *Juvenile transfers to criminal court in the 1990s: Lessons learned from four studies.* Retrieved online January 2, 2005: http://www.ncjrs.org/html/ojjdp/summary/08_2000/jtcc_6.html

106. U.S. Department of Justice: Office of Juvenile Justice and Delinquency Prevention (2000, June). *Juvenile transfers to criminal court in the 1990s: Lessons learned*

from four studies. Retrieved online January 2, 2005: http://www.ncjrs.org/html/ojjdp/summary/08_2000/jtcc_6.html

107. *The 'Lectric Law Library's Legal Lexicon.* Retrieved online January 16, 2005: http://www.lectlaw.com/def/h001.htm

108. Sources: *Oklahoma Publishing Co. v. District Court, 430 U.S. 308, 97 S.Ct. 1045, 51 L.Ed. 2d (1 977); Smith v. Dai@ Mail Publishing Co., 443 U.S. 97,99 S.Ct. 2667,61 L.Ed. 2d 399 (1979); Fare V. Michael C, 442 U.S. 707, 99 S.Ct. 2560 (1979); Eddings v. Oklahoma, 455 U.S. 104,102 S.Ct. 869, 71 L.Ed. 2d I (1 982); Schall v. Martin, 467 U.S. 253,104 S.Ct. 2403 (1984); Newjersey v. TL.O., 469 U.S. 325, 105 S.Ct. 733 (1985); Thompson v. Oklahoma, 487 U.S. SI S, 108 S.Ct. 2687, 101 L.Ed. 2d 702 (1988); Stanford v. Kentucky, 492 U.S., 109 S.Ct. 2969 (1989); Vernonia School District v. Acton, 51 5 U.S. 646 1 1 5 S.Ct. 2386,132 L.Ed. 2d S64 (1995); Wilkins v. Missouri, 492 U.S. 361, 109 S.Ct. 2969 (1 989); United States v. Lopez, 1 1 5 S.Ct. 1624 (1995).*

109. Howard N. Snyder and Melissa Sickmund. (1999), 91.

110. Douglas C. Dodge (1997). *Due process advocacy. Series:* OJJDP. Retrieved online March 24, 2004: http://www.ncjrs.org/txtfiles/fs9749.txt

111. Dennis J. Stevens (2006). *Community corrections: An applied approach.* Upper Saddle River, NJ: Prentice Hall.

112. Dennis J. Stevens (2006). Community Corrections: An Applied Approach. Upper Saddle River, NJ; Prentice Hall.

14

WOMEN, ELDERLY, AND THE DISABLED

After you finish reading this chapter, you should be better prepared to:

- Identify special correctional populations and their effect upon correctional systems.
- Explain the reason for the current increases in female conviction rates.
- Characterize initiatives in the justice community that victimize women offenders.
- Explain the justification that supports the justice community's victimization of women.
- Describe classification recommendations that would better serve female offenders.
- Characterize the experiences of female offenders while incarcerated.
- Describe the issues related to released incarcerated females.
- Characterize justice policy recommendations that would better serve female offenders.
- Describe program recommendations that would bring corrections closer to its mission.
- Identify obstacles to efficient female correctional programs.
- Provide a description of elderly offenders under correctional supervision.
- Describe some solutions that would aid elderly offenders.
- Describe issues associated with disabled correctional populations.
- Identify some recommendations that would aid a disabled population under correctional care.

KEY TERMS

Dementia

Disabled

Developmentally
   Challenged

Elderly

Feminization of Poverty

Gender neutral

Male Trait Dominated

Prisonization Effect

Over-classify

Repetitive Strain Injury

> Four score and seven years ago our fathers brought forth on this continent a new nation,
> conceived in liberty, and dedicated to the proposition that all men are created equal.
>
> —Abraham Lincoln

INTRODUCTION

In the last decade, correctional populations expanded beyond reasonable expectations and among these increases, new admissions by female offenders grew, the current correctional population aged, and developmentally challenged and disabled offenders brought serious issues to bear upon the correctional community (and rightfully so).[1] In addition, these stretched populations brought with them different experiences than previous corrections populations. For instance, among new admissions, many had failed while participating in diversion, probation, and parole than previous correctional populations, which is one reason these special groups are discussed in detail.[2] Also, these individuals affect correction systems in different ways than typical offenders and equally important, their experiences within correction programs both in and out of prison tend to be remarkably different than others. According to Abraham Lincoln's address, our nation is dedicated to the proposition that all men are created equal, but for women, the elderly, and the disabled it is unlikely that many of them can be equal because productive lives for them are strongly linked to social forces and social services outside and inside the criminal justice community. For example, poor women, who tend to have a greater reliance on the public welfare system to support their families, have been linked to high divorce rates, lower wage scales, and lower income job options or what can be referred to as the "feminization of poverty."[3] This notion holds significant meaning when maintaining female offenders and their families in the community because women are frequently single parents with sole parental responsibilities for their children and sometimes extended family members. The elderly have issues associated with correctional supervision because they tend to lack resources, especially when paroled, to find housing, employment, and health services that can aid them in the quality of life amenities many of us take for granted. There is also a chilling litany of incidents in which factory workers and other workers in hazardous jobs have been paralyzed, burned, blinded, deafened, lost limbs, lost physical or mental function, or have otherwise been rendered disabled. When some of these disabled workers are apprehended for a crime and convicted, CC is enormously challenged in providing quality services to these participants in an already tightly budgeted system.

Therefore, planning intermediate sanctions for special groups of offenders such as women, the elderly, and the disabled must include the social systems such as child protective services, parental education, health services, shelter assistance, employment assistance, possible skill or trade updating, child care, and family planning support that can address special needs of these offenders. Without help, these individuals can easily be returned to prison for parole violations or simply come to the attention of law enforcement because they have few opportunities to lead a productive life without help. What will be revealed in this chapter is that most special groups of offenders such as women, the elderly, the disabled, and in the next chapter the mentally ill and sex offenders, have less rights, more needs, and more demands upon them than other offenders.

FEMALE OFFENDERS

Few female offender and correctional outcome studies exist in the literature. Criminal sanctions including confinement and community supervision are meant to exact retribution for crimes and rehabilitation of their character.[4] Since 1990 the number of female defendants convicted of felonies in state courts has grown at more than two times the rate of the increase in male defendants and appropriate studies have not been forthcoming. Yet most of the available rhetoric tends to ignore much of the common ground about women offenders, both those incarcerated and those in community correctional programs. Before we begin a journey through government statistics, classification opportunities, prison experiences, and programs, it will prove helpful to describe exactly what we are talking about:

> Women (offenders) in the criminal justice system (prison and community programs) have a multiplicity of problems. They are overwhelmingly poor and substance abusers. They are also victims of abuse and violence. Many are depressed and suffer from various forms of mental illness. They experience a high rate of HIV infection, other sexually transmitted diseases, tuberculosis and untreated chronic diseases. A high percentage are homeless or marginally housed. Typically, they are undereducated, unemployed, and have minimal legitimate work histories. On average, 75 to 80 percent of them are mothers, statistically, of 2.4 children. If women are to live healthy, sober, law-abiding lives in the community, all of these issues must be addressed in some manner.[5]

Specifically, nearly 6 in 10 women in state prisons had experienced physical or sexual abuse in the past, just over one third of imprisoned women had been abused by an intimate in the past, and just under one fourth reported prior abuse by a family member.[6] With that said, we can move forward.

Female Offender Statistics

Overall, in 2003, an estimated 1.3 million women (or approximately 1 woman for every 109) in the United States were under correctional supervision. Women have increased among all correctional populations largely because of drug and alcohol violations.[7] Women represented the following estimates:[8]

- 24 percent of all arrests (3.5 million)
- 7 percent of the nation's prison population (101,000)[9]

- 13 percent of the nation's jail population (82,000)
- 23 percent of the nation's probationers (930,000)
- 13 percent of the nation's parolees (97,000)
- 24 percent of female state prisoners were mentally ill (largely white, between 35–54)[10]

Female Offenders and Correctional Outcomes

Most first-time, female offenders, especially nonsubstance abuse participants, complete the conditions of probation and parole successfully more often than female property of-fenders (also true of male offenders). But, white female parolees and probationers com-pared to black females succeed more often. Overall, females in general succeed at a higher rate than males, but when compared to females, men were more likely to receive parole.[11] Females tend to be incarcerated for more serious offenses than males, those researchers argue, but females tend to receive less prison time than men for similar crimes.[12] However, poor women, especially those with children, tend to revoke parole and violate probation conditions more often than other women. In a closer look at the process of female offend-ers, it becomes clear that many differences exist between male and female offenders.

Female Defendants

Women account for:[13]

- 16 percent of all felons convicted in state courts in 1996.
- 8 percent of the convicted violent felons.
- 23 percent of the property felons.
- 17 percent of drug felons.
- 41 percent of all felons convicted of forgery, fraud, and embezzlement.

Since 1990 the number of female defendants convicted of felonies in state courts has grown at more than two times the rate of increase in male defendants.[14] The majority of female felony defendants in the 75 largest counties in the United States were either charged with violence or were recidivists. An estimated 27 percent of male and 42 percent of female felony defendants in state courts in large counties had no history of prior con-victions. More female first-time offenders are convicted than male first-time offenders.[15]

The characteristics of adult women on probation, in jail, and in prison are shown in Table 14.1. For instance, of white women, 62 percent of women offenders were on probation, 36 percent were in jail, 33 percent were in state prisons, and 29 percent were in federal prisons. A similar breakdown is available for black, Hispanic, and other women. Other characteristics include age, marital status, and education.[16]

Table 14.1   Percent of Adult Women Supervised in Corrections

Characteristics of Women	Probation	Local Jails	State Prisons	Federal Prisons
Race/Hispanic origin (%)				
White	62	36	33	29
Black	27	44	48	36
Hispanic	10	15	15	32
Other	1	5	4	4
Age (%)				
24 or younger	20	21	12	9
25–34	39	46	43	35
35–44	30	27	34	32
45–54	10	5	9	18
55 or older	1	1	2	6
Median age (in years)	32	31	33	36
Marital status (%)				
Married	26	15	17	29
Widowed	2	4	6	6
Separated	10	13	10	21
Divorced	20	20	20	10
Never married	42	48	47	34
Education (%)				
8th grade or less	5	12	7	8
Some high school	35	33	37	19
High school graduate/GED	39	39	39	44
Some college or more	21	16	17	29

Printed with permission of the U.S. Department of Justice.[17]

An Explanation of Female Conviction Rates

Is the justice system gender biased? Knowing that female first-time offenders are convicted more often than male first-time offenders implies that the justice system practices a gender bias toward women and probably toward other special groups as well. This conclusion is consistent with findings revealing that women who utilize self-defense strategies after the justice system failed to protect them and their children are victimized again by the justice community. For instance, failure of the justice community to protect some women from a chronic aggressor who abused them and their children led to the murder of the aggressor.[18] Those women were convicted of first-degree murder and incarcerated for life sentences. One implication arising from those findings is that women are devalued in the American society at large and that convicted females carry their cultural baggage with them into CC programs and prison. The system continues to diminish female rights and moral responsibility toward women (and other special groups) as evidenced by strip-searches, female classification, over-classification, prison experiences including health care among pregnant women, and POs' view of girls.

Strip-Searches

A different set of arrest practices are used for female suspects compared to male suspects. At the time of an arrest, females taken into custody for nonviolent crimes are strip-searched, whereas males are rarely strip-searched at the time of an arrest for any crime. For example, the *Boston Globe* reports that women are routinely strip-searched after being charged with drunken driving.[19] Specifically, Massachusetts officials agreed to pay $10 million to settle a class-action lawsuit filed on behalf of an estimated 5,400 women who were routinely and illegally strip-searched over a four-year period at Nashua Street Jail in Boston. U.S. District Judge Nancy Gertner ruled that the city and the county engaged in a blanket strip-search policy that violated the constitutional rights of thousands of women who were ordered to strip naked and bend over while a female officer searched their vaginas and rectums. This problem is not an isolated problem as lawsuits have been filed in numerous jurisdictions across the country.

Female Classification

It is easy to assume that females and males should be similarly evaluated when they first enter a corrections system. The purpose of classification as you recall is twofold: (a) to keep order and ensure safety within institutions and communities and (b) to determine both risk and needs of an offender. "Risk" relates to personal and institutional possibilities of danger associated with supervision; "needs" relates to services and programs required by an offender. Supervision, services, and programs are centered in the outcomes of classification assessment strategies. You will probably agree that the more standards used to evaluate offenders are appropriate, the more likely supervision strategies will enhance public safety, and services and programs will be made available to offenders who require them.

However, one reality of most classification systems for female offenders is that they were designed for male offenders.[20] Another way to look at this finding is to say that because most correctional strategies and practices for women are patterned after male experiences, assessment of women offenders and levels of their success are also based on male standards. Female classification systems focus on male issues that frankly, are different for females such as mental health issues, health issues, social history, and relationships. Consequently, correctional services, both those in prisons and in the community, for female offenders might be lacking in the quality of assessment and the services and programs provided. Why? Because "throughout most of our nation's history, women offenders have been largely invisible or forgotten in a system designed to control and rehabilitate men."[21] Therefore, it would stand to reason that outcomes for women could be improved as correctional assessment changes to meet female issues.[22]

Two important conclusions are revealed through the research of Burke and Adams:[23]

1. There is no single model for correctional classification that can be successfully used nationwide, whether for men or women. Classification is an activity so central to each agency's objectives, population, and resources that each should undertake the development of its own approach to classification for both female and male offenders.

2. Within every jurisdiction, classification should be gender-neutral, both on its surface and in its effect. Gender should not be used as a classifying principle, largely because of parity issues and the danger of a legal challenge.

What is suggested is not a gender-based approach to classification, but an approach to classification associated with a corrections system's objectives regardless of an offender's gender.

Also, there is a tendency of corrections to treat women offenders like children with an emphasis on domesticating them.[24] Add to this perspective the notion of early policy makers who saw women offenders as a pathetic group of people, and decision makers focused on their precocious sexual development as the root cause of their delinquency.[25] Barbara Zaitzow reminds us that this issue of "rehabilitation has undoubtedly been the single most damaging influence on female corrections," largely because the treatment for women tends to:[26]

- Foster sexual morality
- Impose sobriety
- Instill obedience
- Prescribe sex-role stereotypes of mother and homemaker

In some jurisdictions, assessment relative to facility assignment hardly matters because most female facilities, community centers, and institutions often have only one facility to choose from. Therefore, a female prison generally houses all custody level offenders and all the services available must be offered at that facility or community center. One result when assigning housing for women prisoners, for instance, might be that a mentally ill prisoner is assigned to a housing unit that also houses women convicted of a minor charge who are mentally healthy.

Over-classifying Female Offenders   Another primary issue in the classification of women offenders is the widespread tendency to over-classify. Current assessment instruments tend to score female inmates into a higher custody level than is appropriate, given their threat to the safety and security of an institution or a community. For a variety of reasons, many classification systems across the country should be fine-tuned or at least assessed for female offenders to ensure validity. Florida offers an example of reforms in classification among women offenders. For instance, Florida's Department of Corrections (FDOC) developed and validated both an internal and external classification system for female prisoners.[27] FDOC also developed a systematic needs assessment process that compiles and rates a female prisoner's mental health, substance abuse history, education, vocation, wellness/life skills, financial management, relationships (both within and outside

Differences between Male and Female Inmates

In recent years, researchers and policymakers have argued that female offenders not only need more services to put them on a par with men, but in many instances women require different services as well. A 1991 survey by the Bureau of Justice Statistic (BJS), which highlighted the following key gender differences among state prison immates, clarifies why women may need different services.[a]

- Female and Male inmates differed in their patterns of drug use and drug-related crime.[b] Women were somewhat more likely than men to have used drugs in the month before the offense that resulted in their incarceration and to have been under the influence of drugs at the time of the offense.[c] They were also more likely than men to have used crack in the month before the incarceration offense. Women were considerably more likely than men to have committed crimes in order to obtain money to purchase drugs. Women were also more likely than men to be serving sentences for drug offenses.

- Female inmates had important, and often unique, health-related needs. At least 2,300 women (6 percent) were pregnant when they entered prison in 1991. Also, a slightly higher proportion of women (3.3 percent) than men (2.1 percent) reported being HIV positive.[d]

- Female inmates were more than three times as likely as incarcerated men to report having experienced physical or sexual abuse at some time prior to incarceration. The BJS researchers discovered that 43 percent of the female immates they surveyed reported having been victims of sexual or physical abuse prior to admission, with most having been victimized before the age of 18.

- Incarcerated women were more likely than incarcerated men to have children for whom they acted as caretakers until the time of their incarceration. They were more likely than man to have children under the age of 18 who were being cared for primarily by their grandparents while their mothers were incarcerated. The data further showed that the burden on grandparents is greater when a child's mother is incarcerated than when a father is incarcerated because mothers usually care for the children of incarcerated fathers.

- Female Inmates were less likely than male inmates to have been sentenced in the past. Of the women surveyed, 72 percent had been sentenced previously. Among inmates with prior records, women inmates were more likely than men to have been sentenced previously for a nonviolent offense.

- Women were less likely than men to have been incarcerated for violent crimes. In 1991, women were about as likely to be serving time for a violent offense (32 percent) as for a property (29 percent) or drug offense (33 percent). In contrast, 47 percent of male inmates were incarcerated for a violent offense. From 1986 to 1991, the proportion of women incarcerated for drug crimes nearly tripled, whereas the proportions of those incarcerated both for violent and property offenses dropped significantly.

- Men and women incarcerated for violent crimes differed in their patterns of violence. Women incarcerated for violent crimes were nearly twice as likely as their male counterparts to have committed homicide, more than twice as likely to have victimized a relative or intimate, and more likely to have victimized men.

[a]Back et al., *Survey of State Prison Inmates, 1991,* Washington, DC: U.S. Department of Justice, Bureau of Justice Statistics, March 1993: 5, NCJ 136949.

[b]Christine Rasche notes several significant differences in the drug use patterns of women and men in the general population as well, including: women tend to be introduced to heroin and cocaine use by a man in their lives, but thereafter tend to become more heavily addicted to greater amounts of the drug in a shorter time; women spend twice as much money per week on cocaine as do men; nationally, heroin addiction has increased at a faster rate for women than for men; and twice as many woman as men and up in hospital emergency rooms because of drug overdoses. See Rasche, Christine E., *Special Needs of the Female Offender.* Tallahassen, FL: Florida Department of Education, Division of Vocational, Adult, and Community Education Sex Equity, 1990, Handout #17B.

[c]These findings parallel those from an earlier BJS survey, which showed that female inmates were more likely than men to have used heroin or cocaine in the month before the incarceration offense, and to have used those drugs on a daily basis; see Greenfeld, Larry and Stephanie Minor-Harper, *Women in Prison,* Washington, DC: U.S. Department of Justice, Bureau of Justice Statistics, March 1991, NCJ 127991.

[d]Among those tested, female inmates were more likely than their male counterparts to report test results; see Back et al., p. 25. Recent studies by the United Nations Development Programme and the Centers for Disease Control and Prevention show that AIDS is growing rapidly among young women in this country and around the world. Although women accounted for just 14 percent of all AIDS cases reported in the United States in 1992, the number of women with AIDS in that year increased four times as fast as the number of men with the disease. See Rensberger, Boyce, "AIDS Spreads Fastest Among Young Women," *Washington Post,* July 29, 1993, A-1.

Source: U.S. Department of Justice.[30]

the penal system), and parenting skills. It also rates refinement of the state's Custody Assessment and Reclassification System (CARS) and Risk and Needs Internal Classification System as appropriate to consider all of the inmate's critical needs.

Finally, as we consider different assessment tools for female offenders versus male offenders, the following data is revealing:[28]

- Three of four violent female offenders committed simple assault.
- An estimated 28 percent of violent female offenders are juveniles.
- Nearly two of three victims of females had a prior relationship with the female offender.
- Four of 10 women committing violent crime were perceived by the victim as being under the influence of alcohol or drugs at the time of the crime.
- Women offenders tend to have a long history of physical, sexual, and emotional abuse.[29]

Classification Recommendations

Recommendations for female classification systems include:[31]

1. Classification of women must be designed by an individual system and its institutions. It should not be imported from another state or institution.
2. Technical standards must be met in the development of risk-based classification tools for female offenders.
3. A different emphasis on classification for women may be in order, an emphasis that grows out of habilitation concerns rather than risk concerns.
4. Any developmental work undertaken to improve classification for female offenders must be "gender-neutral" both on its surface and in its effect on offenders.

This argues for both gender-neutral risk classification tools and the development of new classification approaches based on habilitation concerns. These approaches could be utilized for both female and male offenders in settings where the profile of the population allows.

Female Prison Experiences

Although confinement is featured in this section, women in community centers experience similar outcomes as locked-up women, it's just to a different degree. With that said, there is little disagreement that every facility and every community center have their own unique features, which among other things are linked to its history, its architecture, its composition of participant demographics, its prior experiences and memories of its staff, and its communities as knowledgeable agents. Therefore, each facility and community center is unique unto itself. But experiences of women are different than experiences of men in America's free population as well as those under correctional supervision. For instance, serious violence is rare among women; as a result there should be different forms of correctional supervision among female than male offenders. The few dangerous women, estimated at 6 percent under correctional supervision, are controlled in environments known as maximum security.

Many women's facilities tend to have the appearance of being a college campus. Women often dress in their own clothes and decorate their rooms, but repression is every bit as strong as in men's facilities; "it is simply more subtle. In fact," reveals Barbara Zaitzow, "Inmates have referred to the social control in women's prisons as 'pastel fascism'— control glossed over and concealed by a superficial façade of false benevolence and concern for the lives of the inmates."[32] The few possessions they do own are confiscated or destroyed and all women are subject to arbitrary body searches.

When a female offender fails to comply with directives, implied or otherwise, physical control is utilized and visitation (especially during holidays with children or family members) is used to obtain further control. Incarceration for females, regardless of their custody level, is far more unusual than for males in that females are not as violent nor have they come up through the "sandlots of crime" or been institutionalized.[33] A recent study of female drug addictions reveals that most incarcerated females have been robbed, raped, or beaten beginning as early as age 8.[34] It goes without saying that victims of early sexual abuse are more likely to experience serious consequences later (e.g., prostitution, psychiatric problems, homelessness, HIV, eating disorders, suicide, substance abuse, self esteem problems, and teen pregnancy) than women who have not experienced sexual victimization.[35] Note: early sexual abuse is not necessarily associated with subsequent crimes of violence among females or males.[36]

Also prior to correctional supervision, unwanted sexual partners and pregnancies, antisocial associates, criminal lifestyles, and poverty dominated the lives of younger females.

Female facilities tend to be physically similar and poorly maintained and experiences of prison are emotionally stressful for most women.[37] For instance, the fear of the unknown, severed ties with children, and loss of financial assets might prove to be so overwhelming that many female prisoners look to staff, as well as to one another, to provide emotional support and nurturing, unlike male inmates who band together in large groups along racial, political, or organizational concerns for different reasons including protection.[38] One reason female prisoners, parolees, and probationers have more difficulty organizing and cooperating with others is that women are largely organized differently than male offenders.[39] Female advocacy is emotion and personal allegiance to a few, whereas male offenders tend to engage in physical advocacy and allegiance to a group of males.[40] A woman's role in the traditional family from one perspective might include her continued devalued or subordinate role and seeking freedom from all institutions might prove a wiser choice, especially after being confined for a long period of time.[41]

> Because women tend to internalize messages that devalue femaleness, suggesting she is irrational, immoral, emotional, dependent, and submissive in the first place, once released or participating in poor quality correctional programs merely confirms her inadequacies all the more and any incentive to succeed may not be as strong a variable as expected.[42]

Nonetheless, most female correctional systems utilize male trait services and programs: from classification to supervision routines to medical and mental health strategies to re-entry programs, female offenders receive similar programs and strategies as that of males.[43]

Females Adapting to Prison Life

A strong attitudinal predictor of lifestyle goal changes for female prisoners (like male prisoners) is associated with the length of time served in prison.[44] That is, options to commit crimes of violence, regardless of the original crime that brought an offender to prison, is greater depending on how many months an offender is confined once released. It might be said that imprisoned defendants (both males and females) tend to become institutionalized and angry due to their prison experiences. This thought is consistent with a "prisonization effect" as advanced Donald Clemmer 65 years ago.[45]

Also, in one study, it was found that over 50 percent of the previously married women with children would pursue a loving and caring family experience less often, based on the length of time served. The more months a female is imprisoned, the less likely she thinks about rekindling family values, if she held any prior to incarceration. In addition, women under correctional supervision were mothers of an estimated 1.3 million minor children in 1998.[46] It appears that once women enter institutions, they and their children often "go from being victims of justice to victims of injustice."[47] For your thoughts, 70 percent of all imprisoned parents (male and female) in the United States do not have a high school diploma and more than one half of the mothers were unemployed in the month before their arrest.[48]

Victimization of Female Prisoners

It probably comes as no surprise that female victimization while incarcerated is common-place. For instance, women often record allegations of serious assaults including sexual assaults by correctional (male and female) personnel and other prisoners. Women in one prison filed allegations that were investigated and shown to be *dubiously* unsubstantiated that prisoners belonging to a gang coerced other women prisoners into drug smuggling. The alleged sexual assaults were of a prison gang carrying out internal searches of other prisoners for drugs with the knowledge of many custody officers. In some facilities, female drug gangs would intimidate female prisoners to have their visitors smuggle drugs into prison. If drugs were not forthcoming, the prisoner was attacked on numerous occasions and in numerous ways. Extortion, blackmail, stabbings, and sexual assaults await those who fail. Additionally, some women who had children prior to incarceration would neglect to report their children to the authorities for fear their children would be taken into custody by DSS or some other public agency. As gang members learned of truths of this variety (and other truths), the information was used to blackmail a prisoner into submission of all sorts of tasks. When female prisoners report fear of an assault much like male prisoners, it is the victim who is placed in protected custody (PC), which usually means a form of solitary confinement. Finally, it is not unusual for female prisoners to experience drug consumption or even addiction and other forms of personal abuse for the first time in their lives once incarcerated. "If she was not a drug user prior to incarceration, she will be by the time she leaves," one correctional officer says.[49]

Pregnant Prisoners and Health Care

Some studies report as many as 25 percent of female prisoners are pregnant at intake or have given birth during the year prior to their incarceration.[50] The children of incarcerated parents are a relatively invisible population and often suffer from neglect and nurturing elements associated with most children.[51] Pregnant women who are incarcerated face even more difficulties in receiving quality care. Their pregnancies are often considered to be high-risk and many are complicated by drug and alcohol abuse, smoking, and sexually transmitted infections (e.g., HIV, Hepatitis B). These factors, if combined with poor social supports and histories of abuse, place these women and their newborns at even greater risk for increased prenatal and postnatal morbidity and mortality. Most female prisoners and

At night, women with infants are confined in this unit at Bedford Hills, Sgt. Williams is the unit manager. Photo by Dennis J. Stevens

many women in community programs including those who are pregnant do not receive "regular pelvic exams or sonograms, that they receive little to no education about prenatal care and nutrition, that they have the inability to alter their diets to suit their changing caloric needs, and that they can be disempowered by remaining shackled during delivery and by being denied labor support from family members."[52] Furthermore, after delivery, incarcerated women might not be permitted to breast feed and they are allotted between 24 and 72 hours "to bond" with their infants before that infant is turned over to a family member for guardianship or enters the state's foster care system. Many jurisdictions will not turn the child over to the father unless he and the mother were married prior to her incarceration. Fortunately, model programs do exist where pregnant, incarcerated women learn about appropriate prenatal care and parenting skills such as at Bedford Hills, NY, through the professional leadership of Superintendent Elaine A. Lord. But these types of programs are few and far between. Superintendent Lord takes great pride in the number of efficient programs designed to aid women while incarcerated.[53] Their Children's Center includes a nursery and pre-teen/teen programs.

There are workshops for female offenders and outside volunteers. In these programs, a pregnant woman is allowed to be with her child during part of her prison sentence, but then the child is sent to its father, her parents, or foster care. The concern is that most of these women are eventually conditionally released into community initiatives and a woman

This teenager and her child are together during the day. Bedford Hills, NY. Photo by Dennis J. Stevens

who loses her children can experience consequences too numerous to mention. There are few programs in the United States to reach the thousands of pregnant women in prison.

Probation Officers' View of Girls

Further evidence that the criminal justice community tends to generally devalue individuals, specifically females, can be found in one study consisting of 174 racially and ethnically diverse girls.[54] The girls were between the ages of 12 and 17 and were referred to juvenile court for person, property, drug, and status offenses and probation violations. The study examines the perceptions of these girls held by juvenile POs, psychologists, and other juvenile court personnel. Three dominant themes emerged from the case narratives among probation officers: (a) a gap between POs' and other court officials' perceptions of the girls as "whiny and manipulative" and the realities of the girls' lives, including sexual abuse and teen motherhood[55]; (b) the disconnect between official perceptions of the girls' families as "trashy" and irresponsible, and the realities of the girls' family circumstances, including situations such as poverty and history of abuse; and (c) a lack of knowledge and understanding on the part of the POs regarding culturally and gender appropriate treatments, consistent with the findings in the earlier section of this chapter.

The researchers also found that the stereotypical images of the girls outweighed any realities. Girls were also referred to treatment services that did not match their needs and

Playroom at Bedford Hills, NY. Photo by Dennis J. Stevens

the probation officers inadvertently "blunder" when attempting to be sensitive to race, gender, and class.[56] Performance of the POs was generally founded on the stereotypical notions about the probationers. What stereotypical notion had the POs implied most often? Girls are criers, liars, and manipulators, reveal Gaarder, Rodriguez, and Zatz.[57] These findings are consistent with other research suggesting that girls on probation have common images typically centered in fabricating reports of abuse, acting promiscuously, whining too much, and attempting to manipulate the court system.[58] One assumption is that male probationers might well experience similar stereotypical notions held by some justice personnel.

VICTIMS OF FEMALE OFFENDERS

About 1 of 7 violent offenders described by victims was a female. Women accounted for 1 in 50 offenders committing a violent sex offense including rape and sexual assault, 1 in 14 robbers, 1 in 9 offenders committing aggravated assault, and more than 1 in 6 offenders described as having committed a simple assault.[59] Violent offenders most often victimized persons of the same gender. More than 3 out of 4 female offenders had a female victim; about 7 out of 10 males had a male victim. Male and female violent offenders differed substantially in their relationship to those they victimized. An estimated 62 percent of female violent offenders had a prior relationship with the victim as an intimate, relative, or acquaintance. By contrast, about 36 percent of male violent offenders were estimated to have known the victim.

Also, 14 percent of the time victims identified women as their attackers. Sexual assault victims identified female offenders 2 percent of the time, robbery victims identified females 7 percent of the time, aggravated assault victims identified females 11 percent of the time, and simple assault victims identified females in 18 percent of the cases.[60] Females as compared to males do not commit crimes of violence as often as males.

Parents Who Kill

Between 1976 and 1997, parents and stepparents murdered nearly 11,000 children. Mothers and stepmothers committed about 50 percent of these child murders. Mothers were responsible for a higher share of children killed during infancy whereas fathers were more likely to have been responsible for the murders of children age eight or older.

Female Offenders and the Federal System

Twenty Federal prisons—including prison camps, correctional institutions, a medical center, and metropolitan correctional centers—currently house female offenders. There are more than 7,000 female offenders—7 percent of the federal prisoner population. To ensure consistency across the system, BOP staff share responsibility in considering women offenders' needs for different medical, psychological, educational, vocational, recreation, religious, and parenting programs. Each discipline is developing measurable objectives to ensure that female offenders have access to programs and services that meet their needs, prepare them to function in an institutional environment, and return to the community.[61] Largely, studies have shown that federal male parolees return to prison at higher rates than female parolees (16 percent as compared to 12 percent).[62] Another study found that female parolees are more compliant with parole conditions than males.[63]

Women Released from Prison

Perhaps Catherine Conly's story about Elise can typify many of the experiences of most females (and males) once released from prison or jail. Elise "walked the winter streets, her hands and face bitterly cold; her mind filled and distracted; her heart brittle.[64] No one had prepared her for the enormity of the challenges she faced—no place to live; no money; her children scattered and angry; no true friends; and that burning desire to get back to (and at the same time avoid) the people, places, and things that had landed her in jail in the first place. Just when success was so important, all she could think of was failure." For females, good paying jobs are hard to come by and safe places to live are even scarcer, especially if you haven't the funds to pay the first month's rent and a security deposit. That is assuming the former convict can pass a credit check, not to mention the difficultly in getting around to find safe quarters in the first place.

As they return to their communities from prison or jail, female offenders like Elise often must comply with conditions of early release. They must achieve financial stability, access health care, locate housing, and commence the process of reuniting with their children.[65] Setting priorities and accomplishing goals can seem overwhelming to anyone locked up for some time, especially those without any support once released. Also, without strong support in the community to help negotiate the rules and regulations of myriad public agencies, many offenders, including women, quickly spiral back into a life of substance abuse and related crimes.

Community Correction Programs for Women

Women are supervised in residential and nonresidential programs. In nonresidential programs, supervision consists more of urine tests and "breathalyzers" to detect alcohol/drug use.[66] Monitoring women's activities in the community through workplace and home visits and telephone checks to verify participants' whereabouts is commonplace among nonresidential programs. Most female CC programs can provide the following services:[67]

- Anger management
- Counseling including crisis intervention
- Cognitive skills
- Educational and vocational skills
- Living skills
- Alcohol/drug treatment
- Parenting
- Job-seeking skills
- Fraud counseling

Services are required to aid women with expressing their anger in nonlethal ways, which were often acquired through negative experiences in a male-dominated lifestyle. This is especially true for younger women whose rap culture glorifies pimps, violence, and freak (sexual) women. Most counselors are unprepared to deal with white middle and upper class females who emulate lower class values but have education and social networks to ensure their safety, up to a point. After that, little matters other than efficient counselors and compassionate jailers.[68] Counseling services, including crisis intervention, consist of individual and group sessions on general life issues as well as domestic violence and sexual abuse. Cognitive skills relate to enhanced methods of thinking and problem-solving techniques, including control management. Educational and vocational skills are linked to formal academic programs and vocational skills relate to learning new job skills. Living skills training is when women learn and practice money management, meal planning and preparation, job and housing search skills, household management, health and hygiene, use of community resources, and other tasks of daily living. AODA treatment tends to be similar to the 12 steps of AA. Parenting is usually around issues of child hygiene and nutrition, conflict resolution and anger management, and child rearing practices. Job seeking skills relate to employment services, which includes a range of activities: vocational assessment, job readiness, job skill training, and job placement. Some programs require offenders to work and/or have stable employment before successfully completing the program. Fewer programs relate to fraud counseling but more should because many women practice chronic theft, including shoplifting and property theft. In the latter case, it should be noted that these offenders pose a significant problem as they tend to be better educated, drug-free, socially skilled, stably employed, and of average or above average intelligence.[69] In addition to residential care, a large number of programs provided case management services by providing or brokering a matrix of treatment services to meet the needs of participants.

Researchers studied numerous public and private CC agencies across the United States and some of their conclusions include the idea that Intermediate sanctions are needed at every point in the criminal justice system from pretrial to re-entry from jail and prison specifically designed for women.[70] Every program for female offenders should be designed to meet their potential risk as well as their critical needs related to addiction, physical/sexual abuse, unemployment, and family relationships.

Female Offenders and System Victimization

Some argue that childhood victimization may prevent girls from learning the social and psychological skills needed for successful adulthood. Abused and neglected females have multiple problems including lower academic and intellectual performance, more stressful life events, more suicide attempts, increased likelihood of abusing alcohol, higher levels of hostility and sensation seeking, and lover levels of self-esteem and sense of control, argues Cathy Spatz Widom.[71] The behavior and health risks of these women are of particular concern because "the environment they create affects the physical and psychosocial development of their children."[72] Widom suggests that most females who first come in contact with the justice community are usually runaways and status offenders. In my own experience, young women in particular enter the system usually because of their relationship with a male who largely used and abused them.[73] It is at that time that nonthreatening intervention opportunities should exist. This thought is consistent with other studies that have found female incarcerated offenders who engage in criminal lifestyles had been apprehended early in the their criminal career but were never prosecuted.[74] Widom's idea is that little if any appropriate intervention was available to aid young women toward societal compliance and subsequently, they continued criminal activities.

Criminal Justice Policy Recommendations

James Austin, Barbara Bloom, and Trish Donahue offer the following recommendations:[75]

1. Increase the number and range of pretrial and community sanctions programs for female defendants and offenders.[76]

Federal, state, and local corrections agencies should consider expanding community treatment and supervision programs for female offenders. Furthermore, pretrial and sentencing options that incorporate the "continuum of care" approach should be expanded to provide services to meet the special needs of female defendants and offenders. Options available to the courts should incorporate nonresidential, less restrictive programs and services (home confinement, intensive probation supervision, day treatment, and substance abuse outpatient treatment) as well as more restrictive residential programs (work release, mother/infant programs, halfway houses, and therapeutic communities).

2. Conduct evaluations of community programs for female offenders.
   Virtually nothing is known about the cost-effectiveness of these programs and intervention strategies. Evaluations are needed to better understand what types of interventions are most effective. Process and impact studies would also provide more accurate information on the characteristics and needs of female offenders, services provided, agency costs, and outcomes. In particular, gender-exclusive strategies, as opposed to coed options, need to be rigorously tested.

3. Improve the collection and dissemination of data on female offenders in both institutions and the community.
   In most jurisdictions, lack of uniform data impedes program and service design for women. Without reliable information on crime patterns and sentencing trends, it is difficult to target programs effectively. To help local jurisdictions, the U.S. Department of Justice, Bureau of Justice Statistics should augment its current reports to provide more timely analysis of female offenders in the community and in jails and prisons. Such reports would provide practical information for planners.

4. Corrections policies regarding female offenders should emphasize family preservation and the needs of children of women offenders.[77]
   When women commit crimes, their children often become the innocent victims of the criminal justice system. These children, many of whom are placed in foster homes away from both parents and siblings, suffer emotional trauma associated with separation and social isolation. Without intervention, these children are at greater risk for involvement in the justice system than their peers. Most mothers and their children will eventually reunite; therefore, correctional programs and policies that emphasize family reunification, parenting skills, and children's services are essential. Currently, few programs provide services to assist in maintaining mother–child relationships.

Program Recommendations

1. Intermediate sanctions for female offenders should include gender-specific services and supervision.
   A strong case management approach should be incorporated into all programs serving women offenders, including screening and intake procedures, individualized treatment planning, referrals to community services, systematic tracking of client

progress, and intensive monitoring of client activities. However, another issue requires some thought. That is, the core concept for developing gender-responsive programs includes the idea that equality does not mean sameness.[78] Equal service delivery of any program is not simply about providing women access to service traditionally reserved for men. Equality needs to be defined in terms of providing opportunities that are relevant to each gender. Why? Because a "females' sense of self is manifested and develops differently in female-specific groups as opposed to coed groups."[79]

2. Management information systems (MIS) need to be developed for community programs.
   Most community programs currently lack the capacity (funding, skills, and equipment) to assess program results. Basic computer information systems can maintain data on clients and aid in measuring recidivism and other outcomes.
   Computer databases would enable programs to develop comprehensive client profiles needed to track completion rates. The database would also allow programs to refine risk/needs screening criteria continually. Programs could identify short- and long-term indicators of program effectiveness, including program progress, recidivism, alcohol/ drug abstinence, and job retention.

3. Training and technical assistance should provide program planners and providers with practical support and information.
   The experience of exemplary programs and experts in the field can assist in the development and implementation of quality programs.[80] Conferences, including transfer of knowledge workshops, site visits to exemplary programs, and onsite assistance can provide training and technical assistance. Specific areas should include screening, client follow-up, information systems, management, and evaluation.

4. Relapse prevention programs.
   Relapse programs and relapse prevention programs are generally missing from corrections programs. That is, in most counseling and intervention strategies, seasoned personnel and volunteers have experienced that most participants fail or come close to failure and require techniques and a "mind-set" of what to do to stay focused on their mission when they do fail. This perspective is so vitally important that without its incorporation into most programs, it is difficult to say what the real outcomes might be, especially because only a handful of programs have followed their participants to determine future outcomes other than recidivism.[81]

A framework for successful intervention regardless of whether a program is offered in prison or in the community is offered by Barbara Bloom and Anne McDiarmid, which includes:[82]

- **Prevent justice system entry**—Create a community response to the issues that impact women's lives and increase their risk for criminal justice involvement. To prevent women from entering the system, community-based substance abuse treatment, economic support, and a community response to violence against women should be provided.

- **Do no harm**—Create alternatives to secure custody for women in the criminal justice system. Modify policies and procedures that often re-traumatize survivors of prior abuse.

- **Create gender-responsive services**—Provide services (both context and content) that are comprehensive and relate to the reality of women's lives. Programs should consider larger issues of poverty, race, and gender inequalities as well as individual factors that impact women in the criminal justice system.

- **Build community support**—Create a system of support within communities that provides assistance (housing, employment, transportation, family reunification, child care, drug and alcohol treatment, peer support, and aftercare) to women who are returning to their communities.

Obstacles to Efficient Programs for Women

Obstacles to efficient programs for female offenders are typical to that of male programs while confined or in the community. Women are often victimized and devalued in mainstream America and often victimization and devaluation continues in correctional programs. Criminally charged women are considered more pathological (uncontrolled—an example might be the witch trials of Salem, MA, in 1692) than men, especially if the crime they committed is associated with a crime of violence.[83] Men in America have, or so they think, a "monopoly" on violence and when women engage in crimes of violence, they commit more than just a violent act, they also break a cultural norm. Breaking a law is serious enough but when that law is associated with strong cultural values, justice outcomes tend to be different.

For instance, just desert perspectives play a significant role in determining how the justice system, including a correctional system, will deal with female offenders. Once convicted, women are typically characterized as having in some way "failed" to meet their adult responsibility, especially if they have children at home. Although correctional policy makers, interest groups, and the public recognize that many of the problems experienced by female offenders are endemic to their social situation outside correctional supervision, they argue that there is little they can do about the big picture of poverty, victimization, housing, and unemployment. On the other hand, some say that the problems of female offenders reflect personal limitations that could be affected by correctional intervention and informal counseling.[84] (There is a ring here that sounds similar to the prosecute versus protect initiatives employed when dealing with children. Should there be some truth to this thought, it could be argued with some degree of confidence that female offenders are treated as though they were children).[85] Note, however, that male offenders might be treated in a similar fashion, which suggests that there is a lot of work to do within the justice community. Nonetheless, women as a group tend to be underserved in both substance abuse prevention and treatment programs, and data remain scarce on women and substance abuse, particularly on prevention throughout a woman's incarceration and community experiences.[86]

ELDERLY OFFENDERS

The population of elderly prisoners under correctional supervision (confined and unconfined) has also increased significantly. Little is known about this group and few studies are dedicated to a better understanding of this phenomenon. The graying of offenders under correctional supervision is a result of tougher penalties advocated by conservatives who see punishment and control as the best responses toward violators.

Elderly prisoners are more likely to have committed crimes such as homicide, manslaughter, and sexual offenses, especially sex crimes against children.[87] For those crimes they are more often imprisoned. However, for crimes such as robbery and burglary and other crimes that bring younger men to prison, these elderly offenders are placed in CC programs. Concerns about the graying of American correctional populations are complicated by the high cost of housing and treating an elderly defendant, which is estimated at three times the cost of housing and treating a younger offender.[88]

Some reasons for the population increase are that despite reports that the percentage of crime attributed to the elderly remains low, the actual number of crimes committed by the elderly is rising.[89] Also, under three-strikes laws such as in California, older men are being given longer sentences and fewer are given probation. This is because admitted third strikers, who are punished most severely, already have a lengthy criminal record. Parole is also less likely to be an opportunity for offenders sentenced under three-strike sentencing.

In California, the average age of a sentenced third-striker is about 36, whereas the average age of non third-strikers is 34. Nationally, the average age of admitted non third-strikers is about 31. Although three-strikes legislation contributes to the aging prison population, it's not the only culprit. Other harsh sentencing policies such as mandatory minimums and truth in sentencing also leave criminals in prison longer.

For instance, as one mandatory state reports (Florida), although there were fewer than 2,000 elderly prisoners who made up less than 5 percent of the total prisoner population in 1990, they expect to house nearly 10,000 elderly prisoners (making up over 10 percent of the total prisoner population) in 2005. As the elderly are released on conditions of freedom, an already rising elderly offender population impacts CC. Punishment advocates who influence sentencing policy take the position that prison is the only answer—the only just deserts for criminals regardless of the expense. Maybe they're right.

Elderly Prisoner Defined

Although there is no definitive, nationwide standard for what constitutes an "elderly prisoner or correctional client," most researchers identify 55 as the threshold age. It must be acknowledged that offenders typically are functionally older than their chronological age because of their offender lifestyles, lack of medical care, and daily routines. Also, a higher percentage of these offenders are substance abuse offenders than in the free society. Additionally, a study reveals that more than half of the elderly prisoners in their sample had a psychiatric diagnosis.[90] The most common diagnoses were personality disorder and depressive illness. The prevalence of depressive illness was five times greater than that found in other studies of younger adult prisoners and elderly people in the community. A retrospective case note study of remand prisoners found that 55 percent (as compared to 10 percent of general populations) of those over the age of 65 years had symptoms of psychiatric disorder and dementia (cognitive and intellectual deterioration).[91] Underdetected, undertreated depressive illness in elderly correctional populations is an increasing public health problem.

Dementia is a syndrome that includes loss of memory, judgment, and reasoning and changes in mood and behavior. These symptoms may affect a person's ability to function at work, in social relationships, or in day-to-day activities. Sometimes dementia-like symptoms can be caused by conditions that may be treatable, such as depression, thyroid disease, infections, or drug interactions. If the symptoms are not treatable and progress over time, they may be due to damage to the nerve cells in the brain.[92] Alzheimer's Disease, the most common form of dementia, accounts for over 60 percent of all dementias. However, an area of equal concern to correctional managers might focus on what Silverstein, Flaherty, and Tobin refer to as wandering behavior.[93]

Description of Elderly Prisoner

A general description of elderly prisoners is a white male, in poor health, often with a history of substance abuse and depression, uneducated, unskilled, with no close family, and serving a long sentence for a major offense.[94]

Typology of Elderly Prisoners

There are three types of elderly prisoners that have been identified, but prison conditions for each group are very stressful.[95] There are "lifers," who have been in prison for their entire adulthood; new elderly offenders, who are sentenced in their 40s or 50s; and third, the chronic reoffender who has been in and out of prison facilities most of their adult life. First time offenders coming into the system at 60 to 70 years of age experience the simultaneous loss of freedom, family members, and amenities, especially health care. Elderly prisoners require more orderly conditions, safety precautions, emotional feedback, and familial support than younger prisoners. They are especially uncomfortable in crowded conditions and tend to want time alone.

Health-Related Experiences

There are vast differences between elderly prisoners who are fit and healthy and those who are unfit and unhealthy. Prisoners who are unfit and unhealthy have a difficult time with younger offenders who exploit and victimize them. Elderly offenders are integrated in prison, jails, and CC programs with other age groups, leaving them susceptible to intimidation and thievery. "The fear of becoming a victim can have an impact on their daily life," Aday says.[96] For example, one Texas facility houses aging prisoners in separate cells from younger inmates but forces everyone to mix in the yard. Many older inmates are so scared of mingling that they don't go outside.

A medical source at the Richard J. Donovan Correctional Facility in San Diego says the most common illnesses among elderly men in prison are diabetes and hepatitis C. Many are on dialysis machines, receive oxygen, or have cancer.[97] Many facilities across the United States do not have separate quarters or cafeterias for older prisoners that tend to have special dietary needs. Prisoners with diabetes usually eat the same food as other inmates—meals full of sugar and carbohydrates. For instance, pancakes loaded with syrup is a common breakfast in many prisons.

Although some prisons in the United States have been designated for elderly inmates or the chronically ill, many elderly and sick inmates remain in prisons that are unable to address their needs, medically and socially. For example, specific end-of-life care protocols or hospice programs are virtually absent in the prison system. And similar to community hospitals in the United States, pain management at the end of life is underutilized. Without such treatment protocols and programs, sick and frail inmates are left to their own resources to receive daily care, including eating, grooming, socializing, finding spiritual outlets, and getting to "sick hall" to see a physician. Often, other inmates, not trained in providing skilled nursing care, may care for a friend, but most often inmates complain of being left alone in a cell, sick and isolated.

Elderly Rights

Emerging from court litigation, health care for elderly offenders under correctional supervision relates to three basic rights that are linked together:[98] (a) access to care must be provided for any condition: medical, dental, and psychological. When denial of care results in pain, suffering, deterioration or degeneration; (b) that right to care is ordered: "Constitutional violation is presented when needed prescribed care is denied to an inmate."[99] The third right is the right to a professional medical judgment. This assures that decisions concerning the nature and timing of medical care are made by medical personnel, using equipment designed for medical use, in locations conducive to medical functions, and for reasons that are purely medical.

Elderly Female Prisoners

Elderly female prisoners are at an even greater health risk than males. Older females, oftentimes grandmothers, have special health care needs that are very distinct from male health care.[100] Necessary health programs like therapeutic services, cervical and breast cancer screenings, and nutritional meals containing calcium and fresh vegetables are not widely available in or out of prison.

Correctional Programs for the Elderly

Prison programs for the elderly should include (but should not be limited to):[101]

1. All existing academic and special education programs that are currently being offered for the general population.
2. Vocational programs such as cabinetmaking, environmental services, and horticulture.
3. Wellness education that provides information pertinent to elders' specific health needs.
4. Wellness facilities that fit their particular fitness capabilities.

5. Substance abuse programming specific to elders' needs.

6. Betterment programs that are age-specific.

Solutions

There are several types of solutions to combat an at-risk, rapidly aging prison population. The most immediate thought is the early conditional release of these prisoners and in CC programs that separate offenders based on an age-range criterion. The literature indicates that elderly prisoners are better behaved than younger offenders.[102] However, once a parole authority learns the type of crime the offender had been convicted of, and sees a very weak opportunity for this prisoner to establish residence and obtain employment, an elderly prisoner is a poor parole risk.[103] Therefore, at-risk evaluations require reexamination and community residence corrections might bring corrections closer to its mission rather than incarceration. It would appear that the most practical solution is to build long-term care facilities for aging inmates, like nursing homes or correctional hospice units, that should be community facilities operated by private providers or government human service agencies. In this manner, preventive care, including instruction on how an elderly prisoner should eat, exercise, and monitor his or her own health, can be accomplished. Special meals, proper cancer screenings, and community interaction through the use of volunteers has a better chance outside of a prison compound. It's also important that elderly offenders receive immediate medical treatment when needed and in a community "home" this is more certain than when confined. Other alternatives include halfway houses or house arrest, both more appropriate for a nonviolent elderly offender than a maximum-security prison. In the long run, the only way to stop the rapid influx of aging prisoners is to reinstate softer sentencing laws and give more power back to judges. A few jurisdictions have initiated softer penalties. As the realities of prison life become clear to policy makers, the political climate is moving toward alternatives. The central argument for releasing elderly inmates is that society cannot afford the medical and personal care they require. If they are physically impaired, they are not a threat to society and should be released to a less costly type of care. Just desert advocates suggest that early release should not be an option. No matter how old and feeble they are, these prisoners were given long sentences and they should serve them. Offenders regardless of their age should pay their debt to society, some think.[104] "With the ready availability of guns, even a person in a wheelchair can be a killer. Society can save money by not coddling these old prisoners so much," Sherry Cashman adds.[105]

Florida's Supervised Population

As of June 30, 2000, Florida had over 120,000 probationers, over 13,000 individuals on community control, and approximately 6,000 on "post-prison release," which includes parole, control release, and administrative control.[106] There were 11,140 elderly probationers (50 and older) on probation in the state of Florida, representing 9.2 percent of the total probation population. Additionally, 791 elderly individuals were on community control, making up 6 percent of the total community control population, and 901 elderly individuals were on postprison release, representing 14 percent of the postprison release population.[107]

Aging While Under Correctional Care

Professor Nina Silverstein

Department of Gerontology
University of Massachusetts-Boston

Aging-in-place is a construct that gerontologists use to describe the desire of community-residing elders to remain independently in their own homes for as long as possible. That construct has added meaning when considering the elder offender who is aging-in-place in a system that may be limited in its ability to respond to the specialized needs and challenges presented by caring for elders both within and outside of the prison walls.

Such challenges are well-known to health and social service professionals in long-term care. Whole industries and professions have emerged to respond to the demographic shift propelled by the baby boomers' emergence on the thresholds of an aging society. Assisted living providers, special care units for dementia care, geriatric care managers, elder law attorneys, geriatric nurse practitioners, and board certified geriatricians are among those that interact with the *aging network of programs and services* to respond to the needs of elders and their caregivers. With each 4-year span, there is a doubling of the older correctional population.

The majority of older prisoners are non-Hispanic white men over the age of 55 without high school diplomas, although African Americans are also overrepresented in this population. Moreover, some studies have found that the average older prisoner has three or more chronic health conditions and may have a history of alcohol abuse.[108] In addition, issues of dementia, whose prevalence is directly related to increased age, is rarely, if at all, addressed in the correctional literature and will certainly impact those systems. The individual who is cognitively impaired (and not likely diagnosed) may have his or her behaviors misinterpreted by correctional staff and other prisoners and may become victimized within that context. For example, the cognitively impaired elder who does not return to his cell within the time allotted may have lost his ability to find that cell (especially because his cell is likely to resemble all of the others).

WHERE ARE THE INFORMAL SUPPORTS?

The informal supports of family and friends that are so fragile and carefully maintained for the community-residing elder are even more tenuous for the imprisoned elder. The importance of such support networks is well known among gerontologists as a critical factor for successful aging. Elders without strong supports are likely to be a greater risk for social isolation, depression, and reduced compliance for following instructions related to medical conditions. One researcher observes that aging inmates who do not have external support cope more poorly in prison than those who maintain external support systems.[109]

Where informal supports do not exist, the *aging network* in the community tries to fill in with formal support such as assistance with *activities of daily living* (ADL; personal care). Special training for prison personnel in elder care, and more specifically, dementia-care, may become necessary in the near future. Some models already show promise in addressing the long-term care need and laws exist that support this direction.

POSITIVE DIRECTIONS

The law advises that correctional populations have the right of access to medical care. They also have rights to:[110] (a) a reasonably safe environment, (b) appropriate treatment, (c) special education, and (d) due process. For the most part, prison administrators largely allocate resources to younger inmates and some administrators openly discourage older prisoners from attending rehab and other educational programs. Physical facilities of most prisons are not structurally designed for older prisoners to: (a) minimize falls; (b) permit older prisoners with mobility limitations or assistive devices barrier free access to bathrooms and other facilities; or (c) allow for short walks to access meals, medical services, social services, and other needed services. The need for such design changes have support through the judicial system citing a 1998 U.S. Supreme Court Decision *(Pennsylvania Department of Corrections v. Yeskey),* which found that Title II of the American with Disabilities Act of 1990 unambiguously extends to state prison inmates.[111]

Although limited, there are several positive initiatives emerging in the long-term care arena. For instance, in 1996, the Pennsylvania system opened SCI Laurel Highlands, a long-term care prison that employs certified nursing aides (CNAs) and contains four skilled nursing units and a personal care unit for inmates with less serious ADL needs.[112] Arizona, South Carolina, and Tennessee also provide assisted living units or facilities. Several other states report using infirmary space for chronically ill care. Skilled nursing is provided in Alabama, Maine, New York, and Pennsylvania. And in 2001, seven states reported having hospice programs: Colorado, Louisiana, Minnesota, Oklahoma, Pennsylvania, South Carolina, and Wisconsin.[113]

THE ELDER AFTER PRISON

Reintegration programs are programs that prepare release plans and assist inmates with their return to the community by setting the stage for employment, financial assistance, and housing. A model program, Project for Older Prisoners (POPS), was originally designed in 1989 by Jonathan Turley but has not as yet been critically evaluated. POPS uses a four-step protocol: (a) identify low-risk/high-cost inmates; (b) assign older prisoners to law students who conduct extensive risk assessments, including interviews and background checks; (c) develop residential and employment financial plans; and (d) prepare reports for parole/pardon board reviews.[114] *Compassionate Release Programs* are for debilitated or dying inmates. These programs accelerate parole while providing case management services to stabilize released inmates in the community after thorough reviews of medical conditions and public safety threats are assessed.

NEXT STEPS

More research, policy development, and program implementation is needed to improve the readiness of the correctional system to respond to the changing demographics of the prison population. Best practice models from community and institutional long-term care might be reviewed and adapted, where appropriate, to the correctional facility.

In addition, more community supports are needed to reintegrate the paroled elder into community life. More counseling programming is also needed to address issues concerning

(continued)

(continued)

chronic illness, death and dying, depression, grief, institutional dependence, isolation, loss, and other concerns pressing older inmates. Such supports might include day treatment, nursing homes, residential care, counseling, in-home support, and increased access to the aging network of programs and services available under the *Older Americans Act.*

Dr. Nina Silverstein, May 5, 2004.[115]

DEVELOPMENTALLY CHALLENGED AND DISABLED OFFENDERS

Few studies exist that provide a real picture of developmentally challenged individuals (DM; learning difficulties, low IQs, and mentally retarded) and disablement (loss of limbs or limb use) among correctional populations but one estimate is that a disproportionate number of persons under correctional supervision have disabilities.[116] Though U.S. Census Bureau data suggests that disabled persons represent roughly one fifth of the total population, prevalence of disability among prisoners is startlingly higher, Marta Russell advises.[117] Hearing loss, for example, is estimated to occur in 30 percent of the correctional population or approximately 2 million offenders.

Disablement in the General Population

Repetitive strain injury debilitates hundreds of thousands of mostly high-tech workers, and accounted for 66 percent of all reported work-related illnesses in 1999.

What is Repetitive Strain Injury (or RSI)?

Repetitive strain injury, repetitive stress injury, or RSI is a term that most people have heard of. RSI is really a blanket name that is used to describe many different types of soft tissue injury including carpel tunnel syndrome and tendonitis. It is usually caused by a mixture of bad ergonomics, poor posture, stress, and repetitive motion.[118]

Only one third of working age disabled individuals are currently employed. Thirty four percent of disabled adults live in households with an annual income of less than $15,000, compared to 12 percent of those without disabilities, a 22-point gap that has remained virtually constant since 1986. Disabled persons are twice as likely not to finish high school (22 percent vs. 9 percent). A disproportionate number of disabled persons report having inadequate access to health care (28 percent vs. 12 percent) or transportation (30 percent vs. 10 percent). It should be acknowledged that the disabled live on the economic margins of all societies throughout the world, not merely in a capitalist country. But wherever they live, they are more likely to come to the attention of the justice community and more likely to be found guilty of crime than individuals without disabilities because they tend to lack resources, networks, and knowledge to defend themselves. But there's more, including the process of social labeling that is strong in our society. Once labeled, the disabled, as well as the mentally ill, a sex fiend, or those who are HIV positive have less change of winning criminal litigation than other defendants.

A few years ago, a group of researchers discussed handicapping conditions and symptoms associated with mental retardation and learning disabilities and the incidence of these disabilities among the adult prison population.[119] They posed problems endured by some prisoners and their programming needs. They also provided a legal analysis of special education in correctional facilities and outlined model programs, options, standards, and policies for special education programming.

Disability Rights

The Americans with Disabilities Act (ADA) was signed into law in 1990. The evidence of its success is everywhere. Handicap parking spaces, Braille instructions on ATMs, and ramps built into sidewalks have all become commonplace fixtures that make an enormous difference in the lives of persons with disabilities. And yet despite ample evidence that the ADA is working, people with disabilities are still, far too often, treated as second class citizens, shunned and segregated by physical barriers and social stereotypes. They are discriminated against in employment, schools, and housing, robbed of their personal autonomy, sometimes even hidden away and forgotten by the larger society. By and large, people with disabilities continue to be excluded from the American dream. And when a disabled person is under correctional supervision, it appears their rights are violated on a continuum.

The ADA of 1990 is the world's first comprehensive civil rights law for people with disabilities. The ADA prohibits discrimination against people with disabilities in employment (Title I), in public services (Title II), in public accommodations (Title III), and in telecommunications (Title IV). Equal Employment Opportunity Commission (EEOC) is responsible for enforcing Title I's prohibition against discrimination against people with disabilities in employment. The ADA has been described as the Emancipation Proclamation for the disability community. In addition, the U.S. Supreme Court ruled that the ADA covers prisoners and offenders under correctional supervision.

For some time, many corrections systems have been under a federal court order to improve the care of offenders with serious mental illness. One court settlement, *Clark v. California*, April 1996, provides special care and treatment for prisoners with developmental disabilities in California.[120]

Prisoners claimed their rights were violated under the federal ADA. The class-action lawsuit filed reported that developmentally disabled inmates had been assaulted by other inmates; taunted by correctional officers; and excluded from medical, work, and education programs. One inmate at the California Medical Facility in Vacaville was stabbed several times after informing on other prisoners. Another inmate with an IQ of 54 told officers he believed he was in danger, but nothing was done to protect him.[121] Subsequently, the disabled inmate was raped repeatedly by his cellmate at R. J. Donovan State Prison in San Diego and had his throat cut.[122]

Cliff Allenby, director of the California Department of Developmental Services, said the state needs more time to develop smaller community facilities to house residents and to create adequate services to support them.[123] Although there are numerous community care homes where developmentally disabled people live successfully, only a limited number can accept the more critically ill. One recommendation is that facilities operated by private home care providers be contracted to provide for these special populations. State and local systems tend to require special legislation to develop specialized facilities, but correctional systems can easily contract private providers without all the "red tape," Allenby clarifies.[124] Correctional officials in many states are watching the developments in California before making decisions in their own jurisdictions.

The Governor of New York, George E. Pataki, took a different approach. He built a 60-bed center for the treatment of developmentally disabled criminals in upstate New York.[125] "This secure facility will expand our ability to protect the public by providing appropriate services for people with mental retardation who violate the law and must be treated in secure settings," Pataki said before the construction of the $18 million facility. One problem with this plan is that family members of inmates living 240 miles away in New York City might find it difficult to visit family members.

Developmentally Challenged Offenders

Developmentally challenged offenders are individuals who have learning disabilities and tend to be mentally retarded. Developmentally challenged offenders can be distinguished from disabled offenders and from the mentally ill. In a review of historical and philosophical trends in the study of developmentally challenged offenders (which is different than a physically disabled individual), before the late 19th century little attempt was made to differentiate between the developmentally challenged individual and anyone who commits a crime. Currently, there is less reluctance to associate "retardation" with delinquency. Nonetheless, Joan Petersilia implies that developmentally challenged offenders are often offenders who have never been accepted by society at large and their social label shapes both society's and correctional response toward them.[126] Although there are few accurate counts concerning developmentally challenged offenders under correctional supervision, one estimate is between 5 and 8 percent, or approximately 350,000 offenders at all levels in correctional services including probation, parole, and incarceration. The landmark *Ruiz v. Estelle* decision set the tone for judicial concerns about developmentally challenged individuals under corrections supervision.[127] The case clarified that developmentally challenged individuals in the Texas system were:

1. Abnormally prone to injuries, many of which were job related.
2. Decidedly disadvantaged when appearing before disciplinary committees.

The implications arising from these findings are that developmentally challenged individuals in a correctional system experience less fairness than others and receive fewer services than others.

SUMMARY

Women, the elderly, and disabled offenders among others are on the rise in correctional populations across America. Drug violations have produced more female offenders under correctional care. The graying of correctional populations is a result of tougher penalties advocated by conservatives who see punishment and control as the best responses toward violators. Elderly defendants are more likely to have committed crimes such as homicide, manslaughter, and sexual offenses, especially sex crimes against children, and are generally imprisoned after their conviction. But, for crimes such as robbery and burglary and other crimes that bring younger men to prison, elderly offenders are placed in CC programs. As for the disabled, many defendants were disabled prior to their conviction due to employment injuries or other conditions in their environment, which could include heredity and injuries. Also, it is likely that many became disabled during their incarceration. Once labeled in our society as different than a typical offender (e.g., marginal, mentally ill, or disabled), advantages and privileges quickly disappear.

Once arrested, female offenders are victimized by the justice community as evidenced through strip-searches, correctional classification systems, and male traits. That is, programs and services designed for the typical male offender are the mainstay of correctional programs. One recommendation is to design classifications on gender neutral criteria.

Some criminal justice policy recommendations for female correctional systems include an increase in programs, program evaluations, improved collection and dissemination of data, and an emphasis on family preservation and child needs. As for program recommendations, they include gender-specific services, development of management information systems, practical training and technical assistance for providers, and relapse prevention programs. Obstacles to efficient programs for female offenders are typical to that of male programs but include society-at-large practices that victimize and devalue females in general.

In regard to elderly and disabled offenders, one common thought is that living criminal lifestyles tends to add health problems to an individual; therefore, elderly is seen as a person over 55 years of age. Early conditional release of elderly and disabled prisoners is one resolution but once a parole authority learns the type of crime the offender had been convicted of, and sees a very weak opportunity for this prisoner to establish residence and obtain employment, an elderly prisoner is a poor parole risk. At-risk evaluations require re-examinations and community residences dedicated to the elderly and the disabled would prove helpful. Another recommendation is that facilities run by private home care providers be created to deal with special populations primarily because state and local systems require special legislation to develop those facilities. Finally, developmentally challenged individuals in correctional systems tend to be treated less fairly than others and receive fewer services than others. One solution is litigation that provides equal services.

DISCUSSION QUESTIONS

1. Identify special correctional populations and their effect upon correctional systems, both from an institutional perspective and a community perspective.

2. Explain the reason for the current increases in female conviction rates. In what way do you agree with those increases? Disagree?

3. Characterize initiatives in the justice community that victimize female offenders. What worthy alternatives does the justice community have to reduce female victimization within the justice community?

4. Explain the justification that supports the justice community's victimization of women.

5. Describe classification recommendations that would better serve female offenders. Provide specific examples in your answer and supporting rationale.

6. Characterize the experiences of female offenders while incarcerated. In what way can some of those experiences be aided by CC programs?

7. Describe the issues related to released incarcerated females. Highlight a plan that might aid female incarcerated offenders from negative experiences while carrying out the sentence of the court.

8. Characterize justice policy recommendations that would better serve female offenders.

9. Describe program recommendations that would bring corrections closer to its mission.

10. Identify obstacles to efficient female correctional programs. How can some of those obstacles be turned into advantages?

11. Provide a description of elderly offenders under correctional supervision.

12. Describe some solutions that would aid elderly offenders. Provide rationale that supports those solutions.

13. Describe the issues associated with disabled correctional populations.

14. Identify some recommendations that would help a disabled population under correctional care. Provide rationale that supports those recommendations.

NOTES

1. Joan Petersilia (2003). *When prisoners come home: Public safety and reintegration challenges.* New York: Oxford University Press. Retrieved online August 24, 2004: http://www.ojp.usdoj.gov/bjs/pub/pdf/ppus03.pdf. Bureau of Justice Statistics (2004, November). *Prisoners in 2003.* Washington, DC: U.S. Department of Justice, Office of Justice Programs, NCJ 205335. Retrieved online January 4, 2005: http://www.ojp.usdoj.gov/bjs/pub/pdf/p03.pdf. Bureau of Justice Statistics Bulletin (2004, May). *Prison and jail inmates at midyear 2003.* Washington, DC: U.S. Department of Justice, Office of Justice Programs, NCJ 203947. Retrieved online August 21, 2004: http://www.ojp.usdoj.gov/bjs/pub/pdf/pjim03.pdf

2. Ann Jacobs (2000). Give'em a fighting change: The challenges for women offenders trying to succeed in the community. *Topics in community corrections: Annual Issue 2000: Responding to women offenders in the community.* National Institute of Corrections (pp. 44–49). Retrieved online January 4, 2005: http://www.nicic.org/pubs/2000/period180.pdf. Also see Joan Petersilia and Michael Tonry (1999). *Prison research at the beginning of the 21st century.* National Institute of Justice. NCJ 184478.

3. Sara S. McLanahan and Erin L. Kelly (2000). *The feminization of poverty: Past and future. Network on the family and the economy.* Retrieved online April 10, 2004: http://www.olin.wustl.edu/macarthur/working percent20papers/wp-mclanahan3.htm. Also see Greg Duncan, Rachel Dunifon, Morgan Ward Doran, and W. Jean Yeung (1998). How different are welfare and working families? *Effects of Welfare Reform on Children, 4*(4), 407–427.

4. Barbara H. Zaitzow (2000). Treatment needs of women in prison. In Dennis J. Stevens (Ed.), *Corrections perspective* (pp. 148–151.) Madison, WI: Coursewise.

5. Ann Jacobs (2000). Give'em a fighting chance: The challenges for women offenders trying to succeed in the community. *Topics in community corrections: Annual Issue 2000: Responding to women offenders in the community.* National Institute of Corrections (pp. 44–49). Retrieved online January 4, 2005: http://www.nicic.org/pubs/2000/period180.pdf

6. Bureau of Justice Statistics (1999, December). *Women offenders.* Washington, DC: U.S. Department of Justice, Office of Justice Programs, NCJ 175688. Revised October 3, 2000. Retrieved online January 4, 2005: http://www.ojp.usdoj.gov/bjs/pub/pdf/wo.pdf

7. James Austin, Barbara Bloom, and Trish Donahue (1992, September). *Female offenders in the community: An analysis of innovative strategies and programs.* National Council on Crime and Delinquency, San Francisco, CA (p. 7). Retrieved online June 30, 2004. http://www.nicic.org/pubs/1992/010786.pdf

8. Bureau of Justice Statistics Bulletin (2004, May). *Prison and jail inmates at midyear 2003.* Relative to their number in the U.S. resident population, men are about 15 times more likely than women to be incarcerated. On June 30, 2003, the rate for inmates serving a sentence of more than 1 year was 61 female inmates per 100,000 women compared to 914 sentenced male inmates per 100,000.

9. Bureau of Justice Statistics (2004, November). *Prisoners in 2003.* Washington, DC: U.S. Department of Justice, Office of Justice Programs, NCJ 205335. Retrieved online January 4, 2005: http://www.ojp.usdoj.gov/bjs/pub/pdf/p03.pdf

10. Bureau of Justice Statistics (1999, July). *Mental health and treatment of inmates and probationers.* Washington, DC: U.S. Department of Justice, Office of Justice Programs, NCJ 174463l. Retrieved online January 4, 2005: http://www.ojp.usdoj.gov/bjs/crimoff.htm

11. Edward J. Latessa and Harry E. Allen (1999). *Corrections in the community.* Cincinnati, OH: Anderson, 415.

12. Bureau of Justice Statistics Bulletin (2004, May). *Prison and jail inmates at midyear 2003.*

13. Bureau of Justice Statistics Bulletin (1999, December). *Women offenders.* Washington, DC: U.S. Department of Justice, Office of Justice Programs, NCJ 175688. Revised October 3, 2000. Retrieved online January 4, 2005: http://www.ojp.usdoj.gov/bjs/pub/pdf/wo.pdf

14. Bureau of Justice Statistics Bulletin (1999, December). *Women offenders.*

15. Bureau of Justice Statistics Bulletin (1999, December). *Women offenders.*

16. Bureau of Justice Statistics Bulletin (1999, December). *Women offenders.*

17. Bureau of Justice Statistics Bulletin (1999, December). *Women offenders* (Table 16, p. 7).

18. Dennis J. Stevens (1999). Interviews with women convicted of murder: Battered women syndrome revisited. *International Review of Victimology, 6,* 117–135.

19. Women get $10m for strip searches at Mass. jail. (2002, May 30). *Boston Globe,* p. A7.

20. Peggy Burke and Linda Adams (1991). *Classification of women offenders in state correctional facilities: A handbook for practitioners.* NICIC. Retrieved online August 20, 2004: http://nicic.org/pubs/1991/010662.pdf

21. Meda Chesney-Lind (2000). Women and the criminal justice system: Gender matters. *Topics in community corrections: Annual Issue 2000: Responding to women offenders in the community.* National Institute of Corrections (pp.7–9). Retrieved online January 4, 2005: http://www.nicic.org/pubs/2000/period180.pdf

22. Merry Morash, Timothy S. Bynum, and Barbara A. Koons (1998). *Women offenders: Programming needs and promising approaching.* National Institute of Justice, NIJ 171668.

23. Peggy Burke and Linda Adams (1991).

24. Joanne Belknap (1996). *The invisible woman: Gender, crime, and justice.* Belmont, CA: Wadsworth. Also see Barbara H. Zaitzow (2000). *Treatment needs of women in prison.* In Dennis J. Stevens (Ed.), *Corrections perspective* (pp. 148–155). Madison, WI: Coursewise.

25. Cathy Spatz Widom (2000). Childhood victimization and the derailment of the girls and women to the criminal justice system. In *Research on women and girls in the criminal justice system* (pp. 27–35). National Institute of Justice: Research Forum, NCJ 180973. Also see A.D. Smith (1962). *Women in prison.* London: Stevens.

26. Barbara Zaitzow (2000), 148. Also see Joan Petersilia (1993). Criminal justice performance measures for prisons. In Bureau of Justice Statistics, *Performance measures for the criminal justice system* (pp. 19–60). Washington, DC: Article prepared for the U.S. Department of Justice, Bureau of Justice Assistance. Retrieved online November 12, 2003: http://www.bja.evaluationwebsite.org/html/documents/measuring_the_performance_of_com.htm

27. Florida Department of Corrections. Retrieved online August 20, 2004: http://www.dc.state.fl.us

28. Bureau of Justice Statistics (2000, October 3). *Women offenders.* Washington, DC: U.S. Department of Justice, Office of Justice Programs, NCJ 175688. Retrieved online January 4, 2005: http://www.ojp.usdoj.gov/bjs/abstract/wo.htm. Also see Louise Bill (1998, December). The victimization, and revictimization of female offenders. *Corrections Today, 60*(7), 106.

29. In many of this author's own studies and professional experiences among female offenders, a common denominator is they had been raped, robbed, and beaten most of their lives from early ages such as three, up to and including while incarcerated. See Dennis J. Stevens (1999) and Dennis J. Stevens (1998a). Incarcerated women, crime and drug addiction. *The Criminologist, 22*(1), 3–14.

30. Catherine Conly (1998). *The Women's Prison Association: Supporting women offenders and their families.* Washington, DC: National Institute of Justice, U.S. Department of Justice, NCJ-172858 (p. 4). Retrieved online January 4, 2005: http://ncjrs.org/pdffiles/172858.pdf

31. Peggy Burke and Linda Adams (1991, March). *Classification of women offenders in state correctional facilities: A handbook for practitioners.* Washington, DC: National Institute of Corrections. Retrieved online June 4, 2003: http://www.nicic.org/pubs/1991/010662.pdf

32. Barbara Zaitzow (2000), 149.

33. J. M. Byrne-Pollack (1990). *Women, prison and crime.* Pacific Grove, CA: Brooks/Cole (pp. 78–84). B. Fletcher and D. G. Moon (1993). Introduction: The population. In B. R. Fletcher, L.D. Shaver, and D. G. Moon (Eds.), *Women prisoners: A forgotten population.* (pp. 67–81). Westport, CT: Praeger.

34. Dennis J. Stevens (1998a).

35. A. W. Burgess and L. L. Holmstrom (1974). Rape trauma syndrome. *American Journal of Psychiatry, 131*(9), 981–985.

36. Cathy Spatz Widom (2000).

37. Larry Muse (2000). Intermediate sanctions for women offenders. A lesson in criminal justice policy-making. *Topics in community corrections: Annual Issue 2000: Responding to women offenders in the community.* National Institute of Corrections (pp. 36–39). Retrieved online January 4, 2005: http://www.nicic.org/pubs/2000/period180.pdf

38. B. Fletcher and D. G. Moon (1993). Ann Jacobs (2000).

39. R. Giallombardo. (1966). *Society of women: A study of a women's prisoner.* New York: Wiley. I. Moyer (1985). *Changing roles of women in the criminal justice system. Offender's victims, and professionals.* Prospect Heights, IL: Waveland.

40. Christine Adler (2003). *Young women and the criminal justice system.* Paper presented at the Juvenile Justice: From Lessons of the Past to a Road Map for the Future Conference convened by the Australian Institute of Criminology in conjunction with the NSW Department of Juvenile Justice and held in Sydney, December 1–2, 2003. Retrieved online January 17, 2005: http://www.aic.gov.au/conferences/2003-juvenile/alder.pdf Also, Dennis J. Stevens (1998b). The impact of time-served and

regime on prisoners' anticipation of crime: Female prisonization effects. *Howard Journal of Criminal Justice, 37*(2), 188–205.

41. R. S. Ogle, D. M. Katkin, and T. J. Bernard (1995). A theory of homicidal behavior among women. *Criminology, 33,* 173–187.

42. Dennis J. Stevens (1998b), 190.

43. The author has experience with this thought in that he taught and conducted group encounters in North Carolina, Illinois, South Carolina, and Massachusetts. If the female correctional systems in those states are typical of other systems, then male-trait-dominated programs are employed in the facilities where I worked.

44. Dennis J. Stevens (1998b), 189.

45. Donald Clemmer (1940). *The prison community.* Boston: Holt, Rinehart, and Winston.

46. John M. Jeffries, Creasie Finney Hairston, and Suzanne Menghraj (2001). *Serving incarcerated and ex-offender fathers and their families: A review of the field.* New York: Vera Institute of Justice.

47. Barbara Zaitzow (2000), 149.

48. C. Mumola (2000, August). *Incarcerated parents and their children.* Washington, DC: Bureau of Justice Statistics, US Department of Justice. Also, C. Beatty (1997). *Parents in prison: Children in crisis: An issue brief.* Washington, DC: Child Welfare League of America.

49. Personal communication between a correctional officer at the women's facility, MCI Framingham, MA, and the writer. This is a similar comment I have heard from other officers in other women's facilities where I have been involved with educational group encounters.

50. Dina R. Rose and Todd R. Clear (2001, December). *From prison to home: The effect of incarceration and reentry on children, families, and communities. Incarceration, reentry, and social capital: Social networks in the balance.* Paper presented at the National Policy Conference. From Prison to Home: The Effect of Incarceration and Reentry on Children, Families, and Communities. U.S. Department of Health and Human Services, The Urban Institute, January 30, 2002.

51. J. Mark Eddy and John B. Reid (2001, December). *The antisocial behavior of the adolescent children of incarcerated parents: A developmental perspective.* Oregon Social Learning Center. Retrieved online July 7, 2004: http://www.selfhelpmagazine.com/articles/child_behavior/treatviolent.html. Mike Stoolmiller, J. Mark Eddy, and John B. Reid (1994). Detecting and describing preventive intervention effects in a universal school-based randomized trial targeting delinquent and violent behavior. *Journal of Consulting and Clinical Psychology, 68*(2), 131–143.

52. Stanford School of Medicine Arts and Humanities Scholars Program. *Understanding prison health care.* Retrieved online July 7, 2004: http://movementbuilding.org/prisonhealth/feedback.html

53. Personnel communication with Superintendent Lord and informal tour of the facility, June 2002.

54. Emily Gaarder, Nancy Rodriguez, and Marjorie S. Zatz (2004, September). Criers, liars, and manipulators: Probation officers' view of girls. *Justice Quarterly, 21*(3), 547–578.

55. Emily Gaarder, Nancy Rodriguez, and Marjorie S. Zatz (2004, September), 555.

56. Marjorie S. Zatz (2000). Convergence of race, ethnicity, gender, and class on court decision making: Looking forward to 21st century. In Julie Horney, Ruth Peterson, Doris MacKenzie, John Martin, and Dennis Rosenbaum (Eds.), Policies processes, and decisions of the criminal justice system (pp. 503–552). Washington, DC: U.S. Department of Justice, Office of Justice Programs, National Institute of Justice. Retrieved online January 17, 2005: http://www.ncjrs.org/criminal_justice2000/vol_3/03j.pdf

57. Emily Gaarder, Nancy Rodriguez, and Marjorie S. Zatz (2004, September), 556.

58. M. Baines and Christine Alder (1996). . . . and when she was bad. Are girls more difficult to work with? Youth workers' perspectives in juvenile justice related areas. *Crime & Delinquency, 42,* 467–485. And L. Bond-Maupin, J. Maupin, and A. Leisenring (2002). *Women and Criminal Justice,* 13, 51–77.

59. Bureau of Justice Statistics (2003). *Crime characteristics.* Washington, DC: U.S. Department of Justice, Office of Justice Programs. Retrieved online August 20, 2004: http://www.ojp.usdoj.gov/bjs/cvict_c.htm

60. Bureau of Justice Statistics (2003). *Victim characteristics. Trends in violent victimization by age—1973–2003.* Washington, DC: U.S. Department of Justice, Office of Justice Programs. Retrieved online August 20, 2004: http://www.ojp.usdoj.gov/bjs/cvict_v.htm

61. Bureau of Prison. Federal. Retrieved online August 22, 2004: http://www.bop.gov/

62. William J. Sabol, William P. Adams, Barbara Parthasarathy, and Yan Yuan (2000, September). *Offenders returning to federal prison, 1986–1997.* Special report. Washington, DC: U.S. Department of Justice, Office of Justice Programs, 1.

63. Leslie Acoca and James Austin (1996). *The crisis: The woman offender sentencing study and alternative sentencing recommendations project: Women in prison.* Washington, DC: National Council on Crime and Delinquency.

64. Catherine Conly (1999, December). *The women's prison association: Supporting women offenders and their families.* Washington, DC: National Institute of Justice, U.S. Department of Justice, NCJ 172858.

65. Catherine Conly (1999, December).

66. M. Kay Harris and Debra L. Stanley (2002, November). *Community corrections programs for women offenders in the United States: An overview of programs and practices.* Paper presented at the 2002 American Society of Criminology Conference, November 12, 2002, Chicago.

67. The following sources were used as a guide in this section: James Austin, Barbara Bloom, and Trish Donahue (1992, September). *Female offenders in the community: An analysis of innovative strategies and programs.* San Francisco, CA: National

Council on Crime and Delinquency. Retrieved online July 4, 2004: http://www.nicic.org/pubs/1992/010786.pdf. Jill Atkinson and Heather McLean (2000). *Women and fraud: Results of a program at the prison for women*. In Dennis J. Steven (Ed.), *Corrections perspective* (pp. 145–147). Madison, WI: Coursewise. M. Kay Harris and Debra L. Stanley (2002).

68. League of women voters: Massachusetts. Retrieved online January 17, 2005: http://lwvma.org/corrections.shtml (pp. 503–552). Also Stephen Walters (1996). Across the border: A comparison of U.S. and Canadian correctional officers. *Journal of Offender Rehabilitation, 23,* 185–195. And J. M. Yeonopolus (*nd*). *Innovative programs for inmates. Oklahoma Department of Corrections.* Retrieved online January 17, 2005: http://www.doc.state.ok.us/DOCS/OCJRC/OCJRC94/940650a.htm

69. Jill Atkinson and Heather McLean (2000), 146.

70. James Austin, Barbara Bloom, and Trish Donahue (1992). *Female offenders in the community: An analysis of innovative strategies and programs.* San Francisco, CA: National Council on Crime and Delinquency.

71. Cathy Spatz Widom (2000).

72. Cathy Spatz Widom (2000), 34.

73. It can be a two-way street but often, young women are under the impression that they can control a man and change him; in reality, if the male has criminal intensions prior to meeting a particular female and appears to be agreeable toward change, that's only part of his technique or manipulation skills. It is likely that female predators operate in a similar fashion among vulnerable males, who are also under the impression that they can change the woman. See Dennis J. Stevens (2000). *Inside the mind of the serial rapist.* Boston: Authors Choice, 81–90.

74. Dennis J. Stevens (1998a).

75. James Austin, Barbara Bloom, and Trish Donahue (1992). *Female offenders in the community: An analysis of innovative strategies and programs.* San Francisco, CA: National Council on Crime and Delinquency.

76. This thought is consistent with Scott K. Okamoto and Meda Chesney-Lind (2000). The relationship between gender and practitioners' fear in working with high risk youth. *Child and Youth Care Forum, 29*(6), 373–383.

77. This thought is consistent with Ann Jacobs (2000), 46.

78. Barbara Bloom and Anne McDiarmid (2000). Gender-responsive supervision and programming for women offenders in the community. *Topics in community corrections: Annual Issue 2000: Responding to women offenders in the community.* National Institute of Corrections (pp. 11–18). Retrieved online January 4, 2005: http://www.nicic.org/pubs/2000/period180.pdf

79. Barbara Bloom and Anne McDiarmid (2000), 13.

80. This thought is consistent with Larry Muse (2000), 36–37.

81. Jill Atkinson and Heather McLean (2000), 147.

82. Barbara Bloom and Anne McDiarmid (2000), 17.

83. Kai Erikson (1966). *The wayward Puritan: A study of the sociology of deviance.* New York: Wiley.

84. Barbara Zaitzow (2000), 150.

85. This thought is simply an interpretation of the information provided by the author.

86. N. Finkelstein, C. Kennedy, K. Thomas, and M. Kearns (1997). *Gender-specific substance abuse treatment.* National Resource Center on Homelessness and Mental Illness and the Health Care for the Homeless Information Resource Center.

87. J. R. Holman (1997). Prison care. *Modern Maturity, 40*(2), 30–36.

88. J. R. Holman (1997).

89. State of Florida. *Florida Corrections Commission 2000 Annual Report.*

90. Seena Fazel, Tony Hope, Ian O'Donnell, and Robin Jacoby (2001, December). Hidden psychiatric morbidity in elderly prisoners. *British Journal of Psychiatry, 179,* 535–539.

91. P. J. Taylor and J. M. Parrott (1988). Elderly offenders. A study of age-related factors among custodially remanded prisoners. *British Journal of Psychiatry, 152,* 340–346. P. Saunders, J. Copeland, M. Dewey, C. Gilmore, B. A. Larkin, H. Phaterpekar, and A. Scott (1993) The prevalence of dementia, depression and neurosis in later life: The Liverpool MRC–ALPHA study. *International Journal of Epidemiology, 22,* 838–847. Also see Nina Silverstein, Gerald Flaherty, and Terri Salmons Tobin (2002). *Dementia and wandering behavior: Concern for the lost elder.* New York: Springer.

92. Alzheimer Society. Retrieved online August 20, 2004: http://www.alzheimer.ca/english/disease/dementias-intro.htm

93. Nina Silverstein, Gerald Flaherty, and Terri Salmons Tobin (2002), 61–63.

94. Kate King and Patricia Bass (2000). Southern prisoners and elderly inmates: Taking a look inside. In Dennis J. Stevens (Ed.), *Corrections perspective* (pp. 66–69). Madison, WI: Coursewise.

95. Ronald H. Aday (2003). *Aging prisoners: Crisis in American corrections.* Greenwood Press.

96. Ronald H. Aday (2003), 91.

97. Stephanie Pfeffer (2002, August). One strike against the elderly: Growing old in prison. *Medill News Service.*

98. B. J. Anno (1991). *Prison health care: Guidelines for the management of an adequate delivery system.* Washington, DC. U.S. Department of Justice, National Institute of Corrections. Also see Kate King and Patricia Bass (2000), 67.

99. B. J. Anno (1991), 36.

100. Ronald H. Aday (2003).

101. Y. Barak, T. Perry, and A. Elizur (1995). Elderly criminals: A study of first criminal offence in old age. *International Journal of Geriatric Psychiatry, 10,* 511–516. Also see Department of Corrections, State of Florida.

102. J. R. Holman (1997).

103. A. Gotting (1983). The elderly in prison: Issues and perspectives. *Journal of Research in Crime and Delinquency, 20,* 291–309.

104. Sherry Cashman (2000, November 10). Should elderly prisoners be released early? *Gazette.* State of Minnesota website. Retrieved online January 4, 2005: http://www.demography.state.mn.us/notyet/nyged01.html

105. Sherry Cashman (2000, November 10), 1.

106. Florida Correction Commission. Official website. Retrieved January 4, 2005: http://www.fcc.state.fl.us/fcc/reports/final00/#28

107. Bureau of Research and Data Analysis, Florida Department of Corrections. Retrieved January 4, 2005: http://www.fcc.state.fl.us/fcc/reports/final00/#28

108. J. J. Kerbs (2000a). The older prisoner: Social, psychological, and medical considerations. In M. B. Rothman, B. D. Dunlop, and P. Entzel (Eds.), *Elders, crime, and the criminal justice system.* (pp. 207–228). New York: Springer.

109. J. J. Kerbs (2000a), 215.

110. *Estelle v. Gamble, 1976.*

111. J. J. Kerbs (2000b). Arguments and strategies for the selective decarceration of older prisoners. In M. B. Rothman, B. D. Dunlop, and P. Entzel (Eds.), *Elders, crime, and the criminal justice system.* (pp. 229–252). New York: Springer.

112. C. M. Mara (2004). Chapter 3: Chronic illness, disability, and long term care in the prison setting. In P. R. Katz, M. D. Mezey, and M. B. Kapp (Ed.), *Vulnerable populations in the long term care continuum.* (pp. 39–56). New York: Springer.

113. C. M. Mara (2004), 39–51.

114. J. J. Kerbs (2000b), 229–252.

115. Specifically written for this textbook by Dr. Nina Silverstein. University of Massachusetts Boston, Department of Gerontology.

116. Marta Russell (2001, July). Disablement, prison, and historical segregation. *Monthly Review.* Retrieved online January 4, 2005: http://www.findarticles.com/cf_0/m1132/3_53/77150231/print.jhtml

117. Marta Russell (2001, July).

118. The Repetitive Strain Injury Association. Retrieved online April 12, 2004: http://rsi.websitehosting-services.co.uk/index.asp

119. Osa C. Coffey, Norma Procopiow, and Neal Miller (1989). *Programming for mentally retarded and learning disabled inmates: A guide for correctional administrators.* Economic and Policy Studies, Inc. National Institute of Corrections, NIC 007380.

120. Keith Hearn (1998, September). Developmentally disabled inmates to receive special care and treatment. CAPT *Outreach.* Retrieved online April 10, 2004: http://www.psych-health.com/inmates.htm

121. Keith Hearn (1998, September).

122. Keith Hearn (1998, September).

123. Keith Hearn (1998, September).

124. Keith Hearn (1998, September).

125. Jennifer Cooper (1998, September 30). Center to treat disabled inmates: Project will create 200 jobs in Norwich. *Tri-Towns Bureau,* 3.

126. Joan Petersilia (2000, May). *Doing justice? The criminal justice system and offenders with developmental disabilities.* California Policy Research Center. Retrieved online April 11, 2004: http://216.239.57.104/search?q=cache: 4GSF31fXxH8J:www.seweb.uci.edu/users/joan/Images/offenders_with_dd.pdf+ Developmentally+Challenged+Offenders++&hl=en&ie=UTF-8

127. *Ruiz v. Estelle,* 503 F. Supp. 1265 (S.D. Texas), cert denied, 103 Ct. 1438, 1980. Other cases that provide protections to developmentally challenged corrections individuals are: *Clark v. State of California,* United States District Court of Northern California, No. C96–1486 FMS, 1998; *Penry v. Lynaugh.* 109 S. Ct. 2934, 1989; *Yeskey v. Commonwealth of Pennsylvania Department of Corrections,* Supreme Court of the United States, No. 97–623, October 1996.

15

MENTAL ILLNESS AND SEX OFFENDERS

LEARNING OBJECTIVES

After you finish reading this chapter, you will be better prepared to:

- Define serious mental illness (SMI) versus mental illness and explain the differences.
- Explain the impact of deinstitutionalization among the mentally ill.
- Provide a rationale for diversionary practices among SMI prisoners.
- Discuss the contributions of Dorothea Dix to the field of mental health.
- Describe correctional services and programs available to the mentally ill.
- Provide a profile of a sex offender and distinguish them from sexual predators.
- Identify the behavioral characteristics of a typical sexual predator.
- Describe some corrections programs available to control sex offenders.
- Characterize and criticize sex offender registration.
- Characterize sex offender community supervision practices.
- Describe the containment approach among dangerous sexual offenders.

KEY TERMS

Civil Commitment Statute	Predict Potential	Dorothea Dix
Community Notification	Dangerousness	Important Court Case
Deinstitutionalization	Mental illness	*Kansas v Hendricks*
Pedophile	Serious mental illness	

Whoever fights monsters should see to it that in the process he does not become a monster. And when you look long into an abyss, the abyss also looks into you.

—Friedrich Nietzsche, *Beyond Good and Evil*

INTRODUCTION

As explored in Chapter 14, female offenders, the elderly, and the disabled have forever changed correctional populations and have fostered new attempts to accommodate those correctional participants in keeping with the correctional mission. Complicating correctional populations and the focus of this chapter are findings associated with offenders who characterize mental illness and sex offenders. You might be surprised to learn that approximately 16 percent of all offenders under the care and custody of corrections are mentally ill offenders. Also, more convicted sex offenders are in CC programs than ever before, and although some sex offenders serve their full prison sentences, they are released (but confined for treatment if evaluated a danger to the community) in some jurisdictions. The number of existing corrections programs for any of these special groups remains insufficient to meet the risks and needs of these growing populations.[1] As Friedrich Nietzsche wonders, are members of a special group staring into an abyss of no return? That is, most jurisdictions have relied primarily on a standardized procedure among correctional participants, often ignoring specialized needs and risk among women, the elderly, disabled, the mentally ill, and sex offenders. In a sense, are members of those groups forced into accepting the abyss of correctional care, never to return to even a modified form of normality?

MENTAL ILLNESS

Serious mental illness (SMI) is defined as an individual having at some time during the past year a diagnosable mental, behavioral, or emotional disorder that meets the criteria specified in the *Diagnostic and Statistical Manual of Mental Disorders,* Fourth Edition (DSM–IV).[2] SMI behavior results in functional impairment that substantially interferes with or limits one or more major life activities.

Caution: "It is now well established that insanity as defined by the criminal law has no direct analog in medicine or science. The divergence between law and psychiatry is caused in part by the legal fiction represented by the words 'insanity' or 'insane' which are kind of lawyers' catchall and have no clinical meaning."

United States Supreme Court Justices.[3]

That is, insanity is a criminal justice perspective and mental illness is a psychological perspective.

There are numerous disorders associated with SMI, such as severe schizophrenia and mood disorders (including bipolar disorders). These disorders can profoundly disrupt a person's thinking, feeling, moods, ability to relate to others, and capacity for coping with the demands of life.[4] Therefore, you could say that it deprives a person of freedom of choice.[5] **Mental illness** can affect persons of any age, race, religion, or income. Mental illness is not the result of personal weakness, lack of character, or poor upbringing.

The relevance of acknowledging the prevalence of SMI in the general population will help you understand how SMI affects corrections. For instance:

- In 2002, there were an estimated 17.5 million adults aged 18 or older with SMI. This represents 8.3 percent of all adults or 1 in 28 Americans.[6]
- Rates of SMI were highest for persons aged 18 to 25 (13 percent) and lowest for persons aged 50 or older (5 percent).
- Among adults, the percentage of females with SMI was higher than the percentage of males (11 vs. 6 percent; females represent 66 percent of total SMI population).[7]
- Up to four million Americans suffer from both SMI and drug addiction.[8]
- An estimated 50 percent of all SMI patients received treatment in 2002.

A substantial amount of media and professional attention has also been devoted to the incidence of sexual abuse in the population at large, but the plight of those who suffer from abuse and SMI have been ignored.[9] Rand researchers agree that the quality of care provided to the mentally ill at large is poor if not inadequate, and efforts to improve access to appropriate treatment for individuals with more than one issue are hampered by barriers between mental health and other human service fields.[10] If these indicators are accurate for a free population, imagine barriers to appropriate care for a correctional population regardless of whether those individuals are confined or in community correctional programs.

Differences between SMI and Mental Illness

For the purposes of this work, SMI can be defined as a severe mental disorder that results in functional impairment that substantially interferes with or limits one or more major life activities for a period of time.[11] On the other hand, mental illness does not necessarily disrupt living cycles. Individuals with mental illness can be highly functioning individuals, unaware of the problem. This description can be criticized by experts, yet even the *DSM–IV*, developed by the American Psychiatric Association, admits that there is no specific definition that can adequately provide specific and precise boundaries for the concept of mental disorder.[12] A consistent operational definition that covers all circumstances is unlikely. Nonetheless, mental illness can be described as a true illness and brain disease. Mental illness is defined as a psychiatric disorder of the mind that causes untypical behavior. People with a mental illness have difficulty in coping with life on a daily basis, and it is fair to say that at the far extreme of these difficulties could be an individual with SMI.

However, unlike the images we often see in books, on television, and at the movies, most people with mental illnesses can lead productive, fulfilling lives with proper treatment and support. On the other hand, most people with SMI require medication to help control symptoms, but also rely on supportive counseling, self-help groups, assistance with housing, vocational rehabilitation, income assistance, and other community services to achieve their highest level of recovery.[13]

Correctional Statistics of the Mentally Ill

It is estimated that there are 283,800 mentally ill (how many suffer from SMI is anybody's guess) offenders incarcerated,[14] which represents 16 percent of the state prison inmates, 7 percent of federal prisoners, and 16 percent of those in jails.[15] An estimated 16 percent or 547,800 probationers reported they had had a mental condition or stayed overnight in a mental hospital at some point in their lifetime.[16] Mental health researchers determined that based on information from personal interviews, state prisoners with a mental condition were more likely than other inmates to be incarcerated:[17]

- For a violent offense (53 percent vs. 46 percent)
- To be under the influence of alcohol/drugs at the time of offense (59 percent vs. 51 percent)
- More than twice as likely as other inmates to have been homeless in the 12 months prior to their arrest (20 percent vs. 9 percent)

Over 75 percent of mentally ill prisoners had been sentenced to time in prison or jail or on probation at least once prior to their current sentence.

Deinstitutionalization and the Mentally Ill

In part, thoughts about the mentally ill are linked to the correctional community in a different way than expected. For instance, from the 1960s to the 1980s, with the advent of new drug therapies that appeared to control or mask most extreme behaviors of the mentally ill, the *deinstitutionalization* movement developed in the United States, demanding that the mentally ill be treated in the community rather than at mentally ill hospitals and facilities.[18] That is, many institutions that cared for the mentally ill downsized and sent patients home.

> **Deinstitutionalization** is defined as: release from institutional care; to discharge someone from institutional care, often to treat him or her through the use of drug therapy in the community.

Court decisions of the day reinforced deinstitutionalization. One result was that the mentally ill were more than twice as likely as others to be arrested, convicted, and sent to prison or jail. One researcher's findings strongly suggest that the reduction in the service capacity of state and county mental hospitals from 1971 to 1996 is directly responsible for a large number of the mentally ill incarcerated in state prisons.[19] Also, because most individuals suffering from a mental illness are without family support or medical insurance, they are more likely to live on the streets or in shelters prior to their arrest than other of-fenders (20 percent vs. 9 percent).[20] Furthermore, when released, they were more likely to return to the streets without appropriate care or supervision. Thus, the mentally ill appeared to be victimized more often than others on the streets and come to the attention of the justice community—time and time again.

Mental Illness and Diversion

When individuals with mental disorders fall through the net of psychiatric services, they tend to gravitate toward the criminal justice system. Therefore, attempts are made to remove individuals, (particularly those with SMI behavioral characteristics) from confinement through diversionary initiatives to CC programs to receive such services. Should the jurisdiction lack such services to provide specialized treatment, contracted providers aid in this endeavor.[21] There are three reasons supporting this diversionary initiative: (a) the standard of health care provided in prison is, generally speaking, poor; (b) prison health care centers are not recognized as hospitals for the purposes of the Mental Health Act (MHA) 1983; and (c) treatment for mental disorder cannot be given against a prisoner's will unless justified under common law.

Mental Correctional Services

At yearend 2000, among prisoners in state correctional facilities, a reported 17,354 (2 percent) were under 24-hour mental health care; 137,395 (13 percent) were receiving therapy or counseling; and 105,336 (10 percent) were prescribed psychotropic medications; or 260,085 (24 percent) total prisoners were aided by mental health services.[22] The U.S. Department of Justice further reports:[23]

- About 10 percent, or 18,900, of the mentally ill inmates were housed in a 24-hour mental health unit.
- Approximately two thirds of all state inmates who were in therapy or receiving medications were in facilities that did not specialize in mental health services.
- Twelve state facilities were primarily for mental health or psychiatric confinement, and an additional 143 state institutions reported they specialized in mental health treatment.
- The percentage of inmates in mental health therapy or receiving medication was higher in female prisons.
- More than one in four female prisoners were in therapy and one in five were on medication.
- One in every 10 state inmates was receiving psychotropic medication.
- States with the highest percentage of inmates receiving such psychotropic medication (Hawaii, Maine, Montana, Nebraska and Oregon) reported that approximately 20 percent of their inmates were receiving medications.

- In Louisiana, Maine, Nebraska, and Wyoming, at least one in four inmates were in mental health therapy or counseling programs.

Mentally Ill and Supermax Facilities

Continuing along this line of thought, the American Civil Liberties Union (ACLU) lobbied the federal court to order the immediate transfer of six SMI prisoners from Wisconsin's Supermax Correctional Institution (SMCI) to an inpatient psychiatric facility.[24] The ACLU also asked the court for an order allowing an independent psychiatric assessment of all prisoners housed at the SMCI. An ACLU attorney, David Fathi, argues that the courts have previously recognized that housing the SMI in supermax facilities amounts to torture and should be stopped.[25] After a medical doctor interviewed 20 prisoners at SMCI, he concluded that 6 of the prisoners should be transferred out of SMCI on an urgent basis.[26]

Mental Health and Correctional Facilities

The U.S. Department of Justice indicates that of the nation's 1,558 adult state correctional facilities, almost 1,400 of them provided mental health services at the beginning of 2001:[27]

- 70 percent reported that they screen prisoners at intake.
- 65 percent conduct psychiatric assessments.
- 51 percent provide 24-hour mental health care.
- 71 percent provide therapy and/or counseling by trained mental health professionals.
- 73 percent distribute psychotropic medications.
- 66 percent help released prisoners obtain community mental health services.
- 1 in every 8 state prisoners received some type of mental health therapy.

Of those assessed to be mentally ill, 80 percent receive therapy or counseling in correctional facilities. About 60 percent of the mentally ill receive psychotropic medications, including anti-depressants, stimulants, sedatives, tranquilizers, or other anti-psychotic drugs. State prisons and correctional systems vary in the way they provide mental health services. Some prisons have professional services available and some use outside providers or independent contractors when providing professional services. How mental health services are delivered to correctional populations depends on many factors, including:

- Number of individuals who require those services in a given system
- Security level of a prison or community center
- Custody level of a correctional participant
- Available resources
- Available resources to a specific prison
- Attitude of policy makers, interest groups, and the public

Often, it comes down to the money or funds available to provide services and what those in charge think about specific groups of individuals. Largely, funds for professional services can depend on the philosophy or belief systems of those who control the purse strings.

There are 155 facilities in the United States that specialize in mental health/psychiatric confinement.[28] General confinement facilities provided most mental health treatment (see Table 15.1). Twelve of these facilities reported that their primary function was mental health confinement. In some states, these facilities are used to house mentally ill prisoners separately from the general prison population. In other states, they are used to remove inmates in response to acute episodes for a short term. The most severely mentally ill are often transported to outside agencies and many others are simply released.

Facilities with mental health confinement as their primary function are typically smaller than other facilities. Between July 1, 1999 and June 30, 2000, these facilities had an average daily population of 690 prisoners, compared to an average of 1,460 in facilities that provide specialized care but hold other inmates as well. On June 30, 2000, the 12 primary facilities listed in Table 15.1 treated more than 8,124 prisoners within a 12-month period.

The majority of prisoners receiving therapy/counseling and medications were housed in facilities with a mental health specialty. Nearly 70 percent of all prisoners receiving therapy and 65 percent of those receiving psychotropic medication were in general confinement or community facilities. It should also be noted that most mentally (and physically) challenged individuals in American society, including those under correctional supervision, are protected by an aggressive set of federal and state laws that aid them on a daily basis.[30]

According to a 1996 Pacific Research Institute for Public Policy report, in 1999 California spent between $1.2 billion and $1.8 billion annually on the mentally ill in its criminal justice system.[31] Comprehensive community treatment programs might reduce

Table 15.1 Characteristics of State Correctional Facilities Providing Mental Health Services (June 30, 2000)

Characteristic	Facilities that Specialize in Mental Health/ Psychiatric Confinement			Other Facilities	
	Total	Primary	Secondary	Confinement	Community Based
Number of facilities	155	12	143	961	442
Mean average daily population	1,400	690	1,460	928	130
Number of inmates held on 6/30/00	217,420	8,124	209,296	902,976	58,411
Number of inmates receiving treatment					
In 24-hour care	13,739	3,335	10,404	3,308	116
In therapy/counseling	38,992	3,373	35,619	83,828	3,876
Psychotropic medications	34,426	3,277	31,149	60,976	2,170

*Printed with permission of the U. S. Department of Justice.[29]

these expenses and help turn some former prisoners into productive members of the community. However, one large problem would be to hire more qualified counselors, professional managers, and prudent administrators and obtain the other resources to conduct professional programs.[32] This thought in itself implies that policy makers, interest groups, and the public do not entirely favor community corrections programs, let alone programs designed for those individuals with mental health conditions.

Mental Health Reform

There was a time when everyone was imprisoned together regardless of gender, age, crime, risk, mental health, disease, and so on. In 1842, Dorothea Dix, a former Boston schoolteacher steeped in Unitarian theology, wrote Memorial to the Legislature of Massachusetts, a 32-page text vividly describing the plight of the impoverished mentally ill.[33] Dix considered herself an instrument of divine will and imbued the text with evangelical fervor. Confining the criminal and the insane in the same building, she wrote, was "subversive of the good order and discipline which should be observed in every well-regulated prison." While campaigning to build a mental institution in New Jersey, Dix wrote that, although jails were built "to detain criminals, bad persons, who willingly and willfully (transgress) the civil and social laws," the mentally ill were innocents, guilty of nothing but "laboring under disease." Jailing them, she wrote, made as much sense as jailing someone for contracting tuberculosis. Through her efforts, mentally ill prisoners were separated from other prisoners but they remained in the same facility. Current mental health reform practices build upon Dorothea Dix's perspective, and her contributions have been celebrated by many.

Goals of the State Planning and Systems Development Branch

The State Planning and Systems Development Branch (SPSDB) was created by the National Mental Health Information Center, part of the United States Department of Health and Human Services, to aid community mental health services.[34] These community services can include CC programs; however, some programs disallow individuals with criminal histories. SPSDB goals include:

- Improve access to community mental health service systems and provide funding for public systems of mental health care when an individual's insurance benefits are exhausted.

- Involve consumers of mental health services, family members, state officials, and service providers in developing community systems of care for people with mental illness.

- Develop a range of services, treatment options, and resources to assist persons with mental illness living in the community.

- Coordinate the delivery of mental health services with other support services such as employment, housing, and education.

- Reduce the use of hospitalization for people with mental illness.
- Address the needs for services among special populations, such as homeless persons with mental illness and people with mental illness who live in rural areas.

In the area of protection and advocacy, SPSDB's goals are:

- Protect and advocate for the rights of people with mental illness in residential treatment facilities and for 90 days following discharge from a facility.
- Investigate, correct, and prevent abuse, neglect, and rights violations of persons with mental illness receiving treatment in residential facilities.

Managing Mentally Ill Offenders in the Community

It becomes clear to probation and parole personnel who supervise mentally ill offenders that most require medication and close monitoring.[35] Program success is based on keeping persons with mental illness in the community so that they can learn to live independently. As you can see, this objective is far different than you might have thought.

> Success of corrections supervisors among mentally ill participants is keeping those participants out of the prison and jail systems.

It should be acknowledged that most mentally ill participants have been in and out of institutions of all types, including jails and hospitals, most of their lives.[36] Few have homes or jobs, and most are drug addicts by the time they participate in a CC program. Often, their own untreated psychotic behavior may have been furthered through their association with the criminal justice process.

One CC Program that Works among the Mentally Ill

The Wisconsin Correctional Service (WCS), a private not-for-profit organization in Milwaukee, has established an innovative Community Support Program (CSP) that adopts a "carrot and stick" approach to managing mentally ill offenders in the community, most of whom are schizophrenic, advises Douglas C. McDonald and Michele Teitelbaum.[37] The program model includes the following five defining elements, all of which can be adapted quite readily to other jurisdictions. These include:

1. *Medical and Therapeutic Services:* Medication is prescribed, administered five days a week, and closely monitored by a pharmacy on the premises. Psychotherapy and group sessions are also available and case management services are provided to all clients to help them obtain primary health care.
2. *Money Management:* The program arranges to be the legal recipient for the client's social security and other disability benefits. The client's fixed expenses (e.g., rent)

are paid directly by the program. The remainder is given to the client in a daily allowance—after clients have taken their prescribed medicine, they receive a chip to turn in at the cashier's window, where they get their daily allowances.

3. *Housing and Other Support Services:* Intensive casework is undertaken to provide for the client's basic needs, either after arrest or upon release from jail or a hospital. This includes referral to other social service agencies if needed. Housing in the community is arranged directly by the program and daily living is monitored by periodic home visits.

4. *Day Reporting and Close Monitoring:* Most clients are required to report to the clinic daily, where they can stay either for a brief period to take medications and get money or for longer periods. The daily observation and interaction with the clients enables staff to monitor behavior and to spot when changes in medications are needed. Failure to report is noted and clients are located.

5. *Participation:* Although clients must agree to enter the treatment program, their choice is constrained by other less desirable alternatives, including jail. Because many mentally ill persons are difficult to manage and resist being medicated, the combination of supportive services backed by firm legal authority is effective in bringing them into treatment.

Program administrators believe that what keeps the mentally ill in the program are the benefits. Prior to coming into the program, many of the participants were homeless and without any means of support. By helping with shelter, income, and medication, the program creates a powerful incentive for staying.

SEX OFFENDERS

Most sex offenders are released into the community—either directly following sentencing or after a term of incarceration. Despite legislative changes and sentencing practices that increase the likelihood and length of imprisonment for those convicted of a sexual offense, most sex offenders are supervised in the community. A recent U.S. Department of Justice study reports that approximately 265,000 sex offenders were under the care, custody, or supervision of correctional agencies in the United States at yearend 2004. Approximately 60 percent of those offenders were on parole or probation.[38] Sex offenders represent almost 4 percent of the estimated seven million convicted offenders yearly. On an average, sex offenders serve three years and six months of an eight-year sentence before a conditional release.[39]

As you can imagine, these offenders present many challenges among correctional personnel charged with their supervision, largely because of the volatile community response to sex offenders and the irrefutable harm to victims stemming from their previous offense and the potential of their reoffense.[40] The mission of correctional personnel is to prevent reoffenses.[41] In most jurisdictions, professional supervisors have learned that no single strategy or plan can prevent sexual assault alone. What holds greater promise of bringing practitioners closer to their mission is the application of multidisciplinary models of sexual offender management.[42] Recent legislation in several states providing correctional supervision, including rehabilitative treatment or "containment," has stirred legal, clinical, and public policy controversies.[43]

Sex Crimes

Although definitions for sex crimes depend on jurisdiction, they can include attempts and conspiracies and can be characterized as:

- "Forcible rape" is forcible intercourse with an adult male or female without the consent (depending on jurisdiction) of the victim.[44]

- "Statutory rape" is the carnal knowledge of a victim usually under 16 years of age and an aggressor over 17 years of age regardless of whether force or lack of force existed.

- "Aggravated rape" is a rape committed upon a person 65 years of age or older or when the victim resists the act to the utmost, but whose resistance is overcome by more force than necessary or the use of a weapon (includes any object used to threaten the victim), and can involve two or more offenders.

- "Lewd acts with children" includes fondling, indecent liberties, immoral practices, molestation, and other indecent behaviors with children. Children cannot give sexual consent.

- "Forcible sodomy" includes deviate sexual intercourse, buggery, and oral or anal intercourse by force.

- "Other sexual assault" includes gross sexual imposition, sexual abuse, aggravated sexual abuse, and other acts such as fondling, molestation, or indecent liberties when the victim is not a child.

Using the Commonwealth of Massachusetts as a guide to provide a better understanding of sex offenses, victims unable to provide consent include victims who are unconscious, alcohol or drug intoxicated, mentally impaired, and children under 16 years of age. There were 1,722 sex offenders incarcerated for a conviction of Sex Offenses Against the Person, associated with Massachusetts General Law Chapter 265 and Chapter 272 Crimes Against Chastity, Morality, Decency, and Good Order on January 1, 2002.[45] There was also an estimated 18,000 offenders who had been found guilty of sex offenses who now resided in the communities of Massachusetts during the spring of 2004. The most frequent sex offense for incarcerated males was rape and sexual abuse of a child (29 percent), followed by rape of a child with force (21 percent), aggravated rape (17 percent), and rape of an adult (16 percent).[46] Of 18 imprisoned female sex offenders in 2004, 9 were convicted of rape and abuse of a child.

Profile of a Sex Offender

Thanks to the media, when we think of sex offenders we think of sexual predators. A sexual predator can be defined as a repeat sexual offender who often uses physical violence and intimidation upon victims, often preys on children, and has many more victims than are ever reported.[47] They are prosecuted for only a fraction of their crimes, if ever prosecuted at all. A typical characteristic among sex offenders and predators is the devastating trauma visited upon their victims.

However, there is significant distinction between a predator and a sex offender—the repetition of the act. An estimated 1 in 10 of all convicted sex offenders can be classified as a chronic sex offender or a predator.[48] Sex offenders of all types vary significantly in age and represent all races, ethnicities, and socioeconomic classes. Females and children can and will commit crimes of a sexual nature.

There are similarities in the behavior of sexual predators who victimize women and children. For example, **pedophiles** or child molesters tend to arrive at deviancy via multiple pathways and engage in many different sexual and nonsexual "acting out" behaviors or episodes with children.[49] However, no single "molester profile" exists. As expected, child molesters are highly dissimilar in terms of personal characteristics, life experiences, and criminal histories. However, the trauma they inflict among victims is similar.

Sexual predators are an extremely heterogeneous population that have not on the whole been subdivided into clinically meaningful groups.[50] (See Table 15.2) A sexual offense, whether pedophilia, rape, or indecent exposure, is a legal term for describing complex behavior. It tells little about the individual who carries out these complex acts. We tend to think in terms of child molesters or sexual predators as members of a group and base our understanding of their behavior on that one aspect of their conduct: victim selection. However, sexual predators, both those convicted and those not convicted of chronic sexual assaults, although individually different from each other, can share the following characteristics.[52]

In a study of 561 compulsive adult offenders, rapists reported a lifetime average of seven incidents and exhibitionists more than five.[66] Some literature reports seven as a very low number of attacks, whereas other literature shows that sexual predators can sexually assault over 100 victims during their lifetime.[67] One point requires clarity, although a detailed discussion is above the scope of this work. Most prisoners convicted of sexual assault are not predators. Many are first-time offenders and over one-half of those convicted of sexual assault had never been arrested of another crime.[68] The data at BJS implies that a very high percentage of sexual assault violators are first-timers caught up in a crime of passion, which could include a status offense.

Personality Tests

Many observers mistakenly hold an assumption that when tested, convicted sex offenders will cooperate with researchers during interviews and while taking a personality test such as the Minnesota Multiphasic Personality Inventory (MMPI) or Millon Clinical Multiaxial Inventory (MCMI).[69] Results from these methods further assumptions about especially high-profile offenders and about treatment. Nonetheless, practitioners such as myself accept the idea that what seems to be ignored is that most sex offenders are criminals—individuals who break laws to get what they want and testing a "norm" or fabricating the truth is not beyond their "routine" grasp. Even the *DSM–IV* advises that a salient characteristic of most individuals with antisocial behavioral patterns is that they are chronic liars. "So why would a predator be truthful with a friggen interviewer or on a personality

Table 15.2   Characteristics of Sexual Predators[51]

Characteristics of Sexual Predators	Source
1. Highly manipulative with public and criminal justice personnel	DSM–IV, 1994[a]
	English, Pullen, and Jones, 1996
2. Victimize in secrecy	Pithers, 1990[53]
3. Secretive lifestyles	Douglas and Olshaker, 1997[54]
4. Well-planned attack strategies	Holmes and Holmes, 1996[55]
5. Highly functional	English, Pullen, and Jones, 1996
6. Excellent social skills	Thornhill and Palmer, 2000[56]
7. Chronic liars and largely loners	DSM–IV 1994; Samenow, 1998[57]
8. Developed complicated and persistent psychological and social systems for purpose of distorting harm they have brought to others	Leberg, 1997; Stevens, 2002[58]
9. Sophisticated rationale to avoid detection	Knapp, 1996[59]
10. Accomplished facades designed to hide the truth about themselves	Strate, Jones, Pullen, and English, 1996[60]
11. Commit a wide range and large number of crimes, including sexual deviance	Gottfredson and Hirschi, 1990
12. Hold a propensity to reoffend	Wakefield and Underwager, 1998[61]
13. Offend against family and nonfamily victims	Abel and Rouleau, 1990[62]
14. Attack without regard for victim gender, age, or social status	English, Pullen, and Jones, 1997
15. Attack without regard for victim's condition or circumstance	Eggers, 2002[63]
16. Sexual assault is their life's work	Michaud and Hazelwood, 1998[64]
17. Best victim profile is vulnerability	Stevens, 2000[65]; Samenow, 1998

[a]Date of publications provide a timeline because new information is a continuum.

test," advises a sexual offender in a group facilitated at a high-priority penitentiary. "Being truthful means they could give themselves away," another sex offender adds. I took that to mean that to avoid detection as a predator carries a harsher sentence than the one imposed upon other offenders.

In addition, correctional systems, including intake assessment initiatives, may have difficulty in identifying sexual predators. Earlier studies[70] find chances are that most sexual predators, including pedophiles, are rarely apprehended and when they are, it is unlikely that they are identified as a sexual predator. There are several reasons for this perspective, including plea bargaining practice, because 95 percent of all felony convictions in state courts were plead out in 2002, suggesting that often little is really known about prisoners.[71] Other factors relate to an "institutional blindness" of the criminal justice community due in part to its bureaucratic hierarchal organization and the sophistication levels of predators.[72] Practitioners imply that sex offenders would more often present positive aspects of their sexual activities or what can be called socially approved scenarios about their motivation because they need to justify their conduct to others and those positive scenarios serve to neutralize their penalties.[73] Furthermore, pedophiles have good reason to want others to believe their lies because those offenders are considered by most cultures, including prison cultures, to be among the most degenerate of all criminals.[74] The bottom line is that most data describing offenders should be suspect based on the imposed naïve perspectives of correctional policy makers as result of institutional blindness, offender observers who believe their own findings, and the sophisticated levels of manipulation of offenders, one correctional manager advises.[75]

Child Abuse Reporting

One theme consistent in the literature on sexual assault of all types is that it is extensively undisclosed and underreported.[76] Why? Victims of sexual abuse tend to have an inability to "trust" others contributive to secrecy and nondisclosure.[77] An implication of this thought is that it is expected that many incarcerated career criminals and many more in CC programs have actually committed a sexual crime that was never reported and therefore they were never charged with a sexual offense but were instead charged with crimes such as aggravated assault.[78] One study shows that of a sample of 61 prisoners, only two had been convicted of a sexual offense, but it was estimated they were responsible as a group for an estimated 1,708 rapes of men, women, and children.[79]

There are other factors associated with the dynamics of the insufferable crime that may impact victim failure to disclose. Victims of sexual abuse frequently experience feelings of shame, guilt, isolation, powerlessness, embarrassment, and inadequacy.[80] Victims can have a feeling that "something is wrong with me" or that the abuse is their fault.[81] They may be embarrassed or reluctant to answer questions about sexual aspects of the abuse.[82] Sometimes, some children often fail to report abuse because of fear that the disclosure will bring consequences even worse than being sexually abused.[83] Also, the victim may feel guilty for creating consequences for the perpetrator and may fear subsequent retaliatory actions from the perpetrator.[84]

Based on research, it is expected that victims' perceptions of guilt and self-blame interfere with their decision to identify themselves as victims.[85] The relevance of this information implies that many sexual offenders are not detected as often as expected. However, because offenders engage in many forms of criminal activities, they are usually detected for crimes of a lesser nature.[86]

Monitoring Sex Offenders

Elaborate strategies across the country have been established to control sexual offenders. For instance, in Tampa, FL, a working partnership was created between several criminal justice agencies and community groups to keep track of released and known sexual predators.[87] One method called for an intensive program of monitoring identified and released predators that included the dissemination of all relevant material to parole officers and POs as well as neighborhood watch groups. With federal funds designated for a community policing initiative, police officials established a Firehouse Unit to conduct personal contact checks several times on a monthly basis with released predators. Here's how it works: an administrative day shift officer is the program coordinator when a sexual predator moves into the city limits and that officer obtains information on every daycare center/nursery school and public/private school within a 1.5-mile radius of the subject's residence. Copies of the predator's photos are provided. Each firehouse officer will make monthly contacts with released predators in their assigned areas. All information is recorded and available to concerned individuals. "This information will contain a myriad of intelligence that can be utilized in future investigations if necessary."[88] To ensure accurate data are maintained, the administrative officer acts as the liaison between the Tampa Police Department, the Hillsborough County Sheriff, and the Florida DOC. Other agencies created an "omnipresent atmosphere" and a database in which pertinent information relates to sex offenders.[89] What have the results in Tampa been like? One way to look at these programs might be to review some dramatic offender self-reported data on victimization rates. For example, from research in which investigators recruited 561 individuals who were not under DOC supervision, 291,737 "paraphilic acts" committed against 195,407 victims under the age of 18 were reported.[90] Not overpathologizing children's sexual behaviors became even more critical in the 1990s when many states were registering youths as sexual predators regardless of age. For instance, Colorado maintains a database in the Central Registry in which all persons who have a sustained petition of sexual abuse against them are registered as sexual predators. A person's name remains in the registry for life. Children as young as six have been listed in the Central Registry.[91]

Sex Offender Registration

Registration or notification proponents believe that by informing the public about the presence of a sex offender, community members will be able to take action to protect themselves from sex offenders by keeping themselves and their children out of harm's way.[92] Notification is also thought to improve public safety because the public can identify and report suspect behavior characterized by those sex offenders (e.g., conversing with children, buying sex-oriented magazines) that might escalate into criminal behavior if ignored.

      Washington state's 1990 Community Protection Act included America's first law authorizing public notification when dangerous sex offenders are released into the community. However, it was the brutal 1994 rape and murder of seven-year-old Megan Kanka that prompted the public demand for broad-based community notification.[93]

      In 1995, a convicted child molester was arrested for the murder and rape of Megan Kanka in a New Jersey suburb. The offender lived right across the street from the Kanka residence, but the police department was prohibited from disclosing the presence of this child molester because at the time the law did not allow the release of sex offender information to the public.[94] On May 17, 1996, President Bill Clinton signed Megan's Law into legislation.

      Community Notification.   Megan's Law allows the States discretion to establish criteria for disclosure, but compels them to make private and personal information on registered sex offenders available to the public. Community notification:

- Assists law enforcement in investigations
- Establishes legal grounds to hold known offenders
- Helps to deter sex offenders from committing new offenses
- Offers citizens information they can use to protect children from victimization

An estimated number of registered sex offenders in each state is provided in Table 15.3. According to the state data, Delaware has 1,080 or the fewest number of registered sex of-

Table 15.3   Number of Registered Sex Offenders in Each Sate and Date Data Were Updated

Alabama—4,757 updated 1/20/04	Louisiana—3,570 updated 7/1/03	Ohio—9,104 updated 2/7/03
Alaska—2,709 updated as of 7/28/03	Maine—1,051 updated 6/17/03	Oklahoma—4,800 updated 5/28/03
Arizona—13,500 updated as of 6/19/03	Maryland—2,576 updated 8/19/02	Oregon—12,137 updated 7/29/02
Arkansas—4,982 updated 1/20/04	Massachusetts—18,000 updated 11/15/02	Pennsylvania—5,500 updated 6/18/03
California—95,401 updated 3/25/03	Michigan—32,424 as of 7/01/03	Rhode Island—1,424 updated 5/16/01
Colorado—8,071 updated 7/25/03	Minnesota—11,000+ updated 7/31/03	South Carolina—5,242 updated 7/29/02
Connecticut—2,443 updated 4/09/03	Mississippi—2,547 updated 8/12/03	South Dakota—1,200 updated 7/01/03
Delaware—1,080 updated 7/17/02	Missouri—8,338 as of 8/19/02	Tennessee—6,176 updated 7/31/03
Florida—25,000+ updated 8/19/02	Montana—2,500+ updated 7/28/03	Texas—28,728 updated 2/18/03
Georgia—2,800 updated 11/12/02	Nebraska—1,658 updated 7/25/03	Utah—5,192 updated 3/20/02
Hawaii—2,177 updated 4/4/01	Nevada—6,000 as of 7/1/02	Vermont—1,701 updated 6/19/03
Idaho—2271 adults; 118 juveniles updated 7/1/03	New Hampshire—2,500 updated 2/18/03	Virginia—11,457 updated 7/01/03
Illinois—12,408 updated 7/17/02	New Jersey—9,161 updated 7/25/03	Washington—16,559 updated 7/28/03
Indiana—# can be researched by Sheriffs' departments; updated 7/25/03	New Mexico—1,490 as of 7/28/03 New York— 14,432 as of 7/29/02	Washington, DC—494 updated 7/1/03
Iowa—5,355 updated 6/17/03	North Carolina—5,915 updated 7/30/02	West Virginia—1,731 updated 8/20/03
Kansas—3,117 updated 11/25/03	North Dakota—1,023 updated 7/25/03	Wisconsin—15,200 updated 8/12/03
Kentucky—4,003 updated 1/20/04		Wyoming—708 updated 7/29/02

Printed with permission of Klaaskids Foundation.[95]

OFFENDERS REQUIRED TO REGISTER:

Any person who resides or works in the Commonwealth of Massachusetts and who has been convicted of a sex offense or who has been adjudicated as a youthful offender or as a delinquent juvenile by reason of a sex offense or a person released from incarceration or parole or probation supervision or custody with the department of youth services for such a conviction or adjudication or a person who has been adjudicated a sexually dangerous person under section 14 of Chapter 123A, as in force at the time of adjudication, or a person released from civil commitment pursuant to section 9 of said chapter 123A, whichever last occurs, on or after August 1, 1981. Offenses that may require full registration are:

- Indecent assault and battery on a child under 14 under section 13B of chapter 265
- Indecent assault and battery on a mentally retarded person under section 13F of said chapter 265
- Indecent assault and battery on a person age 14 or over under section 13H of said chapter 265
- Rape under section 22 of said chapter 265
- Rape of a child under 16 with force under section 22A of said chapter 265
- Rape and abuse of a child under section 23 of said chapter 265
- Assault with intent to commit rape under section 24 of said chapter 265
- Assault of a child with intent to commit rape under section 24B of said chapter 265
- Kidnapping of a child under section 26 of said chapter 265
- Enticing away a person for prostitution or sexual intercourse under section 2 of chapter 272
- Drugging persons for sexual intercourse under section 3 of said chapter 272
- Inducing a minor into prostitution under section 4A of said chapter 272
- Living off or sharing earnings of a minor prostitute under section 4B of said chapter 272
- Second and subsequent adjudication or conviction for open and gross lewdness and lascivious behavior under section 16 of said chapter 272, but excluding a first or single adjudication as a delinquent juvenile before August 1, 1992
- Incestuous marriage or intercourse under section 17 of said chapter 272
- Disseminating to a minor matter harmful to a minor under section 28 of said chapter 272
- Posing or exhibiting a child in a state of nudity under section 29A of said chapter 272
- Dissemination of visual material of a child in a state of nudity or sexual conduct under section 29B of said chapter 272
- Possession of child pornography under section 29C of said chapter 272
- Unnatural and lascivious acts with a child under 16 under section 35A of said chapter 272
- Aggravated rape under section 39 of chapter 277
- Any attempt to commit a violation of any of the aforementioned sections pursuant to section 6 of chapter 274 or a like violation of the laws of another state; the United States; or a military, territorial, or Indian tribal authority.

INFORMATION COLLECTED

Fingerprints and a photograph, date of birth, social security number, current residence and employment addresses, physical description, date of conviction, and a description of the offense or offenses for which the offender was convicted or adjudicated delinquent.

Source: Commonwealth of Massachusetts Sex Offender Registry Board.[96]

fenders while California has over 95,000 registered sex offenders. The population of any given state influences the number of sex offenders as do the efforts of the criminal justice system which has to detect, prosecute, and convict sex offenders. Keep in mind, these numbers do not reflect those sex offenders who have not be detected and convicted.

Although the requirements of each jurisdiction vary, the policy outlined by the Commonwealth of Massachusetts appears to be consistent with many states. See Massachusetts' requirements for offenders required to register.

Criticism of Sex Offender Registration

The dilemma facing many states is that of finding a balance between the public's right to know a sex offender has moved into their neighborhood and the need to successfully reintegrate the offender back into the community.[97] Although the primary goal of community protection is being served, law enforcement and corrections agencies bear a high cost in terms of personnel, time, and budgetary resources. Notification requires a great deal of work related to identifying which offenders will be subject to notification.[98] Also, determining the geographic scope and recipients of notification, scheduling hearings for offenders to contest notification, and actually doing the notification hold their own set of problems. Furthermore, there is little question that the public requires instruction about the nature and purpose of notification including the prevention of a false sense of security, Peter Finn adds.[99]

Community notification is also found to carry a personal cost for the sex offender. Probation/parole field units bear the onus of locating housing in the community for sex offenders, a time-consuming and frequently frustrating task. Supervision; home visits; collateral contacts with landlords, employers, and so forth; and escorting sex offenders also consume a large portion of agents' workweeks. Also, agents are now directly involved in community meetings for sex offenders in notification programs. In short, probation/parole caseloads are already large and sex offender supervision demands an inordinate amount of time.

Concerns About Notification

Criticism of notification arises, in part, from due process concerns. Thirty two states, as well as dozens of local governments, have posted the mandated registries on the Internet so parents and schools can check for sex offenders in their midst. Recent court challenges argue that the online lists violate three constitutional rights: the right to privacy, the right to due process, and the right not to be punished after completing a sentence for a crime (ex post facto). The Supreme Court has agreed to hear two challenges brought by the ACLU against online sex offender registries in Alaska (arguing unfair punishment) and Connecticut (arguing due process), resulting in some jurisdictions closing down their notification system all together. On the other hand, the legal director of the New Jersey ACLU, Ed Barocas, argues that sex offender notification encourages vigilante acts and violates privacy rights.[100] The state of New Jersey's online registry now divulges offenders by county, not by street address.

Finally, some argue that sexual registration aids the false security of a community in the sense that registration and reoffending might be two different perspectives.[101] That is, because a previous offender registers, is that an assurance that she or he cannot or will not reoffend? Actually, there is little empirical evidence available regarding notification's impact—notification has not shown that it reduces recidivism among sexual predators.[102]

An Emerging Approach to Sex Offender Supervision

Challenges and Responses

Probation/parole agencies are faced with a number of significant challenges in their efforts to supervise sex offenders safely. These include:

- Victims are usually sexually assaulted in or near their homes by individuals they know.
- Offenders are often supervised in the same community where they committed their offense and where their victims and potential victims also reside.
- Offense patterns that are characterized by deceit, secrecy, repetitiveness, and extreme trauma to victims.
- Offense patterns that include a variety of offenses, making potential victims harder to identify and protect.
- A fragmented criminal justice and social service system in which responsibility for investigating, prosecuting, sentencing, supervision, treatment, and monitoring of sex offenders is dispersed across agencies, disciplines, and branches of government.

It is not surprising that in many jurisdictions, an approach to sex offender supervision is difficult and at the same time different strategy than supervising other offenders. It is recommended that a consistent philosophy and strategy for the supervision of sex offenders be developed across jurisdictions. Because so many agencies are involved in the identification, assessment, supervision, and treatment of these offenders, a common philosophical framework and set of expectations would aid public safety and possibly aid in the reoffending behavior of sex offenders.

Sex Offender Treatment Centers

Most sex offenders, regardless of whether they are male, female, or juveniles, are treated in facilities that are not dedicated solely to sex offender treatment. There are only 11 dedicated correctional facilities in the United States to specially treat sex offenders and only 1 exists in Iowa for females.[103] In some systems, sex offender treatment is mandatory for all prisoners convicted of a crime of a sexual nature. Largely, this treatment is generally in a group format and includes a facilitator who is generally employed by a private provider (outside contractor). This treatment lasts somewhere around two to three hours a day for 6 to 10 months. For an offender to be eligible for early release or once their prison term has expired, they must successfully complete these programs. In the Virginia prison system, for instance, all juvenile females with a history of violence, especially of a sexual nature, are required to complete a nine-month moral reasoning program that focuses on understanding the impact of their violence on the victim and victim's family and it deals with their own attitudes and beliefs. In New York's system, there are prisons that primarily house only youthful (18 to 35 years of age) sex offenders (nonheinous) such as Groveland in western New York. New York learned that youthful sex offenders tend to be victimized in prisons with general populations.

Sex Offender Community Supervision

Researchers who evaluated sexual offender programs found that:[104]

- The most commonly reported special conditions for sex offenders on probation or parole were court-or officer-ordered treatment requirements and no-contact-with-victim provisions.
- Probation and parole agencies with specialized caseloads were more likely to report use of such community-safety approaches as emphasis on after-hours monitoring of offenders and an orientation focusing on victim protection.
- More than 80 percent of probation and parole respondents stated that mental health treatment is mandated for sex offenders under community supervision.

As you already know, sex offenders (both male, female, and juveniles) under correctional supervision are most often found on probation or parole residing in residential correctional facilities in the community, including halfway houses or in their own residence. It is recommended that an enhanced supervisory strategy be developed on a case-by-case basis to enhance public safety and to provide greater surveillance of a sexual offender, largely because each sexual offender and the community in which she or he makes their residence is different. Often, volatile community responses to sex offenders and the irrefutable harm that reoffense would cause potential victims, the many issues surrounding the community supervision of sex offenders, and how best to ensure public safety are of critical importance. The primary concern, of course, is preventing sexual reoffense by the offender, but often sex offenders can become victims in the community. Developing an appropriate balance of public safety and supervision practices that serves everyone's interests is a huge but necessary task. Therefore, the caseload for each officer should be less than other officers supervising typical offenders. It is recommended that sexual offender caseloads should not exceed 30 offenders, and depending on the geographic location, as few as 15 to 25 offenders. It is also recommended that sexual offender probation and parole officers do both—supervise their caseloads and participate in the treatment process of their clients. These officers would have different training and skills than typical officers and their expertise would be in demand in other justice agencies such as developing PSIs for the court and evaluating prerelease concerns of prisons and jails.

Equally important, it has been found that jurisdictions across the country that apply a multidisciplinary model of sex offender management have learned that no single entity can prevent sexual assault alone. Only through the use of collaborative approaches can those responsible for sex offender supervision attempt to control sex offenders and minimize the risk of future sexual victimization. Victims and victim advocates are an essential part of this equation, some argue. That rationale goes something like this: when probation and parole officers and offender treatment providers engage victims and victim advocates in their work, the goal of victim and community safety is served. Yet, experienced officers suggest that most victims want little or no contact with the individual who violated them, nor do they wish contact with other violators. Nonetheless, a set of idealized supervision standards follows for your thoughts.

Contact Standards.   Arguably, each sexual offender has his or her own unique set of circumstances that require supervision officers to adjust the level of supervision necessary to assure the greatest level of public safety, but contact standards should be set as a minimum and agents should expect to maximize contact as time and circumstances permit. There are three phases used as guidelines in this program that help CC move to their correctional mission:

> **PHASE I-**A minimum of one face-to-face contact per week; two contacts a month should occur at the offender's residence. Contacts while facilitating groups count towards these standards. Phase I should continue until the offender is successfully participating in treatment and making positive progress toward completion of his or her case plan. Offenders not participating in treatment groups should remain in Phase I for the duration of their supervision unless the officer recommends and perhaps a supervisor or cofacilitator approves advancement to the next phase. Offenders should be required to provide daily schedules. Electronic home monitoring (the bracelet) and curfews should be included as an additional structure during this phase.
>
> **PHASE II-**A minimum of two face-to-face contacts per month; one of these contacts should occur in the home. Offenders should be making positive progress in treatment and on their case plan. Phase II should continue until primary group treatment is completed and positive progress with the case plan has occurred.
>
> **PHASE III-**A minimum of one face-to-face contact a month. One of these face-to-face contacts every three months should be at the residence of the offender. Offenders should be making positive progress in aftercare and with the case plan. Phase III should continue until aftercare is completed. Upon completion of Phase III, the offender should be transferred to a regular supervision caseload. In no case should offenders be transferred from the enhanced supervision caseload if they have had a major violation. Transfer to regular supervision should be reviewed by other team members.

Minnesota Department of Corrections Sexual Offender Program

This idea is consistent with the Minnesota DOC, who developed a model for the enhanced supervision of sex offenders in the community in addition to current DOC policy. This model focuses on a programmatic approach that emphasizes both treatment and supervision. Under this model, sex offender treatment becomes an integral part of the treatment process. Where possible, corrections agents participate with therapists and offenders in treatment groups. The agent does not provide therapy but is involved as a co-facilitator, bringing a unique perspective to the group that relates to the realities of the community and correctional supervision. Involvement in sex offender treatment is an integral part of holding offenders accountable for their crimes. In treatment, the offenders are required to address the behaviors that brought them into the criminal justice system. Participation in treatment and other sex offender programming is usually mandated as a condition of probation or supervised release. This model partners the agent and the treatment provider in an integrated collaboration of treatment and supervision that is preventative and works against further victimization.

Containment Approach

Kim English, Suzanne Pullen, and Linda Jones developed what they call a containment approach to manage sexual offenders.[105] The model process for managing and containing sex offenders on probation or parole values public safety, victim protection, and reparation for victims as paramount. The model process seeks to contain offenders in a triangle of supervision:

- Treatment to teach sex offenders to develop internal control over deviant thoughts.
- Supervision and surveillance to control offenders' external behaviors.
- Polygraph examinations to help design, and to monitor conformance to, treatment plans and supervision conditions.

Other aspects of the process are (a) collaborative strategies relying on intra-agency, interagency, and interdisciplinary teams to develop a unified approach to sex offender management; (b) consistent public policies supportive of sex offender-specific containment practices; and (c) quality control measures that include monitoring and evaluation to guide continuous improvement in sex offender management.

Treating Imprisoned Dangerous Sex Offenders after Prison Terms Expire

A new trend in controlling dangerous sex offenders begins once a prisoner serves his or her prison sentence. Rather than releasing the offender, corrections keeps the sex offender in custody based on a prediction potential of dangerousness. That is, once a sexual offender is ready for release, he is evaluated based on his potential of reoffending. If he appears to be a likely candidate for sexual assault, he is released but held for treatment. The job for some specialized practitioners in corrections is to motivate a prisoner away from years of experiencing pleasure from a sexually deviant lifestyle prior to incarceration. Those practitioners must help change nonmainstream attitudes and behavioral patterns of a convicted sexual offender after years of imprisonment, and it goes without saying that many of them are angry about placement in a program after serving his or her "time," and who now sees no clear release date.

The Kansas' Sex Offender Treatment Program was the first program to pass a U.S. Supreme Court Challenge in 1997 associated with *Kansas v Hendricks*[106] Currently, prisoners near release deemed at high risk to reoffend are held until their "mental abnormality no longer exists." Technically, these former prisoners are not incarcerated but remain under the supervision of the department of corrections. Can sex offenders be effectively treated under these conditions? One theme taken by many practitioners who treat prisoners in general is:

- Changing your thinking, changes your life.

The Kansas Sexual Predator Treatment Program (SPTP) keeps prisoners after their release date if they are considered a risk to society and likely to reoffend. As with most sexually violent persons (SVP) laws, the Kansas law came into being as a legislative response to a brutal, heinous crime that provoked a public outcry.[107] The case that powered Kansas' SPTP into being is linked to Donald Ray Gideon, who was released early from prison after serving 10 years for the rape and aggravated sodomy of a college student. Gideon offered Stephanie Schmidt a ride home after her birthday party in a local bar. She was a student at Pittsburg State University in Pittsburg, KS. Both of their whereabouts were unknown for 26 days until America's Most Wanted aired his picture on television. He was apprehended, tried, and convicted of the kidnapping, rape, sodomy, and murder of Schmidt. He received a 40-year sentence. As a result of this case, the SPTP was developed to keep other predators off the streets. Many states are following Kansas' lead.

The SPTP of Kansas empowered the state's attorney general to bring civil commitment actions against individuals deemed as a high risk to reoffend within 90 days of their release. Justice Clarence Thomas indicated in a majority decision by the U.S. Supreme Court that the constitutional protections imposed by Kansas among sexual predators were not in violation of criminal law because the state was committed to reform the offender.

The SPTP operates on the premise that once behavior change is demonstrated, success is achieved and release for the offender is possible. The emphasis is on changing behavior, not on putting in prison time. There are five stages in their program.

Stage One's goal permits the "client" to familiarize himself with the program, rules, and expectations. Because sex offenders see themselves as a victim of the system, they are persuaded to see the merits of new thinking. This stage also gives staff time to familiarize themselves with the client.

Stage Two teaches critical concepts to identify typical thoughts and behavioral patterns. The focus of this stage is on learning what thoughts and behavior the offender experienced as they were:

- Building toward a sexual offense
- During the sexual offense
- How they justified the sexual offense
- How they returned to a "normal state" before the next attack

Stage Three consists of a 12-month curriculum whereby the offender learns how to control sudden uncontrollable impulses. They learn how to internalize the concepts learned and their progress depends on demonstrating consistent application. Also, they must develop a draft **relapse prevention program** that they present in a group setting with other offenders in the program. Needs and/or fears powering attacks of individual offenders are also identified at those group encounters.

Stage Four's focus is on fine-tuning their individualized relapse prevention plan.

Stage Five is a transition stage whereby an offender is moved to a halfway house in the community.

Shortcomings of Civil Commitment Strategies

It is the expectation that even a trained professional has the ability "to see the future" that makes this process so questionable. Who can predict with accuracy that another human being will engage in future crimes such as sexual homicide? One noted psychiatrist remarks that "the belief in the psychiatrist's ability to predict the likely dangerousness of a patient's future behavior is almost universally held, yet it lacks empirical support." He adds, "Labeling of deviancy as mental illness or predicting dangerousness is just a convention to get someone to treatment. Once in treatment the concept of dangerousness is forgotten."[108]

The difficulties in predicting dangerousness have not stopped courts from using such predictions in sex offender commitment proceedings and it is well-established that there is no constitutional barrier to using such predictions in legal proceedings, including those that result in loss of liberty.[109]

The California Department of Mental Health provides the intensive five-phase treatment in the state's program for sexually violent predators.[110] In 2002, it cost the state 60 million dollars to operate. One twist is that released prisoners who successfully complete the in-hospital treatment are moved into the closely supervised community treatment phase, called conditional release. In part, due to media attention, they are met by protesters and local officials who pressure them to leave any temporary shelters they try to call home. On the other hand, prisoners who refuse treatment and sit around playing cards and watching television must be reevaluated "a danger" every two years at a cost of $2,500 for each psychiatric evaluation. With a price tag that hovers around $110,000 per offender per year to maintain, former incarcerated sex offenders are released with little notice.

In 2003, there were nearly 100,000 registered sex offenders in California. Under Megan's Law, they are required to register with the law enforcement agency in the community in which they settle. But in 1996, state law created a new, more visible category of sex offender, called "sexually violent predators." These inmates have two or more convictions for rape or child molestation. Under the "civil commitment" statute, after their prison terms, these convicts may remain confined in the state's high-security psychiatric facility in Atascadero if it's deemed they pose a likely danger of reoffending. The director said that of the 5,321 convicts referred for civil commitment since 1996, only 462 had met the legal requirements: two psychiatric evaluations, a court ruling, and a jury or judge's decision. As long as the burden of proof is on the state to justify keeping someone in a "civil commit-ment (program)," it is likely that little will change. In fact, in California's program in 2002, 19 of the 30 men released unconditionally were still deemed as likely to commit more acts of sexual violence. In California, approximately 60 percent refuse any therapy.

Recidivism Levels of Sex Offenders

In 1994, prisons in 15 states released almost 15,000 male sex offenders,[111] of which:

- 3,115 released had been convicted of rape
- 6,576 released had been convicted of sexual assault
- 4,295 released had been convicted child molesters
- 443 released had been convicted of statutory rape

They were traced for a three-year period. Compared to non sex-offenders released from state prisons, released sex offenders were 4 times more likely to be rearrested for a sex crime. And 40 percent of those crimes occurred within the first 12 months of their release. Within the first three years following their release from prison in 1994, 5.3 percent (517 of the 9,691) of released sex offenders were rearrested for a sex crime. The rate for other prisoners was lower or 1.3 percent.

A first-time offender who "made a mistake" and wants to reform is more likely to re-form than an offender who has experienced life-long attacks as a sexual predator. Rehabili-tation and recidivism levels are "tied" variables in that quality rehabilitation would seem to be measured more often by lower recidivism levels. Some argue that in reality, rehabilita-tion is not an instrument for encouraging good works but a "noble lie"–an ideology that al-lows coercion to flourish behind a mask of benevolence.[112] Many understandably argue that given the seriousness of the crimes committed by recidivist sex offenders, mandatory treatment for these populations might not be the best answer, especially because there are a few programs that exist and the clinicians working hard in them are not bragging about re-sults.[113] Is this true of most correctional programs from substance abuse to vocational train-ing, regardless of whether those programs and services are provided in the penitentiary or in the community? That is, the "nothing works" syndrome among correctional programs is well-represented in the literature, in the popular media, and by the decision makers.[114]

However, there is another side to the argument about the success rates of correc-tional programs that should be considered. The truth is that many programs fail to work because they are ill-conceived (not based on sound criminological theory), have little ther-apeutic integrity (lack professional management and appropriate support), or the method-ological evaluation is highly suspect (lacks appropriate evaluation designs and often inadequate variables are measured to determine success, which should mean more than merely recidivism).[115] We need to move beyond the naiveté and exuberance that blem-ished the advocacy of rehabilitation in the 1950s and early 1960s, and beyond the cyni-cism, pessimism, and retributive responses that powered correctional policy and practice in the 20th century.[116] The challenge is to escape ideology, rhetoric, and ignorance and do the job expected of a modern society.

How Well Do Sex Offenders Respond to Treatment?

The question in itself is one that is difficult to answer because not all sex offenders are predators. One study tested 48 male patients with longstanding histories of deviant sexual behavior.[117] The participants received doses of "medroxyprogesterone acetate" (a hormonal product generally used to treat cancer—Depo-Provera) and milieu therapy for up to 12 months. Forty subjects responded positively, all within 3 weeks, with diminished frequency of sexual fantasies and arousal, decreased desire for deviant sexual behavior, increased control over sexual urges, and improvement in psychosocial functioning.[118] The participants were all volunteers and it may be difficult to predict long-term functioning.

Actually, it is difficult to achieve studies that will measure what we would like to measure, especially in light of the large number of sex offenders who are rarely detected. Trying to compare treated and untreated sex offenders has not really been accomplished.[119] The few tests that have tried to make comparisons were flawed, with recidivism rates underestimating actual recurrence of the pathological behavior.[120] Some research suggests a reduction in recidivism of 30 percent over seven years, with comparable effectiveness for hormonal and cognitive-behavioral treatments. Institutionally based treatment is associated with poorer outcomes than outpatient treatment and the nature of the offender's criminal record is an important prognostic factor. The problem is that treatment does not eliminate sexual crime.[121] Professional treatment can decrease sex offense, but that depends on the offender,[122] doesn't it?

SUMMARY

The problem of mental illness among correctional populations is a serious problem that has yet to be resolved, although many correctional professionals keep trying. Understanding the problem is always the first step toward resolution. SMI is described as a severe mental disorder that results in functional impairment that substantially interferes with or limits one or more major life activities for a period of time. Mental illness is defined as a psychiatric disorder of the mind that causes untypical behavior. People with a mental illness have difficulty in coping with life on a daily basis and it is fair to say that SMI is the far extreme. Individuals with mental illness can be highly functioning individuals who are unaware of the problem, but most individuals characterized with SMI require medication to help control symptoms, and rely on supportive counseling, self-help groups, assistance with housing, vocational rehabilitation, income assistance, and other community services to achieve their highest level of recovery.

In the 1960s through the 1980s, new drug therapies that masked extreme SMI characteristics sent patients out of the hospitals for treatment to the community or *deinstitutionalization.* Many patients did not have homes and those that did lacked appropriate care or supervision. Former patients came to the attention of the justice community as victims and offenders and many were incarcerated in high-custody facilities.

There are diversionary initiatives in place to remove the mentally ill from confinement because the standard of health care provided in prison is usually poor. Prisons do not qualify under the MHA of 1983 as providers, because treatment for mental disorder cannot be given against a prisoner's will.

Dorothea Dix, a former Boston schoolteacher, described the plight of the impoverished mentally ill to the Massachusetts Legislature in 1842. Jailing them made as much sense as jailing someone for contracting tuberculosis. The legacy of Dorothea Dix lives today among most social service organizations and influences policy and practice.

An effective CC program for the mentally ill is patterned after the Wisconsin Correctional Service, which utilizes a "carrot and stick" approach to managing mentally ill offenders in the community. The program model includes: medical and therapeutic services, money management, housing and other support services, day reporting and close monitoring, and patient participation.

The second part of the chapter defined sexual predators as repeat sexual offenders who have many more victims than ever reported. Predators are prosecuted for only a fraction of their crimes. There is a significant distinction, however, between a predator and a sex offender—the repetition of the act. An estimated 1 in 10 of all convicted sex offenders can be classified as a predator. Sex offenders of all types, ages, and gender vary significantly and represent all races, ethnicities, and socioeconomic classes.

Sexual predators can be characterized as highly manipulative; highly functioning; having high social skills; likely to victimize in secrecy; having secretive and manipulative lifestyles; being involved in well-planned assaults; having complicated and persistent psychological and social systems; committing a wide range and large number of sexually deviant acts; having a propensity to reoffend; offending against both family and nonfamily victims; attacking without regard for victim gender, condition, or position in the community; and making sexual assault their life work.

CC initiatives such as registration and containment have been developed to control sex offenders. Registration proponents believe that by informing the public, the public will be able to protect themselves. The dilemma facing many states is that of finding a balance between the public's right to know and the need to successfully reintegrate an offender into the community. Carrying out notification bears a high cost in terms of personnel, time, and budgetary resources and provides a sense of community security, but some argue it's a false security. Notification carries a personal cost for the offender and presents issues of due process.

Containment seeks to keep offenders in a triangle of supervision after the offender has served his prison sentence and is released to the program. It includes treatment to teach sex offenders to develop internal control over deviant thoughts, supervision and surveillance to control offenders' external behaviors, and polygraph examinations to help design, and monitor conformance to treatment plans and supervision conditions.

DISCUSSION QUESTIONS

1. Define serious mental illness versus mental illness and explain the differences between the two. In what way might serious mental illness lead a person to crime?

2. Explain the impact of deinstitutionalization among the mentally ill. Who benefits from this policy and in what way?

3. Provide a rationale concerning diversionary initiatives among SMI prisoners. In what way do you agree with this strategy?

4. Discuss the contributions of Dorothea Dix to the field of mental health.

5. Describe correctional services and programs available to the mentally ill. In what way would correctional personnel be trained differently than personnel providing services to typical offenders in a CC system?

6. Provide a profile of a sex offender and distinguish them from sexual predators.

7. Identify the behavioral characteristics of a typical sexual predator. In what way might these individuals differ from a typical sex offender, especially a first-timer?

8. Describe some corrections programs available to control sex offenders.

9. Characterize and criticize sex offender registration and explain the benefits of this strategy.

10. Characterize sex offender community supervision practices.

11. Characterize the civil commitment actions used among dangerous sex offenders after their prison term is completed. In what way do you agree and disagree with this practice? What other recommendations might you have to control dangerous sex offenders?

NOTES

1. James Austin, Barbara Bloom, and Trish Donahue (1992, September). *Female offenders in the community—an analysis of innovative strategies and programs.* National Council on Crime and Delinquency. Retrieved online April 14, 2004: http://64.233.167.104/search?q=cache:j_Osps8aMkwJ:www.nicic.org/pubs/1992/010786.pdf+Austin,+Bloom,+ percent26+Donahue,+1992&hl=en&ie=UTF-8

2. *Diagnostic and statistical manual of mental disorders,* 4th edition (1994). Washington, DC: American Psychiatric Association (APA). College students tend to link mental illness with the "insanity plea" associated with litigation; however, mental illness and the insanity plea are two different variables. An insanity perspective is a criminal justice perspective and less likely found within the psychological community.

3. *Foucha v Louisiana,* 504 U.S. 71 (1992), Justices Kennedy and Rhenquist's dissenting opinion. Findlaw. Retrieved online January 5, 2005: http://caselaw.lp.findlaw.com/scripts/getcase.pl?navby=search&linkurl=<%LINKURL%>&graphurl=<%GRAPHURL%>&court=US&case=/data/us/504/71.html

4. National Association of Mental Illness. Retrieved online August 24, 2004: http://www.nami.org

5. Curt R. Bartol and Anne M. Bartol (2005). *Criminal behavior: A psychological approach* (7th ed.). Upper Saddle River, NJ: Prentice Hall, 188.

6. Joan Epstein, Peggy Barker, Michael Vorburger, and Christine Murtha (2004). *Serious mental illness and its co-occurrence with substance use disorders, 2002.* Department of Health and Human Services (SMA 04-3905, Analytic Series A–24). Rockville, MD: Substance Abuse and Mental Health Services Administration, Office of Applied Studies.

7. Joan Epstein, Peggy Barker, Michael Vorburger, and Christine Murtha (2004). Section 2.3.3

8. Harold Pincus, Audrey Burnam, Susan Ridgely, Michael Greenberg, Katherine Watkins, and Nancy Pollock. (2004, February). *Helping people with mental illness and drug addiction.* Rand Corporation Study. Retrieved online February 2004: www.rand.org

9. M. Harris and C. Landis (Eds.). (1997). *Sexual abuse in the lives of women diagnosed with serious mental illness.* Netherlands: Harwood, 2.

10. Harold Pincus, Audrey Burnam, Susan Ridgely, Michael Greenberg, Katherine Watkins, and Nancy Pollock (2004, February).

11. Ronald C. Kessler, Shanyang Zhao, Steven J. Katz, Anthony C. Kouzis, Richard G. Frank, Mark Edlund, and Philip Leaf (1999, January). Past-year use of outpatient services for psychiatric problems in the national co-morbidity survey. *American Journal of Psychiatry, 156,* 115–123.

12. *Diagnostic and statistical manual of mental disorders,* 4th edition (1994).

13. National Association on Mental Illness (2004). Retrieved online January 5, 2005: http://www.nami.org/

14. Bureau of Justice Statistics (1999, July). *Mental health and treatment of inmates and probationers.* Washington, DC: U.S. Department of Justice, Office of Justice Program, NCJ 174463. Retrieved online January 4, 2005: http://www.ojp.usdoj.gov/bjs/pub/pdf/mhtip.pdf

15. Canada reports that 20 percent of their prisoners also display characteristics of mental illness. Operation statistics: Institutional health care centres and major psychiatric facilities. Medical and health care services. Correctional Service of Canada, 1980–86: Updated. (2004, October 13). *A Five-Year Historical Profile of Canadian Regional Psychiatric Centres Forum on Correctional Research,* 2(3), 141–152.

16. Bureau of Justice Statistics (1999, July). *Mental health and treatment of inmates and probationers.*

17. Bureau of Justice Statistics (1999, July). *Mental health and treatment of inmates and probationers.*

18. Steven Raphael (2000, September). *The deinstitutionalization of the mentally ill and growth in the U.S. prison populations: 1971 to 1996.* Retrieved online January 5, 2005: http://ist-socrates.berkeley.edu/~raphael/raphael2000.pdf. Raphael's findings are consistent with an earlier study that provides a time series analysis of aggregate

national data for the United States between 1926 and 1987, revealing significant negative correlations between the size of mental hospital population and prison and jail populations. George B. Palermo, Maurice B. Smith, and Frank J. Liska (1991). Jails versus mental hospitals: A social dilemma. *International Journal of Offender Therapy and Comparative Criminology, 35*(2), 97–106.

19. Steven Raphael (2000, September), 13.

20. Bureau of Justice Statistics (1999, July). *Mental health treatment of inmates and probationers.*

21. Luke Birmingham (2001). Diversion from custody. *Advances in Psychiatric Treatment, 7,* 198–207. Retrieved online August 20, 2004: http://apt.rcpsych.org/cgi/content/full/7/3/198

22. Bureau of Justice Statistics (2001, July). *Mental health treatment in state prisons, 2000.* Washington, DC: U.S. Department of Justice, Office of Justice Programs, NCJ 188215. Retrieved online January 5, 2005: http://www.ojp.usdoj.gov/bjs/pub/pdf/mhtsp00.pdf

23. Bureau of Justice Statistics (2001, July). *Mental health treatment in state prisons, 2000.*

24. Disability rights (2001, August 10). *ACLU requests transfer of mentally-ill prisoners from supermax.* American Civil Liberties Union. Retrieved online January 5, 2005: http://www.aclu.org/DisabilityRights/DisabilityRights.cfm?ID=10301&c=74

25. Disability rights (2001, August 10).

26. Terry Kupers (1999). *Prison madness: The mental health crisis behind bars and what we must do.* San Francisco: Jossey-Bass. Retrieved online January 5, 2005: http://www.etext.org/Politics/MIM/agitation/prisons/controlunits/kupers.html

27. Bureau of Justice Statistics (2001 July). *Mental health treatment in state prisons, 2000.*

28. Bureau of Justice Statistics (2001 July). *Mental health treatment in state prisons, 2000.*

29. Bureau of Justice Statistics (2001 July). *Mental health treatment in state prisons, 2000.*

30. See U.S. Department of Health and Human Services. Center for mental health services division of state and community development systems. State planning and systems development branch—protection and advocacy. Retrieved online January 4, 2005: http://www.mentalhealth.org/publications/allpubs/KEN95-0021/default.asp. National Institute of Mental Health. Retrieved online January 4, 2005: http://www.mentalhealth.samhsa.gov/_scripts/redirect.asp?ID=24

31. Lance T. Isumi, Mark Schiller, and Steven Hayward (1996). *Corrections, criminal justice, and the mentally ill: Some observations about costs in California.* Pacific Research Institute Study, Pacific Research Institute for Public Policy. Retrieved online January 5, 2005: http://www.mhac.org/pristudy_01.html

32. Arthur J. Lurigio and James A. Swartz (2000). Changing the contours of the criminal justice system to meet the needs of persons with serious mental illness (pp. 503–552). In Julie Horney, Ruth Peterson, Doris MacKenzie, John Martin, and Dennis Rosenbaum (Eds.), *Policies processes, and decisions of the criminal justice system.* Washington, DC: U.S. Department of Justice, Office of Justice Programs,

National Institute of Justice. Retrieved online January 17, 2005: http://www.ncjrs .org/criminal_justice2000/vol_3/03c.pdf

33. Spencer P. M. Harrington (1999 May). *New Bedlam: Jails—Not psychiatric hospitals. Now care for the indigent mentally ill.* Retrieved online January 4, 2005: http://www.findarticles.com/

34. National Mental Health Information Center. Retrieved online January 6, 2005: http://www.nmha.org/infoctr/index.cfm

35. Douglas C. McDonald and Michele Teitelbaum (1994, March). *Managing mentally ill offenders in the community: Milwaukee's community support program.* National Institute of Justice, NCJ–145330. Retrieved online January 5, 2005: http://www .ncjrs.org/txtfiles/menill.txt

36. Douglas C. McDonald and Michele Teitelbaum (1994, March). Also, Joan Nuffield (2005). Diversion programs for adults 1997–05. *Forum of Corrections Research.* Retrieved online August 19, 2004: http://www.psepc-sppcc.gc.ca/publications/ corrections/pdf/199705_e.pdf

37. Douglas C. McDonald and Michele Teitelbaum (1994, March).

38. Bureau of Justice Statistics (1997, February). *Sixty percent of convicted sex offenders are on parole or probation: Rapes and sexual assaults decline.* Washington, DC: U.S. Department of Justice, Office of Justice Programs, NCJ–163392. Retrieved online January 5, 2005: http://www.ojp.usdoj.gov/bjs/pub/press/soo.pr

39. Bureau of Justice Statistics (2002, June). *Recidivism of sex offenders released from prison in 1994.* Washington, DC: U.S. Department of Justice, Office of Justice Programs, NCJ 193427. Retrieved online January 5, 2005: http://www.ojp.usdoj.gov/ bjs/abstract/rsorp94.htm

40. Kim English, Suzanne Pullen, and Linda Jones (1997, January). *Managing adult sex offenders: A containment approach. American Probation and Parole Association.* Washington, DC: U.S. Department of Justice, Office of Justice Programs, NCJ–163387. Retrieved online January 17, 2005: http://library.lp.findlaw.com/ articles/file/00007/000875/title/Subject/topic/Health_Mental%20Health/filename/ health_2_3889

41. D. D'Amora (1999). Center director: Special services, center for the treatment of problem sexual behavior. Presentation during the training program *In defense of the community: Effective community-based responses to sex offenders.* Westchester County, NY.

42. *Dangerous sex offenders: A task force report of the American Psychiatric Association* (1999). Washington, DC: American Psychiatric Association (pp. 44–50).

43. L. S. Grossman, B. Martis, and C. G. Fichtner (1999). Are sex offenders treatable? A research overview. *Psychiatric Services, 50*(3), 349–361.

44. Bureau of Justice Statistics (1997, February). *Sex offenses and offenders.* Washington, DC: U.S. Department of Justice, Office of Justice Programs, NCJ 163392. Retrieved online January 5, 2005: http://www.ojp.usdoj.gov/bjs/pub/pdf/soo.pdf. More

specifically, BJS defines rape as: "Forced sexual intercourse including both psychological coercion as well as physical force. Forced sexual intercourse means penetration by the offender(s). Includes attempted rapes, male as well as female victims, and both heterosexual and homosexual rape. Attempted rape includes verbal threats of rape." Retrieved online January 5, 2005: http://www.ojp.usdoj.gov/bjs/glance/rape.htm

45. Massachusetts Sex Offender Registry Board. Retrieved online August 21, 2004: http://www.mass.gov/sorb/community.htm

46. Massachusetts Department of Corrections. Retrieved online August 21, 2004: http://www.mass.gov/doc/

47. The author facilitated a group encounter among high-custody prisoners and trained them to conduct research in a prison program among other inmates. One finding was that sexual predators indicated that most avoided violence and preferred various methods of intimidation to sexually assault their victims. In addition, in most high-custody penitentiaries, known sexual offenders are segregated from other prisoners due to their potential victimization by other inmates who see them as weak and childlike. See Dennis J. Stevens. (2000). Most correctional personnel say that sex offenders are fearful of violence. "They talk a good game," says a custody captain at Elmira Corrections in NY. Also, this definition is consistent with many state definitions including Florida's Statutes, Section 775.21(3).

48. Kim English, Suzanne Pullen, and Linda Jones (1997, January).

49. *Child sexual molestation: Research issues* (2000). Retrieved online January 5, 2005: http://www.ncjrs.org/txtfiles/163390.txt

50. D. H. Grubin and H. G. Kennedy (1991). The classification of sexual offenders. *Criminal Behaviour and Mental Health, 1,* 123–129.

51. In this sense, most characteristics of predators are centered in convicted known predatory acts. The characteristics offered here include largely those inmates who were not convicted of predatory crimes. See Stevens (2000). This table was developed by the author for this chapter.

52. Dennis J. Stevens (2005). *Community corrections: An applied approach.* Upper Saddle River, NJ: Prentice Hall.

53. W. D. Pithers (1990). Relapse prevention with sexual aggressors: A method for maintaining therapeutic gain and enhancing external supervision. In Marshall, Laws, and Barbaree (Eds.), *Handbook of sexual assault: Issues, theories, and treatment of the offender.* New York: Plenum.

54. John Douglas and Mark Olshaker (1997). *Journey into darkness.* New York: Scribner.

55. Ronald M. Holmes and Stephen T. Holmes (1996). *Profiling violent crimes: An investigative tool.* Thousand Oaks, CA: Sage.

56. Randy Thornhill and Craig R. Palmer (2000). *A natural history of rape.* Cambridge, MA: MIT Press.

57. Stanton Samenow (1998). *Before it's too late.* New York: Basic Books.

58. Eric Leberg (1997). *Understanding child molesters: Taking charge.* Thousand Oaks, CA: Sage. Also see Dennis J. Stevens. (2002b).

59. M. Knapp (1997, January). *Treatment of sex offenders.* In English, Pullen, and Jones (Eds.), *Managing adult sex offenders: A containment approach.* Lexington, KY: American Probation and Parole Association.

60. Linda Jones, Suzanne Pullen, and Kim English. (1997, January). Criminal justice policies and sex offender denial. In Kim English, Suzanne Pullen, and Linda Jones (Eds.), *Managing adult sex offenders: A containment approach.* Lexington, KY: American Probation and Parole Association.

61. Hollida Wakefield and Ralph Underwager. Paper presented at the 14th Annual Symposium of the American College of Forensic Psychology, San Francisco, CA, May 3, 1998.

62. G. Abel and J. L. Rouleau (1990). The nature and extent of sexual assault. In W. I. Marshall, D. R. Laws, and H. E. Barbaree (Eds.), *Handbook of sexual assault: Issues, theories, and treatment of the offender.* New York: Plenum.

63. Stephen A. Egger (2002). *The killers among us.* Upper Saddle River, NJ: Prentice Hall.

64. Stephen G. Michaud and Roy Hazelwood (1998). *The evil that men do.* New York: St Martin's.

65. Findings show that most predators will attack a victim based upon victim vulnerability as perceived by the offender (as opposed to what the victim thinks).

66. Kim English, Suzanne Pullen, and Linda Jones (Eds.). (1997, January). *Managing adult sex offenders: A containment approach.* Lexington, KY: American Probation and Parole Association.

67. Dennis J. Stevens. (2000). The problem is that most sexual predators do not keep count after reaching a certain number of victims. One predator tells the author at a high-custody penitentiary group encounter, "Who keeps score, ya know?" Leberg (1997) implies a higher number of victims.

68. Katharine K. Baker (1999). What rape is and what it ought not to be. *Jurimetrics, 30*(3), 233. Craig T. Palmer, David N. DiBari, and Scott A. Wright (1999). Is it sex yet? Theoretical and practical implications of the date over rapists' motives. *Jurimetrics, 39*(3), 281–283. Bureau of Justice Statistics (2005). *Sourcebook of criminal justice statistics online* (Table 5.53). Retrieved online January 5, 2005: http:// www.albany.edu/sourcebook/1995/pdf/t553.pdf. Table 5.53 shows that of the estimated 27,000 arrests in 2003 for rape, 26 percent of those defendants had a prior felony conviction and for 50 percent of those defendants, this was their second felony arrest. Some would argue that because most predators are not detected, it would be hard to say that 74 percent of those arrests were actually first-timers. Because predators engage in many types of crime, they would have been arrested in the past more than once on other charges.

69. The MCMI consists of a 175-item, paper-and-pencil self-report questionnaire designed to measure psychopathology. The MCMI produces a personality profile

based on 20 personality dimensions. Also see Stevens (1999b), whereby Myers–Briggs Personality Tests failed to identify significant differences between convicts, cops, and college students.

70. Dennis J. Stevens (2000a). *Inside the mind of the serial rapist.* New York: Authors Choice (pp. 14–16). Also see Dennis J. Stevens (2000b). Identifying criminal predators, sentences, and criminal classifications. *Journal of Police and Criminal Psychology, 15*(1), 50–71.

71. Bureau of Justice Statistics (2004, December). *Felony sentences in state courts, 2002.* Washington, DC: U.S. Department of Justice, Office of Justice Programs, NCJ 206916. Retrieved online January 6, 2005: http://www.ojp.usdoj.gov/bjs/abstract/fssc02.htm

72. G. M. Sykes and D. Matza (1988). Techniques of neutralization. In James M. Henslin (Ed.), *Down to earth sociology: Introductory readings* (pp. 225–231). New York: Free Press.

73. G. M. Sykes and D. Matza (1988).

74. C. D. Bryant (1982). *Sexual deviancy and social proscription: The social context of carnal behavior.* New York: Human Sciences Press.

75. Personal communication with author when asked about these findings in this section. February, 2004. Also see Sam S. Souryal (2003). *Ethics in criminal justice: In search of the truth* (3rd ed.). Cincinnati, OH: Anderson (pp. 380–387). Souryal answers his own question of what can be done to restore ethics in criminal justice, which can include community corrections. One interpretation of his argument is to cut through the institutional blindness influenced by personal egos of policy makers, interest groups, and the American public. Also, for sophistication of chronic offenders, see Eric Leberg (1997), 17–28.

76. C. Bagley (1992). Development of an adolescent stress scale for use of school counselors. *School Psychology International, 13,* 31–49. Also see C. Bagley (1991). The prevalence and mental health sequels of child sexual abuse in a community sample of women aged 18 to 27. *Canadian Journal of Community Mental Health, 10,* 103–116.

77. Nancy Faulkner (1996). *SARANDI: The Sexual Abuse Recognition and Non-Disclosure Inventory.* Ann Arbor, MI 48106–1346, 1-800-521-0600. Dissertation.

78. Dennis J. Stevens (2002a). Pedophiles: A case study. *Journal of Police and Criminal Psychology, 17*(1), 36–51. Dennis J. Stevens. (2002b). Three generations of incarcerated sexual offenders. *Journal of Police and Criminal Psychology, 17*(1), 52–59.

79. Dennis J. Stevens. (2000a).

80. C. A. Courtois and D. L. Watts (1982, January). Counseling adult women who experienced incest in childhood or adolescence. *The Personnel and Guidance Journal,* 275–279. N. Faulkner (1996). *Sexual abuse recognition and non-disclosure of young adolescents.* Ann Arbor: University of Michigan Press. OCLC 35693021.

L. Swanson and M. K. Biaggio (1985). Therapeutic perspectives on father-daughter incest. *American Journal of Psychiatry, 142*(6), 667–674.

81. B. B. Johnson (1987). Sexual abuse prevention: A rural interdisciplinary effort. *Child Welfare, 66,* 165–73.

82. *Sex offender treatment skills for corrections professionals* (2001). Washington, DC: U.S. Department of Justice, National Institute of Corrections (pp. 1–17). Retrieved online January 6, 2005: http://www.nicic.org/downloads/pdf/2001/sexoff-files/PartSec1Offenders-Programs.pdf.

83. Nancy Faulkner (1996, October). Pandora's Box: The secrecy of child sexual abuse. *Sexual Counseling Digest.* Retrieved online January 6, 2005: http://www.prevent-abuse-now.com/pandora.htm

84. Nancy Faulkner (2003). *School based research on undisclosed sexual abuse. Shouldn't children have the right to speak out anonymously?* Retrieved online January 6, 2005: http://www.prevent-abuse-now.com/shouldntChildren.htm

85. Michael J. Jenuwine, Ronald Simmons, and Edward Swies (2003, December). Community supervision of sex offenders. *Federal Probation, 67*(3), 20–32.

86. Michael R. Gottfredson and Travis Hirschi (1990). *A general theory of crime.* Stanford, CA: Stanford University Press (p. 16). Also see Dennis J. Stevens (2000b).

87. G. M. McNamara (2000, April). Sexual predator identification notification. *Law and Order, 48*(4), 60–62.

88. G. M. McNamara (2000, April), 61.

89. G. M. McNamara (2000, April).

90. G. G. Abel, J. V. Becker, M. S. Mittelman, J. Cunningham-Rathner, J. L. Rouleau, and W. D. Murphy (1987). Self reported sex crimes of nonincarcerated paraphilics. *Journal of Interpersonal Violence, 2*(1), 3–25. Also see G. G. Abel, A. Jordan, C. G. Hand, L. A. Holland, and A. Phipps (2001). Classification models of child molesters utilizing the Abel Assessment for sexual interest. *Child Abuse & Neglect: The International Journal, 25*(5), 703–718.

91. T. C. Johnson (1999). Development of sexual behavior problems in childhood. In Jon A. Shaw (Ed.), *Sexual aggression* (pp. 41–74). Washington, DC: American Psychiatric Association.

92. Peter Finn (1997, February). *Sex offender community notification.* Washington, DC: U.S. Department of Justice, Office of Justice Programs, National Institute of Justice, NCJ 162364. Retrieved online January 5, 2005: http://www.ncjrs.org/txtfiles/162364.txt

93. Jeremy Travis (1997, February). *Sex offender community notification. Series: NIJ research in action.* Washington, DC: U.S. Department of Justice, Office of Justice Programs, National Institute of Justice. Retrieved online January 6, 2005: http://www.ncjrs.org/txtfiles/162364.txt

94. Megan Nicole Kanka Foundation (2003). Retrieved online January 6, 2005: http://www.megannicolekankafoundation.org/mission.htm

95. Klaaskids Foundation (2003). Retrieved online January 6, 2005: http://www .klaaskids.org/pg-legmeg.htm

96. Commonwealth of Massachusetts Sex Offender Registry Board (2004). Retrieved online January 6, 2005: http://www.mass.gov/sorb/community.htm

97. Richard G. Zevitz and Mary Ann Farkas (2000, December). *Sex offender community notification: Assessing the impact in Wisconsin.* Washington, DC: U.S. Department of Justice, Office of Jusice Programs, NCJ 179992. Retrieved online January 5, 2005: http://www.ncjrs.org/txtfiles1/nij/179992.txt

98. Peter Finn (1997, February).

99. Peter Finn (1997, February).

100. Michael Symons (2003, September 27). Addresses listed online. *The Journal News.* Retrieved online January 5, 2005: http://www.nynews.com/newsroom/092703/b0527megan.html

101. James Alan Fox. Northeastern University Boston. ABC Radio Report. December 18, 2003.

102. Peter Finn (1997, February).

103. American Correctional Association. 2002 Directory. Page 28.

104. Kim English, Suzanne Pullen, and Linda Jones (1997, January). *Managing adult sex offenders in the community—A containment approach.* NCJ 163387. Retrieved online January 4, 2005: http://www.ncjrs.org/pdffiles/sexoff.pdf

105. Kim English, Suzanne Pullen, and Linda Jones (1997, January).

106. *Kansas v Hendricks:* No. 95–1649. June 23, 1997. Kansas' Sexually Violent Predator Act establishes procedures for the civil commitment of persons who, due to a "mental abnormality" or a "personality disorder," are likely to engage in "predatory acts of sexual violence." After Hendricks testified that he agreed with the state physician's diagnosis that he suffers from pedophilia and is not cured and that he continues to harbor sexual desires for children that he cannot control when he gets "stressed out," the jury determined that he was a sexually violent predator. Finding that pedophilia qualifies as a mental abnormality under the Act, the court ordered him committed. 1. The act's definition of "mental abnormality" satisfies "substantive" due process requirements. An individual's constitutionally protected liberty interest in avoiding physical restraint may be overridden even in the civil context. *Jacobson v Massachusetts,* 197 U.S. 11, 26. This Court has consistently upheld involuntary commitment statutes that detain people who are unable to control their behavior and thereby pose a danger to the public health and safety, provided the confinement takes place pursuant to proper procedures and evidentiary standards. *Foucha v Louisiana,* 504 U.S. 71, 80. . . . additional requirements serve to limit confinement to those who suffer from a volitional impairment rendering them dangerous beyond their control. 2. The act does not violate the Constitution's double jeopardy prohibition or its ban on *ex post-facto* lawmaking (pp. 13–24).

107. Austin T. DesLauriers (2002, October). Kansas' sex offender treatment program. *Corrections Today,* 118–123.

108. Bernard Rubin (1972). Prediction of dangerousness in mentally ill criminals. *Archives of General Psychiatry, 27,* 1, 397–407. Supporting information: Robert Prentky, A. Lee, and R. Knight et al. (Eds.). (1998). Recidivism rates among child molesters and rapists. *Law and Human Behavior, 21*(6), 635–659. Abstract available. Retrieved online January 5, 2005: http://www.ncbi.nlm.nih.gov/entrez/query .fcgi?cmd=Retrieve&db=PubMed&list_uids=9418384&dopt=Abstract. Also, Harry E. Allen, Clifford E. Simonsen, and Edward J. Latessa (2004). *Corrections in America,* (10th ed.). Upper Saddle River, NJ: Prentice Hall, 360.

109. D. M. Doren and D. L. Epperson (2001). Great analysis, but problematic assumptions: A critique of Janus and Meehl (1997). *Sexual Abuse: A Journal of Research and Treatment, 13,* 45–51. Also see E. S. Janus and P. E. Meehl (1997). Assessing the legal standard for predictions of dangerousness in sex offender commitment proceedings. *Psychology, Public Policy, and Law 3*(1), 33–64. Douglas L. Epperson et al. (2003, December). *Minnesota sex offender screening tool–Revised (MnSOST–R) technical paper: Development, validation, and recommended risk level cut scores* (p. 5). Retrieved online January 6, 2005: http://www.psychology.iastate.edu/faculty/ epperson/TechUpdatePaper12-03.pdf

110. Suzanne Bohan. (April 6, 2004). These sexual predators go free and unnoticed. *Sacramento Bee.* Retrieved online January 5, 2005: http://www.sacbee.com/content/ news/

111. Bureau of Justice Statistics (2002, June). *Recidivism of sex offenders released from prison in 1994.*

112. Francis T. Cullen and Paul Gendreau (2000). Assessing correctional rehabilitation: Policy, practice, and prospects. *Criminal Justice, 3,* 109–114. Retrieved online January 5, 2005: http://www.ncjrs.org/criminal_justice2000/vol_3/03d.pdf

113. *Managing adult sex offenders. A containment approach* (1996). Washington, DC: American Probation and Parole Association (pp. 298–307). Sex offender treatment skills for corrections professionals (2001). Washington, DC: U.S. Department of Justice, National Institute of Corrections (pp. 1–17). Retrieved online January 6, 2005: http://www.nicic.org/downloads/pdf/2001/sexoff-files/PartSec1Offenders-Programs .pdf.

114. Douglas Young (2002). Impacts of perceived legal pressure on retention in drug treatment. *Criminal Justice and Behavior, 29*(1), 27–55.

115. Francis T. Cullen and Paul Gendreau (2000). p. 21. Mark W. Lipsey (1999). Can rehabilitative programs reduce the recidivism of juvenile offenders? An inquiry into the effectiveness of practical programs. *Virginia Journal of Social Policy and Law, 6*(Spring), 611–641. Wayne N. Welsh and Gary Zajac (2004). A census of prison-based drug treatment programs: Implications for programming, policy, and evaluation. *Crime & Delinquency, 50*(1), 108–133.

116. Francis T. Cullen and Paul Gendreau (2000). p. 24. Ted Palmer (1992). *The re-emergence of correctional intervention.* Newbury Park, CA: Sage.

117. P. Gagne (1981). Treatment of sex offenders with medroxyprogesterone acetate. *American Journal of Psychiatry, 138,* 644–646. Martin P. Kafka (2003, August). Sex offending and sexual appetite: The clinical and theoretical relevance of hyper-sexual desire. *International Journal of Offender Therapy and Comparative Crimi-nology, 47*(4), 439–451.

118. P. Gagne (1981).

119. Linda S. Grossman, Brian Martis, and Christopher G. Fichtner (1999, March). Are sex offenders treatable? A research overview. *Psychiatric Services, 50*(3), 349–361.

120. Linda S. Grossman, Brian Martis, and Christopher G. Fichtner (1999, March). Martin P. Kafka (2003, August). Sex offending and sexual appetite: The clinical and theoretical relevance of hypersexual desire. *International Journal of Offender Ther-apy and Comparative Criminology, 47*(4), 439–451.

121. Linda S. Grossman, Brian Martis, and Christopher G. Fichtner (1999, March).

122. Martin P. Kafka (2003, August).

INDEX